THE AMERICAN STATES
DURING AND AFTER THE REVOLUTION

1775-1789

THE MACMILLAN COMPANY
NEW YORK · BOSTON · CHICAGO · DALLAS
ATLANTA · SAN FRANCISCO

MACMILLAN & CO., LIMITED
LONDON · BOMBAY · CALCUTTA
MELBOURNE

THE MACMILLAN CO. OF CANADA, LTD.
TORONTO

John Adams	John Hancock	James Bowdoin
George Clinton	Alexander Hamilton	John Dickinson
George Mason	Patrick Henry	Charles Cotesworth Pinckney

NINE GREAT STATE LEADERS

THE AMERICAN STATES

DURING AND AFTER THE REVOLUTION

1775-1789

BY

ALLAN NEVINS

AUTHOR OF "ILLINOIS"; "THE EVENING POST: A CENTURY OF JOURNALISM";
"AMERICAN SOCIAL HISTORY AS RECORDED BY BRITISH TRAVELLERS," ETC.

New York

THE MACMILLAN COMPANY

1924

All rights reserved

Printed in the United States of America by
J. J. LITTLE AND IVES COMPANY, NEW YORK

In Memory of
JOSEPH A. NEVINS
1845-1916

"This study in American history was written for the non-competitive program of the Knights of Columbus to encourage investigation into the origins, the achievements and the problems of the United States; to interpret and perpetuate the American principles of liberty, popular sovereignty and government by consent; to promote American solidarity; and to exalt the American ideal."

PREFACE

The design of this volume is to present a conspectus of State history, as distinguished from national history, from the organization of the first independent State agencies at the beginning of the Revolution until 1789. In general, American historiography has treated each Colony separately till 1775, but with the year of independence has suddenly ceased to regard the thirteen commonwealths as separate entities, and followed only their collective fortunes. No real attempt has been made to synthesize State history for this period, or any other. For that matter, the work of the local historian, refusing to look beyond his State boundaries, has been distressingly uneven. Many states have no good historical record. The seminary studies initiated at Johns Hopkins by Herbert Baxter Adams, those of the Columbia department of history, the better volumes of the American Commonwealth Series, and such works as General Edward McCrady's history of South Carolina till 1783, and Mr. H. J. Eckenrode's history of Virginia during the Revolution, represent genuinely scientific research and skilled interpretation. But they leave wide fields of State history quite unexplored.

While to a large extent this volume is a correlation of monographic material and the best State histories, it is also built upon extensive research in the sources, and for a number of States supplies a historical record not to be had in any other form. It is hoped that it will both furnish a background to the study of national history, and contribute to a stronger interest in State history merely as such. The whole State field has been unduly neglected. Important provinces of legislation belong largely to the States—education, transportation, suffrage, control and protection of labor, crime and punishment, the regulation of business, public amusements and morals. The development of constitutional ideas within the States is as interesting as changes in the Federal Constitution and its interpretation. In politics, State and Federal influences constantly interact. Who can understand Calhoun's career without a knowledge of

South Carolina politics, and particularly the compromises between up-country and low-country interests, which made him the consistent enemy of any system which gave tyrannical power to a mere numerical majority? Who can understand Thaddeus Stevens's career in Congress without knowing something of his conduct in the Buckshot War in Pennsylvania?

The author believes that this book possesses a greater unity than might appear at first sight. In the introductory chapter an effort is made to furnish some essential information upon the thirteen Colonies and their governments. Then follow two chapters tracing the origin and early growth of independent agencies of State government. The crystallization of governmental ideas into written constitutions is described in chapter four, and the development and revision of the constitutions in chapter five. Few Americans know very much about politics in the various States during and just after the Revolution, and chapters six to nine inclusive treat the subject in detail. The financial history of the States has never before been explored save in those aspects which bear directly upon national finance, and the sweeping change in social outlook and social legislation which accompanied the Revolution has also been neglected; each is given a special chapter. There naturally follows a discussion of the relation of the States to one another and the central government, leading to the formation of a really integrated nation. The outstanding fact emphasized by the whole survey is that State history was much less confused and chaotic in this period than is usually supposed, and that it showed a fairly orderly and systematic march toward important goals.

To weave thirteen strands into a single fabric without confusion is a difficult task. Narrative and exposition must frequently double and redouble upon themselves. The Greek poetess rebuked Pindar, when he celebrated all the Theban gods and goddesses in a single hymn, by saying that he should sow with the hand and not the sack. No one believes more than the author in the selective rôle of the historian. But in this instance he has thought it best to aim at thoroughness, and to omit no State in any department of the book. The volume is meant to serve as the cornerstone of a series, and will shortly be followed by a treatment of State history 1789-1815 in which the selective principle will be given full play.

For the errors which the book contains the author is alone to be held responsible. But he wishes to acknowledge gratefully the assistance and counsel he has received from many scholars, and in especial from Professor Evarts B. Greene, Professor Dixon R. Fox, Professor Samuel F. Bemis, Professor Richard Purcell, and the late Mr. Gaillard Hunt. Constant aid has been given by Miss Gertrude M. Carey of the Knights of Columbus Historical Commission, and Chairman Edward F. McSweeney has been unfailing in his encouragement. The index is the work of Mr. David M. Matteson, who has given valuable advice in many particulars.

TABLE OF CONTENTS

CHAPTER I

THE COLONIES BEFORE THEIR UNION

CHAPTER II

BEGINNINGS OF THE TRANSITION FROM COLONIES TO STATES

CHAPTER V

THE CONSTITUTIONS IN OPERATION: THEIR REVISION

CHAPTER VI

POLITICAL DEVELOPMENT IN NEW ENGLAND

CHAPTER VII

POLITICAL DEVELOPMENT IN THE MIDDLE STATES

CHAPTER VIII

POLITICAL DEVELOPMENT: THE UPPER SOUTH

CHAPTER IX

POLITICAL DEVELOPMENT: IN THE LOWER SOUTH

CHAPTER X

PROGRESS IN LIBERALISM AND HUMANITY

CHAPTER XI

The States and Their Money Affairs

CHAPTER XII

State Quarrels and State Friendships

CHAPTER XIII

THE RELATIONS OF THE STATES WITH CONGRESS

CHAPTER XIV

FACING WESTWARD: CONCLUSION

THE AMERICAN STATES
DURING AND AFTER THE REVOLUTION

1775-1789

THE AMERICAN STATES

1775-1789

CHAPTER ONE

THE COLONIES BEFORE THEIR UNION

"On their late revolution," wrote Jefferson of the States when the war was safely over, "the changes which their new form of government rendered necessary were easily made. It was only necessary to say that the powers of legislation, the judiciary and the executive powers, hitherto exercised by persons of such and such descriptions, should henceforth be exercised by persons appointed in such and such a manner." This is not the exaggeration it may seem. The student of early State institutions is struck by the fact that almost all of them descend directly from Colonial institutions. From the national point of view a true revolution occurred between 1776 and 1789. That noble china vase, the British Empire, to use Franklin's image, was broken; and a new nation was established. But from the point of view of each separate State there was not so much a revolution as an evolution.

Governmentally the Colonies were a diverse family before they cut their mother's apron strings, and the new States showed the same diversity. In Pennsylvania the pre-Revolutionary government had only one legislative chamber, and so had the post-Revolutionary government. In Connecticut and Rhode Island the highly prized Charters of Colonial days were preserved to be used as Constitutions in independence, and the faults and merits of the olden time were transmitted side by side to the new. In South Carolina and Virginia there were glaring inequalities in the legislative representation of the different sections, and both States after 1783 presented these same inequalities. In Colonies where the King's Governor was weak, like North Carolina, as the people's Governor he was weaker than ever, and in one where he had been strong, New York, he retained a comparatively large part of his strength. Some inhabitants of New

Jersey saw the evil of having the Governor in Colonial days a powerful judicial officer, but he remained the Chancellor after Yorktown.
The necessity for making the State governments more fully answerable to the new democratic theories, and for making them adequate
to the stern practical demands of the time, dictated changes and
amplifications of the Colonial governments; but no understanding
of State polity is possible without some understanding of Colonial
polity.

Four main types of Colonial government were distinguishable just
before the Revolution.   Massachusetts stood alone as a Province
having a Crown-controlled executive, but possessing a much-cherished
Charter. Her neighbors Connecticut and Rhode Island boasted of
Charters, and in addition controlled their own executive branches.
There were three Proprietary Provinces, Pennsylvania, Delaware,
and Maryland, the executive administration of which, with many
other rights and benefits, was vested in the Penn and Calvert families.   The other seven Provinces were administered by Crown-
appointed Governors, and they had no Constitutions save those of
an unwritten nature fixed by tradition, practise, and the customary
form of the instructions sent the Governors from London.

The 300,000 people who lived in Massachusetts in 1770 were as
pure a racial stock as could be found in the world, remarkably
homogeneous in their customs, manners, and habits of mind as
well as in blood and language. They had a sturdy pride in their
purity of race, high intelligence, and the choiceness of the grain
"sifted," as old Governor William Stoughton said, to send "over into
this wilderness." [1] Since the rocky and largely infertile country
neither attracted many men of wealth nor made them, extremes of
riches and poverty were uncommon, and social differences had less
opportunity than in other sections to root themselves in material considerations. A fierce democracy, feared outside New England as
"leveling," was the result.[2] There was indeed a careful social grada-
tion, but it arose in the main from a regard for ancestry, service to
the state, ability, and education. At Harvard to the eve of the
Revolution the students' names were arranged in the order of the

---

[1] Quoted by Lodge, "English Colonies in America," 409.
[2] Cf. *Mass. Hist. Soc. Colls.*, series V, Vol. II, 313, where Jeremy Belknap writes
(March 3, 1784): "Where shall we look for an equal division of property? Not
in the five Southern States, where every white man is the lordly tyrant of an
hundred slaves. Not in the great trading towns and cities, where cash in funds
yields thirteen or sixteen per cent., and in trade much more. The yeomanry of
New England are, in point of *equality,* the fittest materials for a republic. . . ."

respectability of their parentage, the leading families including the Hutchinsons, Saltonstalls, Winthrops, and Quincys. It was the glory of the Province, as of Scotland, that intellectual distinction really distinguished. The educational system of New England, the best in America, was better before than just after the Revolution. Nowhere else in America was there such a body of high-spirited, intelligent liberals as the tradesmen and mechanics of Boston, and the townsmen and yeomen of eastern Massachusetts, save in the Merrimac Valley of New Hampshire, where they had spread northward. Hilly western Massachusetts, like western New Hampshire, showed the radicalism and equalitarianism that almost always mark a frontier.

Though saddled with a government designed to check them, the people of Massachusetts had won a fairly satisfactory self-expression in politics by 1765. The Crown appointed the Governor, Lieutenant-Governor, and Secretary; and the Governor could veto any legislation, disapprove any choice for Speaker, summon, prorogue, or adjourn the House, and—with the consent of the upper chamber, or Council—make important appointments. But the House, to which each town was entitled to send up two delegates annually, always showed a self-assertion which boded ill for any Crown official who trenched upon the people's rights. At the beginning of the eighteenth century it refused to fix a permanent salary for executive officers, and within twenty years it had made the annual allowances so shabby and precarious that the Governor refused to accept his stipend. Defending itself in a formal statement in 1728, the House asserted the "undoubted right of all Englishmen, by Magna Charta, to raise and dispose of money for the public service of their own free accord, without compulsion"; [3] and this position, identical with that of the House of Commons, it maintained.

The Legislature established the judiciary, and in spite of opposition from England, managed to keep it under a certain degree of popular control. The House, sitting each year with the old Council, elected the new Council of twenty-eight, subject to the Governor's consent. Decade after decade the representatives of the people engaged in new quarrels with the Governors. In the time of the very first Crown appointee, Sir William Phips, an energetic, hotheaded native of Maine who favored some unpopular measures, we

[3] This document is given in full in Hutchinson's "Hist. of Mass.," II, 309 ff. (third ed., 1795).

read of the "friends of Phips" and the "court party" as opposed to the popular party. We need mention only the most prominent executives thereafter—Dudley, Stoughton, Burnet, Belcher, Shirley, Pownall, Bernard, Hutchinson—to recall the harsh quarrels connected with each; a series of quarrels the dramatic quality of which Hawthorne caught in his tale of the ghostly procession of Governors which appeared to Gage on his last night in the Province House. Finally came the popular disturbances of the period following the Stamp Act and Townshend Impost Act, and the punitive measures of the British Government with which all are familiar. Troops were poured into Boston as if it were a conquered city, the trials of British officers for capital offenses were transferred out of the Province, Boston harbor was closed, and the fisheries on the Newfoundland Banks, which provided the Colony with much of its food, were forbidden to New Englanders. Worst of all, the Charter, the shining palladium of Massachusetts liberties, was altered by giving the Crown the right to appoint the Council—a right it already possessed in New Hampshire—and by increasing the powers of the Crown Governor.

When we turn to Rhode Island and Connecticut, we turn to Provinces governed under Charters to which they were justified in holding tenaciously throughout and after the Colonial period. Had all the Colonies been under such rule, there might have been no Revolution. Under Rhode Island's Charter of 1663, and Connecticut's of 1662, there was no point at which the authority of the British Government directly interfered with the administration of the Colonies. The freemen of each Province in May annually chose a Governor, Deputy-Governor, and an upper house; the towns chose deputies to sit in a lower house; and in May and October the Governor and two houses sat as a General Assembly. These General Assemblies proceeded, to all practical purposes, as if the two Provinces were self-contained republics. In both governments the salient characteristic was the dominance of the Legislature over the executive and judicial branches, a dominance that endured long after the Revolution. In both the upper house was composed of "Assistants," who in Connecticut were twelve in number, elected on a general ticket, but in Rhode Island were one for each town, or by 1790 thirty in all. As for the lower chamber, in Connecticut each town sent it not more than two deputies, while in Rhode Island not more than six were sent by Newport and either four or two by other cities or towns.[4]

The most interesting and the unique feature of Connecticut's government was the close connection between it and the ecclesiastical power, making the Colony almost a theocracy. This connection was regarded with not merely complacency, but pride. The churches and government used the same assessment lists in levying rates and taxes; the civil power collected the church rates by distraint where necessary; if the church neglected to support its minister, the General Assembly decided the proper scale of maintenance; and if any congregation remained without a minister for a year, the civil authorities could compel it to fill the pulpit. The binding together of all the Congregational or Presbyterian churches upon the Saybrook platform (1708) was followed by a legislative decree that the churches so united should be considered thenceforth "established" by law. Generation after generation the political leaders and ecclesiastical leaders maintained their firm alliance, bulwarking each others' power. Just as civil officers took pains to see that Congregationalism was protected and financially nourished, so the clergy saw that public opinion was molded to the support of a trusted Governor and Assistants. Yale College was kept under church influence, and made a feeder for the church and the civil service alike. Thus was built up a Standing Order, so-called, that was unshakable. Rhode Island's perfect religious freedom stood in sharp contrast with it.

As time wore on, the taxation of dissenters in Connecticut for the Congregational Church was partly halted. But serious additional limitations upon the excellence of the government lay in the fact that the Legislature had complete control of the judiciary, while the upper chamber itself enjoyed large judicial powers; in the possession by this upper chamber, the Assistants, of a larger share in the executive power than was proper; and in an unfair procedure in the election of Assistants, tending to keep veterans in office against the rivalry of younger men, no matter how much abler. A dangerous authority was thus given to a dozen men, who held office year after year until worn out in harness.

Upon the whole, however, Connecticut's later Colonial history is a history of consistent prosperity, progress, and harmony. In the

[4] See Thorpe, "Constitutions and Charters," for text of all Colonial and State Constitutions.

century following the grant of the Charter, she had but nine Governors, the general rule being for each to serve until he died or was superannuated. The people learned to administer their finances wisely and frugally; to adjust executive power to the demands of the changing times; to pass wholesome laws, and to interpret them wholesomely in the courts. Crime was rare, and order was rigidly preserved. Any youth of parts could rise through the local schools to the well-supported college at New Haven. The Colony was checkered by small farms, so well cared for that the people boasted they made more profit from mowing land than the New Yorkers made from wheat land, and that the butter, cheese, and packed meats of Connecticut were esteemed by the West Indies the best to be had. This prosperity encouraged a rapid growth of population, so that by the Revolution Connecticut not only had more inhabitants to the square mile than any other Colony—there were 198,000 in 1774—but was known for the settlers whom it sent north and west. Rhode Island also prospered in material ways, but her history was troubled, being disfigured in especial by persistent paper money follies. Unfortunately for her general progress, and for the character of her government after 1776, little of her wealth was put into schools.

We meet a different kind of government when we turn to the three proprietary Provinces, and especially to the greatest. The taint of feudalism was upon the colonial system of Pennsylvania. It was impossible for the later Penns to take anything but a selfish view of the great domain of which they were proprietors—to look upon it other than as an estate from which they were to wring the utmost revenue. Contention, said Franklin, was "radical, interwoven in the Constitution, and so became of the very nature of proprietary governments." [5] The Constitution, the latest of William Penn's Charters, was simple enough. The executive branch consisted of a Governor and of an advisory council which was kept at the Governor's beck and call. The legislative power was vested in the unicameral Assembly, chosen yearly by a broad electorate. The Governor's powers were large, for he possessed a veto, and made all judicial and most civil appointments. But the cardinal element of contention to which Franklin referred was not the Governor's

---

[5] Franklin's "Cool Thoughts on the Present Situation of our Public Affairs," 1764 ("Works," Bigelow Ed., III, 286 ff.) analyzed the government of Pennsylvania fully.

wide authority, but the fact of the Proprietary's ownership. He had the rights and revenues of a mediæval baron centuries after the reasons for a feudal establishment had ceased to exist in Europe, and held them in a new, untamed country, amid a population whose civil and religious convictions were opposed to them. These overseas potentates, inheriting the government, owning millions of acres of wild land and enormous areas from which they drew quit-rents, and able in scores of ways to interfere with the people as no Crown Governor could, too often wished to give nothing, and to take everything.

The fact that the Legislature consisted of only one house simplified the constant struggle between it and the Governors. The Quakers were the most powerful and long the dominant group in the Assembly, but in spite of their innate conservatism they stood firmly for the colonists' rights. The principal bones of contention till near the end involved money considerations. They included the revenues of the Proprietor, the question of his right to participate with the Assembly in disposing of the money raised by taxes and otherwise, the question of the exemption of his estates from taxes, and his greed in laying hands upon the Indian country. The Assembly always tried to protect itself from any unjust clauses in the Proprietary's instructions to the Deputy-Governor by insisting upon a knowledge of them, and only a few Deputy-Governors proved defiant. It also maintained that the Deputy-Governor must disregard the instructions if they violated the Charter as the Assembly interpreted it. But what cost the Assembly its hardest struggle was its attempt to vindicate a right to appropriate and use the public moneys without interference from the executive.

In the spring of 1764 the Legislature, goaded beyond endurance by the efforts of the selfish Thomas Penn to take advantage of the Seven Years' War and its perils to wring concessions for his purse and his authority, passed a set of condemnatory resolutions without a single dissenting vote.[6] It denounced Penn's claim for special tax exemptions. It accused him of making great land purchases from the Indians, holding these lands vacant for a better market, and thus keeping the frontier so thinly settled as to invite Indian attacks.

[6] These twenty-six "aggrievances" are in the "Votes and Proceedings" of the House, 1758 and succeeding years (1775 ed.), 337-339; and in *Pa. Mag. Hist. and Biog.*, V, 70 ff. For the enduring memory of the Proprietary's responsibility for the Indian massacres, see a letter of the Phila. Committee of Safety, Pa. *Packet*, June 17, 1776.

The exorbitant prices he demanded for his acres, it added, had driven thousands of Pennsylvania families to the cheap lands of the South. To swell his revenues by license fees, Penn had encouraged dram-shops until they were a serious element of moral corruption. He had tried to gain absolute control over the judges, and to render his command of the militia so complete that it would endanger the popular liberties. The Proprietary's wealth would grow with that of the Province, the Assembly stated, until it became a menace to the Crown and the people alike. Some of these charges were exaggerated, and in justice to even Thomas Penn, it must be remembered that with a good opportunity, the Assembly might have overtaxed his estates; but the gravamen of the indictment was sound. For various reasons, however, the movement to supplant the Proprietary Government by Crown Government failed.

The most scandalous feature of Pennsylvania's government was the frequent bargaining between people and Governors for the passage of useful laws. Franklin has succinctly described it: [7]

Ever since the revenue of the quit-rents first, and after that the revenue of tavern licenses, were settled irrevocably on our Proprietors and Governors, they have looked on those incomes as their proper estate, for which they were under no obligations to the people: and when they afterwards concurred in passing any useful laws, they considered them as so many jobs, for which they ought to be particularly paid. Hence arose the custom of *presents* twice a year to the Governors, at the close of each session in which laws were passed, given at the time of passing. They usually amounted to a thousand pounds per annum. But when the Governors and Assemblies disagreed, so that laws were not passed, the presents were withheld.

The fencing between the Assembly and Governor was sometimes finely humorous. On one occasion, several bills desired by the people were, when the session neared its end, in the hands of Governor Thomas. The House informed the Governor that it awaited his "result" upon the bills, and he sent back word that he was considering them, and meanwhile awaited the "result" of the House. Further interchanges led the Governor to state that as he had received evidence of a "good disposition" on the part of the Assembly, he would show the like himself by sending down the bills without any objection. This was not equivalent to saying that he would approve them, and the cautious Assembly therefore passed a resolution that when the Governor signed the bills before him, and such others as might yet be presented, it would pay him, in two orders, £1,500. The orders were drawn, the Governor arranged a meeting,

[7] "Works," Bigelow ed., III, 311.

and while he signed with one hand, he took the money with the other. [8]

Yet after all, many of the grievances of the popular party were allayed just before the Revolution. When Thomas Penn, "a miserable churl, always intent upon griping and saving," as Franklin said, gave way to John Penn, who had many fine traits and himself came to America to govern, Pennsylvania entered upon a fairly placid phase of proprietary rule. The Quakers were not only peaceful by religion, but were attached to England by blood and tradition, while the Germans of the country districts were a slow, cautious race, so that the people as a whole, more than a quarter million in 1775, seemed conservative in their attitude towards the Revolutionary movement. By the property qualification for the ballot, fifty acres or fifty pounds, and by the fact that before the Revolution the five frontier counties—Lancaster, York, Cumberland, Berks, and Northampton—had only ten Assemblymen, while Philadelphia, Chester, and Bucks counties had twenty-six, this conservatism was strengthened. Delaware, which had its own Assembly and Council —a bicameral Legislature—but shared Pennsylvania's Governor, was similarly conservative. As for Maryland, the popular house or Burgesses there had gained a power considerably greater than that of the Pennsylvania Assembly, and maintained entire control over the public moneys, while it even denied the Governor's right (after 1733 the proprietors ruled only through deputized Governors) to veto legislation.

The governments of the seven Royal Provinces had much in common. In all the Governor was appointed by the Crown, and the other executive officers, with a few exceptions, were named either by the Crown or the Governor. In all the Legislature consisted of a House and Council, the former popularly elected and the latter appointed with an eye to the strengthening of the Governor. The history of all seven is largely a history of quarrels between the Governors and Houses. New York had probably the most unfortunate government, a government arbitrary, corrupt, and inefficient. There, and there alone, the Governor usually had a considerable wing of the Assembly under his influence, partly because the southern part of the Province contained a warmly loyal population, partly because he added to his other means of obtaining support the power

[8] W. C. Bruce, "Benjamin Franklin Self-Revealed," II, 106.

of granting land-patents at low quit-rents to favorites. In Virginia the Governor's authority was equally great. There he was executor of the laws, commander of the militia, Chancellor and Chief Justice, and virtually head of the established Anglican Church, for though he did not appoint the clergy, he inducted them into their charges. He could propose legislation, veto bills, convoke, prorogue, and dissolve the Assembly, and pardon minor criminals. He had a wide patronage, and he added to his income and his political power by his control over quit-rents, the disposal of unpatented lands, and the exchange of public money.[9] In no Crown Colony was the authority of the Governor weak, and in all his social dignity was very great. In even poor New Hampshire Governor Benning Wentworth wished to found a family supported by great landed estates, and he built at Portsmouth one of the largest mansions in the North—the mansion celebrated, as the scene of his romantic second marriage, in Longfellow's poem "Lady Wentworth." In Virginia, Botetourt was given his coach by George III, and made a great show of reflected royal glory as he took office.

The differences among the seven Legislatures were more salient than among the seven Governors. They varied greatly in size. Virginia counted 110 Burgesses in 1760, two being elected from each county and one each from the three borough towns and the College of William and Mary. New York's lower chamber contained fewer than one-third that number, New Jersey's had only 24 members, and South Carolina's consisted in 1770 of only 48, elected triennially by the parishes. There were fairly wide discrepancies in the property qualifications for the ballot, and wider ones in the property requirement for a seat in the House. Thus in New Hampshire voters had to have a £50 estate, in Virginia 50 unsettled acres or 25 acres and a house, in North Carolina or Georgia 50 acres, and in South Carolina 100 acres. In North Carolina any man with 100 acres might sit in the House, while in South Carolina he had to have 500 acres and 10 slaves, or to be worth £1,000 in land, houses, and other property. As for the Council during late Colonial times, in Virginia and New Hampshire a Governor was more likely to count on its opposition in any quarrel with the House than on its support. In New York and South Carolina, however, it was almost consistently with the Crown, while in North Carolina, one of the keenest observers

---

[9] But see P. S. Flippin, "Royal Govt. in Va.," 211, for the encroachments of the Virginia Burgesses on the Governor's power.

just before the Revolution tells us, the chief defect of the Constitution was the fact that the Councilors were the tools of the executive; they "always advised as they supposed the Governor desired, and acted even in their legislative capacity as the merest servants of his will."

In one important respect the lower houses of the Southern legislatures were alike: the scheme of representation was inequitable. The apportionment of two Burgesses to each county in Virginia was unfair, for the counties varied widely in size and population, and they were smallest in the Tidewater section of great plantations and rich planters. The gentry hence enjoyed a decided advantage over the small farmers of the uplands and Shenandoah. In North Carolina Governor Tryon complained of a similar injustice, stating that in 1767 the counties of the coastal region north and east of Cape Fear sent five members each to the Legislature, Bertie County sent three, and all the counties of the western reaches only two each. The establishment of new counties in western North Carolina was much too slow to meet the needs of the swelling population. In South Carolina the upland settlers had practically no representation, for they were afforded a semblance of local government and of a voice in the Legislature only by the makeshift extension of the nearest lowland parishes 200 miles west to the Cherokee country. They long clamored in vain for the creation of upland parishes, which would save them the necessity of traveling perhaps many scores of miles to court, and would automatically give them seats in the Commons House. Instead, as a concession just before the Revolution, the upper country was divided into four judicial districts, Orangeburgh, Camden, Cheraws, and Ninety-Six, so that justice at least was somewhat nearer the settlers. Georgia was too young a Colony to feel distinctly any sectional inequality, but the injustice was taking root.

Almost everywhere from Pennsylvania to Georgia a struggle between east and west, Tidewater and uplands, cut in the later Colonial period across the alignment between people and Crown. In each larger Province the self-assertion of the democratic, individualistic settlers of the hill and inland regions marked the decade 1760-1770. The border ravages of the Indians in Pennsylvania during 1763 were followed by the disorders of the "Paxton boys" from near the present city of Harrisburg. They massacred some Christian Indians,

and by an angry march upon Philadelphia, which they thought indifferent to their sufferings, threatened a civil war, which Franklin
and others averted. This episode marks the beginnings of the pre-
dominance of the Ulster Scotch and other Calvinists in Pennsylvania
affairs, replacing the old Quaker supremacy. In Virginia the planter oligarchy ruled almost unchallenged until in 1765-66 there transpired a scandalous mismanagement of the treasury by a rich representative of this class; and the explosion threw the House into the
hands of the uplanders. In North Carolina the sufferings of the
inland population from corrupt sheriffs, court officials, and tax
collectors, from heavy taxes, charges for land-patents, illegal fees, and
quit-rents, caused graver and graver disturbances as the sixties
wore on. These culminated when the backwoodsmen of a territory
comprising all or part of seven counties in what is now the north
central part of the State rose in the Regulators' Rebellion; and the
vigor with which the lowland militia under Tryon crushed this
outbreak at the battle of the Alamance (1771) bred an intense
hatred for the coast country among the discontented settlers.
Similar disorders in upper South Carolina reached a crisis in 1769,
but here bloodshed was averted.

Outside of New England no Colony, not even North Carolina,
closely approached a true democracy in its social conditions. In New
York, Cadwallader Colden in 1765 distinguished four different
classes. First, of course, came the great landholders, some of whose
estates comprised tens and hundreds of thousands of acres, on which
the tenants were counted by villages. Those of the Van Rensselaer,
Van Courtlandt, and Livingston families were each entitled to a special representative in the Assembly, while the Schuylers, Cuylers,
Philipses, Morrises, and others lived in almost feudal state. Then
came the lawyers, to whom much deference was paid; then the merchants, many of them enriched by illicit trade in the French War;
and finally, the farmers and mechanics, who "are the most useful and
the most moral, but allwise made the dupes of the former."[10] New
Jersey boasted of one estate with a private deer park; and in Pennsylvania there was an impassable gulf between the rich landholders
and merchants of the southeast, and the poor Ulster Scotch frontiersmen. In Virginia great tobacco plantations of from 1,000 to 50,000
acres lined the James, Potomac, Rappahannock, and other rivers.

[10] N. Y. Hist. Soc. Colls., 1876-77, II, 68 ff.

The large-scale employment of slaves under the supervision of alert overseers made holdings that had cost their original owners almost nothing productive in favorable years of £10,000, £20,000, and sometimes even more. The rich planters were country gentlemen recognizably akin to the Squire Western of Fielding's England, though with more pride and intelligence. They lived with profusion but usually without taste, they were often self-indulgent, and they treated the common folk with condescension. Some scholars were found among them, and some large libraries—the Byrds of Westover owned 4,000 volumes; but what redeemed them as a group was the shrewd and deep interest they took in public affairs. It was this interest which made them merit their long control of the Legislature. A similar position was taken in South Carolina by the wealthy rice and indigo planters of the lowlands, and the Charleston merchants. The affluent South Carolinians recognized the value of education. In the quarter century 1759-1786 more South Carolinians were admitted to the Inns of Court in London than citizens of any other Colony—46 in all, against 20 from Virginia.

Throughout British America the governments were governments by parties, and the Legislatures came to be run with nearly as much wire-pulling, log-rolling, party bossism, and political bargaining as would exist in American communities of the same size today. Adam Smith spoke in his "Wealth of Nations" (1776) of "the little prizes which are to be found in what may be called the paltry rabble of colonial faction," and these little prizes were zealously sought. In Massachusetts before 1765 there was formed the "Junto," led by Samuel Adams, and including James Otis, John Hancock, Thomas Cushing, Joseph Hawley, and Samuel Dexter. It held the Assemblymen almost in the palm of its hand. Beyond doubt it was modeled after the famous Caucus Club which, controlling the affairs of Boston in late Colonial times, gave America one of its familiar political terms. This Caucus Club, according to John Adams, met in the garret of Adjutant Tom Dawson, a large room, where they smoked, drank flip, and made their choice of the men to be elected selectmen, collectors, assessors, and legislators.[11] In New Hampshire a compact group of squires year after year drafted the legislative program. The Virginia House of Burgesses was controlled for many years by a ring of Tidewater representatives of wealth, family, and brains,

[11] Cf. Gordon, "Hist. of the . . . Independence of the U. S." (1788), I, 365.

the Speaker-Treasurer being its head in Governor Dinwiddie's time. In all three of these Provinces the lower house was large.

Governor Clinton, of New York, complained to the Board of Trade in 1747 concerning the "constant meeting of a committee of the Council and Assembly, who never make any report of their proceedings, tho' the resolutions of both Council and Assembly were directed by them." A little later, Lieutenant-Governor Colden described a combination of lawyers which had been formed to dominate the Assembly, though only a few Assemblymen belonged to it. Thus "they rule the House of Assembly in all matters of importance," he observed. "The greatest numbers of the Assembly being common farmers who know little either of men or things are easily deluded and seduced. By this association, united in interest and family connections with the proprietors of the great tracts [of rich land], a domination of lawyers was found in this Province, which for some years past has been too strong for the executive powers of government." In North Carolina, again, not long before the Revolution there existed a junto composed of four members of the Council and a little knot of the House, with one of the Treasurers for leader. This Treasurer, John Starkey, was paymaster of the Assembly, and Governor Arthur Dobbs wrote that he used his powers in such a manner that "all the low members who want a supply follow him like chickens, so that he sways the House against the most sensible members in it." Even in half-formed Georgia, which was only a row of dotted settlements along the coast and three rivers, such a directing committee or ring was formed, the most prominent member being the Speaker, Noble Wimberly Jones.[12]

[12] Clinton's fullest description of the New York caucus is in "Docs. Rel. Col. Hist. N. Y.," VI, 354; for Colden's words, see *Idem.*, VII, 796; for Dobbs's, "Col. Recs. N. Ca.," V, 948-49.

CHAPTER TWO

BEGINNINGS OF THE TRANSITION FROM COLONIES TO STATES

During the sessions of the Continental Congress in June, 1775, it was considered expedient to issue a declaration of the causes for taking up arms. Jefferson prepared a draft, but it met with such vehement objections from John Dickinson that the latter was requested to write a declaration suiting his own cautious views. He did so, and Congress, actuated by a desire not to move too fast for any considerable group of members, approved it almost without change. When this was done, Dickinson expressed his joy, adding: "There is but one word, Mr. President, in the paper which I disapprove, and that is the word 'Congress.' "[1] Thereupon Benjamin Harrison lifted his tall, spare figure and replied: "There is but one word in the paper, Mr. President, of which I approve, and that is the word 'Congress.' " The division between the forces of radicalism and conservatism which this incident illustrates was as wide as the American Colonies in the years 1774-76. In every Province the patriot party was split into two wings, one wishing at first to make an unqualified, defiant assertion of American rights, and later to hasten the assertion of independence; the other eager at first to emphasize the hope for reconciliation with Great Britain, and later to delay the total break with the mother country. To the radical side belonged the Adamses, George Clinton, Joseph Reed, Patrick Henry, and Christopher Gadsden; to the conservative side equally sterling Americans like James Bowdoin, John Jay, Robert Morris, Edmund Pendleton, and John Rutledge.

Another division between somewhat different groups of radicals and conservatives was sharply defined upon domestic issues. When the time came to frame State constitutions, the conservatives in general wished for balanced and rather aristocratic forms; the radicals for a highly popular form—one in which the legislature, directly representing the people, would dominate the executive and judicial

[1] Jefferson's Writings, Memorial Ed., I, 17.

branches, while property qualifications for the ballot would be low or absent. The radicals aligned themselves against special social, economic, and religious privilege. They attacked the church establishment, primogeniture and entail, methods of taxation which favored the rich, and the discrimination against new settlements in the apportionment of representation. But the conservatives were usually ready to support the old order. In the South, they staunchly defended the Anglican Establishment, the preservation of ancestral estates intact, and the favored position of the lowland planters in the legislature. A struggle between radicals and conservatives upon imperial questions was thus rapidly followed by another upon State questions.

I. GRIEVANCES OF INDIVIDUAL COLONIES

As every Colony was more or less distinctive in its government, so nearly every Colony found some distinctive fault with British authority, and cherished its hope of distinctive reform. The greater discontents were those common to all the provinces. Franklin expressed them in his "Causes of the American Discontents," and the American leaders in 1774-76 enumerated them in a series of noble state papers. From the time the colonists lost their first fear of the forest and the savage the central grievance was simply, as the Massachusetts legislators told Cromwell's Parliament, that they wanted to live "under the government of a governor and magistrates of their own choosing, and laws of their own making." This goal was attained only by Connecticut and Rhode Island. The aspiration produced friction so early that the Puritans were thought by John Locke, and the Virginians by Stuart observers, to be planning independence. But all the Colonies, save autonomous Connecticut and Rhode Island, and the two weakest Provinces, Delaware and Georgia, had separate reasons for restiveness. We can hardly understand the spirit with which men of every section sprang forward in 1775 unless we take account of such facts as the irritability of New Hampshire under the arbitrary management of the Crown lands, the resentment of South Carolina when the Crown denied the right of its house to send money to John Wilkes, and the anger of Maryland over rapacious fee charges.

In some Colonies the special irritations were so numerous that one no sooner lost its force than another appeared. This was notably true of the fastest-growing Southern commonwealth. North Carolina before the Revolution had received successive waves of immigrants from the north and the seacoast, until it had become one of the most populous Colonies. These rugged, individualistic small farmers had distinctive economic interests, and were not men to let their liberties be abridged. Just before the war the little capital of New Bern witnessed four marked disputes, involving finances, boundaries, representation, and the courts.

The most important of these controversies arose from the determination of the royal authorities to extricate North Carolina from her financial embarrassments by heavy taxation. The population was poor; it groaned under the costs of the French war, the campaign of 1771 to suppress the western malcontents or Regulators, and the redemption of former issues of paper money. Under pressure from the farmers, the legislature tried to stop the collection of certain onerous taxes. The Governor, a stiff, unimaginative, conscientious officer named Josiah Martin, disallowed the bill, the legislators tried to override him, and their quarrel continued till the very beginning of the Revolution, involving repeated prorogations of the Assembly. As for the boundary, the Crown had fixed a disputed line with South Carolina in a position unfavorable to the claims of the northern Colony, and had instructed Governor Martin to mark it. The Assembly, unwilling to lose a rich territory, open to land-hungry North Carolinians, declined to pay the surveyors a shilling; and Martin, to the general resentment, appointed his own commissioners to run the line.

This controversy had no sooner been thus summarily disposed of than there arose a graver dispute concerning the courts. The Assembly of 1773, aware that the law which established the judicial system was to expire that session, framed an enactment to replace it, and inserted a clause which made the North Carolina property of persons who had never resided in the Colony attachable for debt. That is, they asserted the right called "foreign attachment." Englishmen objected to such a clause for several reasons, the chief of which was that it gave to American claimants a prior lien upon the American property of foreign debtors who owed money both in England and America. Martin was bound by his instructions to refuse assent to the law as framed, a deadlock ensued, and the greater part of the court system went out of existence. For a full year the

Colony was left dangerously unprotected against lawless men. At the same time, the legislature evinced its jealousy for its own rights by halting what it regarded as a step towards packing the lower house. Governor Martin, pleased by the hospitality offered him at Tarboro, a Tar River hamlet of some importance as a centre of export for tobacco and pork, chartered it as a borough town, with a special seat in the legislature. The Assembly refused to admit the member elected, on the ground that Tarboro did not have the population required by law for borough towns.[2]

We are not here concerned with the merits of these controversies; the important fact is that within a few years North Carolina was disturbed by four separate collisions. And beneath these disputes smouldered on the old persistent quarrel regarding the Governor's powers over the legislature, a spluttering little fire ever ready to help light other blazes. The colonists wanted an Assembly chosen at fixed intervals, not at the arbitrary will of the Governor; a body able to sit at stated periods, free from the fear of being prorogued as soon as it met. In 1773 the legislature discussed a bill to establish triennial elections for the Assemblies, though everybody knew that such a bill would be vetoed. "Such was the ardent and unanimous desire of the people of the Province," we are told by a historian acquainted with the leading figures of the day, that these bills were frequently drafted although "they stood no chance of becoming a law."[3] Martin took pains to conciliate the Regulators, with such effect that, smarting with resentment against the lowlanders, they rallied to his side; but the rest of the Province remained hostile.

The Colonies had many and protean money quarrels with the Crown authorities in the period immediately preceding the Revolution. We may instance only the most picturesque, furnished by South Carolina—a dispute so debatable that the two chief historians of the State have disagreed upon it.[4] The South Carolina Whigs became passionately interested in the crusade of John Wilkes, the English agitator, for freedom of speech and elections. When Wilkes was prosecuted for his writings in the 45th issue of the *North Briton*, they made as much of that magic numeral as the English Whigs, drinking 45 toasts at tables bearing 45 lights and 45 bowls. Like most Americans, they believed the cause of Whiggism identical in

[2] Martin's "North Carolina," II, 306.
[3] Jones, "Defence Rev. Hist. N. C.," 80.
[4] See McCrady, "S. C. Under the Royal Government," 663, 690 ff.; D. D. Wallace, "Life of Henry Laurens," ch. 13.

England and America. When in 1769, after Wilkes was barred from Parliament, Chatham took sides with him, and an English society was formed to aid him in his fight, South Carolina flew to his aid. The Commons House impulsively ordered £1,500 to be sent to London for Wilkes and his friends. This was a slap in the face of the Crown; it was also a slap at the Governor and the dependents who formed the Council, since they insisted that their approval was necessary for any vote of money. The British Attorney-General ruled that the House could not legally appropriate money from the treasury without the consent of the Governor and upper chamber, and that its act had been unconstitutional; a doctrine which the House flatly rejected, declaring that it had the right to grant money for any purpose and at any time.[5]

This quarrel became ugly, and inflamed public sentiment in a half dozen directions. It involved the colonial treasurers, whom the House ordered to jail when they refused to pay out another sum, this time for silk manufacture, without the consent of Governor and Council. It involved the tax bills, for the angry Council refused to approve any taxes levied for the replacement of the money sent to Wilkes. It involved the press, which took sides. Governor Montagu, a young English lord, fatuously called a session of the legislature at an inconvenient, unhealthy spot, Beaufort, hoping the stubborn Charleston members would not attend.[6] He little knew the temper of the patrician merchants and planters, and on the very first day he was greeted by the fullest house in the history of the Colony. Thereafter he was an exile in a hostile land, resisted politically and ignored socially by the once affable society of Charleston. Thus South Carolina, entering the lists in behalf of a man who, however disreputable personally, was called by Gladstone one of the great champions of British liberty, received a preliminary training for the Revolution.

But the Wilkes affair was by no means South Carolina's sole dispute with the crown authorities. In the uplands a population of small farmers, similar to that across the line in North Carolina, and now constituting a majority of the white population, had long demanded the establishment of new parishes to give them local government and legislative representation. When the legislature

[5] Smith, "S. C. as a Royal Province," 373-4.
[6] D. D. Wallace, "Const. Hist. S. C.," 73.

finally created two such parishes, the King's ministers decided in 1770 to veto the act.[7] Both the uplands and lowlands were still further irritated by another royal negative, that of a bill to emit £106,500 in paper currency to exchange for a former issue; and there were still other disagreements.

Disputes over the position of the judges and courts were all too common. New York preceded North Carolina, just as North Carolina preceded Massachusetts, in contesting this issue with the Crown authorities. Cadwallader Colden—"Old Silverlocks"—a Scotch-born physician whose achievements as a student of Indian life, natural science, and philosophy made him one of the worthiest intellectual figures of the Colonies, a man Benjamin Franklin was proud to know, was acting-Governor of New York during most of the troubled sixties. We soon find the patriots levelling against him three positive indictments: that he had refused to grant the judges commissions during good behavior, that he had supported the claim of litigants in civil cases to an appeal from the Province courts to the Governor or King in Council, and that he had approved the Stamp Act.

Colden indeed insisted, in accordance with British instructions, upon limiting the freedom of the courts. He maintained that the right of appeal to the Governor or King in Council was requisite for the preservation of justice, since the courts were in a confused state, and subject to pressure from the wealthy landholders—both reasons possessing real force. The Assembly resolved that the practise was a dangerous innovation, tending to promote litigation, and subject the people to arbitrary power; but the Crown authorities stood firm. So, too, the royal officers maintained their right to give the judges commissions revocable at will. It became impossible to obtain a chief justice except by going to Massachusetts for a favorite of Thomas Pownall's, and popular discontent with the dependent character of the judiciary remained high till the Revolution.[8]

Ecclesiastical questions were a source of constant friction, for large bodies of the colonists entertained an inveterate suspicion of the Anglican church, particularly where it was the legal establishment. Archbishop Thomas Secker of Canterbury made a proposal in the sixties regarding King's College in New York which some men

[7] McCrady, "S. C. Under the Royal Government," 640; Wallace, "Henry Laurens," 171.
[8] See Colls. N. Y. Hist. Soc., 1877 (Colden "Letter-Books," II), 452-467 *et passim.*

regarded as a project for maintaining an Anglican school at public expense; and as late as the end of 1774, John Adams tells us, the radicals and conservatives in the Province were known respectively as the Presbyterian and Episcopalian parties.[9] When John Cam, the head of William and Mary College, tried to give impetus to an old scheme for the establishment of an Anglican bishopric in the Colonies, not only the Virginia dissenters, but a majority of Episcopalians as well, opposed the episcopate as likely to afford support for undesirable Crown measures.[10] This was despite the obvious arguments, from a religious standpoint, for resident bishops.

Two disputes over the maintenance of the Anglican clergy, in Virginia and Maryland, were particularly noteworthy in that they helped to bring to the front a pair of the ablest Revolutionary leaders, Patrick Henry and Charles Carroll of Carrollton. In Virginia the controversy, the famous "Parson's Cause," arose during the last French war, when the price of tobacco soared sharply. With it soared the salaries of the clergy, who were each paid eight tons of tobacco annually. Feeling that the ministers received too much, the legislature ordered them remunerated in cash at the rate of twopence a pound of tobacco, or much less than the market price. The ministers protested, the Crown vetoed the law, and several parsons began suing for the arrears of pay. In one case in Hanover County the parishioners retained as counsel young Patrick Henry, who, though an Anglican, had a Presbyterian mother, and sympathized with the poor and independent-spirited upland farmers. He made such an effective attack on the Established clergy, many of whom were too nearly worthless to deserve a salary at all, that the jury—swayed by popular feeling and the young lawyer's eloquence—gave the parson suing only a penny in damages.[11] In Maryland also the Anglican clergy were grossly overpaid. In 1767 the annual income in sixteen parishes exceeded £200 each, while in All Saints Parish of Frederick County it was £450, and increasing at the rate of £50 a year. We are told that the place-hunting minister who wrung this fat living out of the hardworking settlers had to carry a pistol into his pulpit. Members of the Baptist, Presbyterian, Catholic, and other churches naturally resented a law which compelled them to contribute so heavily to the

[9] John Adams, "Works," II, 345 ff.; Jones, "Hist. N. Y.," I, 12 ff.; Docs. Rel. Col. Hist. N. Y., VI, 913; Flick's "Loyalism in N. Y.," 18.
[10] Eckenrode, "The Revolution in Va.," 30 ff.
[11] Eckenrode, *Idem*, 12 ff.; Tyler's "Henry," ch. 4; Hening's Statutes, VI, 82 ff., 568 ff.

Episcopalian faith. The issue, however, did not become acute except as part of a larger controversy.

It happened in Maryland that the exorbitant and often wholly illegal fees levied for the payment of government officers had become very oppressive. Some officers, such as the judges of the land court, could become rich in a few years. The assembly wanted the fees reduced, and when the act of 1763, which regulated their amount, expired in 1770, it took a firm stand for revision, pointing out that the annual income from the greater offices had increased by more than one-half in twenty-three years, that charges were made where no service had been performed, and that for some services there was a double charge. Governor Robert Eden thereupon prorogued the legislature and fixed the amount of the fees by proclamation. His act was regarded as a gross usurpation, for in effect it was an arbitrary exercise of the power of levying taxes. To add to the discontent, the lapse of the fee law brought into force an old enactment for the payment of Anglican ministers, under which they became entitled not to thirty pounds of tobacco·per poll, as in recent years, but to forty pounds. The result was a popular uprising against both the Governor and the clergy.

The election of May, 1773, one of the most heated contests in Maryland history, turned upon this question of the fees. From the beginning of the year a vigorous debate was carried on in the *Maryland Gazette* of Annapolis, the most important newspaper. On the Governor's side "Antillon," later identified as Daniel Dulany, the Attorney-General and leading lawyer, stepped forward to defend the proclamation, and presented his case with argumentative skill. But he met more than his match in "The First Citizen," soon known to be Charles Carroll of Carrollton, a wealthy young Catholic who had enjoyed an excellent education in France and England. Carroll's letters continued till midsummer. Meanwhile, the legislative elections ended in a complete triumph for the anti-proclamation party, whose victory was jubilantly celebrated. In Annapolis the proclamation, carried in a coffin labelled "The Child of Folly and Oppression," was interred under the gallows; in Baltimore the proclamation was hanged in effigy and buried, while Carroll received votes of thanks from all over the Province. Governor Eden was able to stand firm and the fees remained in force. But the Assembly resolved that their collection was arbitrary, unconstitutional, and oppressive, while in a final *Gazette* article three of the leading patriots, Thomas Johnson, William Paca, and Samuel Chase, solemnly asserted that ultimate sovereignty lay in the freemen of Maryland, not in the Crown.

The ebullition of indignation which, as every schoolboy knows, occurred in Massachusetts when the British troops were quartered upon Boston, had been preceded by similar outbursts in other Colonies. In New York, during 1765 the British Government asked the legislature to provide quarters, firewood, bedding, provender, soap, and candles for as many British troops as might be stationed in the Colony. The Assembly declined, replying that the several counties made provision for the troops barracked within them, and that if any general supply were required for soldiery on the march, the legislature would consider the question of payment after the costs had been incurred. Under the insistence of the London authorities, the demand was twice repeated, and twice refused. Parliament finally forbade the New York legislature to pass any more laws until it had made provision for the troops, and for two years, 1767-69, legislation was suspended while the Assembly stood fast. At the end of that period a new election gave control of the Assembly to the moderate party, which acceded to the requirement.[12] Popular anger rose high when £2,000 was appropriated in September, 1769, for the troops, and it was intensified by the Assembly's prosecution of Alexander McDougall for libelling it. In the same year Governor Montagu asked the South Carolina house to supply fuel and other barrack necessities to the royal troops in Charleston, and met with a sharp rebuff. Here the dispute had a happier ending, for the forces were soon sent to Florida.

We have touched upon only some of the more typical disputes in individual Colonies. Many other causes of ill-feeling between the colonists and Crown, operative in single Provinces or groups of Provinces, but not in British America generally, might be enumerated. One lay in the appetite for land exhibited by some royal officers. We have mentioned the deep antagonism to the Proprietary's land policy manifested in Pennsylvania in the fifties. A different manifestation of this greed was presented in New Hampshire. Governor Benning Wentworth, a Harvard graduate and typical colonial aristocrat, granted himself more than 100,000 acres in the

[12] Roberts's "New York," II, ch. 22.

course of a long administration which closed in 1765. His tracts were scattered all over the Colony, so that no matter which section grew fastest, the old Crown Governor would be enriched. After his death his nephew and successor, John Wentworth, a handsome, shrewd, polished young man, was suspected of planning to lay hands on this property, which had gone to Benning Wentworth's widow. Nothing that we know of John Wentworth's character, save his desire to pose as a man of wealth in a luxurious manor house, justifies this suspicion; and the Crown authorities finally dismissed the charge. But the memory of Benning Wentworth's land-grabbing endured till the eve of the Revolution.[13]

Much might be said, also, of the perennial friction in the South, especially Virginia, between the planters and their British creditors, a friction which grew acute in years of poor crops and low prices. The hard-pressed planters tended to look upon the English merchants and factors as extortionate plunderers. Several Colonies, notably the Carolinas, felt acutely the British law of 1764 forbidding the issue of legal-tender paper money. In other Colonies a decided contribution was made to the Revolutionary spirit by the impatience with which various groups regarded the obstacles laid by the Crown in the path of westward expansion. These obstacles began with the royal proclamation of 1763, which converted most of the trans-Allegheny territory into an Indian reservation, in which further grants of land were forbidden. This was a temporary administrative measure, intended to control, not to prevent, emigration westward, but it angered men interested in the irresistible westward movement. The climax was reached in the Quebec Act of 1774, extending the boundaries of that Canadian Province southwest to the Ohio and Mississippi, thus transgressing the charter claims of many Colonies and again thwarting numerous schemes for land development.

The principal causes of the Revolution were of course the general causes, affecting the whole continent. Differences between the character of the American and British peoples, and between their political and social ideas, were of the utmost importance. There were radical defects in the entire plan of colonial administration. The economic factors were numerous. Historians still dispute the exact rôle played by the mercantile system, which, beginning with

[13] N. H. State Papers, XVIII, 616-624; Mayo's "John Wentworth," ch. 7. Complaints regarding the Governor's land policy continued till in 1773 the British government forbade grants without the King's express permission. Prov. Papers, VIII, 320.

the first Navigation Act under Cromwell, was embodied in more than a hundred Parliamentary statutes, designed to give effect to the principle that trade within the empire should benefit the citizens thereof, not foreigners. Some of the acts injured the colonists, some benefited them. But inevitable collisions grew out of the British effort, after the close of the last French war, to stop smuggling and establish an effective customs service—an effort tantamount to the reënactment of a series of navigation and tariff laws which had been allowed to fall into harmless desuetude. Colden wrote from New York in the fall of 1765 that "the merchants in this place think they have a right to every freedom of trade which the subjects of Great Britain enjoy." [14] Then came the attempt to collect new taxes, direct and indirect, from the colonists. Throughout America the effect of the Sugar Act of 1764, which placed a tariff on various commodities imported by the colonies, the Stamp Act, the subsequent Townshend duties, the stiffer customs collections, and the tea duty of 1773, was to unite the substantial merchant classes with the unpropertied radicals in opposition to the Crown.

We cannot deny the paramount importance of the general causes. We cannot forget that in the years 1773-75 the other Colonies, whatever their special complaints, more and more gave them a secondary place as they watched events in Massachusetts. Pennsylvania a decade before had been wrought to a high pitch of feeling by the "twenty-six aggrievances" which it used as an argument for the abolition of the proprietorship. But it was not these grievances which impelled John Dickinson, a successful lawyer trained in the London Inns of Court, to write his "Letters From a Farmer" attacking British policy—it was Townshend's tariff, and the opposition to this tariff came to a head most dramatically in Boston. The coercive enactments by which Parliament punished the Boston tea-party centred all eyes upon Massachusetts. Nevertheless, the special grievances of the several Colonies, as distinguished from their common grievances, may easily be underrated. Each Province entered the Revolution as an individual community, with its distinct hopes for change and reform as well as its share in the general American aspirations.

In the very multiplicity of the disputes between the British Government and the Colonies we see an evidence of the fact that funda-

---

[14] He added: "But the inhabitants of the country are absolutely free of the seditious spirit which rages in this town." Colden, "Letter-Books," II, 62.

mentally two ideas, two entire tendencies, were in conflict. The Crown administration, perceiving after the Seven Years' War that imperial polity was crude and rudimentary, and that the empire had no constitution worthy of the name to knit it together, thought that the remedy lay in a firmer central authority. The Colonies, awakening at the same time to their wealth, strength, and energy, felt a new self-reliance, and concluded that they ought to enjoy a greater freedom. The American idea of a colony was in the main the old Greek idea—a plantation which in due time should grow into almost complete independence; the British held rather to the Roman conception, that of a dependent part of a cohesive empire. Very little large statesmanship on either side was addressed to the problem of a proper imperial organization. It was not until too late that England's rulers were willing to listen to Chatham's proposal for a compact delimiting and guaranteeing the rights both of the Colonies and Parliament, a proposal the spirit of which, at least, was sound. In Great Britain statesmanship was confined to the opposition; in America circumstances forced it into nationalist, not imperial, channels.

II. Organization of Provincial Congresses

In all the non-autonomous Colonies except New York the beginnings of the Revolution were first discerned in a clash between the legislature and the royal officers; in New York the legislature was on the royal side. In a few Colonies, most notably Maryland and South Carolina, the upper chamber was loyalist, but in general the popular branch at least was thoroughly Whig. These Assemblies were effective instruments up to a certain point—well organized, experienced in struggles with the Crown, and able to maintain a tight grip on the treasury. Their limitations were that the Governor could usually dissolve or prorogue them when he liked, that he could sometimes manipulate a minority, subservient to himself and the Crown, for his own ends, that they could seldom keep any secrets from him, that they could not move with dispatch, and that they were hampered by a sense of their oaths and legal position. The early history of the Revolution is largely a spectacle of these half-fettered bodies struggling to effect what they could, until most of them were pushed out of the way by a new set of patriot agencies, openly defiant of the Crown.

In Virginia the fencing between the House and Governor entered upon a sharp phase at an earlier date than in the other important Provinces. In 1769 the Burgesses passed resolutions protesting against the taxation then just planned by the British Ministry, whereupon Lord Botetourt promptly dissolved them. Outwardly, the members accepted dissolution. In reality, they simply proceeded to a private house, chose as chairman Speaker Peyton Randolph, a rich planter, as cautious as he was patriotic, and agreed that public-spirited men would no longer buy imported slaves, wines, or British manufactures. Washington, who was a Burgess, moved the agreement, but its author was the scholarly planter of Gunston Hall, George Mason, who was not a member of the House. This agreement was broadened the following year into an "association." The principal political leaders, including Randolph, Washington, Jefferson, R. H. Lee, and Richard Bland, signed it, and the important merchants formed an organization at Williamsburg to enforce it. A committee of 125, including merchants as well as planters, was appointed to watch over both its observance and the general political situation.[15]

A similar flare-up occurred early in 1773. The Burgesses, sitting in February, received from Massachusetts a statement of colonial grievances, including the recent efforts to tax the colonies, the act of Parliament for sending certain classes of accused persons to England for trial, the movement to establish bishoprics in America, and the restraints upon manufactures. Thereupon, led by a radical group including Patrick Henry, Jefferson, and R. H. Lee, they appointed a committee of intercolonial correspondence, and wrote to the other Provinces asking for the establishment of similar bodies.[16] This was one of the most important of the early steps of the Revolution. It meant that the Continent would be knit closely together, while each Province would have a watchful junta at work between legislative sessions. The Governor, Lord Dunmore, dissolved the Assembly, but too late.

The final crisis commenced a year later. In May, 1774, the news of the Boston Port Act arrived, electrifying Virginia as it did all the other Colonies. The radicals, under Jefferson, Henry, and Lee, were again ready for action. These men, with four or five others, held a

[15] Eckenrode, "The Revolution in Va.," 29, 30.
[16] Journal, House of Burgesses, 1773-76, p. 12. For a defence of Virginia's title to this honor, see Va. Hist. Colls., n. s., I, 19. R. H. Lee was author of the proposal; Letters, I, 29. See also J. M. Leake, "The Va. Committee System," 60, 61.

conference in the Council chamber, where they had the benefit of a small library, and decided that to arouse the people to the emergency, a day of fasting and prayer should be proclaimed.[17] There had been no such solemnity since the Seven Years' War had opened in gloom. There is something incongruous in the spectacle of these sons of a Cavalier Colony, the Lees being members of one of the proudest Cavalier families, rummaging over the precedents of the Puritans under Cromwell. But they did so, and induced the Burgesses to appoint June 1 as a fast day. The expected result occurred. Lord Dunmore again dismissed them.[18] This time the Burgesses, 89 strong, marched down the long street to the Apollo Room of the Raleigh Tavern, for a generation the scene of balls, banquets, and political gatherings.[19] Putting Speaker Randolph in the chair, they not only drew up a new agreement for the non-importation of East India goods, but they took another important step in the leadership of the Colonies—they instructed their corresponding committee to propose an annual Continental Congress. The Connecticut Legislature had suggested the same measure three days earlier, but without communicating it directly to the other Colonies.

Thus far the Legislature had been able to serve the Colony well, despite the fact that Jefferson thought the older members not "up to the point of forwardness and zeal which the times required." But it was not in a position to meet when it wished, and even in these preliminary measures it had been hampered by a sense on the part of some members that they were acting illegally. At the Raleigh Tavern R. H. Lee had wished his companions to take additional steps, but "a distinction was set up between their then state and when they were a House of Burgesses," as he disgustedly wrote Samuel Adams.[20] However, the logical new move was now near at hand. Most of the Burgesses had just left town when on a quiet Sunday afternoon, May 29, a messenger from the north rode into Williamsburg with a packet of letters from Boston and other colonial capitals. Peyton Randolph at once sent out a call for all the members within reach, assembled twenty-five the next day, and took

[17] "The lead in the House on these subjects being no longer left to the old members," Jefferson explains; "Writings," Memorial Ed., I, 9.
[18] Dunmore had hitherto evinced a disposition to get on amicably with the House, and no quarrels had been serious. See P. S. Flippin, "Royal Govt. in Va.," 144; Journal, House of Burgesses, 1773-76, Introduction.
[19] "Memoirs of Elkanah Watson," 35, describe Williamsburg in 1777; a town of 320 houses, mostly wooden, on one street three quarters of a mile long, with the Capitol at one end and William and Mary College at another.
[20] Letters, I, 111 ff. See Schlesinger, "Colonial Merchants and the Amer. Rev.," 362 ff.

up the plea of the Bostonians for a stoppage of all trade with England. It was decided to convoke the members of the late House in Williamsburg on August 1, and with this decision the first Provincial Convention or revolutionary legislature was born.[21]

Massachusetts exhibits the same cycle of legislative insubordination and executive chastisement, ending in the creation of a wholly new body; but its several phases were more acute because Massachusetts was the storm-center of the continent. In the Bay Colony by 1770, both houses were firmly Whig, while both were supported by energetic local organizations—the alert town-meetings—for which Virginia had no real counterpart. On the other hand, the royal governor of Massachusetts was a man of much greater ability than the Scotch earl, Lord Dunmore, who sat in the Governor's Palace at Williamsburg. Thomas Hutchinson, who entered office in 1770, was a member of one of the best Boston families, a descendant of Anne Hutchinson, and a graduate of Harvard. He had shown high qualities as a legislator, helping to put the Colony's finances on a sound basis, and he had been for a time an impartial chief justice. Like Cadwallader Colden, he was a genuine scholar, as he showed in his history of Massachusetts Bay; and like Colden again, he was an ingrained conservative, who disliked all radical leaders and radical tendencies.[22] But despite his ability, activity, and public spirit, Hutchinson was quite overmatched as a political tactician by Samuel Adams and other Whig chieftains.

The most vigorous assertion of the popular liberties in Massachusetts came from the Boston town meeting. The year 1728 is a milestone in Massachusetts history because it witnessed the earliest such meeting to take a strong stand against the Governor. "The chief cause of the mobbish turn of a town inhabited by twenty thousand persons," wrote Governor William Shirley some years later, "is its constitution, by which the management of it is devolved on the populace, assembled in their town meetings." [23] The workmen had a self-assertiveness that was rude and turbulent, but healthy. In the sixties the gatherings of the citizens began to play a prominent

[21] See C. R. Lingley, "Transition in Va.," 48; Calendar Va. State Papers, VIII, 52. During the summer of 1774 the Whig leaders all over Virginia called county meetings at which committees were chosen to enforce the non-importation agreement. Washington presided June 18 over one in Fairfax County. All over the Province the voters also approved the plan for the attendance of their late Burgesses at the Williamsburg Convention on August 1.

[22] See James K. Hosmer, "Life of Thomas Hutchinson"; John Fiske, "Essays Historical and Literary"; M. C. Tyler, "Literary History of the American Revolution."

[23] Cf. the declaration of a Tory, "Sagittarius," that the town meeting was "the hotbed of sedition"; Frothingham, *Atlantic Monthly*, November, 1863.

part in stiffening the Assembly's stand against the Crown. When the enforcement of the Townshend Act was impending in October, 1768, the people voted in town meeting to dispense with many imported articles of British manufacture, and appointed committees to obtain signatures to the agreement.

Samuel Adams, though a poor man—he was an unsuccessful maltster—laid aside all personal business, and thenceforth devoted himself wholly to public affairs. Under his leadership, the town never looked back. When in September, 1769, a large consignment of goods arrived at Boston in charge of a factor, they were ordered to be locked up, and the keys given to a committee of patriots. If Boston had been governed by a mayor and council, the radicals would have found it much harder to throw into the revolutionary movement, but in the town-meetings the ship mechanics and shop-keepers could carry all before them. One day Adams might be presiding over a gathering at Faneuil Hall, and the next be in his seat in the General Court, so that the two bodies had in him a satisfactory link.[24] All over the Province towns little and big tended to catch the spirit of Boston.

Many acts of the Boston town-meeting were highly dramatic. We have a number of such grim stories as that of the Scotch merchant who, brought before 2,000 earnest men in Faneuil Hall, and stubbornly refusing to accede to the non-importation agreement, was panic-stricken when Samuel Adams rose and moved that the crowd resolve itself into a committee of the whole to call upon him and urge him to yield. Reverting to his native accent, the culprit hastily stammered, "Mr. Moderator, I agr-r-ree, I agr-r-ee." On the afternoon following the Boston Massacre (March 6, 1770), the town meeting was attended by every man who could leave his employment, while many citizens had flocked in from neighboring towns. When a committee which had called on Governor Hutchinson to demand the immediate removal of the troops returned to Old South Church to report, Samuel Adams whispered right and left to those densely crowded at the door: "Both regiments or none! Both regiments or none!" Hutchinson's reply, that he would send one regiment to the Castle in the harbor, but keep the other in the city, was no sooner read than the shout, "Both regiments or none!" filled the street, and to this demand the Governor had to yield.

[24] Hosmer's "Samuel Adams," ch. 10.

But the most significant action of the town meeting was not dramatic at all. It was so quiet that few could have thought of it in its true aspect—the raising of the curtain on the first act of the Revolution. During the summer of 1772 the House learned with alarm that the Crown had granted the Governor a permanent salary, and resolved that such a provision, independent of the grants of the General Court, was an infraction of the charter rights of the Colony.[25] Then came the news that the royal government had gone further and had offered the judges of the Superior Court independent salaries, to attach them to it rather than the legislature. A town meeting held on November 2 angrily took the step which "included the whole Revolution." At the instance of Samuel Adams, a committee of correspondence, with twenty-one members, was appointed to communicate with other towns upon the maintenance of "the rights of the colonists, and of this Province in particular."[26]

The significance of the corresponding committee in Boston was that it led at once to the organization of all the patriot forces of the commonwealth. It held its first meeting, with the brilliant but already partly insane James Otis as chairman, on November 3, 1772, and drew up the report upon British encroachments which we have already mentioned. This paper, sent in the closing days of the year to all Massachusetts towns, found a ready response from the marsh flats of Cape Cod to the hills of Berkshire. Almost every town formed its own corresponding committee, so that the Province, humming like a hive, was soon a closely-bound unit. The smaller communities naturally looked up to Boston. There were to be found the ablest men of the Colony—the Adamses, Otis, James Bowdoin, John Hancock, Josiah Quincy, and Thomas Cushing—to whom outlying leaders like James Warren of Plymouth and Joseph Hawley of Northampton deferred; there were the citizens boldest in opposing the Crown. By Samuel Adams's proposal the people had been brought into a well-marshalled array. In each town the local committees could educate the public in the principles of the radicals, enforce the trade agreement, and push forward defensive measures.

[25] Governor Hutchinson first gave definite announcement on June 13, 1772, that the King had provided for his full support. The House vigorously protested, declaring that it alone had a right to determine his salary. Hutchinson, waxing indignant, thereupon accused the legislators of trying "to alter the constitutional dependence of this Colony upon the Crown and upon the Supreme Legislative authority of Great Britain." His reply to the House, July 14, 1772, set forth the historical and constitutional arguments for the Crown's action. See his "History of Massachusetts Bay," III, 357 ff.

[26] For a study of all Revolutionary committees of correspondence see E. D. Collins's essay in Annual Report Amer. Hist. Assn., 1901, I, 243 ff.

John Adams wrote that the communities "have been wonderfully enlightened and animated. They are united in sentiment, and their opposition to unconstitutional measures of government is become systematical."

This work of organization, a Tory remarked a few years later, was "the source of the rebellion. I saw the small seed when it was implanted; it was as a grain of mustard. I have watched the plant until it has become a great tree." [27]

Meanwhile, the Provincial legislators had observed the action of the towns with sympathy. When news reached Boston early in 1773 that the Virginia Burgesses had proposed a system of inter-colonial communication through committees of correspondence, it was hailed with satisfaction. Here was an opportunity to do for all the Provinces what had been done for all the Massachusetts towns. The General Court accordingly established at its spring session a corresponding committee, with Cushing as chairman and Samuel Adams as the leading spirit. The Crown authorities were exceedingly hostile. They considered the step, Governor Hutchinson says, "a most glaring attempt to alter the constitution of the Colonies by assuming to one branch of the legislature the powers of the whole; by continuing, by delegation, the powers of government after the authority from which the delegation had derived had expired; and by uniting in one body a number of bodies which, by their constitutions, were intended to be kept separate and unconnected." That is, although they might not strongly have opposed a correspondence with other Colonies while the legislature sat, they objected to a permanent body carrying on communication between sessions, and exercising important powers. The house made a defiant reply to Hutchinson's objections, pointing out that American rights were constantly being attacked in the intervals when Assemblies stood prorogued or adjourned.[28]

During this session, the House also resorted to stern measures to try to keep the judiciary dependent on itself rather than on the Crown. The justices had accepted only half of the grants made them by the Assembly, from which it was inferred that they intended thereafter to take the newly-offered Crown salaries. The House resolved that any such action would convict them of hostility to the Constitution and friendship to tyranny, and it demanded of

[27] Massachusettensis, ed. 1819, 159 ff.
[28] Hutchinson's "History," III, 398-99.

them, under threat of impeachment, an immediate and explicit declaration of intention. Hutchinson thereupon carried out a previously announced determination of proroguing the House. Its demeanor and spirit, he tells us, had become far more defiant in the course of the preceding five years: [29]

> That which used to be called the "court house" or "town house" had acquired the name of the "state house"—"the house of representatives of Massachusetts Bay" had assumed the name of "his majesty's commons";—"the debates of the assembly" are styled "parliamentary debates";—"acts of Parliament," "acts of the British Parliament";—"the Province laws," "the laws of the land";—"the charter," a grant from royal grace or favour, is styled the "compact," and now "impeach" is used for "complain," and the "house of representatives" are made analogous to the "commons," and the "council" to the "lords," to decide in cases of high crimes and misdemeanours, and, upon the same reason, in cases of high treason. Another instance of the same nature was attempted in this session. The year of the King's reign, and the royal style, had always been prefixed to the laws of the Province in Latin, as they are to acts of Parliament; and in this style the royal authority over the whole dominion is expressed; but in all the bills prepared in the house this session, the prefix was altered from the old form in Latin, to these English words, "In the thirteenth year of King George the third."

The next session of the General Court, in January, 1774, naturally produced quarrel after quarrel with the Governor. It occurred just after the Tea-Party, which had caused much new excitement; it occurred also after Samuel Adams had published in the Boston *Gazette* a series of essays in which he went to extreme lengths, proposing that a Continental Congress be assembled, that it draw up a bill of rights, and that it send an ambassador to the British Court to act for the united Colonies.[30] Both the dispute over the committee of correspondence and that over the judges were renewed. Four of the magistrates, under popular pressure, refused the Crown's offer, but Chief Justice Peter Oliver took a different stand, declaring that he had sat upon the bench for seventeen years, that his salary had always been insufficient, and that now he intended to accept the King's bounty. The House at once undertook to make good its threat by impeaching him before the Governor and Council; and when Hutchinson tried to block this procedure by absenting

[29] *Idem*, III, 413. Hutchinson on Feb. 4, 1773, had confirmed the fears of the House by stating that a Crown order for the allowance of salaries to the judges of the Superior Court had actually been made. This news, as Hutchinson later wrote in his "History" (III, 387) was "resented with much warmth" by the legislators. The House at once expressed its hope that no judge who had a due regard for independent justice, or his own character, would choose to be placed under such an "undue bias" as acceptance of the Crown's money would imply. After some delay, Hutchinson replied defiantly. The House then passed a set of resolutions, while it and the Council together appealed, but in vain, to Lord Dartmouth for a recall of the warrants for the judges' pay. "Speeches of the Governors of Massachusetts," 365-67, 397-98.

[30] Adams waxed bold in these letters. Answering in October the question how the colonists should "force their oppressors to proper terms," he said that the only method had often been suggested: it was to "form an independent state," "an American commonwealth." Boston *Gazette*, September 27, October 11, 1773. Other radicals might have used such an expression to alarm the Crown agents; Adams used it sincerely.

himself from the Council meeting, the indomitable Samuel Adams, who was with the House committee, told Bowdoin, the presiding officer of the upper chamber, that the Governor was presumptively present, and entered the fact of the impeachment in the House journals. Before any further steps could be taken, the Governor prorogued the General Court by messenger.

Meanwhile, the news of the Tea-Party had reached England, and before the General Court met again in its regular May session the Ministry had brought into Parliament a series of enactments to punish the stiff-necked Americans. They were passed rapidly and by large majorities. The general view in Parliament was that of General Thomas Gage, soon to be military governor of Massachusetts—that the colonists would be "lyons, whilst we are lambs; but, if we take the resolute part, they will undoubtedly prove very meek." [31]   One bill closed the port of Boston, which Lord North said had been a place of riot and confusion for seven years. Another, much less censurable, allowed a transfer of the trials of any accused royal officials out of the Colonies in which they were accused. A third was the Quartering Act. But the most important was the bill to alter the Massachusetts Constitution, embodying a direct attack upon both the legislature and the sleepless town meetings which stood behind it. "At present, their Assembly," argued Lord George Germain, then as later doing all that folly could suggest to rive the Empire asunder, "is a downright clog upon all the proceedings of the Governor." [32]   Under the terms of the measure, the Crown, not the General Court, was thereafter to choose the Council or upper house, while town meetings were not to be held, except for the annual elections, without the Governor's consent. The passage of this law committed Parliament to the principle that the Constitution of the Colony was not a compact, unalterable except by consent of both parties, but a document which the British government could alter at will. Nine tenths of the people of Massachusetts would not admit such a principle for a moment.

The people were equally determined not to allow the upper house to be prostituted to the Crown. For long years it had once been a tool of the royal authorities, and at the time of the Stamp Act a very dangerous one. But since James Bowdoin, a patriotic merchant, had become its leader, it had acted as a valuable ally of the

[31] M. A. M. Marks, "England and America 1763-83," I, 308.
[32] *Idem*, I, 309. Ex-Governor Pownall made a warm protest against the bill.

representatives, and they meant it to remain so. When the list of new royal appointees, or mandamus Councilors, was sent out to Hutchinson, the people showed a passionate determination never to let them take office.[33] Actually, the Governor's authority had now declined to a point where it possessed no real effectiveness. "All legislative, as well as executive, power was gone, and the danger of revolt was daily increasing," wrote Hutchinson later of this period when the news of the punitive acts arrived.[34] "The inhabitants, in many parts of the Province, were learning the use of firearms, but not under the officers of the regiment to which they belonged. They were forming themselves into companies for military exercise, under officers of their own choosing." The real authority now lay in the local committees of correspondence and the town meetings. Exhausted by his trials, Hutchinson resigned as soon as a successor could be found; and on April 2 Thomas Gage, the commander-in-chief in America, was nominated to supersede him, while to emphasize the military character of the new administration, four regiments were ordered to Boston.

By a final dramatic stroke the legislature promptly showed the new Governor how unmanageable it was. On May 26, a fortnight after word of the final passage of the Port Act had kindled the people to unprecedented anger, the General Court convened in its usual spring session, only to be prorogued by Gage to meet at Salem early in June. When it reopened, the public anger was still intense and Samuel Adams and his radical co-workers were in full control. Both chambers adopted indignant addresses to the Governor. All the while the leaders were mindful of the preparations they must make for the Continental Congress proposed by Virginia. Adams watched his chance; he gathered his followers in hand; and on June 17 he had the doors of the House suddenly locked. Resolves were brought in appointing five delegates to the Congress. A Tory escaped on a pretext, and bore the news to Gage, who at once hurried the secretary of the Colony over to the House to dissolve it. He arrived panting for breath, but the patriots would not open the door. While he contented himself with reading the Governor's message to a few members and idlers gathered on the doorstep, the House imperturbably went on with its business. To pay the expense of the delegates, £500 was voted, and since no money could be taken from

---

[33] Hutchinson's "History," III, 156; 4 Amer. Archives, I, 741.
[34] Hutchinson's "History," III, 455.

the treasury without the Governor's consent, this sum was assessed upon the towns in proportion to their last tax list. Then the members went home.[35]

It was only a short step now to a revolutionary legislature and the complete paralysis of the old agencies of government. The news of the Port Bill and of the alteration of the Charter galvanized the town committees all over the Province into a rapid movement towards a more inclusive and energetic organization for defense. County and district units began to form. On May 12 the committees of Boston and eight neighboring towns met and drew up resolutions intended to inspire popular resistance. Far to the west, on July 6 sixty delegates from towns in Berkshire County convened at Stockbridge. On August 9, more than half a hundred delegates from a score of towns and districts in Worcester County met at a Worcester inn, and later that month another convention of 150 assembled there. At the same time an equal number of Middlesex County delegates gathered at Concord. In September a half-dozen other counties held meetings. From these bodies there came a series of resolutions attacking the punitive acts of Parliament and virtually declaring that they must not come into effect. The resolves of the Suffolk County convention were of special importance because they were subsequently endorsed by the Continental Congress. They summed up a plan of resistance, declaring bluntly that the Parliamentary acts should be disobeyed, the payment of taxes stopped, and the new judiciary disregarded.[36]

While this was going on, the events following Gage's dismissal of the General Court showed that the old government had utterly broken down. The Governor had a heavy pretorian guard of veterans of famous European battles at his command; six regiments lay at Boston, and one was camped at his residence in Salem. But they were useless, and in flat defiance of a proclamation which he issued, a town meeting gathered at Salem within the very sound of their drums. Popular threats caused the effort to organize a

[35] John Adams, "Works," I, 144-45.
[36] The proceedings of these bodies are in the "Journals of the Provincial Congress," 601-660. The first Worcester meeting adopted resolutions denying the jurisdiction of Parliament, attacking its measures, and called for a non-consumption agreement. The second Worcester gathering declared for the free convocation of town meetings and proposed that town taxes should be collected but withheld from the Provincial Treasury. It also recommended that fit persons be sent to a Provincial Convention "to resume our original mode of government . . . or some other which may appear to them best calculated to regain and secure our violated rights." The Middlesex delegates also asserted the free right to call town meetings and voted in favor of sending delegates to a Provincial Congress.

Council by royal appointment to fail, and even had it succeeded, the House would never have acted with that body. More threats forced the Lieutenant-Governor to resign; and Gage wrote despairingly to Lord Dartmouth that "we shall shortly be without law or civil power." [37] When on September 1 the Governor issued writs for the election of a House to meet at Salem on October 8, every leader saw that the meeting would lead to another quarrel and another dissolution.

Already a Provincial Convention had been suggested from several quarters, and the people now made use of the idea. It is the universal opinion, the Boston committee wrote to outlying communities, "that 'tis best to send as many representatives as the Charter and Province laws allow and then to instruct not to dissolve themselves, but to form a provincial congress there to consult and execute measures that concern the internal government of the Province." [38] When the towns elected the Assemblymen, with a uniformity that points to a few directing minds, they therefore empowered them, if a break with Gage occurred, to resolve themselves into an irregular legislature. A number of towns also chose delegates to act in the irregular body alone. While the Province thus trembled on the brink of complete governmental revolt, the perplexed Gage on the late date of September 28 withdrew his call for the General Court.

But his hope thus to delay the movement was in vain. The Continental Congress had met September 5, with the eyes of all Americans upon it, and a Provincial agency to coöperate with it was imperatively needed. On October 5, 1774, ninety representatives gathered at Salem just as if the Governor's call were still valid. They courteously awaited the appearance of Gage, and finally came to a temporary organization, with the rich merchant, John Hancock, whom Samuel Adams had brought into the radical camp some years before, as chairman. Two days later they adopted ominous resolves, treating the Governor with a new harshness. Recalling the explicit provisions of the charter safeguarding their legislative rights, they denounced his annulment of the writs of election as not merely insolent, but unconstitutional, inasmuch as his power to prorogue a General Court was not valid until the body actually met.

[37] Parliamentary History, XVIII, 96 ff.
[38] Cushing, "Transition from Provincial to Commonwealth Government in Massachusetts," 114. There had been a Provincial Congress of 96 towns and districts in 1768, when the British troops had been sent to Boston.

Then they voted to resolve themselves into a Provincial Congress, to determine on such measures as would promote the true interests of the King and Colony in this dangerous juncture.[39] By an orderly process, a body of both great legislative and executive powers had been created.

So it was in all parts of America. During the spring and summer of 1773 the atmosphere of the continent had been one of growing tension. Before midsummer five legislatures, those of New England and South Carolina, had replied with enthusiasm to the proposal of the Virginia Burgesses for uniting the Colonies by corresponding committees. In the autumn the news that the Tea Act was to be carried into effect transferred at one stroke the resentment of all Americans from local issues and fixed it upon the great imperial issue of taxation. Popular indignation was carried at a bound to a pitch higher than in Stamp Act times. "I have not known so sudden and so universal an appearance of discontent," wrote an observer in Philadelphia on October 25.[40] Angry mass-meetings were held in Boston, New York, Philadelphia, and Charleston, and the destruction of the tea in the first-named city was greeted with exultation by the Whigs throughout the country. During the fall and winter all the other Colonies save Pennsylvania chose corresponding committees, and at the same time similar bodies were organized in many towns. It was while this violent agitation was still unabated that in the spring of 1774 intelligence of the coercive measures directed against Massachusetts reached the Colonies, acting as a final precipitant of radical determination. The immediate results were the birth of the Continental Congress and the general emergence of revolutionary legislatures. The latter process has particular interest for us.

In New Hampshire repeated prorogations forced the popular leaders to exchange the regular Assembly for a revolutionary body several months before Massachusetts. The patriots here possessed a leader with some of Samuel Adams's boldness and alertness in their Speaker, who bore the same name as the Governor, John Wentworth. The Governor, always a man of energy and decision,[41]

[39] "Journals of the Provincial Congress," 6.
[40] Frothingham, "Rise of the Republic," 299.
[41] Governor John Wentworth had to play much the same rôle as Hutchinson. He was American-born and was graduated at Harvard with John Adams—when Adams was President of the United States, Wentworth was royal governor of Nova Scotia. He had a tact which made him popular in spite of his aristocratic tastes, genuine sagacity, and force of character. Though still a young man, he had caused the Province to be surveyed, had laid it out into five counties, which he named after as many

tried throughout 1773 to make a stand against the mounting Whig spirit, which found expression not only in the appointment of a Provincial committee of correspondence, but in vigorous town meetings. He was able to prevent a duplication of the Boston tea-party when a ship reached Portsmouth with the hated commodity,[42] but could do nothing with the Assembly. Accordingly he dismissed it in March, 1774, when it was about to discuss some letters from other Colonies, in the hope, as he wrote Lord Dartmouth, that a few weeks would bring it to a more moderate temper.

However, when a fresh Assembly met just a month later he found that it included new men of ability to fortify its radical temper— men like Meshech Weare, Josiah Bartlett, and his long-time enemy, Woodbury Langdon. The legislators again misbehaved so badly, in his view, that as soon as they had finished the urgent Provincial business he once more dismissed them. It was a futile act, for the popular leaders, now aroused by the news of Lord North's program in Parliament, repeated the procedure of the Virginia Burgesses. They agreed to meet in their usual chamber for an extra-legal session, and had gathered in their seats for business when the angry Governor, supported by the sheriff, arrived and ordered them to disperse. Admitting that they had no right to sit in a government building, they simply marched over to the leading inn of Portsmouth, ordered a good dinner, and over their roast beef decided to summon the towns to elect a Provincial Congress. Eighty-five members duly appeared at Exeter on July 21, only one Congress having met earlier—that of Maryland.[43]

The majority of the Colonies early in 1774 needed only an electric shock to fuse them into a patriotic whole, and that shock, the passage of the Boston Port Bill, ran from north to south in May and early June. The news reached Boston on May 10, New York on May 12. Paul Revere rode into Philadelphia with full details on May 19, carrying letters to Thomas Mifflin and Joseph Reed, the one a wealthy Quaker merchant, the other the foremost

English noblemen, had undertaken to provide better roads, and—with results unexpected by him—had improved the military strength of the Colony. He wished to please his own people, and counselled the Crown authorities to be moderate. When driven into exile, he wrote: "I will not complain, because it would be a poignant censure on a people I love and forgive." Mayo's "Wentworth," 157.

[42] On the day of the Boston tea-party, a Portsmouth mass-meeting sent resolutions to all the towns denouncing the British taxes and expounding the principles which the British government had transgressed. Prov. Papers, VII, 333-34; cf. Adams's "Annals of Portsmouth," 239-40.

[43] Prov. Papers, VII, 352-400 *passim*. Each town was asked to select "one or more persons" for the Provincial Congress. For its proceedings, see Prov. Papers, VII, 407 ff.

lawyer of the Province. All three hurried out to "Fairhill," the home of John Dickinson, a rich retired lawyer, though still in his forties, whom the Province counted its most distinguished citizen after Franklin. His "Letters From a Farmer," attacking the Townshend Act, had won him a continental reputation.

The city had already been aroused by the news, and other Whig leaders, such as Charles Thomson, a brilliant young scholar and missionary to the Indians, soon to be noted as the secretary to Congress, joined in taking appropriate steps. Two representative mass-meetings were held in Philadelphia, the second attended by 8,000 people; [44] a city committee of correspondence was created, keeping in close touch with county committees; and the counties were asked to send delegates to a Provincial conference on July 15 in the building now known as Independence Hall—the first step toward a regularly organized Provincial Congress. This body met on the date set, and proved to be a gathering of seventy-five members, representing all eleven counties, and able to speak with authority. It asserted the rights of America, pledged the coöperation of Pennsylvania with the other Colonies, and requested the Assembly to appoint delegates to a Continental Congress—which the Assembly did. Pennsylvania, because of its wealth and of the intrenched position of the peace-loving Quakers and loyalist Anglicans, was one of the most conservative of the Provinces, and it waited for Congress to act upon commercial non-intercourse.[45]

In Maryland the news of the Port Act burst like a thunderclap in an atmosphere already made sultry by the quarrel over the executive regulation of fees and the excitement arising from the Tea Act. Observers wrote that they heard "strange language every day," and that a popular majority seemed ripe "for any measure that will tend to the preservation of what they call their natural

[44] The first mass-meeting, held at the City Tavern, was addressed by Dickinson, Reed, and Charles Thomson, and Thomson spoke so impetuously that he fainted. See Scharf and Westcott, "Memorial Hist. Philadelphia," I, 289-90; Stille's "Dickinson," I, 107-8.

[45] Even if the Assembly could have been called at once, it would have been difficult to make it a revolutionary agency. Conservative by tradition, elected by conservative voters who had to be worth fifty pounds each, with the radical new counties of the west grossly under-represented, and responsive to the conservative lawyer, Joseph Galloway, its speaker, it was certain to hang back. The creation of the Philadelphia committee of correspondence was a step of almost as great significance for Pennsylvania as the appointment of the Boston committee had been for Massachusetts. The Whig leaders had for some time encouraged the formation of a system of county committees, and they now obtained a committee-in-chief. They hoped that as events wrought upon the public mind, the Provincial Conference or Convention would exert a growing influence, and, without jostling the Assembly out of place, lead the Colony forward. As Thomson said, the Province would move slowly but surely to maintain its rights. But the radical extremists did not want to wait for the Assembly. Thomson Papers, N. Y. Hist. Soc. Colls., 1878, 280-81.

liberty." Governor Sir Robert Eden was as helpless in the face of the situation as Wentworth was in New Hampshire. Personally he was well liked by the Marylanders. He was a man of moderate views and winning bonhomie, with just the touch of the aristocratic dignity required in a planter society; moreover, he was noted for his hospitality, and tradition states that Washington more than once rode over from Mount Vernon to dine and spend the evening with him.

Now he could be but little more than a passive spectator of the storm. Mass-meetings were held in Baltimore and Annapolis on May 25, to choose committees of correspondence. Annapolis declared for ending all trade with England, and for stopping intercourse with any Colony which did not coöperate to obtain a repeal of the Port Act. It was Baltimore, however, the rising trade center of the Province, which set in motion the machinery of revolutionary organization. At a second meeting, May 31, her people proposed a Continental agreement on trade, and called for a general congress of county deputies at Annapolis. Other counties immediately assented, and ninety-two delegates organized as the first Provincial Convention, under Matthew Tilghman, in the aristocratic little capital on the Severn, June 22, 1774.[46]

In the Carolinas the story of the revolutionary legislatures is particularly interesting. Governor Martin, after renewed quarrels with the North Carolina house over taxation and the court bill, had summarily dismissed it at the end of March, 1774, and let it be known that he would issue no call for a new body, though urgent business remained unperformed. At this John Harvey, the Speaker, flamed up with the assertion, "Then the people will convene themselves!" Early in April Harvey conferred with three Whig leaders, Willie Jones of Halifax, Samuel Johnston of Edenton, and Colonel Edward Buncombe of Tyrrel County. He was in "a very violent mood," Johnston reported, and declared that he was ready to issue handbills over his own name for an independent convention.[47]

The news from Boston kindled an indignation that gave Harvey and his associates their opportunity. The people of Cape Fear sent a shipload of provisions to the Bostonians. William Hooper, whose New England birth and Harvard training made him feel the

[46] See Scharf's "Maryland," II, 146, for the letter of a Baltimore committee to the Bostonians; see also J. A. Silver, "Provincial Government of Md., 1774-77," Johns Hopkins University Studies, Series 13, No. 10.
[47] N. C. Col. Recs., I, Introduction.

more strongly, but who was always a moderate leader, hostile to reckless measures, wrote that the Colonies were striding fast toward independence, and would ere long build an empire on the ruins of Great Britain.[48]   Most North Carolinians had so little sentimental regard for the British connection that nearly fifteen years earlier Governor Arthur Dobbs had spoken of "the rising spirit of independence stealing into this Colony."   During June there came news that one Province after another was choosing delegates to a Continental Congress.   Finally, Hooper, Richard Caswell, Harvey, and others made arrangements for calling a Provincial Convention in a more dignified manner than by handbills; this was by a circular letter sent out July 21 from a general meeting in Wilmington district, asking all the counties to send deputies.[49]   The body duly met on August 25 at New Bern, under the very eyes of the Governor.

In South Carolina we find a conservatism which closely resembled that of the lowland planters of Virginia, but was decidedly more intense.   The Province was governed by an aristocracy of planters and merchants which had felt strong social and intellectual bonds with Great Britain.   The Rutledges, Laurenses, Bees, Pinckneys, and Draytons looked to London much as did the wealthy county families of Norfolk, or cultured merchants of Bristol and Chester. They regarded England as "home"; they thought a season at the center of empire an incomparable diversion; they felt that their sons were not well educated until they had finished at an English university or the inns of court; and they had a fervent admiration for Chatham, Burke, Wilkes, and the other great English Whigs. England was their chief market for cotton and indigo, and from England they bought books, clothing, furniture, pictures, and the other elegances of life.[50]

Conjoined with this love of England was a settled aversion to disorder.   The Charleston leaders permitted nothing like the exploits of the Mohawks in Boston or the Sons of Liberty in New York. "It may be asserted with the greatest truth," one of them wrote after the Revolution, "that no kingly-ruled Province in America had less of mobbing in it, than this; though we had many disputes of great consequence with all our last British governors, yet not the

[48] E. W. Sikes, "Transition of N. C.," Johns Hopkins University Studies, Series XVI, Nos. 10, 11.
[49] N. C. Col. Recs. IX, 1016-18.   See also Schlesinger, *op. cit.,* 370.
[50] McCrady, *passim;* Wallace's "Laurens," chs. 2, 3, 14, 15; Ravenel's "Charleston," chs. 9, 11.

least symptom of mobbing appeared; not even when, to try their tempers and bring them to improper compliances, the Assembly was most haughtily and provokingly ordered to sit at Port Royal, and that too at the most unhealthy season of the year." As men of property, whose prosperity depended upon order, the planters and merchants resisted a complete revolution so long as they could do so consistently with their principles. When Christopher Gadsden later produced a copy of Paine's "Common Sense" in Charleston, most of his fellow-legislators were horror-stricken; and John Rutledge said that he would ride night and day to Philadelphia if thereby he could avert a final rupture with England.

The revolution in aristocratic South Carolina found its beginnings in city mass-meetings, just as in democratic Massachusetts it originated in the town meetings. The first one, called in the closing days of 1773 when the ship *London* arrived at Charleston with nearly three hundred chests of tea, showed the ability of the conservative leaders to control the situation and prevent violence. They kept the extremists in hand until the collector of the port seized the cargo for debt, stored it in safe vaults, and thus cut the Gordian knot. Several other meetings followed, until on January 20, 1774, the "general meeting" became an established institution. That is, a committee of substantial, cool-headed citizens was placed in charge, and soon after was empowered to call it at any time. The ruling order knew not only that it would be useful in safe Whig hands, but that it would be dangerous in the hands of the ignorant retailers, mechanics, and waterfront workers. New England travelers before the Revolution tell us that the laboring groups of Charleston, Philadelphia, and New York were inferior to those of Boston, and there is reason to believe the workmen of Charleston the most irresponsible of all. The established leaders, thus keeping the "general meeting" under control, called one at the City Tavern when news of the Port Bill arrived, and used it to take the next step in the Revolution—that is, to send out a call for a general Provincial gathering. This conference, for such it was, met July 6 in Charleston with 104 official members.[51]

One Province in which the organization of the new revolutionary

---

[51] It was attended by delegates from all but a few localities. For the early Revolutionary movement in South Carolina see, besides McCrady's, Drayton's, and Ramsay's histories, Wallace's "Arrival of the Tea and Origin of the Extra-Legal Organs of Revolution," Pubs. of Vanderbilt Southern Hist. Society, No. 4 (1900).

machinery followed a remarkably methodical course was New
Jersey; and, we may add, in which it was remarkably rapid, considering all the obstacles. These obstacles were varied. Governor
William Franklin, the wayward but able son whom Dr. Franklin
later disinherited, was liked by all classes and parties. The Province
had few commercial interests, and little share in the commercial
grievances of New York and Philadelphia. The people were
thoroughly provincial—"they are a very rustical people, and
deficient in learning," Governor Belcher had correctly written some
twenty years earlier—while in race and creed they lacked unity.
There were Dutch inhabitants sprinkled thickly through the beautiful region of hills and streams in the northeast, along the Hudson
and Kill van Kull; there were Palatinate Germans along the upper
Delaware; enterprising New England farmers had begun to migrate
to some fertile spots; there were a few French Huguenots and
Scotch, and of course many English. A majority of the Episcopalians were staunch Tories, while the Quakers whose prim meeting-
houses were found everywhere from Burlington down the Delaware
to its mouth manifested a conservative, peace-seeking spirit. However, the loyalists of the Colony were scattered, and therefore at a
disadvantage as compared with the loyalists of New York and
Philadelphia, whose strength was concentrated in the two cities
which were both capital and metropolis, and in the surrounding
countrysides. The patriotic leaders could not force the pace too
fast, but they did force it steadily.

The eastern section of New Jersey made New York city its
market and in politics and manners followed its guidance, while
the southwestern section, with its Quaker communities, was distinctly under Philadelphia's influence. Naturally, it is the former
that we find leading the revolutionary movement. The London
ship that brought word to New York of the passage of the Boston
Port Act aroused an outburst of indignation among the radicals
which had an immediate effect also across the Hudson. The first
committee of correspondence was appointed by a popular meeting
at Lower Freehold, a town near the future battlefield of Monmouth,
on June 6. A more important gathering, representing all Essex
County, which lies within sight of the towers of New York, was
held at Newark five days later, where it advanced the idea that
each county should choose a committee, and that county repre-

sentatives should meet in a Provincial conference at the earliest feasible date. The response was gratifying—Governor Franklin wrote to England in alarm that all the leading men approved the proposal. One after another, in June and July, the people of the various counties gathered at their courthouses, and took the desired action by appointing committeemen to attend. Thus the movement bore fruit in a Provincial conference that sat briefly at New Brunswick on July 21, 1774, only six days after the similar Pennsylvania meeting.[52]

That Essex County should furnish the leaders of the conference was another evidence of New York's influence. They were Stephen Crane, the chairman, William Livingston, soon to be Governor, and Isaac Ogden and Elias Boudinot, all living within a short ride of the Hudson ferry. All could have communicated constantly with New York radicals like John Morin Scott and George Clinton, while Livingston had long lived in New York, and was in touch with not only his influential family there, but with his son-in-law, John Jay.

In three other Colonies the crisis of May and June, 1774, saw the tiller of government seized firmly by the patriots without the necessity of establishing revolutionary legislatures; for in these three—Connecticut, Rhode Island, and Delaware—the Whigs were in full control of the ordinary mechanism of administration, and no royal official was able to interfere. Connecticut boasted in Jonathan Trumbull the only Colonial Governor who stood staunchly by the American cause. This sterling merchant-statesman, born in Connecticut and educated at Harvard, had served a half dozen years before the first bloodshed of the Revolution. He had been one of the leaders of the movement against the Stamp Act in Connecticut, and as a member of the Council had refused to witness Governor Fitch's acceptance of the prescribed oath that he would execute all the clauses of the hateful enactment. Under Governor Trumbull, the non-importation agreement of 1769-70 had been better observed than in some other northern Provinces.[53]

Connecticut was one of the first Colonies to appoint a committee of correspondence, and to see that the Tea Act raised anew the

[52] N. Y. *Journal*, June 30, 1774; N. J. Archives, Series I, vol. 29, 409-32. This gathering was called "the committee of 72"; L. Q. C. Elmer, "Const. and Govt. of N. J.," ch. 2. As Elmer says, it exercised no legislative powers. Governor Franklin's comments on its proceedings are given in Colls. N. J. Hist. Soc., V, 438 ff.
[53] Johnston's "Connecticut," 288.

whole question of imperial taxation. The spring of 1774 found her legislature passing resolutions declaratory of colonial rights, authorizing the dispatch of delegates to the Continental Congress, and taking the first steps to organize the militia for emergencies.[54] It found the towns resenting Lord North's attacks upon Boston and Massachusetts in the spirit of hardy little republics. They were condemning the Ministry in formal resolves, appointing local committees of safety, and buying arms and munitions. In Farmington the Port Bill was burnt with fitting ceremony; in Norwich a generous gift to Boston was collected, consisting of grain, money, and a flock of nearly 400 sheep; in Windham, emblems of mourning marked the day the Port Act became effective, and the same week a Boston Tory named Green, traveling there on business, was mobbed.

Such was public sentiment that in various Connecticut localities where Crown sympathizers were tarred and feathered it was impossible for the magistrates to enforce the laws against assault. The fall meeting of the General Assembly took the foremost place on the continent in the preparations it made for war. Militia officers were appointed where needed, men who absented themselves from muster were fined, and the towns were required to provide a double quantity of powder, balls, and flint. A general muster was ordered for the end of November, and during the winter drill went steadily on.[55] Connecticut was preparing to furnish far more than her share of the American forces.

Rhode Island's record during 1774 was equally good, for the popularly-elected Governor, the aged Joseph Wanton, as yet showed no lack of firmness. Early in the year the leading towns appointed committees of correspondence, and as soon as they heard of the passage of the Port Act, Providence and Newport instructed their Deputies to do their utmost to promote a Continental Congress. The House during the middle of June declared for a firm and inviolate union of all Colonies, in council and measures, and appointed two delegates to the Continental Congress. Aid was promised the people of Massachusetts, and the Providence Light Infantry was established. Other steps for arming the Colony followed that fall, companies of militia being authorized in a number of localities, and the same preliminary measures for defense taken

[54] Public Records of Conn., XIV, 264-75.
[55] The legislature sat October 13-November 4, 1774; Public Records, XIV, 325 ff.

as in Connecticut.[56]   These autonomous Provinces, being free
agents, and closely united by blood and sentiment with Massachusetts, had every reason to keep in the van of the revolutionary
movement, and they did so.   As for Delaware, it was of course not
autonomous.   But there was no Governor resident in the Colony,
which made the progress of the revolutionary movement much
easier; while the ability of the Proprietary to interfere with the
legislature was strictly limited—it had the right to meet on a certain
day annually, and could not be prorogued or dissolved.   When news
of the punitive British legislation of the spring of 1774 reached
Delaware, mass-meetings were held in all three counties.   The
people knew that Governor Penn would not call the Assembly before
the date to which it stood adjourned, so they simply requested
Cæsar Rodney, the speaker, to do so.   The legislature, or, if we
deny it that name, a convention of legislators, met at New Castle
on August 1.[57]

Thus far nothing has been said of two Provinces, New York and
Georgia, for the reason that both were laggards, and in neither did
the Whigs try to erect a revolutionary legislature or employ any
other adequate agency during 1774.   The tardiness of Georgia in
joining the Revolution was inevitable.   She was the youngest and
most nearly isolated of all the Provinces.   The population was only
about 17,000 whites, and all the militiamen of from 16 to 60 who
could be collected from St. Mary's on the coast up to Augusta
numbered only 2850.   Within the borders or along the frontier lay
powerful tribes of Creek, Choctaw, Cherokee, and Chickasaw
Indians, 10,000 of whom were warriors, and all of whom had been
attached to the Crown through the presents and influence of British
officers.

On the south was the well-garrisoned Province of Florida, from
which royal troops under Governor Tonyn, aided by loyalist volunteers, might be brought up to harry Georgia.   Naval raids would
be easy.   The prosperous colonists remembered with gratitude
England's generous bounties upon the culture of silk, indigo, and
other products, and the million dollars she had given in Parliamentary grants.   Governor Wright, who had served fifteen years,

[56] R. I. Col. Recs., VII, 280; Staples, "R. I. in the Cont. Congress," 10; Foster,
"Stephen Hopkins," II, 232; Field, "R. I. at the End of the Century," I, 225 ff.
[57] Scharf's "Delaware," I, 186-87, 215 ff.; W. T. Read, "Life and Corr. of George
Read," ch. I, II; Agnes Hunt, "Provincial Committees of Safety," 98; L. P. Powell,
"Historic Towns of the Middle States," chapter on Wilmington.

was liked and respected; for he had labored ceaselessly to undo the evil wrought by incapable trustees under the old Proprietary government, had won the amity of the Indians, and by negotiation had added millions of acres to the lands open to settlement. The metropolis, if we may so name the village of Savannah, was filled with placemen, and except in a few localities, Georgia had stronger bonds with England than with the sister colonies.[58]

There was no lack of radical agitators, or what Governor Wright called "liberty people," in Georgia. They found it easy to set up a standard, but a more difficult matter to obtain recruits. The news of the Port Bill aroused Archibald Bulloch, Noble Wimberley Jones, John Houstoun, and George Walton, four men of property and dignity who had taken part in certain bickerings between House and Governor. The result was a notice in the only journal, the Georgia *Gazette*, on July 20, 1774, denouncing the bill and summoning all patriots to attend at the liberty pole at Tondee's tavern in Savannah a week later. The first meeting was quite unsatisfactory because the outer parishes had received insufficient notice. A second gathering a fortnight later was more representative, but it failed to take the essential step of choosing delegates for the Continental Congress.[59] The most fervent center of Whig sentiment at this time was a seaboard community of Massachusetts folk called St. John's parish, below Savannah, and it was so bitterly disappointed that for a time it thought of sending its own representative to Philadelphia. Yet leaders like Bulloch and N. W. Jones are not to be blamed because Georgia alone was unrepresented there. As judicious observers, they knew that the people were as yet little shaken in their faith in the Crown, and would resent precipitate action. Governor Wright had much justification for informing Lord Dartmouth that the two Provincial meetings were not the voice of the people, but only that of a small and precipitate junto.[60] Indeed, the loyalists met in various localities to express their dissent from the resolutions passed under the liberty pole, and showed an impressive strength. Thus the year passed with nothing substantial achieved.

[58] Stevens's "Georgia," II, *passim;* Ga. Rev. Records, I, Introduction.
[59] Ga. Rev. Records, I, 11-17.
[60] Colls. Ga. Hist. Society, III, 180-81. But Wright remarked that as long as the agitators continued busy, "I apprehend there will be nothing but Cabals and Combinations and the peace of the Province and minds of the People continually heated, disturbed, and distracted." See Schlesinger, *op. cit.,* 379 ff.

New York, however, stood foremost in 1774 among the Provinces of which Ministers could think without a sinking heart. Nowhere else was the Tory party quite so militant and effective. The aristocratic element, powerful in the whole Hudson valley, headed the opposition to the radical patriots, and this opposition, though composed of many groups, was surprisingly cohesive. It included most of the great landowners, such as the Van Cortlandts, Crugers, De Peysters, Cuylers, Roger Morris, Frederick Philipse, the Jessups, and the De Lanceys, men with wide estates, retinues of slaves, and roomy manor houses; most of the rich merchants; a large proportion of the professional men; many prosperous farmers; and lovers of the good old order generally. Members of the Anglican church, the most extensive and opulent of the denominations, formed in the main a phalanx of loyalists, and the loyalists, led by James De Lancey, were long called the Episcopal party.[61] Those who depended upon the merchants or patroons for a living frequently shared their attachment to the Crown.

And as a whole, the royalists were as respectable for their character and convictions as for their numbers. New York as much as any Colony shows us that the Tory party was long unjustly besmirched in reputation. The great body that was ably and honestly captained by Hutchinson and Oliver of Massachusetts, Galloway and Chew of Pennsylvania, De Lancey and Jones of New York, was not a body of time-serving cowards. Not only were many Tories men of the highest principle and courage, but they were swayed by a logic that Americans frequently honor. They held that if the colonists would dismiss needless anxieties, give over provocative measures, push aside all selfish agitators, and appeal to the British to do the same, then the genius of the race for compromise would assert itself, British statesmen would cease to insist upon legalistic claims, and the development of the Empire would proceed to a glorious future.

The population of the Province in 1771, the year Tryon arrived as Governor, was 168,007, of whom some 150,000 were whites. New York city, still a perceptibly smaller seaport than Boston, had 21,863 people. With three newspapers, a few fine shops and residences, and King's College to diffuse a classical tone, it was the only town of size or social gaiety in the Province. Albany, the

---

[61] Jones, "Hist. N. Y. During the Rev. War," I, 2 ff.

seat of the fur trade and Indian traffic, had about 3,000 inhabitants, and Kingston was a straggling hamlet of fewer than two hundred houses. Little more than the southeastern part of the Province could be called settled—that is, Long Island, the districts on both sides of the Hudson, and small areas along the eastern part of the Mohawk. The most populous county on the east bank of the Hudson above New York city was Dutchess (22,404 people), with many settlers from across the Connecticut line; the most populous county on the west bank was Ulster (14,000 people), almost directly opposite. Albany County, including the vast territory north and west of the town of that name, had more inhabitants than both combined.[62]

Plausible evidence has been adduced for the assertion that more than half the people of the Colony, when the time came to cast the die, were either open Tories or too conservative to assist the patriot cause. The radical Whigs were represented everywhere, and were very powerful in Ulster County, eastern Long Island, and some other rural districts; but their stronghold was the poorer wards of the metropolis. Here the mechanics and artisans, who had many of the crude, turbulent, and, to the aristocratic party, offensive ways of the Boston harbor-workers, formed a compact mass of patriots.[63]

Tryon, landing during a hot July week, and greeted by parading soldiers and applauding townsfolk, by merchants offering their congratulations and citizens joining with the King's officers in drinking his health, took particular pleasure in one fact. He had learned in North Carolina what it was to have a legislature hostile to him, and he was delighted to be welcomed by a friendly Assembly as well as Council. The character of the lower house had been decisively changed by an election two years earlier. The Whig or Presbyterian party had gone down in defeat, all its prominent members save Philip Livingston, George Clinton, Nathaniel Wood-hull, the patriot general later killed near the outset of the war, and Philip Schuyler, losing their seats. The victorious Tory party had made immediate use of its victory to choose John Cruger, of New York city, speaker.[64] Twenty-seven members sat in the

---

[62] Roberts's "New York," I, ch. 21; Winterbotham's "View of the United States," II, 297 ff.
[63] Flick, "Loyalism in N. Y.," *passim.*
[64] For this disastrous election of 1769 see G. W. Schuyler, "Colonial N. Y.," II, 262. For the sectarian controversy over King's College that made the terms Episcopalian and Presbyterian party labels, see Jones, "Hist. N. Y.," I, 12-17; Docs. Rel. Col. Hist. N. Y., VI, 913; and histories of Columbia University.

Assembly when Tryon opened it, four for the city and county of New York, two each for the other nine counties, and one each for the borough of Westchester, the town of Schenectady, and the three great manors, Livingston, Cortlandt, and Rensselaerwyck. The Tories counted the entire city delegation, consisting of Cruger, James De Lancey, Jacob Walton—all three of rich landholding families—and James Jauncey, as well as a majority of the remaining representatives. In 1772 the Assembly was swelled by members from two new counties, and the newcomers were Tory also. Inasmuch as its conduct was perfectly satisfactory to the Crown, this legislature was never dissolved, and held its place from the spring of 1769 until it was overthrown in the Revolution.

From the names of George Clinton and Philip Schuyler it must not be inferred that all the advantages of brains and energy were on the side of the Whigs. John Cruger and James De Lancey were Tory leaders of education and skill, and their followers included some able men. Nor is it to be thought that loyalists like Cruger and Pierre Van Cortlandt did not resent the arbitrary acts of Parliament and desire a reform. They differed from the Whigs not so much in the goal they sought as in the method by which they proposed to gain it. The tact with which they acted made it possible for thousands of moderate patriots to stand by them. As for the Council, it was staunchly loyalist. It had just one bold Whig member, William Smith, jr., and his boldness declined till he also took the King's side.

At first the two chief sources of agitation were the Tea Act and the presence of British troops in New York city. Non-importation was the natural weapon of the people against the hated excise laws, but the strength of the moderates prevented a thorough use of it. Two parties arose in 1772, after the British duties had been removed from everything but tea. The radicals wished to continue a sweeping non-importation policy; the merchants were willing to exclude tea alone. The latter canvassed the city, found about 3000 out of 4150 men on their side, and carried their point.[65] As for the troops, wise old Cadwallader Colden had reported to the British government early in 1770 that a violent faction was trying to arouse the passions of the town against the infantry, and to provoke riots, but that

[65] Colden, "Letter-Books" (N. Y. Hist. Soc. Colls., 1876-77), II, 221-24; Docs. Rel. Col. Hist. N. Y., VIII, 218-220. Colden wrote July 7 that the canvass showed 1180 for importation, about 300 neutral or silent, and few men of any prominence opposed. Flick, "Loyalism," 21, gives the above figures.

the responsible population was unmoved. The townspeople, on the other hand, complained of provocation by the soldiery. The most important clash was the so-called Battle of Golden Hill, fought this year amid the January drifts of John Street. "An ill-humor had been artfully worked up between the townspeople and soldiers," Colden wrote, "which produced several affrays, and daily, by means of wicked incendiaries, became more serious. At last some towns-people began to arm, and the soldiers rushed from their barracks to support their fellow-soldiers." [66]   In this encounter the troops did not fire, the civilians used clubs alone, and only one man was slain. But the important fact was that the more belligerent part of the people and the infantry had for the first time faced each other in arms.

The acts by which the Assembly showed its hostility to all who wished to push New York along the radical road taken by Massachusetts and Virginia were emphatic. It met each January in 1773, 1774, and 1775, and its sessions always lasted between two and three months. In the first year the question whether a further money grant should be made for the accommodation of the British troops was carried in the affirmative by a close margin. Next year a committee of correspondence had to be chosen, but it was so constituted that it was safely loyalist in character, Cruger being its chairman. A supply was granted His Majesty's troops by the decisive vote of 18 to 2,[67] and £5000 was appropriated to Governor Tryon in compensation for the burning of his house by incendiaries, 14 to 11. George Clinton, it may be noted, showed his fairness by standing with those who wished the Governor reimbursed. At both sessions the Assembly steadfastly refused to protest against the Parliamentary enactments. It was prorogued too early in 1774 to discuss the Boston Port Bill or the proposal for a Continental Congress, but it would have been little stirred by either. It was firmly on the Crown's side.

Yet among the general populace the Port Act aroused the same excitement that was felt in other Colonies; and the best measure of the strength of the moderates and Tories is the ease with which they brought this excitement under control. Nearly every tongue denounced the Act. But when a public meeting was called for

[66] Colden, "Letter-Books," II, 210-12; Feb. 21, 1770.
[67] Votes and Proceedings of the Gen. Assembly, 1774, p. 43 (February 8).

May 16, 1774, at the Exchange, the cautious element in the city resolved to obtain the upper hand. "The loyalists made a point of attending," says one Tory writer. Colden wrote to England:[68]

The men who at that time called themselves the committee who dictated and acted in the name of the people, were many of them of the lower rank, and all the warmest zealots of those called the Sons of Liberty. The more considerable merchants or citizens seldom or never appeared among them; but I believe were not displeased with the clamor and opposition that was shewn against internal taxation by Parliament. The principal inhabitants being now afraid that these hotheaded men might run the city into dangerous measures, appeared in a considerable body at the first meeting of the people, after the Boston Act was received here. They dissolved the former committee, and appointed a new one of fifty-one persons, in which care was taken to have a number of the most prudent and considerate persons of the place. Some of them have not before joined in the public proceedings of the opposition, and were induced to appear in what they are sensible is an illegal character, from a consideration that if they did not, the business would be left in the same rash hands as before.

There were actually two public meetings, the first at which a committee of fifty was nominated, and the second at which the public approved it and added a fifty-first member.[69] An overwhelming majority of the committee was composed of conservatives, and the chairman, Isaac Low, a rich and able but opinionated and conceited merchant, was a moderate. No fewer than twenty-one of the members later adhered to the British side. The Tories and moderates rejoiced openly. Thus Rivington, the Tory editor, whose weekly *Gazeteer* was the leading loyalist organ in America, circulating in every Colony and having 3600 subscribers, wrote Henry Knox that it was now absolutely certain that neither non-importation nor non-exportation would be approved in New York or Philadelphia. The influence over the general public once wielded by the various "demagogues of a very turbulent faction in this city," he said, had "expired instantly upon the election" of the new committee, which was made up chiefly of "inflexibly honest, prudent, and loyal citizens." Colden thought the same.[70] The Tories and moderate Whigs had seized the helm in New York in just the same way that the moderate Whigs had done in Charleston.

The radicals of New York were unfortunate not only in being numerically weak, but in having at first no great leaders like John Adams or Patrick Henry. Their resentment at being set aside was immediate. Four members of the Committee of Fifty-one were deputed to draft an answer to Boston's request for a renewal of

[68] Colden, "Letter-Books," II, 339-41.
[69] 4 Amer. Archives, I, 293 ff.
[70] *Idem*, I, 293-302; Jones, "Hist. N. Y.," I, 438 ff., 467; Colden, "Letter-Books," II, 342. Schlesinger, *op. cit.*, 329.

the non-importation agreement—Chairman Low, John Jay, James Duane, and Alexander McDougall. Jay and Duane, two leading barristers, were then regarded as safe conservatives. McDougall was a young radical, the son of a poor Scotch milkman, who four years previously had published violent attacks on the Assembly for voting a supply to the British military forces, had been clapped into jail, and had become a popular idol, fêted and praised as a second John Wilkes.[71] The answer to the Boston communication, probably written by Jay, approved of a Continental Congress, but refused the request as to non-importation, declaring that so important a question should be left to Congress for a decision. When the Committee of Fifty-one approved this paper, the anger of the radicals instantly flared up. It was a piece of selfish cowardice, dictated by the mercantile interests, they said. They held a meeting, decided that the Boston plan of stopping imports should and could be enforced, and set to work to give it effect by using the machinery of threats and spying which had been employed for the same purpose at the time of the Stamp Act. The merchants, thus beset, took a protest to the Committee of Fifty-one, and the latter body flew to their rescue, denouncing the action of the hotheads. Simultaneously the radicals demanded that their Committee of Mechanics share in the naming of delegates to Congress.

Who were the principal hotheads? As Colden says, they were the leaders of the Sons of Liberty. This organization had first been formed in the thirties, when the printer Zenger had been tried for seditious libel in assailing the colonial governor and council, the founders being a triumvirate of brilliant young Yale men: John Morin Scott, William Smith, and William Livingston, lawyers all. It was revived during the Stamp Act agitation, lapsed again —though the three were consistently active with their pens in behalf of a larger colonial autonomy—and was reorganized on November 29, 1773. This time its leaders were McDougall, Isaac Sears, John Lamb, and Marinus Willett. They were all substantial men in the little city. McDougall had become an affluent merchant. Sears, who was the oldest and a Yankee by birth, was a prosperous participant in the coastwise trade; his influence over the common folk gave him the nickname of "King Sears." Lamb, the son of

[71] For the famous trial of McDougall for his libel against the Assembly, see Jones, I, 29-33; Colden, "Letter-Books," II, 211 ff.; Docs. Rel. Hist. N. Y., VIII, 213 ff.

an English optician, had amassed a considerable property in liquor importing.[72] It is significant that three of the extremist chieftains in New York should have been of the mercantile group chiefly injured by British taxes and restrictions.[73] Marinus Willett, the youngest, was in his early thirties.

All four were men of great boldness and energy. In the French and Indian War Sears had commanded a privateer, McDougall with a little six-gun sloop had taken valuable West Indian prizes, and Willett had been with Abercrombie at Ticonderoga. All had been active in opposing the Stamp Act.

McDougall caught John Adams's fancy as the latter passed through New York to the first Congress. "He is a very sensible man and an open one," Adams's diary runs. "He has none of the mean cunning which disgraces so many of my countrymen." Washington called him a brave soldier and a disinterested pariot.[74] His imprisonment in 1770 had been an ovation rather than an ordeal. Ladies and gentlemen flocked to breakfast and dine with him, he was overwhelmed with gifts of wine and food, and he was obliged to publish a card fixing his hours for public receptions. Of Sears we have an amusing commendation from General Charles Lee. "He is a creature of much spirit and public virtue, and ought to have his back clapped," wrote Lee in 1776. But the most striking personality was the wealthy Lamb, a man at once shrewd, generous, irascible, and stubborn-willed. He commanded the party which early in 1775 seized the British stores at Turtle Bay on the East River, and the squad which fired the first shots of the war in New York, killing and wounding sailors of the British warship *Asia*. No patriot leader was more insistent upon his own dignity. When he marched under Montgomery against Quebec, as a captain of artillery, Montgomery found him insubordinate but invaluable. He was a man of bad temper, turbulent and troublesome, reported Montgomery, but one who could simply not be spared.

In the second and more cautious rank of the radicals appeared men of greater abilities. John Morin Scott engaged in the plans of the republicans, the Tory historian Jones tells us, with all the

---

[72] Leake, "Life of Lamb," 9, 10. The first seven chapters of this valuable work cover the period till the overthrow of the royal government; the remaining eighteen deal with Lamb's Revolutionary and wrongheaded post-Revolutionary career.

[73] "The merchants in this place think they have a right to every freedom of trade which the subjects of Great Britain enjoy. But the inhabitants of the country are absolutely free of the seditious spirit which rages in this town." Colden, II, 62.

[74] John Adams, "Works," II, 345; Washington, "Works," Sparks Ed., IX, 186.

violence and acrimony of a madman,[75] but this is an exaggeration.
He was a man of principle, a strong Whig from youth, frank and
open in his manners, convivial in his habits, and possessed of a
wide circle of acquaintances. A leading lawyer of the Province,
he had made a small fortune at the bar. At his seat three miles
out of town on the Hudson he dispensed a generous hospitality.
"A more elegant breakfast I never saw," wrote one plain Yankee
visitor; "rich plate, a very large silver coffee pot, a very large silver
teapot, napkins of the very finest materials, toast, and bread, and
butter, in great perfection. After breakfast a plate of beautiful
peaches, another of pears, and another of plums, and a muskmelon,
were placed on the table."[76] Peter Livingston, a retired merchant,
called "Jew Peter" for his avarice, had the same firm but not
intemperate zeal as Scott. Philip Livingston, a rough, blustering
man, was also a staunch Whig, his ardor tempered by an inordinate
prejudice, fairly common in the Middle Colonies, against all New
Englanders. This second rank of the radicals was steadily recruited
from the list of conservative Whigs. It was not long before Jay,
with the best brain of all, and Duane, who owned a hundred thousand acres in the north, were ready to join it.

When Lamb and his fellow agitators found themselves denounced
by the Fifty-one, they took the bit between their teeth. By an
unsigned press advertisement, they called a meeting for the hour
after work on the evening of July 6, in "the Fields" or common,
an open grassy space now directly overlooked by the Woolworth
Tower. The crowd, enthusiastic and determined, was presided over
by McDougall, and addressed by extremists, with one new orator
of note—Alexander Hamilton, seventeen years old, a student at the
royalist King's College. As the fine summer evening closed, resolutions were adopted denouncing the Port Act, promising help to
Boston (coins and bills were there dropped into a hat), and above
all, declaring for non-importation. The temper of the gathering
was bitterly hostile to the Fifty-one, and the Fifty-one responded
with dignified anger. In a meeting the next day, they declared a
firm enmity to any extremist program against the British Government. The result was a split in the Fifty-one. Eleven members
affiliated with the Committee of Mechanics, including McDougall,

[75] Jones, "Hist. N. Y., I, 4 ff.
[76] John Adams, "Works," II, 349.

Sears, and Peter Livingston, withdrew and published an appeal to the people.

A Continental Congress had now become a certainty, and the Committee of Fifty-one assumed the right to superintend the sending of delegates from the metropolitan district.[77] It nominated Philip Livingston, Jay, Duane, Low, and John Alsop, the last-named another wealthy merchant, known to love both bishops and kings— a thoroughly conservative ticket, with Livingston's name as a sugar-coating for the radicals. This ticket was submitted to all male freemen of the city on July 19, 1774, the mayor and aldermen supervising the counting of the votes. A stormy debate occurred, and the extremists, who were out in force, tried unsuccessfully to substitute McDougall's name for that of Jay.[78] They did succeed, however, in defeating resolutions which the Committee of Fifty-one simultaneously proposed, again affirming that non-importation should be left for Congress to decree or reject. A week of confusion ensued. Jay and two of his colleagues refused to accept their election on the ground that the meeting had not been representative and that they approved of the rejected resolutions; and simultaneously the Committee of Mechanics demanded that the workmen be given a fuller voice in affairs. A new election by wards had to be held. The old ticket was again successful, emphasizing the fact that the so-called Patricians, not the Tribunes, were in control. Jay and Duane did yeoman service that fall in Philadelphia, alongside Galloway of Pennsylvania and other conservatives, in restraining the radical delegates of the first Congress and laboring for reconciliation.

The farmers and villagers of most rural sections had watched the actions of the radicals in the city unresponsively. "The present political zeal and frenzy is almost entirely confined to the city of New York," wrote Colden in July. In October he added that a great deal of pains had been taken to persuade other counties to send delegates to Congress, or adopt those sent by the city, but that several had refused to be concerned in the measure. This was true. Ulster, Westchester, Dutchess, and Albany asked the city delegates to act for them, Kings, Suffolk, and Orange chose their own delegates, and the other counties ignored the invitation. In

[77] But only after considerable delay; Colden, "Letter-Books," II, 346.
[78] 4 Amer. Archives, I, 320-21; Jones, "Hist. N. Y.," I, 464; Flick, "Loyalism," 23. New York City alone took a keen interest in this election; most of the rural districts were indifferent or hostile.

the counties immediately surrounding New York city the loyalists were especially strong and active.[79] Just a month after Congress opened, Colden reported an incident which dramatically proved the continued loyalty of the city itself. Certain New York merchants had received contracts for articles needed by the British troops in Boston. The radicals called a meeting, attended by few but the poorer classes, and warned the merchants to desist; whereupon the Committee of Fifty-one summoned a larger gathering, which silenced the turbulent minority and authorized the filling of the contracts.[80]

Yet as the fall of 1774 passed the situation began gradually to change. As the crisis in Massachusetts waxed, and as one Province after another shook off the old governmental vestures and put on new garments, many New Yorkers began to awaken from their apathy and many more to lose their conservatism. Fragmentary reports came from Philadelphia of the proceedings of Congress and of the speeches of its ablest members, acquainting them for the first time with the determined temper of other Colonies. Even men like the rich and snobbish Gouverneur Morris, who had been filled that spring with a horrified apprehension of mob rule, began to catch a perception that the convictions which the untutored city populace shared with such leaders as John Adams, Benjamin Franklin, and George Washington, might be essentially sound after all.

One reflection of this change is to be seen in the flock of alarmed pamphlets and addresses which came flying thick from New York presses. Dr. Cooper of King's College, Samuel Seabury, later the first Episcopal bishop in America, Isaac Wilkins, one of the Tory Assemblymen, and other alarmed loyalists, in these publications attacked the Continental Congress with vehemence, while Rivington's *Gazetteer* spoke out as hotly for the Tories as John Holt's *Journal* did for the patriots. Many loyalists had hoped that Congress would prove to be for all British America what the Committee of Fifty-one had been for the Province of New York, where the violent radicals were driven from the field. Instead, they had seen an association for non-importation drawn up; Galloway's plan for a British-American legislature to solve the problem of colonial

[79] See, e.g., Onderdonk's "History of Queens County" for the hostility of the Queens loyalists.
[80] Colden, "Letter-Books," II, 367-68.

government totally suppressed; and cautious New Yorkers like Duane and Alsop overruled by zealots like Samuel Adams and R. H. Lee. The radicals in New York took courage from the bold stand of Congress and the bustle of revolutionary activity all over the continent. Many of the Provinces were now beginning to arm and drill.

The recommendation by Congress of a non-importation agreement made necessary the creation of a patriot machinery to enforce it, and was accompanied by the request that county and town committees be chosen to carry it out. The New York radicals, who rightly regarded this recommendation as a heavy moral victory, took prompt action to force the choice of an energetic body. Lieutenant-Governor Colden still tried to take a hopeful view of the situation. Writing to London on November 2, he declared that the measures of Congress had elicited more dissatisfaction than applause in the Province, and that a great majority of the people, far from approving the dangerous and extravagant measures of New England, desired nothing so much as to put an end to the unhappy dispute with the mother country.[81] Nevertheless, when the new committee of observation, called the Committee of Sixty, was elected, he could not prevent a note of keen anxiety from creeping into his dispatches: [82]

> The first thing done by the people of this place in consequence of the resolutions of the Congress, was the dissolution of the Committee of 51, in order to choose a new Committee of Inspection, to carry the measures of the Congress into effect. A day was appointed by advertisement for choosing 60 persons to form this new committee. About 30 or 40 citizens only appeared at the election, and chose the 60 who had been previously named by the former committee. I can no otherwise my lord account for the very small number of people who appeared on this occasion, than by supposing that the measures of the Congress are generally disrelished. . . . The non-importation association affects the smugglers as well as the fair traders. . . .
> In the present committee of this place there are several gentlemen of property, and who are esteemed to favor moderate and conciliatory measures.. . . . I have at length discovered that they act with a view to protect the city from the ravages of a mob. For this purpose they say that they are obliged at present to support the measures of the Congress—that if they did not, the most dangerous men among us would take the lead, and under pretence of executing the dictates of the Congress, would immediately throw the city into the most perilous situation. . . . I fear, my lord, there is too much truth in this representation. It is a dreadful situation.

A dreadful situation!—so it seemed to any Tory with courage to look it in the face. The new committee, though also headed by Isaac Low, contained more radicals and fewer conservatives than the old Committee of Fifty-one. Moreover, the Committee of

---

[81] Colden, "Letter-Books," II, 369-70.
[82] *Idem,* 372-73.

Mechanics coöperated heartily in enforcing the non-importation agreement, and did it with a roughness which frightened the propertied loyalists into silence. Brilliant young men like Jay and Gouverneur Morris, with some of the merchants, were moving farther to the left. The King's appointees and the aristocratic Tory element, recently so confident, felt the ground trembling beneath their feet.

Thus it was that the momentous year 1774 closed, in England and America, amid uncertainty and gloom. The King and Parliament had loosed their bolt against the colonists in the punitive acts, all passed before the end of June. The colonists had replied by two great achievements, the establishment of a Continental Congress, and the erection in every Province save two of nascent agencies of government wholly in the hands of the progressive patriots. The rapidity with which these new agencies had come into being, and with which the royal authority had dropped like a palsied arm, was ominous. Three months had not elapsed from the receipt of the Port Act before seven Colonies—New Hampshire, New Jersey, Pennsylvania, Delaware, Maryland, Virginia, and South Carolina—had brought together congresses, conventions, or conferences representing the whole commonwealth. North Carolina and Massachusetts had soon followed.

These bodies plainly contained the embryo of a complete revolutionary government for every colony. American administration, as the blindest might see, was beginning to slip wholly and perhaps irretrievably into the hands of the American people. As yet the transference was but tentative. The great majority of the inhabitants hoped that it would be arrested by a compromise, and that the old royal agencies, though modified in form, would be restored. But the current of events was already carrying the colonists out of sight of the old landmarks, the stream was hurrying them on, and some believed they already heard in the distance the roar of that ocean called independence.

III. Work of the Provincial Congresses

As the creations of haste and anxiety, most of the early Provincial Congresses were crudely constituted. They were chosen in the most convenient way, and with no attempt to conform to a careful plan of representative government. In even the second New Jersey Congress, for example, we find the county delegations varying egregiously in size, Hunterdon sending fifteen men and Cape May only one. To the first Maryland Congress some counties dispatched a few delegates, others a small troop. If the radical farmers of a North Carolina county thought it cheapest and most convenient to content themselves with a single representative, well and good; but in some countrysides it seemed politic to honor all the leading families by membership. As for the Provincial conferences first held in Georgia and South Carolina, they were little better than mass meetings. In the former, "all persons within the limits of this Province" were asked to brave the July heat by gathering at Tondee's Tavern, and many did so, but with unsatisfactory results. In South Carolina a queer hybrid meeting was held. The parishes outside Charleston sent uneven groups, and the Charleston leaders should have added a small deputation of their own to make up a deliberative body. Instead, they allowed the radical tradesmen and mechanics of the town and its conservative merchants and planters to crowd in indiscriminately. The gathering resembled a mob rather than a representative assemblage, and though it outstripped Georgia by choosing a delegation to the Continental Congress, it accomplished little else.[83]

In other Colonies, however, the Congresses from the outset had a clear-cut form, following the general model of the old Provincial House or Assembly. Thus in Virginia in the summer of 1774 each county chose two members, just as it had long elected two Burgesses. Most counties simply designated the former legislators. The first Congress in Massachusetts was largely identical with the old General Court. The chief difference was that it was somewhat larger, for each town was allowed to send as many delegates as it pleased; three days after steady sittings began at Concord in October, there were 260 members, more than the General Court had ever seen.[84] Resentment had long existed over the desire of the Crown authorities to keep the membership of the House low, and their consequent reluctance to allow the incorporation of new settlements as towns. The Province chafed under any limitation upon the representation of its migrating population, and one of the first benefits which new com-

[83] Stevens's "Georgia," II, 77; N. C. Col. Records, X, 37, 38; Silver, "Provisional Govt. of Md., 1774-77"; Drayton, "Memoirs of the Amer. Rev.," I, 113, 126.
[84] Journals Prov. Congress; Cushing.

munities seized from the Revolution was a seat in the patriot legislature. The same privilege was eagerly grasped in New Hampshire.
Here the first Provincial Congress contained 85 delegates, and the
fourth 131, the last including men from many towns theretofore
barred, and boasting itself "the fullest representative body this
Province ever had." [85]

Caution was the keynote of the revolutionary congresses or conferences which met in the summer of 1774, and they confined themselves to two or three main tasks. Where delegates to the Continental Congress could not be appointed by the regular legislature, as
they were in Massachusetts and Pennsylvania, these irregular bodies
had to name them. Virginia, for example, chose seven men of a
high average of ability, four of whom were conservative Whigs, and
three—Patrick Henry, George Washington, and R. H. Lee—progressives. North Carolina's Provincial Congress elected three men, who
were all radicals, though Joseph Hewes of the rather aristocratic
Edenton community was of a less ardent temperament than William
Hooper or Richard Caswell. New Hampshire sent two men, one of
them John Sullivan, a lawyer whose success at the bar, where he
had amassed a fortune of ten thousand pounds in a few years, was
the envy of John Adams. Sullivan had been a favorite both of
Governor Wentworth and the people, and was destined to be a
patriot general of high usefulness. Maryland chose five sons, representing her advanced section of opinion by the radical and impetuous
Samuel Chase, and the more moderate majority by the wealthy
Thomas Johnson and Matthew Tilghman. New Jersey also elected
five delegates, with William Livingston at their head.

These men were given brief instructions by every Colony. It
happened that in Virginia Jefferson, who was absent because of
illness, wrote a set of proposed instructions which attracted wide
attention for the vigor with which they attacked the Crown's measures. They declared that the relation between England and America
was identical with that which had subsisted between England and
Scotland after James I became king but before their union, and
asserted that England had no more right to govern America because
she had colonized it than the Danes and Saxons had to govern
England because their forefathers had settled the island. These

---

[85] Each New Hampshire town was originally asked to select "one or more persons";
N. H. Prov. Papers, VII, 400, 401.

resolutions were too revolutionary to have a chance of passage, for even R. H. Lee believed that Britain possessed the right to regulate American trade; but when printed in pamphlet form, they circulated extensively in both England and America.[86]

The two other tasks of these first revolutionary legislatures were to offer moral and material aid to Massachusetts, and to strike back at Great Britain with the old economic weapon, non-intercourse. We need not pause over the resolutions passed to cheer New England, nor the steps taken to send money and provisions to Boston. As for trade warfare, systematic non-importation had been tried in 1765-66 in answer to the Stamp Act, and in 1769 in answer to the Townshend taxes, half ruining many British merchants and contributing much to the partial reversal of British policy which followed. It was hoped that it might now help obtain a withdrawal of the punitive measures.

At first the Colonies presented a ragged, uncertain alignment. The upper South went the farthest, partly because the planters of Maryland and Virginia, and the planters and farmers of North Carolina, were becoming passionately aroused by the issues of constitutional and personal liberty; partly because many of them, always deep in debt to British merchants, with their crops pledged for seasons to come for goods already received, had no objection to a relief from the pressure of debt-collectors. Virginia led the way. After the Burgesses had stopped the trade in East India goods in May, the August Convention decided upon a sweeping interdiction of British commerce, widely influential in other Colonies—no goods or slaves were to be imported after the beginning of November, and if American grievances were not previously redressed, the shipment of all goods to Britain was to cease Aug. 10, 1775.[87] The closing of the courts amounted to a moratorium for debts. Maryland's Congress in July endorsed an association for stopping both importation and exportation. North Carolina was not a heavy user of the imported luxuries demanded elsewhere in the South—of furniture, wines, books, silks, carriages, and china; but she followed Virginia's example, deciding to stop buying British imports with the New Year, and to cease shipments to England October 1, 1775.[88]

[86] Jefferson's "Works," Memorial Ed., I, 181 ff.
[87] 4 Amer. Archives, I, 688; Leake, "Va. Committee System," 146. Richard Bland, though a conservative, was the reputed author of this sweeping non-intercourse plan.
[88] Proceedings of the N. C. Convention are given in Col. Records, IX, 1043-49.

In the two leading Middle Colonies the great merchants had little inclination to ruin themselves by cutting off the overseas trade. We have seen how the propertied leaders of New York City organized to meet the radical movement for non-importation there, and quashed it. Both there and in Pennsylvania it was decided to wait for the Continental Congress to pronounce upon the question. In South Carolina similar friction promptly developed. When the Provincial conference was held in July, the merchants opposed an interruption of commerce with Great Britain, while the mechanics and shop-keepers favored it. A decade earlier, following the Stamp Act, that born radical Christopher Gadsden had led the workmen to victory against the mercantile class on the same issue, but now it was left to the Continental Congress. Four of the five South Carolina dele-gates in Philadelphia that fall were at first unwilling to agree to the stoppage of exportation unless rice and indigo were excepted, and in the end they signed the Continental Association only after a com-promise had been effected, the shipment of rice being allowed, that of indigo barred. The discrimination between the two products at once produced a quarrel in South Carolina, the indigo growers demanding a compensation for their loss, and eventually receiving it. But in general all differences between the Colonies on this subject were ironed out by the action of the Continental Congress in October. It drew up an agreement by which all British imports were to be rejected beginning December 1, 1774, and by which exportation was to cease September 10, 1775.

This measure was modeled on the Virginia agreement, and the Virginia plan of enforcement was also adopted. Throughout the summer and fall the counties of the Old Dominion had been ap-pointing committees, to which the Provincial Convention deputed the task of seeing that the trade boycott was observed by everyone, willing or unwilling. They differed from the older local committees, set up in various parts of America since 1772, in that their chief duty was inspection, not correspondence. Congress now called for such bodies in every county, city, and town, and a host of them sprang into being as if by magic. In most localities the radicals rallied with enthusiasm, like the mechanics behind the Committee of Sixty in New York, to make the word of these bodies law. The drastic way in which the county committees of Maryland dealt with anyone who tried to bring forbidden commodities into the

Province was well illustrated by the affair of the brig *Peggy Stewart*. When it arrived in October with more than a ton of tea, the public indignation was intense; the owners and the consignees, humbly apologizing, offered to burn the cargo, but without satisfying the people; and finally the former, after consulting with sober leaders, stated their willingness to burn the vessel too—which was done!

In North Carolina the organization of committees proceeded all fall, and in some counties they reached enormous size, a hundred members or more being chosen to prevent any jealousy among rival families, and to bind them all to the Whig cause. At Charleston there was also a huge committee, at first constituted upon occupational lines—15 merchants, 15 mechanics, and 69 planters—which took charge of the city and harbor, while smaller bodies formed in every parish and district. On February 16, 1775, a vessel from Glasgow arrived at New York, and the Sixty forbade it to unload. When the lieutenant of a British warship tried to interfere, the committee instantly seized the warship's captain and made him order his subordinate aside.[89]

At first the object of these committees was simply to enforce the boycott, but in many towns and counties they quickly took over nearly all governmental powers, acting like the vigilance committees of a later day. This was equally true in large ports like New York, Baltimore, and Charleston, and in rural communities. In such Provinces as Virginia, North Carolina, and New Jersey, every county was a little world of its own, in which the authority of a determined group might be absolute. "Everything is managed by committee," we soon find one Virginia loyalist lamenting, "setting and pricing goods, imprinting books, forcing some to sign scandalous concessions, and by such bullying conduct they expect to bring government to their own terms."[90]

What were the penalties they imposed? Congress, which was in a milder mood than most of the Provincial and local bodies, expected them simply to exert the power of public sentiment, stamping every recreant citizen with infamy. But these revolutionary bodies, num-

[89] For growth of the non-intercourse movement, see Schlesinger, Chs. 8 and 9.
[90] Eckenrode, 45; by imprinting books is meant the approval of account-books. In North Carolina the insistence of the committees of safety upon oaths of loyalty and their rough treatment of suspicious persons made the Tories reluctant to lift their heads. We find the Wilmington authorities ordering the return of a cargo of tea to England; disapproving a horse-race as too frivolous for the times; and encouraging the distribution of powder. Later in the winter, several county committees sometimes united in a district conference.

bering rough and irresponsible men as well as patriots of the highest
type, could not always be restrained within neat paths of decorum.
Civil wars are not made with eau de cologne, and the contest between
Whig and Tory was fast verging upon civil war.   There had been
not a little mob violence even before the middle of 1774.   John
Adams, in a letter of July 7 evoked by an outrage upon a merchant
of Scarborough, Massachusetts, had bitterly denounced "these tar-
rings and featherings, this breaking open houses by rude and insolent
rabble." [91]   Mob activity throughout America increased during the
autumn and winter, and frequently was approved or even instigated
by the local committees.   Everywhere the committees encouraged
Whig sentiment, warned the loyalists to be quiet, deprived them of
their arms, and compelled them to sign the Association.   The indefensible acts of which some committees were guilty soon led to a
movement among moderate men, particularly marked in Virginia and
North Carolina, to bring them under the rigid supervision of the
Provincial Congresses or Conventions.

It became evident in the fall and winter of 1774 that the arbitra-
ment of arms was only too probable.   As a consequence of the non-
importation agreement, the merchants of London, Bristol, and
Glasgow petitioned Parliament for a reconciliation with America,
pointing out that millions of pounds were due them from the American people, and that thousands of ships and sailors were normally
employed in the trade now stagnant.   But these petitions, like the
pleas of Fox, Wilkes, and Burke, were little heeded by the Ministry.
Lord North's conciliatory resolutions passed in the early spring of
1775, proposing an exemption from imperial taxation to any Colony
which should voluntarily make a contribution to the common defense
satisfactory to the Crown; but the futility of any such offer excited
ridicule in England as well as America.   The Commons on February
2 passed an address to the King so angry in tone that Horace Walpole
called it a vote for a civil war.   And more alarming still were the
events in and about Boston.   When Gage at the beginning of September, 1774, sent a party of troops to seize a store of powder at
Medford, the result was a rally of thousands of militia and other
armed men at Cambridge, who were with difficulty dissuaded from
marching upon Boston.   After the annual muster of the Massachusetts militia that fall the companies never really disbanded, remain-

[91] C. F. Adams, "Familiar Letters of John Adams and His Wife," 20; see S. G.
Fisher, "True Hist. of the Amer. Rev.," ch. 8.

ing ready to spring to arms. Gage, beginning to fortify Boston Neck, was unable to obtain American carpenters for the work even by sending to New Hampshire and New York. The reconnoitring by British troops in the vicinity of Boston, the continued seizure of munitions wherever practicable, and such menacing demonstrations by the Crown forces as accompanied the anniversary of the Boston massacre, March 5, 1775, increased the tension day by day.

As Massachusetts was the storm center, naturally the Provincial Congress of Massachusetts led the continent in making military preparations. As early as October, 1774, when it was sitting at Concord, committees were appointed to find out just what armed forces were available, and to draft a plan for strengthening them. It was decided to appoint a Committee of Safety, which was immediately named; to commission three generals; and to organize the militia in companies and regiments for equipment and intensive instruction. The three generals named were Jedidiah Preble, Artemas Ward, and Seth Pomeroy. Pomeroy was the old Northampton gunsmith who, a veteran of King George's War and the Seven Years' War, was later hailed at Bunker Hill by Putnam with the gleeful shout, "By God, Pomeroy, you here! A cannon shot would waken you out of your grave!" Ward had fought under Abercrombie in Canada; and Preble had been present as a major when the Acadians were expelled from Nova Scotia. On every village common the quiet training of militia was taken in hand by commanders who pushed any old militia officers thought to be attached to the Crown brusquely aside. Efforts were made to obtain a sufficiency of arms and ammunition, and the small game of the Province rejoiced in a sudden immunity from hunting.[92]

The second Provincial Congress, meeting at Cambridge on February 1, 1775, took every possible step to prepare the Massachusetts army for the hostilities now imminent. Two new generals were appointed, John Thomas and William Heath, and were directed to oppose by force two of the recent acts of Parliament.[93] A committee ascertained the exact number of officers and men, and the quantity of ammunition and general equipment in the town storehouses, as a basis for the effective redistribution of the Colony's munitions. The British knew that stores were being concentrated, and did their best,

[92] Journals Prov. Congress, 21 ff.; Frothingham, "Siege of Boston," 41 ff.
[93] Cushing, 133-34.

which was little, to interfere with the patriots' plans. On March 18 the redcoat guard at Boston Neck seized nearly 13,500 cartridges, with a ton and a half of balls, and though this was private property, refused to give it up.

A few days earlier a symbolic incident had occurred. When on March 6 the Old South Church was crowded with people to hear Dr. Joseph Warren's oration on the anniversary of the Boston Massacre, forty or fifty British officers pushed their way into the place, and were installed by Samuel Adams in the front pews. At one of the orator's passionate appeals, an officer seated on the pulpit stairs held up a handful of pistol bullets before Warren, who calmly dropped his handkerchief over the open palm and proceeded.[94] On April 5, the Congress adopted articles of war. Two days later, it called upon the people of each county to put their militia and minute-men in a posture for immediate action. The next day, with Lexington less than a fortnight away, it resolved that the dangerous situation of public affairs made it necessary to put an army into the field at once; and delegates were sent to the three neighboring provinces to enlist their aid.

Immediately after Lexington the Massachusetts Congress voted unanimously that America ought to muster an army of 30,000, and that Massachusetts must contribute 13,600 men. The Committee of Safety and four other members were set to work on a plan of organization. Handbills were distributed, and each county was asked to suggest the men best fitted for positions of command. Thereafter the Congress labored unremittingly to keep its force ready for action. It ordered enlistments, built fortifications, commissioned officers, and made rules of discipline. It entered into the pettiest details of military equipment. In the middle of May, it requested the Continental Congress to take some measures for directing and regulating the American forces. By this time they consisted of 20,000 men, stretching in a line thirty miles long from Cambridge around Boston to Roxbury. The leaders included Putnam, of Connecticut, who had fought at Ticonderoga with Lord Howe, Stark, of New Hampshire, who had also made a brave record in the last French war, and Ethan Allen, the dashing colonel of the Green Mountain boys. The commander was Artemas Ward, and his subordinate next in rank was John Thomas, who had served as a

[94] Frothingham's "Warren," 430 ff.; Hutchinson's "Diary and Letters," 528-29.

surgeon at the capture of Louisbourg. Meanwhile, the Congress had to provide for the refugees from Boston, of whom 5,000 were soon distributed among the villages.[95]

The principal arm of the Provincial Congress in administering affairs was the Committee of Safety, of which the most prominent members were John Hancock and Dr. Warren. In its hands were placed the direction of enlisted men, the care of military supplies, and the guarding of suspicious persons. Twice during the spring its powers were enlarged, while its membership was increased from nine to thirteen. This small body was expected to summon and control all armed forces, to look after the equipment of the soldiers, and for the time being, to commission the officers. The flocking of raw volunteers from all parts of New England to Boston made the responsibility heavy. Many of the field officers were totally incompetent, for the Congress had invited any one who could enlist fifty-nine men to take a captaincy, and any one who could organize ten companies a colonelcy. A motley array of a few veterans and many inexperienced farmers and fishermen, shopkeepers and artisans, had to be whipped into shape, fed, and sheltered.

The Committee gave careful attention to interminable lists of items —food, picks, wagons, tents, shells, powder, medicines, and artillery. It decided how much codfish, bacon, and meal made a ration. It was feverishly busy before and after Lexington in concentrating munitions where they could most effectively be used. It tried to enlist as many men as possible for a definite term of seven months. The little army over which Washington took command at Cambridge was not well furnished—John Adams, who saw it, said so, and the British called it "a rustic rout with calico frocks and fowling pieces." It lacked blankets, clothing, and fuel, the quarters were a picturesque array of tents, cabins, sail-cloth shelters, and brush-thatched huts of turf or stone, it had not five rounds of powder a man, and it was fed largely by gifts from the far-stretching farms of New England. But that it was sufficiently well equipped to be effective was attributable to the foresight and unwearied labor of the Committee and the Provincial Congress.[96]

In war every community inevitably tries to make itself a great

[95] Parkman, "Montcalm and Wolfe," ed. 1914, I, pp. 291, 428, 441 ff; II, 94, 123.
[96] See letters from Boston the summer of 1775 in Almon's "Remembrancer"; Marks's "England and America, 1763-1783," I, 380; Lodge's "Story of the Revolution," I, 71 ff.

workshop. The Provincial Congress had little need to concern itself with the boycott of English imports, for that was already almost complete, but from the beginning it labored to make the Province self-supporting. It early appointed a committee to report upon the best means of increasing native manufactures, while it also arranged for a thorough census of the population and its finished products. The people were urged to turn energetically to the making of nails, gunpowder, steel, tin plates, and other articles, and to the raising of large crops. Directions for making saltpeter were scattered throughout the Province, and the Congress offered a high price for all that was turned over to it during 1775, while a similar guarantee was given the makers of firearms and bayonets.[97]

The rest of New England kept almost equal pace with Massachusetts in her early preparations for war. We have noticed that the Connecticut Assembly, adjourning November 4, 1774, had previously ordered a general muster and arranged for carrying on drill all winter. When it met again on March 2 it could not have acted more wisely had it foreseen that fighting would begin the next month.[98] It at once directed that one fourth the militia, or six regiments, be assembled and equipped for active service, and fixed the men's pay. It ordered 3,000 stand of arms, 1300 axes, picks, and spades, and 500 tents, and made the Governor's son commissary-general. A few important cases of Toryism that had cropped up, chiefly along the New York border, were dealt with by the Provincial authorities, but the Whiggism of Connecticut was so uniform that from other Colonies loyalists were later exiled to the land of steady habits.

In both Rhode Island and New Hampshire also men drilled all winter. The Assembly of the former Colony in December appointed a committee of five to revise the militia laws, one of the five being a studious young forge-master, a private in the Kentish guards who had lately gone to Boston to buy a musket and some military books— Nathanael Greene.[99] On the fourteenth of the same month, a drum began to beat in the streets of the little New Hampshire capital, a a force of 400 patriots collected in the cold, and they marched against Fort William and Mary, overwhelming the four or five defenders without loss of life, though several cannon were discharged from

[97] Journals Prov. Cong., 52, 61, 62-5, 103.
[98] Conn. Public Records, XIV, 388 ff.
[99] F. V. Greene, "General Greene," 17.

the ramparts. Governor Wentworth was now quite helpless. He ordered the enlistment of thirty men to guard the fort, but nobody responded, he commanded the magistrates to jail the offenders, but not a warrant was sent out, and he had to content himself with dismissing a few officeholders concerned in the attack.[100]

Farther south men did not rankle under the presence of a grim imperial force camped on their own soil, and imperial ships ranging their own coast; they could not so easily look down the road and imagine a force of redcoat invaders topping the hill. Yet some Provinces were preparing to fight in the same spirit as New England. Lord Dunmore of Virginia occupied a sad Christmas eve in 1774 in writing to Lord Dartmouth that every county was arming an independent militia company. All British authority had been set aside, he testified, so that there was not even a justice of the peace active; his own power had grown so feeble that he could not issue a single order, for it would only be laughed at and humiliate the Crown; and he saw no hope for the future save a faint possibility of dissension among the patriots.[101] In Virginia the non-importation agreement was rigidly maintained, partly because the planters had so long smarted under a sense of economic vassalage to the British. When the merchants and factors tried to resist it by forcing up prices, the county committees resorted to price-fixing decrees, and sternly enforced them.

Whig agitators were busy calculating just how much Virginia's past dependence upon England in all commercial operations had cost her. One newspaper writer estimated that in every £100 of non-British goods imported from England—silks, or Madeira wines, or French jewelry—the colonists lost £75 in profits to English middlemen. As such importations normally amounted to at least £350,000 a year, the Britons were gainers by £262,500 annually. Again, he computed that there were at least fifty flourishing British mercantile companies with Virginia agencies, and that their average net profits were £15,000 a year apiece, or £750,000 in all. The salaries of their factors alone were £120,000 a year. This ingenious statistician put the British profit in buying Virginia's tobacco at £2,200,000 a year, and the whole annual toll of the mother country,

[100] Belknap's "New Hampshire," Farmer's Ed., 353; Proceedings N. H. Hist. Society, IV, 18-46; Parliamentary Register, I, 101; N. Eng. Historical and Genealogical Register, XXII, 277.
[101] 4 Amer. Archives, I, 1062.

apart from the wages of place-hunters, at just short of £6,000,000.[102] Such an estimate was preposterous, but it helps explain why the Association was so well observed, and why every muster field was echoing with commands.

No legislature met during the winter or early spring, for Dunmore repeated his prorogations, but the Provincial Convention held its second session in March, 1775.[103] This new gathering was called in the village of Richmond, far up the James, where the members would enjoy more freedom than at the capital. It brought the sharpest clash between the radical and conservative Whigs that the Colony had yet seen. The Convention on its third day took up military affairs, and Patrick Henry offered a resolve "That this Colony be immediately put into a posture of defense," and proposed a committee which should prepare a plan for enlisting and arming a force.

There was nothing extreme or illogical in this, yet the conservatives rose in angry opposition. St. George Tucker, who watched the proceedings as a visitor, says that there occurred an animated debate, in which Richard Bland, R. C. Nicholas, Benjamin Harrison, and Edmund Pendleton opposed the resolution as premature. These men believed that a threat of armed force might so antagonize the moderates and Whigs in England as to make all hopes of a peaceful agreement vain; while Patrick Henry was convinced that such hopes were fatuous, and that war was at hand. He listened with unconcealed impatience as Bland and the others argued. Then he rose, and in the most famous speech of the Revolution, declared that it was insane to temporize; that judging from the past, the colonists had nothing to hope for in British forbearance; that the Crown was marshaling its forces, and the next wind from the north might bring the clash of arms; and that as for any fear to test the youthful strength of the Provinces against Great Britain, others might hesitate, but he would have liberty or death. Washington, Jefferson, and R. H. Lee supported him, and his resolution passed by the close vote of 65 to 60.[104]

[102] "A Planter," Virginia *Gazette,* April 13, 1776. "You are without merchants, ships, seamen, or shipbuilders. . . . Your trade is confined to a single spot on the globe, in the hands of the natives of a distant island, who fix the market of all commodities at their pleasure, and we may be very sure will rate yours at the lowest, and theirs at the highest, they will in any conscience bear. Every article of merchandise, that is not the produce of Britain, must first pay its duties to the Crown, perhaps must be increased in the price a very large per cent. there, and then be re-exported to Virginia, and undergo an additional advance of 75, or sometimes near 150 per cent. here." The planter wrote that he hoped independence would not be prevented by negotiation.
[103] See Virginia *Gazette,* February, for elections to the March Congress.
[104] Tyler's "Henry," ch. 9.

The committee chosen to prepare the plan of defense was brilliantly able; and in the main it was composed of radicals, for it included Henry, R. H. Lee, Washington, and Jefferson. It lost no time. A day later it brought in its report, which after a few amendments was immediately approved. Before the Convention closed, it also appointed a committee to prepare a program for stimulating manufactures, while it adopted a new Association. Had Patrick Henry completely had his way at this March session, Virginia would have been thrown into open rebellion. He would not only have raised troops, but would have appointed civil officers under new commissions, levied taxes, and treated the Crown government as totally overthrown—perhaps have expelled Dunmore. This was too much for the conservatives and moderates, but they had yielded to Henry's insistence that the Province be made ready for instant hostilities.[105]

South Carolina, which was not behindhand, offered a dramatic illustration of the spirit of the people. In March the revolutionary authorities there appointed an important secret committee of five to provide for defense, and a committee of intelligence to collect information. The former body included two prominent radicals— William Henry Drayton, a gifted young judge whom the Crown had just suspended from the bench, and Arthur Middleton, who had been educated in Whig principles in England.[106] The committee of defense acted at once. The night after its appointment it superintended the seizure of the public powder in two Charleston magazines, and of the arms and stores in the State House. Many prominent men were present, including President Charles Pinckney of the Provincial Congress and Chairman Henry Laurens of the Charleston general committee. The Commons House being then sitting, the perplexed Lieutenant-Governor Bull appealed to it. Some of the very men who had engaged in the raids concurred in voting an investigation, which resulted in the farcical report that no certain intelligence of the affair was obtainable, but that there was reason to think that it had been inspired by the late alarming news from England. Of the remaining Colonies, Maryland's Provincial Convention acted energetically in December, 1774, when all males between sixteen and fifty were called upon to form companies and

[105] Eckenrode, 96 ff.
[106] McCrady, "S. C. Under the Royal Govt.," 786 ff.

begin drilling; while the county authorities were authorized to raise by subscription a total of £10,000 for expenses.[107]   In Pennsylvania, North Carolina, and New Jersey the county authorities were drilling and outfitting troops during the winter, and the first-named Province gave special attention to the manufacture of ammunition, firearms, and bayonets.

Thus it was that most of the Colonies were zealously preparing for the event when the 19th of April arrived—the day that dawned with a crackle of musketry about Lexington, and that closed with an exhausted British column crawling back into Boston, the country for miles around pouring troops toward the city, and couriers already started for the neighboring Provinces.   American communications were slow, a fact which hampered all efforts for a continental union, but the spring season saw the Fiery Cross sent around with unexampled rapidity.   Lexington was fought on Wednesday.   On Thursday morning Major Israel Putnam, ploughing his farm at Pomfret, Connecticut, caught the irregular beat of a drum coming down the road, and heard a horseman, his bridle wet with foam, shout the news across the furrows.   Putnam unharnessed, paused a moment at his house, and was off for Boston.   A year earlier, he had replied with ready humor to the query whether 5000 British regulars might not march from one end of America to the other: "Yes, if they behave and pay their way; but if they make any disturbance, our housewives will knock them on the heads with their ladles."   On Sunday the news was known in New York.   In little more than a fortnight every American, to the backwoods of North Carolina and Georgia, had heard the alarm.

[107] "Proceedings of the Conventions of the Province of Md., 1774-76," *passim*.

CHAPTER THREE

THE EMERGENCE OF POPULAR GOVERNMENT

The repercussion of Lexington throughout America sent half of the royal governors scurrying for safety. The debonair and once popular John Wentworth of New Hampshire, for all his intrepidity, was one of the first to go. Though after Lexington 1200 New Hampshire men at once set out to join the forces about Boston, Wentworth for a time still hoped and labored for peace. Following the receipt of Lord North's conciliatory proposal, he had called a new Assembly which, containing the Colony's leading men, met May 4, 1775. Unfortunately for the Governor, the House not only returned an unfavorable reply to Lord North's offer, but it evinced a warm resentment of Wentworth's attempt to give three new towns the right of representation by the King's writ, as a special gubernatorial authorization was called.[1] The House had always resisted efforts to interfere with its exclusive power to control representation, though Governor Benning Wentworth had beaten it upon this question about 1750, and now it emphatically bade the three claimants begone. Meanwhile signs of increasing violence had appeared. At the end of May there had been mild rioting in Portsmouth over the seizure of two provision ships by a British frigate, and many conservatives—such men as Benjamin Thompson, later Count Rumford —were being driven from the rural districts. On June 13 one of the royalists whom Wentworth had tried to assist to a seat in the Assembly was espied calling at the Governor's fine house, and a mob besieged the mansion, threatening to batter it down with a cannon. The crowd dispersed when the loyalist was given up, but the episode showed Wentworth how much danger he ran, and he withdrew to Fort William and Mary, where he was safe under the guns of a British warship.[2]

[1] N. H. Prov. Papers, VII, 370, 383 ff; Stackpole, II, 77 ff.
[2] On July 18, 1775, he adjourned the House to September 28, and it never met again. N. H. Prov. Papers, VII, 385-86. Wentworth joined Howe in Boston, went to New York, and after giving up hope of an invasion of New Hampshire, sailed to England in 1778. Mayo's "John Wentworth," 163 ff.

In Virginia the news of Lexington and Concord reached the ears of the patriots at a moment when they were agitated by stirring events at Williamsburg. Lord Dunmore committed the same folly that Gage had committed at Boston, and at almost the same time. On the night of April 20 a party of British marines from the schooner *Magdalen* in the James landed and in Lord Dunmore's wagon carried off fifteen half-barrels of powder from the round ammunition storehouse in Williamsburg. At this highhanded act many of the people in and about the town caught up their arms as those about Boston had done the day before, but the town officials —who, with many other conservatives, were eager to have the peace maintained—quieted them by offering assurances that the powder would be restored. The Provincial Council protested, but being also conservative, accepted the Governor's flimsy excuse that the seizure had been a precaution against an apprehended slave rebellion.

Meanwhile, more distant communities received the news of Dunmore's act, and thousands of armed men prepared to march on the capital, one Fredericksburg company notifying George Washington that it was ready to advance within a few days. For a time it seemed dubious whether Peyton Randolph and other conservatives would quell the rising storm or not. But while others hesitated, Patrick Henry caught up the gauntlet. He at once summoned a company of his own Hanover County militia to meet him on May 2, 1775, set out for Williamsburg with several thousands more flocking to his standard, and frightened Governor Dunmore into a hasty payment of £330 for the powder on May 4. Two days later, when Henry was far on his road home, Dunmore issued a proclamation denouncing him as a rebel and warning all citizens not to aid or countenance him. Many counties responded by votes of thanks to Henry, but as yet the peace remained unbroken.[3]

Events now moved rapidly in Virginia. The Assembly, meeting on June 1, rejected Lord North's offer in a drastically hostile message written by Jefferson and carried by him to the new Continental Congress.[4] It voted its approval of the acts of the Provincial Convention, and refused to pass fee bills to permit the reopening of the courts.[5] All the while, as one item of news after another arrived from the North, public sentiment was growing angrier. The Vir-

[3] See Eckenrode, "The Revolution in Virginia"; 4 Amer. Archives, II, 390, 395, 426, 443, 510, 529, 539, 641, 667, 710.
[4] Jefferson's Writings, Memorial Ed., I, 14; Letters of R. H. Lee, I, 136 ff.
[5] Journals; Lingley, "Transition in Virginia," 71.

ginians heard that the siege of Boston had begun; they heard that Generals Howe, Clinton, and Burgoyne had arrived there to prosecute a vigorous campaign.

The extent of the revolution in sentiment became plain when the moderate Peyton Randolph took his uncompromising stand with the radical Jefferson, and when it began to be gossiped that the conservative Richard Bland had proposed that Dunmore be hanged.[6] Williamsburg was filled with knots of patriot soldiery, who had come in as escorts for several of the members, and some not only of the soldiers but of the Burgesses wore the homespun hunting shirts of the western troops. When Lord Dunmore received a letter from General Gage informing him of the latter's hope to capture Samuel Adams and Hancock, he reflected that if these two patriots were actually taken, the Virginians would probably seize him as a hostage on the other side. Moreover, he was apprehensive of the "blind and unreasoning fury," which had, he said, unaccountably fallen on so many. At night he slipped out of town and took refuge on the *Fowey*, a man-of-war on the James. Here he had the effrontery to invite the House to meet him, and the Burgesses replied that his invitation was an impudent breach of privilege.

But it was in North Carolina that the complete debacle of the Crown's authority after Lexington first occurred. Here Governor Martin had been trying to cope with a situation which grew rapidly worse after he called a new Assembly to meet March 29, 1775, at New Bern, and found that the ingenious Speaker Harvey had summoned the second Provincial Convention to sit at the same place at almost the same date, April 3.[7]

This was a direct challenge to Martin, for the membership of the two bodies would be almost identical, and he drew up another proclamation forbidding any one to support the Convention. It was largely ignored, nearly every county and borough town choosing delegates. In most instances they were the same men as the Assemblymen, though some counties elected additional members. The Convention and the Assembly made a quorum and organized on the same day. The outraged Governor Martin, who opened the latter with a warm denunciation of illegal gatherings, found himself mocked by the fact that although there were two bodies in appearance, in fact

---

[6] Mag. of History, III, 160; cf. 4 Amer. Archives, 465, for Washington's view.
[7] N. C. Colonial Records, IX, 1125.

there was but one. The Assembly had 52 members, while the Convention numbered 67; and every Assemblyman except one, who later became a noted Tory, was also a deputy to the second body. The two met in the same room and almost at the same time, with John Harvey, under the alternate name of Mr. Speaker and Mr. Moderator, presiding. Ordinarily the business of the Convention had precedence, but whenever the Governor's messenger was announced at the door, the protean Convention became the Assembly, the extra delegates turned into mere spectators, and His Excellency's communication was gravely received. The functions of the two bodies were not always strictly separated, and those of the Convention alone had much significance. It subscribed to the Continental Association, reëlected the former delegates to the Continental Congress, and strengthened and directed the work of the county committees.[8]

Governor Martin dissolved the Assembly on April 8, after a stormy session of four days; it had returned a defiant answer to his message calling on it to resist the illegal body sitting in the town. The Convention had adjourned the previous day. The whole episode showed just how dead the old instruments of government had become in a typically radical Colony by April, 1775. Then swiftly followed the denouement in their utter collapse. Martin, pathetically defiant to the last, called his council together, struck Harvey's name from the list of magistrates, and planted a half dozen cannon before his palace. During a council meeting on April 24, men representing New Bern's town committee, whom Martin described as pot-valiant, carried off the guns. That night the Governor and some of his followers fled in haste to Wilmington, and when the news from Boston further excited the Colony, they took refuge in Fort Johnston on the Cape Fear.[9]

The two autonomous Colonies of New England, which had no royal Governors to drive out, of course made an instant response to the call of Massachusetts for help in besieging Boston. Couriers with the news of Concord reached New Haven April 21, and that day a special session of the Connecticut legislature was called, which

[8] Governor Martin wrote Lord Dartmouth that 10 of the 34 countries—actually 9—sent no delegates, that in many others the committees arrogated the choice of delegates to themselves, and that in the remainder they were not chosen by one-twentieth the people. Martin viewed "the inhabitants of the western counties who were for the most part concerned in the late insurrection" as especially likely to be loyal—the Regulators. The proceedings of the Convention are in N. C. Col. Recs., IX, 1178-85; Martin's letter *idem*, 1223-28; proceedings of the legislature *idem*, 1187-1205.

[9] E. W. Sikes, Transition of North Carolina, Johns Hopkins Studies, Series XVI, Nos. 10, 11.

brought the Province wholeheartedly into the conflict. Eight regiments were ordered enlisted from the militia, an act was passed to encourage the manufacture of arms and military stores, and articles of war were adopted.[10] Not only did the siege of Boston begin with 2300 Connecticut troops in the line of 16,000 men, not only did a great share of the munitions come from Connecticut, but the credit for Ticonderoga belongs to her. A cordial relationship had always existed between Connecticut and the Vermont settlers, many of them Connecticut-born. At the end of April a committee consisting of Silas Deane and ten other patriots who knew the possibility of a successful attack on the post signed notes for some £800 on the treasury to equip the expedition. They were assured of the approval of the Governor and Assembly, though both were glad to be excused from officially authorizing the attack. It was impracticable to send a force from Hartford to Ticonderoga, for secrecy was essential, but Connecticut volunteers were among Ethan Allen's force, and Benedict Arnold of Connecticut was second in command, when on May 10 the key to the northern lakes fell.

An important addition was made to the wartime government in May, the Connecticut Assembly appointing nine men to assist Governor Trumbull when it was not sitting. They were virtually a Council of Safety, resembling the Bay Colony's useful body of that name, for their function was to supply the troops and direct their movements; but they were destined to a greater usefulness than any other body of the kind in the country. They sat until the end of the war—all but one of the members were neighbors of Trumbull, and his little store became known as the War Office—and in all held almost twelve hundred meetings. It was they who at the dark period of Valley Forge gave two agents $400,000 for the purchase of cattle for the starving army.[11]

Had Rhode Island possessed a Trumbull, her record might have been a duplicate of Connecticut's. The steady flow of the revolutionary current was at this critical moment interrupted briefly, but only briefly, by the Toryism of the Governor. Joseph Wanton, a representative of one of the wealthy, distinguished families of the

[10] Public Records, XV, 15-31.
[11] The powers of this important body may be noted precisely. It was to help the chief executive "to order and direct the marches and stations of the inhabitants enlisted and assembled for the special defense of the Colony, or any part or parts of them, as they shall judge necessary, and to give orders from time to time for furnishing and supplying said inhabitants so enlisted with every matter and thing that may be needful." Public Records, XV, 39; for early proceedings, see *Idem*, 84-530.

Province, had lived for nearly seventy years under the British flag, and like many merchants of the thriving seaport towns, knew that a war would bring commercial disaster. When elected a half dozen years earlier as a result of a truce between the factions of the rival Hopkins and Ward families, he was regarded as a sterling patriot, and for some years his attitude was all that the progressive Whigs expected. But he was unwilling to go the whole road to independence. At the special legislative session which met three days after Lexington, he watched the House uneasily while it armed the troops, prepared 1500 men for service elsewhere, and named a committee to consult with Connecticut upon defense. Greatly alarmed, the old Governor and three members of the upper house protested against these measures as likely to be fatal to the Charter and leading toward civil war. Yet the speaker had testified that the House had scarcely ever in its history shown greater unanimity.[12]

Had Wanton contented himself with a mild expostulation all might have been well, but when the legislature met in regular session on May 2 he showed an obstructive spirit. It authorized the issue of paper money, chose a Committee of Safety, and elected Nathanael Greene a brigadier-general in command of the little army. The inauguration of the newly-elected legislature should fully have taken place by this time, but Wanton showed his Toryism by blocking it. He asked to be excused from attending its sessions on account of illness, recommended a careful consideration of Lord North's offer, and declared that if Rhode Island were "torn from the body to which we are united by our religion, liberty, laws, and commerce, we must bleed at every vein." He also refused to sign the military commissions, or to proclaim a fast day. The House thereupon pushed the old executive out of the way by suspending him from office until, that fall, his seat was declared vacant, and the patriotic Deputy-Governor, Nicholas Cooke, was installed in it. Being now in unhampered control of Rhode Island, the legislature drove the conduct of the war with energy.[13]

In the Colonies where the moderates and conservatives were strongest—that is, in all of them south of New England save Virginia

[12] For Wanton's creditable espousal of the patriot side in the Gaspee affair, see I. B. Richman's "Rhode Island," 204 ff.
[13] Records Col. R. I., VII, 312 ff., 325-334, 393. Cooke, though capable, was given nothing like independent war powers; the Assembly kept them firmly in its own or its committees' hands. Stephen Hopkins and Nathanael Greene early in 1775 were advocating independence; see Bates, "R. I. and the Union," 62; 4 Amer. Archives, IV, 571.

and North Carolina—the royal and proprietary governors remained in their seats even after Bunker Hill, but as impotent spectators of a rapid strengthening of the revolutionary governments and the fighting forces. Sir Robert Eden, of Maryland, actually managed to stay till the very eve of the declaration of independence. This was because he had always been personally popular, because a considerable group of Annapolis and Baltimore townsfolk and of wealthy planters protected him, and because he had tact enough to efface himself.[14] When the news of Lexington and of Dunmore's rape of the powder arrived in Annapolis, the third Provincial Convention, with a hundred members, was sitting there. It at once demanded that Eden surrender the Provincial arms and munitions, and although the Governor expostulated, he yielded, doing so with all possible dignity by agreeing to hand over the military stores to certain colonels of the militia regularly appointed by himself, but perfectly trusted by the Whigs. This course, he wrote his brother rather uneasily, satisfied every one save perhaps "some of our infernal independents, who are in league with the Bostonians."

But as Eden found, henceforth the sensibilities of British officials were given little consideration. A month after Bunker Hill, Maryland's first troops set out for the seat of war, two companies of hardy riflemen from Frederick County, dressed in hunting shirts, trousers, and moccasins, and able to hit a squirrel without a rest at a hundred yards. The Fourth Provincial Convention, which met in midsummer, did everything possible to place the Province upon a war footing. To this end, it provided for the enlistment of every able-bodied effective freeman between sixteen and fifty, the organization of forty companies of minute men, the purchase of munitions and erection of a powder mill, and the issue of $266,666 in bills of credit.

The shot heard round the world did not reach South Carolina till May 3, but it brought that Province also into a posture for immediate hostilities. A meeting of its Congress was called for June 1, 1775. Old Charles Pinckney, too loyal yet for a total break with England, resigned, and his place as president was taken by the rich merchant-planter Henry Laurens, who had just returned from a

---

[14] Eden's tact and popularity were more effective in restraining the radical Marylanders than the good qualities of Governor Wentworth in New Hampshire. See the biography, by B. C. Steiner, "Sir Robert Eden," John Hopkins Studies, Series XVI, Nos. 7, 8, 9.

period spent in England to educate his children. Laurens stood midway between the moderates and the radicals, but the news of Lexington caused him to move toward the latter. A clash between the two wings at once occurred over an Association which it was proposed the Congress should compel all patriots to sign—a pledge which bound its subscribers to fight to the death in defending the freedom and safety of America. The moderates were overborne, and the Association was ordered used throughout the Province as a test; President Laurens, however, making an address in which he pleaded that the honest Whigs who refused to accept it should be treated with fairness and respect. The Congress proceeded to raise three regiments, to issue a million pounds in paper, and to appoint treasury commissioners, while it, like the Maryland Convention, appointed a Council of Safety which became the executive head of the government.[15]

When all pressing revolutionary business had been finished, on a fine afternoon in mid-June the Congress sent a committee to address Lieutenant-Governor Bull, at his neighboring country seat of Ashley Hall, in explanation of their proceedings and motives. The warship *Scorpion*, bearing the new Governor, Sir William Campbell, was off the coast, and as the deputation offered its paper, the Charleston guns saluting the incoming executive were heard. The brave Lieutenant-Governor, sick at heart, alleged the fact that he had now been supplanted in office as a reason for refusing to accept the address; he really was unwilling to have this token of the virtual end of the Crown régime come into his hands.[16]

We need not pause long over the events of the spring in New Jersey, Pennsylvania, and Delaware, where the same preparations were taken in hand as in other Colonies. Governor Franklin wrote Lord Dartmouth from the first-named Province on May 6 that all hopes for a restoration of harmony had been defeated by the news of Lexington.[17] Companies were drilling everywhere, militia officers had resigned their connection with the Crown, and an effort had been made to carry away the Provincial treasury-chest and public records. Four days before the Governor mailed this ominous report,

---

[15] The Journal of the Council is in the Colls. of the S. C. Hist. Soc., III, 35-372.
[16] See Drayton, "Memoirs of the Amer. Rev.," I, 255 ff.
[17] Colls. of N. J. Hist. Soc., V, 445. The counties had acted promptly upon receiving the news from the north. Thus Morris County on May 1 entrusted nine men with raising men, arms, and money, and this committee next day took all steps requisite for outfitting 300 troops. On May 4 Upper Freehold township subscribed £160 for ammunition. Lee's "New Jersey," II, ch. 3.

another general conference of county committeemen began at New Brunswick, and in view of the fighting near Boston, issued a call for a regular Provincial Convention at Trenton. This second body voted measures of military organization similar to those we have noticed elsewhere, though it protested its entire loyalty to the King. In Pennsylvania the Assembly sat within a week after the news that hostilities had begun, and pushed to completion certain undertakings which an emergency mass meeting and the city committee had already initiated. Troops were enlisted, a census of arms was taken, £200c was set aside to pay for munitions already bought, and a committee which included Thomson, Dickinson, and Anthony Wayne was charged with procuring needed stores. Lord North's offer was emphatically rejected, and the delegates in Congress were instructed to take vigorous measures for obtaining a redress of grievances. Later, at the end of June, when the subject of fortifying the city and taking further military steps had been pressed by the radicals, the Assembly appointed a Committee of Safety under the chairmanship of Dickinson.[18] He held this post throughout the summer, when Dr. Franklin superseded him.

But it was in Georgia and New York, the two laggard Provinces, that the effect of the first fighting in the north was most stunning, for in both it brought over a great number of moderate Whigs to the side of the radicals and encouraged the latter to a new boldness. The overturn in Georgia was almost amazing, for the revolutionary movement had seemed pitifully weak there. The effort to hold a Provincial Congress in January had been almost abortive, only five of the twelve parishes sending delegates. This rump body had chosen three men to the Continental Congress, but had been too timid to endorse the Continental Association, and its pusillanimous conduct, as they deemed it, had outraged the New England settlers of St. John's Parish.[19] It had also angered the patriot authorities of Charleston, who early the next month resolved to have nothing to do with Georgia; whereupon St. John's protested, set itself apart from the rest of the Province, and elected Dr. Lyman Hall its own delegate to the Continental Congress. The three other delegates did

[18] Votes and Proceedings, VI, 584 ff. Early in June Congress was impressed by a glittering field day of 2,000 troops in Philadelphia; Adams, "Familiar Letters," 61.
[19] See Rev. Records of Ga., I, 34-63. The proceedings of the first Provincial Congress are in the Colls. of the Ga. Hist. Soc., V, pt. I. The Congress would perhaps have gone further in coöperation with the Assembly, but that the latter after showing a mildly patriotic temper, was suddenly dissolved by Wright.

not go to Philadelphia in May, but sent instead a full explanation of the recent events in Georgia.

Admitting that the Province seemed to have played a contemptibly unworthy part, they pointed out that the recent Provincial Congress could not call itself representative of the whole people, and that it lacked the strength to enforce the Association. The people of Savannah were not ready for non-importation. "The importers were mostly against any interruption, and the consumers very much divided. There were some of the latter virtuously for the measures; others tremulously against them; but more who called themselves neutral than either." They had, they concluded, naturally decided to await the drift of events and the further measures of Congress.

But the opening of war in New England had its natural effect upon the waiting Georgia neutrals. At the beginning of May the Assembly refused to make a quorum. Immediately afterwards the news of Lexington produced a burst of excitement in Savannah, in the midst of which the radicals took from the royal magazine a quarter ton of powder.[20] The King's birthday was celebrated by setting up a fine liberty pole and flag, a parade, and a dinner at which the first toast was the King and the second American liberty. The enforcement of the Association was made so rigid in Savannah that notorious violators had to clear out at dead of night.[21] The patriot leaders assumed control, and a call was sent broadcast for the election of delegates to a new Provincial Congress to meet July 4, 1775. In despair, Governor Wright wrote that "all law and government . . . here as well as elsewhere, seems now nearly at an end. And it has been debated whether or not to stop the courts and shut up the port, but this I am assured is laid aside for the present although very probably will be resumed hereafter." When the Congress met on the date set, every parish and district was at last represented, and Georgia could consider herself one of the thirteen embattled Colonies.

The work of this Congress, which under President Bulloch sat at intervals until the fall of 1776, resembled that of the like bodies elsewhere.[22] At its first session it elected delegates to the Continental Congress, including one, the Rev. Dr. Zubly, who later proved

[20] Rev. Records of Ga., I, 66, 67.
[21] Colls. of the Ga. Hist. Soc., III, 183-4. Many inhabitants of Savannah and the surrounding country met at the Liberty Pole in that town on June 22, 1775, to elect a Council of Safety. Rev. Records, I, 67.
[22] Cf. C. C. Jones, "Hist. of Georgia," II, 197 ff.; Schlesinger, 546 ff.

to be a Tory and resigned; it strengthened the executive Council of Safety;[23] it adopted a new Association; and it resolved upon raising £10,000. This so placated the other Colonies that a resolution which the Continental Congress had passed, setting all Georgia except St. John's outside the pale of commercial intercourse, was rescinded. The courts were closed during the summer, and that winter were placed under the jurisdiction of the Provincial Congress. "In short, my lord," Wright wrote to London on September 16, 1775, "the whole executive power is assumed by them, and the King's Governor remains little else than nominally so." He asked to be taken home, since a Crown officer "has little or no business here."[24]

The news of Lexington fell upon New York at a critical and interesting juncture, the moment when a Provincial Congress was at last taking the place of the regular legislature. When the Assembly had met for the last time in January, 1775, with the loyalists still in firm control, its conduct had totally disgusted the patriots. One by one it had defeated every undertaking of the progressive members. By a vote of 15 to 9 it rejected Schuyler's motion to thank the New York delegates to the first Continental Congress, and by 17 to 9 it refused to appoint delegates to the second Congress. A set of much-amended resolutions was finally allowed to pass as a milk-and-water expression of the attitude of moderate Americans toward the aggressions of Parliament. These went so far as to speak of the punitive acts as grievances, but they asserted that the colonists owed the same obedience to the Crown as if they lived in England, and that Parliament, so long as it did not tax them without their consent, had a right to regulate colonial trade and to lay duties on American imports from foreign lands. A memorial to the King was adopted, admitting that some of the colonial measures "are by no means justified," and begging His Majesty to regard them as "the honest, tho' disorderly struggles of liberty." Colden, rubbing his hands with satisfaction over these measures, wrote home throughout the first three months of the year praising the steadfastness of the people.[25]

[23] The minutes of this Council are in the Colls. of the Ga. Hist. Soc., V, 3333, pt. I. It emitted paper money, delivered commissions to officers, collected funds for the Provincial treasury, and directed the movements of troops. Early in January, 1776, it made arrangements to obtain extensive military stores; on January 8 it took control of Indian affairs.

[24] Colls. of the Ga. Hist. Soc., III, 209-210.

[25] One member of the Assembly, Simon Boerum, had been a delegate to the Continental Congress. The petition to the King referred to some acts of the colonists as

Long before the Assembly broke up on April 3 the thoroughly disgusted radicals were taking steps to set it aside. Its refusal to elect delegates to Philadelphia brought the demand for a Provincial Congress to a head, and the Committee of Sixty ordered an election.[26] When the *viva voce* balloting took place early in March at the Exchange, a pitched battle of Whigs and Tories with staves and bludgeons preceded it, creating such an uproar that the choice of the delegates virtually fell upon the Sixty. The Congress held its first brief session at the Exchange on April 20-23, 1775, its forty-two members representing all the counties but three, though in Westchester hundreds had protested against the sending of delegates, and in Dutchess three fourths of the people were said to be in opposition. Its roster was highly creditable. It included Jay, Duane, Low, McDougall, Philip Livingston, and Isaac Roosevelt, from New York City; Philip Schuyler and Abraham Yates from Albany; George Clinton from Ulster, and Robert R. Livingston from Dutchess.[27] Its chief act, however, was merely the choice of delegates to Philadelphia.

Before the Congress had adjourned there came the news of fighting, and after that events crowded rapidly upon each other. Business was suspended on April 23, the followers of "King" Sears and John Lamb paraded the town with drums and colors, the city armory was broken open, arms were distributed, drilling began, and the Sons of Liberty took over the local government.[28] For the temporary administration of the city a Committee of One Hundred was chosen

unjustifiable, but begged His Majesty to consider them "the honest, tho' disorderly struggles of liberty." Votes and Proceedings of the General Assembly, 1775, 109 ff.; see also 4 Amer. Archives, I, 1188-91; Docs. Rel. Col. Hist. N. Y., VIII, 532, 543; Colden's "Letter-Books," II, 381-400.

[26] Colden's "Letter-Books," II, 389-90. The proposal to call this body came from the Whigs alone, the loyalists opposing it, but not daring to show enough energy to defeat it.

[27] See Journals N. Y. Prov. Congress. The city and county of New York cast four votes in the Congress, Albany County three, and the other counties two each. Philip Livingston was chosen president. In New York city and county the delegates were elected by the voters on the regular poll lists; in Albany county by the local committee of correspondence; and in Ulster by the committee of the towns and precincts

[28] See William Smith's Ms. Diary, N. Y. Public Library, entry of April 29, for a vivid account of the excitement of the city, the buzzing of the taverns, and the stoppage of the courts. Colden noted that the agitation of the radicals had been rising to a climax. "Every species of public and private resentment was threatened to terrify the inhabitants of this Province if they continued disunited from the others. The certainty of losing all the debts due from the other colonies, which are very considerable, and every other argument of private interest that could influence the merchants, or anyone, was industriously circulated. The minds of the people in this city were kept in constant agitation by riots and attempts to stop the transports loading here with stores . . . for the army." Then the news of Lexington was "spread with horrid and aggravating circumstances. The moment of consternation and anxiety was seized, the people were assembled, and that scene of violence and disorder was begun which has entirely prostrated the powers of government. . . ." "Letter-Books," II, 401-02; May 3, 1775.

on May 5, at the instance chiefly of Jay and Duane, and it received implicit obedience from the patriots. This body contained many conservative members, its head was Low, and more than one third of its number was usually absent, but under it New York City drove forward steadily into the Revolution. It assured the people of London that the inhabitants were as one man in the cause of liberty, took arms and munitions under strict control, and surveyed the ground for city fortifications.[29] Suspected loyalists found themselves under sharp surveillance. All over the Province after Lexington the enforcement of the non-importation rule was stiffened; within a short time some 12,000 persons had agreed to it, while only about half as many refused.

Almost immediately the second Provincial Congress was held (May 22, 1775), and sat, with short interruptions, for almost a year. It was chosen, like the first, in response to an appeal from the New York City committee, addressed to the county committees or prominent citizens, and it again represented eleven counties out of fourteen. The large conservative element for a time prevented the formulation of any aggressive policy. When in June Governor Tryon returned from a business trip to England, it happened that he arrived at Sandy Hook on the very day upon which Washington passed through the city to take command at Cambridge. Washington was met with a cautious address by the Provincial Congress, even the most radical of whose members still professed nominal loyalty to the Crown, while the mayor, corporation, and most influential inhabitants received Tryon with marked cordiality.[30] But by the time Bunker Hill was fought the Province was being unmistakably committed to the Revolution under its own Congress. In June steps were taken to build up a military force, and were followed by the familiar measures. Officers were commissioned, ammunition collected, an issue of paper money voted, and the Tories dealt with harshly. A committee of safety was appointed in July, and in September Tryon took refuge on a man-of-war in the harbor.

[29] After a time the city committee surrendered its functions to the Provincial Congress. For their activities just after Lexington see 4 American Archives, II, 529-535, 1574 ff.; III, 15-21.
[30] Many hoped Tryon would be more liberal than Colden. Colden's authority had been paralyzed and he admitted that the Province was in a state of "anarchy and confusion." "A committee has assumed the whole powers of government," he said, retiring to his Long Island farm. "Letter-Books," II, 404, 406.

Roughly speaking, the transition between Colonies and States was now more than half completed; the colonists stood between two worlds in midsummer of 1775, the one quite dead, the other in its birth throes. From the Continental point of view, independence was a year distant, but from the point of view of the single Province, it was already being grasped in at least ten Colonies of the thirteen. John Adams wrote his wife some months later that he firmly believed that no Province which had assumed a government of the people would ever give it up. There was something unnatural and odious in a government a thousand leagues distant, he said, something sweet in a government of their own choice; and a perception of this fact was just beginning to steal over multitudes of patriots. In New York the loyalist Councillor William Smith was impressed by the attitude of some of his colleagues at the first Council session after Lexington. "Jauncey apart told me he now saw the end of the quarrel," he wrote in his diary; "that the union was complete against taxation, and no power in Europe was strong enough to subdue a country three thousand miles off." [31]

It remains for us only to trace two movements—the rapid assumption of a fixed and fairly well developed form by the rudimentary revolutionary governments, and the triumph in the several Colonies of the demand for a formal assertion of independence.

I. Patriot Agencies Take Regular Form

For the American people to live under the rule of agencies which had an indefinite tenure, a vague authority, and an irregular mode of functioning was impossible, while to try to carry on war through such agencies was preposterous. A process of regularizing the new Provincial authorities manifested itself throughout the continent during the spring and summer of 1775. The way was being paved for the writing of Constitutions and the full emergence of new States.

This process is most fully illustrated by the four Provinces of Massachusetts, New Hampshire, New Jersey, and North Carolina, representing each section. Massachusetts naturally led the way. The flash of muskets at Concord and Lexington lit up the future sufficiently for men to see that they would long be estranged from England, and that the emergency government furnished by the

[31] Adams's "Familiar Letters," 174; Smith's Ms. Diary, N. Y. Public Library.

Congress and Committee of Safety must be improved. Even before the fighting, a conflict of opinion had manifested itself upon the subject. The great majority favored the simplest possible course. If the Provincial Congress was truly the legal continuation of the General Court, why not simply resume government under the old Charter? The recent British alterations, the patriots had always argued, were null and void, inasmuch as the Charter was a compact which could be changed only by the two parties in agreement. A number of citizens wished to go a little farther; they proposed revising the old charter to suit the popular taste. Finally, the radicals urged a wholly new framework of government.[32] The course followed was the first. A request was made to the Continental Congress for an authorization to exercise the powers of government in some more satisfactory form, and that body in June recommended that an Assembly and Council be chosen in the old fashion to take charge of affairs, the Governor's chair being regarded as vacant until the King appointed another incumbent.

In midsummer of 1775, therefore, Massachusetts slipped easily back under her Charter of 1691, now administered wholly by the people. A house was elected on the former basis, almost immediately to be enlarged, and it in turn chose a Council of twenty-eight. The ballot was given all freeholders who owned realty worth 40 shillings a year, or other property worth £40. It would have been well if the General Court had arrogated to itself the right to name an acting Governor, for though the Council tried to exercise the executive functions of a civil character, it was too unwieldy a body to move effectively. This interim government went into operation when the new legislature met at the safe inland village of Watertown on July 19, 1775, and was destined to endure the surprising space of five years.[33]

New Hampshire showed somewhat greater boldness. After Lexington her hardy farmers had no intention of allowing any of the old departments to remain outside their control. The Congress

[32] Cushing, 164-65, quotes Joseph Warren and Thomas Young as writing as early as September, 1774, that the mass of the people were for resuming the old Charter and organizing a government immediately. But in May, 1775, Joseph Warren wrote Samuel Adams that they awaited the advice of the Continental Congress. "We cannot think," he added, "that you will advise us to take up that form established by the last Charter, as it contains in it the seeds of despotism, and would, in a few years, bring us again into the same unhappy situation in which we now are." See Journals Prov. Congress, 219-220. The advice of Congress is in 4 Amer. Archives, II, 1845.
[33] Journals Prov. Congress, 359; for John Adams's warm praise of the second legislature elected under the revised Charter, see Works, IX, 392.

which sat in May, 1775, had no sooner met than it sent a committee to Portsmouth for the records of government and turned them over to its clerk as a new secretary of state, while it obtained from the former treasurer his accounts and public moneys, and gave them to a new officer.[34]   The Committee of Safety which was appointed on May 20 served as an executive, especially in military affairs.   Still, the people had an uncomfortable sense that they were without a real government, and after Governor Wentworth fled they demanded that their representatives take the subject in hand.   The result was that in November a committee brought in a plan for electing a new Congress empowered to establish some form of administration. Every legal taxpayer should have a vote; every man possessing realty worth £200 should be eligible to a seat, and eighty-nine representatives should be apportioned among the counties by population. For this apportionment a special census was taken. Much to the disgust of the smallest communities, no town was allowed a separate representative unless it had a hundred freeholders, while some larger towns were given two seats, and Portsmouth three.   When the fifth Provincial Congress met on Dec. 21, 1775, under this plan, it proceeded to design a rough Constitution.[35]

This framework, adopted January 5, 1776, may be briefly described.   The Congress received the name and authority of a House of Representatives; it was to choose twelve freeholders, apportioned among the counties by population, to be a Council; and the Council was to elect its own president, and to exercise equal powers with the House except in the framing of money bills.   Most civil officers were to be elected by the two houses.   If the dispute with England did not close in 1776, the two houses were to prescribe a method by which the Council should be elected by the counties.   A new legislature was to be chosen at the close of each year, in a manner to be determined by the Council and Assembly.   In short, the little northern Province set up a government in which the legislature was almost absolute, and limited in power only by being chosen anew yearly.   No mention was made of a Governor or judiciary, and the president of the Council was given no more authority than the Speaker of the House.   A Portsmouth oligarchy of men like Judge Weare, Squire John Wentworth, and Dr. Thornton had governed

[34] Proceedings scattered through N. H. Prov. Papers, VII, 468-669. The proceedings of the Congress which met in April are in *Idem*, 452-67.
[35] Stackpole's "Hist. N. H.," II, ch. 5; N. H. Prov. Papers, VII, 690-710.

the Colony so far as it could in the old days, and the people were glad to see the legislature supreme in the new.

No other Province went quite so far before the close of 1775. We have seen that in New Jersey, as in various other Colonies, the first revolutionary legislature was a motley array of county delegations, some large and some small. But before the middle of August in 1775, the increased gravity of the crisis caused the Provincial government to draw up what was in effect a rough sketch of government. The qualified voters of each county, who had to be worth £50, were directed to hold a meeting the next month, and choose not more than five deputies to a new Congress which was to sit October 3 at Trenton. At the same time they were to elect their county committees of correspondence and inspection, while in March yearly the people of each township were to choose a committee to assist the county authorities.[36] The crown officers, who had been relaxing their grip on the administration, now almost wholly lost it, while the militia were organized on a Province-wide scale, and paper money was issued to pay for outfitting the troops. Since each county sent its full quota of five members to the Congress which met the spring of 1776, it was possible to vote there by individuals, instead of counties, a great improvement. New Jersey's Committee of Safety had meanwhile been appointed, with the usual executive powers, in the early autumn of 1775. This was the normal type of governmental development in 1775.

But it was North Carolina which in the late summer of 1775 established the most elaborate provisional government on the continent, a carefully graded system of committees. The radicalism of the individualistic, aggressive small farmers had been well expressed by the militia companies of Mecklenburg County, which held a meeting at Charlotte on May 31, and resolved that all royal commissions were null, that the government of each county was now vested in its revolutionary legislature under the Continental Congress, and that the county ought to form at least a temporary government of its own. After Governor Martin had fled, the demand for a systematic administration became irresistible, and was met by a Provincial Congress which Samuel Johnston called at Hillsborough, in the heart

---

[36] "By these means the government was to a great extent taken out of the hands of the officers holding under the King; and by the coöperation of most of the people, the committees thus chosen arrested and imprisoned persons believed to be disaffected to measures of resistance . . . ; and they became, in most parts of the Colony, the governing power." Elmer, "Const. and Govt. N. J.," ch. 2; born in 1793, Elmer had talked with many Revolutionary survivors.

of the regulators' country, beginning August 21.[37]   The Province was divided into six military and judicial districts, each to be controlled during the recesses of the Congress by a committee of thirteen, chosen by the district's delegates in the Congress.   Above these six committees there was placed a grand Provincial Council, composed also of thirteen members—two from each district, with a thirteenth appointed by the Congress—which during the recesses was to command the troops, draw on the treasury at will, and in fact do anything for the public security which did not contravene an act of the legislature.   The Provincial Congress of course retained paramount powers.   By this governmental plan the direction of affairs was well centralized, and the county committees, which had indulged in some shameful excesses against the Tories, were brought under restraint. War measures, too, could be more effectively pushed.[38]

The development of the revolutionary government in Maryland during 1775 is also sufficiently interesting to repay examination. During the summer it was arranged that each county should elect five delegates annually to the Provincial Convention (four had been the number in the old popular chamber), and that when this body was not sitting, authority should be vested in a Council of Safety of sixteen men, half from each shore of the Chesapeake.   Thus the revolutionary legislature, previously a gathering of uncertain size, was placed on almost the same basis as the House under the old régime—a little larger, that was all.   At the same time two treasurers, one for each shore, were appointed.

The Provincial Convention heard judicial cases, presented by the county committees, thus acting as a supreme court, and in one instance it banished a sheriff and confiscated £500 of his property. Each county committee was instructed to appoint a board to license or refuse licenses for civil suits.   Governor Eden remained virtually

[37] No fewer than 214 delegates had been elected, representing every county and borough town.   The Convention sat for three weeks; N. C. Col. Records, X, 164-220. It ordered 4,000 troops raised, and sent missions to plead with the former Regulators and Scotch Highlanders.   The plan of temporary government was devised by a committee of 46.
[38] See J. S. Bassett, "Const. Beginnings of N. C.," Johns Hopkins Studies, Series XII.   Among the members of the first Provincial Council were Cornelius Harnett, who had been in public life since 1730, Thomas Person, Willie and Thomas Jones, Abner Nash, and Samuel Ashe—an able roster.   But the government proved wretchedly poor.   The Provincial Council, which did not have to meet oftener than four times a year, and when it did meet sat only a few days, made an inadequate executive.   The district committees, also meeting at wide intervals, were equally weak.   The county and town committees, while less irresponsible than before, were by no means rendered fully trustworthy.   Not one of the governmental agencies knew the precise extent of its powers.   Naturally, the demand for a better framework of administration grew constantly.

undisturbed, and his nominal powers were still extensive, for provincial officers yet held their commissions from him, while the patriot leaders counselled outward obedience to his administration. But with his usual tact, he avoided a collision with the revolutionary agencies. We find him interceding with the committee of Ann Arundel county to obtain a mitigation of a harsh sentence upon a scow which brought, along with seventy indentured servants, a cargo of porter, coal, and cheese. The sentence was that the ship should put back to England, servants and all, but Eden obtained the admission of the immigrants.[39]

In most other Colonies the county committees were at least given closer coördination and clearer method by the councils of safety, which became feverishly busy the latter half of 1775. This was the fact in Pennsylvania, where the Committee of Safety was appointed June 30. The Virginia Convention elected its Committee of Safety, an executive junta of eleven members, on August 17, 1775, and at the same time undertook vigorous governmental measures, establishing a permanent provincial army, voting £350,000 in treasury notes, and laying taxes upon a considerable variety of objects. South Carolina had earlier chosen thirteen men as a Committee of Safety. As for Georgia, so tardy in entering the revolutionary movement, she now showed a highly creditable enterprise. Early in the summer her Provincial Congress established a committee of intelligence, and conferred upon the Council of Safety (created June 22) full recess powers of government, while near the end of the year it appointed a committee of fifteen to sit quarterly in Savannah as a court of appeal. Before the year 1775 closed the Council of Safety had been organized as a body sitting almost continuously, with George Walton as president, and swaying the widest authority. It was the real government, enforcing the non-importation agreement and the suspension of horse-racing, cock-fighting, and gaming.[40]

As the Colonies thus passed under temporary governments of a rudimentary form, nearly all the remaining British officials either departed or became virtual prisoners. Governor Wright of Georgia, without money, dignity, or authority, was glad to seize an opportunity early in 1776 to escape on board a British ship cruising off the coast, and the Georgians were glad to see him go. Lord William

[39] J. A. Silver, "Provisional Govt. of Md., 1774-1777," Johns Hopkins Studies, Series XIII, No. 10, ch. 1; B. C. Steiner, "Life of Sir Robert Eden," ch. 10, 11.
[40] Steven's "Hist. of Ga.," II, 121, 127.

Campbell of South Carolina had taken refuge on a warship the previous September, and thence had dissolved the Commons House, thus ending its one hundred and fifteen years of history. He was well liked and well connected, for he had married one of the most aristocratic daughters of the Colony, a young lady with a dower of £50,000.[41] His departure disturbed the conservative South Carolinians, who still hoped for a reconciliation, and the Charleston General Committee asked him to return, but he refused. Farther to the north, the only governors left in their capitals when the year 1775 closed were Eden of Maryland, John Penn of Pennsylvania, and Franklin of New Jersey, all of whom were by now totally impotent.

Penn, who more than half sympathized with the revolting colonists, was never expelled from the country. Franklin remained quietly in Perth Amboy, pacing his garden with increasing anxiety until in March, 1776, Lord Stirling with some patriot troops rode into the town and made him a prisoner in his house, taking his parole not to escape. In June the Provincial Congress ordered his arrest, for he had been corresponding with the British authorities, and he was soon sent up to East Windsor, Connecticut, for safety. But it was the position of Governor Eden which was the most remarkable.[42] He stayed on in Annapolis; though he deplored the crisis, he lived comfortably; and though he called the Council of Safety "a real and oppressive tyranny," he made no overt attempt to oppose it. In March, 1776, the interception of a letter sent him by Lord George Germaine showed that he had been in communication with England, and led the Continental Congress to ask the Council of Safety for an immediate seizure of the Governor and his papers. But this the Council, as anxious as the South Carolinians to maintain the ostensible forms of the old government, refused to grant.[43] Not until May did the considerate Provincial Convention go so far even as to declare that the public tranquility required Eden's departure, which should be allowed with all his personal property. He lingered on until June 24, when he left Annapolis in the frigate *Fowey*, but without his effects, as the ship harbored some deserters, and his

[41] McCrady, "S. C. Under the Royal Govt.," 709.
[42] B. C. Steiner, "Life of Sir Robert Eden," ch. 11.
[43] It declared that it could not act without the instructions of the Maryland Convention; and asserted that "'tis the peace and happiness of the Province we wish to preserve, and we are persuaded that it will be best done by keeping up the ostensible form of our chartered government."

possessions were detained on the wharf in an effort to compel their surrender.

II. CHARACTER OF THE NASCENT GOVERNMENTS

In one respect these simple provisional governments of 1775 were disappointing to some progressive thinkers. They showed a powerful tendency to follow the old colonial practise with respect to property qualifications for suffrage and the inequitable representation of sectional divisions. The time was too hectic for any innovations beyond those dictated by the plainest expediency. In Virginia and Maryland, for example, only men qualified to vote for the former legislators were now permitted to help choose the Provincial Conventions, and the qualification included possession of at least twenty-five settled acres in Virginia, and fifty acres (or £40) in Maryland. In both Colonies, again, all counties were granted uniform representation—the little tidewater Colonies of a small planter population in Virginia sent two delegates just as did the large western counties filled with small farmers. Throughout America the colonists were inclined, as English-speaking peoples always are, to build their new political institutions upon the old.

Nevertheless, certain distinct advances were being made in every section of the continent. We meet them during 1775 in New Hampshire and Massachusetts, in New Jersey and Pennsylvania, in North and South Carolina; Massachusetts, for example, gave every settlement of thirty or more freeholders a seat in the General Court.[44] In the two northernmost Colonies many towns were given a representation they had not previously enjoyed. In New Jersey, by a vote of five counties to four in the Provincial Congress, the old freehold qualification for the ballot was abolished, and anyone worth £50 was granted the right of suffrage. In Pennsylvania, as we shall see, large new elements, including many immigrants not born under the British flag and previously debarred by a naturalization requirement, were admitted to the polls, while the representation of the western counties in the revolutionary legislature was made much fairer than in the old Assembly.

Previous to the Revolution, no North Carolinian was allowed to

[44] This was done by an enactment of the July session, 1775; Acts and Laws of that year, p. 4.   In passing it the legislature took occasion to attack the practise in colonial days of incorporating certain towns without giving them the right of representation, saying that this was contrary both to common right and the charter. Thus was a large population, especially in the west, gratified by a notable reform.

vote unless he owned fifty acres. Naturally, in choosing members to the Provincial Convention the Whig leaders did not care to incur needless enmity by denying a voice to poor but zealous patriots. They wooed every element in the Colony—the disgruntled Regulators, the loyal Scotch Highlanders, and so on—and they did not forget the landless. When the provisional government of the late summer of 1775 was instituted, the suffrage was restricted to freeholders, but without stipulation as to the size of their estates. Almost everywhere the Revolution opened up a hope of political participation to men who had been denied it. The voteless mechanics of New York and Charleston, the Virginia shopkeeper, servant, or tenant, and the unnaturalized German of Philadelphia, wanted the ballot; while the frontier farmers wanted a representation which was totally denied them in South Carolina, and partly denied in Pennsylvania. These desires were among the springs which gave the revolutionary movement its irresistible power.

South Carolina admirably illustrates the difficulty of instituting a completely liberal system, and the inevitability of compromise. In arranging for the first Congress the question of representation was found perplexing. The populous upland country would expect to be represented, but as it had never been given membership in the Assembly, there were no fixed precedents. The only units of apportionment available were the four great judicial districts erected above the "fall line" a few years earlier—Cheraws, Camden, Orangeburgh, and Ninety-Six. The Charleston committee seized upon these divisions and decided that in the Provincial Congress Charleston should have thirty delegates, each parish six, and the four districts ten apiece. The upland country was thus allotted only 40 delegates out of 184. Yet at this time it had much more than half the population of the Province, even counting the slaves, who were far more numerous in the lowlands than elsewhere. An Assembly committee in 1769 had estimated that it contained three fourths of the white people. Unquestionably the lowlands did not believe that the disproportion was so great, while they also believed in the principle that wealth, of which they had the great preponderance, ought to be well represented. As for the up-country farmers, they had so long endured a virtual exclusion from the legislature that they were glad to win any concession. But an unjust precedent, destined to be effective generation after generation, and to be a source of discord until

Ben Tillman's time, was set in this limited apportionment to the rugged majority of the interior.[45]

The principal element excluded from the new governments, however, as the British executives were rowed to the nearest warships, and one regular legislature after another flickered out, was the ultra-conservative element—the Tories and those Whigs whom John Adams called timid, fearful, and skittish. The Tories showed apprehension wherever they were in a minority, inertia where they had a majority. A few attempts at Tory organization were made in the uplands of the Carolinas, on the western shore of Maryland, and in several New York counties, notably Albany and Westchester, but as a whole they were abortive. In the old Provincial Assemblies the conservatives had some opportunity to make themselves heard. But in the South not one of these legislatures met after those of South Carolina and Virginia broke up in June, 1775; in the North, outside the proprietary Colonies, none met after that of New Jersey adjourned in November.

The tendency of the conservatives was to abstain sullenly from participation in the choice of the Provincial Congresses and local revolutionary committees even where they would have been allowed to enter. But one Congress after another during the summer of 1775 drew up a test-oath or Association. That of Maryland pledged its signers to repel force by force, while it promised adherence to the new revolutionary agencies in a section which significantly set them upon a parity with the old civil government. That of South Carolina declared that all persons who refused to subscribe would be regarded as enemies to the liberty of the Colonies, a clause which Henry Laurens, always a defender of freedom of thought, courageously denounced.[46]

In the Colony where the Tories were strongest, New York, they were for a time mercilessly disciplined by the Provincial Congress. In August this body decreed that any loyalist who gave information

---

[45] Schaper, "Sectionalism and Representation in South Carolina." Attention being centred mainly on relations with England, this injustice did not arouse much immediate resentment. Note what the contemporary annalist Ramsay says of South Carolina in 1775 ("Hist. of S. C.," I, 251): "Legislative, executive, and judicial powers were insensibly transferred from their usual channels to a Provincial Congress, Council of Safety, and subordinate committees. . . . The power of these bodies was undefined; but by common consent it was comprehended in the old Roman maxim: 'To take care that the commonwealth should receive no damage.' The ardor of the people and their jealousy of the designs of Great Britain, gave the force of laws to their determinations. The voice of an approving country gave efficiency to the proceedings of the committees."

[46] See *S. C. Hist. and Genealog. Mag.*, VIII, 142, for Laurens's address.

to the enemy should be punished by the local committee; those who gave supplies to the enemy were to be fined double the value of the goods and jailed; those who denied the authority of the Congress were to be disarmed, and if they persisted, imprisoned. A few weeks later an order went out for the seizure of the arms of all who failed to swear their friendship to the American cause. Many outrages followed, and intense bitterness was generated. Just a year previously McDougall had cautioned the Massachusetts delegates, en route to Philadelphia, not to hint in New York City at war or independence, for the result would be disastrous. Many men were beginning to think of non-intercourse as a peace measure, he said, and would oppose it if it were called a war measure. Many others hated the "levelling" democracy of the Yankees and feared it would gain a foothold; a third element was imbued with an Episcopalian prejudice against Congregational New England; and a large mercantile party wanted continued commerce and amity with England.[47] Now in the fall of 1775 all these loyalist groups were held in submission, and the radicals spoke frankly of the possibility of independence. But a large and powerful section of the population, in both the city and rural counties, awaited only the British invasion to rally to the royal standard.

There were fewer Tories in Pennsylvania, and more of the extremely cautious Whigs typified by John Dickinson. John Adams tells us that when many citizens there "began to see that independence was approaching, they started back." It was in Pennsylvania that the final struggle between conservatives and radicals was most protracted, most intense, and most disastrous in its after-effects upon the patriot resistance to Great Britain.

We have seen that Pennsylvania came spiritedly to the aid of New England after the passage of the Boston Port Act, that a Provincial Conference was at once convoked, and that an energetic network of county committees was created. After Lexington, we have also noted, the Assembly coöperated vigorously with the Philadelphia and other committees in the ordinary measures of military preparation. The great question was whether the Assembly should be allowed to continue at the helm, as in Connecticut and Rhode Island, or whether it should be pushed aside by a Provincial Congress, as in most Colonies. For the Assembly was decidedly con-

[47] Adams's "Works," II, 350.

servative, while the Provincial Congress would be as radical as progressives like Reed and Bryan could desire. John Dickinson, born to great wealth and of a Quaker family, educated in England, deeply versed in the cool philosophy of law, and as moderate in temperament as Samuel Adams was bold and ardent, was the foremost defender of the Assembly's leadership, and was supported by Charles Thomson, Robert Morris, and James Wilson. Thomson has declared that caution was indispensable: [48]

A great majority of the Assembly was composed of men in the Proprietary and Quaker interest, who [though] heretofore opposed to each other were now uniting, the one from motives of policy, the other from principles of religion. To press matters was the sure way of cementing that union, and thereby raising a powerful party in the state against the cause of America. Whereas, by prudent management, and an improvement of occurrences, as they happened, there was reason to hope that the Assembly, and consequently the whole Province, might be brought into the dispute, without any considerable opposition. And from past experience it was evident that though the people of Pennsylvania are cautious and backward in entering into measures, yet when they are engaged none are more firm, resolute, and persevering.

Throughout 1774 the Assembly was still fully in control of the government, with entire popular confidence. The people and legislators were at one in abhorring extreme measures. The Assembly met a fortnight after the Continental Congress opened on September 5, and when Congress broke up near the end of the following month, tendered it a dinner at the City Tavern, then reckoned the finest hostelry in America. At the dinner, as John Adams relates, "a sentiment was given—'May the sword of the parent never be stained with the blood of her children.'—Two or three broadbrims were over against me at the table. One of them said, 'This is not a toast but a prayer; come, let us join in it.' And they took their glasses accordingly." Adams also tells us that when the resolution of October 10, approving Boston's resistance to the late acts of Parliament, was passed in Congress, the resolution whose tone did so much to harden the heart of George III, "I saw the tears gush into the eyes of the old, grave, pacific Quakers of Pennsylvania."

One passage of his diary lets us into the secret of a considerable amount of the Quaker dislike of New England radicalism. One evening he, with Hopkins, and Ward of Rhode Island, and other New Englanders, were invited by some Quakers to a meeting at Carpenter's Hall. They found it crowded; and the leading Friends, seated with their large beaver hats on, informed them that they wished to discuss certain complaints received from Baptists and

[48] Thomson Papers, N. Y. Hist. Soc. Colls., 1878, 280-81.

Quakers in Massachusetts, relative to restrictions upon freedom of conscience there. Rich old Isaac Pemberton spoke at length upon the obstacles to Continental union in any such religious discrimination. John Adams flushed with anger. The suspicion leaped to his mind that Pemberton was "endeavouring to avail himself of this opportunity to break up the Congress, or at least to withdraw the Quaker and the governing part of Pennsylvania from us; for, at that time, by means of a most unequal representation, the Quakers had a majority in the House of Assembly." But he mastered his resentment, and made a tactful defense of the Massachusetts laws, which Cushing and Samuel Adams supported.[49]

Yet even John Adams in the fall of 1774 trusted that the Assembly would maintain a firm Whig stand. Elections were held at the beginning of October, and when the forty members for the twelve counties and the city met, it was found they included such able men as Dickinson, Wayne, Ross, Mifflin, and Thomson. They unanimously approved the report of the Pennsylvania delegates in the Continental Congress, and reappointed substantially the same delegation.[50] The following March a majority of the forty showed their sturdy Whiggism when they received from Governor Penn a message expressing the belief that all grievances should be humbly represented to his Majesty by the various colonial assemblies, not through a general Congress. The Assembly voted a defiant answer, defending Congressional action, 22 to 15. Joseph Galloway, the most prominent Pennsylvania Tory, led the opposition, which consisted of all Bucks County members, three in four of those from Lancaster County, and half the Philadelphia County delegation, but Thomson, Mifflin and other soberly progressive men were too much for him.[51] Above all, when the news of Lexington arrived, as we have seen, the Assembly acted with surprising ardor and resolution. Dickinson, like such other conservatives as Rutledge and Jay, was a man of spirit, who roused instantly when his countrymen were attacked. He was the foremost leader in the legislature, and when it appointed a

---

[49] Adams's "Works," II, 398-400.

[50] A second provincial conference was called by the Philadelphia committee of safety late in 1774. The principal objects were set forth as a stiffening of the enforcement of the non-importation association, and the stimulation of domestic production. Reed presided over the brief five-day session. As yet no really warlike measures were under consideration; people were discussing enterprises which implied a faith in continued peace, such as the bridging of the Schuylkill. Votes and Proceedings Pa. H. of Representatives, VI, 573; "Stille's "Life of Dickinson," I, 150; Reed's "Reed," I, ch. 4.

[51] Votes and Proceedings, VI, 577; March 9, 1775.

Committee of Public Safety (June 30), he was made chairman. So effectually did he and others labor that troops by the thousand were soon under arms. When the Assembly met on September 20, 1775, following a recess, it was pleased to hear from him that the Province was more than half prepared for war. He himself was colonel of the first regiment raised, and so ranking officer for all Pennsylvania.

But throughout the summer of 1775 the atmosphere of Pennsylvania had been growing more electric. A domestic storm was brewing, as those could perceive who stopped to look and listen attentively. The tension was by no means caused by the unwillingness of much of the Quaker population to take up arms; its principal source lay in the anger and consternation aroused by the radical hints of approaching independence. Men like Dickinson were willing to fight to their last drop of blood, men like Morris to spend their last penny, in defense of their rights, but the idea of breaking from England they abhorred. A great number of these moderates began to take fright during the summer; they were thorough patriots when it was a question of defending America within the Empire, but they did not want to see her thrown outside the Empire. They were vigorously supported by Quakers conscientiously opposed to war.[52]

Amid his multifarious Provincial duties, Dickinson was laboring throughout the summer in the Continental Congress to promote reconciliation with England. He prepared the second petition to the King, adopted by Congress in July, 1775. Thomson tells us that it was necessary to make this experiment, for "without it it would have been impossible to have persuaded the bulk of the people of Pennsylvania that a humble petition drawn up without those clauses against which the Ministry and Parliament had taken exception in the former petition, would not have met with a favorable reception."

The debate on the document aroused a violent animosity between Dickinson and the New England delegates. John Adams and Sullivan made speeches in opposition, taking little pains to conceal their opinion that America ought already to have destroyed all the British commissions, to have drawn up a Continental constitution, formed a navy, and arrested every crown officer. Dickinson, in a towering

[52] The Quakers were a serious problem to military authorities. On grounds of belief, the more orthodox refused to give direct assistance to fighters in any form. Since many who were not Quakers objected to making heavy sacrifices if the prosperous Friends were not to lift a finger, the Committee of Safety recommended to the Assembly that all able-bodied citizens be made liable to military service, except the conscientious objectors, who should be required to pay a fixed sum in lieu of it. This was Franklin's idea. Votes and Proceedings, VI, 601.

rage, one day met Adams in the hallway of Congress. "Look ye!" he burst out, "If you don't concur with us in our pacific system, I and a number of us will break off from you in New England, and we will carry on the opposition by ourselves in our own way." Adams, finding himself in "a happy temper," was able to answer coolly. But he at once wrote a friend denouncing the conservatives, and referred bitterly to Dickinson as "a certain great fortune and piddling genius." This letter fell into the hands of the English, who published it; so that when Dickinson read it, he cut Adams in the street. The downright Braintree lawyer informs us that during some of his public harangues in Philadelphia at this time, "on looking round the assembly I have seen horror, terror, and detestation strongly marked on the countenances" of many of his auditors.[53]

When a new Assembly met in October, it found the spirit of factionalism growing more pronounced in the Province. It was hardly as able an Assembly as before, though Franklin and Robert Morris as well as Dickinson, Mifflin, and Ross were present. A new Committee of Safety was appointed.[54] The Quakers brought forward a careful explanation of their objections to any share in the war, which angered the city committee of observation and the troops now drilling everywhere. Indignant public protests came from these patriots, and the pressure upon the Assembly grew stronger than ever from the radical side. The result was that late in November, after prolonged debate, a special tax was levied upon those who for conscience's sake refused to bear arms, while new war measures were voted. After the session ended, the storm rose constantly higher. The conservatives and extremists were becoming irreconcilable. Most alarming of all to Dickinson, Morris, and Thomson, the question whether the Charter and Assembly should be suppressed was becoming the central issue.[55]

The struggle of the right and left wings of the Whigs in Pennsylvania was largely a reflection of the same increasing struggle in Congress and a half-dozen other Colonies. As 1776 began, those who believed in independence and those who did not openly clashed. Thomas Paine published his powerful argument for it, "Common Sense," from a Philadelphia press on January 9, 1776. Some had

[53] Adams's "Works," II, 407-13; Cf. Austin's "Life of Gerry," I, 194.
[54] Votes and Proceedings, VI, 626; it had 32 members.
[55] Stillé's "Life of Dickinson," I, 172-75; the radicals, as in New York, were sometimes called "the Presbyterian party."

previously held that separation from Britain was inevitable, while many were convinced by his pamphlet. Congress tended to be more conservative than General American opinion, but in Congress the same sentiment began to find vigorous expression, the New England Colonies and Virginia being now for a total breach. Of the Pennsylvania delegates, Franklin alone was at first boldly for independence, and his stand made him the object of no little abuse. A Marylander wrote from Philadelphia on February 4 that "Franklin has hurt himself much here, and reigns only with the Presbyterian interest, which is much stronger than I could wish it to be." It was realized that so far as independence went, Pennsylvania probably held the scales; that when Franklin and the Adamses won her over, the step would be taken. But the Pennsylvania delegates were bound by instructions, drawn up the previous November by Dickinson, which enjoined them to reject all proposals leading to a separation from England.[56]

The press of the Province warmly took sides upon this contest in Congress. The chief leaders of the conservatives remained Dickinson, Mifflin, Morris, and an exceedingly able young Scotch-born lawyer of Carlisle named James Wilson; those of the radical party were Dr. Franklin, Thomas McKean, and such frontier chieftains as Robert Whitehill. But among the radicals at Philadelphia new men were coming to the front, some of them military officers, like the fire-eating Colonel Daniel Roberdeau of the city battalions, and some civilians like Judge George Bryan. The newcomers were for the most part men of the same ultra-democratic principles as Samuel Adams and Thomas Jefferson. They disliked British rule, and also disliked the somewhat aristocratic character of the Province Charter, which gave the western population an inadequate representation in the Assembly, and denied the ballot to unpropertied freemen. Paine's remarks upon State government were written to please such leaders. John Adams, as probably the most determined leader of the movement in Congress for independence, was glad to ally himself with them to overthrow the Assembly, and thus bring Pennsylvania into line.[57] Naturally, his exertions were resented by all conservatives as an impudent meddling in Province affairs.

The angry excitement, the uncertainty of the outcome, and the

[56] Reed's "Reed," I, 155; Cf. Austin's "Life of Gerry," I, 179.
[57] Adams did not like their governmental ideas, however, nor they his. When he published his "Thoughts on Government" in 1776, they were alarmed, and Paine came to Adams's lodgings to remonstrate.

dependence of the government upon it, made Pennsylvanians feel during the late winter that a kind of anarchy had fallen upon the Colony. But the march of events favored the radicals. Sporadic fighting from New Hampshire to Georgia, rumors of a British attack on New York, and above all, the evidence that the British Ministry would be unyielding, strengthened the sentiment for more extreme measures. It encouraged the democratic element and the frontier counties to demand immediate reforms in the structure of the government.

In the midst of the turmoil, the Assembly sat from the middle of February until April 6, 1776, and resumed its labors May 20.[58] It was bewildered. Animated by a keen sense of duty to the conservatives they represented, still strongly attached to the past, not comprehending the drift of the times, its members found it painful to make concessions to the radical clamor. The city extremists in disgust called a new conference of the county committees, intending to create a powerful Provincial Congress, a move which greatly alarmed all the moderates.[59] But Dickinson, laboring frenziedly, succeeded in postponing the crisis. The insistent western demand for a fairer Assembly representation was met in March, when by a heavy majority, 21 to 9, the legislature provided for admitting seventeen additional members—four from the city and the remainder from eight counties—almost balancing the two sections.[60] The city committeemen, thus mollified, revoked the call for a new Provincial conference.[61]

But two other insistent demands of the radicals and democrats remained unsatisfied. The more important was for the abolition of the property qualifications for the ballot. Do not farmers and mechanics constitute ninety-nine parts in a hundred of the American people? asked one writer. Do not half the brains and character of

---

[58] Votes and Proceedings, VI, 726.

[59] Voting in the Convention would be by counties, and hence the radicals would control it. Paine in "Common Sense" had attacked the Assembly as unrepresentative, and not a real spokesman for the Colony. But Reed "applied himself earnestly to obviate the necessity or pretext for precipitate action by procuring the redress of the two great grievances of which the popular party complained—the non-revision of the articles of the Association, and the inadequacy of representation in the Assembly." Reed, "Reed," I, 162. Reed was in the legislature at the time. The city committee of inspection had been authorized by the previous provincial conference to call another conference at any time it chose. See the Pa. Packet, March 18 ff., for a wordy war between "Cato" and others. "Cato," accusing the committee of wishing to destroy the Charter Constitution, said that not more than 200 electors had participated in its choice.

[60] Two each from Lancaster, York, Cumberland, Berks, and Northampton, and one each from Bedford, Northumberland, and Westmoreland Counties.

[61] "Cato" declared that public sentiment had forced this step. "I know of some counties where the whole committee was named by six or seven voices only."

Philadelphia belong to men with leather aprons and the rest to sons of such men? [62] If the poor are not to vote, America had better acknowledge the jurisdiction of the gentlemen who make up Parliament. Again, in the press and on the street corners, a noisy clamor was raised against the oath of allegiance to the King which all Assemblymen, as for seventy years previous, had taken. This oath had no real importance, yet it was called an inconsistency and an obstacle to patriotic action. Finally, many radicals were deeply offended when on April 4 the Assembly, following Dickinson's lead, refused to rescind the instructions to the delegates in Congress, keeping them bound to oppose independence. [63]

As May opened, it was plain that the slow-moving Assembly and the Charter were in dire peril. On the first of the month, elections were held for the seventeen additional members. In Philadelphia there was a little disorder by the Germans, upon whose right to vote unless naturalized some doubts had been expressed. The Quakers, Anglicans, and Proprietary party united there to beat the radicals, and won three of the four seats, the fourth being taken by George Clymer, a sober, responsible member of the progressive faction. This victory in the metropolis assured the conservatives of a continued control of the House. [64] But in the western and northern counties the radicals made such a sweep that all the moral advantage of the election was theirs—only one of the thirteen men chosen seems to have been a distinct conservative. They were jubilant, declaring that the Province was with them, and that they would have won even in Philadelphia had so many of their party not been in the army. Radical leaders like Roberdeau and Whitehill saw that an alliance between the mechanics in Philadelphia and the Irish, Scotch, and other frontiersmen would give them control of the Colony; a sweeping control if they could broaden the ballot. In the neighboring Provinces they beheld the Provincial Congresses ruling unfettered. They therefore determined to obtain authority from the Continental Congress to change the framework of government, and to sweep the Assembly forever into the waste-basket.

[62] *Pa. Packet*, March 18, 1776.
[63] C. H. Lincoln, "Rev. Movement in Pa., 1760-1776."
[64] The contest was remarkably close in Philadelphia, the head of the poll receiving 941 votes, and Daniel Roberdeau, at the foot, 890. See the "Remembrancer" of Christopher Marshall, 67, 68; a volume that contains much material upon Cannon, Young, Matlack, and Paine. Paine thought that the defeat of the radicals in the city was due to the absence of many Whig voters with the armed forces, and was doubtless right. See Phila. *Journal*, May 8; C. H. Lincoln, "Rev. Movement in Pa."; Reed's "Reed," I, 184.

It was therefore Congress, the Virginians and New Englanders leading, which brought Pennsylvania's affairs to a crisis. On May 10 it passed John Adams's resolution urging the Colonies which had no adequate governments to form them, and five days later it declared against oaths of allegiance to the Crown. The radicals quickly responded. On May 20, the day the Assembly reconvened, they held a mass-meeting in Philadelphia with Roberdeau as chairman. It drew up a manifesto, which recited that as Congress had asked for new governments under the authority of the people, and as the Assembly derived its powers from the Crown, it should not be allowed to frame the new government; moreover, its members were chosen by too narrow an electorate, and some of them were too closely connected with the Proprietary. The mass-meeting did not deny the right of the Assembly to sit for a short time merely as a legislature.[65] But it assumed that the Charter, as an antiquated relic of British authority, would have to be replaced by a Constitution, and it wished the conference of county committees to summon a constitutional convention. Trusty agents were sent to Lancaster and other towns to arouse sentiment for this plan.[66]

The friends of the old order, Dickinson and Thomson at their head, rushed to the defense. Could intelligent men at one stroke surrender the venerated and time-tested Charter? It was rooted in the popular affection. With its provision for an annual Assembly, the election of which was fixed upon a certain day, and its refusal to allow the Governor to dissolve or prorogue the legislature, it fully safeguarded the public liberties. A great mass-meeting of the conservatives drew up a counter-manifesto, praising the Assembly, and prophesying that the radicals' plan would damp the zeal of multitudes for the American cause. Even Joseph Reed, an able popular leader on the progressive side, joined in the protest.[67]

The Assembly tried to ride out the tempest, making one new concession after another. It took steps to repeal the naturalization requirements and the oath of allegiance to the King. On June 5 a

[65] Many radical leaders, however, did deny this, and wished a convention to pass upon the status of the Assembly. Reed's "Reed," I, 185 ff.
[66] Cf. *Pa. Packet,* May 20, 1776, letter by "Forester"; the text of the manifesto is in Votes and Proceedings, VI, 726-27. It states that "we have very alarming apprehensions, that a new government modeled by persons so inconsistently circumstanced, would be the means of subjecting ourselves and our posterity, to greater grievances than any we have hitherto experienced."
[67] The text of the counter-petition is in Votes and Proceedings, VI, 732 ff.; see also Harley, "Life of Charles Thomson," 78, 79. A remonstrance in favor of the Charter was signed by 6,000 citizens of the city and adjacent counties; *Pa. Gazette,* June 12, 1776.

committee headed by Dickinson was asked to draft instructions giving the delegates in Congress carte blanche to vote for independence, and they were approved on the fourteenth.[68] But the radicals would now be satisfied with nothing less than the surrender of the Charter. They alleged that some of the Assemblymen had shown themselves absolute Tories by their stubborn opposition to independence, that the majority had treated Congress with impertinence, and that they had tried to heighten a local quarrel between different revolutionary agencies. A wave of patriotic feeling was sweeping the continent. Nearly all provinces had now been won to independence, and Dickinson and Robert Morris, still averse to it, were by many regarded as virtual traitors. Some radical Assemblymen, new and old, began to stay away from the legislature, so that it became harder and harder to find a quorum. The local military forces denied the right of the Assembly to appoint the two brigadier-generals for which Congress had called. Finally, on June 14 the Assembly adjourned; it intended to meet again in August, but was never able to organize.[69] The old order was dead.

The sequel needs hardly to be described. Already the Philadelphia committee, under McKean, had summoned a conference of the county committees, which, four days after the adjournment of the regular Assembly, came to order in Carpenters' Hall.[70] It stopped short whatever was left of the old Provincial administration, notifying the judges, for example, to suspend the courts until a new government could be devised. Rules were laid down for electing delegates to a constitutional convention, to gather on June 15, and the overturn in Pennsylvania was complete.

But the manner in which the overturn had come chagrined a large part of the population of Pennsylvania. The triumph of McKean, Bryan, Franklin, and Roberdeau was the defeat not only of Dickinson, Wilson, Morris, Thomson, and Mifflin, but of the great majority of the Quakers and Anglicans. Many looked upon the Assembly with an esteem that dated from the years in which, under Speakers Lloyd and Kinsey, it had resisted Proprietorial tyrannies; many regarded Penn's Charter with deep reverence. The destruction of both seemed wanton. Had not the Assembly, step by step, met

[68] Votes and Proceedings, VI, 740.
[69] *Idem*, 743.
[70] The call for the conference is in the *Pa. Packet*, June 17, 1776; see also an "Address to the People" in that paper, June 24; and the report of the conference in the issue for July 1.

every demand made upon it? Was not the Charter one of the best in America? Both, a multitude of patriotic Pennsylvanians felt, should have been preserved.[71]

III. The Decision for Independence

Thus ended the last phase of the revolutionary transition in the Colony where the conservatives showed the most tenacious resistance to the radicals; what of this phase elsewhere? Up to the spring of 1776 the Provinces had been a straggling file. Massachusetts and Virginia had kept to the front, with the other New England Colonies and North Carolina close at their heels and sometimes even for a few paces ahead. Far to the rear at first had limped Georgia, taunted and scolded by her sisters, but by a sudden spurt in the summer of 1775 she had taken her place well forward. New York was still, from the radical point of view, one of the laggards, and South Carolina another. Just how were all brought up to the mark of independence in July, 1776?

The war had become general by the close of 1775. The British were pent in Boston by an army, now under Washington, which had cheered enthusiastically one summer day when 1400 riflemen, tall, keen-eyed men in hunting shirts, had marched in from the inland districts of Virginia, Maryland, and Pennsylvania. Falmouth, now Portland, Maine, had been reduced to smoking embers by a bombardment in October. Montreal had fallen to the Americans in November, and Quebec had repulsed them the following month. In Virginia Patrick Henry, who cherished military ambitions, had been appointed commander-in-chief, and during the late summer and autumn of 1775 troops had filed into Williamsburg and bivouacked behind William and Mary College. Fighting began there the middle of November, when virtually forced upon the Virginians by Dunmore's provocative raids from Norfolk. The Virginia Committee of

---

[71] Charles Thomson wrote that Pennsylvania had a liberal Charter-Constitution, admirably adapted for independence. It should have been kept. "The Assembly of Pennsylvania, if they could be brought to take a part, supplied the place of a Convention, with this advantage, that being a part of the Legislature, they preserved the legal forms of government, consequently had more weight and authority among the people. . . . The cause of America was every day gaining ground, and the people growing more and more determined. The timid were acquiring courage, and the wavering confirmed in the opposition. Hence, it was apparent the election would soon be wholly in the power of the patriot and Whig party. For these reasons, the Whigs who were then members wished to temporize, and make use of the Assembly rather than a Convention, but unhappily they were thwarted. . ." Thomson Papers, N. Y. Hist. Soc. Colls., 1878, 282-83; *Pa. Mag. of Hist.*, XIII, No. 4, where Charles J. Stillé attacks the work of the radicals as a misfortune to Pennsylvania.

Safety, headed by Edmund Pendleton, a conservative barrister more than fifty years of age and of infirm health, had prevented an attack upon the governor when he could easily have been crushed. Now, a brilliant little victory won at the Great Bridge near Norfolk by Colonel William Woodford, whom Pendleton had pushed to the front while holding Henry back, showed that the Americans were masters of the situation.[72]   There was fighting in Georgia at the beginning of March, 1776, when a British demonstration against Savannah was repelled. During the winter the Tories of the back country in the Carolinas showed increasing restiveness, and those of North Carolina were bloodily defeated at Moore's Creek in February.

The more radical colonists, by the end of 1775 inclining strongly towards independence, were eager to give their governments a still greater regularity and permanence of form. The influence of New England lent a powerful impulse in this direction. Massachusetts in the summer of 1775, and New Hampshire at the close of the year, had taken their places beside Connecticut and Rhode Island with wholly popular governments sufficiently good to last for a long time. Virginia and South Carolina followed their example by asking the Continental Congress for advice on the subject, and were counselled to call a full and free representation of the people whenever they liked, to draw up a framework that would best secure peace and good order during the continuance of the dispute with Great Britain.

Both early in 1776 were almost ready to take that step. Georgia's Provincial Congress did come near taking it in April. Sitting at Savannah, the members enacted a set of "Rules and Regulations" which provided a crude government as a temporary expedient. A President and commander-in-chief was to be elected by the Congress for six months; he was to be assisted by a Council of Safety; and subject to the advice of the Council, he was to have all the executive powers of government. Courts were erected, and the office of Attorney-General was created. The Provincial Congress of course retained all the legislative powers, and had supreme control of the Colony.[73]

[72] Henry warmly cherished his military aspirations, and his chagrin when he was denied a brigadiership by the Continental Congress was as deep as Hancock's chagrin when John Adams nominated Washington to head the Continental army. Washington expressed a widespread view when he wrote that "I think my countrymen made a capital mistake when they took Henry out of the senate to place him in the field"; "Writings," III, 463.   For the spirit in which Henry resigned his colonelcy, see 4 Amer. Archives, IV, 1516 ff.

[73] Text of the "Rules and Regulations" is in Stevens's "Georgia," II, 292 ff.

In South Carolina the final decision for independence followed a struggle almost as interesting as that in Pennsylvania. The patriots there had shown a fighting spirit during 1775, but they did not want a total severance from England. John Drayton, a close observer, says that even after Bunker Hill the Council of Safety was almost evenly divided between the radicals and conservatives, with its head, Laurens, apparently siding with neither. When the radicals wished the harbor fortified, Laurens defeated their first proposal, and in September, 1775, he opposed a scheme for blocking up its entrance by sinking vessels. Holding this balance, and representing a great body of educated middle opinion, he wrote his brother in October that though he would stake everything upon resistance to British tyranny, he had always believed that the "taking the reins of government into our hands" was an "injurious determination." The introduction of the subject of independence into the Congress of February, 1776, caused such an outburst of indignation that if the radicals had pressed it, the Congress would have dissolved then and there. Laurens that month compared himself to a child violently thrust from his father's house, and declared that the word independence "cuts me deep—has caused tears to trickle down my cheeks." [74] John Rutledge, the foremost citizen, also wept; he was emphatically against separation from the Empire to the last, and there is reason to believe that as late as 1778 he cherished a faint hope of friendly reunion. Many lowlanders felt precisely as he did.

Nor was loyalism confined to Charleston and the educated, aristocratic lowland planters. Up-country were elements which July 4, 1776, found indefeasibly attached to the Crown—some of the Scovilite Regulators, the Scotch who had seen enough of rebellion in '45, a few Ulster Scotch who disliked the lowlanders, and Germans who still thought of George as Elector of Hanover. In September, 1775, a bloody battle at Ninety-Six between thousands of Whigs and Tories was barely averted, and in November a conflict there between 2000 Tories and 600 Whigs resulted in thirty-four fatalities. [75] It was necessary for the Provincial Congress at the close of 1775 to send a force northwestward to traverse the Province from end to end and overcome the Tories.

When 1776 opened there was still a powerful weight of sentiment against even a temporary new Constitution, as opening the door to

[74] Wallace, "Life of Henry Laurens," 224, 225.
[75] Drayton, "Memoirs of the American Rev.," II, 72, 73; 118-122.

independence, yet a committee was appointed on February 11 to report the draft of one.[76] While this committee was at work, almost all opposition was swept away in a night by the news of the enactment of Parliament on December 21, authorizing the confiscation of certain American property as that of rebels. On March 5 the new plan of government was received, and three weeks later was adopted. It was hardly a Constitution in the modern sense, for those who, like Rutledge and Lowndes, clung to the belief that they might soon return amicably under the unquestioned sovereignty of the Crown would hear of nothing but a framework of provisional government. That belief floated away with the smoke of the battle of Fort Moultrie three months later, and most citizens received with outward jubilance the news of independence.

None of the other Colonies south of the Potomac stood in any doubt as the spring of 1776 advanced. Georgia was stung to anger by the attack on Savannah. Similarly, North Carolina was thoroughly aroused by the Tory peril that was stemmed at Moore's Creek, and by the presence of a hostile force under Sir Henry Clinton on the Cape Fear River. Her Provincial Convention was the first body of the kind to give explicit approval to the proposal of independence (April 13, 1776), and the same day it appointed a committee to prepare a tentative draft of a constitution. In Virginia the first shots that Dunmore's and Woodford's troops exchanged near Norfolk were virtually a volley across the grave of the old crown régime, and most patriots recognized that it was dead. The Convention called upon all citizens to rise in resistance to Dunmore, threatened with death all loyalists who fought against their fellow Virginians, and supported Woodford as he pushed rapidly forward and captured Norfolk. When a little later the town was destroyed by fire following a British bombardment, and when Virginians heard that Dunmore had proclaimed freedom to the slaves of all rebels, almost the last vestiges of the desire for a compromise disappeared. Most of the counties were eager for full political freedom. The final and most important Provincial Convention, met on May 5, 1776, at Williamsburg, with the fixed purpose of declaring for American independence, and forming a new government. Its first days were

[76] A committee on February 10 had reported "that the present mode of conducting affairs is inadequate to the well governing of the good people of the Colony" and that the Congress should immediately undertake a new government. Drayton, "Memoirs of the American Rev.," II, 171-73.

devoted to a variety of war measures, but on the 15th it instructed
the Virginia delegates at Philadelphia to propose independence, and
appointed a committee to prepare a constitution.

New York hesitated a little longer than the radicals allowed even
Pennsylvania to do. When Washington, with his army following
him over the muddy roads from Boston, reached the city early in
April, he found that, as he put it, he would have a difficult card to
play. The Tories were numerous, in constant communication with
the British ships in the harbor, and so bold that they had recently
proposed sending out writs for a new Assembly. But the chief
difficulty was presented, as in South Carolina and Pennsylvania, by
the conservative Whigs, who were ready to fight but as yet not ready
to cut all the old ties with the motherland.

After the harsh measures taken against the Tories during the fall
and early winter, a certain reaction had occurred among the Whigs.
Men like Jay were disgusted by such episodes as the destruction of
the press of the Tory editor Rivington. The elections to the Provincial Congress in May, 1776, the same month that the radicals
were beaten in the Assembly elections in Pennsylvania, showed that
the moderates were still in control, and that they resented the
excessive fervor of leaders like Lamb and McDougall. There was
no doubt that most of the inhabitants were opposed to any summary
change in the political position of the Province. When in June the
question of independence was presented at Philadelphia by R. H.
Lee, and the New York delegates wrote home for instructions. the
Provincial Congress passed a resolution, moved by Jay, which declared that the people had not yet authorized a declaration of independence.[77] However, late in May it had been determined that a
new government should be framed, and the voters had been asked to
send delegates to a new Congress, to be also a constitutional convention—a virtual notice that independence was at hand. This new
Congress ratified the national declaration on July 9, a week late.

Each of the three smaller Colonies touching Pennsylvania waited,
like her, until June before giving their decision. New Jersey was
the most progressive in temper. President John Witherspoon of the
college at Princeton, who had come from Scotland less than a decade
before, had been asked whether he thought the colonists ripe for
independence. "Ripe? Rotting!" he rejoined. All his undergradu-

[77] 4 Amer. Archives, VI, 1212; Journals N. Y. Prov. Cong., II, 236 ff.

ates were Sons of Liberty, he had told John Adams the fall of 1774.[78] Here it was the third Provincial Convention, meeting at Burlington, the nearest suitable town to Philadelphia, on June 11, 1776, which finished converting the Colony into a State. It at once sent to Philadelphia the five staunch believers in independence whose names appear under the Declaration, ordered Governor Franklin's arrest, and began the drafting of a State Constitution.

In Delaware the result was long in doubt, for the Tories were almost as powerful as in New York. As the discussion in Congress grew warm, with Caesar Rodney and George Read at first holding the Colony against independence, while McKean labored for it with indomitable zeal, party feeling was intensified. Many Quakers and Episcopalians felt as averse to it as their brethren higher up the Delaware, but the defeat which the conservatives suffered in Pennsylvania decisively weakened them. Their overthrow was followed, as in the larger Colony, by the overthrow of the Charter, and in August a Constitution was drafted.[79] As for Maryland, as late as May 21 the Provincial Convention was still "firmly persuaded that a reunion with Great Britain on constitutional principles would most effectually secure the rights and liberties" of the people. The chief factor in altering that conviction, apart from the pressure of events, was a whirlwind campaign waged by Samuel Chase. On June 28 the delegates in Congress were finally ordered to join in approving the Declaration.[80]

IV. FUNCTION OF REVOLUTIONARY GOVERNMENTS

Roughly speaking, it had taken one year, from the spring of 1773 to the spring of 1774, to arrange a system of steady communication among the various Colonies. It had taken another year, from the spring of 1774 to the spring of 1775, to give the Colonies revolutionary congresses, conventions, or conferences, prepared to exercise some of the powers of government. It had taken a half year, to the fall of 1775, to drive out several governors, take over more powers, and prepare to fight; and another half year to determine upon independence. The revolutionary movement was an accelerating stream.

[78] C. H. Hunt, "Life of Edward Livingston," 38, 39. In the month of independence Witherspoon was one of three Americans selected for effigy-burning by the British and Tories on Staten Island.
[79] J. T. Scharf, "Delaware," I, 186-87, 215 ff.; W. T. Read, "Life and Corr. of George Read," ch. 1 and 2; Agnes Hunt, "Provincial Committees of Safety," 98; L. P. Powell, "Historic Towns of the Middle States," chapter on Wilmington.
[80] 4 Amer. Archives, VI, 1491; Proceedings of Md. Convention, 176.

The next six months was to see a marked burst of activity in the drafting of State Constitutions.

Regarding the Revolution from the provincial point of view, we are impressed by the logical sureness with which it passed from stage to stage, the regularity of the steps taken. First we see the scattering local committees; then a legislative committee of correspondence; then a congress starting up side by side with the legislature; then the disappearance of the latter and the rough elaboration of the new government to cover executive and judicial functions; and finally the drafting of a new and free constitution. One reason for this regularity and logic was the fact that in many Provinces the conservatives fought every inch of the way, and gains had to be made rather by converting than by coercing them. A greater reason lay in the ingrained political sagacity of the Americans, inimical to unnecessary violence and hurry. Violence there was, and even some local mob-government and brief reigns of terror; but taking the Colonies as a whole the revolution was effected, in so far as a revolution can be, with remarkable moderation.

The significance, in this revolution, of the emergence of serviceable popular governments before the end of 1775 can hardly be exaggerated. It meant that the people had committed themselves to political liberty while they were still largely protesting their loyalty to the old order. It meant that, as John Adams said, they would never bear to go back to governments dependent on the crown and otherwise so defective as the former governments had been. Great was the satisfaction taken in the new legislatures by many of those who had participated fully in the old—the merchants of Boston, the planters of Virginia. But far keener was the satisfaction taken by men who had been excluded under the previous régime.

The majority of the colonists who thus felt a direct incentive to push the revolutionary movement through till all its fruits had been gathered comprised two main groups. One was the alert, irrepressible proletarian element of the seaports from Boston to Charleston, who had been largely debarred from the ballot by a property qualification for voting. The other was the settlers of the back country, a great homogenous population, rapidly increasing, but deprived of due political rights by unjust discrimination in the matter of representation. They had grievances also in the unfair administration of taxes and of justice. From the valley of the Susquehanna to that of the Savannah these inland settlers, in whose breasts a powerful individualism was nurtured by frontier conditions, were alike in two salient respects. Nearly all dissenters, having little formal education, and being of many European strains, they felt little attachment to England; while economic and other reasons made them eager for a due share in the government. They welcomed the opportunity the revolutionary movement gave them. In Pennsylvania they turned the scale for independence, and in South Carolina greatly assisted in doing so. But independence for them meant only the first milestone on a long road.

Just how great should be the representation of these elements, the city workers and tradesmen and the small farmers, in the new State governments? Should democracy as these radical classes defined it come into being? Their kind of democracy allowed no place (outside New England) for a state-subsidized church; it was hostile to primogeniture and entail; it objected to taxation based on land-acreage irrespective of value, or upon a poll tax irrespective of how much the poll owned; it wanted justice to be convenient, and thought that the seat of government should be central, not on the coast. In short, was special privilege, as well as British privilege, to be extirpated? The paradoxical fact stands out that if the old British governments had been more abusive, the new governments might have been more liberal than they immediately became. The work of destruction would have been more ardent and complete, and reconstruction would have commenced nearer the foundations. As it was, in a State like Connecticut most good citizens would have stared had such a radical as Jefferson told them that any reforms were needed. But the new order and the old order were meeting on a far broader front than that comprehended in a conflict between American Whigs and British and American Tories. That had become impressively evident as the States took up the task of constitution-making.

Three main facts, then, are impressed upon us by a study of the transition from Colony to State in the thirteen individual members of the American family. We realize that when Americans thought of independence in 1775-76, they usually thought of it in terms of their own commonwealth, of Massachusetts, New Jersey, or Georgia, rather than in terms of the nation. The future form and character of the nation, even if one survived, were hazy and inchoate.

But it was a splendid certainty that the Provinces had slipped their shackles, and were stretching their unfettered limbs in a new political freedom. In the second place, we realize with new force the intensity of the clash between radical and conservative groups. In our national history the resistance made to independence by the Quakers, Anglicans, and other propertied folk of southeastern Pennsylvania, or the planters and merchants of South Carolina, bulks small. It is only when we give close scrutiny to the separate history of Pennsylvania and South Carolina that we envisage its true importance, and its complex economic and political causes. Finally, it becomes clear to us that the years of transition, 1774-76, were not so much years of destruction as construction. While the old Provincial governments were being slowly overturned, in their stead new and independent governmental structures were steadily rising. They were awkward, but vigorous. We are now to examine the final and most important phase of this process of government-building—the writing of formal Constitutions.

CHAPTER FOUR

THE WRITING OF THE STATE CONSTITUTIONS

Even if we make allowance for the fact that the main elements of the new governments were simply adapted from the old colonial forms, the labor of writing the State constitutions in 1776-77 was one of forbidding magnitude. In the State that was the very keystone of the Union, Pennsylvania, the party animosities aroused during this task brought on a convulsion which threatened civil war. In another rich and powerful State, New York, the perplexities of constitutional theorizing gave birth to several institutional monstrosities that it required two generations of bitter experience to wipe out. In still other States, such as North Carolina, the glaring imperfections of the new government half disabled it during the Revolutionary struggle. But the task was approached with ardor, for the radical patriots saw in it the chief opportunity and reward of the early phase of the revolutionary conflict.

It was the first time in the world's history that a large group of communities had begun the formation of their own governments under written constitutions. It gave such instruments, indeed, an importance they had never before possessed. We are taught to look upon the written political compact, embodying the two ideas of representative government and full equality before the law, as Anglo-American in origin, the Mayflower Compact being its first true exemplification. Certainly no other people had ever regarded their written constitutions with quite the proud jealousy with which the eighteenth century Americans regarded their charters. According to John Locke, political rights existed independently of the mere scratches of ink and pen on paper, but in practice, the charters had been the bulwarks of the people against oppression, the stepping stones to a larger freedom. The settlers did not look upon them as revocable grants, but as agreements inviolable except by mutual consent. It was precisely because the three leading New England Colonies had been founded upon the charter principle and had retained their charters that New England was more secure in her freedom than other sections. Having asserted their independence, the colonists' first thought was to guarantee it by documents having the nature of fundamental law.

Many students will accept Lincoln's statement that "The Union is older than the States, and in fact created them as States;"[1] for no permanent changes looking towards the substitution of State for colonial forms took place until the Continental Congress had suggested a procedure. Patrick Henry declared in the first Congress that with independence at hand, the colonies were at an end, and the nation alone existed. "Government is dissolved. . . . Where are your landmarks, your boundaries of Colonies? . . . The distinctions between Virginians, Pennsylvanians, New Yorkers, and New Englanders are no more. I am not a Virginian; I am an American. . . . I go upon the supposition that government is at an end. All distinctions are thrown down; all America is one mass."[2] When the fighting near Boston in the spring of 1775 made it clear that the separation from the mother country would be long-continued if not final, the colonists turned to the Continental Congress for advice upon more permanent governments. Massachusetts, New Hampshire, Virginia, and North Carolina in rapid succession requested instructions. And the Provinces did not become States till Congress declared the national independence in 1776.

I. How the Constitutions Were Written

When Herbert Spencer visited the United States in 1881-2, he expressed the opinion that our governmental system was not working well, declaring that this proved the truth of his conviction that no Constitution could be an artificial creation, like ours, and succeed; it must be an organic growth. Lord Bryce exposed the error in this view when he explained to British readers how the State Constitutions grew out of the colonial governments, and how the national Constitution in turn was largely founded upon the State Constitutions.[3] Two States, Connecticut and Rhode Island, kept their charters not for a brief period, but well into the nineteenth century.

[1] Special message to Congress, July 4, 1861.
[2] Adams's "Works," II, 365 ff.; N. Y. Hist. Soc., Duane Papers, IV, 189.
[3] Bryce, "The American Commonwealth," 19 ff. (1888 ed.); E. L. Youmans, "Herbert Spencer on the Americans."

The Pennsylvanians, having for decades maintained a unicameral legislature, in the face of efforts by certain interests to make the Governor's Council a true upper house, now resisted for fifteen stormy years the movement for a bicameral legislature.

Everywhere the main outlines of the State governments followed those of the colonial governments. An elective Governor succeeded the appointive Governor, though he invariably lost some of the old powers; the legislatures functioned precisely as in the later days of the colonial régime; and the judiciary suffered few changes save in mode of appointment for many years. The State governments of 1776-77, in short, were the fruit of a growth which had begun when, under the King's charter, the Governor, Council, and Burgesses of Virginia met in the little Jamestown church in 1619 to hold the first representative legislature on American soil. This growth differed almost as profoundly from the British system of government as the latter differed from the despotism of France, for the great principle of the separation of powers was an impassable gulf between them. Since Walpole had established ministerial government, the separation of powers had no actual existence in England, while the general hostility between Governor and legislature had confirmed it in America. The American growth was unique, distinctive.

Not only upon the practice of a century and a half, but upon the political theorizing of the same period—the writings of Harrington, Milton, Hume, Locke, Blackstone, Montesquieu, and others—were the new American constitutions built.

> Hands that penned
> And tongues that uttered wisdom, better none
> The later Sidney, Marvell, Harrington,
> Young Vane and others, who called Milton friend.

Locke, the great expositor of the principles of the Whig Revolution of 1688, struck the very keynote of the American Revolution when he maintained that the supreme function of the state is to protect life, liberty, and property, which are the natural rights of all men; that political authority is held in trust for the public benefit alone; and that when the natural rights of mankind are violated by it, the people have the duty of altering or abolishing the government, and erecting a better in its place. "The true remedy of force without authority is to oppose force to it," he declared, naming a series of governmental transgressions, such as the corruption of parliament, the betrayal of a nation to its enemies, or the exercise of a personal tyranny in the stead of law, which dissolved the contract between sovereign and subject, and justified revolution.[4] In his noble "Letter on Toleration" he stated the great principle of the distinction between the spheres occupied by church and state, and the propriety of their separation. He showed that religious persecution is wicked folly, and that in its healthy, normal condition the church is purely a voluntary organization. Locke was but one of the greatest liberal thinkers in a long line, owing much to predecessors like Richard Hooker and Algernon Sidney, while successors of such diverse views as Montesquieu, Burke, and Rousseau corrected and enlarged his doctrines; but he was the principal foundation stone on which the Revolutionary thinkers built.

In the constitutional sphere, Locke's and Montesquieu's insistence upon the separation of powers into tight compartments corresponded with all the predilections of Americans. Unlike Harrington, Milton, and other republican writers, Locke wished to preserve the kingship, declaring only that Hobbes's vicious theory of divine right should be discarded. But as a full believer in democracy, this rendered him only the more emphatic in asserting that the legislative authority must be maintained in careful separation from the executive, with the legislature normally supreme. If the executive could make laws, it would have the powers of a despot. If the legislators could execute laws, they might exempt themselves from obedience to them, and "thereby come to have a distinct interest from the rest of the community." Only in emergencies, as in time of war, might the two departments be merged—as several American States during the Revolution temporarily merged them. Montesquieu adopted this doctrine of the separation of powers, defining it as the very root of liberty. In "The Spirit of the Laws" (1748) he asserted that when the legislature and executive were united in the same person or body of magistrates, there could be no freedom, while the judicial power must similarly be held apart. In Turkey and the Italian republics, where all three branches were joined, the people groaned under a terrible oppression; in most European governments the ruler was invested with the first two powers alone,

---

[4] Locke, "The Two Treatises of Government," Book II, ch. 18. Repeatedly Locke makes assertions that were used by the American patriot leaders almost without verbal change; e. g., in Book II, ch. 11, "They must not raise taxes on the property of the people without the consent of the people given by themselves or their deputies."
[5] *Idem*, Book II, ch. 12.

so that the government was more moderate; but the ideal form was one in which the three were rigidly separated.[6]

This doctrine has had a long, and in the opinion of some critics, an unfortunate history, since it was applied in the United States. Montesquieu's careful analysis of the English government as an illustration of the dependence of political liberty upon checks and balances naturally appealed to Anglo-American readers. There were few New World students of politics who had not a thorough acquaintance with both Locke and Montesquieu. John Adams hailed Locke in 1760 as the discoverer of a new sphere, while in 1790 Jefferson, advising his youthful friend Thomas Mann Randolph on a course of reading, wrote that "Locke's little book on government is perfect as far as it goes." [7] The writings of both men contain numerous detailed references to Montesquieu. The tendency of Americans to attribute maladministration to a want of separation between the departments of government is illustrated by a letter of R. H. Lee in May, 1776. The British government, he said, though admirable in design, lacked balance, for the prerogative of making peers and boroughs destroyed the independence of the legislature and opened the way to rank corruption. "However imperfect the English plan was, yet our late government in Virginia was infinitely worse. With us two thirds of the legislature, and all the executive and judiciary powers were in the same hands—in truth it was very near a tyranny, altho' the mildness with which it was executed under Whig direction, made the evil little felt." [8]

With independence in view, a wide debate upon the proper form of the new State governments at once began, and was carried on principally through pamphlets and newspaper essays. Since New England had enjoyed the most republican administration, men elsewhere looked to the New Englanders to lead this debate. Above them all towered the author of the "Novanglus" papers and the best part of the arguments used by the Massachusetts General Court against Governor Hutchinson—John Adams.

In his early twenties Adams had formed the ambition of gaining distinction by his knowledge of the roots and theory of law and

---

[6] "The Spirit of the Laws," Book XI, especially ch. 6. Cf. H. J. Laski, "Political Thought from Locke to Bentham," 162 ff. Montesquieu's system of course differed greatly from Locke's. The former distinguished between executive, legislative, and judicial powers; the latter between executive, legislative, and "federative"—i.e., power over foreign affairs.

[7] Adams's "Works," I, 53; Jefferson's "Writings," Memorial Ed., VIII, 31.

[8] Lee, "Letters," I, 190.

government. He admonished himself at twenty-three to be diligent. "Study Seneca, Cicero, and all other good moral writers; study Montesquieu, Bolingbroke, Vinnius, &c, and all other good civil writers." The passage in his diary which describes how one week in October, 1758, he labored to translate Justinian, chiding himself because he wasted too much time with "chores, chat, tobacco, tea," and putting all light volumes out of reach, is an amusing illustration of his application; [9] he formed the habit of careful legal analysis; and he blamed himself on the eve of the Revolution because he had spent an estate in books. His chief worry when he rode away to the Continental Congress was that he did not have a wider "reading in law and history, that I might appear with less indecency before a variety of gentlemen whose education, travels, experiences, family, fortune, and everything will give them a vast superiority to me." [10] Burke once asked who had read Bolingbroke's works through; yet Adams could truthfully say he had done so three times. By 1765 he and the ill-fated Josiah Quincy stood foremost among all the Massachusetts lawyers on the popular side, and he was the best legal and constitutional adviser the revolutionary movement in that Province had. Now he entered a larger arena.

To the discussions which John Adams and R. H. Lee held at Philadelphia in the fall of 1775 we owe the first important publication upon the best form for a State government. Struck by the vigor and originality of Adams's ideas, Lee suggested that he reduce them to paper. The two men thought alike, for since Congress had reassembled in 1775, both had been expounding the view that timid efforts at reconciliation would only encourage the British to greater exertions against America, and that the Colonies should act vigorously. Adams met Lee's request by addressing to him on November 15, 1775, a short letter suggesting the main features for a Constitution, and Lee carried this letter to Virginia and showed it in manuscript to his friend.

The scheme outlined was rough. Adams proposed the free choice of a House of Commons by the people; the choice of an upper legislative chamber by the House; and the election of the Governor and other executive officers annually by their joint ballot. The Governor's powers were to be extensive, comprising a veto on legislation, command of the armed forces, and the appointment of

[9] Adams's "Works," II, 36, 37.
[10] Cf. "Familiar Letters of John Adams and His Wife," 31 ff.

subordinate officers and magistrates, subject to the consent of the upper chamber. Adams wrote to Lee that by his plan a single month would be sufficient, without the least convulsion, to effect a total revolution in the government of any Colony, and that if they wished, as soon as affairs became more tranquil the legislators might pass a law giving the people the annual election of the Governor and upper chamber.[11]

The second important proposal for a constitution was less finished and far less sound. On January 10, 1776, Thomas Paine's "Common Sense" appeared in Philadelphia, producing instantly by its force of style and radical ideas a profound impression, finding readers everywhere, and running through edition after edition. One section, devoted to ill-digested ideas upon State and national government, led Adams to call Paine "a disastrous meteor." This brilliant writer, he said, had a better hand in pulling down than in building; and he resented the rumor that he had written the pamphlet. Although he knew he was not the master of so simple and manly a style, he flattered himself that he should have made a more respectable figure as an architect. The writer seemed to have very inadequate ideas of what would make a proper State or national constitution.[12] No contrast, in fact, could be more striking than that between Adams and Paine. The one was a careful, methodical lawyer, Harvard-trained, deeply versed in political philosophy; the other a dismissed exciseman, with only a common school education, who had come to the Colonies from England but two years before, and had been glad to find employment with the Philadelphia book-seller Aitken at £25 a year. The one was a true statesman, who had to weigh every word he uttered; the other a genius whose pen was almost as irresponsible at times as it was brilliant.

Paine's notions of government were indeed erratic, though he had shrewdness enough to point out that the American strength was continental, not provincial. He advocated giving each Colony an annually elected legislature of one chamber, very numerous, and representing the parts of the commonwealth much more equitably

---

[11] Adams's "Works," IV, 184-87.
[12] Adams wrote Gates on March 23, 1776, that all the American misfortunes arose from the reluctance of the Southern Colonies to republican government. Each Province should establish its own government preparatory to a general "league." "This can be done only on popular principles and axioms, which are so abhorrent to the barons of the South, as to the proprietary interests of the Middle States, as well as to that avarice of land which has made on this continent so many votaries of mammon, that I sometimes dread the consequences. . . ." "Works," I, 205-07; II, 507.

than had been the fact in Pennsylvania, Virginia, and South Carolina. Each legislature should elect its own president, its business should be wholly domestic, and it should be subject to the authority of the Continental Congress. Adams was contemptuous of the sketchiness of these rapid proposals, while he was offended by the folly of the plan for a unicameral legislature engrossing all the executive powers of government. Though a radical in national politics, he was a conservative in this field; his conception of a good State government was one like Connecticut's, but "not quite so popular." [13]

This same month Adams published as a pamphlet a fuller expression of his opinions upon a model State Constitution, in the form of a letter to George Wythe, bearing the title "Thoughts on Government." Herein he argued at length against a unicameral legislature, and developed his old ideas regarding the legislative and executive branches. He believed that the lower house should be directly elected, but that it should choose from itself, the people at large, or both, a council of twenty or thirty men, to have a negative upon all legislation. All important executive officers should be chosen, during the crisis with Great Britain, by joint ballot of the two houses. Again, and with a sagacity rare in his generation, Adams declared for granting the Governor very wide powers. All elections, in his view, ought at first to be annual, for there was nowhere a more infallible maxim than that where annual elections end, there slavery begins. To this maxim the Bay State was to cling for more than a century and a quarter. He saw no objection, if the state had a sufficiency of men, to rotation in office—that is, to a rule that each man who had served for a definite period of say three years, should be ineligible during another period of equal length.[14]

Only one other theoretical plan for State government attracted national attention. Adams's "Thoughts on Government," issued anonymously, was forwarded to Virginia, where R. H. Lee, Patrick Henry, and Jefferson were exerting their influence in favor of a democratic but well-balanced constitution, and it created a stir. The aristocratic party was so alarmed that it had an anonymous

[13] Moncure D. Conway's edition of Paine's writings was issued in four volumes immediately after the publication of his admirable biography of Paine. In addition to "Common Sense," see the letter to George Washington dated Paris, July 30, 1796, wherein Paine attacks the Federal Constitution, and declares that he has always preferred a plural executive to a single executive.
[14] Adams's "Works," IV, 193-200.

answer prepared in Philadelphia, and sent to Williamsburg for publication in the *Virginia Gazette* on the day on which the Convention met to prepare the State Constitution. This contemptible little tract, as R. H. Lee called it, was too confused and conservative to appeal to many.[15] Its ideas were taken, in a rough way, from the colonial form. It advocated the direct election of the lower house by the people; the election of an upper house of twenty-four by the lower chamber for life; and the appointment of all judges, military officers, and inferior civil officers by the Governor. The pamphlet, attributed to Carter Braxton, found readers in Philadelphia and other cities, but it found no applause. Adams meanwhile had seized upon an opportunity of reiterating his views. In January, 1776, the North Carolina delegates in Philadelphia had been authorized to ask his advice upon State government, and he reëmbodied his counsel in a letter to John Penn.[16]

Meanwhile, as independence came nearer, the whole question became more urgent. When the spring of 1776 arrived, the New England and Virginia delegates believed that Congress ought to go much further than it had done the previous autumn in advising the formation of governments merely to serve during the continuance of the dispute with Great Britain. Adams, urging the necessity of realizing the theories of the wisest writers and erecting the whole building upon the broadest foundations, wanted a more advanced stand. Pressure from him and others, with the insistent attitude which several provincial governments were taking, led Congress finally to make the plunge. On May 10, 1776, it passed Adams's resolution that all Colonies as yet unprovided with a permanent constitution suited to the new conditions should adopt such a government as would best conduce to the happiness and safety of their people. Five days later it added a preamble to this resolution which evinced a thorough-going hostility to the continuance of any British power in the Colonies. We have noted how gravely these acts affected the history of Pennsylvania.[17]

The work of making the new State Constitutions had already commenced. On the whole, it was not accompanied by prolonged heart-searching and deliberation. The debates were in most instances moulded by the general struggle between the radicals and

[15] Lee, "Letters," I, 190-92; Henry, "Henry," I, 411-13.
[16] Adams's "Works," I, 209; IV, 203 ff.
[17] Cf. the Warren-Adams Letters, vol. 72 of the Mass. Hist. Soc. Collections, I, 245.

conservatives. Moreover, and fortunately, the ideas of Adams or any other single American did not so much affect these instruments as to give them uniformity and prevent healthy experimentation. Jefferson states that the exchange of Provincial for State governments was easily made, it being necessary to do little more than declare that the existing powers should be transferred to such and such new agencies. In a colony like Virginia or New York the mass of citizens had never given ten minutes' thought to abstract governmental theory; Jefferson tells us that despite all the discussion of "Common Sense," which sold 100,000 copies, the majority of men had never even heard of its ideas. The time for drawing up the new instruments was limited, the environment turbulent, and there were few practical guides, apart from the existing governments and charters, except the procedure and work of the English revolutionists of 1653 and 1689. The radicals were eager to gather the fruits of independence, and scholarly leaders like George Mason and John Adams applied their theories under many difficulties.[18]

What was the public attitude toward the initial efforts in Constitution-making? The two first Constitutions, those of New Hampshire and South Carolina, were especially hasty. This was because they were avowedly designed for the emergency, to last only until an accommodation with Great Britain could be obtained. In both Provinces there was strong conservative opposition, which had to be overcome by assurances that the step was merely temporary. New Hampshire had many men of substance, especially in Portsmouth and Dover, sincerely attached to Great Britain, who grumbled that the Constitution adopted on January 5, 1776, "appears to us too much like setting up an independency on the Mother Country."[19] In South Carolina the objections were equally vigorous. When a committee of the Provincial Congress reported February 10 in favor of a Constitution, a hot debate ensued. The reason given for the recommendation was that the existing mode of conducting affairs did not fully secure peace and good order, which was true. But the fiery Christopher Gadsden was betrayed by his feelings into an avowal of approbation for Thomas Paine's arguments in behalf of independence, and his speech was like a clap of thunder; even Henry Laurens, the chief advocate of a Constitution, protested

[18] Cf. F. N. Thorpe, "Const. Hist. of the Amer. People," I, 64 ff.
[19] Stackpole's "New Hampshire," II, ch. V.

against the "indecent expressions" of Paine.[20] After the Constitution had been prepared, some of the conservatives were still deeply loath to approve it, and were persuaded to yield only by the news that Parliament had passed an act of confiscation and seizure against the Americans as rebels. The instrument was finally accepted on March 26, when Rutledge was chosen President.[21]

The two other Colonies which drew up their Constitutions before the Declaration of Independence regarded them not as temporary, but permanent, instruments. When the Virginia Convention voted on May 15, 1776, to undertake the task, with not a dissenting voice, the popular approval was unmistakable. The Constitution was unanimously adopted on June 29. Next day the troops at Williamsburg were paraded and put through their maneuvers, a Continental flag was raised over the capitol, and in the evening the principal houses were illuminated. In New Jersey the Provincial Congress which met on June 10 at Burlington found a majority of members eager for independence and certain that it was coming. Petitions arrived from many towns praying for the establishment of a new government, and though other towns sent counter-memorials, representing that any such step would obstruct a reconciliation with Great Britain, the weight of public opinion was clearly with the radicals.[22] The Provincial Congress decided June 21, by a vote of 54 to 3, that a Constitution should at once be written. Although it contained a clause declaring that it should become null and void if the old relations with the mother country were reëstablished, its authors knew that it would be final. As a matter of fact, while the Constitutions of New Hampshire and South Carolina lasted only a few years, those of Virginia and New Jersey both endured more than a half century.

Rapid action was made imperative in the remaining States by the Declaration of Independence. There were only six of these States, for the other three in New England had simply retained their

[20] Drayton's "Memoirs of the Amer. Rev., II, 173; Wallace's "Laurens," 221.

[21] McCrady, "South Carolina in the Revolution, 1775-80," 115.

[22] Cimon in the *Pa. Packet* of April 15, 1776, made a long appeal to the people of New Jersey for a new government. He wrote: "While we are groaning under a load of debt and grappling with the iron hand of oppression, the officers of the British government, which is employed in oppressing us, are maintained at the expense of the people in a splendor fit to dazzle the weak and timid, with a power of distributing profitable employments among a numerous class of dependents; so that the property and very sustenance of a large part of the community, in some measure depend upon them. In the meantime, the friends of liberty, employed in the greatest and noblest of all causes, crouch and wind through indirect paths. Resolves and recommendations of congresses and committees are put in place of the commands of a Legislature; the punishment of crimes is reserved to a standing committee, who are often feeble, sometimes oppressive. The boasted trial by jury is sinking to decay. Anarchy threatens us."

charter governments, though Massachusetts did not regard hers as more than a stop-gap. By the end of August popular Conventions were at work writing Constitutions in the three adjoining States of Pennslyvania, Maryland, and Delaware, while a call had gone out for the election of such a body in North Carolina. New York and Georgia framed their instruments in 1777, the delay in both being due to the exigencies of the war.

In New York especially the delay was quite accidental. The fourth Provincial Congress of that commonwealth began work upon a Constitution early—July 9, 1776—and had the times been favorable, would have carried its labors to a conclusion before any other State of the middle group. But in midsummer Howe's army carried the war into New York, and the Congress was harried northward from town to town. Georgia was not actually invaded, but her exposed position invited the rapid and easy conquest which came two years later; and faced by perils from without and a Tory menace from within, she could not move fast. In midsummer of 1776 President Bulloch initiated action looking toward a true Constitution in place of the rough set of "Rules and Regulations" under which she was then governed. He proclaimed the election of a convention to meet in Savannah in October, but though the body sat at the appointed time, its other duties were pressing, the existing machinery functioned well, and nothing was accomplished for some months.[23]

In no State was the new fundamental law the work of a specially elected Constitutional Convention, such as is now usually entrusted with revision in this country. The war would have made the creation of any such body difficult, even had the plan occurred to the people; but the idea had no currency. It was a conception of slow development, just as was the conception of a State Constitution as something rising far superior to statutory law. The Virginia Constitution was simply Chapters I and II of the legislative statutes, and naturally could be written by a legislative body. Americans then believed that the framing of a State government required only a little more deliberation than the framing of a civil code. Nor did a single member of the Union submit its Constitution to popular vote. The Continental Congress did impress upon the State, as the compact theory of Locke obviously required, the desirability of calling a

[23] Stevens's "Hist. of Georgia," II, 297-98.

"full and free representation of the people" to draft the new organic laws; but that was all.[24]

Three States, however, did not even call a full and free representation in the sense of holding a special election, with the work of Constitution-making in view. In South Carolina, Virginia, and New Jersey, revolutionary legislatures which had been chosen without general thought of constitutional tasks decided, under the pressure of events, to undertake them. Some members of the South Carolina Congress wanted a new election, but they were overruled; after all, the body was writing only a temporary instrument. In New Jersey nobody thought of protesting that the legislature lacked proper authority. It had just been chosen, and if a special election for a constitutional convention had been held, the counties would probably have returned the same men. The situation was the same in Virginia. The election of April, 1776, witnessed a warm contest for many seats, and the people perfectly trusted the delegates who next month decided to draft an organic law for the Old Dominion.

In no fewer than seven States, however, during 1775-77, a special election in contemplation of the writing of a Constitution was actually held. Though New Hampshire acted so early, she took special pains to make her election (November, 1775) successful, a committee of the Provincial Congress drawing up an elaborate plan for equitable representation. New York's Congress of May, 1776, hesitated, some members, like John Morin Scott, wishing it to draft a Constitution without further delay, while others thought it would be sufficient to arrange for the election of additional delegates. But it was finally decided to hold a new election, for in that manner the unmistakable assent of the patriot citizens would be obtained, and it duly took place at the end of the month.[25] In Pennsylvania, as we have seen, a city committee thrust the Assembly aside and called a Province-wide conference which sat in Philadelphia on June 18, and laid down regulations governing the election of a State Convention which was to meet within a month—a body chosen primarily to write a Constitution, but also to make laws. Little Delaware was hard on her sister's heels. The Provincial Assembly in July asked the three counties to send ten

---

[24] Cf. R. S. Hoar, "Constitutional Conventions," ch. 1.
[25] C. Z. Lincoln, "Constitutional History of New York," I, 478 ff.

delegates each to a convention meeting at Newcastle on August 27, and a warm contest was waged between the radicals and conservatives to gain control of it. Maryland's Convention early in July coupled its own declaration of independence with a call for a new Convention which was to begin work the middle of following month at Annapolis upon a Constitution. President Bulloch of Georgia, in giving notice of an election that autumn, impressed upon the voters the fact that the new body would open "business of the highest consequence for the government and welfare of the people." [26]

But it was in North Carolina that the special election had, next to Pennsylvania, the greatest significance and heat. That State attempted at first to dispense with it, and like her neighbors on each side simply allow her revolutionary legislature to undertake the task offhand. After passing its resolutions of April, 1776, declaring for a severance of the ties with England, North Carolina's Congress appointed a committee (April 13) to prepare a Constitution. But this move proved abortive. After a bitter struggle the radicals in the Congress showed the greater strength; their committeemen determined that it would be best to draw up what one spectator called a purely democratic form of government; and on April 25 they laid before the Congress certain resolutions as a foundation for the Constitution. They seemed about to press ahead of all the rest of the South.

Then, suddenly, at a show of intense opposition in some quarters, their leaders concluded that it would be unwise to press so controversial a subject. They could not afford, they decided, to risk antagonizing, by a hasty move, a large group of influential and comparatively wealthy conservatives both within and without the Congress. The committee had discovered that there were many complexities in Constitution-making. Wise Samuel Johnston has left us a letter picturing it sitting nightly, cudgelling its brains over proposal after proposal too tedious to name, and unable to overcome the primary obstacle—"how to establish a check on the representatives of the people, to prevent their assuming more power than would be consistent with the liberties of the people." One motive of the committee in abandoning this first effort was the feeling that the Province was too inexperienced to proceed until

[26] Stevens's "Hist. of Georgia," II, 297.

the greater Colonies had shown the way; but the chief reason was its fear of a schism in the patriot party.[27]

It was unquestionably to the advantage of the radicals to wait, for they grew constantly stronger. In the late summer (August 9, 1776), the Council of Safety recommended that the people pay the closest attention to the coming election of a new Congress, for it would not only make laws but form a new Constitution.[28] A vigorous contest followed. One issue between the radicals and conservatives, between men like Thomas Person and Samuel Johnston, lay in the question how far the right of suffrage ought to be restricted by property or other qualifications. The radicals wanted the judges under close popular control, and the Governor a mere figurehead, to which aims the conservatives objected. A good deal of bad temper had already been displayed, for Johnston, William Hooper, James Iredell, and other conservatives voiced a frank contempt for the provisional government. Its leaders, they said, were a set of demagogues, sacrificing every principle for popular support, and they would give such men no aid. One argument on the radical side was that the success of the Revolution might depend upon the adoption of a government that would enlist the enthusiasm of the poor. Should men be asked to die for freedom, and yet be told they could not vote? The property restrictions in the temporary government had helped the Tories to gain a hold upon excluded groups, but a reform might win over even the Highlanders of Cape Fear. With a treasury empty, and the army ranks to be filled, should they write a Constitution unacceptable to the common people? But other and less fair appeals were used. On the one side, speakers asserted that a conservative victory would mean little less than a monarchy; on the other, that a radical victory would mean the rule of the mob. On election day, October 15, 1776, the radicals decisively triumphed, winning four seats in five.[29]

But even where a special election was held, just how "full and free" was it; how far did it go in recognizing previously neglected sections and classes of the commonwealth? The answer reveals some striking contrasts. In several States the revolutionary legis-

[27] N. C. Records, X, 1034-1037; Sikes, "Transition in North Carolina," 60; Ashe, "Hist. of N. C.," I, 527 ff.; McRee's "Iredell," I, 276-79.

[28] N. C. Records, X, 696. The electorate could have been trusted to keep this in mind. The object of the radical Council was rather to put its adherents on guard against any attempt by the conservatives to carry the election.

[29] James Sprunt Hist. Publications, XI, No. 2 (Frank Nash, "The North Carolina Constitution of 1776 and its Makers"). There was some disorder on election day; N. C. Records, X, 933.

latures which wrote the Constitutions were thoroughly democratic bodies, representing every section; in others they showed no advance beyond the undemocratic colonial legislatures.

New Hampshire set an admirable example in the pains she took to be fair in apportioning representation. A committee which planned the election gave every adult male taxpayer the vote, made every man possessing £200 in real estate eligible to a seat, and arranged for the distribution of 89 members in such a manner that each of the five counties would enjoy a voice commensurate with its population. The limitation of membership to this number was in itself healthful, for many of the smallest towns demanded one delegate apiece, which would have swollen the Congress to unmanageable size. New York's Congress by July of 1776 had also become a much more truly representative body—if we exclude consideration of the Tories—than the old Provincial Assembly. The latter had contained 35 members; the Congress had 107, although one county—Richmond, or Staten Island, which was loyalist and the hills of which were white with British tents when the session opened—was not represented at all.[30] Moreover, the Assembly had been arbitrarily constituted, New York county having four members and the others two each. In the Congress which wrote the Constitution there happened to be a juster approximation of county membership to county population, New York county having 25 members, Albany 11, Ulster 8, and the thinly settled counties of Cumberland and Gloucester 3 and 2 respectively. Every patriot freeman in New York city and Albany, and every freeholder outside, had a vote.

In Pennsylvania there occurred a dramatic rectification of the injustice so long done the frontier counties. In 1775 the Colonial Assembly had contained 41 members, of whom 26 were from the southeastern section, the old, long-settled, wealthy part of the Province, and fifteen from the newer western counties, although the latter now held a majority of the people. The addition of 17 new members early in 1776, as an incident of the tense struggle between radicals and conservatives, raised the western representation to 28 and that of the east to 30, almost a balance. Now, in apportioning representation in the convention to frame a Constitution, the radical leaders gave each county and the city of Phila-

[30] C. Z. Lincoln, "Constitutional History of New York," I, 484-86.

delphia six members. This meant that Philadelphia and the three eastern counties had 24, the eight western counties 48. The situation had been almost completely reversed in the two years, for whereas a third of the members had come from the newer counties under the former régime, now they sent two thirds. As for the qualifications of voters, in one respect they were liberalized. Any taxpayer, or small property holder, could cast his ballot for members of the Convention. But it was added that none might vote save those who approved the movement for a new Constitution, a stipulation that shut out great numbers of conservatives.[31]

Virginia, however, and more notably still South Carolina, illustrated all the old injustices in representation. In the Old Dominion each county, whether its population was large or small, sent two members to the Constitution-making body, just as it had done to the Colonial legislature. This practice was so palpably unfair that it had been condemned by Ward of Rhode Island in the first Continental Congress.[32] The first national census gave to Berkeley County, west of the Blue Ridge, a total population of 19,713, of whom only 2,932 were slaves; it gave to Elizabeth City County, between the James and the York, only 3,450 people, of whom 1,876 were slaves. Other discrepancies as great or greater could be named, and their total effect was much to the advantage of the Tidewater section, where the counties were smaller than in the west, and—with their large plantations—had fewer people. In South Carolina the same sectional injustice was still more glaringly evident. The revolutionary legislature which drafted the Constitution had 144 members from the lowlands, and 40 from the uplands, though the latter region contained three fourths of the white population. Maryland constituted her Convention in the same artificial manner. Each county was allowed to elect four delegates, except Frederick, which was given more; yet the first national census showed that Maryland had five counties of more than 20,000 people, and three of fewer than 10,000.

Yet after all, it was much less important that the constitution-making congresses be carefully representative of every class and section than that they should contain the ablest leaders and thinkers of every State. Representation of brains, not polls, was wanted. It did not greatly matter in Virginia whether Fairfax and Albemarle

---

[31] "Proceedings Relative to Calling the Conventions of 1776 and 1790."
[32] Burnett, "Letters of Members of the Continental Congress," I, 65.

Counties had delegations strictly proportioned to the number of their voters; it mattered immensely whether Fairfax chose some insignificant delegate, or the learned George Mason, and whether Albemarle sent a nonentity up to Williamsburg, or named Thomas Jefferson. Two of the States which had the most democratic conventions, Pennsylvania and North Carolina, adopted Constitutions defective in comparison with Virginia's.

Upon the whole, the personnel of the several congresses was very high, including the most distinguished men available, and the brightest luminaries of the Revolution. In two States, and two only, Pennsylvania and North Carolina, factional quarrels kept some of the best Whig leaders out of the assemblages. The former included Franklin, and the latter Richard Caswell, but no others of distinction. New Hampshire's Congress was also mediocre in membership. The historian Belknap, who was acquainted with many of the delegates, tells us that most of them "knew nothing of the theory of government, and had never before been concerned in public business," which was true.[33] The president was a practising physician and man of substance, Matthew Thornton, the most influential member was the experienced squire and legislator, Meshech Weare, the most active was the handsome merchant John Langdon; but only John Sullivan was then or later a figure of Continental prominence.

But South Carolina's Constitution-makers included the whole roll of scholars and gentlemen who had guided that State as it entered upon the Revolution—John Rutledge, the most eminent statesman south of Virginia; the irrepressible Gadsden; Henry Laurens, who in youth had been a warm friend to Gadsden, but was of a contrastingly cautious, thoughtful temperament, and had bitterly quarreled with him before the Revolution; Charles Pinckney, still more conservative than Laurens; Rawlins Lowndes, a bold and brilliant planter, who as speaker three years before had signally vindicated the dignity of the House in opposition to the Council; and W. H. Drayton, who had done so much to see that South Carolina played a spirited part in the continental crisis.[34] Similarly, the best brains of the State were employed in Maryland. The committee appointed to draft the bill of rights and plan of govern-

---

[33] Jeremy Belknap, "History of New Hampshire."
[34] McCrady, "South Carolina in the Revolution, 1775-80," 110; Drayton, "Memoirs," II, ch. 3.

ment included Matthew Tilghman, Charles Carroll of Carrollton, Charles Carroll the barrister, William Paca, later Governor, and the energetic, erratic Samuel Chase.[35] The conventions of Delaware and Georgia each included one figure of more than local importance, Thomas McKean and Archibald Bulloch. As we shall see later, New York called together a body of strikingly able men, including Jay, Duane, Robert R. Livingston, and Gouverneur Morris.

Somewhat strangely, the personnel of the Virginia Convention was thought by several contemporary judges to be disappointing. Patrick Henry and Thomas Ludwell Lee said so. George Mason feared "a thousand ridiculous and impracticable proposals" from the body, and a heterogeneous, jarring result, while Landon Carter despondently wrote Washington that ignorant men from all over the Colony had pressed forward to claim seats, and that the Convention showed an appalling lack of experience. Superficially, there was a good deal to support this dark view. Peyton Randolph was now dead; Washington was at the head of the army; Jefferson, R. H. Lee, Harrison, and Wythe were kept away by their duties in the Continental Congress, though Lee visited Williamsburg before the convention finished its work. Nevertheless, the body included and in the end was guided by a group of the highest capacity.[36]

Among the conservatives were the veteran Edmund Pendleton, who presided over the gathering with a dignity which impressed Madison and others; R. C. Nicholas, who so long before as 1765 had stood with Pendleton in opposing Patrick Henry's resolutions on the Stamp Act; and Richard Bland, who also had then supported the Crown. The progressives came forward in high spirits, eager for the victory they were destined to win. Among them was Patrick Henry, whom all respected and many admired, but who was not a great constructive statesman; he had mastered Adams's pamphlet, and was determined to attack any "bias to aristocracy." There was James Madison, a new member, not long previously graduated from Princeton, who in spite of his painful diffidence and insignificant stature quickly made a deep mark. "In Convention debate," said Edmund Randolph, also a young member, "his lips were never unsealed except to some members who happened to sit near him;

[35] E. Boyle, "Distinguished Marylanders" 60, 88.
[36] Rowland's "Mason," I, 226; 4 Amer. Archives, VI, 390.

and he who had once partaken of the rich banquet of his remarks, did not fail to wish to sit daily within reach of his conversation." But above all the others there towered George Mason. The wealthy owner of Gunston Hall, a mansion that looked south over the Potomac just off the main road that traversed the province from Maryland to North Carolina, the close neighbor and friend of Washington, a descendant of Cavaliers, Mason was by no means a radical. But he had read and thought much on political questions, and had imbibed liberal ideas. He had made himself master of the English historians and writers on government. Free from personal ambition, he stood unflinchingly by his convictions. His wealth, social position, learning, experience—he had been in the House as early as 1759—and his ability, made Virginians instinctively look up to him.[37]

All these Constitution-making bodies were at times painfully preoccupied with the exigent business of making laws, raising funds, levying war, and carrying on the other activities of the States. Not one was able to devote itself exclusively to the drafting of the fundamental law. The New York Convention was assisting Washington with all its energy till he was driven from the State, and then had to devote itself to rallying the patriots in the fastnesses of the upper Hudson. Not only did the British invasion present a multitude of urgent problems, but it drew members away from the convention to their threatened home communities. In November, 1776, the body had to send a special notification to the county committees requesting the attendance of all delegates without delay, and in general, its business was done by about one-third the members.

The Pennsylvania Convention was bitterly attacked by the conservatives for its extensive use of the lawmaking power, to retain which it was accused of prolonging its session unconscionably. It controlled the militia, appointed a Council of Safety, dropped the conservative Dickinson from the Continental Congress, and made a temporary boundary agreement with Virginia. In Virginia the Convention raised 1,300 men, issued treasury notes for £100,000, annulled certain great private land purchases recently made from the Indians, initiated a revision of the laws, compensated one

---

[37] Lingley, "Transition in Virginia," ch. 7; Rowland's "Mason," *passim;* Eckenrode, ch. 6. See the full pen-portraits of the Virginia leaders in H. B. Grigsby, "The Virginia Convention of 1776."

Lucretius Pritchett for the killing of a slave, and delivered one Moses Riggs from jail—a queer medley of functions. The strangest combination of rôles, however, was that of the South Carolina Congress, which was at once the old revolutionary legislature, the constitutional convention, and the new legislature. On the morning of March 25, 1776, the gentlemen gathered in the Charleston capitol were acting in the first two capacities; that afternoon they had become an Assembly under the new government, and a body of electors for the Legislative Council, or upper house.[38]

Partly because of this necessity of dividing their time between legislative and constitutional tasks, partly because it was the natural procedure, the conventions or congresses deputed the drafting of the new basic instruments to select committees. In some States there were two committees, one to prepare the Constitution proper and one the Bill of Rights. It was in this same manner, of course, that the Declaration of Independence was written. The Continental Congress appointed a committee of five to bring in a draft of it. Of these five, Jefferson was induced to take up the pen, Adams arguing that three reasons pointed to him as the man for the task; he was a Virginian, he was popular and trusted, and he was a finished writer. In a majority of States we can trace the main features of the Constitutions to a few hands, and no part of their story is more interesting than that which exhibits the actual mode of composition.

Eleven men formed the committee chosen to prepare the first draft of the South Carolina Constitution. There is every reason for believing that John Rutledge dominated it, and that its moderate majority followed his ideas. He had been in Congress and talked interestedly with John Adams upon constitutional questions; and the careful conservatism which the Constitution expressed in all its terms harmonized with his views. In New Jersey, by contrast, the dominating figure—if we may trust tradition, our only guide— was not an eminent State leader, but a humble cleric and scholar. The committee of ten there appointed included the Rev. Jacob Green, its chairman, who was pastor of the Presbyterian Church at Hanover, and a man of varied talents; John Cleves Symmes, later a leader in the settlement of Ohio; Lewis Ogden, Jonathan D. Sergeant, and Theophilus Elmer. Green is reputed to have been

[38] McCrady, "South Carolina in the Revolution, 1775-80," 115.

the principal author, receiving assistance from a more noted Presbyterian divine, Dr. John Witherspoon.[39] We do not know which particular member of the Maryland committee deserves most of the credit for that State's instrument. But we may be sure that the strong personalities of Charles Carroll of Carrollton, William Paca, and Samuel Chase all had some share in the result. To Chase has been ascribed the most prominent feature of the new government, the indirect election of the Senate.[40] As for Delaware, the honor of the authorship of her Constitution has been disputed by admirers of George Read and Thomas McKean. Read was president of the convention and chairman of the drafting committee, while McKean was the leading radical. The best evidence supports the claim of McKean, who himself explicitly told Cæsar Rodney years later that he wrote the draft at Newcastle "in a tavern without a book or assistance." [41]

Virginia appointed a committee larger than Delaware's whole convention, thirty-two, but as we shall see, a single hand wrote most of both the Constitution and Bill of Rights. North Carolina imitated her more powerful sister by choosing another large drafting committee, at first of eighteen and later twenty-eight members. It is probable that Willie Jones, in whom were combined an Eton education, good general capacity, a marked taste for horse-racing, hunting, and other sports, and a flaming radicalism, did as much to shape the instrument as Caswell. This was the same Jones who a dozen years later, when North Carolina was debating the adoption of the Federal Constitution, set up as a very mischievous authority on constitutional matters. Other radicals, such as Thomas Person and Abner Nash, doubtless also had a finger in the pie.[42] Georgia made an appallingly simple job of her first Constitution, merely perpetuating, with a few changes and additions, the rough temporary government under which her affairs were already being administered. If the framework had been more creditable, we would be more willing to credit the sagacious Archibald Bulloch with it.

In general, the Constitutions were put together with amazing rapidity, though the necessity of attending to other affairs sometimes made the lapse of time between the commencement of the

[39] Elmer, "Constitution and Govt. of N. J.," 21 ff.; Lee's "New Jersey," II, ch. 25.
[40] Annual Report Amer. Hist. Assn., 1895, p. 129 ff.
[41] Read, "Life of Read," 182-83; Papers Hist. Soc. of Del., II, No. 17.
[42] Cf. North Carolina Booklet, No. 7; "Our First Constitution," by E. W. Sikes.

task and its completion very long. New Hampshire required only a week—the undertaking was begun December 28, 1775, and finished January 5, 1776. New Jersey was almost equally rapid. Her Convention voted on June 21 to essay a Constitution, the first draft was reported for debate June 26, and on July 2, after discussion in committee of the whole, it was accepted. This speed owed something to the pressure of events, for the debate was interrupted by the news that Howe had landed his army at Sandy Hook. Some were for adopting the instrument at once, while others were for deferring it until further consideration was possible, and it bore the marks of haste.

In Maryland the actual committee-work of drafting the Constitution, with its Bill of Rights, consumed almost a month, but it was two months later before the Convention, which was in adjournment part of the time and busied with war problems, finally accepted it. South Carolina required six weeks to frame her Constitution, and North Carolina only five. In Pennslyvania the labor, intermittently pursued, endured from the heat of midsummer to the cold of winter (July 18-November 7, 1776). But Delaware needed less than a month: her Convention met August 27, the draft of the instrument was ready in not quite three weeks, and only five days' debate was given to it before it was approved. Virginia, moreover, with one of the best Constitutions of all, and a Bill of Rights that served as a model for the rest of the nation, required but six weeks (May 15-June 29, 1776), interrupted by other activities. The time consumed was no index of the merits of the different instruments.[43]

II. CONSTITUTIONS OF A RADICAL CHARACTER

Everywhere from north to south the debate on the Constitutions evoked a struggle between ultra-democratic and aristocratic opinion. To define the precise tenets and composition of these radical and conservative parties is difficult, for in a time of crisis men's views alter rapidly, and there were many varying shades of sentiment. But in general the aristocratic element believed in a careful balance of the powers of government, so that the executive would possess a genuine ability to direct the administration, while the judiciary

[43] N. H. Provincial, State, and Town Papers, VIII, 1 ff.; Minutes of the New Jersey Provincial Congress and Council of Safety, 445 ff.; N. C. Records, X, 913 ff.; etc. Georgia required four months; Revolutionary Records, I, 282 ff.

would be capable of a firm protection of property. It held that in the arrangements of government a due respect should be paid to wealth: that property qualifications for the ballot and office, such as had prevailed in most Colonies, were indispensable, and that it would be well if the old propertied governing classes—the rich Virginia planters, the merchants and planters of South Carolina, the merchants and large landholders of southeastern Pennsylvania—continued to hold the tiller of state. To this element the inequalities of representation in some Colonies, the denial of the ballot to many freemen in others, were not abuses but time-tested and valuable features of government.

The ultra-democratic leaders gave these conservatives the contemptuous appellation of dons, patricians, or nobles, the devotees of a vicious class tyranny. They invited them to emigrate to England, where there were real gentlemen, not cheap imitations. Radicals like George Bryan, Willie Jones, and Alexander Gillon proclaimed the sentiment which has so often been used as a battle-cry in our politics: "Let the people rule!" This could be effected, they believed, by a concentration of governmental power in the legislature, and especially its popular house, which colonial experience had shown to be always with the people. Annually elected, the legislators could be trusted to attempt no tyranny, while the governor would be dangerous unless he were given a brief term and made a mere figurehead, and the judges unless their removal was made easy.

John Dickinson, Carter Braxton, and Samuel Johnston denounced the advocates of universal manhood suffrage as the sponsors of a "mob" government and of "levelling." John Adams, who wanted all government well-balanced, but also wanted it moderately democratic, replied by adducing such terrible examples as the republic of Bilbao, where the officers, popularly elected, had to have property worth a thousand ducats, and an unstained lineage. "Thus we see the people themselves have established by law a contracted aristocracy, under the appearance of a liberal democracy," warned Adams. "Americans, beware!" [44]

One of the sharpest struggles occurred in North Carolina, where the election of the constitution-making body, as we have seen, resulted in a sweeping victory for the radicals. They even defeated

<hr>

[44] Adams's "Works," IV, 312, 313.

Samuel Johnston in Chowan County, an exploit which they celebrated by burning him in effigy. When the 169 members met in
the village of Halifax on November 12 they chose Richard Caswell
and Cornelius Harnett, two leaders in the revolutionary movement,
and men of democratic leanings, president and vice-president. The
conservatives were represented by such gentlemen as William
Hooper and Allen Jones, while Samuel Johnston himself was in
Halifax near the end of the session, on business for the State
treasury. But the conservatives were not listened to. "Everyone
who has the least pretensions to be a gentleman," reported Johnston,
"is borne down *per ignobile vulgus*—a set of men without reading,
experience, or principles to govern them." [45] In the drafting committee the radical element was much the stronger. The one strong
conservative influence present lay in the models which the Congress
had before it—the plan drawn up by John Adams, which called for
a careful separation of departments, the New England charters,
the new Constitution of New Jersey, and probably those of Maryland and Virginia as well. Careful study was given these models,
but they were not followed.

Democracy here overleaped itself, and to an excess of radicalism
we must ascribe the highly unsatisfactory nature of the North
Carolina Constitution. Its chief fault was that it gave the Governor
altogether too little power. No more helpless executive existed
anywhere south of Pennsylvania. The Congress was at pains to
make sure that he would be a fit man—he had to be at least thirty,
a resident of North Carolina for at least five years, a sound stipulation in a State receiving heavy immigration, and the owner of a
£1000 freehold. But this carefully selected gentleman was hedged
about by a thousand restrictions. His term was one year only, and
he was not to enjoy more than three terms in any six successive
years, lest he become another Cæsar; while he was surrounded by
an executive council, which was required to keep a journal and on
demand lay it before the House. He had not even a suspensive
veto, nor could he appoint a single officer of importance. In short,
he was simply an ornament, with authority to grant pardons and
reprieves, temporary powers as commander in chief, and a vague
general dignity. All this indicates in part a natural reaction from
the difficulties of the colonists with the old royal governors, Tryon

[45] McRee's "Iredell," I, ch. 9.

and Martin, and in part the radical theory that all authority should be centered in the direct legislative representatives of the people.[46]

"What powers, sir," inquired one of Hooper's constituents after the Congress rose, "were conferred upon the Governor?" "Power," snorted Hooper, "to sign a receipt for his salary." [47]   The first man to luxuriate in this power was Richard Caswell, who was given a temporary appointment till the first Assembly met in 1777.

All officers of importance were elected by the legislature, including judges and even the justices of the peace. The legislature was to issue military commissions, and one clause suggests that it was intended that after a time it should name a commander-in-chief to take the place of the Governor at the head of the armed forces. The Governor had not even the right to call the legislature in special session in time of emergency, a gross defect in the organic law of a State liable to attack at any hour. We shall see how bitterly it rued this omission when the army of Cornwallis stood upon its borders. Apart from these fundamental faults, the Constitution had certain good features. One was the grant to the judges of a tenure during good behavior. Another was the clause inserted in the bill of rights guaranteeing religious freedom. Thomas Jones, a conservative, had provoked an angry debate by demanding a favored position for the Episcopal Church, but this was defeated; the only bit of illiberalism permitted in this connection being a provision that none but Protestants might hold office. Another commendable feature, a true evidence of democracy, was the enlargement of the electorate. Any adult freeman resident in the State for a year could vote for members of the lower house, while any freeholder owning fifty acres—a trifle in that half empty State—could vote for a Senator. Members of the House had to possess one hundred acres, and those of the Senate three hundred; for not even North Carolina could yet waive this restriction on office.

But it was not in a State where the great mass of the people were upon almost the same economic and social level, but in States of heavy inequalities of wealth and culture, that the struggle between men of aristocratic and ultra-democratic views was fiercest. We meet it in its tensest form in Virginia and Pennsylvania. Here, moreover, it found a spectacular stage. These were the two greatest

[46] F. N. Thorpe, "Federal and State Constitutions, Charters, and Other Organic Laws," V, 2787 ff. This set, giving the text of all Constitutions, will not be quoted again.
[47] Wheeler, "Historical Sketches of N. C.," II, 288.

and richest States, to which, since Massachusetts postponed her Constitution until near the close of the Revolution, all eyes were turned.

The result of the contest in the two was strikingly different. In Virginia it gave birth to a partly balanced government, and in Pennsylvania to a shockingly unbalanced form. In Virginia the really unhealthful abuses in the colonial laws and institutions were for the most part singled out and attacked; in Pennsylvania new abuses were planted in the name of democracy. This difference arose in part from the fact that in Virginia the progressive Whigs had early gained control of the Province and guided it steadily towards a total revolution, while in Pennsylvania the radicals and conservatives were more evenly matched, and the latter were overthrown by a violent coup just before the Constitution was adopted. It was a natural birth in the one State, a convulsive production in the other. In part the difference arose from the fact that Virginia's colonial constitution, with its bicameral legislature, offered a better foundation than Pennsylvania's unicameral legislature. But this is to be said for Pennsylvania, that her innovations were highly valuable as experiments.

The Americans as a whole had reason to echo John Adams's statement that "we all look up to Virginia for examples." Her Constitution was written at just the moment the State was ripe for it. With Dunmore's forces defeated in the field and expelled from Norfolk, the revolution there had swept into a calmer current. The once unchecked county committees, ruling in many communities with a high hand, began to be superseded by courts of inquiry, and juries were summoned as in the old days of British rule. Men could stop to think of the future government of Virginia.[48]

As this lull fell in the conflict between the patriots and British, there came into distinct view the clash between the conservative and radical parties. Should the new government be friendliest to the rich or the poor, to the lowland planters and churchmen or the small farmers and dissenters of the uplands and Shenandoah? The aristocratic landholders who dominated Tidewater Virginia would have been well satisfied with the Crown government had only the London authorities pursued Walpole's *noli tangere* system, had the

---

[48] Eckenrode, 147 ff. The courts of inquiry had the same connection as the committees with the central Committee of Safety.

governors kept on dozing, and the tax measures been left to originate exclusively in the colony. But by 1775 the radicals of both the Tidewater and the uplands would have found the domestic government highly irritating even had the Crown kept its hands off. It was a government of inequalities in taxation, representation, and economic opportunity—a government sheltering unhealthful growths like the church establishment and the laws of primogeniture. The progressives did not intend to lose their opportunity to give Virginia a system fostering greater political and social equality. The "vicious points" in State affairs, as Jefferson put it, "urgently required reformation."

John Adams's plan and that attributed to Carter Braxton [49] by no means stood alone as proposed outlines when the Virginia Convention set to work. R. H. Lee, then in Congress, drew up a brief scheme, and Meriweather Smith a more ambitious one, but neither survives. We can best judge of Lee's views by a sentence in one of his letters: "Abridged duration, temperate revenue, and every unnecessary power withheld, are potent means of preserving integrity in public men and for securing the community from the dangerous ambition that too often governs the public mind." Throughout his life, Lee feared and hated centralized government, as he showed when he opposed the Federal Constitution. He would have made the legislature all-powerful, and wished the Governor surrounded by a council of state; but he would have partially checked the legislature by carefully differentiating the two houses.[50] Jefferson, also in Congress, sent an outline of his ideas to Williamsburg, but it arrived too late to exert much influence. A "Government Scheme" was published in the *Virginia Gazette* for May 10, and supposition, but nothing more, assigns it to Patrick Henry. It called for a popularly elected lower house, chosen as in the old colonial days, an upper house of 24, chosen for seven years by the lower, and a Governor, chosen for one year only by the two houses. The Governor was to have little power, and the author of this scheme, much like Lee, wished him hampered by a council. This plan went as far towards ultra-democracy as Carter Braxton's went toward aristocracy.

When the Convention was midway in its work, still another plan

---

[49] We have already described both; the text of Braxton's is in 4 Amer. Archives, VI, 748 ff.

[50] Lee's "Letters," I, 176-80.

was offered in the *Virginia Gazette* (June 7) in an article headed "Loose Thoughts on Government" by "Democraticus." It also carried the principles of democracy to an undue extreme. A lower house elected annually by the people, an upper house elected by committees of twenty-one in each county, and a figurehead of a Governor, chosen out of the upper house by the committees—such were the main agencies suggested. But it was notable for the vigor with which it called for a fair apportionment of legislators, and the abolition of primogeniture and entail. The propriety of an equal representation must occur to every one who does not favor one part of the community over another, it said; and it proposed putting "an end to proprietaries, entails, and other monopolies of land, those remains of ancient tyranny, which will always be incompatible with the spirit of equality and right government." Strangely, however, its author held that land would be a better basis of representation than the number of freeholders.

The large committee appointed to draft the Constitution included Henry, Lee, R. C. Nicholas, Madison, and Mason. Chairman Archibald Cary reported the Declaration of Rights on May 27, and it was unanimously adopted June 22, while the plan for the Constitution was submitted June 24. Over both, the struggle between the conservatives and progressives was spirited. In debate on the floor Patrick Henry naturally captained the democratic faction, while Pendleton and Nicholas led the conservatives. Henry distrusted the wealthy class in a double sense, as undemocratic and but tepidly Whiggish. To R. H. Lee he wrote on May 20 that all the powers of mind and body had now to be collected for one grand effort. "Moderation . . . hath nearly brought on us final ruin. And to see those, who have so fatally advised us, still guiding, or at least sharing, our public counsels, alarms me." To John Adams he wrote that "my most esteemed republican form has many and powerful enemies," that the Braxton pamphlet was an affront and disgrace to the country, and that it would be "my incessant study so to form our portrait of government that a kindred with New England may be discerned in it." Adams replied: [51]

The dons, the bashaws, the grandees, the patricians, the sachems, the nabobs, call them by what name you please, sigh, and groan, and fret, and sometimes stamp, and foam, and curse, but all in vain. The decree is gone forth, and cannot be recalled, that a more equal liberty than has prevailed in other parts of the earth, must be

[51] Adams's "Works," IX, 386-88; Cf. Tyler's "Henry," 178 ff.

established in America. That exuberance of pride which has produced an insolent domination in a few, a very few, insolent and monopolizing families, will be brought down nearer to the confines of reason and moderation than they have been used to.

When the Declaration of Rights was taken up by the Convention, the opposition of the conservative minority to its first clause disgusted Thomas Ludlow Lee. This clause, made immortal when touched by Jefferson's pen, declared that "all men are by nature equally free and independent, and have certain inherent rights . . . namely, the enjoyment of life and liberty, with the means of acquiring and possessing property, and pursuing and obtaining happiness and safety." To many literal-minded men the assertion seems absurd even now, and it might have been expected to meet vehement opposition among Virginia aristocrats who ruled over scores of slaves apiece. Lee wrote his relative, R. H. Lee: [52]

A certain set of aristocrats—for we have such monsters here—finding that their miserable system cannot be reared on such foundations, have to this time kept us at bay on the first line, which declares all men to be born free and independent. A number of absurd or unmeaning alterations have been proposed.

In the museum of the Virginia Historical Society at Richmond is fitly preserved the table on which George Mason wrote his draft of the Declaration of Rights, fourteen of the sixteen sections adopted being his. The document was a notable victory for true democracy. In the main, it was a restatement of English principles—the principles of Magna Charta, the Petition of Rights, the Commonwealth Parliament, and the Revolution of 1688. It of course laid down the necessary stipulations regarding jury trial, cruel and unusual punishments, search warrants, freedom of the press, and the subordination of military to civil power. It asserted that all authority is derived from the people, who, when a government becomes evil, have an inalienable right to reform it. It formulated the doctrine of the separation of executive, legislative, and judicial powers. It stated that all men who had sufficient evidence of permanent common interest with the community should enjoy the ballot. Another important section declared for a full grant of religious freedom; this was originated by Henry, and broadened by Madison, and the conservatives, seeing that it would be the basis for an attack upon the Anglican Establishment, fought it tooth and nail. The first section of the document was also sure to be used in an attack upon entail. Indeed, the Declaration was a remarkable charter of

[52] Henry, "Henry," I, 425.

liberties. It still stands at the head of Virginia's fifth Constitution, and it was the model for all the many similar American documents.[53]

The Constitution proper, though less clearly advanced, was democratic in tendency. Its outline was reported from the drafting committee on June 24, was considered in committee of the whole for parts of three days, and after extensive changes, was unanimously adopted June 29. Few records exist of the debates in the Convention, but there is no doubt that Mason dominated them. There is also no doubt that the original draft of the Constitution was his work. Madison and Edmund Randolph both speak of him as the author, while Jefferson is even more explicit in assigning it to him, adding that he was "one of our really great men, and of the first order of greatness." It is probable that Mason laid a resumé of his ideas before the drafting committee, and that it was used with little change as its report. This report was brief, and had to be expanded; its several articles were in recommendatory form—"Let the legislative, executive, and judicative departments be separate and distinct," and so on—and had to be made declaratory. In addition, Mason's plan was a little too well balanced to suit a period which distrusted all governmental agencies except the legislature.

The important amendments made in the original draft were not, on the whole, improvements. The Convention refused to extend the suffrage quite as far as Mason wished, keeping the colonial property qualification. It made the Senate the direct choice of the people, whereas he had devised an indirect mode of electing it. It more carefully defined the powers of the executive, and in opposition to Patrick Henry, who wished the Governor given the veto power, more sharply limited them. It excluded ministers of the gospel from the legislature. It confirmed the boundaries with the neighboring States, and asserted a claim to the Northwest. But the broad outlines remained Mason's still. The instrument was greeted with satisfaction by all Whigs except the most bigotedly conservative, and though we can hardly believe that Jefferson and Madison were wholly pleased, R. H. Lee breathes general approval in his letters.

Evident as were the faults of the Constitution, it marked a salutary advance for Virginia upon the road to that broad democracy

[53] Rowland's Mason, I, ch. 7.

for which the names of Mason and Jefferson later stood in the South and Southwest. The right of suffrage was left unchanged; it was held by every freeman with fifty acres, and land was then dirt cheap. Both houses were to be chosen by the entire body of voters. Each county was annually to elect two members of the lower house, and Williamsburg and Norfolk one member each, while the Senate was to consist of twelve men chosen from as many specially formed districts, one-fourth going out annually by rotation. The Governor was to be elected annually by joint ballot of both houses, and he might hold office for three successive years, but should then not be reëligible for four years. There was to be an executive council of eight, which Jefferson later called a fifth wheel to the wagon, and Madison a grave of useful talents, but which was more, an unnecessary clog upon the Governor. At every point, it will be seen, the administration could be held responsible to the voters who yearly sent up all the Delegates and part of the Senators to Williamsburg.

One of the two gravest defects of the Constitution, a sin against sound government, was its grant of disproportionate powers to the legislature, and especially to the lower chamber. The latter alone could originate enactments, and though the Senate could defeat any bill, it could not amend appropriation measures. The two houses elected the principal State officers, including judges, and determined all salaries. The governor was pitifully weak, and could not even call the legislature without his council's consent. The other chief fault was a sin against democracy, the unfair apportionment of representation in the lower house. Small counties like Warwick, with a few hundred voters, could choose two delegates just like the great western counties of several thousand voters. The westward drift of population accentuated this injustice, and it soon produced acute discontent. To this limited extent, the Constitution tended to perpetuate the old oligarchy of rich Tidewater planters. [54]

It is plain that these two faults in a limited degree nullified one another. Had the constitution-makers given every important power to the House, and then made the radical element of small farmers, professional men, artisans, and western pioneers dominant in the House, unwise legislation would have been much more frequent than it was. Virginia's government might have resembled North

[54] Ambler, "Sectionalism in Virginia, 1776-1861," ch. 1 and 2; McGregor, "The Disruption of Virginia," 27-30. By 1810 the 49 counties of the east and south had less than one half the white population by 72,138 souls; but they had an easy majority of the lower house.

Carolina's. The partial dominance by the sober conservatives for several decades, without actually blocking progressive legislation, did block much unwise, precipitate action. On the other hand, had the Constitution-makers entrenched the Tidewater representatives in the House, given the Senate more power, and entrusted all appointments and an absolute veto to the Governor, progressive legislation would have been much harder to obtain than Jefferson and Madison found it. Better for Virginia had neither defect been present, but the two together were perhaps to be preferred to one alone.

News of the adoption of the Virginia Constitution had barely reached Philadelphia when on July 8 the polling took place there for its own Convention. In Philadelphia the election, held at the State House, passed off quietly. "Fine starlight, pleasant·evening," wrote one observer that night. "There were bonfires, ringing bells, with other great demonstrations of joy upon the unanimity and agreement of the Declaration." [55] However, there was no unanimity or joy over the step which the State was just taking. The election laws had been in one sense so far liberalized that a very heavy vote should have been cast. The property qualification of fifty pounds or fifty acres, and the obnoxious naturalization requirements which had excluded many Germans, had been swept away; but so deep was the repugnance which many citizens felt for the destruction of the Charter, a destruction for which they had to declare their approval before they could vote, that in the entire State only 6000 went to the polls.[56] The hundred delegates met just a week later, on a hot July 15, in a room just across the hall from the Continental Congress.

The Convention, destined to produce the most peculiar of all the early Constitutions, had just one great name, that of Franklin, now nearly seventy, who was chosen its president. With him were associated David Rittenhouse, the astronomer, a mathematical genius whom the radicals liked all the more because he had been born a poor farm lad; James Smith, a lawyer of York and a signer of the Declaration; Thomas Smith, who had been a small officeholder in Bedford County; George Ross, an able lawyer and experienced legislator from Lancaster; and George Clymer, a Philadelphia merchant of wealth and brains. Special mention must be made

[55] "Diary of Christopher Marshall," 83.
[56] *Pa. Packet*, Dec. 25, 1787, quoting Col. Hartley.

of two Convention leaders who stood apart, both extreme radicals —James Cannon, an ingenious Scotch professor of mathematics in the college in Philadelphia, and Timothy Matlack, a fiery Quaker of middle age, born in New Jersey, who was disowned by his sect for the fighting part he took in the Revolution. Most of the others were men of slender parts and education. Not one-sixth of his fellow-members, wrote Thomas Smith, had ever read a word upon constitutional topics. A powerful influence was exerted upon the Convention by one man not a member, George Bryan. One of the most active leaders of the radical party, Bryan was a Philadelphian of Irish birth and blood, intensely earnest and idealistic, with an active but rather shallow mind, who was possessed of a keen instinct for public life which had made him an assemblyman and judge long before. Bryan was intimate with Cannon, and found a mouthpiece for his views in the latter.

The procedure of the Pennsylvania Convention was simple. On July 18 a drafting committee, which included Matlack, Cannon, the two Smiths, Ross, and Rittenhouse, was appointed. Franklin could not serve, for much of his time was occupied by the Continental Congress. By September 5 the Convention had finished its preliminary discussion of the instrument, and ordered 400 copies distributed for criticism by the public. After only ten days, however, it resumed debate, punctuating the discussion with other business, and on September 28 it unanimously approved the form of government.[57]

The minutes tell us this, but nothing more. Just who was writing the Constitution during these ten weeks? All the evidence points to Franklin, Bryan, Cannon, and Matlack as the foremost contributors to this remarkable instrument. Alexander Graydon, author of one of the most interesting American autobiographies, says that it was understood to have been principally the work of Bryan, in conjunction with Cannon, but that Dr. Franklin was also implicated in its production. He attributes one of its peculiar features, the Council of Censors, to Cannon and Bryan, while an anonymous pamphlet of eight years later traces this to the "fanatical schoolmaster," Cannon, alone. John Adams was in Philadelphia during the summer, and intensely interested in the State Constitution, for the Pennsylvania radicals had been offended by his plan for a government com-

[57] Proceedings Relative to Calling the Conventions of 1776 and 1790, 48-55 *et passim.*

prising three well-balanced branches. He tells us that not Franklin, but Matlack, Cannon, Thomas Paine, and Dr. Thomas Young, a physician of the city, were the authors. Adams of course condemned the Constitution. Again, it was men like Cannon and Matlack whom Thomas Smith must have meant when he wrote General St. Clair: "We might at least have prevented ourselves from being ridiculous in the eyes of the world were it not for a few enthusiastic members who are totally unacquainted with the principles of government. It is not only that their notions are original, but they would go to the devil for popularity, and in order to acquire it, they have embraced leveling principles, which you know is a fine method of succeeding." [58]

The Constitution bears several of Franklin's hallmarks. Three of his peculiar political ideas were the desirability of a plural executive, of a unicameral legislature, which Pennsylvanians had long maintained, and of gratuitous public service, and we find the first two embodied in the new government. His little story to illustrate the defects of the bicameral system is well known. "Has not the famous political fable of the snake, with two heads and one body, some useful instruction contained in it?" he asked. "She was going to a brook to drink, and in her way was to pass through a hedge, a twig of which opposed her direct course; one head chose to go on the right side of the hedge, the other on the left; so that time was spent in the contest, and before the decision was completed, the poor snake died of thirst." [59] Franklin had presented to Congress, a year previously, a plan for a union of the colonies, which called for one legislative house, and an executive council of twelve. Timothy Matlack wrote a friend some years later that when the debate on the form of the legislature was almost ended, Franklin was asked to speak and made a vigorous plea for a single house.[60] As for the Council of Censors, Graydon was no doubt right when he named Bryan and Cannon as its parents. To the former, who was an omnivorous reader, and knew so many recondite facts that a bet was once offered by a friend that he could name the town crier of Bergen-op-Zoom, the Roman flavor of the Council doubtless appealed as

[58] For the above see Graydon's "Memoirs," 266-268; Konkle's "Bryan," ch. 9; Adams's "Works," II, 507 ff.; *Pa. Mag. of Hist. and Biog.*, IV, 92, 93; XVI, 315; XXII, 265-300; Konkle, "Life of Thomas Smith." Rittenhouse's biographer states that he had no appreciable share in the Constitution; Barton's "Rittenhouse," 336 note.
[59] Cf. William Cabell Bruce's "Benjamin Franklin Self-Revealed," II, 249 note. The decision of the French Constituent Assembly in 1790, after hot debate, was for a unicameral legislature.
[60] *Pa. Packet*, March 30, 1779; Journals Cont. Cong., II, 195 ff.

much as to the academic-minded Cannon. But Franklin also probably approved it. With the Constitution as a whole Franklin was so well pleased that he carried a copy to France, and exhibited it to Turgot, La Rochefoucauld, Condorcet, and other admirers.

The first three sections of the Constitution proper—for there was also a bill of rights—contained the gist of the instrument. "The supreme legislative power shall be vested in a house of representatives . . ." they began; "the supreme executive power shall be vested in a President and Council;" and, "Courts of justice shall be established in the city of Philadelphia and in every county of this State."

There was to be no Governor, and no upper house! The members of the single legislative chamber were to be elected annually by the counties and metropolis, no property qualification being required of them or the voters. A blundering effort was made to supply the place of an upper house by requiring that every bill be printed for the consideration of the executive and people before it was brought up for final debate, and that only urgent temporary legislation should be passed by the same session of the legislature at which it was introduced. Naturally, to propose legislation at one session and enact it at the next was found so troublesome that in practice nearly all bills were treated as temporary, and at the ensuing session were declared permanent. The people every three years were to choose an Executive Council of thirteen, one from each county and the city of Philadelphia. However, its President and Vice-President were not to be popularly elected, but chosen annually from the Council by joint ballot of it and the Assembly. The President was little more than the presiding officer of the Council, and even its authority was closely restricted. That favorite demand of the radicals, rotation in office, was embodied in a rule that Assemblymen might not serve more than four terms, and councilors not more than one, in seven years.

The crowning eccentricity of the Constitution, however, was the provision that for seven years no alteration was to be permitted, but that at the end of that time—in October, 1783,—and every seven years thereafter, a Council of Censors was to be elected by the freemen to examine the operation of the government and inquire whether the Constitution had been violated. If they thought it in need of amendment, they had the power to call a State Convention to sit within two years, for the purpose of passing upon a program of alterations suggested by the Censors.

The instrument was received with a perfect storm of opposition. All loyalists and conservatives, all lovers of the old Charter, would have denounced it even had it been perfect, and its glaring faults made it an easy target. John Adams's converts to the gospel of a well-balanced government were outraged by this quite unbalanced form. The provision for a single chamber of paramount powers struck many as dangerous,[61] and that for a many-headed executive as absurd. And who had ever heard of Censors? The Romans, to be sure, had possessed officers of that name, with duties of a varied nature, including the right of disqualifying men from public functions upon moral grounds, and of selecting the Senate. Montesquieu, in his "Spirit of the Laws," had praised the Roman censorship and Spartan ephorate as a method of keeping government uncorrupted, while Rousseau in his "Social Contract" had spoken highly of the former. A pamphlet just published in Philadelphia had advised a decennial meeting of delegates to examine the State Constitution, and to see that it was kept pure and vigorous. But to many Pennsylvanians the Council of Censors seemed eccentric, impracticable, and totally inadequate to keep such an unbalanced government in the straight path.[62]

Above all, the complete abandonment of the past by the Constitution-makers offended all conservatives, who felt that Thomas Smith had been right when he accused his colleagues of determining to reject everything in the Charter simply because it had been part of the old government. Observers from other States shared these views. Thus Hooper of North Carolina wrote home ridiculing the Constitution as a beast without a head, a motley mixture of limited monarchy and execrable democracy, in which the mob was made the second branch of the legislature, and taverns and dram-shops became the councils to which the State laws were to be referred.[63]

Even before the Constitution was finally adopted, savage attacks began appearing upon it in the press. One critic said that he saw no powers delegated to the executive, and yet it was surrounded by a hundred barriers; while he saw all possible powers given the legis-

[61] See typical denunciation in *Pa. Packet,* September 24, 1776.
[62] L. H. Meader, "The Council of Censors," discusses this institution in Pennsylvania and Vermont; see W. E. Heitland, "The Roman Republic," *passim,* for the censors in ancient times.
[63] Jones, "Defence of the Rev. Hist. of N. C.," 325.

lature, and not a single safeguard there from abuse. Had not all nations found compound legislatures the most favorable to liberty? The Rump Parliament, which sat nearly twenty years, "Scipio" warned his readers, was a unicameral legislature. After the adoption of the Constitution these attacks were redoubled. Finally, the excitement culminated in general mass-meetings held in the State House Yard on the nights of October 21 and 22.

Ostensibly, these mass-meetings were held for debate. Colonel John Bayard presided, and a set of resolutions attacking the new Constitution was advocated by Dickinson, McKean, and others, and opposed by Cannon, Matlack, and Dr. Thomas Young. But the real design of the conservative leaders was to use the meetings to overthrow the Constitution. The elections for the new legislature were now near at hand. The leaders were already urging the voters to refuse to name any Councilors whatever, and to elect Assembly-men opposed to the Constitution; then, they said, the government would break down, the Assembly could resolve itself into a convention to recast the Constitution, and it would be submitted to the people for final action. The resolutions skilfully outlined this purpose. The first half dozen hinted nothing of it, but simply constituted a thorough assault upon the instrument. They were passed with a shout, for as one Anti-Constitutionalist wrote, "we had all the rich great men and the wise men, the lawyers and doctors on our side." [64] Written by an expert pen, they lent themselves to a succinct indictment of the Constitution: [65]

1st. It establishes only a *single* legislative body. 2dly. It renders the *judicial* [department] dependent on that *single* legislative body, who may remove any judge from his office *without* trial, for anything they please to call "misbehavior." 3dly. It renders the executive dependent on that *single* legislative body; by whom alone the *executive* officers are to be paid for their services—and by whom, from the great disproportion between the members of the Assembly and Council, the President and Vice-President must always be annually chosen—besides that, every officer, executive or judicial, may be impeached *by the Assembly,* before six of the Council *thus dependent on the Assembly,* and be tried or condemned. 4thly. It erects no court of appeals, more necessary here than in some other States, as our Supreme Court may try causes in the first instance.

But it was the final resolutions that really counted for the future. They declared that amendments were absolutely and immediately

[64] *Pa. Gazette,* November 13, 1776; Marshall's "Diary," 98, 99. One resolution was devoted to omissions in the Constitution; that is, its neglect to state which of the Colonial laws should remain in force, to fix the property qualification of the Assembly-men, to say what judges should sit in certain courts, and so on. Another complained that the constitution treated many subjects properly left to the legislature—the control of fishing and hunting, the status of insolvent debtors, and so on.
[65] This is a footnote published with the resolutions; *Pa. Packet,* October 23, 1776.

indispensable. They urged the voters at the approaching election to refuse the oath accepting the Constitution required by the Convention, and asked the Assemblymen not to take the oath to maintain the instrument intact. No Councilors, it was advised, should be elected. The twenty-seventh resolution asserted that the Assembly should consider itself empowered to make changes in the Constitution, and the twenty-ninth that it should submit such amendments to the people. The plan, in fine, was to prevent the creation of an effective government, and to force the new Assembly to remake the Constitution.

For a time the Anti-Constitutionalists seemed likely by these aggressive tactics to carry the day. Their ticket in the city and county of Philadelphia, headed by John Dickinson, was elected by a vote of two to one over the radicals. Only Assemblymen were chosen there, for the Anti-Constitutionalists were insistent that the Council must not come into existence. Within a few days (November 8) another mass-meeting adopted instructions to the Philadelphia Assemblymen. It asked them to propose to the Assembly the amendment of the new fundamental law; to oppose, in this revision, any unnecessary changes from the government offered by the late Charter, confining themselves in the main to the simple extinction of the royal and proprietary powers; and to take special care that the legislature be bicameral. Their final injunction is of importance as showing the growth of the constitutional idea that the people should be allowed to ratify or reject the organic law: [66]

. . . You are to remember that the consent of a majority of the poeple alone can render a frame of government, as well as laws, valid, and therefore you will propose that the frame of government be submitted to the consideration of the people a reasonable time, and after having collected their opinions in such a manner as shall be most expedient, you are to alter or confirm the same as shall be found necessary.

As the news of the election came in from other counties it appeared that the vote had been remarkably light—only about 1500 votes all told; that not enough supporters of the Constitution had been elected to the Council to enable it to reorganize and sit; and that the Anti-Constitutionalists, though a minority, constituted more than one-third of the Assembly. They could prevent it from reaching a quorum, and thus possibly dictate their own terms to it. The Anti-Constitutionalist members, including Dickinson, Clymer, and Robert Morris, were jubilant.

[66] *Pa. Packet,* November 12, 1776.

When the Assembly vainly tried to organize on November 28, Pennsylvania's affairs were in dire confusion. There was no executive; there was no Legislature, the minority resolutely preventing it from sitting; and half the State was bitterly opposed to the new régime. Dickinson's ultimatum was soon prepared. He and the minority would agree, he said, to the choice of a speaker and the transaction of business, provided the majority would call a constitutional convention before the end of January, leave the existing Constitution in abeyance, and dissolve before the convention met. The majority leaders indignantly refused, and the deadlock dragged on, until in December the Assembly broke up, the majority agreeing to meet again a month later. Once more, when they convened, efforts to give the State a legislature utterly failed.

But the dark aspect of national affairs now compelled Congress to intervene, and it intimated to Pennsylvanians that if they could not bring this stupid contest to an end, it would have to take over the government of the State. Thus admonished, the Anti-Constitutionalists, Dickinson and their other leaders being patriots through and through, began to give up their attempt to kill the Constitution. In February, 1777, elections were held for new Asssemblymen in place of several who had refused to act, and Philadelphia consented at last to name a Councilor. On March 4 the new government was finally set in motion by the organization of both Assembly and Council; they elected Wharton President, and George Bryan Vice-President, and next day these men were inaugurated.[67]

In these six months of turmoil and uncertainty Pennsylvania paid part of the cost of the reckless precipitancy with which the radicals had torn the government from the Provincial Assembly in May, 1776, and framed it anew; part of the bill was still to pay. The deadlock which had paralyzed the State for several months at a time when Howe seemed about to fall upon it was ended, but the ill-feeling persisted. It was bound to increase, not to decrease. Party antagonisms in Pennsylvania from 1776 to 1787 were more consistently violent than in any other State, and more injurious to it and the nation.

[67] *Pa. Gazette*, February 25, 1784; Stillé's "Dickinson," 207-10; *Pa. Mag. Hist. and Biog.*, V, 426-39; *Idem*, IX, 188 ff. (Diary of James Allen).

III.   CONSTITUTIONS OF A CONSERVATIVE CHARACTER

The two brilliant victories of the conservatives were won in Maryland and New York, which as Colonies had been governed by an aristocracy, and as States were to continue under aristocratic rule for another generation.   Maryland's Constitution was made especially interesting by its provision for the indirect election of the upper house.   Here the electoral college, which Mason had suggested in Virginia, made its bow in American politics.   It was well to have it tried in at least one State, though as adopted by the nation the use to which it has been put signally disappointed the intention of its originators.

The convention, presided over by the head of one of Maryland's most aristocratic families, Matthew Tilghman, began its work at Annapolis August 14, 1776, finished it September 17, adjourned for a fortnight after sending a dozen copies to each county for consideration, and finally adopted the Constitution on November 11.   That is, at least a show of ascertaining public opinion upon the instrument was made.   Of the actual course of debate and of the inside history of the convention's procedure, we know almost nothing.   Within a fortnight after the work began a disagreeable incident occurred— Samuel Chase and Charles Carroll, barrister, resigned as a consequence of receiving from their constituents in Ann Arundel County instructions to adhere to points which they believed incompatible with good government.   A decade later Chase was praised for having defeated radical constitutional notions "similar to those which have divided and distracted a neighboring State," which implies that the majority in Ann Arundel may have wished a unicameral legislature.[68]

The chief distinction of the Constitution lay, as we have said, in the careful differentiation in the choice of the two legislative branches. The House of Delegates was to consist of four members from each county, and two each from Annapolis and Baltimore, elected annually by freemen having £30 or 50 acres.   Members of the Senate, however, were to be chosen for five years, and by an indirect system then quite new.   In September, 1781, and every fifth year thereafter, the voters were to name two persons for each county, and one each for the two cities, to be electors of the Senate.   Three weeks later

---

[68] See *Maryland Journal*, November 8, 1785, on Chase's part in the Convention.

this electoral college was to meet and select from its own ranks or from the people at large fifteen Senators, nine from the western and six from the eastern shore. To be eligible to the Senate, a man must have resided in Maryland three years, and must own £1000 worth of property. The whole arrangement was most conservative, making it certain that the upper house would represent the wealth, position, and caution of the State; it was the antithesis of the system which the Pennsylvania radicals were adopting at the same time. Hamilton more than a decade later singled out this feature for praise in the Federalist, stating that "the Maryland Constitution is daily deriving, from the salutary operation of this part of it, a reputation in which it will probably not be rivaled by that of any State in the Union." [69] The electoral college had its drawbacks, but the chief danger in most States after 1776 arose from the rash legislation demanded from vociferous, ill-educated voters, and against such demands Maryland was well protected.

Another conservative, and in this instance really undemocratic characteristic of the Constitution was the high property qualification demanded for any civic participation. Each member of the House had to have property worth £500; each Senator twice as much; and the Governor real and personal property of no less than £5000 value, of which at least £1000 had to be in a freehold estate. The first governor was a very rich lawyer, able to equip and maintain at his own expense a considerable military force to join Washington in the retreat through the Jerseys.

Nowhere was a Constitution adopted under more difficult circumstances than in New York, and nowhere was one better written until Massachusetts performed the task in 1780. The Provincial Congress which acted as Constitutional Convention met first at White Plains; then, as the British advanced northward, it moved from Harlem successively to King's Bridge, Philipse's Manor, Fishkill, Poughkeepsie, and at last Kingston, well up the Hudson. It was a government on the run.[70] Immediately after meeting, and approving the Declaration of Independence, it resolved that the dangerous situation of the state demanded its undivided attention, and that consideration of a Constitution should wait until August 1. Jay at this moment felt the military prospect so hopeless that he was for ravaging Long Island, burning New York City, and retiring into the

[69] Federalist, No. 63.
[70] Lincoln, "Const. Hist. of N. Y.," 491, 492.

Highlands. But on the appointed day, a committee of thirteen was chosen to draft the instrument.[71]

This committee was remarkable for the youth of most of its members, and the high proportion of names destined to fame. It is well established that John Jay, with some help from Gouverneur Morris and Robert R. Livingston, produced the first draft of the Constitution. All three were young lawyers of prominent family. Jay, the eldest, was not quite thirty-two—a handsome man, with dark hair and classic features. His great abilities were partly concealed by his modest, self-effacing disposition, but he had made such a record at the bar that he was highly regarded. He belonged to a family of Huguenot merchants which had sent a scion to America in 1686, and his ancestors had intermarried with aristocratic Knickerbockers, while he himself had recently taken as wife the daughter of William Livingston. As a member of the Continental Congress, he had distinguished himself by the papers he had drafted —letters to Canada, Ireland, and Jamaica, the famous circular letter to the Colonies, and the address to the people of Great Britain, which Jefferson called a production of the finest pen in America. He was conservative, thoughtful, scholarly, and inventive, the best man available for the place. Robert R. Livingston, of the Scotch family which held the great manor comprising most of what are now Dutchess and Columbia Counties, was thirty, had been at King's College with Jay, and was for a short time his law-partner; in the first days of the Revolution Jay still remembered the very date in 1765 when the two had "particularly professed" their friendship, and hoped that their "unbounded confidence" in each other might be perpetual. Livingston was soon to become the State's first Chancellor, and to hold that position close upon a quarter-century. Gouverneur Morris, of English descent, had been born in the old manor house of Morrisania, and now only twenty-four, was just beginning to make his name as a lawyer. Of the other committee-men, William Duer, who had been an aide to Clive in India, was twenty-nine, and Robert Yates, John Broome, and John Sloss Hobart were each thirty-eight.[72]

Jay wrote Rutledge early in July that the drafting of the Constitution would take only a month or two. "We have a government,

[71] *Idem,* 490.
[72] Cf. D. S. Alexander, "Pol. Hist. N. Y.," I, 5-9; J. H. Daugherty, "Const. Hist. of the State of N. Y.," ch. 3.

you know, to form; and God only knows what it will resemble. Our politicians, like guests at a feast, are perplexed and undetermined which dish to prefer." [73]   He was inclined to believe that the movement for a Constitution was premature, and that it would be best to wait for a period of greater tranquility.

As a matter of fact, it was to be weary months before he was free to think in a sustained way of constitutional affairs, for even after August 1 it proved impossible to begin work on the instrument. On that day Jay, Robert R. Livingston, and Robert Yates of the drafting committee were absent from the Convention as a secret deputation charged with obstructing the Hudson and otherwise annoying the British ships. The Convention tried to recall them, so that they could whip together a tentative framework before August 26, but their return was delayed. September slipped away, while the military situation grew steadily worse, and on October 14 the Convention definitely shelved its constitutional work by resolving itself into a committee of safety. At that moment Washington, holding the hills between Kingsbridge and White Plains, was in a precarious position, and before the end of the next month his defeated, dispirited troops had abandoned New York soil and were retreating through New Jersey. The Convention sat again early in December. But it was not until March 12, 1777, that the committee's draft of a Constitution was at last brought in, and, in the absence of Jay, was read by Duane in his place, delivered at the table, and thence again read. Debates upon it commenced the next day.[74]

Our chief authority for believing Jay the author of the greater part of the New York Constitution is his son, who had ample means of obtaining the facts from his father. Jay's field service in obstructing the Hudson and fortifying West Point, and his work upon a committee for defeating conspiracies against the patriot cause, occupied much of his time until the end of February, 1777. His son states that to design the new government, he retired the early spring of

[73] Jay, "Correspondence," I, 68.
[74] Lincoln, "Const. Hist. of N. Y.," 499. The Convention's Journals do not show the nature of the debates or even give the votes with fulness. The original draft provided for calling the upper house a Council, the colonial name, but the Convention changed it to Senate, which Jefferson had first suggested. It was originally proposed that the Assemblymen be chosen by districts, but the Convention preferred the colonial plan of election by counties. The first draft provided for voting at elections by ballot, instead of *viva voce,* a desirable reform. Gouverneur Morris defeated this plan, but Jay was able to obtain a clause providing that after the peace voting by ballot should be given a fair trial. The Convention also refused to allow all taxpayers to vote for Assemblymen, as was first suggested, and limited the ballot to propertied men.

1777 to some place in the country. "Upon reflecting on the character and feelings of the Convention he thought it prudent to omit in the draft several provisions that appeared to him improvements, and afterwards to propose them separately as amendments. . . . It is probable that the Convention was ultra-democratic, for I have heard him observe that *another turn of the winch would have cracked the cord.*" [75] We know that Jay was well pleased with the finished work, rejoicing that it had met universal approval, even in New England, where few New York productions were liked. John Adams boasted in his old age that, according to Duane, Jay had left Congress to return to New York for the work of Constitution-making with Adams's letter to Wythe in his pocket for a model.[76] Jay certainly would not have neglected to study Adams's pamphlet, as well as other helpful treatises, but it is doubtless quite too much to say that he made it his model.

With great merits, the Constitution as at last adopted united great defects, and defects unique among those of the early State Constitutions. At the time, and with reason, it was widely regarded as the best of the organic laws, and it exerted a considerable influence upon the Federal Constitution. It was the first Constitution to provide for popular election of the Governor, and to grant him an approach to adequate powers, while it refused to hamper him with an executive council. It was the first which gave a fair balance to the three departments of government, executive, legislative, and judicial. Its treatment of the judiciary, though not far-sighted, was better than that of most States. The Constitution was well-arranged, well-written, and brief, something which could be said of few. Its main faults, which it was impossible to perceive in advance, were connected with two remarkable innovations, the Council of Revision and the Council of Appointment.

The Legislature was to consist of an Assembly and Senate, of which the Assemblymen were to have annual and the Senators quadrennial terms, one fourth of the latter body retiring each year. The Assembly consisted of seventy men elected from the counties in proportions constitutionally fixed, but subject to correction by septennial censuses; and the Senate of twenty-four members elected from four great State districts. In forming the Legislature, Jay

[75] Pellew, "John Jay," 76.
[76] Adams's "Works," X, 410.

and his associates built upon the foundation afforded by the Provincial Legislature.[77]   Voters for the Assembly had to be freeholders, and Gouverneur Morris, an aristocrat to his finger-tips, was responsible for a provision that the freehold must be worth at least £20; but Jay carried an amendment preserving the ballot to all the existing freemen of Albany and New York City.   A voter for the Senate and the Governor had to own a freehold worth £100 clear.   The Governor was given a term of three years, in itself an unheard-of act of generosity, and powers similar to those of the Crown Governor.   He commanded the armed forces, he could convene the legislature, and prorogue it for limited periods, and he had a limited power of pardon. He was to correspond with Congress and the other States, and to recommend legislation.   The fear of his power was greatest with respect to appointments and the veto, and in trying to hedge it in at these points the Convention opened the way to gross future misgovernment.

A few members wished the Governor to make all appointments; others, of the ultra-democratic stamp to which Jay referred in his talk with his son, wished to empower the legislature to make them. Jay probably approved the objection that the first method would give the Governor too much power, and undoubtedly believed that the second would too greatly strengthen the legislature.   The original draft-Constitution proposed that the Governor should make a nomination, that the legislature should approve or veto it, and that when the Governor had made four nominations to one place without success, then the legislature should proceed with its own choice.   A protracted discussion arose.   While the disagreement was at its height, Jay spent an evening at the lodgings of Morris and Robert R. Livingston, proposed a plan for a Council of Appointment, and arranged with them to bring it forward the following day.[78]   This plan was that the legislature should yearly name four Senators, one from each district, as a Council to sit with the Governor for the appointment of officers; the Governor to have only a casting vote, and to preside.   As an after-thought, Jay suggested that the Speaker be added, so that the casting vote would be less frequently needed, but this suggestion was overruled.

It took many years to show just how extremely bungling this

[77] See Memorial Hist. N. Y., II, 610.
[78] Jay, "Correspondence," I, 128.

star-chamber arrangement was. Jay had intended that the Governor should make the nominations, and that the Council should confirm or reject them, but this was not stated in the Constitution. In practice, whenever a majority of the Assembly was politically opposed to the Governor, it chose four Councillors who tied the latter's hands, and made all appointments from among his political enemies. In order to do this, the Council was led to assert that the power to nominate was vested concurrently in the Governor and each of the four Senators, thus virtually stripping the Governor of all appointive power unless he happened to be of the same political party as at least two of its members. Every new Assembly election meant a new division of the spoils. The appointees were very numerous, the patronage enormously valuable in New York. The mistake here made, as to some extent ten years later in drafting the Federal Constitution, was in failing to foresee how powerfully the two-party system would shape all political institutions.[79]

The Council of Revision was similarly intended as a check upon both the legislature and the Governor, this time to solve the perplexing question of the veto. The Convention was afraid on the one hand that the Governor would interdict useful legislation, and on the other that a legislature might sometimes wish to pass rash bills. A Council was therefore created of the Governor, Chancellor, and three judges of the Supreme Court, or any two of the four acting with the Governor, to "revise all bills about to be passed into law by the legislature." The exercise of the veto might be grounded upon either the unconstitutionality or the inexpediency of the bill. The suggestion for this section probably came from a memory of the King's Privy Council, which had enjoyed a veto upon colonial legislation. But if the Council of Revision took no action upon a bill within ten days, or if each house could repass it by a two-thirds vote following a veto, it became law. The chief defect of this feature was that it gave a bulwark to the standing order and to conservatism, since the landed proprietors could often control the Council; while many thought that the body improperly united legislative and judicial powers.[80]

Still another unfortunate feature of the New York Constitution

[79] For Hamilton's exposition of the early defects manifest in the New York system of making appointments, see the Federalist, No. 77. The Council, he said, was "a small body, shut up in a private apartment, impenetrable to the public eye," and hence open to cabal and intrigue.
[80] Pellew's "Jay," 81; Daugherty's "Const. Hist. of the State of N. Y.," 86 ff.

lay in the close restriction of the suffrage, for conservatives like Morris, Livingston, and Yates never believed in a really popular government. As late as 1790 only 1303 of the 13,000 or 14,000 male residents of New York city possessed enough property to vote for Governor.[81] Any elector qualified to vote for an Assemblyman was eligible for that office, while the Senators and Governor had merely to be freeholders. Men could thus run for these two higher offices even if they could not vote for them. But the restriction of the electorate meant that none but men of large property were likely to be placed in any of the higher positions. In too large a degree the government was made of, by, and for the landholders. "It was a favorite maxim with Mr. Jay," writes his son, "that those who own the country ought to govern it." [82] We shall see that it was the landed class, as opposed to the mercantile class, which for years did govern New York.

The Constitution was finally approved April 20, 1777, by a vote of 32 to 1, less than one third the Convention then being in attendance.[83] Even Jay, after arriving about the middle of March, had been called away a month later by his mother's death. As Georgia's Constitution—an instrument which, like Pennsylvania's, gave despotic authority to a unicameral legislature—had been completed on February 5, New York had the honor of closing the whole original phase of constitution-making. This period had lasted sixteen months, beginning with New Hampshire's rudimentary instrument and ending with New York's comparatively finished and symmetrical design; and as a whole the patriots were well pleased with its fruits.

IV. DEFECTS OF THE EARLY CONSTITUTIONS

It is remarkable that of these first Constitutions, four lasted more than a half century: North Carolina's seventy-five years, New Jersey's sixty-eight, Maryland's sixty-five, and Virginia's fifty-four. The Charter of Connecticut served as a State Constitution for forty-two years, and that of Rhode Island for no less than sixty-four. New York's Constitution, though mulled over by a convention in 1801, endured substantially unaltered, its faults becoming ever more flagrant, for forty-five years. The others, including the temporary

[81] Alexander, "Pol. Hist. of N. Y.," I, 15.
[82] William Jay's "Jay," I, 70. One good feature of the Constitution was its guarantee of freedom of worship.
[83] Lincoln's "Const. Hist. of N. Y.," 556 ff.

instrument of Massachusetts, had comparatively brief careers, some being discarded almost immediately—and not one too soon.

Four main sets of precautions were taken to assure the continuance of popular control over the State governments. In the first place, the Constitutions made it clear that the civil officers were instruments of the whole people: "Magistrates are their trustees and servants, and at all times amenable to them," the Virginians put it. Again, tenure of office was held within close bounds, for almost all terms except those of judges were made exceedingly brief. There were few exceptions to the rule of annual election for Governors or legislators. In the third place, the Constitution-makers acted upon the Whig theory of political dynamics in providing for a theoretically careful balance of powers. As the planets are poised against each other, and between centripetal and centrifugal forces, so the colonists, following Locke and Montesquieu, sought to poise the executive, legislative, and judicial branches. The Virginia convention required that "the legislative and executive powers of the state shall be separate and distinct from the judiciary." The Georgia Convention declared that "the legislative, executive, and judiciary departments shall be separate and distinct, so that neither exercise the power properly belonging to the other." The Massachusetts Convention of 1780 stated the same demand even more explicitly. The Federalist contains no stronger piece of exposition than that setting forth this theory of checks and balances.[84]

That the theory is in considerable part unworkable has been repeatedly pointed out. A hostile poise between the departments is an outgrown ideal; partly because party government makes a close harmony between the executive and the legislative majority often as natural as it is desirable, and more largely because of a fundamental reason which one American President has stated in cogent language: [85]

Government is not a dead thing, but a living thing. It falls, not under the theory of the universe, but under the theory of organic life. It is accountable to Darwin, not to Newton. It is modified by its environment, necessitated by its tasks, shaped to its functions by the sheer pressure of life. No living thing can have its organs offset against each other as checks, and live. On the contrary, its life is dependent upon their quick coöperation, their ready response to the commands of instinct or intelligence, their amicable community of purpose. Government is not a body of blind forces; it is a body of men, with highly differentiated functions no doubt, in our modern day of specialization, but with a common task and purpose. . . . There can be no successful government without leadership or

---

[84] See especially Madison's essay, Federalist, No. 47.
[85] Woodrow Wilson, "Const. Govt. in the U. S.," 56, 57.

without the intimate, almost instinctive coördination of the organs of life and action. This is not theory, but fact, and displays its force as fact, whatever theories may be thrown across its track.

Yet the theory of checks and balances was, despite all the insistence upon it, by no means given true effect, for the first Constitutions provided no real equality of powers. As a fourth precaution to ensure popular control, the makers left the preponderance of authority to the legislature, which dominated the executive and shaped the judiciary.

The subordination of the executive branch to the legislature grew out of the memory of hated British executives, and out of precedents set in the hurried work of retiring troublesome governors and giving their authority to servants of the people. The Americans of 1776 thought that it was easy to keep the legislature a truly popular agency, but they knew no way of holding a powerful governor responsive to their will. They were unable to distinguish properly between a Crown governor and a popularly elected governor, and they had not learned the value of a concentration of responsibility. Each Constitution except New York's made the Governor elective by the legislature. Maryland spoke for most of her sisters when she asserted that "a long continuance, in the first executive departments of power or trust, is dangerous to liberty." Hence in all the States the Governor or President was given a one-year term, save in New York and Delaware, where he had three years, and in South Carolina, where he had two. In most States a marked check upon the Governor was provided in the shape of an executive council, varying in number from four to thirteen. In no State did the Governor have a final veto upon legislation, and in only three did he have a partial veto power. No State allowed him to adjourn the legislature, and the few which permitted prorogation, like New York, placed limitations upon the right. None of the States gave him any patronage for independent distribution. South Carolina, in a quaintly timid clause, specially forbade him to make war or peace or to enter into any treaties. In four States there was not even a Governor at all in the ordinary sense—Pennsylvania, Delaware, New Hampshire, and Massachusetts, where the real executive was simply a council. The Charter-Constitutions of Rhode Island and Connecticut made the Governor elective by the people, but they also kept him quite secondary to the legislature.

As for the judiciary, it was as lamentably dependent upon the assemblies as the executive branch. In Connecticut and Rhode Island the judges were chosen by the legislature, and held office for only one year. In Massachusetts also, under the revamped charter, the legislature elected the judiciary. The arrangement in New York seemed better, for all the jurists, from the Chancellor and Supreme Court justices to officers of the petty courts, were named by the Council of Appointment. But here again the legislature might exercise indirect control through its hold upon the Council. In Pennsylvania, the Executive Council and its President appointed the judges, and in Maryland they were given their commissions by the Governor with the consent of the Council. This was a great improvement upon a legislative election, but in the former State complaints soon arose that the legislators had failed to provide a fixed salary. In all other members of the Union the legislature elected the judges directly, though in Delaware the President sat with the General Assembly when it did so. It was usually easy for a legislature to effect the removal of any judge whom it disapproved. In Massachusetts (by the Constitution of 1780) and in Maryland, Delaware, and South Carolina, a judicial officer could be unseated by address of the two houses followed by formal action by the Governor. In Pennsylvania and Vermont the single house might remove judges without the assistance of the executive. In New Jersey the judges were removable by one branch of the legislature upon impeachment by the other.

In all, it is not strange that Jefferson burst out in indignation at the Constitution of his own State because "all the powers of government, legislative, executive, and judiciary, result to the legislative body." He added, in his "Notes on Virginia," that "the concentrating these in the same hands is precisely the definition of despotic government. It will be no alleviation that these powers will be exercised by a plurality of hands, and not a single one. One hundred and seventy-three despots [the number of the Virginia legislators] would surely be as oppressive as one. Let those who doubt it turn their eyes on the republic of Venice. As little will it avail us that they are chosen by ourselves. An *elective despotism* was not the government we fought for, but one which should not only be founded on free principles, but in which the powers of the government should be so divided and balanced among several bodies of magistracy, as that no one could transcend their legal limits, without being effectually checked and restrained by the others.[86] We have noted that a critic made precisely the same objection to the Constitution drafted in Pennsylvania in 1776: "In the Assembly I find the most *unbounded liberty,* and yet no kind of barrier to prevent its degenerating into licentiousness."

It was partly in reference to this legislative domination that Madison declared in the Federalist that "the accumulation of all powers, legislative, executive, and judiciary, in the same hands, whether of one, a few, or many, and whether hereditary, self-appointed, or elective, may justly be pronounced the very definition of tyranny." He went on to show, by reference to one State after another, that in not a single instance had the three departments been kept absolutely separate and distinct, and that in nearly all the legislature had obtained a marked ascendancy. Upon New Jersey's Constitution he was particularly severe. In New York alone, he suggested, was the government fairly free from the reproach outlined by Jefferson. In the Empire State it was not a lack of balance that was to prove objectionable, but the fact that the agencies devised for the mutual checking of the three departments were not rational, but irrational. Madison wisely pointed out that even if the executive and judicial departments had initially been made about as strong as the legislative branch, the latter would be likely to gain at their expense. "Its constitutional powers being at once more extensive and less susceptible of precise limits, it can, with the greater facility, mask, under complicated and indirect measures, the encroachments which it makes on the coördinate departments." [87]

A fact which contributed greatly to the early supremacy of the legislatures was the general assumption during the years 1776-87 that they were the sole judges of their own constitutional powers. Few Americans believed that any State court had the right to declare an enactment invalid on the ground that it violated the Constitution. New York, in creating her Council of Revision, implied that whenever a legislative enactment was approved by the Council, it was thenceforth subject to no question. The Chancellor and two or more judges of the Supreme Court had places on the Council, and possessing this opportunity to review legislation, were certainly not expected to have any other; it would have been fatuous to have

[86] "Writings," Memorial Ed., II, 162, 163.
[87] Federalist, No. 48.

given them a judicial review of acts passed over their disapproval. As for the two States which had Councils of Censors, Pennsylvania and Vermont, the provision for these bodies—"whose duty it shall be to inquire whether the Constitution has been preserved inviolate in every part"—seemed to vest in them the whole judicial function of interpreting the constitutionality of the laws. These two remarkable institutions had the same influence in both States: they delayed the recognition of a distinction between the Constitution and statutes, and the development of a judicial enforcement of that distinction. As early as June, 1777, the Pennsylvania Legislature was grossly transgressing the limits set up by the Constitution. The Pennsylvania, Delaware, and Georgia Constitutions were flagrantly violated in the very provisions which referred to the writing of fresh Constitutions.

The Massachusetts Constitution of 1780 also showed that the State courts were in no instance expected to annul a statute, for it provided that in 1795 there should be a popular vote upon the calling of a Convention to remedy any transgressions of the fundamental law—"to correct," stated the Constitution, "those violations which by any means may be made therein." Moreover, the legislative and executive branches were authorized, before the former acted upon any bill, to "require the opinions of the justices of the Supreme Judicial Court upon important questions of law and upon solemn occasions." This demonstrates that the legislature's action, after such an opinion was given, was to be considered final. But New Jersey surpassed all her sisters in offering her legislature *carte blanche*. The Constitution required each legislator to swear not to assent to any proceeding which annulled certain specified portions of it; so that by implication, the other portions were left quite open to violation! Delaware also marked certain parts of her Constitution as inviolable.[88]

As a matter of fact, the inevitable reaction against this legislative dominance became a strong motive for giving the courts that judicial review which is now such a universal feature of American government. "Experience in all the States," said Madison in the Federal Convention, "has evinced a powerful tendency in the legislature to absorb all power into its vortex. This was the real source of danger to the American Constitutions; and suggested the necessity of giving

[88] Cf. J. A. Jameson, "Const. Conventions," 135-36.

every defensive authority to the other departments that was consistent with republican principles." Madison himself, however, thought it undesirable to make the judiciary paramount in the Federal Government, and wished to avoid this by establishing a Federal Council of Revision. The first partial assertion of the right of a State court to set aside a statute as unconstitutional occurred in New Jersey in 1780. The Legislature did not fully assent to it; nor were such assertions fully accepted in the two or three other States where they were made before 1787, though there was a steady and powerful development toward establishment of the right.[89]

Thus one great eighteenth century principle which the constitutions were supposed to vindicate, the principle of the balance of departments, they signally failed to apply. Another great principle, that of democratic equality, they equally violated by their property requirements for voting and office-holding. In order to enjoy the right of suffrage, a man in New York (with the urban exceptions already noted) had to have a freehold of £20 or one paying a rent of 40 shillings; in Maryland to have 50 acres or other property worth £30; in South Carolina 50 acres, a town lot, or property paying equivalent taxes; in Connecticut and Rhode Island property worth £40, or 40 shillings a year in rent; and in Virginia 25 acres settled, or 500 unsettled. In Pennsylvania, Delaware, North Carolina, and Georgia any taxpayer might vote, and in Vermont not even this much was required, but these States were exceptions. To be a member of the lower legislative house a very considerable property was usually demanded—£500 worth in New Jersey and Maryland, £250 worth in Georgia, 100 acres in North Carolina, and so on. The Constitutions were ill-arranged, and several showed a tendency to embody extensive codes of law as well as the bare framework of government. Nevertheless, as a whole they did credit to the political sagacity of the people, and most of them served their purpose well.

[89] For Justice Brearly's decision in New Jersey, see Austin Scott, *Amer. Hist. Review,* IV, 456 ff. Jefferson took the view in his "Notes on Virginia" that State Constitutions might be changed by an act of the legislature, but St. George Tucker, in his "Commentaries on Blackstone" (I, Part I, Appendix, 83-95), combated this view; Howison's "Virginia," II, 138. James Iredell published in the summer of 1786 an argument for the right of the courts to decide the constitutionality of laws, and pronounce them null and void if unconstitutional; McRee's "Iredell," II, 145-49. A year later a decision in North Carolina was largely founded upon his argument; Martin's Reports, I, 42. For action of the Rhode Island and New York courts whose tendency was to nullify a State law, see pp. 230, 270, of this volume. Much was said upon judicial review in the Federal Convention. For recent discussion see Charles Warren in the *Nation,* Vol. 118, p. 526 ff.; Beard's "Supreme Court and the Constitution," 1 ff.

CHAPTER FIVE

The years immediately following the drafting of the first Constitutions were a period of rapid experiment and change. By 1800 the sixteen States then composing the Union had adopted twenty-six Constitutions. The year 1793 found three, New Hampshire, Vermont, and South Carolina, under their third form of organic law, and four others, Massachusetts, Pennsylvania, Delaware, and Georgia, under their second. These rapid substitutions were necessary. Jefferson said, in explanation of the defects of Virginia's Constitution, that "the abuses of monarchy had so filled all the speeches of political men that we imagined everything republican that was not monarchical. We had not yet penetrated to the mother principle that governments are republican only in proportion as they embody the will of the people and execute it." [1] In general, it was found that the crude early Constitutions were most workable in those features in which they followed the colonial governments, and least practical when they departed widely from them.

While it required a good many years to demonstrate the inutility or danger of such innovations as the Council of Censors in Pennsylvania or the Council of Appointment in New York, the errors made in the application of old principles of government were soon evident. A series of wartime shocks taught the States that their legislatures were much too strong, their executive departments too weak. The principle of balance had suffered no more than that of democracy. The constitutional definition of the new electorate, it was found in many States, was too narrow. Complaints arose, again, that important liberal principles had been stated and then not applied at all. The bills of rights in particular laid down generalizations upon equality of representation, religious freedom, and the debarment of property from special privilege, which the Constitutions failed adequately to put into effect. A number of

[1] Thorpe, "Const. Hist. of the Amer. People," II, 62.

rising young radicals showed an embarrassing tendency to accept them as truths to be carried out to the letter. Later on, the Western and Southwestern States used them with few reservations as a basis for their fundamental laws. When the Revolution ended, throughout the South the conflict between the uplands and lowlands was suddenly thrust into the foreground, while in the north new economic problems affected the outlook of the people upon their Constitutions.

Fortunately, the rapid development of better State Constitutions was facilitated by the free interchange of constitutional ideas, and the popular willingness of most States to hold revising conventions. The obstacles to the calling of such bodies were decidedly fewer than today. Outside the South, the vested interests that might be injured by alterations were not so powerful as they became within a few decades. Men were accustomed to the idea of constitutional change, while most of the original instruments had been adopted informally, and formalities took root only slowly. When later the tide of constitutional revision ebbed, it was in part because a tendency had arisen to look upon the "fathers" with peculiar reverence —a tendency which Jefferson before his death deprecated. "They ascribe to men of the preceding age more wisdom than human, and suppose what they did to be beyond improvement," Jefferson complained. "I know that age well. I belonged to it and worked with it. . . . It was very like the present, but without the experience of the present, and forty years experience in government is worth a century in book-reading." But in the first three decades after 1776, constitutional evolution led the country toward a uniform type of State government, with future lines of progress clearly indicated.

I. Revision in New England

Three stages disclose themselves in this evolution as it was presented before 1790. The first was the substitution of permanent for temporary constitutions in the three States which had adopted imperfect instruments before the Declaration of Independence— South Carolina, New Hampshire, and Massachusetts. The second was the appearance of constitutional reform as a bitter political and sectional issue in Pennsylvania, Virginia, South Carolina, and Georgia. The third was produced by the impact of the Federal

Constitution upon the people, giving them a clearer idea of constitutional perfection; it merged with the second, and in Pennsylvania and the two southernmost States it helped to effect an actual revision. The first stage would be intrinsically of the least importance were it not that it witnessed the development in New England of the modern process of Constitution-making. We have seen that not one of the original constitutions was made by a special convention, and that none was submitted to the people, though in Pennsylvania and Maryland an imperfect effort was made to obtain an inkling of public sentiment while the instrument was still unratified. By 1780 a more finished method had appeared.

We need not linger long over South Carolina's adoption of a revised Constitution in 1778, a step necessitated by the fact that her original instrument was simply a stop-gap. Before three years had passed a majority of the legislature saw that it must be replaced. Sentiment was particularly aroused in favor of two reforms, the disestablishment of the Anglican Church, and the creation of a popularly-elected Senate in place of the Legislative Council. In the days preceding March 3, the legislature, under the leadership not only of radicals like Christopher Gadsden and W. H. Drayton but of such conservatives as Rawlins Lowndes, debated and passed a new Constitution. It was treated in all respects as if it were merely a complex legislative measure. On the date named, it was sent to President Rutledge, and five days later Rutledge vetoed it, giving his reasons in an able speech to the two houses. He had sworn to support the old Constitution, he said, and he did not believe that the people had delegated to the legislature the power of making a new one. From one passage in his address some inferred, doubtless mistakenly, that he still thought it wrong to close the last door to a reunion with England.

But the main reason for Rutledge's veto was his thorough-going conservatism, which inspired his dislike for any marked innovation. The people, he said preferred the existing mode of electing the upper house, because men of higher integrity and ability would be chosen by and from their representatives, when assembled, than by a popular vote in the several localities. He ventured farther: "The people also preferred a compounded or mixed government to a simple democracy, or one verging toward it, perhaps because however unexceptionable a democratic government may appear at first view, its effects have been found arbitrary, severe, and destructive"—a remark pointing at North Carolina. Then Rutledge resigned, to the relief of the legislature, which immediately repassed the Constitution and sent it to Rawlins Lowndes as the new President for his signature. It went into effect that fall, and the people showed that honest John Rutledge was still their most popular leader by electing him the first Governor.[2]

The new Constitution was in some respects a measurable improvement over the first. The religious section guaranteed tolerance and equality to all Christian Protestant sects, though the Anglican Church was secured in all its property. It was wise also to arrange for direct popular election of the upper house, thus relieving it of dependence upon the lower.

However, the instrument remained essentially aristocratic in character, and some of its most glaring defects were in no wise softened. The newer section of the State was still treated unjustly. The representatives were apportioned among the parishes and western districts by the Constitution just as before—the lowlands electing 144 members, the uplands 58; but in 1785 and every fourteen years thereafter, they were to be reapportioned according to the number of white inhabitants and the value of the taxable property. There was no assurance that this reapportionment, which would be carried out by the legislature, would be fair, and the history of the past was good reason for believing that the arbitrary discriminations against the west would be repeated. Moreover, the double basis of representation stipulated by the Constitution offered a broad ground for quarrel. Anyone could see that the lowlands would try to place the emphasis upon property, and the plateau country upon population, and that the lowlands would win.

As for the Senate, most parishes were given the right to name one member. The Governor was still to be elected by the legislature for two years, still allowed only the slenderest appointive powers, and lost his veto—there was no improvement here. One important change, confirming the aristocratic nature of the government, lay in the high property qualifications required for any official participation.

[2] McCrady's "S. C. in the Rev., 1775-80," 235 ff.; Van Santvoord, "Lives of the Chief Justices," 121-22. For young Col. John Laurens's indignation over the legislature's action, as tending to the erection of an oligarchy or aristocracy, see "Army Correspondence of John Laurens," 172-73; Wallace's "Henry Laurens," 476. Christopher Gadsden was the foremost leader in carrying the new Constitution through and if the State had been converted to radical political views it would have made him President; but it was not.

The Governor, Lieutenant-Governor, and privy councillors had to own plantations worth £10,000 or more in currency. A Senator had to own an estate in his parish or district worth £2000, or, if he were not resident in the parish he represented, to be worth £7000; a representative had to possess fifty acres, a town lot, or equivalent taxable property in his own parish, or if he sat for another parish, to possess an estate there worth £3500. These provisions, it will be seen, gave rich Charlestonians owning country estates a right to represent the communities in which these plantations lay. Every voter had to have fifty acres, a town lot, or their equivalent, and as he did not have to reside where he voted, plural suffrage was legal. It was distinctly a government for the rich, well-born lowlanders, who had made it for themselves, and meant to keep it their own.

Fortunately, the constitutional labors of Massachusetts had a better direction and result. Here it was that two momentous ideas —that of the independent constitutional convention, and that of the submission of its handiwork to the people—were first insisted upon. The special convention was proposed by Concord on October 21, 1776, with the cogent argument that the legislature was not at all a proper body to form a constitution, since the instrument it made would be alterable by later legislatures. Even earlier, the town of Norton had proposed a convention as an alternative to legislative action. The first demand for the submission of any constitution to popular vote came from the poor, hardy settlers of Berkshire County in the west. They feared that an aristocratic form of government would be imposed upon them by the commercial and professional groups of Boston, which they knew were conservative and inclined to press special economic interests. Led by the fighting parson who later fired the first shot at the battle of Bennington, they held a mass-meeting at Pittsfield and sent a memorial to the General Court. They argued that the people were the fountain of all power, that the revolutionary legislature had no right to impose a Constitution upon them, and that it should devise a new government and then refer it to the State, for only majority-consent could give life and validity to it.[3]

The leaders of the State tried at first to grant but half this popular demand—to agree to a referendum on the Constitution, but to deny the people a special convention. There was no question when inde-

[3] Mass. Archives, CLVI, f. 182; Cushing, "Transition from Province to Commonwealth," *passim;* "Manual of the Mass. Convention of 1917-18."

pendence was declared but that the old Charter made an unsatisfactory organic law, and would have to be replaced as soon as possible. As we have said, the council of twenty-eight constituted a slow, cumbersome executive. The legislature yielded to the temptation of appointing its own members to paid offices, until one Pooh-Bah from Falmouth, Maine, held six at once. In the west the Charter was so unpopular, and the awkwardness and cost of the judicial system were so great, that the Berkshire towns erected their own courts, almost openly defied the State authorities, and for some years were practically autonomous. If the General Court had tried to enforce its enactments, the dismemberment of Massachusetts might have resulted. Even in the east, the government was hardly in operation before the movement to supersede it began.[4] As early as September 17, 1776, the House therefore asked the town meetings to say whether they would consent to a conversion of the legislature into a constitutional convention, and whether they wished the new Constitution published for their inspection before it was ratified by the Assembly.

Most of the towns which replied declared that the Constitution should not merely be published, but submitted to popular vote. The opposition to anything but a special constitutional convention independent of the legislature was so strong, moreover, that a House committee recommended (January 28, 1777) that the towns be asked to elect delegates to such a body. But the House, unfortunately, was determined to undertake the task itself. On May 5 it and the Council urged the voters, at the election that month, to choose representatives who would not only perform the ordinary legislative work, but would unite with the Council to draw up a Constitution for submission to the voters.[5]

This proposal aroused widespread indignation. The legislature promised that the new instrument would be sent to the town meetings, and duly established only when approved by two thirds of the adult freemen present, but this was not enough. A meeting of representatives of a number of towns had already been held in Worcester County, and had voted that only a special convention ought to undertake the task. Boston now voted that her representatives must take no part in a Constitutional Convention formed out

[4] "Manual of the Mass. Convention of 1917-18," 13 ff.
[5] Mass. Archives, CLVI, f. 199.

of the General Court. Nevertheless, the program was carried out. The elections were held; the new House met, concluded that most of the people had acquiesced in the short-cut method of Constitution-making, and set to work. Some of the best men in Massachusetts thought this method the proper one. John Adams, for example, who had feared a year earlier that a spirit of "leveling as well as innovation" was afloat, now wrote to James Warren that it was a pity the legislature was obliged even to lay the Constitution before the towns; for it would divide and distract them.[6]

But the short-cut method ignominiously failed. The first draft of the Constitution was drawn up by a committee of twelve, in which Robert Treat Paine was the leading spirit, and James Warren, James Prescott, and Thomas Cushing were prominent. The work went forward slowly, and not until February 28, 1778, was the finished instrument approved. Yet it was so poor a Constitution that the chaplain of the House expressed the opinion that it had been drafted with the deliberate purpose of having it rejected, so that the Charter authorities might continue in power. It had no bill of rights, though this alone was enough to seal its fate. It provided for a legislature of two branches, but the Senate was to be indirectly elected, and was to be the Governor's council as well as the upper house. All the acts of the Governor were to be dependent upon the advice and consent of the Senate, in which he had a voice. He was of course given no veto power. The weakness of the Governor and the contrasting strength of the legislature especially alarmed the conservatives, who feared disorder and license. In short, the new form found friends neither among the radicals, who condemned the method of drafting it, nor the cautious. Boston was unyieldingly hostile. On March 4, the constitution was submitted to the freemen, and defeated by the crushing vote of 9,972 to 2,083.[7]

The conservatives followed this election with a manifesto. Twenty-seven leading men of Essex County, led by Caleb Cushing and Theophilus Parsons, held a meeting the next month at Ipswich, and published a document stating the chief objections to the defeated

---

[6] Boston Record Commissioners, XVIII, 284-86; see Adams's "Works," index under "Massachusetts," for his writings regarding the Massachusetts Constitution; also Bradford, II, 188 ff.; Journal of the H. of Reps., 1777, 15 ff.; Morison, *Mass. Hist. Soc. Proceedings,* April, 1917.
[7] *Continental Journal,* October 8, 1778; *Mass. Spy,* Oct. 15, 1778; Barry, "Hist. of Mass.," III, 175; Bradford, "Hist. of Mass.," II, 158-59.

Constitution, and the principles on which they deemed a sound instrument should rest. Its author was Parsons, later chief-justice of Massachusetts, then a young man of twenty-eight. The Essex Result, as the paper was called, represented the conservative standpoint. Its twenty-eight articles demanded a bill of rights; a fuller independence for each of the three departments of government; exclusion of the Governor from the legislature; fairer apportionment of representation; and a better mode of electing the Senators. It went on to discuss, with much sense and clear logic, the characteristics of a truly sound, balanced government. Especially notable was its emphasis upon the necessity for safeguarding the rights of property. Parsons suggested that the lower house, to number not more than a hundred, should represent population alone, and that the upper, to number perhaps forty, should represent that part of the population possessing a certain amount of wealth. He wished both branches, and the Governor as well, chosen not directly but through county conventions. To the Governor he would give broad powers, including the right—with the consent of his council—to veto any bill.[8]

This pamphlet showed the existence in Massachusetts of the same cleavage between ultra-democratic and conservative parties that existed in Pennsylvania, Virginia, and North Carolina. The Essex Result evinced an exaggerated respect for wealth and leisure. It assumed that only "men of education and fortune," with time for study, could exhibit high wisdom in legislation; it frankly declared that "the bulk of the people" could not possess an adequate knowledge of the interests of the State. The idea that a self-educated rail-splitter might rise to a position of supreme governmental power would have staggered its authors. But on the other hand, Samuel Adams, his homespun Boston supporters, and many voters in Berkshire County and other remote districts, were too impatient of mere property rights; Parsons and Cushing merit high praise for their agitation in favor of a more complex, carefully balanced form of government.

The defeat of the first proposed Constitution made the legislature docile. It took the sense of the town meetings again,[9] and in June,

---

[8] Parsons, "Memoir of T. Parsons," 46 ff.; the text of the Essex Result is given, p. 359 ff.
[9] Nearly one-third of the towns neglected to give an answer; but the vote was 6,612 to 2,639 in favor of a new Constitution and a special Constitutional Convention. Adams's "Works," IV, 215.

1779, directed that a special constitutional convention be elected, giving every adult freeman, resident in a town, the right to vote.[10] Amid general satisfaction this convention opened on September 1 in Cambridge at the old First Church Meeting House, whose site is now marked in Harvard Square by a tablet. Though nominally it had 293 members, in fact there were never more than about 250 in attendance. The period was the darkest in the Revolution, with Clinton victorious in the South, Washington inert on the Hudson, and the Massachusetts troops just defeated on the Penobscot. Yet its membership made it one of the two strongest conventions in Massachusetts history; John Adams, John Hancock, Samuel Adams, Theophilus Parsons, George Cabot, Robert Treat Paine, Samuel A. Otis, Increase Sumner, James Sullivan, Levi Lincoln, and Caleb Strong were all there. On the first day James Bowdoin was elected president, and three days later a committee of thirty was appointed to prepare a first draft of the Constitution.

As a matter of fact, the task fell to John Adams. He wrote the bill of rights entire, save for the article on religious freedom; while he was the chief architect of the Constitution proper, the committee and convention making only a few changes in the report which he drew up. For two reasons he was above all others the man for the task. He stood intermediate between the radicals and conservatives, between the Boston merchants and the Berkshire farmers, between James Bowdoin and fiery Samuel Adams; when he first entered the convention he made a powerful speech to smooth over their differences. In the second place, no man in America had given so much sound thought to constitutional problems. He was the foremost American champion of the bicameral legislature, a staunch believer in giving the State Governor nearly all the powers of the old colonial governor, and an advocate of an assured tenure for the judiciary—three principles which greatly needed emphasis in America.[11]

The convention, meeting in October after a recess, took up Adams's drafts of the bill of rights and the constitution, and continued to debate the former until another adjournment on November 12. The next day Adams was on the deck of the *Sensible*, bound for

[10] The Constitutional Convention was thus elected by a decidedly wider electorate than the State government itself. Morison, *Mass. Hist. Soc. Proceedings*, May, 1917.
[11] It should be added that he believed in general education, and wrote the section of the Constitution which enjoined the government to cherish literature and science, encourage humanitarian societies, and countenance all virtues, including "good humor." See "Works," IV, 216.

France, and was sorely missed during the third and concluding session, from January 5 to March 2, 1780. On account of the intense cold and heavy snowstorms, for the winter was the bitterest since the great frost of 1717 of which Cotton Mather left such a vivid description, the real opening did not occur until January 27, and the number of members voting never exceeded 82. For a time there were hot disputes upon several points, notably over the article regarding religious freedom. The instrument having been agreed upon, there still remained the problem of submitting it to the people. It was determined that it should be printed and distributed to the towns; that it should there be discussed in the town meetings; that the townsmen should vote upon it clause by clause and state their objections to any article that did not obtain a majority; and finally, that the people should grant the adjourned convention authority to meet again, to tabulate the results of the voting, to ratify the Constitution if there were a two-thirds majority for each part, and if not, to alter the Constitution in accordance with the popular will, and ratify it as amended.

In brief, the delegates made sure that their labor would not be lost, and yet that the popular will could not be openly defied. What a contrast this presents to the arbitrary action of the Pennsylvania constitution-makers in 1776! The ingenious plan was unsatisfactory in just one particular. How could a clause be amended if, for example, one fourth the voters approved it, another fourth disapproved it for one reason, still another fourth for a second reason, and the third fourth for no declared cause at all? [12]

Newspapers took little notice of the convention, few pamphlets were printed upon its work, and the public mind must have been greatly depressed by the war, yet a vigorous debate on the Constitution occurred in most towns. The 16,500 voters of the State had fourteen weeks in which to discuss it. It has been said that this opportunity for debate was a safety valve for the discharge of democratic prejudices which otherwise would have destroyed the instrument, and there is no doubt that if it had been left to a yes-or-no decision, it would have failed ingloriously. But the citizens displayed much grasp and shrewdness. The convention's request for a reasoned statement of objections evoked a criticism that was constructive as well as destructive, and that showed a remarkable

[12] Morison, op. cit.; Manual of the Mass. Convention of 1917-18.

appreciation of the basic principles of government. It anticipated most of the amendments made before the Civil War. The criticism prepared by Joseph Hawley for Northampton, in twenty-three closely written quarto pages, has in our time been published as a distinguished piece of political thinking.[13] He was an ardent democrat, and his objections to the property qualification for the ballot, the imperfect guarantee of religious freedom, the small size of the Senate, and other sections, were shared by many radicals. The Boston town meeting, after a day and a half of debate, recommended that on a third day the shops be closed. Most of the discussion throughout the State centered in the religious article, the separation of departmental powers, the reduction of the legislature's importance, the qualifications for office, and the position of the judiciary.

The final meeting of the convention began June 7, 1780, in Boston, and eight days later it formally accepted the Constitution. It was by now plain that a strong State government was an imperative necessity, since in political, financial, and military affairs the central authority needed much more power. Nothing but an energetic government could enforce the laws, collect taxes, and prosecute the war. "Never was a good Constitution more needed than at this juncture," wrote Samuel Adams.[14] In some western communities the cry, "No Constitution, no law," was being raised by rascals who wished to evade their due burdens, and even radical Pittsfield was so alarmed that it cast its whole vote for the unamended instrument. This critical aspect of affairs made the committee which scanned the votes a little careless of the details, a little eager to gloss over the objections. At least two articles, by a strictly fair count, would not have had a two-thirds vote, though they probably had more than half; but the committee reported all as having the necessary two-thirds majority, and the convention accepted the statement.[15] One of the two was the article on religion, and the other was the provision that in 1795 a vote should be taken on the calling of a new Convention, for there was widespread sentiment in favor of making a revision compulsory. On June 15, 1780, the convention formally accepted the Constitution.

The instrument thus adopted was admirable, and a great majority

[13] Smith College Studies in History, III, No. 1. The procedure in most towns was to appoint a committee to draft amendments and to debate its report at a subsequent meeting.
[14] Wells's "Life of Samuel Adams," III, 103.
[15] Morison, *op. cit.*; some town returns were hard to decipher and many were chaotically arranged.

of its provisions have endured to our own day. It was excellent,
first, in that it provided a true balance of powers, for it made the
Governor, as Hancock and Bowdoin soon showed, as powerful an
officer as in New York. He had a veto,[16] which could be overridden
only by a two-thirds vote; he had wide appointive functions, naming
—with the consent of his council—all judicial officers, the Attorney-
General and Solicitor-General, sheriffs, coroners, and registers of
probate. For the time being, he was commander-in-chief. Like
New York's Governor, he was chosen by the people, not the legislature. Radicals and conservatives each found something to please
them in the legislature. The former could rejoice over the perfect
democracy and large size of the House, for every town had at least
one representative; only the fact that till 1811 no State salary was
paid these men kept the House manageable in size, for many poor
western hamlets thought they could not afford to send members.
The conservatives could take pleasure in the fact that the forty
Senators were divided among thirteen districts in proportion to the
State tax paid by each district, the body thus, as the Essex Result
demanded, having a special relation to property. Judges were
appointed by the executive, and held their places during good
behavior. Thrifty Massachusetts insisted that each vote should
have a freehold estate of £3 income a year, or any other estate
worth £60; each representative a freehold worth £100 or other
estate of £200; each Senator thrice as much; and the governor
a freehold worth £1000.[17]

Meanwhile, New Hampshire had been watching the course of her
southern neighbor with interest. Here, too, the original constitution
was quite unsatisfactory, principally because a many-headed executive could not take the place of a real Governor; here, too, there
sprang up an agitation for a special mechanism to ensure meeting
the popular will; and here, too, there was a long delay before a
Constitution was drawn in such form that the people would accept it.

If it was difficult in the Bay State to write a constitution satisfactory alike to the rich Boston shipowner and the poor Berkshire
farmer, it was equally hard in New Hampshire to please discordant

[16] Not exercised until after Governor Lincoln was inaugurated in 1825; *Mass. Hist.
Soc. Proceedings,* XI, 64-66.
[17] These clauses, with the faulty article on religion, were the chief defects of the
Constitution. Three Maine counties in 1785 asked for separation from Massachusetts,
in part upon the ground that "A great part of the inhabitants of these counties are
deprived of representation in the popular branch of the legislature, where all the
money bills originate. . . ." Williamson's "Maine," II, 521-27.

elements of the population. The people in and about Portsmouth were very largely aristocratic, those of the Merrimac Valley were principally Massachusetts emigrants conservative in politics, though socially democratic, and those of the western towns were radicals. No fewer than three false starts were made. The legislature in the early spring of 1778 summoned a special Constitutional Convention, which met at Concord in June, the first such body in the United States or the world. It drew up a Constitution of a rather sorry kind, the chief defect of which was that it failed to provide an efficient executive, the legislature remaining all-powerful; and in their plebiscite the towns made short work of it. As the end of the war approached, the need for a better government became still more pressing, and a second convention sat in June, 1781. It laid before the towns a trial constitution which closely followed that just adopted in Massachusetts. There was to be a senate of twelve, a house of fifty, elected, as the Essex Result had suggested, by conventions of town delegates held in each county, and a governor vested with the veto power. Once more the proposed instrument met a decisive defeat, for it was quite too conservative to please the people. The opposition to the limited house was especially marked, for the towns wanted a larger body, elected directly by the voters, and felt that the choice by conventions would open a door to political manipulation. Not at all daunted, the convention met again, and made an effort in the latter half of 1782 to patch up its rejected handiwork. Hundreds of copies were once more scattered over the State, the towns debated it, and the convention reopened to find that for the third time it had been rejected.[18]

The situation was now becoming anxious, for it was generally understood that the original constitution was valid only until peace had been made with Great Britain. In June, 1783, a convention met for a fourth and final effort, and laid before the towns a form of government which they ratified that fall. It became effective in June, 1784, and that month the General Court met in Concord, where old Meshech Weare, the political Nestor of the State, was chosen President.

[18] In rejecting the second framework, many towns were actuated in part by dislike of the high property qualifications demanded for office, which were substantially identical with those asked in Massachusetts. Concord cast every vote against the third Constitution, demanding that the Legislature be granted many of the powers which the Constitution-makers had tried to give the Governor. See Manual of the N. H. Constitutional Convention of 1918, *passim;* Stackpole's "New Hampshire," II, ch. 8, 9.

The Constitution was frankly based upon that of Massachusetts, which had been read with admiration by New Hampshire men, most of whom held John Adams in high regard. Thanks to this fact, and to New Hampshire's own ripe experience, the legislature was not allowed to dominate the government so completely as before. The President presided over the Senate, enjoyed the pardoning power, and could make a considerable list of appointments, though he did not have the limited veto allowed the Governor of Massachusetts. The General Court consisted of a very large house elected by the towns, and a very small senate, the seats of which were filled by districts. As in Massachusetts, all elections were annual; while also as in the Bay State, the judges were to sit during good behavior, but were removable, as in England, upon an address voted by both houses. In one respect it was an unusually democratic constitution for the time, since it gave the ballot to every man who paid a poll tax, and required a property qualification of no official save the Governor, who had to be worth only £500. The article upon religious freedom was only slightly better than that of Massachusetts, for while it seemed fair to all faiths, it actually left it difficult for members of the smaller denominations to escape the payment of tithes to the Congregational Church. Upon the whole, however, it was a far better Constitution than the first one.[19]

The two New England States had now provided themselves with permanent Constitutions; more than that, they had been instrumental in developing the standard method of constitutional revision in America. By calling special conventions to write their Constitutions, they had lifted them far above the level of statutory law, and given the courts a basis for that doctrine of judicial review which was soon to be formulated.

II. REVISION ELSEWHERE BEFORE 1788

From this exhibition of method and reason it is something of a shock to turn to Pennsylvania, whose constitutional history presents a record of such intense bitterness and party antagonism. The United States has witnessed many violent constitutional struggles, but none ever aroused a deeper rancor than that which agitated the once-placid Quaker commonwealth from 1776 to 1789. Radicals and doctrinaires, defending the new instrument, were pitted against

[19] Plumer's "Life of Plumer," 115 ff., deals with its faults.

the conservatives, who attacked it. The western counties supported the new government, which had given them their due in representation; the old settled part of the State hated it. It was justly assailed for its inherent faults, unjustly assailed as a symbol of the revolutionized order.

For the first seven years all the attacks launched against it were futile, and we may pass rapidly over their failure. Dickinson, in petulance and disgust, retired to his lands in Delaware, leaving the leadership of the conservatives to Dr. Benjamin Rush, Robert Morris, Mifflin, Thomson, and Clymer. These men did what they could against the "red republicans," led by Bryan, Cannon, Matlack, and Dr. Young. For a time in 1777 the acrimony of the contest paralyzed the efforts the State was making in the war. Dr. Rush wrote General Wayne that the radicals "still hold back the strength of the State by urging the execution of their rascally government in preference to supporting measures for repelling the common enemy." He regarded the new Constitution as intolerable, he explained, because "it has substituted mob government for one of the happiest governments in the world. . . . A *single legislature* is big with tyranny. I had rather live under the government of one man than of seventy-two." Wayne replied that at the first view of the sickly Constitution he had decided that it was not worth defending; he was too good a patriot not to defend anything American, but his opinion was one that many Pennsylvanians acted upon literally.[20] The weight of intelligent sentiment was clearly against the Constitution. Even the radical Joseph Reed found fault with the provision forbidding any but a septennial revision, saying that the government might go to pieces before a necessary reform could be effected.[21]

But the "red republicans" were able politicians, adroit in rallying the public; they had the advantage of position, for they needed only to stand fast; and they were favored by fortune. Early in 1777 the pressure for revision became so exigent, and was so emphatically backed by the Board of War, which realized that the dispute was hampering the conduct of hostilities, that the legislature partially yielded. On June 17, at the recommendation of the Executive Council, it voted to ascertain the wishes of the people for a new

[20] C. J. Stillé, "Wayne and the Pennsylvania Line," 68, 69.
[21] Reed, "Reed," I, 302 ff.

Convention.[22] Luckily for Bryan and Cannon, Howe's invasion prevented further action. After Howe evacuated the State, the subject was taken up again. The Legislature once more (November 28, 1778) set a date for ascertaining the popular will;[23] and the Anti-Constitutionalists, forming a "Republican Society" to give vigor to their campaign, again felt confident of victory. But the Constitutionalists set to work with even more vigor and decidedly less scrupulousness. They organized a rival "Constitutional Society," with Charles Wilson Peale as president, and zealously circulated petitions against the proposed plebiscite. Office-holders under the Constitution procured signatures or even forged them, and some 16,000 names, out of an electorate of 50,000 or 60,000, were obtained. The willing legislature was so impressed that it rescinded its call for the election a few weeks before the date set. An angry cry of betrayal went up from the Anti-Constitutionalists, but they were helpless.[24]

More petitions came from this discontented party, and their ablest writers bombarded the newspapers with criticism of the Constitution; but nothing could now be done until the first septennial meeting of the Council of Censors in 1783. The two sessions of this body afford one of the most interesting episodes in Pennsylvania history. Everyone knew that the Constitution was very faulty. How a majority of the Council, but not the two-thirds majority needed, fought for revising it and failed, is a story eloquent of the party passion which the issue aroused.

Two Censors were duly chosen from each of the twelve counties and the city of Philadelphia. They met on November 13, 1783, and chose Frederick A. Muhlenberg, of the revisionist majority, president. Little was done till after the new year.[25] Then on January 2, after warm debate, it was resolved by a vote of 13 to 10 that some articles of the Constitution "are materially defective, and absolutely require alteration and amendment,"[26] and a committee of five, including Arthur St. Clair, was asked to draw up a report singling out these articles and recommending substitutes.

---

[22] Pa. Archives, Series II, vol. I, 53, 54; Series IV, vol. III, 655-56.
[23] The legislature even specified the subjects which would come before the Convention: the creation of a bicameral legislature, the grant of wider appointive powers to the executive, a more secure tenure for judges, and the abolition of the Council of Censors. Proceedings Relative to Calling the Conventions of 1776 and 1790, p. 111 ff.
[24] Cf. *Pa. Packet*, March 24, 25, 1779.
[25] A newspaper campaign for revision was in full swing; on the other side, see articles by "Constitutionalist" in the *Freeman's Journal*, Dec. 24, 1783, and after.
[26] *Pa. Gazette*, Jan. 7, Jan. 14, 1783.

Fifteen days later the Council received this report, which was taken up by paragraphs, debated, and with some changes adopted. On every paragraph the ayes were twelve, including the three ablest members, Muhlenberg, St. Clair, and Wayne, and the nays were nine. The adoption of the document occupied only one day, but it generated enough anger to excite the State for months.[27]

For what did the report ask? St. Clair's committee demanded a single chief executive, instead of the Executive Council. It of course wanted a bicameral legislature, consisting of a house and a legislative council. As for the other two branches, it asked for decided improvements in the position of the judiciary, and it asserted that the Governor should be chosen by popular vote, should have larger powers of appointment, and should possess a limited veto. Representation, it recommended, should still be according to the number of male taxables, but the House should be limited to 100 members, and the Council to half that many. Judges should be appointed by the Governor, should hold office during good behavior, and should have fixed salaries. Very sensibly, the committee recommended that the Council of Censors be abolished forthwith. All in all, it was an admirable report, and every step which it urged was salutary; Pennsylvanians had only to look at the better governments of Massachusetts or New York to perceive that.

But the report, however wise, could not clear away the murky vapors of prejudice and malevolence which surrounded the issue. Whereas by section 47 of the Constitution a two-thirds vote of the Council was required to call a revising convention, the revisionists had only twelve of the twenty-one or twenty-two men usually present. An angry quarrel sprang up on the floor. Convinced of the justice of their position, and of the fact that a majority of intelligent Pennsylvanians were with them, the revisionists deemed it outrageous that they should be checkmated by the blind provision of an instrument which few respected. The minority stood stoutly for adherence to the strict letter of the organic law, stating that if section 47 were now violated, other dangerous innovations would follow. The advantage was clearly with them, for the majority knew that it could not legally issue a call. It was finally decided that the

---

[27] The minutes of the Council of Censors may be found in the Proceedings Relative to Calling the Conventions of 1776 and 1790. As other authorities, see S. B. Harding, "Party Struggles Over the First Pennsylvania Constitution," in Annual Report Amer. Hist. Association, 1894; L. H. Meader, "The Council of Censors"; Reed's "Reed"; Stillé's "Dickinson"; and Konkle's "Life of Bryan," ch. 17.

Council should adjourn, with the understanding that the question of a convention should be referred back to the people, for an informal expression of a decision before the members met again. The body then broke up, to reconvene on June 1.

Throughout the spring the debate convulsed the State. The minority argued that the true task of the Censors was to reveal and rebuke the infractions of the Constitution, not to rewrite it; that it had proved a satisfactory instrument, and that it would be criminal to evade its prescription of the manner of amendment. They contended that the single executive would prove tyrannical, and that an upper house would be a privilege-seeking House of Lords. The conservatives, on the other hand, appealed to the public with careful arguments, filling the *Gazette* and *Packet* with their articles. The real question, they maintained, was the Constitution itself, so obviously faulty. It had been adopted at a time of party passion, when many able citizens were in military service, while others had assented to it only upon the understanding that it was to be amended at the first good opportunity. A majority of the Council now wished to change certain parts of it in a manifestly wise way. Yet after seven years of struggling, a minority which probably did not represent one third the voters, for the plan of representation in the Council gave a thinly settled frontier county equal weight with the most populous, tied the arms of the majority. The Council of Censors was itself an irrational institution, for its correction of infractions would always be too late, while sometimes its septennial meetings might produce a needless convulsion.[28]

Public feeling was deeply aroused, and the weight of numbers proved to be with the radicals. The resignation of one of Philadelphia's Censors brought on a direct test of the city's sentiment, and a spirited contest resulted in the choice of the noted Constitutionalist leader, George Bryan. Another Censor died, and he also was succeeded early in June by a man opposed to revision. It thus became evident before the middle of the year that the radicals would have at least fourteen votes, or a majority. At the same time petitions, circulated by the ruling political machine, poured in against a Convention, until in August some 18,000 signatures had been obtained.[29]

[28] See papers in the *Pa. Gazette,* in February, March, and April for revision by "One of the Majority" and "A Citizen of Pennsylvania," and in the *Pa. Journal* of June 19, June 23, July 7, and July 10.
[29] *Freeman's Journal,* Sept. 29, 1784.

All plans for a new Constitution perished forthwith. Frederick Muhlenberg declared that his side had been beaten by the "blind passion and party spirit of the common crowd," which was true; but Joseph Reed spoke more to the point when, admitting defeat for the revisionists, he attributed it to the fact that they had attempted too much—if they had urged fewer changes, they might have called a Convention by a two-thirds vote.

The final activities of the Council nevertheless remain of interest, for on August 16 it took up the long-delayed report of a committee on violations of the Constitution. Bryan's Constitutionalists controlled this committee, and labored ingeniously to do two incompatible things—first, to whitewash the Constitution, and second, to show that it had been outrageously violated by the Anti-Constitutionalists when they had held the government. The report stated that the frame of government appeared "clear in its principles, accurate in its form, consistent in its several parts, and worthy of the veneration of the good people of Pennsylvania." But the chief test of a Constitution is its correctness of operation. The committee had to confess that it had found various and multiplied instances of departure from the instrument, and though it selected only such instances as were necessary to illustrate and reëstablish the leading principles of the Constitution, they filled many pages. Everyone knew that it was ridiculous for it to try to explain this by implying that most of the violations resulted from the malignancy of the conservatives. Its list of infractions laid emphasis on those occurring in and after 1781, when the Anti-Constitutionalists had attained power; this was manifestly unfair, for if the breaches made in the Constitution by its enemies were the more numerous, those by its friends were the largest.[30]

Overwhelming evidence was presented that the legislature had irresponsibly trenched upon the field of the executive and judiciary, and exceeded its already exorbitant powers. It had even broken three sections of the Bill of Rights. That for the protection of private property had been transgressed by acts authorizing its seizure, at a fixed price, for army use, and by absurd attempts to regulate the price of commodities. That for preserving men's private possessions from search and seizure had been transgressed by an act

---

[30] See letters in the *Pa. Gazette*, Sept. 1 and 8, 1784, demanding an explanation for the failure to criticize Bryan's three-year administration.

for county levies and other tax laws. That guaranteeing jury trial in suits over property had been nullified by an act summarily settling one such civil suit.

As for the Constitution proper, the legislature had riddled it with violations. Several representatives had been county treasurers, though the Constitution forbade them to hold any office except in the militia. The House, in legislation upon land cases, in dissolving marriages, and in vacating roads alleged to be useless, had infringed upon the functions of the judiciary. The *Gazette* at this time charged one Censor from Bucks with voting in the Council that the legislative stoppage of highways was unconstitutional, although "this old hypocrite addressed the House five months since for a law to vacate a road running through his plantation in Bucks County, and the House consented." [31] The legislature had allowed some members to make reservations in taking the oath prescribed by the Constitution. It had usurped the appointment of revenue officers, county lieutenants, a collector of the port of Philadelphia, and other functionaries. Whereas the Constitution explicitly gave the President and Executive Council the right to submit bills, the House in February, 1779, had declined to receive a proffered measure. It had pardoned criminals, including three Italian seamen convicted of murdering their captain, although pardons were the sole prerogative of the Executive Council. It had made drafts upon the Treasury, another act which the Executive Council alone was authorized to perform.

Of course, a multitude of violations of the section which demanded that all bills not introduced under stress of an emergency should be held over for vote by the following Assembly, and meanwhile be printed for public consideration, were alleged. An important section required that all State charges should be paid from the State treasury. Yet the House had seized Hall's Stables, in Philadelphia, for the horses of its members, and had authorized the officers defending the Delaware River to draw their moneys from the naval authorities collecting certain revenues, without letting the revenues pass into the State treasury. It had restrained a duly erected county, Fayette, from electing assemblymen, Censors, or a Councilor. The constitutional injunction that all judges should be granted fixed salaries had been disobeyed; while many acts—as one affecting those who

[31] Sept. 1, 1784.

harbored army deserters—had violated the provisions regarding jury trial. Although the Philadelphia newspapers had criticized nearly all the forms of constitutional infringement during the years 1776-83, they had been most severe upon the interferences with the judiciary. In 1781 a bill before the House to give the Chief Justice £800 for one year only was attacked as violating the requirement of fixed salaries. In 1781 the *Freeman's Journal* censured a resolution of the Assembly, laid before the Executive Council, declaring that a court fine against a certain woman ought to be remitted, as an interference at one stroke with the executive and judiciary.[32]

In short, the Censors agreed that the Constitution had been treated with gross disrespect, and that the legislature—never the Executive Council or judges—had been the guilty agent. The committee report was an implicit admission that the government was dangerously lop-sided. Because it embodied much Constitutionalist propaganda, it was adopted by a vote of only 14 to 9, Wayne, Muhlenberg, St. Clair and six others explaining that while they approved part of it, other parts were foreign to the real object of the Censors. The final action of the Council was taken September 16, 1784, when it resolved, 16 to 10, that there was no necessity for calling a convention. Its sessions had cost Pennsylvania nearly £20,000, and its main accomplishment was to fan higher than ever the flames of party and sectional feeling.[33]

This struggle of 1783-84 should not be regarded as a mere contest over the Constitution, for new factors of the greatest importance were tacitly involved. The Anti-Constitutionalists were now identified with the party which supported the Bank of Pennsylvania and the Bank of North America, both recently founded through the efforts of Robert Morris and the commercial community of Philadelphia. The mercantile and propertied interests which disliked the State Constitution also felt a growing aversion for the weak Articles of Confederation, and wanted a more vigorous, responsible national government as well as State government. This fact was grasped by the radicals of Philadelphia and the western counties, who fiercely opposed the grant of a power of taxation to the Confederation, and who wanted no nationalization

[32] See the issues of June 6 and December 19, 1784.
[33] See the *Pa. Gazette's* review, March 11, 1789.

of the great open west. Battle was thus really being joined on a wide front—the fight for revision of the Constitution was but one episode. A number of purely State issues added fervor to the struggle, for the conservatives wanted the charter of the college in Philadelphia, recently revoked, given back again, and the civic persecution of the great mass of neutrals and conscientious objectors in the late war stopped.

Simpler but hardly narrower implications stamped the struggle for constitutional reform in Virginia and South Carolina. Here the rivalry between uplands and lowlands offered the central issue. In both States the war had produced changes favorable to the western region. Many Tidewater communities were half ruined by the stoppage of exports and the trampling of the armies. The population of the long settled districts stood still, while immigration into the up-country rapidly accelerated after 1781. Despite all the old bickerings, the Crown Government had acted as a pillar of support for the conservative lowlanders, and they keenly felt its removal. In Virginia new civil leaders, like Patrick Henry, Jefferson, and Madison, and new military leaders, like Daniel Morgan, came from outside the Tidewater. After Charleston was conquered and shackled by the British in South Carolina, the up-country rallied and waged a victorious warfare under such bold leaders as Sumter, Pickens, and Hampton. A demand arose from one end of the South to the other for the removal of the State capitals westward, for Williamsburg, New Bern, Charleston, and Savannah no longer suited the majority. Western Virginia and South Carolina were anti-federalist in their instincts, and the eastern sections federalist, but in both States there were central districts which held the balance of power.

South Carolina's second Constitution was not long satisfactory. Men justly complained that it displayed religious intolerance, since none but Protestants were guaranteed equal religious and civil privileges; that a House of more than 200 members was unnecessarily large; and above all, that the west was unjustly treated. Immediately after peace came, a revision began to be discussed. In 1784 Governor Guerard recommended measures to amend and perfect the Constitution.[34] The question was discussed by the legislature, and a bill for a convention passed the House only to

[34] *S. C. Gazette,* February 10, 1784.

meet defeat by a large majority in the Senate. The opposition came from the aristocratic lowland group in both chambers, and in the Senate it was accentuated by the fear that a constitutional convention might abolish the upper branch.

But in the years following, the demand for a new Constitution sturdily persisted. During 1786 the low-country element was forced to consent to the temporary location of the capital at what is now Columbia, a central position. Charleston had ceased, while the British held it, to be all that counted in the State. After the evacuation, while it was recovering from its prostration, the plateau region made great gains in population. The site of Columbia in 1786 was not marked by even a village, and it was said that the capital had spoiled the best cotton plantation in the State, but the legislature was able to meet there four years later. Its removal was an outward sign of many deep economic and social changes which justified the progressives of the up-country in calling for constitutional revision.[35]

Early in the same decade the demand for a revising convention in Virginia became equally marked. In his "Notes on Virginia" (1781-82), Jefferson wrote that time had already revealed capital defects in the Constitution. The majority of freemen in the State were unrepresented, for the roll of citizens entitled to vote—it was limited to men owning 500 acres unsettled or 50 acres settled with a house—did not generally include half the militiamen or taxpayers. Among those who did vote, the legislators were apportioned very unfairly. Thus Warwick County, with a hundred fighting men, had as large a voice in the legislature as Loudoun, which could muster 1750. In the Tidewater section, according to Jefferson, 19,000 fighting men elected 84 legislators; the whole remainder of the State, with 31,000 fighting men and an area ten times as great as that of the Tidewater, had but ninety legislators. What if the Tidewater did not possess a clear majority? This disadvantage it so generally overcame by its proximity to the capital, and the consequent promptness with which its members could attend the sessions, that it governed the commonwealth.[36]

Again, various critics thought the Senate too nearly homogeneous with the House, for it was chosen by the same electors at the

[35] For this removal see Ravenel's "Charleston," 344; *S. C. Gazette*, March 6, 1789; Schaper, "Sectionalism and Representation in S. C.," 377.
[36] Jefferson's "Notes on Virginia," Ford's one-volume ed., 157 ff.

same time; and Jefferson adverted with implied approval to the
example of States in which the House represented population,
while the Senate in some degree represented wealth. A more valid
criticism of the legislature was that its powers were excessive.
Jefferson spoke none too strongly of the impropriety of its authority to alter the Constitution itself, and its right to determine its
own quorum, declaring that the former particularly was one of
the potentialities of a despotism. Edmund Randolph declared
that the legislature had repeatedly violated the Constitution, till
"everything has been drawn within the legislative vortex"; this
was a rhetorical exaggeration characteristic of Randolph, but it
had a germ of truth.[37]

At the close of the Revolution constitutional questions were
thrust sharply forward in Virginia. In the spring of 1783 a campaign for a revising convention was organized under Jefferson's
leadership; it was a year in which a wave of reform seemed flooding the State, for a new attack was being made on the vestiges
of the Anglican establishment, a law was passed encouraging the
manumission of slaves, and petitions were circulated for the abolition of slavery. Thomson Mason brought the subject before the
legislature, but marked opposition was expressed to any hasty
consideration of it; his brother, George Mason, thought it should
be deferred for several years, till the excitement of the war had
passed.[38] After the session ended, Jefferson went to the trouble
of drafting a plan for constitutional revision, which was full of
faults, but had the signal merit of apportioning members of the
lower house among the counties according to the number of voters.
Jefferson would have pressed the campaign at the spring meeting
of the legislature in 1784, but was kept in Congress till the end
of May, and then left immediately as an envoy to France.

The task was entrusted to his chief lieutenant. While Jefferson
was preparing to depart, Madison had a set of resolutions introduced in the House, and put his best energies behind their passage,
dwelling in a long speech upon eleven salient defects of the Constitution. Some of them were important, such as the confusion

---

[37] H. B. Grigsby, "Hist. of the Va. Convention," I, 122-23. Note that the grand
jury of Richmond, Va., presented as a grievance in 1787 "the great number of representatives in the General Assembly; also the contracted powers of the judiciary department, directed by the Constitution of the State, and earnestly recommend an alteration of the same on a model more easy and less expensive." *Pa. Packet,* Feb. 2, 1787.
[38] Rowland's "Mason," II, 43, 66.

of the three departments of government, the dependence of the executive and judiciary upon the legislature, the inequitable apportionment of representation, and the denial of the ballot to large groups. Some were comparatively trivial, such as the bad footing on which impeachments were placed. He brought up the great question of the lack of any mode of interpreting the Constitution, and thus checking the legislators. Some of his opinions upon the Constitution differed materially from Jefferson's, and they were generally sounder. Nevertheless, the resolutions failed by a vote of 57 to 42. One all-sufficient reason was the unexpectedly vehement opposition of Patrick Henry, and another was the fact that R. H. Lee, who was to have been a leading advocate, was taken ill.[39]

Georgia was still, save possibly for North Carolina, the most democratic State of the South. Her population was small, her problems simple, and despite the faults of the Constitution—its single house, its weak Governor, its dependent judiciary—the instrument served fairly well. One minor complaint was that the legislature was too numerous. In 1784 the Chatham County Grand Jury was told by a circuit judge that an agitation had arisen over a supposed infirmity of the Constitution, and that if they wished to comment upon it, "it should be with great good temper." With great good temper, the jury presented as a grievance the heavy expense occasioned by the excessive number of legislators.[40] Every county of more than a hundred voters, and by 1789 there were eleven counties, had ten representatives, save Liberty, which had fourteen, yet the whole population in 1784 did not reach 70,000. In 1784 the legislature tried to meet at Augusta. It was expected, however, said a newspaper, "that as soon as a house was formed, they would adjourn to Savannah, as there were not by any means sufficient accommodations for so numerous a body. . . ." But the chief cause of discontent was the same as in Virginia and South Carolina, the unfair apportionment of representation. The first Constitution gave the five seacoast counties 36 legislators, and this number was increased as two of the counties filled up; the two middle counties were given 20 legislators; and

---

[39] Rives's "Madison," I, 555-60. Few legislators were in favor of a convention possessing unrestricted powers; the majority would have been willing to authorize a body to alter the Constitution in certain specified ways, but neither Jefferson nor Madison wanted this.

[40] *Pa. Journal,* June 19, 1784.

the one upland county, 10. Yet at the first census the total population of the uplands was 37,946, that of the middle district 25,336, and that of the lowlands 21,536. This injustice, accentuated by the fact that most of the numerous slaves were included in the lowland population, the upland farmers owning few, grew more and more irritating.[41]

III. Influence of the Federal Constitution

Thus in four States—Pennsylvania, Virginia, South Carolina, and Georgia—the era of the Confederation witnessed a growing bitterness over the defects and injustices of the constitutional system. Left to itself, perhaps not one of the four would have attempted a revision. The lowlands were too well entrenched in the South, while the agitators for reform in Pennsylvania could be fobbed off with the statement that the Council of Censors would meet again in 1790. But the Philadelphia Convention of 1787 and the State ratifying conventions of 1788 concentrated the thought of the nation upon constitutional questions; and when the "new roof" was actually raised, its symmetry and strength stood in striking contrast with the ill-shaped Constitutions of some States. The year 1788-89 saw revised conventions sitting in rapid succession in Georgia and Pennsylvania, while delegates to such a convention had just been elected in South Carolina. In Pennsylvania the Constitutionalists had rendered their position precarious by their insolent behavior after they had gained complete control of the Council of Censors in 1784 and had followed that feat by a smashing victory in the fall Assembly elections. Flushed with success, they had indulged in legislative follies, including an annulment of the charter of the Bank of North America, which had produced a strong revulsion against them. The adoption of the Federal Constitution was a second stunning blow to them, for they were the party of opposition. George Bryan, one of the chief authors of the Constitution of 1776, toured the State in 1787 to arouse sentiment against the Federal instrument. William Findley, another of the Constitution-makers of 1776 and an anti-revisionist member of the Council of Censors, was one of Bryan's chief lieutenants. The southeastern part of the State was federalist, while the rural districts and newer counties were principally anti-federal-

<hr />

[41] Cf. U. B. Phillips, "Georgia and State Rights," 88, 89.

ist. The decision was not long in doubt, and ratification was effected as early as December, 1787, by the decisive vote of 46 to 23.

By the middle of 1788, Pennsylvania knew that the Constitution had been ratified by ten States. The demand for a State government in harmony with it, and of greater intrinsic merits, now became irresistible. The ridiculous features of the Bryan-Matlack instrument, men said, had long enough rendered the great centre of the Union ridiculous. The administration was steadily growing more unwieldy and costly. Every county elected two members of the quaint executive, so that there were already 18, there would soon be 22, and in a few decades there might be 50 or 60. To pay each Councilor fifteen shillings a day, with £1500 for a President, was ruinous—the whole expense when two new counties came in would be $24,000 a year. Under the pernicious requirement as to rotation in office, many valuable members of the Assembly that very year would automatically be debarred from giving Pennsylvania the continued benefit of their experience. Did anyone still believe in a unicameral legislature? It was idle to say that Pennsylvania must wait for the Council of Censors, for the seven least populous counties could block any action by that body, although they had only 13,000 electors, and the rest of the State 56,000. Moreover, sections of the Constitution of 1776 and the Declaration of Independence showed that the people had an inherent right to alter a bad government when and how they pleased.[42]

Pennsylvania's second Constitutional Convention—called by the legislature on March 24 by a vote of 41 to 17—formed a quorum November 25, 1789, and proved a body of high ability. Among the members from Philadelphia were James Wilson, William Lewis, and Thomas McKean; James Ross sat for Washington; William Findley for Westmoreland; and two men destined to achieve a national reputation, Albert Gallatin and Timothy Pickering, for Fayette and Luzerne. Gallatin, who had tried to organize an opposition in the western section, wrote in old age that it was one of the ablest bodies with which he had ever been acquainted. "Indeed, could I except two names, Madison and Marshall, I would say that it embraced as much knowledge and talent as any Congress from 1795 to 1812.

---

[42] *Pa. Gazette*, June 20, 1787, quoting Dr. Price; March 11, April 1, 1879, on defects of the Constitution; January 14, 1789, on costs of government. The text of a widely circulated petition in favor of a Constitutional Convention is in the *Pa. Gazette*, March 11, 1789.

But the distinguishing feature of the Convention was that, owing perhaps to more favorable times, it was less affected by party feelings than any other public body I have known. The points of difference were almost exclusively on general and abstract propositions; there was less prejudice and more sincerity in the discussions than usual, and throughout a desire to conciliate opposite opinions by mutual concessions." [43] Thomas Mifflin was elected president. The first act of the delegates was to lay down a general programme, upon which they showed a remarkable unanimity. They voted 56 to 5 for a legislature of two branches, 64 to 0 for a one-man executive, 56 to 8 for granting the judges a securer tenure, 60 to 4 for giving the governor a limited veto, and 64 to 0 for amending the bill of rights. A committee of nine, of which the best-known members were James Wilson, William Lewis, James Ross, and Findley, was then appointed to draft the new Constitution.

The mandate thus given the drafting committee was one which Franklin, on the edge of the grave, raised his voice to oppose. In reply to the revisionists, he wrote an essay in which he staunchly defended the plural executive and single-chambered legislature, while he also objected warmly to the proposal to elect the lower house on the basis of population and the upper house on a basis of wealth. Such a plan he regarded as the omen of a tendency among some Pennsylvanians "to commence an aristocracy, by giving the rich a predominancy in government." He hoped that the State would not rush into these innovations, but remember the Prophet's words: "Stand in the old ways, view the ancient paths, consider them well, and be not among those that are given to change." Justice Bryan, whose days were also numbered, was expressing the same view. [44]

The debates in the convention were long-continued, but they were dominated by a few members. The principal directing mind on the majority side was that of James Wilson, a man whose commanding achievements in national history have been inadequately recognized. Born in Scotland and given a university education there, Wilson came to America when the Stamp Act agitation was at its height, became a teacher in the college in Philadelphia, and studied law with Dickinson. He practiced for a time at Carlisle, but his brilliant talents before long made him one of the leaders of the conservative faction

[43] Adams's "Gallatin," 79-83. Graydon's "Memoirs," 317-30, gives an invaluable account of the Convention of 1790.
[44] Franklin's "Works," Bigelow Edition, X, 184 ff.; Konkle's "Bryan."

in Philadelphia, and he was as much trusted by the national bank group after Yorktown as Morris. He it was who in 1783 wrote the resolution of Congress asking the States for the power of the purse, which was a foundation stone of the movement for a Federal Convention. He was one of the most active members of that Convention, and labored tirelessly to induce Pennsylvania to ratify its work. Now he was acknowledged the best-trained debater and most powerful orator of the State Convention, more than a match for Lewis, who had only a country-school education. Gallatin, as he himself confessed, took a minor rôle in the proceedings, and so did Mifflin. Pickering was energetic, and is to be credited with the provision made for education.

Agreement upon the main features of the revision being secured in advance, the two issues most mooted were not of great intrinsic importance. One was the mode of electing senators, the other the freedom of the press. The drafting committee wanted the Senate chosen through an electoral college, and Lewis supported this proposal; but Wilson took the other side, and carried the day. As for the press, the issue was whether the truth should be received in libel suits as a justification for damaging utterances. The Convention's decision marked an important advance in the power of the press. It was asserted in the new declaration of rights that any citizen might speak, write, and print on any subject, being responsible for abuse of the privilege. In suits regarding the publication of matter on the conduct of public officials, or where the statements about private persons were proper for public information, the truth might be given in evidence; and in all indictments for libel the jury should determine the law and the facts as in other cases. The central principle of this section was in time accepted in both the United States and England, though in neither country till later.[45]

The new Constitution—finally voted September 2, 1790—reflected everywhere the influence of the Federal Constitution. The two greatest improvements, of course, were the bicameral legislature and the creation of a single Governor vested with adequate powers. Members of the House were to be elected annually, and apportioned among the counties by population in such manner that they should never be fewer than sixty or more than one hundred; members of

---

[45] Douglas Campbell, "Origin of American Institutions," Proceedings Amer. His. Association, 1891. Fox's Libel Act of 1792 in England authorized the jury to give a general verdict on the whole matter put in issue.

the Senate were to be chosen triennially from districts. As for the. Governor, he was now to be chosen for three years by the people, not for one year by the Legislature. The old scheme of rotation was wisely dispensed with, a mere vestige of it surviving in the provision that no man could be Governor for more than nine years in twelve. The Governor had the same veto power as the President of the nation, and wide powers of appointment; he could pardon all offenders save impeached officials, and could convene the legislature in extra session. In short, his authority equaled that given the Governor of Massachusetts, and exceeded that vested in New York's Governor. No more notable reaction from a headless form of government occurred anywhere in the United States.[46]

While just and progressive principles of government were thus winning a complete victory in Pennsylvania, in the two southernmost States they were being thrown back in partial defeat. Revising conventions in both South Carolina and Georgia completed their work during the years 1789-90. Georgia very willingly, and South Carolina after a contest between lowland federalists and upland anti-federalists, had ratified the Federal Constitution in January and May of 1788 respectively, and they at once found the demand for better State frameworks becoming irresistible. Georgia's convention met at Augusta on November 4, 1788, and South Carolina's at Columbia in May, 1790. In each State the structure of the Constitution was improved, and liberalism won certain advantages; but the central issue was whether the populous uplands should be granted an equitable representation in the legislatures, and both States decided it in the negative.

When the South Carolina legislature issued a call for a convention, it debated acrimoniously the proper apportionment of delegates. The uplands argued that whenever a people undertook the drafting of a new organic law, they reverted to the first principles of society, according to which, as expounded by Locke and Rousseau, all men are equal; so that the delegates should be apportioned according to the white population. But the lowland legislators, arguing that property as well as population should be represented, had a heavy majority and of course triumphed. When the conven-

[46] In the spring of 1790 the convention took a recess of about five months to give the State time for consideration of the instrument. When it resumed its sessions, only one member voted nay. Gallatin tells us that the Constitution was everywhere liked—"no public act was ever more universally approved"; and the first Governor, Mifflin, testified that it had diffused confidence and concord. *Papers of the Governors of Pa.*, IV, 192 ff.

tion met it contained the same number of members as did the legislature—239—apportioned in the same way. Of the 209 who actually
attended, 104 usually voted on the upland side, and 105 on the lowland side. Of the 30 absentees, 22 were low-country men, so that
had the situation demanded it, the lowlands could have mustered a
majority of a full score; while its actual advantage was greater than
the working majority indicates, for its representatives had more
unity, tenacity, and education. Upon several reforms in which the
Federal Constitution and the newer State Constitutions had pointed
the way, there was general agreement. But apart from this, the
session was simply a bitter conflict between the two great sections,
one democratic, one aristocratic.[47]

Upon the most vital issue, the distribution of representation, the
lowlands would not budge. With desperation it fought both a
proposal to base the representation upon population, and a suggestion
that it be based upon population and property combined in fair proportions. It knew that the uplands, spacious, fertile, and healthful,
their population fast increasing, would shortly gain control of the
State under even the second plan. By sheer doggedness it held its
own and kept control of both houses. According to the final arrangement, the House membership was reduced from 208 to 124. In
general, the representation of each district and parish was halved,
Charleston receiving eighteen members instead of thirty, and most
parishes three instead of six. The uplands were allotted thirteen
more than half of the former representation, and the lowlands, where
some new local divisions were created, seven more. That is, the low
country was left in control of the House by 70 votes to 54. The
membership of the Senate was increased from 31 to 37, of which
number the lowlands were given 20, and the uplands 17. At this
time, we must remember, while the white population of the low
country was only 28,644, and its negro population 79,216, the white
population of the upper country was no less than 111,534, and its
negro population 29,679. In other words, a dominant position in
the government was retained by a little more than one-fifth the
whole white population.

The lowlands received a further advantage in that the qualifications of members of the legislature were kept excessively high. Each
Senator had to be at least thirty, to have been for five years a

[47] Schaper, "Sectionalism and Representation in South Carolina," 369 ff.; an indispensable monograph.

citizen and resident of the State, and to own a freehold estate worth
£300; if he did not reside in the parish he represented, he had to
own an estate of £1000 there. All representatives had to own freeholds of 500 acres each, with ten slaves, or real estate worth at
least £150; and if non-residents of the parish or election district
for which they sat, freeholds worth at least £500. Absentee representation of a community by wealthy Charlestonians thus remained
possible. The Governor was required to have a settled estate worth
£1500.

Some concessions the poor farmers of the uplands nevertheless
won, the most substantial of which was the removal of the capital,
as a permanent measure, to Columbia. A frank delegate stated that
the question was whether the legislators should meet "amongst the
opulent at Charleston, which to the up-country members is a different
climate, or amongst those who are styled a plebeian race." Unfortunately, the lowlands consented to the change only with reservations
which gave the State almost two centers of government. There were
to be two treasurers, one at Charleston and one at Columbia, the
surveyor-general was to have his office at Columbia but to keep
copies of his plots with a Charleston deputy, the secretary of state
could maintain his office in either place provided he kept a deputy
at the other, and the Governor might live at Charleston except when
the legislature was in session. The aristocratic old capital was
loath to part with its dignities.

One democratic reform of marked importance, moreover, was the
injunction laid upon the legislature to abolish the right of primogeniture, which meant that some of Charleston's richest ancestral
estates, kept intact generation after generation, were now slowly to
be broken up. It was a heavy blow to the patrician customs of the
lowlands. No longer could the leading families build great houses
like "Fairlawn Barony" of the Colletons, "Drayton Hall" of the
Draytons, and "Newington" of the Blakes, assured that they would
descend from eldest son to eldest son. A somewhat better balance
was given the government, for the Governor gained in power by the
abolition of the hampering executive council, and a more explicit
definition of his authority and duties. The judiciary, too, attained
a better footing. But upon the pivotal issue of the day and of the
next generation the revision was a failure.

An analogous set of conditions existed in Georgia, and an analogous result occurred. Here, too, the lowlands were divided into great plantations of rice—the staple crop—and indigo, worked by slaves; the uplands were being settled by small farmers and cattle-raisers, who did much of their labor with their own hands, owning comparatively few negroes. Savannah was by no means another Charleston; it was a small center of not 1000 white souls when the Federal Constitution was ratified, and seemed likely to be overtaken soon by the new town of Augusta. But the lowlands were firmly entrenched in the legislature, preserved the same advantage in the revising convention and took care to maintain it in the new Constitution. By this time there were eleven counties, five on the seacoast, three in the middle district, and three in the uplands. The lowlands contained only 8475 whites and 13,261 slaves; the middle counties had 18,134 whites and 7202 slaves; and the uplands had 29,145 whites and 8801 slaves. Yet it was decided that of the 34 members initially constituting the House, the five seacoast counties should send 15, the three middle counties (which inclined toward the low-lands) 10, and the three upland counties—with more whites than the other two sections put together—only 9. In the Senate the division was even more unfair, for each county sent one member. The economic interests of the uplands being markedly different from those of the rest of the State, they were bound to suffer in any conflict over such a subject as the basis of taxation. Moreover, the property qualifications for office were set at an undemocratic level, ranging from 200 acres, or £150 in other property, for Assemblymen, to 500 acres and additional property worth £1000 sterling for the Governor.[48]

Yet in Georgia also something was gained. The substitution of a bicameral for a unicameral legislature was a genuine blessing. A queer arrangement was made for the choice of the Governor, the House nominating three men, and the Senate, with its heavy lowland strength, choosing one of them; but his term was wisely lengthened to two years, and he was given a limited veto. In neither of the southernmost States, of course, could the revised Constitution be submitted to the people—the uplanders might have risen in anger to reject it. But while South Carolina's convention simply promulgated the new instrument, Georgia's was at curiously elaborate pains to consult the public. The first convention, after deliberating

[48] Winterbotham's "View of the United States," III, 273-74.

less than three weeks, agreed to an instrument and adjourned. Half a thousand copies were scattered throughout the state, the justices and militia officers reading them to knots of citizens, and the legislature provided for a new ratifying convention. This, consisting again of three members from each county, popularly elected, made certain amendments. Then a third convention was called by the Governor, as the legislature had directed, made a few more changes, and gave a final approval to the instrument. The proclamation of the new Constitution was accompanied by the discharge of eleven cannon in honor of the federate States, and the Governor, with the members of the convention, repaired to the Government House and drank a glass of wine to its prosperity.[49] They little realized what was in store for their weak commonwealth.

No other State revised its fundamental law in this period. Only Virginia, where the old discontents smoldered on, and Delaware, which rewrote its Constitution in 1792 on the general model of Pennsylvania's, were in a mood seriously to consider doing so. In North Carolina there was much opposition to the Constitution, but no organized movement to replace it—its radical supporters were far too strong. The great fault, as R. D. Spaight wrote Iredell in 1787, was that there existed no "sufficient check to prevent the intemperate and unjust proceedings of our legislature," though such a check was "necessary to our well-being." The government was indeed ill-balanced, but it was to be decades before the State had a new Constitution. In Maryland an agitation commenced in 1789 for removing all restrictions upon manhood suffrage except a condition as to residence, and for apportioning senators and representatives according to population instead of arbitrarily by counties; but neither of these sound reforms received marked attention for several years. New Jersey's hasty Constitution of 1776 was under no severe strain in a State small in size, population, and wealth, and was to undergo no real overhauling for seventy years. Yet intelligent citizens recognized that the legislature had far too much power, and the other two departments of government far too little; while a study of the Federal Constitution emphasized other errors. In 1790 an attempt was made in the legislature to call a revising convention, but it failed. New York was still quite content with her frame of government. Few and bold, of course, were the citizens of Connecticut

[49] *Georgia Gazette,* May 9, 1789; *American Museum,* V, 310, 608.

and Rhode Island who dared breathe upon the name of the Charter-Constitutions.[50]

A fresh period in constitution-making was soon to be opened. It was to begin with the drafting of an organic law by Kentucky, the first western State to be admitted to the Union; for these new commonwealths wrote their constitutions, in one sense, *de novo*, while they fitted them to a social structure quite unlike that of the thirteen original States. A formative period had ended, and an era of growth and adaptation was to begin.

[50] See McRee's "Iredell," II, 169-70, for Spaight's views of North Carolina's government; for the complaints in Maryland, see *Maryland Journal,* September 1, 1786; for the effort at revision in New Jersey, *N. J. Hist. Soc. Proceedings,* Series II, vol. II, 135 ff.; Report of the Committee of the Legislative Council on the Proposed Alteration of the Constitution, 1841.

CHAPTER SIX

POLITICAL DEVELOPMENT IN NEW ENGLAND

THE government carried on under the new State Constitutions was better than their crudity might lead us to expect. Disastrous mistakes were made in many States in the issue of paper money, and made repeatedly in some; in nearly all States the Loyalists were treated too harshly; and in more than half of them the executive branch lacked the authority necessary to a vigorous administration. Party quarrels often generated excessive heat. The States which show the most shameful pages were Rhode Island, where a selfish and narrow-minded State Rights party plunged into deplorable financial heresies; Pennsylvania, where constant turmoil attended a long struggle over a wretched Constitution; North Carolina, where the government was largely in the hands of ignorant, unlettered men; and Georgia, where many in each of the two factions would rather have seen the British conquer than their rivals win. At a period when watchwords of democracy were glib on every tongue, in several States scheming cliques used the government for their special interest. But in general, though the new vehicles, moving on new roads, lurched from side to side, they recovered themselves buoyantly. It is sometimes said that the adoption of the Federal Constitution saved the States from ruin. It did save the Union from decay, but as for the States, they were better-governed in 1788 than ever before, and their financial position was steadily growing stronger. It must be reiterated that most of the governments were not so new as they seemed—they were old in their main principles; and we must also remember that in many States the property qualifications excluded the most irresponsible element from the polls.

Again, the headless nature of the State governments was sometimes more apparent than real. The ablest men of the States were as eager to serve them as to serve the nation. Jefferson forsook the Continental Congress after 1776 to return to Virginia, with the feeling that the nearer duty lay there. Cæsar Rodney, of Delaware, ordered to Europe to find treatment for a cancer that was killing him, refused to leave his post as President of the State till the disease drove him to his death-bed. Franklin was proud, on returning from the French court, to be President of Pennsylvania for three years. When Madison left Congress in 1784 to lead the progressives in the Virginia House, he thought his new position hardly less conspicuous or responsible than the old. Men of marked talent like Clinton, Hancock, Mifflin, and Lowndes devoted themselves almost exclusively to State duties, and many more, like John Adams, Gouverneur Morris, Charles Pinckney, and Henry Laurens, though giving most of their time to the nation, kept a watchful eye on their home States. The Governors or Presidents were treated with a popular deference which helped to weaken the constitutional restrictions on their authority.

In Virginia, Jefferson and Henry at different times held the government, even without special grant of powers, in the hollow of their hands. And during the Revolution, extra-constitutional allotments of authority to the chief executive were frequent, for the State governments simply had to be more flexible than a literal interpretation of the Constitutions allowed. Virginia, Maryland, Pennsylvania, and Georgia gave to Patrick Henry, Thomas Johnson, Joseph Reed, and Archibald Bulloch at various times wide emergency powers. The Virginia Legislature explained that its grant of "additional powers" to Governor Henry was necessary to meet "the present imminent danger of America, and the ruin and misery which threaten the good people of this commonwealth." The Constitution-makers of New Jersey might write an instrument filled with suspicion of the Governor; but the people and legislators were actually filled with the warmest regard for Governor William Livingston.

Not more than a dozen figures stand out saliently in the government of the New England States. Massachusetts had one leader, John Hancock, able to hold the tiller from 1776 until his death in 1793, almost continuously Governor. Hancock at the time independence was declared was not quite forty, the owner of one of the most flourishing businesses, as an importing and commission merchant, in Boston. He was as proud and ostentatious as he was wealthy, fond of the richest wines and food, of silver and china table-furnishings "the most genteel in the country," of silk and velvet garments, and of a fine equipage; his mental powers did not merit comparison with those of John Adams or James Otis, but behind his strut he was the shrewdest of politicians, skilled in ingratiating himself with the Boston voters. Able to take or refuse the Governorship almost as he chose, and to make or unmake subordinates, he became one of the first three great "bosses" in America. Another chieftain, a purer patriot and abler man, Samuel Adams, who had introduced Hancock into politics, was in State affairs after 1776 for the most part in opposition to him and out of power. But immediately after the adoption of the Federal Constitution, they became reconciled. With Adams and the opposition was associated Elbridge Gerry, a wealthy young merchant of Marblehead known as an enthusiastic exponent of democracy; for though changeable, Gerry in general held that government must at all costs be kept close to the plain people. He was in Congress till near the end of the Revolution. James Bowdoin for a time led a third faction, one thoroughly conservative, and at the severest crisis of the State's early history, he was given an opportunity to display marked courage, tact, and vigor.

None of the other New England States produced such a galaxy, for despite Hancock's political opportunism and Samuel Adams's lack of constructive talent, the Bay State group represented high ability and character. In New Hampshire the leaders were of rougher fiber and inferior training in affairs. John Pickering was a Harvard graduate who became a lawyer at Portsmouth before the Revolution, and when the war began was already noted for his fluent tongue, social tact, and wide legal practice. A man of second-rate abilities, he performed his greatest service to New Hampshire when he did more than anyone else to induce the State to ratify the Federal Constitution. Old Meshech Weare was another Harvard graduate, who became prominent when chosen Speaker in 1752, and thereafter was active in Provincial affairs. During the Revolution he was the principal single force in the government, for besides being President of the Council, and Chief Justice, he was the best-trusted leader in the State. His correspondence with Washington was extensive. We may accept Belknap's characterization of him as a man not of brilliant originality, but of "clear discernment, extensive knowledge, accurate judgment, and calm temper." When chosen the State's first head under the Constitution of 1784, Weare was already past seventy and died two years later. John Langdon, a wealthy ship-owner and sea-captain, who was acquainted widely in England as well as America when the war opened, was made useful by his sanguine, businesslike temper and great energy. He threw himself into the war with extraordinary activity, serving in Congress and the Legislature; building warships for the nation—on Langdon Island he launched the *Raleigh, Ranger,* and *America;* commanding a regiment at Saratoga; and taking the Presidency of New Hampshire in succession to Weare. He capped his career by becoming a United States Senator, and so ardent a Republican that he expressed the wish that Washington could be removed from office. John Sullivan is best known for his military exploits, but he also served as State President and in the Continental Congress, posts for which his legal training helped qualify him.

Connecticut's history exhibits men of sturdy sense and moral fiber, but none of genius. Roger Sherman was more prominent in national than State affairs, though he was a member of the Committee of Safety in 1776-77 and 1782, and mayor of New Haven for nearly a decade following 1784. Jonathan Trumbull had become Governor long before the war broke out, in 1769, and remained in the office till old age forced him to retire, in 1784. There was no more sterling patriot in America. His successors were two men of sense but of common-place parts, Matthew Griswold and Samuel Huntington. As in Colonial days, governmental promotion was regular: a man rose from minor offices to be Deputy-Governor, and when the Governor retired, he stepped by universal consent to the higher place. Of the three men, Trumbull alone had a college education, having entered Harvard to fit himself for the ministry, but the other two were thoroughly self-tutored, and all three were members of the bar. They were democratic, hard-headed representatives of a democratic, hard-headed, thrifty commonwealth. In the instance of Trumbull, Washington paid tribute to "a long and well-spent life in the service of his country." As for Rhode Island, it produced no leaders of preëminent ability. The three Governors whose terms cover the years 1775-1790, Nicholas Cooke, William Greene, and John Collins, were certainly not men of distinction. The two Rhode Islanders who made the chief reputations in their generation were Gen. James Varnum and David Howell, the protagonists of the struggle over the Federal Constitution. The former was one of the State's badly-supported delegates to the Continental Congress, a man sincerely attached to the idea of a strong Federal union; the second was a lawyer of Providence, a professor in the institution now called Brown University, and an ardent believer in State Rights.

Faction rather than party shaped the politics of New England from 1776 to 1789, and many factions were purely personal. In Massachusetts, though there was a shadowy alignment between conservatives and radical democrats, we strive in vain during most years to discern any true party, animated by enduring principles. The followers of the various leaders frequently excited themselves over mere trivialities while substantial political issues lay unnoticed. Did Bowdoin have a less patriotic record in 1775 than Hancock? Was Hancock too luxurious in style of his habits? One writer said in 1786 that the two parties in Connecticut were simply "Commutation" and "Non-Commutation." "Great numbers of people were angry with Congress for promising more extra pay to officers and soldiers; but when they found that the five years' pay, even in cash, would not make good the original contract with the army, and especially when they found that the securities were likely to depreciate, the murmurs ceased—the army was cheated and the people satisfied." [1] Only the intensification of the conflict between the rural and the mercantile or maritime interests in 1785-6—born of the "hard times" following peace—and the clash between federalist and anti-federalist opinions, crystallized the New England factions into true parties.

I. MASSACHUSETTS POLITICS TO 1787

The revolutionary extremists led by the Adamses and Hancock having effected the total rupture between Massachusetts and England, for five years, or until 1780, the government of the Bay State was wholly confided, under the Charter, to the Legislature. The chief issue during the five years was just how the Charter should be replaced by a Constitution, and whether the Constitution should be radically or conservatively democratic. Apart from this, the principal question was whether the personal ambitions of Samuel Adams or of Hancock for the leadership of the State should be gratified. Samuel Adams was in Congress, but in his absence from home able lieutenants, the foremost being James Warren, looked after his political interests. Hancock, who also sat in Congress 1775-80, had agents in Boston as adroit as those of Adams, and Hancock won the

[1] Connecticut *Courant*, Nov. 20, 1786.

first skirmish. In 1778, during an interval of residence at home, he was elected Speaker of the House in place of Warren, who was not even chosen to the General Court by his own town, Plymouth. The chagrined Warren wrote to Samuel Adams to explain this defeat, and gives us an inkling of how keenly party rancor was felt during even the darkest days of the Revolution:

It may not satisfy you to carry it to the account only of the versatility and caprice of mankind. They have had their effects, but they would not do alone. Envy and the ambition of some people have aided them, and the policy, or rather what you will call the cunning of a party here, who have set up an idol [Hancock] whom they have determined to worship, has had the greatest. They have even made use of the Tories to prevent my being chosen by my town, who made their appearance on this occasion for the first time for seven years. The partiality of you and the rest of my friends made me an object of great importance with this party, and everything is done to get me out of sight. In short, the plan is to sacrifice you and me to the shrine of the idol.[2]

We can readily believe that as between Samuel Adams and the rich Hancock, loyalists and men of moderate opinions would choose the latter. But the factions behind both men, as distinguished from other groups in the State, worked to give Massachusetts an ultra-democratic government. Their ideas were met by the instrument which Robert Treat Paine and others wrote in 1778.

We have seen that the opposition to this Hancockian Constitution crystallized in the spring of 1778 in a convention at Ipswich, where the Essex Junto was born. The State's conservatives—when the Junto was fully launched, it included Fisher Ames, Timothy Pickering, George Cabot, Theophilus Parsons, and Caleb Cushing—were able to rally in a successful defensive struggle, and pass from it to offensive warfare. The defeat of the proposed Constitution was due largely to them; and, with Parsons leading, they also offered Massachusetts a constructive design possessing great merits. In the reaction against the Hancockian instrument, the two radical factions had to accept a subordinate position in the next Constitutional gathering. Samuel Adams returned from Philadelphia to attend the Convention of 1779-80, received the highest vote in the election of delegates at large for the committee which was to draw up a tentative Constitution, and played some part in laying the foundations of the new government, while Hancock also was a member. But thanks to John Adams, the Constitution was a marked victory for conservatism, and by basing the upper house upon property, it bulwarked the power of the prosperous merchants and shippers. Samuel

[2] Adams MSS., New York Public Library.

Adams went back to the Continental Congress in June, 1780, and was there when the first elections under the new basic law were held. Hancock stayed in Massachusetts to gain possession of the government framed by his adversaries.[3]

This was an easy task, and Hancock walked away from other aspirants for the Governorship. The election of 1780 showed three distinct factions, one led by Hancock, one—the followers of Samuel Adams—by James Warren and Elbridge Gerry, and one by the chieftains of the Essex Junto. The whole opposition to Hancock tended to group itself behind Bowdoin. Samuel Adams wrote to John Adams in Europe that the responsibility of the Governorship would "fall on the shoulders of one of two gentlemen whom you know." One reason for Hancock's easy victory was the unscrupulous adroitness of his adherents' campaign. Turning on Samuel Adams, they had the effrontery to whisper that not only was he, the most unflinching of patriots, connected with the Conway Cabal, but that he had joined a British party, along with Laurens and the Lees! Turning on Bowdoin, they insisted that his share in the Revolution had been much less spirited than Hancock's.

But the principal reasons for Hancock's victory lay in his splendid record as a patriot and benefactor of his fellow citizens. It was recalled that as a rich merchant he had lost thousands of pounds in the war; that he had been bracketed with Samuel Adams in the famous British order which, in June, 1775, exempted these two leaders from Gage's pardon; and that he had been the first to sign the Declaration of Independence. In Philadelphia he had sat as president of Congress for more than two years, and had made an imposing return in the autumn of 1777, escorted part of the way by dragoons. Chosen moderator of the first subsequent town meeting in Boston, he had been thanked for a gift of 150 cords of wood to the poor, one of many generous acts. In the following May he had received a higher vote than anyone else as Boston's representative in the General Court; and in the same year he had notified his debtors that he wished to be paid in paper money and not silver, though a dollar in silver was worth at least $3.50 in bills. It was later said that he had lost £26,000 by thus doing poor debtors a favor and proclaiming his belief in the paper currency. He had commanded the Massachusetts militia in their expedition with D'Estaing against

[3] A. E. Morse, "Federalist Party in Mass. to 1800," p. 19 ff.; Barry's "Mass.," III, 180.

Newport, and upon his return took the lead in entertaining D'Estaing's men, dining about forty officers at his home each day, and paying for a banquet of five hundred covers in Faneuil Hall. Bowdoin, on the other hand, had refused to accept a nomination to the first Continental Congress on account of his ill health, and had since taken little part in public affairs. As for personal popularity, Hancock's qualities gave him all the advantages of an Alcibiades. He was a handsome man, in the prime of life, he was eloquent, and about him hung the engaging air of the old aristocracy.[4]

Less than 12,300 ballots were cast—not one fourth of the electors voted[5]—and of these Hancock received about 11,000, sixteen other men dividing the remainder. His choice gave general satisfaction, and he received a number of flattering addresses. Even Samuel Adams wrote his wife that "many circumstances have combined to make this election appear to be politically necessary." The Governor was inaugurated with a pomp that dismayed Puritans and sticklers for republican simplicity. The bright October day was ushered in with ringing bells and firing cannon; the Legislature met at ten, and after Hancock had taken the oath, he was proclaimed to a rejoicing crowd from the State House balcony; the militia were paraded, thirteen guns were fired, and the troops and shipping discharged a salute; and then the Legislature and Governor Hancock heard Dr. Samuel Cooper discourse in the Old Brick Meeting House from the text: "And their congregation shall be established; and their nobles shall be of themselves; and their governor shall proceed out of the midst of them." A sumptuous dinner followed in Faneuil Hall, where thirteen toasts were drunk in the best Madeira.[6] Thereafter, the Governor usually went out in an elegant chariot which had caused much stir in Philadelphia. His Beacon Street home—"the Stone House"—was fine, it was finely furnished, and he and his wife, Dorothy Quincy, dressed finely. But those who took offense were few. So effectually had the opposition been stamped out that in the fall of 1780, when Samuel Adams was put up for the Secretaryship of the Commonwealth, he was beaten by a Hancockian named Avery.[7]

[4] See the resolutions praising Hancock voted by the Boston town meeting on Oct. 16, 1780; Boston *Gazette*, Oct. 23, 1780. The Chamberlain MSS., Boston Public Library, contain (No. 255) a statement of some £4,737 damage done Hancock's estate by the British.

[5] Boston *Gazette*, April 2, 1781.

[6] *Idem*, Oct. 30, 1780.

[7] Shortly after Hancock became Governor, General Sullivan wrote him from Philadelphia in congratulation. He expressed some surprise that Bowdoin, apparently so lukewarm at the crisis of the Revolutionary uprising, should have received such a

And very popular for a time the Hancock régime remained. In 1781 Bowdoin was again defeated, by the smashing vote of 7966 to 304, and in 1782 by a smaller but no less eloquent majority—5855 to 1155. Nevertheless, the opposition slowly developed a material strength. Hancock, true to his radical democratic principles, failed to press for adequate steps to restore the depreciated currency and to establish the public credit; and the creditor class thus grew more and more dissatisfied. He was one of the most prominent American believers in State autonomy, and the merchants saw clearly that they would gain if, in defiance of his wishes, Congress were given more authority. In the spring of 1781, his opponent Samuel Adams received a remarkable vote in Boston for the General Court,[8] and he was repeatedly chosen president of the Senate. Hancock was reëlected Governor in 1783 and 1784, by unknown majorities, for the vote was not recorded.[9] But we do know that in the latter year, the election developed violent party feeling, involving both State and national issues. The question of the impost amendment to the Articles of Confederation was then coming before the Legislature, and the party representing trade took the Congressional side of the issue, while Hancock leaned to the other. In the gubernatorial campaign, both sides resorted to every possible weapon, even bringing charges of Toryism against the other. The contest showed a growing conservative strength, and it alarmed the Governor.

Moreover, as the year 1784 passed, Hancock saw that trouble was brewing among the poorer folk of the western part of the State. Especially in the Berkshires, there was already rampant the discontent soon to explode in Shays's Rebellion, alarming all America; discontents arising partly from the State Constitution, for the radicals objected to the existence of the Senate, the fact that the principal officers of government were not annually dependent upon the General Court for their salaries, and other "aristocratic" features, but chiefly proceeding from the sore economic straits of the people. The State treasury was nearly empty, the taxes not having been collected during the past year, and only partly collected for preceding years; the

large vote. The letter was captured, and published first in Rivington's *Gazette,* New York, and then in a Boston paper. A warm controversy followed, and Judge James Sullivan took his brother's part, though he discountenanced the slur upon Bowdoin. Amory's "Sullivan," I, 109.

[8] Boston *Gazette,* May 21, 1781.

[9] The Mass. *Centinel* of April 7, 1784, simply says that the people met at Faneuil Hall at nine to elect the State officers, that the poll closed at one, and that Hancock and Cushing were chosen "by a vast majority of votes."

State's creditors were becoming impatient; and the commercial men and moneyed interests of Boston were rebellious over the economic situation, opposing bitterly the paper-money and other measures of relief asked by the western farmers and villagers. European creditors were demanding money of them, and they could not be cheated of their own unpaid accounts by stay laws and depreciated currency.

Hancock was infirm, and amid these difficulties his physician helped him find an escape; he resigned January 29, 1785, upon the ground of illness. We can only guess whether his plea of ill health was a valid excuse. John Adams has written that Hancock had "a delicate constitution," and that "a great part of his life was passed in acute pain." In the fall of 1785 he was undoubtedly so sick at his country home that he feared he might be prevented from going to Philadelphia.[10] But Hancock frequently used a minor malady as an excuse for avoiding a difficult decision or duty. In 1781, during an agitation over a repeal of the State tender act, Mrs. John Adams wrote: "The Governor, as has been heretofore predicted, when anything not quite popular is in agitation, has the gout and is confined to bed." Years later he used his gout to explain his rudeness in failing to call upon President Washington during the latter's visit to Boston, and finally had himself carried into Washington's presence, swathed in flannels. His resignation in 1785 was quite unexpected, even by close friends, and a source of great joy to his opponents. They could not believe that he was sincere, and accused him of expecting the General Court to refuse his resignation and to direct him to keep his position, while recovering his health, by letting the Lieutenant-Governor perform its duties. When Hancock came to the floor of the House to take leave, his supporters shed tears, while his political enemies showed what the former called an "indecent" pleasure.[11] But the resignation was a shrewd political move.

Upon Hancock's retirement, which took place just before the spring election, there occurred a hot contest between the conservative candidate, Bowdoin, and the Hancockian candidate, Lieutenant-Governor Cushing. Cushing was assailed as a mere seat-warmer for Hancock, whose weaknesses were unsparingly set forth. The

[10] See James Sullivan's letter upon his illness, "Life and Corr. of Rufus King," I, 111.
[11] Gerry, who with C. Gore tells this, "Life and Corr. of King," I, 75-6, 80-1, says that when "his proposition to resign was in polite terms *encouraged* by the Legislature, he was much chagrined and disgusted, but delayed his resignation three weeks, and was then under the necessity of proffering it, as all resources failed him for making retreat." Cf. Adams, "Three Episodes in Mass. Hist.," II, 892.

luxurious extravagance which the Governor had shown in "the Stone House" was rebuked. It was said that while it was a recognized duty of the Governor to prepare a comprehensive, accurate statement of the condition of the commonwealth for each Legislature, the indolent Hancock had not done so, and that he had failed to correspond with General Washington and other national leaders, leaving Massachusetts in want of valuable military and other information.

Bowdoin, on the other hand, was assailed for his alleged lukewarmness during the Revolution. Had he not refused to go to Congress, or to accept the Lieutenant-Governorship in 1780? "Shall we confer dignities on a man who withheld his services from his country at a time of her distress?" It was said that Tory factors, British agents who had come to Massachusetts to collect old debts, and Boston merchants who wished to trade with England on any terms, were assisting Bowdoin, and that his election would be a bodyblow to independence. In the west, the natural tendency of those who hoped for paper money and stay-laws was to vote against the Governor. The local retailers and money-lenders, pressed by Boston creditors, were requiring payment from the farmers, and beginning to threaten foreclosure and distraint. Tax-collectors were demanding cash. The agrarian party knew that Cushing and the House would take their side, while Bowdoin and the Senate would oppose soft money or a moratorium. In Boston, Bowdoin naturally polled almost two votes to one over Cushing, but outside the two ran neck and neck. The vote given General Lincoln prevented either from receiving a majority, and threw the election into the legislature.[12]

This result was known finally on May 11, 1785, and between that date and May 25, when the Legislature settled the contest, the campaign between Bowdoin and Cushing raged more fiercely than ever. British favors, said Bowdoin's opponents, were being planned by his faction—British commerce, the admission of British refugees from American soil, British claims, and "in short, British everything." In retaliation, Bowdoin's party declared that Hancock's plan was to have the Legislature elect Cushing as Governor, to have Cushing refuse the post, and then to leave it unfilled for another year, when Hancock could be called upon to save the State from grave embarrassment by reclaiming it. During the year the seat was empty,

[12] Mass. *Centinel,* April 2, 6, 16, and May 11. In the whole State, Bowdoin had 3502 votes, Cushing 2997, Lincoln 1141, and Oliver Prescott 298.

Cushing as Lieutenant-Governor would perform the duties of Governor, and receive the emoluments of both offices.[13] The heat of the contest in Boston alarmed some country towns. When the House met, it named Cushing by 134 votes, and Bowdoin by 89, as candidates to be presented to the Senate; and the Senate sensibly chose Bowdoin by a vote of 18 to 10.[14]

Bowdoin made an excellent Governor during the trying year which followed, a year in which the social discontent rose steadily towards a climax. To his reëlection in 1786 there was no real opposition outside of the western districts. In Boston on the April election day he received all the votes save a complimentary baker's dozen cast for Hancock. In the whole State he was given no fewer than 6,001 votes out of a total of 8,231.[15] His victory naturally intensified the discontent of the radical agrarians, while it left the seaport towns well satisfied.

Already the storm in the western counties was beginning to mutter threateningly. Money was so scarce that in the rural regions the general payment of taxes and debts was out of the question. When the creditors called upon sheriffs and courts to help them collect their debts, and mortgages were foreclosed upon the property of the poor, popular wrath rose against the law and its agents. Poor citizens grumbled that the costs of State government were excessive. The spring session of the Legislature in 1786 rejected all petitions for an issue of paper money, and at the same time granted the supplementary funds asked by Congress, thus increasing the tax burden. The cry went up from desperate farmers and villagers that the Legislature was corrupt or prejudiced, and that it must sit in some small town, not under the influence of Boston merchants and lawyers. Riotous attacks upon the courts occurred, and before the end of summer it was plain that harsh measures were required. Governor Bowdoin's foresight and energy anticipated every demand, and when Shays's Rebellion came to a head early in 1787, it was instantly crushed by an armed force. Arrests were made, the courts were put in rapid motion, and fourteen ringleaders were convicted of treason. Meanwhile, commissioners were sent into the rebellious counties, and they received the submission, with promises of good

---

[13] Mass. *Centinel*, May 14, 21, 25. The agitation against British "factors" led to a meeting in Boston on April 15 to consider what to do with them; Morse, "Fed. Party," 29-31.

[14] "Life and Corr. of King," I, 100-101; Mass. *Centinel*, May 28.

[15] Mass. *Centinel*, March 25, 1786; April 1, April 5, June 3.

behavior, of most of the insurgents. Men of property and sense had reason to be highly grateful to Bowdoin, whose judicious measures had upheld the Government without needless bloodshed.

However, the very firmness of Governor Bowdoin's course gave offense to large classes, and this discontent offered Hancock his longed-for opportunity to become Governor again. Partly because of the numerous casualties among the rebels, partly because of the feeling that the Boston merchants were bleeding the rural poor, Bowdoin had no chance of carrying the western counties. Friends of the fourteen men from that section sentenced to death feared that his election would seal their fate, while they hoped that Hancock would pardon them. Conservatives like Chief Justice Parsons and Sedgwick were for executing the prisoners, and even Samuel Adams sternly asserted that "the man who dares to rebel against the laws of a republic ought to suffer death." It was feared that Bowdoin sympathized with this view. Moreover, many who had no particular pity for the condemned rebels believed that under Hancock's mild sway the State would return more rapidly to general harmony than if Bowdoin remained in the chair. The newspaper war in the campaign of 1787 was as feverish as in 1785. While Samuel Adams and Stephen Higginson led the supporters of Bowdoin, James Sullivan, who had defended some of the prisoners professionally, again exerted his influence for Hancock. Hancock had by no means been laid on the shelf during the last two years; he had been chosen a member of the House in May, 1785, by Boston, a little later he was elected delegate to Congress, and he had again become its President, so that his prestige was undiminished. Said a Boston paper at the end of March:[16]

All accounts from the country agree, that the electioneering mania never raged with greater violence in this commonwealth than it does at the present moment—the insurgents in all parts seeming determined to effect by law, that which they could not by conventions and arms.

Friends of Bowdoin charged Hancock with wasting his estate; not so, said defenders, he reduced it by charity and patriotism. Some declared that Hancock, who was reputed to be much involved in debt and unable to pay, would bring in paper money; not so, averred his supporters, he had opposed paper money in the House. Bowdoin's friends urged his reputation for boldness as the best guarantee that the revolt would not break forth again, and asserted that be-

[16] Mass. *Centinel,* March 28, 1787. See also issues of March 21, 24, and 31.

lievers in sound government in other States awaited the issue "with an anxiety not to be described." They made political capital of the fact that Bowdoin had put forth an earnest effort to collect the tax arrears, which Hancock's good nature had allowed to pile up to an enormous figure. The first attempt in the State at a political roorback was their circulation of a handbill a few days before election, stating that Hancock had surrendered to the insurgents. "It is said, that a committee from their body has waited upon Mr. H—— to request his acceptance of the chair, if their influence could effect his choice to it, and also to know his mind with respect to the introduction of a paper currency: to both which propositions he has given his assent." Far from stooping to such weapons, Bowdoin himself did not solicit a vote. The queer issue of the Governor's salary played a slight part in diminishing his support. The Legislature had passed a bill reducing the stipend from £1100 to £800, and this Bowdoin courageously vetoed, to the resentment of some rural districts, because he thought it wrong to curtail his successors' income.[17]

If ever a Governor deserved reëlection it was Bowdoin, but circumstances were too much for him. Even some supporters of his administration, like Stephen Higginson, thought it had been rather too harsh. In Boston the two men ran neck and neck, but Hancock led, 775 to 724,[18] and when the heavy western returns came in, Bowdoin was found to have a total of only 6,394 votes, as against 18,459 for Hancock. As the excitement of Shays's Rebellion passed away, the State was thus again headed by its original executives, Hancock and Cushing. The agrarian radicals had failed in their legislative program through the opposition of the Senate, though at the fall session of 1786 their tax burden had been lightened. They had failed in the field because of Bowdoin's energy. Now they found what consolation they could in setting up the old Governor again.[19]

The election left the Bowdoin party—a party which comprised those opposed to unrestrained democracy, and which became the nucleus of Federalism in Massachusetts—bitter over what naturally seemed a gross injustice.[20] They vehemently assailed their rivals, and the newspaper warfare was maintained till late in the fall; the

[17] Holland, "Hist. Western Mass.," I, 282 ff. See Mass. *Centinel*, March 24 and 27, for charges of Hancock's connection with the rebels. Cf. Sparks, "Letters to Washington," IV, 239, for Jonathan Trumbull's low opinion of Hancock and high esteem for Bowdoin.
[18] Mass. *Centinel*, April 4, 1787.
[19] *Idem*, May 24, 1787; Conn. *Magazine*, June 14, 1787.
[20] Morse, "Fed. Party in Mass.," 41.

acrid diary jottings and letters of young J. Q. Adams show with what indignation thoughtful Bostonians generally regarded this exhibition of "the caprice of an ungrateful populace." [21] But thenceforth the Hancockian party controlled the State until its chieftain's death, the personality of the proud, gouty old leader dominating every other political force. During the summer after his election everyone was eager to learn what his attitude would be toward the Federal Constitution, then being written.

II. Other New England States to 1787

In New Hampshire no one man came so near controlling State politics as Hancock did those of the southern neighbor; and political currents flowed much more equably, except when the State was agitated by the paper money question. During the Revolution the inchoate government was nominally in the hands of the lower House, but as a matter of fact it was left to Meshech Weare, Matthew Thornton, and a few others whom the people trusted, and who in stormy days had arrogated to themselves extensive powers. For nine years Weare was the principal figure in the State. Year after year the upper house chose him its president, and in the popular elections under the new Constitution of 1784, he was made President of the State by a great majority.[22] Physical disability forcing his retirement in 1785, there appeared a number of aspirants, the chief being George Atkinson, John Langdon, and General John Sullivan. In Sullivan the State saw its chief military hero. He had been a rising young lawyer when the war began, a rollicking, bustling Irishman, as tough and staunch as a blackthorn, who had served in the militia and attained the rank of major; and he was chosen a delegate to the first Continental Congress. At the close of 1774, he and Langdon led the expedition which bloodlessly captured Fort William and Mary, in Portsmouth harbor. First as a brigadier and later as a major general, he served with great credit in a number of campaigns, particularly when Washington's discretion controlled him, and in 1779, for his operations against the Tories and Iroquois in New York, received the thanks of Congress.

---

[21] *Mass. Hist. Soc. Proceedings,* Series 2, Vol. XVI, 404. For Samuel Adams on Shays's Rebellion, see Fiske, "Critical Period," 184; for the views of Stephen Higginson, Rept. Am. Hist. Assn. 1896, p. 754.
[22] For this election, see Portsmouth corr. of *Md. Journal,* July 16, 1784.

But it was also felt that the State owed much to John Langdon, the bluff sea-captain, whose personality was more dashing than Sullivan's. His supporters recalled that he had distinguished himself in opposition to the royal Governor; that "his complaints of our oppressions once reached the royal throne"; that he ventured his fortune in building warships, thus providing employment as well as defense; that he had contributed a 20-gun ship to the expedition against Penobscot, and uncomplainingly, after long delay, received pay for it in depreciated paper currency; and finally, that after the war "his enterprise gave to business a spring, when it was in a state of almost total stagnation." [23] The popular vote was indecisive. The House then sent the names of Atkinson and Langdon up to the Senate, which chose the latter (June, 1785).[24]

Sullivan's opportunity came the next year, when he was elected President (June, 1786) by a clear popular majority.[25] As in Massachusetts, the paper-money agitation made the close of 1786 and the opening months of 1787 critical, and Sullivan, like Bowdoin, discharged his duty with discretion and vigor. When in September a mob menaced the members of the Legislature at Exeter, Sullivan placed himself at the head of the militia, and quickly dispersed them. The good sense of New Hampshire rapidly asserted itself against the unwise agrarian scheme for a new paper issue. But Sullivan, like Bowdoin, had offended too many voters to receive the endorsement of an immediate reëlection. John Langdon and Judge Samuel Livermore stood for the Presidency against him, each with a loyal following among those who had not countenanced the riots. The rioters and their friends sought their natural revenge at the polls. Sullivan, wrote the correspondent of the New York *Journal*, "has lost a great number of votes by his . . . patriotic efforts in support of the government of this State, when attacked by a lawless and insulting rabble; all the towns from whence the mob came, which attacked the General Court at Exeter, having generally voted for another candidate." [26] In even the two principal towns, both conservative, Sullivan made a poor showing. The election was thrown into the Legislature, which once more chose Langdon.[27] He suited the discontented element in the State better than any other man,

[23] N. H. *Mercury*, March 2, 1785, essay by "Candidus."
[24] *Idem*, June 14, 1785.
[25] *Idem*, June 21, 1786.
[26] N. Y. *Journal*, June 14, 1787.
[27] N. H. *Mercury*, March 14, 28; Pa. *Packet*, March 29, June 13, 1787.

but as in Massachusetts, this element could do nothing but settle down and wait for better times.[28]

In Connecticut there were even fewer political antagonisms than in New Hampshire, for the State showed a remarkable degree of unanimity in its attitude towards all political questions. It was little troubled by governmental errors in financial policy, and their consequences upon the people. The people were ardently patriotic during the war, and after it showed zeal in supporting the erection of the Federal Government. They were largely of one religious faith, one economic condition, and one social view. The commonwealth had the advantage of passing from the Colonial status to full Statehood not only without change of fundamental law or Governor, but without having to displace more than a few subordinate officers.

When the Revolution began, Governor Trumbull was so universally liked that "it was a rare thing to see a counting of the votes," as the leading Connecticut journal said, his annual reëlection being a matter of course. Trumbull was the ideal man for the place, a practical, hard working, versatile Yankee. He had been in public life since the early thirties, when he had been chosen to the Legislature and commissioned lieutenant in the "Troop of Horse"; he had been Governor since 1769; his early training for the ministry was a decided asset in a State where church and government were so closely linked; and being a farmer and merchant, and the son of a cooper, he had the confidence of agricultural, mercantile, and laboring interests. He had a store, warehouse, and wharf at Haddam, on the Connecticut, others at Norwich, and ships to carry his own goods. From the prosperous farmers of Windham County he bought cattle, sheep, horses, salt meat, and grain, collected them, and sent them by long wagon trains to the two towns, where they were taken by his vessels to the West Indies, and exchanged for sugar, salt, molasses, rum, and cotton. Long before the Revolution Trumbull had become one of the rich men of New England. He owned a spacious mansion on the main street of Lebanon, and a store, grist-mill, and several farms in that township. When the news of Lexington reached Connecticut,

[28] The House decidedly preferred Langdon, who was especially popular in the interior, while the Senate insisted upon Sullivan. Langdon's following in many ways resembled that of Hancock in Massachusetts; Sullivan was popular with the merchants of Portsmouth and Dover much as was Bowdoin with those of Boston. See the Portsmouth correspondence of the Providence *Gazette*, April 2, 1785, for Langdon's strength in the inland towns. Portsmouth gave Sullivan 120 ballots, almost exactly half her vote; Dover 169 ballots; and Concord only 6. The whole State vote was: Langdon 3619, Sullivan 2850, Livermore 583, Bartlett 457, Atkinson 100.

the Governor hastily converted his Lebanon store into a supply-depot, and for days worked feverishly, coatless and hatless, his gray locks loose in the breeze, giving tents and rations to the train-bands that came through, and packing wagons with munitions, provisions, and clothing for the camps about Boston. This little shop throughout the war was one of the government centers of Connecticut. Hundreds of meetings of the Governor and Council were held there, and within its walls at various times stood Washington, John Adams, Hancock, Jefferson, Greene, and Rochambeau. Trumbull was as able as Governor Clinton or Governor Bowdoin, more unselfish and purer than the former, and more energetic than the latter.[29]

Yet in the darkest years of the Revolution Trumbull's popular vote (the choice of the Governor was by secret vote in town meetings, or if no man had a popular majority, by the Legislature) fell to remarkably low levels, and that for his rivals rose high. The discontent of the electorate under the heavy load of taxes and army service found a natural vent in blaming the honest Governor. Why not meet these terrible expenses, frugal-minded Yankees asked, by other means than immediate taxation? Friends of the prominent younger men of the State, as Samuel Huntington and Oliver Wolcott, both "signers" and long delegates to the Continental Congress, could hardly help feeling that Trumbull by 1782 had held office long enough. The British took pains to spread slanders adroitly designed to injure him. Tavern gossip and Tory rumor accused him of sharing in the illicit trade with the King's army in New York, a trade which he of all men was doing the most to disrupt and punish. The enemy exposed cases ostensibly containing smuggled commodities on the New York docks, marked with Trumbull's name; and they shipped similar boxes on vessels bound up the New England coast, so that American officers held captive by them became convinced of Trumbull's guilt.

In 1780 the vote for Trumbull was only 3598 as against 3668 for all other candidates combined; the Legislature, however, sensibly reëlected him by a ballot of 107 to 9. The spring session of 1781 chose him again by a vote of 104 to 18, William Pitkin, Wolcott, and Huntington being his principal rivals. In the next few months the silly stories about the Governor's share in smuggling spread until even his quiet disdain was disturbed, and on January 29, 1782, he

[29] Stuart's "Trumbull"; Trumbull's "Trumbull"; Todd, "In Olde Conn.," Ch. 10.

requested the General Assembly to conduct an official investigation. The Legislature appointed a committee, with Wolcott as chairman, which of course reported that the charges were "false, slanderous, and altogether groundless," and in all probability originated by enemy agents. A fuller vindication was granted Trumbull in the election of 1782, when the people gave him a generous majority.[30] He was now about to retire, and he prized this victory. No man in the State had voluntarily sacrificed so large a part of his wealth in the Revolution as Trumbull. A story is told how, in the winter of 1780, when the army was in dire need, Governor Trumbull ordered contributions for relief taken in the churches on a Sunday; how in the meeting-house at Lebanon his call was read from the pulpit; and how Mrs. Trumbull rose and laid on the altar a fine scarlet cloak she wore, a gift from Rochambeau. For eight years the Governor paid no attention to his business, and allowed it to sink into ruin.

Yet at the close of the Revolution, as during it, many voters somehow connected Trumbull with their tax-burdens. We have quoted the statement of one observer that the State was divided between two parties, "Commutation" and "Non-Commutation," and that numbers of farmers and townsmen were angry with Congress for its grant of half-pay to officers. This observer mentions also the existence of a post-Revolutionary faction which hated the Cincinnati. The industrious, saving people of Connecticut abominated anything which looked like avoidable expense, and equally detested anything that savored of aristocracy. Governor Trumbull, like most other men of station in Connecticut, unquestionably agreed with Washington that the officers ought to be given a generous grant in commutation of their claims. He wished for a stronger, closer Union, and in both a suitable reward to all veterans, and State payments into the national treasury to make that reward, he beyond doubt acquiesced. But the General Assembly in 1780 instructed Connecticut's delegates in Congress to oppose the half-pay plan, and when in 1782 it passed an act empowering Congress to collect import duties in the State, it added the provision that no money so collected should be used for a half-pay grant. There was a small body of anti-federalist sentiment in the State, and it was of course aligned against Trumbull. The Governor's son Jonathan was a charter

[30] Trumbull's "Trumbull," 288 ff.; Corr. and Journals of S. B. Webb, II, 260-61; III, 14.

member of the Cincinnati, and Trumbull's approval of the order is shown by his later acceptance of an honorary membership. It is not at all strange that when the annual election was held in May, 1783, he once more failed of a popular majority. The Legislature, however, reëlected him without hesitation, 96 to 22.

Trumbull was now seventy-three, and when the General Assembly met in October, he resigned. He dwelt on the fact that his life was "worn out almost in the constant cares of office." Indeed, he saw only one more autumn. Characteristically, he struck a religious note in his last message: "I think it my duty to retire from the busy concerns of public affairs; that at the evening of my days, I may sweeten their decline, by devoting myself with less avocation, and more attention, to the duties of religion, the service of God, and preparation for a future happier state of existence."

The old Governor was succeeded by Matthew Griswold, who had begun life as a poor boy, had prepared himself for the bar by unremitting labor, and in 1765 had been one of the Councilors who had refused to swear support of the Stamp Act. As Deputy-Governor he had been at Trumbull's elbow throughout the war, shared his views, and was his natural successor. Although he had a plurality of the popular vote, he received less than a third of it, and was chosen by the Legislature. Two years later Samuel Huntington took the office and held it for a decade—another fine example of the self-taught man of rural origin, a Norwich lawyer who had once been president of the Continental Congress. He proved an energetic friend of the Federal Constitution, and it was in part owing to his efforts that Connecticut was the first New England State to ratify it. During his and Griswold's administration political feeling over even the paper money question did not rise high.[31]

When we turn to Rhode Island, we turn to a much stormier record, though for some time there were few divisions among the patriots. Nicholas Cooke, chosen Governor when Wanton was deposed, was of unassailable Whig principles. He had acquired a fortune and respect as a merchant. But the real Revolutionary leader had been and for several years continued to be Stephen Hopkins, of Providence, who had been a good Governor in the fifties and sixties, and who in his radical temperament was not unlike Samuel Adams. He shared with Nathanael Greene the chief burden of directing the con-

---

[31] For sketches of Griswold and Huntington, see *Conn. Magazine*, VII, 170 ff.

flict in the desperately beleaguered State. Newport, the fourth city in the nation, was lost to the enemy early in 1777, and thereafter the southern towns were incessantly harried. The attack of Sullivan and D'Estaing on Newport was an ignominious failure, and Rhode Island was not free from the enemy until the fall of 1779, when Clinton voluntarily evacuated it. The patriots saw that stern sacrifices were so indispensable for victory that internal bickering would mean ruin. Cooke, worn out, resigned in the spring of 1778, and William Greene, another rich merchant, the son of a Colonial Governor, was chosen in his stead, holding the office for eight years.

Before the final signing of peace with England, a struggle opened in Rhode Island over the requests of the Continental Congress for proper financial support, while after the peace the paper money question grew steadily more acute. The cleavage between the two parties, one for sound money and Federal measures, and one against both, would not have been so well-defined but for certain economic facts. As in Massachusetts and even in the two other New England States, the war brought prosperity to a considerable group of merchants and shippers. There were fat war contracts to be filled; there was the usual trade for supplying a growing population with overseas commodities; and for the boldest spirits there was a perfect mine of riches in privateering. In Newport the British occupation ruined many substantial citizens, and drove away most of the Hebrew traders who had helped give the city its reputation for commercial enterprise. But Providence grew the richer by the transfer of Newport's commerce, and by engrossing nearly all the privateering enterprise. Moreover, the depression in Newport was brief: a steady recovery followed the British evacuation, so that by 1784 much new wealth had been created there. Unfortunately, not only was the wealth confined to a few groups even in the towns, but all the while, as in the other New England States, the rural population grew poorer, fell deeper into debt, and began to regard the future with more and more desperation. Taxation to pay the public debts seemed especially severe in Rhode Island, for the State was small, well settled, and without claims to western lands. It could not assist itself by the sale of large land-grants to settlers, and it could not hope for a rapid expansion of its population.

The "country party" born out of this discontent was a State Rights party, opposed to a firmer national union. It did not wish Congress given control over imports, with the right to lay even a five per cent. duty, for this would raise the price of the imports used; it did not wish to pay the money requisitions constantly made by Congress. Many townspeople shared these views, while some intelligent farmers doubtless opposed them, so that the title "country party" was not wholly accurate. But it is significant that David Howell, the Providence lawyer, who led the opposition in 1782 to the impost amendment, took the pseudonym of "A Farmer."

Howell's essays against the impost plan appeared in the leading Rhode Island newspaper, the Providence *Gazette,* in March and April, 1782. An equally able series of rejoinders was published by General James M. Varnum, a member of Congress, in the same sheet in March, April, and May. To a certain extent, the issue figured in the Assembly elections that spring, and so far as it did, the country party was victorious. When the Assembly met, it promptly retired the three delegates then sitting in the Continental Congress, Varnum, Daniel Mowry, and William Ellery, and elected four men who were less favorable to the impost amendment—Howell, John Collins, General Ezekiel Cornell, and Jonathan Arnold. Howell was at once sent on to Philadelphia to defend the position of the State there, for it was now alone—except for Georgia, expected momently to yield—in denying the impost to Congress. When the Rhode Island Assembly re-convened in the fall of 1782, it voted unanimously against the impost plan, and by its decided stand alone prevented the fulfillment of all the hopes of Congress. Furthermore, in the spring of 1783 the legislature again rejected the impost; "by so great a majority, and from such false reasoning," General Greene dolefully wrote, "that I begin to despair of their coming into the measure at all; at least in season to save us either from convulsions or bankruptcy."[32]

However, the opposition to the State Rights party began to gain strength. This very spring of 1783 Varnum, making a gallant fight, had seemed for a time to win over the majority sentiment. General Greene had written Robert Morris that the impost plan would succeed if the Assembly could be persuaded first to pass it in qualified form, and then be led to perfect its grant. In February, 1785, the Legislature was actually induced to make a concession. It laid a State duty precisely like the national duty Congress had proposed,

[32] Greene, "Life of Nathanael Greene," III, 523 ff.

and provided that $8000 annually of the proceeds should be used to pay the State's share of the foreign debt of the nation; while at the same time, it granted Congress the power to regulate the importation of foreign goods in foreign ships. The commercial interests of Rhode Island were awakening to their stake in the whole question, and that fall they were able to push the Assembly a step further: it gave Congress power to prohibit foreign importations in American ships. Finally, in March, 1786, the Assembly took the long-desired step, and adopted the new impost plan, on condition only that the other States should consent to Congressional regulation of interstate trade. Little Rhode Island wished for such regulation because while it was lacking her stronger neighbors had it in their power greatly to injure her commerce by discriminatory duties.

But after having thus triumphed, the commercial party, favorable to a strong national government, was suddenly overthrown by a political revolution—the great paper-money earthquake which shook the country from end to end. The farmers thought it bad enough to be bowed to earth by a crushing load of taxes and mortgages. It was worse to see the merchants and shippers rolling in prosperity, fattening upon the same circumstances which ruined the tillers. The latter had been growing more and more surly, and now, in 1785, they perceived the commercial class get its way in spite of all opposition, and give Congress certain privileges which seemed certain to increase the cost of living. It was too much.

In the fall of 1785, a few paper-money advocates had seats in the Assembly. During the February session of 1786, members of six towns brought instructions to the Legislature calling for an emission of bills. The merchants of Newport and Providence took alarm, and submitted remonstrances, arguing that there was no real scarcity of money, and that if the paper were printed, it would drive coin from circulation. A paper money law, they predicted, would ruin Rhode Island's commerce with other States, which would not accept payment for their goods in rag money. In March the Assembly voted on the question, and the country party lost, 43 to 18. However, because of the scarcity of currency, an act was passed—the Providence remonstrants had themselves suggested it, and it was genuinely expedient—making real property and certain kinds of personal property a legal tender for debts on execution. This act of course gave the poor debtor only a shadowy protection.

The result was a spasmodic and startling successful movement at the polls for the defeat of the commercial and capitalist party. At the April election in 1786, to which mortgaged farmers went with the same feeling that they took to the polls in Kansas in 1896, Governor Greene and Deputy-Governor Jabez Bowen were overthrown. Greene was a rich merchant, while Bowen had made himself obnoxious to the country party when, two years before, he had quashed at the outset an attempt at resistance to the collection of the taxes. Two tried representatives of the country party, John Collins and Daniel Owen, were chosen to the Governorship and Deputy-Governorship, positions they were to hold four years each. No less than 45 new members appeared in a House of 70, and five new Assistants in a total of ten. Newport, Providence, and Bristol held firm, but the character of the Legislature was at one stroke degraded and debased. "I never saw so great a proportion of ignorant men in a public body," says one observer. "There are but four or five that appear to understand the nature of money and the operation of the law; and but a few of these can express their sentiments with propriety. You never heard language and common sense so tortured and murdered as in this House." [33]

The victorious country party lost no time. On May 5, on the ground that the money in the State was "quite insufficient" and that the farmers were losing their all at forced sales, an act was initiated for emitting £100,000 in bills, to be loaned at interest on landed security. It passed by a large majority. Its worst features were the provisions forcing the circulation of the bills, and especially one which, if a creditor refused them, enabled any debtor to discharge his debt by depositing the required sum with the county judge, who should give notice of the fact in the press. Depreciation of the paper was instant and swift. By the fifth of August, it was passing at four to one, and many honest men would have nothing to do with the "rags and blacking"; rogues and unprincipled debtors, however, hastened to fill their pockets with it to pay their obligations, and a neat brokerage business sprang up to assist them.

During August the Assembly was called in special session to hit upon further measures for compelling the circulation of the paper. The law was amended to make any person who refused to accept the bills finable from £6 to £30 for a first offense, and from £10 to

[33] Newport letter to the N. H. *Mercury*, Oct. 25, 1787.

£50 for a second; while to make it easier to deal with these offenders, they were deprived of trial by jury. The paper was also made a tender in payment of Continental taxes, an act which dishonored the State and called forth a protest in writing from the Newport, Providence, Warren, Bristol, and New Shoreham representatives. The activity of the debtors was extraordinary; one issue of the Providence *Gazette,* that of September 23, contained twenty-seven advertisements giving public notification that as many men had lodged sufficient sums in paper with the authorities to cover what they owed. However, it soon became plain that the advocates of inflation and repudiation could not carry everything by force of law. A general stagnation of business set in. Shops in all towns shut their doors rather than sell their wares for paper; the good people of Connecticut and Massachusetts—particularly after it was learned that a boy driving over the line with a load of potatoes had been compelled by force to sell them for paper—refused to dispose of their livestock, grain, apples, and homely manufactured products in Rhode Island or through Rhode Island traders. Many merchants began to flee from the seaport towns to other parts of the Union as if a plague were behind them. And, most hopeful of all, the courts revolted.[34]

In September, 1786, a test case—the famous case of Trevett *vs.* Weeden—was carried to the Superior Court by a refractory Newport butcher, who was defended by General Varnum, and the members of that tribunal defied the Legislature by refusing to punish the culprit in any way, declaring that they lacked jurisdiction. A month later the House summoned the justices before it, and reprimanded them, but it could do nothing more, and the precedent stood.

Opposition to the forcing-law insanity was by no means dead in the legislature, the larger towns standing firm. But the majority was not checked in the least by the arguments of the shippers, traders, and propertied men generally. The assembly lost the appearance of a deliberative body at its regular October session, for secret conclaves decided upon most measures and hurried them through without real debate. On Sundays and at night little juntas canvassed proposed bills, determined which should be enacted into law, and next day marshalled the rank and file to carry out the program. A com-

---

[34] See the Rhode Island correspondence of the N. Y. *Daily Advertiser,* especially in the issue of Sept. 14. R. I. Acts and Resolves, October, 1786, p. 6.

mittee actually drafted a statute to destroy the negotiability of notes, and under certain circumstances to outlaw them in six months, and eight men had the effrontery to vote for it. Early in October a secret caucus prepared a bill which its opponents promptly dubbed "the bloody act." It required every citizen to take an oath to support the paper money as equal in value to cash, suspended every office-holder who should refuse the oath, denied permission to any non-juring shipmaster to load or unload his vessel, prohibiting non-juring lawyers from practicing, and disfranchised these men and all other non-jurors. This bill was sent to the towns to be submitted to the voters in town meeting for their instructions. It met almost no favor; Providence promptly called it "unconstitutional, unjust, impolitic"; and it was never passed.

During 1787 the hold of the paper-money party seemed outwardly as strong as ever, though in reality it was weakening. The force acts, thanks to the Superior Court, were practically inoperative, and the injustices and distresses of the previous summer had produced their natural effect on the consciences of all good citizens. Still, however, paper sufficed to pay a debt. The ticket or "prox" of the country party at the spring election was headed by Collins and Owen, and bore the legend: "Liberty and Property secured by Persever-ance." It was a balanced ticket, for while Owen was the leader of the faction in its most radical stronghold, Gloucester, Governor Collins held more moderate views, and wavering men might easily be attracted by him. The opposition "prox" bore the names of William Bradford for Governor and John Malbone for Deputy-Gover-nor. The former had been an early leader in the Revolution, having served on the Committee of Safety in 1775; while he represented also the new federalist movement, for he had succeeded Stephen Hopkins in Congress and believed in a closer national union. This was im-portant, for the country party and town party had just found a further theme of dispute in the recommendation of Congress that each State appoint delegates to a convention for revising the Articles of Confederation. By a large majority, the Legislature had declined to send delegates. As for Malbone, he was a member of one of the oldest mercantile houses in Newport, and represented the commercial interests.[35]

The acts of the recent paper-money sessions were subjected to a

[35] Bates, "Rhode Island and the Formation of the Union," 144-45.

raking fire. Their impolicy and injustice were alike clear. Business was now at a total standstill; the merchants and farmers alike had been struck a grievous blow. One wag said that the next money of the State would be rope, cut into fixed units, and that if a man depreciated it, it would first be used to whip and then hang him. The sound-money campaigners called attention to the public sentiment of other States, disgusted by Rhode Island's acts; "the quintessence of knavery," a New York journal had termed the policy. They showed that while in part the paper money agitation had been founded upon real distress, in part its supporters had been rascals who had used the bills as easy way of paying debts; and that since the paper had depreciated, the tender clauses were sheer swindle-breeders. A moderate writer, who took the tactful name "A Farmer," stated that he had at first advocated paper, but that the emission had been too large, and the supporting measures too harsh.

Nevertheless, the sound money party failed. The vote in Newport, Providence, and Bristol strongly supported it. The first-named city, still the largest in the State, had a peculiar grudge to satisfy, for the paper money party, upon the petition of some of Newport's irresponsible citizens, had revoked its charter;[36] and this despite the fact that these petitioners did not constitute one-fourth of the freemen, that their property was not assessed for one-seventeenth the city taxes, while from some of them no taxes at all could be collected, and that the city administration had been excellent. Moreover, the Newport postmaster had been dismissed on a trivial pretext. In their wrath the Newporters gave Malbone and Bradford 243 and 211 votes respectively, and Owen and Collins only 63 and 83.[37] However, the rural returns snowed under these city majorities. When both houses met at Newport on May 2, the correspondent of the *Connecticut Magazine* reported that matters had gone from bad to worse in the upper branch. "Those who had in many instances opposed, or dissented from the proceedings of the late administration," he said, "were superseded by the avowed partisans of their favorite system. In the lower house, the division was nearly as last year." [38] The correspondent of the Massachusetts *Centinel* described the majority of the upper chamber as "a most curious medley of Know Ye justices, horse jockies, and so on." Their prox, he added,

[36] Pa. *Packet,* April 5, 1787 (Newport dispatch dated March 22).
[37] N. Y. *Advertiser,* April 30, 1787.
[38] Conn. *Mag.,* May 31, 1787.

had been headed by the word "perseverance," an accurate motto if men added, "in villainy." [39]

The government of the State under the new Legislature of 1787 was of course not a whit improved. Repudiation was allowed to run its course. Payment of the State debt in paper was continued, and during the summer three-fourths of it was wiped off the books. The night before the Assembly organized, a program was blocked out by a caucus, made up of paper-money legislators and some private citizens, "as good friends to the cause as ever broke bread"; and a salient feature of the agreement reached was that no functionary should be reappointed who was not of the country party. The electorate had already punished the Superior Court, for virtually declaring the forcing act unconstitutional, by displacing the four subordinate justices and reëlecting the Chief Justice alone. Newcomers, sometimes grossly unfit, always inexperienced, now replaced a number of well-equipped officials. To crown its perversity, the Legislature again declined to send delegates to attend the Constitutional Convention in Philadelphia: the upper house in May refusing to concur when the lower house passed the needed measure, and in June the lower house failing to consent to action by the upper.

III. New England and the Federal Constitution

At this point we may turn to the neighboring States for a moment. While Rhode Island under Governor Collins had been declining to coöperate in the Constitutional Convention, the majority of intelligent men elsewhere in New England had been looking expectantly toward Philadelphia. To understand the isolation of Rhode Island after 1787, we must take note of the attitude of Massachusetts under Hancock, New Hampshire under Langdon, and Connecticut under Huntington, toward the effort for a better national Constitution.

Connecticut was everywhere expected to be one of the first States of the nation to ratify. This was in spite of the fact that a clear division of opinion on the question of federalism had arisen before Trumbull's resignation, and had grown more prominent. Thus a political essayist wrote in the Connecticut *Courant* of November 20, 1786:

There are two parties in the State, jealous of each other—federal and anti-federal. The federal men suppose the anti-federal to be knaves, artful designing demagogues.

[39] *Mass. Centinel*, June 20, 1787; R. I. Records, X, 239 ff.

The anti-federal suppose the federal to be ambitious tyrannical men who are aiming at power at the expense of the people at large. . . . The anti-federal think as they have been bred—their education has been rather indifferent—they have been accustomed to think on the small scale—they can think on no other without an enlargement of their minds. Besides, most of them live remote from the best opportunities of information, the knowledge they acquire is late, and is longer in producing conviction in their minds than in more enlarged minds. . . . Were the anti-federal men in this State to travel, to sit in Congress, to converse with men who understand foreign policy, in short, were they to view this State and the continent in their true connection with other nations, they would think like the federal men and join in their measures. The system of measures now pursuing by the majority of the Legislature would, if carried through, inevitably bring disgrace, poverty, and ruin upon this State —and at any rate would produce embarrassments innumerable.

But as the paper-money agitation ruffled Connecticut politics but little, so this antagonism of federal and anti-federal men did not greatly disturb its placid surface. The *Connecticut Magazine* in June, 1787, when the Constitutional Convention was well launched, took occasion to "congratulate our fellow citizens on that spirit of candor and unanimity, which has signalized the House of Representatives. No spirit of party or faction has appeared." The people of Connecticut were often tight of pocketbook, sometimes provincial of mind, but on the whole they were too public-spirited not to approve of an energetic national government even if it meant sacrifices.

The State convention of January, 1788, spent only a few days in debate, and voted 128 to 40 for ratification. Among the opponents were a few who had sympathized with the Shays insurrection. These dissenters were strengthened by a number of Revolutionary officers, led by General James Wadsworth, who had sat in the Continental Congress, and who objected to giving Congress both the sword and the purse. The senior member of the Council, William Williams, at first was unfavorable because the instrument imposed no religious test, but gave over his objection. Two men who had helped write the Constitution, Oliver Ellsworth and Roger Sherman, spoke for it in the Convention with effect, and Gov. Huntington seconded them, taking pains to express his faith in the high motives of the opposition. At the next State election the voters significantly left Wadsworth out of the government.[40]

Massachusetts sent four men to the Constitutional Convention— Elbridge Gerry, the trusty henchman of Samuel Adams; Rufus King, a young man; Nathaniel Gorham; and Caleb Strong, yet little known, but a hard-headed Puritan who was to be ten times Governor. Gerry sat in the Convention till it ended, and assisted it materially, but

[40] B. C. Steiner, "Connecticut's Ratification," *Proceedings Amer. Antiq. Soc.*, April, 1915.

refused to sign the Constitution. When he returned home to oppose ratification, it was plain the fight would be intense. As Knox wrote Washington after study of the situation in the final months of 1787,[41] three parties might be distinguished. One, the weightiest, included all engaged in commerce, all men of large property, the clergy, the lawyers, and the officers of the Revolution; it represented three-sevenths of the population, and was emphatically for ratification. Another was composed of the people of the district of Maine, nearly two-sevenths of the population, who would be for or against the Constitution as it promised to impede or help their plans for a new State—chiefly against it. A third party consisted of the recent insurgents and their friends, some of whom wished to see public and private debts abolished or reduced, and all of whom opposed ratification. The great question was, what would be the position of Governor Hancock and Samuel Adams? No one knew, but it was suspected that, opposed though the two men were in politics, at heart they agreed in disliking the Constitution.

The State convention opened upon January 9, 1788, in Boston, and numbered many of the most distinguished men of Massachusetts. Governor Hancock, richly dressed, his position unknown, presided. On the floor were his lofty, reserved rival, the federalist Bowdoin; the leader of the Boston commonalty, Samuel Adams, who was hesitant; two Revolutionary generals, Heath and Lincoln; three of the delegates to Philadelphia, Gorham, Strong, and King; and several young men of note, as Fisher Ames, Theophilus Parsons, and Theodore Sedgwick—all three federalists and conservatives. The evidence is that at the outset a majority of the 360 members were ready to vote against the Constitution. James Madison wrote Washington from New York on January 20 that "the intelligence from Massachusetts begins to be very ominous to the Constitution." But the indispensable foundation for ratification was laid by searching debate upon one provision of the Constitution after another.

A great success was scored when Samuel Adams, after listening in silence to the discussion for a fortnight, was brought over—in part by an enthusiastic mass-meeting of Boston mechanics—to the advocacy of the "new roof." The important question of Governor Hancock's position remained, and he, when the moment for answering it came, was suddenly confined to bed by his painful but indispensable

---

[41] Drake, Knox, 97-8.

gout. Some ardent supporters of the Constitution did not reflect that Hancock's political future depended on whether his decision was shrewd, but Hancock never forgot it. How would his answer affect the April election for Governor? Was he to bring his personal following into support of a new national government, or to lead an irreconcilable State Rights party? The friends of the instrument helped him decide. A deputation sought his home, induced him to reappear as an advocate of compromise—that is, of ratification with a request for changes—and furnished him nine proposed amendments called the "conciliatory proposition," written by Theophilus Parsons. One inducement offered by the Federalists was a promise of support for the Governorship, even from Bowdoin's friends. Another, as Rufus King told Knox, was the prospect that if Virginia did not enter the Union, Hancock might become the first President of the United States. The effect of Hancock's advocacy of ratification was all that was expected, and the Constitution was accepted (February 6) by a majority of less than twenty—187 to 168.

Besides Rhode Island, New Hampshire remained to ratify. The issue arose there simultaneously with the annual election, and the attitude of the rival candidates, Sullivan and President Langdon, was of interest. Sullivan was firmly federalist. He was quoted in January as saying "that although he did not doubt New Hampshire, singly considered, might have found a better Constitution for themselves, yet when the whole of the thirteen States were considered; that it was to unite them, jarring in interests, in politics and prejudices, he was bold to say, it was one of the best systems of government ever devised; and all the objections which have been raised against it are no more than what might be brought against any form of government whatever." [42] When he made this emphatic declaration, the State Convention to debate the Constitution had not met, and when it did meet in February, it adjourned till June, 1788, to see how the other States would act. President Langdon, who had been one of the two delegates to Philadelphia (Nicholas Gilman the other), was also rated a supporter of the Constitution. But his opinions gave a larger place to State Rights—a dozen years later he had become an ardent Jeffersonian—and men suspicious of the Federal instrument would be more likely to vote for him. The elections were held in March, and an unusual number attended the polls.

[42] Portsmouth dispatch in Pa. *Journal,* Jan. 2, 1788.

Concord went overwhelmingly for Langdon. He was soon known to have an overwhelming plurality, but it was long doubtful whether he would attain a majority. Finally, at a late date in June, the Legislature ascertained that Langdon had received 4421 votes, Sullivan 3664, and scattering candidates 753.[43] If three men had changed their votes against Langdon, the election would have gone to the Legislature.

Before the news that Langdon was again President had reached Philadelphia and Richmond, the question of ratification also had been decided. The Convention met on June 17, and finding that eight States had acceded to the Constitution, it could hardly hesitate longer. After four days of debate, approval was voted by a small majority.

Meanwhile, the outlook for ratification in Rhode Island seemed hopeless. It was true that the meeting of the Constitutional Convention, and the failure of the Legislature to send delegates, were the means of showing again that the commercial leaders were almost unanimously for a stronger Union. They asserted their federalism in the press. General Varnum sent a letter to the Constitutional Convention in which he declared that the measures of the Legislature grossly misrepresented the State:

> They are equally reprobated and abhorred by gentlemen of the learned professions, by the whole mercantile body, and by most of the respectable farmers and mechanics. The majority of the administration is composed of a licentious number of men, destitute of education, and many of them void of principle. From anarchy and confusion they derive their temporary consequence; and this they endeavor to prolong by debauching the minds of the common people, whose attention is wholly devoted to the abolition of debts, public and private. With them are associated the disaffected of every description, particularly those who were unfriendly during the war. Their paper-money system, founded on oppression and fraud, they are determined to support at every hazard and . . . they trample upon the most sacred obligations.[44]

The commercial and professional groups owned most of the State's wealth, but their antagonists were far too numerous for them. There was no ground for optimism in Varnum's statement. Rhode Island was reaping the harvest inevitable from her lack of schools, the distinct cleavage between her small body of educated townspeople and her large body of ignorant laborers and farmers, and her failure to nip the paper money folly in the bud. Madison in distant Virginia perceived that she would offer one of the stubbornest obstacles to complete acceptance of the Constitution.

[43] Pa. *Journal*, July 2, 1788; N. Y. *Journal*, June 26.
[44] Text in Updike, "R. I. Bar," 300; Cf. Bates, "R. I. and the Formation of the Union."

With brave promptness the friends of the Constitution, who were also the sound-money followers of Bradford and Varnum, began a newspaper battle for it. When the Legislature met in October, 1787, the debate was led for them by representatives of the chief towns—Marchant and Champlin of Newport, Arnold and Bowen of Providence, and Bradford of Bristol; while the chief opposition speakers were from rural districts like Joslin, Charlestown, and East Greenwich. The anti-federalists saw that they could best prevent ratification by preventing a special Convention, for as they said, in a Convention the artful lawyers might talk over the opponents. Their plan was to arrange for a direct vote upon the Constitution in the towns, and after some delay they carried it, 43 to 15 in the lower house. The day set for this referendum was March 24, 1788. Indignant that discussion by thoughtful leaders and a deliberate decision by them had thus been frustrated, the federalists showed their resentment by staying away from the polls. In Providence not one vote was cast for the Constitution, and in Newport only one; in the whole State the result was 2708 against and 237 for, though fully 6000 men were eligible to vote. This month, it may be noted, the State finished the "payment" of its debt in its depreciated paper, and thus lightened the tax burden.[45]

For two years after the disastrous referendum the "country party" maintained its bitter resistance to the Constitution; for eighteen months it maintained its refusal to modify the iniquitous paper-money measures. During the spring and summer of 1788 the news of the last needed ratifications came in, till finally only North Carolina and Rhode Island were hesitating. Yet the autumn session of the Legislature failed to call a Convention, and in December a renewed effort for one failed. In March, 1789, when the Federal Government went into operation, still another attempt proved fruitless. Worst of all, when the elections for the Legislature were held that spring, it was found that the country party had again decisively triumphed, though the federalists had gained strength. In their jubilation the majority took an insolent step. Since no one knew when in old Colonial days, it had been the immemorial privilege of the Assemblymen for each town to nominate the justices of the peace for their own community. Now a country member proposed a list of "country party" justices for Providence, and the Providence repre-

45 Bates, 164.

sentatives had to sit in helpless rage and see it approved; while another country member played the same trick upon Newport.[46]

But when the regular fall meeting of the Legislature came, the country party exhibited less confidence. Even North Carolina was now on the point of ratifying the Constitution, and did ratify in November. Little Rhode Island was out in the cold, an object of scorn to her neighbors, and her people began to feel the position a bleak one. Thirty towns and a few hundred square miles were too small a territory to set up as an independent nation. As for the paper money, the bills had long since begun passing at twelve to one, and it was useless to affirm that business could be done upon any other basis.[47] Dishonest debtors were still dogging and cheating a few creditors, and the scandal of this legalized robbery was plain to the very children. The adjoining States had with Puritan anger placed the Rhode Islanders, as regarded the collection of debts within their borders, in the position of outlaws. A pirate had as much chance of getting a sum of money through the Hartford courts as a merchant of Newport. The Legislature in September so far recognized the hard facts of the financial situation as to suspend the tender act, saving a last handful of men of property from the clutches of debtors. At the next session it repealed the tender legislation, and recognized fifteen to one as the scale of depreciation (October, 1789).[48] These steps led up to an equally important move affecting the Constitution: in January, 1790, a bill summoning a Convention passed, though only after Governor Collins's intervention in its behalf. It came to nothing, for the Convention failed to ratify, but it showed that the tide had turned.

With the surrender of the country party to the inevitable now near, the election of the spring of 1790 was a curiously mixed affair. For three years the two factions had hated each other intensely, but the hatred had burnt itself out, and from the isolation of the State was born a sense of the need for compromise and peace. Disgusted with Governor Collins because he had supported the Convention, the anti-federalists tried first to nominate Deputy-Governor Owen instead,

---

[46] Newport correspondence in N. Y. *Advertiser,* May 20, 1789.
[47] So the town meeting of Providence had said in its spring instructions to its legislator, which declared: "Viewing as we do a further continuance of the law, making the paper bills a tender in payment of specie contracts at par, in the form and manner as now established, to be abominably wicked and unjust, we do again instruct you, as we have done repeatedly before, to exert your influence . . . to obtain a repeal or alteration. . . ." S. Ca. *Gazette,* April 29, 1789.
[48] Providence *Gazette,* Oct. 24, 1789.

and when Owen refused, took Arthur Fenner of Providence, a scion of one of the most respected families in New England. Fenner was regarded as hostile to the Constitution, but very mildly so, and some even believed him a lukewarm friend to ratification. The federalists, who held their nominating convention on the same day, named the same two men to head their ticket, but offered candidates of their own for the attorney-generalship and a half-dozen assistantships. This ticket they called the "Coalition or Federal Prox." The anti-federalists were generally successful, electing their special candidates, but the maneuver of the federalists in endorsing Fenner greatly lessened the strife of the two parties. In May, immediately after the election, another Convention voted to ratify the Constitution, by the narrow majority of two.

IV. NEW ENGLAND POLITICS AFTER 1788

The year 1789 found the political currents in all New England profoundly affected not only by the new Federal Government but by the marked prosperity which set in after 1787. Below the surface, the foundations for this prosperity were being laid even in the black years 1785-6. The ravages of the war were then being steadily repaired, debts were being liquidated, the American marine was regaining the seas, and markets were being found for American products. Everywhere in New England this economic rebound assisted the federalist sentiment, for federalism found its chief strength among the prosperous classes. In Connecticut, Governor Huntington continued until 1796 to preside over a population which was from the first patriotically eager to support the Constitution. One citizen wrote after ratification that he would never vote for any candidate who had opposed it, "for they fight against God." Many of the objections to the Constitution had been ridiculous, and Simeon Baldwin, a lawyer of New Haven, satirized them by suggesting as fit amendments that the fees of all officers, including doorkeepers of Congress, should be regulated by those of the State officers of Connecticut, and that Congress should be required to reject all petitions for Revolutionary pensions without reading them.

In New Hampshire the strongest public men were drawn into Federal office, the long rivalry of Langdon and Sullivan for the chief magistracy thus being ended. In the fall of 1788 Langdon was elected Senator by the Legislature, and in the following spring he resigned the Presidency of the State to take his place in Congress. For the year 1789 Sullivan had a clear field for the Presidency, distancing a few such opponents as John Pickering. But he also soon accepted Federal office—a district judgeship—and gave place to Josiah Bartlett, a federalist who was not only chosen President year after year, but was elected the first Governor under the new Constitution of 1794.

In Massachusetts, narrow as had been the margin between victory and defeat for the Constitution, the federalists at once and rapidly grew in strength. The eastern section, with its large population devoted to commerce, was in the main thoroughly federalist in feeling, while in the west, now more prosperous, a reaction against the Shays folly was evident. Elbridge Gerry, by nature and education a hater of federalism, and one of the Northern leaders in the fight against the Constitution, was embittered by this growing sentiment. He wrote a friend in 1788: "The vigilant enemies of free government have been long in the execution of their plans to hunt down all who remain attached to Revolution principles. They have attacked us in detail, and have deprived . . . Mr. S. Adams and myself, in a great measure, of that public confidence to which a faithful attachment to the public interest entitles us; and they are now aiming to throw Mr. Hancock out of the saddle, who, with all his foibles, is yet attached to the Whig cause." He complained that the federalists were trying to identify themselves with the brains and property of Massachusetts, and to create an impression that any anti-federalist was of the rabble poor, and forfeited "all title to the respect of a gentleman." He was right as to the concerted attack upon Hancock for his instinctive adherence to the anti-federalist side, but wrong if he feared that the gouty leader could be easily displaced. Hancock, while accepting the Constitution, did not wish the State government which he headed to be more eclipsed by the power and glory of the Federal Government than was unavoidable. He was still a thorough democrat in principles. But Massachusetts voters saw no reason why their Governor had to be a strict federalist; they applauded his plans for economy in State affairs and his long record of service even while they grew in liking for the new national system.

In the election of 1788 the two chief State parties united in supporting Hancock, who received an overwhelming vote—17,841 ballots in a total of 22,157.[49] In considerable part it was a "delivered" vote. Everyone knew that the federalist and conservative leaders, in return for Hancock's support in the ratifying convention, had intimated their willingness to sustain him for the Governorship and later for high Federal office.[50] But the two parties did hotly contest the Lieutenant-Governorship. Cushing, who was awaiting his ninth reëlection, had just died. The federalist vote was divided between two patriots who had never been decently rewarded for their services to America—Samuel Adams, who had fired New England to fighting temper, and Benjamin Lincoln, who had fought a hopeless fight at Charleston, taken Cornwallis's sword at Yorktown, and suppressed Shays's Rebellion. Most anti-federalists supported James Warren, whose Revolutionary record had been much more modest. No one received a majority, though Lincoln came very near doing so, with Adams in second place. The House sent the names of these two ageing leaders to the Senate, which elected Lincoln. Both chambers were now warmly federalist, and the choice pleased the State.[51]

The election of 1789 was more spirited. Bowdoin again entered the lists against Hancock, and Stephen Higginson, his old Achilles, made the *Centinel* ring with attacks upon the Governor. He recalled how Hancock's wealth rather than his native ability had first lifted him to prominence. He taunted him with having been unduly slow to embrace the patriot cause against the Crown. He revived the old charge: "At one period, and that a distressed one, too, nothing was heard of from Mr. Hancock but balls, routs, and all the various fascinating pleasures of European courts." [52] Hancock's inattention to State business, he asserted, had doubled the length of the legislative sessions in his first five years, thus costing the State £10,000 or more. His correspondence with other Governors and Congress had been so slender that the Legislature knew more about British than American affairs in that period; while his appointments

---

[49] Result given in Mass. *Centinel*, April 4, 1789.
[50] In November, 1788, the two chambers in Massachusetts quarreled violently over the choice of a United States Senator to be colleague to Caleb Strong. The House wanted to name Dr. Charles Jarvis; the Senate wished to select either Azor Orne, or Tristram Dalton. By persistence the Senate carried its point, and Dalton became Senator. Boston dispatch to Pa. *Journal*, Dec. 10, 1788.
[51] For the peculiar Yankee quarrel over a question of salary—whether the Lieutenant-Governor should continue to hold the command of the Castle, in Boston Harbor, a well-paid sinecure—see Amory's "Sullivan," I, 242 ff.: *Independent Chronicle*, Jan. 15, 1789. Hancock wanted it abolished, and thus incurred the increased hostility of Lincoln's friends.
[52] Mass. *Centinel*, Feb. 25, 1789; see also Feb. 18, Feb. 28, March 4, etc.

had been made for political reasons only. "Laco" also charged that the Governor's resignation in 1785 had been a maneuver to restore his waning popularity, and that he had hoped to "make a merit of continuing in office." Finally, he accused Hancock of selling his support of the Constitution in 1788 to the highest bidders. The Governor's friends, called the Club of the Stone House, shared in the abuse directed against him.

But such attacks were ably answered by James Sullivan and others; and the election was humiliating to Bowdoin. In Boston he had 569 votes against 1265 for Hancock, and in the State as a whole he received only 3457 votes, or about half the total given him in 1787.[53] With Bowdoin, Lieutenant-Governor Lincoln also went down in defeat. A notable feature of the preliminaries to the campaign had been the full reconciliation of Hancock with Samuel Adams, who was now made Lieutenant-Governor in Lincoln's place. The two old patriots had begun meeting each other on a cordial social footing again in 1787, when they finally stood together in accepting the Constitution with reservations; and they steadily drifted together politically. The public was for the most part delighted in seeing the names of the leaders of the Revolution in Massachusetts joined on one ticket. Lincoln had been so popular that the Federalists had entertained a firm expectation of his election, and his failure to run well was a severe blow. In Boston he received only 617 votes against 1219 for Adams.

Thereafter Hancock was reëlected Governor annually, without any real opposition, till his death. In 1790 Bowdoin withdrew from the canvass, and was given but 1884 votes. Along with Hancock, Samuel Adams was four times reëlected Lieutenant-Governor, and when Hancock died on October 8, 1793, Adams succeeded him. Stately, vain, Hancock in these last years had been called "a handsome figurehead for the ship of state," and his failing health, though he was younger than Washington, made it impossible for him to show much executive energy. He had been keenly disappointed in his ambition for higher office, having failed in the first Presidential election

[53] There was no disorder. The Boston dispatch to the Pa. *Packet*, April 21, 1789, said: "If the public papers proclaimed ruthless and implacable hostility in the course of our late electioneering speculations, we have the more reason to congratulate the friends of America on the exemplary good humor which appeared on the floor of the (Faneuil) hall, in the moment of the contest. Scarcely an angry word was heard, and the victor and the vanquished have each their title to the warmest encomiums; the former, for suppressing every emotion which could indicate the insolence of success; and the latter, for the manly patience with which they have borne their disappointment." See also *Amer. Museum*, V, 415.

to obtain a single vote for even the Vice-Presidency, and both he and Samuel Adams took much pleasure in an attitude of stern loyalty to State sovereignty. There was a considerable popular acquiescence in this, for of all the States Massachusetts had most developed and was most proud of efficient local and State government.

An interesting parallel can be traced between political events in New York and in Pennsylvania from 1776 to 1790. It is true that in New York there existed general unanimity on constitutional questions, and there was only one Governor; while Pennsylvanians quarreled constantly over their Constitution and in this period had a half dozen Presidents. But in both States all political differences had for a time to be sunk to deal with British invaders. In both occurred a deplorably extreme vendetta against loyalists and neutrals. This bitter persecution began in Pennsylvania as soon as the chief city was evacuated in 1778, and in New York reached its height soon after the British took ship from the chief city in 1783. The reaction also occurred first in Pennsylvania, where Dickinson, with other mild leaders, gained control of the State in the fall of 1782. It was not till the beginning of 1784 in New York that the champion of moderation, Hamilton, fully opened his campaign. In both States the party chiefly responsible for Tory-baiting, the Constitutionalists in Pennsylvania and the Clintonians in New York, furnished most of the recruits for the party which opposed strengthening the government of the Confederation. In both, the fight for a stronger union had been well begun by 1785.

I. The Active War Period in New York

The roster of New York's second Provincial Congress, which was driven from town to town by the British advance during the summer and fall of 1775, includes all but a few of the names prominent in State politics for the next twenty years. Mention has been made of John Jay, Gouverneur Morris, and Robert R. Livingston, the youthful trio who wrote almost all the Constitution. There was also George Clinton, who nearly a decade before had begun to champion the patriot cause in the Assembly, and had lately gone to the Continental Congress. John Morin Scott, aristocrat and radical, had come up from his mansion on the outskirts of New York city. There was Philip Schuyler, representative of a patrician Dutch family which owned enormous tracts near Albany, who for his varied experience in the Seven Years' War had been named one of the four Continental major-generals, and who would have led the expedition against Quebec had he not been crippled by the gout. Three representatives each of the wealthy Yates and Van Cortland families were present, the most prominent of the former being Robert Yates, an esteemed Albany lawyer. William Duer, a young man who had been on the Committee of Safety, hailed—like Clinton—from the newer regions of the State. He had been in India; he had helped Clive defeat Dupleix, and now drew his sword with men who had helped Wolfe defeat Montcalm. A few men only do we miss. Hamilton was not there, but at the head of the artillery company he had organized; Aaron Burr, with his usual impetuosity, had tossed aside his lawbooks at Litchfield, Conn., to share the attack upon Quebec; Robert Troup, one of Jay's protégés, was a lieutenant in the army; and Egbert Benson had not yet become prominent.

Hot political contests began early in New York, and from the first struggle sprang the man who was to hold the leadership in State affairs during his generation. George Clinton is so bold and picturesque a figure that it is strange the fame of his nephew De Witt Clinton has overshadowed him. A descendant of a gentle English family, whose head had abandoned his estates in a flight to Ireland when the Puritans defeated the Cavaliers, and which had later migrated to America, he had been born in the up-Colony hamlet of Little Britain. Study was interrupted by the Seven Years' War, and at sixteen he served aboard a privateer at sea. Finding a sailor's life distasteful, he joined his father's regiment, and at eighteen fought as a lieutenant in the expedition which took Fort Frontenac. In his later twenties, having been admitted to the bar and found a practice in Ulster County, he was sent to the Assembly, and seized the opportunity to lead the minority opposition to British aggression. Without the profound intellect of Jay, without the family dignity of Gouverneur Morris, without the riches of John Morin Scott or the magnetism of Hamilton, he had qualities of daring, decision, and imperiousness which made him an irresistible political leader.[1]

[1] Gouverneur Morris, "Oration in Honor of George Clinton," 1812; Prime's "Clinton"; Clinton Papers, Vol. I.

Clinton's very vices were those of a born party general. He was occasionally rash. He had a tendency to domineer—his political enemy, Hamilton, truly said that he was distinguished for his firmness of will, and that it sometimes became sheer obstinacy.[2] His self interest sometimes swayed him from the path of strict rectitude; Hamilton again truly remarked that from his earliest years he had borne a reputation for artfulness and cunning. He had the virtues of quick generosity and engaging human kindliness, mingling readily with cartmen and farmers, rich merchants, or cultivated professional men, and turning a warm side to the most diverse characters. Not an eloquent speaker, he still had a fluent and ingratiating tongue. In short, he could create popularity, hold it, and use it dexterously. His career was built largely upon the sterling record he made as a patriot in the early Revolutionary days. He fought hard, made his subordinates fight hard, and was exceedingly harsh to cowards, failures, and Tories. Men gave him greater credit than Schuyler for the self-assertion of the patriot group in the Legislature in 1770-75; and he was so energetic that at one time in 1776 he was in the Continental Congress, the Provincial Congress, and head of a brigade.

Immediately after the adjournment of the Constitutional Convention in May, 1777, the Council of Safety ordered the election of State officers. The prominence of Clinton and Schuyler in the patriot agitation, and their military rank, made them the inevitable candidates for Governor. Some, however, thought that the service and ability of Jay should, despite his excessive modesty, be rewarded with the Governorship, and some declared for John Morin Scott. Scott's ability as a lawyer was unquestioned; both John Adams and the Tory historian Jones state that he was an unusually ready speaker and a jovial, attractive man in company; and he had made heavy sacrifices for the cause. In New York city he was respected by both his brother aristocrats and the people at large, but he was little known elsewhere, and could not have been elected. As for Jay, he protested that he did not want the office, and asked his supporters to vote for Schuyler for Governor and Clinton as Lieutenant-Governor. There was a distinct feeling among men of wealth and family that "Clinton's family and connections do not entitle him to so distinguished a preëminence," as Schuyler—whose own relationship with

---

[2] Hamilton's "Works," I, 539 ff. Hamilton praised the administration of Clinton during the war, with some reservations, but says that after the war it was negative or mischievous.

the Van Rensselaers, Van Cortlandts, and other Dutch landed gentry gave him an advantage—wrote when the election was over. Even some men who had not a trace of snobbery shared this belief. Four or five families, one of the Livingstons tells us, could almost control the wealth of the State, and it was thought politic to conciliate the class to which they belonged. But Clinton, as Schuyler admitted, "played his cards better than was expected." [3] Few men could speak to him without liking him for his open, energetic, democratic ways, while few could know Schuyler without deploring a certain brusqueness and arrogance in that worthy general.

In those perilous times there could be no thought of electioneering. Clinton was charged with the defence of the lower Hudson, and from his Highland strongholds was watching Sir Henry Clinton's British forces like an eagle; Schuyler was in the north, preparing to meet Burgoyne. The two hostile armies threatened to crush New York State as in a vice. The general expectation was that Schuyler would win the election, and for years it was declared that Clinton obtained his victory only because the ballots of the militia under his immediate command and influence turned the scale in his favor. At any rate, when the Council of Safety counted the votes, it was found that Clinton had been elected both Governor and Lieutenant-Governor by a considerable plurality, Orange County and other southern districts not yet in British hands having gone heavily for him. Jay's disappointment was keen, but Schuyler admitted that the new Governor was able, brave, and patriotic, and Washington wrote the State authorities that the choice was excellent.

Clinton was inaugurated at Kingston on July 30, 1777, in his Continental uniform, standing atop the barrel from which the State Constitution had been promulgated three months previous. Within two months thereafter, Sir Henry Clinton had pushed up the Hudson, stormed or flanked the Highland posts, and putting Governor Clinton and the Legislature to flight, had burned Kingston to ashes.

This was an augury of the immediate future difficulties of the State government. Till after Burgoyne's surrender, Clinton's duties were almost exclusively military, and they continued to be largely so throughout the Revolution. He acted as commander-in-chief of the militia, with the rank of brigadier-general, and held the same rank in the Continental army; he executed the defensive and offensive measures approved by the Legislature; and he took charge of the State's policy towards the loyalists, who were more openly hostile in New York than elsewhere in the North. In October, 1777, he fought at Fort Montgomery until to escape he had to leap down precipitous rocks. In 1780 he commanded the forces sent to check Sir John Johnson, the Tories, and the Indians in the Mohawk Valley, and made a successful stand. During the three years 1777-79 there was only one party in the State, and Clinton, fighting it as he would fight a frigate, commanded its unanimous confidence and support. Hamilton admitted later that "Mr. Clinton's zeal and activity in forwarding the Revolution were unquestionably conspicuous." But the circumstances of the time, with New York city in the grip of the British, and the constant possibility that he would have to take his militia into the field, forced him to share governmental responsibilities with others. Egbert Benson, who had studied law under John Morin Scott, became Attorney-General in 1777, and was Clinton's most prominent adviser.[4]

II. The Active War Period in Pennsylvania

In unhappy contrast with the initial harmony in New York was the party turmoil which rent Pennsylvania. We have seen how the first threat of British invasion could not force an artificial unity, and how the stern demand of the Continental Congress finally sent one faction, the opponents of the Franklin-Cannon-Bryan Constitution, sulking into retirement. Dickinson, its principal leader, had been defeated in national politics by John Adams, whom he hated; he had been defeated in State politics by Matlack and Roberdeau, whom he despised. He had been humiliated when he turned to military ambitions; for while he was at the head of his regiment in New Jersey in the summer of 1776, and as colonel of the first battalion was the ranking officer of all the Pennsylvania militia, his enemies had nominated two brigadier generals over his head. But Dickinson's bitterness when he saw the new State government become operative early in March, 1777, was as nothing beside that of many conservatives—the wealthy merchants of Philadelphia, the

[4] The introduction to Egbert Benson's "Vindication of the Captors of Major Andre" states that while in the Assembly, Benson "drafted almost every important bill" that passed it; and Hamilton ("Works," I, 545) gives him equal credit. Benson's political path parted from Clinton's, and he warmly supported the Constitution.

great landholders in adjoining counties, the thousands everywhere in the southeastern part of the State with a deep sentimental attachment to the ancient order.[5] In no other large State did the British invasion find so many friendly or neutral inhabitants, and many dated their Toryism from the moment the radicals slew the Charter.

The selection of Wharton as the first President of Pennsylvania was a tactful step. A man of moderate views, he would be more acceptable to the disgruntled Quakers and Episcopalians than Reed or Mifflin, whose abilities were greater; a member of a wealthy Philadelphia family, he carried reassurance that "levelling" had not triumphed everywhere. He had helped draft the Constitution, but he frankly acknowledged its defects. "There are many faults which I hope one day to see removed," he wrote St. Clair, "but it is true that if the government should at this time be overset, it would be attended with the worst consequences." . . . This spirit, this eagerness for harmony, pervaded his whole Administration, and he spent much effort in trying to restrain precipitate Assemblymen.[6] Restraint was much needed. The richest, most powerful State in the Union, Pennsylvania should have been the leading commonwealth in prosecuting the war; but in spite of Wharton and Reed, in spite of the spasm produced by the British irruption, internal quarrels palsied her strength. It was the radical measures of the Legislature which did most to keep old animosities alive and growing. The radicals were naturally irritated when they saw many prominent men, like Galloway, Chew, and William Allen, go over to the British, and a great part of the population of Philadelphia insist on a timid neutrality; nevertheless, they should have acted more moderately.

Throughout the spring and summer of 1777, debate upon the revision of the Constitution continued with acrimony, a minority in the Assembly attacking the instrument, a majority defending it.[7] Public antagonisms had been increased by the Test Act, which made anyone who refused to take an oath or affirmation of allegiance to

---

[5] See John Adams, "Works," III, 44, 45, for the anger of the Pennsylvania conservatives at him. "Millions of curses were poured out upon me for these exertions. . . ." Duer wrote R. R. Livingston from Philadelphia in May, 1777, that "a languor of the most alarming nature prevails in this city and State—principally (from what I can judge) to be imputed to the dispute about their government." He added that Philadelphia had attracted the disaffected and the monopolisers of all the States. Livingston MSS., New York Public Library.

[6] See *Pa. Mag. of Hist. and Biog.*, VI, 91 ff., for a sketch of Thos. Wharton, Jr., by Anne H. Wharton. Minutes of the Supreme Executive Council, XI, *passim*.

[7] "The party who believe the government to be a good one is too inconsiderable to be noticed," says a pamphlet of 1777, "Observations on the Present Government of Pennsylvania."

the new government incapable of holding office or voting. The mere form of the oath was repugnant to Quakers and to some German religious sects. Many believed it was just a barefaced attempt to keep a large part of the intelligent, wealthy population away from the polls, and a number of Wharton's friends warned him of the public wrath with which it was received. A York correspondent wrote Bryan soon after its passage that it had weakened the patriot cause: "Not one fourth part of the inhabitants hath, or will take it." [8] Where effective—for in some places it was not—the law threw all oath-takers into one dominant group, and into another and hostile body all the non-jurors, splitting the community in two. Another law, passed in June, 1777, sprang from the view that the inflow of refugee Tories from other States had reached alarming proportions, and that safeguards must be erected against the spread of discontent and disloyalty. The safeguard adopted worked a keen hardship upon non-jurors, for any adult travelling outside his own county or city without a certificate had to take the oath or go to jail.[9]

For the central purpose of such enactments a certain plea of necessity could be made. Throughout 1777 the military outlook was gloomy, and the reverses which culminated in the capture of Philadelphia impressed patriots with a sense of desperation. They felt a clear demarcation between friend and foe necessary; they knew that Philadelphia Tories were referring to 1777 as the year with the three gallows, and discussing who should hang. But the Legislature should have gauged better the psychology of large parts of the population. Not merely were thousands embittered by the precipitation with which the breach with the past was widened in 1776 and 1777. Other thousands, ready enough to give mild support to the patriot leaders, were offended to learn that the radicals suspected them of being traitors. Below this feeling lay the sulkiness of large groups of wealthy Quakers and Episcopalians who had controlled the Colony, and now had to take orders from the upstarts. A typical expression of this spleen may be found in the grumbling of James Allen (son of the rich and respected Chief Justice of Colonial days)

[8] He added: "It rendering the number of electors to be so very few, Government will be thereby weakened, and all offices being thrown amongst a party through the conduct of the disaffected, doth greatly alarm some well-wishers, both to the general cause and to [the Constitutionalist] Government"; Pa. Archives, Series I, Vol. V, 661-63. A resident of Lancaster similarly wrote Wharton: "You will hear a loud cry against this tyrannical oath, that it was intended for naught but to hinder substantial, good disposed people to elect or be elected; depriving them of the rights of freemen, etc."; *idem,* 427.
[9] Pa. Archives, Series I, Vol. V, 479-80.

early in 1777. He burst out [10] against the oppression of Pennsylvania: "It may be divided into two classes of men, viz., those that plunder and those that are plundered. No justice has been administered, no crimes punished for nine months. All power is in the hands of the associators, who are under no subordination to their officers."

The Quakers were exhorted by their Yearly Meeting in 1776 to hold to the quiet path of neutrality. By the fall of 1777, about one-fifth of the adult male Quakers in Philadelphia had joined the American army or taken patriot offices, a few had joined the British, and the great majority had refused to be drawn into the war. Their attitude aroused a considerable popular outcry, and they were naturally accused of cloaking Toryism with assumed impartiality. A forged paper of disloyal character purporting to come from their "Spanktown Yearly Meeting"—there was no such meeting—was circulated the summer of 1777, and for the moment added to the feeling against them.[11]

The more radical wing of Congress during 1777, as in the crisis of 1776, lent support to the radical wing in Pennsylvania. In one harsh step Congress led the way. When the British army approached Philadelphia, Congress thought it dangerous to allow the loyalists at large, and on Aug. 28, 1777, passed a resolve warning the Pennsylvania executive that various Quakers hated the American cause, and recommending that ten men, including John Pemberton, author of "a certain seditious" publication, be seized. Under cover of this resolution, the Supreme Executive Council made out a list of suspects, and arrested some two-score men, for the most part grave, harmless Quakers. Their houses were rifled and desks opened, and though a number were paroled upon their promise to support the Revolution, about half of them were jailed, without the slightest trial, in the Freemasons' Lodge. Here they were asked to sign a written promise of good conduct, but declined, on the ground that they had never had even a hearing, nor been convicted of any offence. Your proceedings, they defiantly told the Executive Council, "have been so arbitrary that words are wanting to express our sense of them." Meanwhile, the British advance had rolled up to the

---

[10] Pa. *Mag. Hist. and Biog.*, IX, 176-96.
[11] R. H. Lee wrote Patrick Henry (Philadelphia, Sept. 8, 1777) of the Quakers that many showed "a uniform, fixed enmity to American measures . . ."; Henry, "Henry," III, 92-94.

gates of the city, and the twenty "mischievous people," as R. H. Lee called them, were hurried into wagons and off to Virginia.[12]

These exiles were substantial citizens, of unquestionable integrity and in many instances of high social station. It was well to secure such men as John Penn, the last Proprietor, who was sent to Fredericksburg, and Benjamin Chew, the recent Chief Justice, but the case was different with the majority who were hurried off south. Among them were Thomas Wharton, first cousin of President Wharton, Edward Pennington, John Pemberton, and Thomas Gilpin, the chief author of an account of the episode called "The Exiles in Virginia." No less than nine of them had signed the non-importation agreement of 1765. Men much more dangerous were left unmolested. The banished suspects were never fully informed of the charge against them; they were packed off without time to make provision for their families; and though they were allowed to select their own boarding houses, they suffered many physical and mental hardships in Virginia. They were not released until April, 1778. This rough act of Congress and the Council, though it had a good effect on some genuine malcontents, aroused bitter feeling, and made the reception of the British more cordial.

For months after the autumn of 1777 the Executive Council was occupied with the military perils of the time. On September 25 Howe and his troops were in Germantown, and on the next day Cornwallis marched down the main street of Philadelphia with 3000 men. Congress had fled to Lancaster, and the Executive Council and Legislature hurried to the same village. The terms of the Assemblymen had almost expired, and it was necessary to take emergency measures to provide a continuing administration. Hence the Legislature appointed the Executive Council, with nine others—the most notable of the added men were Rittenhouse and Cannon—a new Council of Safety, of which only seven men were required to make a quorum. This new dictatorship entered upon its work under Wharton, and in its meetings those of the Executive Council as such were briefly

---

[12] For this affair of the Virginia exiles see Sharpless, "Hist. of the Quaker Govt. in Pa.," II, Ch. 7; Pa. *Mag. Hist. and Biog.*, VI, 91 ff.; Pa. Archives, Series I, Vol. VI, 111 ff., 509-10; contemporary press. Light is thrown on the severity of Congress by a letter of E. Rutledge to R. R. Livingston, Philadelphia, Oct. 21, 1776. "We have great reason to think that the Quakers have determined to refuse our Continental Currency. If they make a point of it, we must make a point of hanging them, which will bring on a storm that will take the wisdom of all our wise men to direct. If the troops under Washington should be defeated, I am satisfied this country will be on the brink of Revolt—Nothing will prevent it, but a great deal more firmness than we at present profess." Livingston MSS., N. Y. Public Library.

merged. It passed out of existence on December 6, a Legislature whose members had been newly elected from most counties having then convened. Meanwhile, Wharton had been reëlected President of the Council.[13] The parts of the State which did not share in the legislative elections because they were in British hands were the most conservative parts, so that the radical Constitutionalists were stronger than ever. For the second time since independence the British menace had given them a fairly free hand.

While in the winter of 1777-78 Washington was suffering at Valley Forge, and Wharton's Council was doing all it could to safeguard the State, the Legislature acted with increasing severity toward loyalists. Howe's capture of the metropolis was followed by the impaneling of five men to seize the personal estates of any people of that county who joined the royal army.[14] Soon after, the existing law dealing with traitors in general terms was followed by one for the attainder of a list of specified persons. If they did not surrender before April 20, 1778, they were to be adjudged guilty of high treason and their property forfeited to the State. Among the men thus proscribed were Joseph Galloway, who had fled to the British while they were still in New York; the influential Allen brothers, John and William, the former a one-time member of the Philadelphia committee of inspection and observation; and Jacob Duché, recently chaplain to Congress, who suddenly turned Tory and wrote Washington a letter advising him to yield. Measures to punish the Quakers and other conservatives for any refusal to accept State or Continental paper money were carried out more drastically than ever. So were the laws imposing extra taxes upon Quakers in lieu of military service. Naturally, none of the restrictions which the patriots could impose upon the lukewarm were relaxed now that the British were ensconced in the chief market town, the surrounding farmers were ready to supply them with food and unwilling to supply Washington, and the danger of a general submission to the Crown seemed great. President Wharton died in office at this strained, critical time (May 23, 1778).

A brief interregnum followed, until December 1, 1778, during which time the capable George Bryan was Acting-President of the Council. Its beginning was cheered by the British evacuation of

[13] For the government of Pennsylvania in this troubled time, see Minutes Supreme Executive Council of Pa., XI, 325-26 ff.
[14] Pa. Archives, Series I, Vol. VI, 13-14.

Philadelphia, and the return of the State officials and the Continental Congress. The appearance of Philadelphia after the invasion did not soften the temper of the radicals. The enemy had left the neatest, cleanest, best-built town in America shockingly dirty and unkempt, had destroyed public and private buildings, had cut down trees and fences, and had filled the streets and gutters with obstructions. In the outskirts and in Germantown were the marks of battle. Most of the fine old country seats surrounding the city had been destroyed—the British had fired seventeen in one day. New-piled mounds in Washington Square showed where the bodies of Continental soldiers, maltreated and starved in their prison by the brutal jailer Cunningham, had been roughly buried.

The British had governed the city in such a manner as to bring to the surface all the elements of Toryism, and these elements had to be dealt with severely. Some 3000 Tories had sailed down the Delaware with the British fleet, but many remained. There were people in the city who had given the enemy willing assistance, and yet seemed to expect the returning patriots to grasp them cordially by the hand. The cry for vengeance was irresistible. Ill-educated and excitable, the mob or "the Furious Whigs," as some observers called the extremists, insisted upon satisfying their resentment. The leaders were for the most part moderate men, but they were unable to restrain their followers. Bryan, who had served on the Supreme Executive Council since its formation, was both farsighted and kindly,[15] while most of the other prominent patriots of the day—McKean, Cadwallader, Ross, Dr. Rush—were opposed to the intemperate demand that the loyalists expiate every sin. Reed, though an enlightened man, went much farther with the majority. An association was at once formed, the signers of which bound themselves to bring all Tories to justice, and Reed's was the one prominent name in the body.

The executive officers, thus spurred, duly took steps to bring notorious loyalists to trial, and in August, the Assembly employed Reed as an extra counsel to help the Attorney-General prosecute them. During the previous year a Philadelphian named Molesworth, who had confessed to being a spy for Lord Howe, had been executed, and the same sentence was now demanded for others. At the fall session of the Supreme Court in Philadelphia forty-five bills for

[15] Konkle's "Bryan," Ch. 12.

treason were sent to the grand jury, and twenty-three cases were tried. Only two men, Roberts and Carlisle, were convicted.[16]

Carlisle was a city carpenter, and Roberts owned a mill about ten miles from the centre of Philadelphia. Both were Quakers, and both had borne excellent reputations before the Revolution. The evidence of their guilt was inconclusive. It was proved before Chief Justice McKean that Carlisle had accepted a commission to keep one of the city gates and issue passes through the lines, and that he had also acted as collector of excise. His chief motive, however, many witnesses testified, was not mercenary or disloyal, but simply a desire to alleviate distress among his neighbors. Roberts had lived sixty years under the British flag, and his sympathies were strongly British. When his Quaker friends were exiled to Virginia, his indignation was such that he visited Howe and offered to lead troops to intercept the convoy. Finding that his neighbors meditated violence against him, he took refuge within the British lines, where he served the British forces by leading parties of foragers out among the farms, and by supplying provisions and enlisted men. His friends said that his worst offences were involuntary. When sentence of death had been passed on the men, a flood of petitions for mercy poured in. They were signed by the best citizens of the town, nearly 400 for Carlisle and nearly 1000 for Roberts. One came from a number of ministers; one for each man was signed by jurymen who had tried them; and letters from persons of prominence were added.

It would have been politic as well as humane to commute the sentences to imprisonment, but the excitement of the "mob" prevented. On November 4, 1778, the men were executed—driven to the common near the city with ropes round their necks, and their coffins before them. There would have been more executions had the moderate leaders not so guided affairs as to satisfy the radicals by the confiscation of loyalist estates, and the publication of long lists of traitor's names.

Meanwhile, marked changes were occurring in the complexion of the Legislature. Throughout the British invasion and the reprisals of the radicals, the Anti-Constitutionalists had remained strong. James Wilson states that their opposition in the Assembly of 1777 had become formidable. The Constitutionalists had been forced to go outside the State to find a fit man for Attorney-General—Jona-

[16] For the hanging of Roberts and Carlisle, see Pa. Archives, Series I, Vol. VII, 21 ff.; Sharpless, "Quaker Govt. in Pa.," II, Ch. 8; contemporary press.

than D. Sergeant, of New Jersey—and a fit Chief Justice—McKean, of Delaware. Especially in Bedford and Philadelphia Counties was discontent with the new Constitution deep-rooted. The Constitutionalists knew this, and just before the annual Assembly elections in October, 1778, they made it known by a legislative resolution that they were willing to take the sense of the voters as to a new Constitutional Convention. As a result, they obtained a decided majority, and even elected one popular Assemblyman from Philadelphia by a vote of four to one. The Anti-Constitutionalists were "satisfied with the late resolve of the Assembly," one of them wrote; "they had no further ends to gratify by putting in persons opposed to the Constitution." The continued disfranchisement of men as loyalists helped the Constitutionalists, and there were other factors. "Since the year 1777," declared a newspaper essayist, "the Constitution has gained *many* proselytes. Some have been seduced by offices; others have been misled by their attachment to the principles of the men who were in power . . .; lastly, some have yielded to the government through necessity, believing no attempts to improve it would ever be made."

Nevertheless, the Anti-Constitutionalists had an Assembly minority strong enough to act as a check upon the Constitutionalists during 1779. Robert Morris, Mifflin, Thomas Smith, and Clymer were all chosen as Anti-Constitutionalists for that year. When the Assembly first met early in November, 1778, many objected to the oath prescribed by the Constitution, declaring it would interfere with their efforts to obtain a new one, and they were allowed to annex a reservation to it. By the close of the month, 23 Anti-Constitutionalists were sitting in a Legislature of 59 members. The Constitutionalists felt the need for a strong leadership to hold their opponents in check.

The first long Administration in the State's history, Joseph Reed's, began the winter of 1778, when (December 1) by a vote all but unanimous, he was elected President of the Council, while George Bryan was again made Vice-President.[17] This choice gave the first place in Pennsylvania to a man of attractive personality, high talents, and unusually good education, but impetuous and lacking in force of will. Educated at Princeton, trained to the law under Richard Stockton and later at the Middle Temple in London, Reed had prac-

[17] Minutes Supreme Executive Council, XI, 632-34.

tised before the Revolution first in his native Trenton and then in Philadelphia. John Adams's Diary does not omit a brief characterization—"a very sensible and accomplished lawyer, of an amiable disposition, soft, tender, friendly"—which suggests his mercurial temper. Washington made him an aide, and learned in the first two years of the war to esteem him highly; Irving tells us that "Reed in fact became, in a little time, the intimate companion of his thoughts, his bosom counsellor." Later he was made Adjutant-General, in which position he addressed a foolish letter to Gen. Charles Lee, intimating a wish that Lee might supersede Washington, the reply to which accidentally fell into Washington's hands and occasioned for a time a marked coolness between the two. A reconciliation followed, however, and Washington again treated him with every mark of friendship and confidence. Reed served in the Continental Congress, and gave valuable counsel upon military affairs. A British attempt to bribe him in 1778 elicited a reply which increased his popularity: "I am not worth purchasing, but such as I am, the King of England is not great enough to do it."

Reed's Administration lasted the three years allowed by the Constitution, for he was reëlected in 1779 by a vote not recorded, and in 1780 by a vote of 59 to 1. It saw Pennsylvania emerge from war into peace, but it was a period of internal storm, and it witnessed a number of rash acts by the Constitutionalist majority which threw them into discredit.

During 1779 Pennsylvania was kept in a turmoil by the discontent of the ill-paid State troops, the social ferment arising from the high price of goods and the depreciation of money, and the continued quarrels of the Constitutionalists and Anti-Constitutionalists. So shabby was the treatment of the Pennsylvania Line by the State government that early in the year the officers as well as men were almost mutinous. New York not only paid her soldiers better, but made special provision for their families, while Virginia was at this time distributing six months' extra pay as a recompense for the declining value of paper money. General St. Clair, commanding the Pennsylvania Line, wrote on March 5 that the pay of the troops "will scarcely purchase anything." St. Clair did not believe that any of the Anti-Constitutionalists (of whom he was one) were making an attempt to draw the officers into the party quarrels of the State, but other men did. General Nathanael Greene, then Quartermaster-

General in the Continental Army, issued a special order warning his subordinates to keep their skirts clear of the struggle between Constitutionalists and Anti-Constitutionalists. The Assembly at once agreed upon measures which partly satisfied the soldiery; nevertheless, a large part of the Pennsylvania Line remained sulky.[18]

By this time the public outcry against speculation and high prices was an old one, but it grew steadily. In November, 1777, Congress had passed a resolution urging the Legislature to take steps against "the spirit of sharping and extortion, and the rapid rise of every commodity." Among Washington's letters to State officers all over the North we find similar exhortations. Nowhere did men suffer more hardship from the rapid rise in prices, and the fall in the value of paper bills, than in Pennsylvania. On January 19, 1779, the Executive Council issued a proclamation threatening men guilty of "forestalling" and "engrossing" with the heaviest penalties.

Sensible men knew that Congress could afford some relief simply by stopping its emissions of Continental bills. But Congress at the moment was much occupied in discussing the charges against Silas Deane; and the defenders of the unpopular Deane, as it happened, were chiefly Anti-Constitutionalists, Robert Morris being among them. During May the public's economic distress reached such a crisis that observers feared an outbreak would result, and on the 26th President Reed, the Speaker of the Assembly, and others presented a memorandum to Congress, asking for some national measure of alleviation. The only response was an address to the people from a Congressional committee, explaining that nothing could be done save what the States would do, and that while the States had already exerted themselves, "we are not yet convinced there has been as much diligence used in detecting and reforming abuses as there has been in committing or complaining of them." This address accused greedy men of monopolizing the necessaries of life, and petty officials of conniving with them. It thus further inflamed the public temper.

On May 27, 1779, a large meeting in the State House yard, presided over by that firebrand of independence, Daniel Roberdeau,

[18] The editor of the St. Clair Papers (I, 488) asserts that most of the Continental soldiers in the Pennsylvania Line were opposed to the Pennsylvania Constitution, but supported it and the State government during the war; St. Clair was of course vigorously against the Constitution, but felt like Edward Biddle, who said: "Our present government is lamentably defective, and has in it the seeds of the worst of tyrannies, but to attempt by force to overturn it, would in my judgment be wicked, as well as impolitic."

resolved to organize two committees. One was to ascertain the prices of articles at periods in the past progressively remote, and then to decree, by progressive future steps, a reduction of rates to these old levels. The other was to investigate alleged abuses in trade and punish them. The meeting declared that profiteering had become intolerable, that large stores of goods had been secreted, and that the time had come for a forcible lowering of commodity prices. Whenever the laws did not suffice, it said, the people should take the regulatory power into their own hands. The whole plan of price reduction was beguilingly simple. Rates were to be held at the level of May 1 until the beginning of July, and then to be reduced to the level of April 1; in August to be brought down to the level of March 1; and so on, turning the wheel backwards.

Of course this scheme failed utterly. Equally of course, in attempting to put it into operation the two committees set up an intolerable tyranny. Leading commercial men were hauled before these committee tribunals, and treated with a total disregard for their rights. Special severity was shown toward Robert Morris, the inquisitors even attempting to interfere with his exertions in supplying D'Estaing's fleet with flour. As the anger on both sides grew, the soldiery took a hand. On June 28, a militia company of artillerymen, just returned from Fort Mifflin, met in the city, praised the committee on prices, and adopted an address declaring that the wicked speculators and monopolists required "something more poignant and striking to bring them to reason." "We have arms and know the use of them," stated the artillerymen; "if by reason of the obstinacy and perseverance of individuals, your committee find themselves inadequate to the task, our drum shall beat to arms."

Meanwhile, on February 27, 1779, the action which the Assembly had taken the previous autumn for submitting the question of a new Constitutional Convention to the people had been rescinded, 47 to 7. The seven legislators who had voted on the Anti-Constitutionalist side included Robert Morris, George Clymer, Thomas Mifflin, and Thomas Smith. The newspapers teemed with articles for and against this rescinding, which was really a gross breach of faith, and feeling between the two parties continued warm all spring. When on March 24 the formation of a "Republican Society" to take the Anti-Constitutional side was announced in an able paper attributed to James Wilson, the writer laid many of the evils of the time to the want of a sound State government, and called on the opponents of the Constitution to redouble their efforts. Among the 82 signers of this paper were, with the men just named, Ross, Cadwallader, Edward Biddle, and Francis Hopkinson. A reply at once appeared, written by Timothy Matlack, which showed none of Wilson's ability, but great acrimony.

When in July Robert Morris explained in a public statement his grievances against the volunteer committees upon prices, he accused them of being in large part actuated, in their spiteful attitude, by their political differences with him. Yet, he added, "my sole object was to obtain such a Constitution as would in my opinion answer the ends of good government." The conservative Anti-Constitutionalists included a majority of the Philadelphians of wealth, and rich merchants were conspicuous in their ranks. Since it was in the rich merchants that the radicals saw the chief obstacle to lower prices, some hotheads leaped to the conclusion that the Anti-Constitutionalists, in revenge for their political failure, were grinding the faces of the poor. Men like Morris, maintained abusive fellows, were indifferent to the public welfare so long as they could extort high profits from the hard-working poor through the derangement of business. Such reckless agitators fomented a popular belief that if the Constitution were revised by the conservatives, the government would fall into the hands of a privileged few. The old feeling against the Tories and neutrals was still powerful, as an amendment stiffening the Test Act in September, 1779, showed; and it and the sentiment against profiteers assisted each other.

A thunder-clap was needed to clear the sultry air, and it came in the "Fort Wilson Riot" of October 4, 1779. The success with which several able lawyers, especially James Wilson, had been defending merchants like Morris in the courts against the price-fixing committeemen had led the radicals to tack up placards all over town denouncing Wilson, Morris, and others as undesirable citizens. On the date named a meeting of the militia was called at Byrne's Tavern at the edge of the city common, and reports spread that its object was to lay plans for arresting the alleged monopolists and forestallers, and for imprisoning or expelling them. A feeling that trouble was imminent seized the city. In alarm, some thirty conservatives, who feared that the meeting would result in an attack upon Wilson, went to that lawyer's house, among them General Mifflin, General William

Thomson, and Colonel Campbell, a one-armed veteran, with other officers and respected citizens.

The house was a large mansion at the corner of Third and Walnut Streets, at no great distance from the City Tavern. While the inmates prepared for defense, word of the imminent clash was sent to President Reed, then confined by an illness. The expected happened. A mixed mob of militiamen and loafers, armed with muskets and bayonets, early in the afternoon moved up Walnut Street, beating drums, yelling, dragging two field-pieces, and carrying a number of prisoners. When it arrived before Wilson's house it surged toward the gate; Colonel Campbell from an upper window ordered it to march past; and shots were exchanged. In the midst of the firing, Mifflin stepped upon the balcony and tried to address the assailants, the window sash being broken by bullets beside him. Scattered for a moment by the fusillade from the house, the mob then turned back and with hammers and bars burst in at one entrance. The fire was renewed, and they again fled. At this moment President Reed, his garments half buttoned and hair flying, galloped up with members of the City Horse hard behind him.

Profound excitement was aroused throughout the city when the news of the outbreak spread. One man had been killed on each side. Arrests were immediately made, some of the mob going to jail, and several defenders of "Fort Wilson" giving heavy bail. The next day President Reed called a meeting in the Supreme Court Room, where both sides aired their grievances and where he made an address that did much to tranquilize public feeling. There were no prosecutions, and by the time the Assembly had passed an act of general pardon it was agreed that Philadelphia was in a better frame of mind than since 1775. The radicals made no more lawless moves, and the attempt at arbitrary price-fixing was abandoned with considerable chagrin.

The session of 1779-80 was remarkable for the emergence of George Bryan as the dominating leader of the Legislature. Bryan, now the most powerful figure in State politics, had served three years as Councilor, or as long as the Constitution allowed. Constitutionalists who had lamented the lack of brains in their party wished his guidance in the Assembly, and he was elected in October, 1779; he had an easy majority to do his bidding, for a vigorous campaign had been waged, and the Anti-Constitutionalist strength fell to a low ebb.[19] With him was chosen Charles Wilson Peale, one of the most versatile of Pennsylvanians—famous as a painter, expert as a silversmith, a soldier who had fought at Trenton and Germantown, and soon to be the proprietor of a museum of natural history.

As the Constitutionalist Society had hoped, Bryan showed splendid parliamentary leadership, and could almost say, *"L'état, c'est moi."* At the autumn session thirty-six committees were appointed, of which he received the chairmanship of twenty-five of the most important, and Peale of five others. Much valuable work was accomplished by the Legislature. Bryan was proudest of the act for gradually abolishing slavery, a noble measure which greatly pleased the Quakers. Another far-reaching enactment was that creating the High Court of Errors and Appeals. An overdue law, surprisingly liberal in terms, stripped the Proprietary family of most of its property, including the quit-rents. Penn was allowed to keep only what could in an intimate sense be called his possessions, as his manors; but he was allowed a compensation of £130,000 sterling, a sum paid soon after the Revolution. The most controversial of the laws passed was that depriving the College of its charter.[20]

The College, till recently the chief pride of all Philadelphia, had taken its origin in a pamphlet which Franklin published in 1749, called "Proposals Relating to the Education of Youth in Pennsylvania." A union of private generosity with an appropriation by the Common Council resulted in the opening of an academy in January, 1751, offering three courses—English, Latin, and mathematical—the success of which was so immediate and full that application was made for a charter. When this was granted in 1753, the trustees determined to enlarge the course of instruction, and elected William Smith to be teacher of logic, rhetoric, and moral and natural philosophy. Dr. Smith, of Aberdeen University, at this time not thirty,

[19] An effort by Bryan to dominate legislation early in 1779, as Vice-President and controller of the Council, had met an immovable obstacle in the Assembly's jealousy of the Executive body. On Feb. 5, 1779, the Council voted a formal message to the Assembly calling attention to the Congressional requisition for $15,000,000, to profiteering, to the Virginia and Connecticut land questions, the need for a Court of Errors, the problem of the proprietary estates, the abolition of slavery, and so on. For abolition, Bryan had drafted a law, which he submitted. For nearly a century the Assembly had struggled to prevent the Council from assuming any legislative functions when it was acting as an Executive Council, the Governor being absent; that ingrown fear was now all-powerful, even against a trusted leader like Bryan. The Constitutionalists in the Assembly meant to have no second chamber. They at once voted a resolution that all bills must originate "in this house." "Minutes of Supreme Executive Council," XI; Konkle's "Bryan," 168 ff.

[20] For the resounding quarrel over the College, see Proceedings Relative to the Convs. of 1776 and 1790, pp. 118 ff.; Provost Smith's petition, Pa. *Gazette,* June 14, 1783; histories of Univ. of Pa.

was a man of energy and learning, and he made the courses so much broader and more thorough that the academy was soon giving instruction equal to Harvard's or Yale's. Having been placed upon a collegiate basis, it deserved, in Smith's opinion, corresponding honors and privileges, application was made for a new charter, and in 1755 one was obtained which gave the power of conferring degrees. The first commencement of the college was held in 1757. Thenceforth it prospered under Provost Smith and its twenty-four trustees, becoming famous throughout the Colonies and drawing students from the South and even the West Indies. In 1765 the teaching of medicine began, and after that date—Dr. Rush joining the faculty in 1769—Philadelphia was the medical center of British North America.

To the Pennsylvania radicals many of the men prominent in college affairs were totally obnoxious. Provost Smith was a Scotchman by birth, and a protégé of the Proprietary family, which had been the chief patron of the College. He and nearly all the active trustees were members of the Church of England. A few, as Richard Penn and William Allen, were Tories. Others belonged to the reactionary faction of the Whigs, struggling to delay independence and to defeat the new State Constitution; among them were Robert Morris, Francis Hopkinson, Alexander Wilcocks, Edward Biddle, John Cadwalader, and James Wilson, a list including three "signers" and one general. When the Test Act was passed, a small group of trustees delayed taking the oath of allegiance, and when the British occupied Philadelphia, three voluntarily remained in the city and accepted British protection. The great mass of Whigs after the evacuation were ready to help attack almost any object labeled "Tory." As a matter of fact, the College was politically harmless, and educationally it was healthy and capable of doing excellent work if well supported; the State should have protected it. But with party feeling so high, it was hard to forget that the Anti-Constitutionalists controlled it.

The repeal of the charter (November 27, 1779) was arbitrary, though not without legal steps or stated reasons. The Assembly had first appointed a committee to investigate the Trustees' conduct and general college affairs, and Dr. Smith prepared a long defensive paper, while counsel was allowed to appear for the College; but there was no judicial hearing, as there should have been. One reason assigned for voiding the Charter was that the trustees, through gaps in their ranks, "had lost their activity and were incapable of exercising their essential functions." Another was that the Charter required each trustee to swear allegiance to King George. A third was that the trustees, by a by-law of 1764, had restricted the original wide foundation. Finally, it was declared that the State was bound to keep public education in patriotic hands.

All these reasons were empty, and a more dishonorable act than the repeal of the charter has seldom stained Pennsylvania's record. As for the alleged impotence of the trustees, twenty-one of them had duly taken the oath required by the patriot government; twelve trustees, the Provost, and all professors had taken it before the summer of 1778. Three—Penn, Allen, and one Dr. Bond—did not take it, and as if to admit its insincerity in this charge, the Assembly appointed Dr. Bond a trustee of the new university it at once erected. In 1764 a fear had grown up that the College might become sectarian, and to combat it, the trustees bound themselves by a by-law to see that the original plan "be not narrowed," and that no man should be given special favors because he was a communicant or non-communicant of the Anglican Church. In asserting that this by-law restricted the foundation, the Assemblymen were flatly contradicting the facts. The Anti-Constitutionalists justly wrote later: "We . . . consider this suggestion but as the specious coloring to a scene of predetermined injustice, which the actors therein could not safely trust to a court of law." To attack the charter because it had required an oath of allegiance to the King was ridiculous, for all such oaths became invalid and a dead letter when independence was declared.

Moreover, the abrogation of the charter was unconstitutional, for at the instance of Franklin and Provost Smith, a clause had been written into the Constitution declaring that all societies of religion and learning should remain endowed with the same rights and privileges they possessed under the laws of the Province. It was, again, in defiance of all principles of law to hold a corporation responsible for the alleged misdeeds of trustees. Finally, whatever action was taken should have been taken by a court, not by the Assembly. In all, the Anti-Constitutionalists were warranted in asserting: "We consider this act as a blind sacrifice to party, of the rights of individuals (many of whom had eminently served the cause of this country in promoting our glorious Revolution); and as an encouraging example to future attempts against whatever may be imagined best secured and fenced by the highest legal sanctions. . . ."

The act abrogating the charter and dissolving the trustees and faculty also vested the College property in a new body called "The Trustees of the University of the State of Pennsylvania," and directed that certain confiscated estates be used for the new University. But the fresh institution failed to prosper. The disruption of the College destroyed for the time being one of the two most democratic and liberal-spirited schools in America, and the damage it wrought was not fully repaired until after the Civil War. When in 1789 another Legislature passed an act restoring the College to its charter and property, the preamble stated that the law of a decade previous had been "repugnant to justice, a violation of the Constitution of this Commonwealth, and dangerous in its precedents to all incorporated bodies."

The year 1780 and the first half of 1781 were a critical season for America, and nowhere in the North were they more anxious than in Pennsylvania. On June 1, 1780, the Legislature at Washington's request vested Reed and his Council with power to declare martial law in any legislative recess, and soon afterwards under his extraordinary authority Reed began the seizure of provisions for the army. On New Year's day, 1781, occurred the mutiny of the Pennsylvania Line at Morristown, N. J., arising from the indefinite length of the enlistments and the lack of food, clothing, and pay. One of Reed's best services to the nation was his prompt action to quell it, when Sir Henry Clinton's emissaries were already among the rebellious men. A few months later the financial straits of Pennsylvania gave birth to a measure upon which the Constitutionalists and Anti-Constitutionalists again sharply divided. The State paper had enormously depreciated, as the Legislature in 1780 recognized when it established a scale of real values in settling with the troops. Yet the Assembly in the spring of 1781 took steps to issue an additional £800,000, of which only £100,000 was safeguarded with any security; and at the same time severely penalized any failure to accept the money at its face value. Not only did the Anti-Constitutionalists, led by Mifflin and Morris, oppose this financial panacea of Bryan's, but one of them, supposedly Morris, wrote an objection to the emission which was quite unanswerable. The event fulfilled his prophecies of disaster. The new bills soon became worthless. As early as June, 1781, President Reed had to write General Greene that the paper "has fairly run its race."

A turn of the political tide in Pennsylvania became evident during the last year of the war. To friends and foe alike, the Constitution-alist Legislature seemed incompetent. It never does anything for the troops, complained General William Irvine in the spring of 1781; it orders the Pennsylvania Line to march and fight, but "are forges, tents, wagons, etc., ever thought of? No." Even Reed admitted that the legislators, intimidated by a fear of popular grumbling, dared attempt nothing vigorous, and that higher taxes, more effi-ciently collected, were an almost imperative need. The Constitu-tionalists had reached their greatest strength in 1779, and it slowly waned. They still held their place partly by virtue of the stringent Test Act, against which in 1781 more and more vociferous protests were made by the disfranchised Quakers and others.[21] Growing bold, the moderates filled the press with stories of the waste of public money, of graft in the disposal of confiscated estates, and of the purchase of city lots with funds stolen from the treasury. When the news of Cornwallis's surrender reached Philadelphia, the radical "mob" suddenly revived in a brief and final ebullition; but in the calm wrought by peace the conservatives prepared to bring Dickin-son back and take over the government.

III. Post-War Rancors in New York

Against the background of Pennsylvania's measures of persecution and repression we can advantageously study the same movement of radical vengefulness against the Tories and neutrals in New York. It had a longer life in New York, which was much longer in British control. As the Pennsylvania loyalists had been most numerous in and around Philadelphia, so in the other Province they were strongest in and near New York city. When the metropolis was delivered into American hands, the rural legislators and the rough, ill-educated city mechanics and clerks were hard to control.

[21] Materials for this reaction had constantly been at hand. Note, for example, the explanation of "Candid" in the Pa. *Packet*, Jan. 21, 1779, of the fact that in the recent Assembly elections the Constitutionalists had four times as many votes as the Anti-Constitutionalists, which he showed to be quite misleading. Ill-feeling over the Test Act was strikingly expressed in the fall of 1778. In Chester County the authori-ties excluded non-jurors from the polls. They outnumbered the jurors and promptly held an election of their own. Livingston MSS., W. W. Livingston to R. R. Living-ston, Philadelphia, Nov. 20, 1778.

The Continental Congress on June 24, 1776, had declared that the property of all adherents to the Crown would be liable to confiscation. Some weeks later the New York Provincial Convention defined allegiance, citizenship, and treason, thus paving the way for the systematic sequestration of Tory property. In March, 1777, commissioners of sequestration were appointed for most of the counties not in British possession, and the seizure of personal possessions began; while many Tories who refused to take the oath of allegiance were expelled or sent within the British lines. All this was proper, but a demand arose for more rigor. In March, 1778, the Council of Revision vetoed an unduly harsh bill to disfranchise all those who, since independence, had denied the authority of the revolutionary government, or had aided the British. The outcry at once redoubled, and in Dutchess County alone 450 citizens signed a petition for drastic measures. In October, 1779, just after the "Fort Wilson Riot" in Pennsylvania, there became law the Confiscation Act, drawn up by John Morin Scott and James Jay. It declared a list of 59 persons, including the former Governors, Tryon and Dunmore, and seven Councilors of the Crown régime, guilty of felony, and their estates forfeit.

Its worst feature, however, was that it empowered the courts, on oath of one credible person, to indict any man as a Tory, and if he failed to appear after four weeks' advertisement, to pronounce his property confiscated. Many a loyal though cautious patriot could thus be robbed of his all by malicious or prejudiced neighbors. The partial motive of greed behind this legislation was obvious, for two-thirds of the property of New York, including the Crown lands, was owned by British or Tory interests. A strong minority in the Legislature opposed the Act, but Governor Clinton supported it. Thereafter the patriots were clearly divided into moderate and extremist factions, the latter the more numerous and sustained by the State Administration, the former possessing the more brains and character.

Alexander Hamilton early appeared as the chief advocate of leniency and justice. The young soldier returned north after the capture of Yorktown, found a home with his father-in-law, General Schuyler, during the winter, took in May, 1782, the petty office of a receiver of Continental taxes, and after a few months of law study, was admitted to the bar. Perhaps in some faint degree because he had begun his career with a tendency towards the Tory side, which a visit to Boston had corrected, in larger degree because his tastes were fundamentally conservative and aristocratic, and in chief part because he knew the importance of respecting our international obligations, and loved fairness, Hamilton became an energetic opponent of Clinton's policy towards the Tories.

The cessation of fighting did not cool the anger of the extremists, which rose higher at the legislative session of 1783 than ever before. Had Clinton had his way, he would have disfranchised every man who had willingly stayed in New York or any other place occupied by the British. He would "rather roast in hell to all eternity than . . . show mercy to a damned Tory," he roughly declared during the war. The Legislature, says a contemporary, was composed of men "fervent, bigoted in their political zeal, and warm in their resentment; their feelings were vindictive; their intemperance and indiscretion banished property and subjects." [22] Early in 1783, this resentful body passed the famous Trespass Act. Its object was to enable any citizen whose property had been occupied or entered upon by British authority during the British occupation to bring suit for damages against such occupant or entrants. Scarce a building owned by patriots on Manhattan Island but had been taken over by new occupants under Sir Harry Clinton, or had British troops quartered in it, or been injured, and all who could fabricate a case prepared to demand high damages or arrears of rent. The evacuation of the King's army from the city took place in November, 1783. Till this time the Confiscation Act had not been given much effect, but now in the metropolis and elsewhere the authorities began to apply it so ruthlessly that between it and the Confiscation Act, it was certain that many Loyalists would be stripped of their last penny.

Simultaneously the most savage deeds were committed by lawless men. When the British evacuated the country north of New York city, "the Skinners" of Westchester followed and, seizing stray Loyalists, brutally misused them; some were beaten to death, while others had the tendons of arms or legs cut and were lamed for life. All the moderate leaders were shocked by such deeds and by the Trespass Act. Jay wrote from Paris denouncing them. The zealots who wish to involve all Tories and neutrals "in indiscriminate punishment and ruin certainly carry the matter too far," he said.

[22] N. Y. *Journal*, April 10, 1788.

"It would be an instance of unnecessary rigor and unmanly revenge without a parallel except in the annals of religious rage in times of bigotry and blindness. . . . Victory and peace should in my opinion be followed by clemency, moderation, and benevolence, and we should be careful not to sully the glory of the Revolution by licentiousness and cruelty." The legislative elections were coming on, and Schuyler accused many noisy politicians of preaching revenge as a means of getting office. But there seemed little hope for such humane counsels. The troops who marched down the Bowery Lane into New York as the British fleet put out to sea, the joyous exiles who flocked in upon their heels, found a scene that stirred deep resentment. A large part of the town was gutted by fire, the rest was defaced and dirty, and on every hand were ruined patriots. The correspondent of the South Carolina *Gazette* wrote just after the evacuation (December 12, 1783) that the spirit of revenge and persecution was "universal." At this juncture Hamilton in his gallant way stepped forward to combat the intolerance, not with words, but with legal action.[23]

One case arising under the Trespass Act, that of Rutgers vs. Waddington, was expedited to furnish a test of the law's force, and Hamilton was announced for the defendant's side, which the attendant circumstances made peculiarly difficult. Elizabeth Rutgers was a widow, who had fled the city on the approach of General Howe, and had been rendered almost penniless. Waddington was a wealthy Tory, representing a firm of brewers into whose hands a brewhouse and malthouse on Maiden Lane, belonging to Mrs. Rutgers, had passed in 1778, and who had paid for three years a rent of £150 annually to a Commissary-General, by order of the British commander; for three additional years nothing had been paid. When the Americans took possession of New York, the brewers were glad to begin paying to Mrs. Rutger's son, as the American authorities ordered, but Mrs. Rutgers wanted arrears of rent also, and filed suit. The statutes seemed, on superficial view, to offer her a plain remedy for a plain injustice. The prosecution was conducted in the Mayor's court, which had jurisdiction, by no less able a man than Attorney-General Egbert Benson.

[23] The story of the case of Rutgers *vs.* Waddington is in some particulars essentially misstated in most histories. The account here given is based upon the legislative journals and contemporary press as well as Hamilton's "Works," and the Papers of Gov. Clinton. See also Leake's "Lamb," 296-98; and a review of the case in *Md. Gazette*, July 19, 1785.

Yet Hamilton's gifts of logic and lucid expression threw the issue into clear relief—the issue whether, after a war had been closed by a solemn treaty, the subjects of one nation could sue those of another for injuries committed while the war was in progress. The captured property of Widow Rutgers had been used according to the rules of international law, just as immovable British property captured by Americans had in innumerable instances been put to patriot uses. The peace treaty had included an adjustment of all claims for damages raised by both sides. Hamilton's brief is of interest for its bearing not only upon the immediate issue but upon the relations between the States and the national government. "The claim to damages for injuries done is in the public, who may agree for an equivalent, or release the claim without it," he said; "and, our external sovereignty existing in the Union, the property of all the citizens, in regard to foreign states, belongs to the United States." The United States had made a treaty which completely exonerated the British from further demands. "Hence to make the defendant answerable, would be a breach of the treaty of peace. It would be a breach also, of the Articles of Confederation." [24] In short, Hamilton skillfully demonstrated that the truer patriotism, the truer national sentiment, would lie in deciding for the Tory, while he above all presented an irrefutable legal argument.

Fortunately, the Mayor's Court was not so much swayed by local rancors as might have been expected; the Recorder or chief judicial officer, Richard Varick, was a man of probity and ability, who had once been Washington's private secretary. Hamilton's argument won the day. The court refused to allow the widow Rutgers any rent for the three years in which Waddington had paid it to the British authorities, holding that the Trepass Act violated the treaty, and that "no State in this Union can alter or abridge, in a single point, the federal articles or the treaty." It did not assert the right of any court to override a law of plain intent, but it did assert that when the consequences of a law had not been clearly foreseen by the Legislature, then the judges were at liberty to expound it by rule of equity, and if they liked, even to disregard it.

A storm of indignation followed this decision. An association of citizens was formed to have it reversed. At the meeting of the Legislature that autumn the Mayor's Court was summoned to appear

[24] Hamilton's "Works," IV, 408.

and explain its action, and a resolution of censure in two parts was introduced by an up-State Assemblyman. The first part declared that the court's decision was in its tendency subversive of all law and order, and led directly to anarchy and confusion, for it would put all the Legislature's enactments at the mercy of the judiciary; the second part demanded of the Council of Appointment that it name as the Mayor and Recorder such men as would uphold the law of the land. By a vote of 25 to 15 the former part was passed, but the latter was easily defeated (31 to 9).[25] Public feeling rose so high that Mayor Duane sent a statement of the case to Lord Mansfield for an opinion. Two successive Legislatures reaffirmed the Trespass Act, and loyalists continued to be mulcted under it.

But Hamilton now boldly entered upon a pamphlet war to support his position. In a letter signed "Phocion" he attacked the intolerance of the radical Clintonians, and both in it and a sequel demonstrated the impolicy as well as illegality of any repudiation of treaty obligations. Suppose Great Britain should refuse any further compliance with the treaty because of the American violations of it, he suggested. Could America renew the war? His readers knew that she could not, and that no European nation would assist the United States to regain rights forfeited by a wanton contempt of international faith. Hamilton defined the character of the true Whig, and by implication that of the opposition party which he led. "The spirit of Whiggism," he stated, "is beneficent, generous, humane, and just. These men [Clintonians] inculcate revenge, cruelty, perfidy, and persecution." He raised his voice also against the plans for arbitrarily exiling or disfranchising great masses of New Yorkers.

Hamilton's vigorous protests were needed. A special election for the State of New York had been held, by Governor Clinton's proclamation, in December, 1783, a few weeks after the evacuation of the metropolis. Naturally, the violent radicals were able to choose their legislative candidates. In at least one county, Orange, when a man unwilling to breathe fire and slaughter against all Tories stood for a seat, a mob forced him to retire. There were three parties in the States, as Robert R. Livingston says—the Tories; the mild Whigs, "who wish to suppress all violences, to soften the rigor of the laws against the loyalists, and not to banish them from . . . social intercourse"; and the violent Whigs, "who are for expelling all

[25] Assembly Journal, Oct. 27, Oct. 29, Nov. 2, 1784.

Tories from the State." The last-named had it all their own way. In New York city they chose such extremists as John Lamb, Marinus Willett, Henry Rutgers, and Isaac Sears. Many of the proscribed citizens had petitioned for permission to return to their homes, but when Gov. Clinton opened the Legislature in January, 1784, it was with a speech to steel it against such pleas. How can we accede to the request, he demanded, "while we recollect the general progress of a war which has been marked with cruelty and rapine; while we survey the ruins of this once flourishing city and its vicinity; while we sympathize with the calamities which have reduced so many of our virtuous fellow citizens to want and distress . . .?"

After formally rejecting the recommendations of Congress for moderation toward the Loyalists, the Legislature proceeded to pass three more iniquitous laws. One was to facilitate the sale of several great Tory properties, like the De Lancey and Bayard estates on Manhattan, and the Rapalje estate in what is now Brooklyn. The second, under date of May 12, 1784, disfranchised and deprived of other civil rights all who had in any way lent comfort to the British forces. Interpreted literally, it excluded from the polls two-thirds of the adult males of New York city, Richmond, and Kings; nine-tenths of those of Queens County; the great majority of those of Westchester; and one-fifth those of Suffolk.[26] Yet the Assembly passed it by a vote of more than three to one, and the Senate of nearly two to one. The Council of Revision, upon which places were held by Chief Justice Lewis Morris and Judge John Sloss Hobart, conservative men, rejected the bill. It argued that the measure retrospectively penalized "the voluntary remaining in a country overrun by the enemy," an act perfectly innocent, that it created a new court in violation of the Constitution, that it flatly violated the peace treaty, and that it was inconsistent with the public good, since in many localities it would "be difficult, in many absolutely impossible, to find men to fill the necessary offices, even for conducting elections, until a new set of inhabitants could be procured." But the bill was repassed over the Council's veto. The third bill made it impossible for attainted loyalists to reënter the State and use the privilege, promised them by the treaty, of re-purchasing their former estates. A resolution was passed calling upon all Governors to interchange lists of banished persons. Indeed,

[26] Flick, "Loyalism in New York," 163-64; cf. Jones's "Hist. N. Y.," II, 249-50.

a proposal was even made for confiscating the estates of the Society for the Propagation of the Gospel.

Hamilton's opposition to these measures made him the target of as great abuse as he suffered when in later years he attacked the excesses of the French Revolution. The first of his letters of "Phocion," early in 1784, drew a reply from one Isaac Ledyard, written over the name "Mentor." Hamilton's second letter demolished Ledyard's argument that all who remained in the British-occupied region thereby became aliens. A tradition runs that it was purposed by a knot of Ledyard's companions that each in turn should challenge Hamilton to a duel, until one was able to kill him, but that Ledyard vetoed this murderous scheme. It is at least certain that an opponent named Oswald challenged Hamilton to a duel which never occurred.

Reflecting men felt the force of Hamilton's appeals, and some hotheads were taught shame by them. The moderate Whigs were by no means ready to erase the line between those who had fought for America and those who had been indifferent or hostile, but they wished the line defined by public sentiment, not by law. Yet after all, the intolerance had to burn itself out. The fear that the Revolution might actually be undone persisted a long while. A meeting of the Sons of Liberty early in April, 1784, resolved that "in our opinion it is impossible that Whigs and Tories can ever associate, or be mingled together, or that government can be considered as completely established, while so great a number of Tories, both of wealth and influence, remain in the metropolis." They ill-naturedly added that where loyalists held positions or had established businesses, they must often exclude patriots from a livelihood—there not being room for all on this vast shaggy continent! Other radicals, in a memorial to the Senate, declared themselves shocked to find that the loyalists, by remaining in the city, had been so "impudent as to expose themselves to the resentment of their injured and incensed countrymen." [27] They could never, even in decades, be good citizens, and an alienation bill must be passed. Yet Jay was able to write Lord Lansdowne just two years later that already some disqualified Tories were sitting in the Legislature, loyalists had been restored to the practice of the law, and the obnoxious statutes were being less and less enforced. [28]

[27] See Pa. *Packet,* April 6, 1784, for the resolve; S. C. *Gazette,* March 25, 1784, for the memorial.   [28] Jay's "Works," III, 191-92.

IV. POST-WAR RANCORS IN PENNSYLVANIA

The process of reconciliation was well advanced in Pennsylvania before it was well started in New York. The former State had not been riven in two during the war; while the people, thanks to the many Quakers, Mennonites, and other peaceable sectarians, and to the responsibility taught by a better diffusion of wealth, were more open to counsels of moderation. No such knightly champion of justice appeared there as Hamilton, but an earnest leader was available in Dickinson, and he had stout aides in Morris, Mifflin, and Wilson.

A transition between the severity of Reed's Administration and the calm of Dickinson's was afforded by the brief term—less than a year—of William Moore, who had been Vice-President, and was a Constitutionalist, but of a more sober temper than most. During his tenure in 1782 the attacks of the Anti-Constitutionalists upon their steadily weakening opponents were maintained. Early in the year Dickinson returned from his long sojourn in Delaware, and was warmly welcomed. All the advantages of intellect were with him, Rush, Morris, and Wilson, for they represented the best abilities of the State; while now that Reed was busy repairing his shattered fortune by law practise, and Bryan had become a judge of the Supreme Court, the Constitutionalists were plainly ill-officered. "They have all the violence of a party, without the abilities to support it," asserted an opponent.[29] Their new leaders coming to the front, of whom the chief were John Smilie, an Irish immigrant, Wm. Findley, an immigrant from Ulster, and Robert Whitehill, born of north Irish parents in this country, were rough and ill-educated men. It was said that their legislators had drawn the laws badly; that the land office act was impracticable; that the act for settling old Treasury accounts on a scale of depreciation was unintelligible; and that most other new statutes were calculated for the profit of the lawyers. Writers like "Candor" in the spring of 1782 justifiably contrasted the evil measures of the Constitutionalists with the sound proposals of the Anti-Constitutionalists. Which party, they asked[30]——

continued the tender law in force, after the Continental money fell to 30 or 40 for one? What party excited and supported a committee with illegal and unconstitutional powers, that had well nigh produced a civil war in this State? What party paid off the Pennsylvania Line with State money, instead of specie, when it was

[29] *Freeman's Journal*, Dec. 5, 1781.
[30] *Idem*, Feb. 6, 1782.

three to one, when several of their own civil officers refused to take it, and by delaying their drafts upon the treasury received their pay in gold and silver, after the repeal of the last tender law? What party set the merchant and farmer at variance, and half ruined the trade of the city, by embargoes? . . .

But again, who instituted the Bank that kept our army from disbanding in 1780? Who protested against the tender law? Who procured the repeal of it? Whose influence opened the ports and revived the industry of the merchant and farmer, by the importation of specie among us? Who instituted the national bank?

The Constitutionalists were sure of an Assembly majority the fall of 1782, but not of a majority of the joint vote of Assembly and Council, which was necessary to elect a President. Dickinson was first chosen to the Council from Philadelphia—"the country will vote *nearly as one man in your favor*," Benjamin Rush wrote him. His only rival in the Council for the Presidency was General James Potter, an ill-educated man who had been Vice-President. Was "a brave honest soldier," asked "Cincinnatus," to be slighted for the "fugitive colonel" who had abandoned the Pennsylvania troops in 1776? Dickinson was also scored for his opposition to the Declaration, and his reluctance to accept paper money. Yet he obtained 41 votes against 32 for Potter (November 7, 1782). He and the other Anti-Constitutionalist leaders were thereby vindicated from the charge of unpatriotic conduct. Dickinson in sulky retirement on his Delaware farm presents no heroic figure, but he had shown himself ready to fight as a private in Delaware and to accept civic responsibilities there; and now he published an elaborate defense of his record during the Revolution.

Dickinson, like Reed, served three years, until the fall of 1785. Sensible men hoped that his administration would effect a rapid dissolution of war-time animosities, together with constitutional revision and liberal legislation, but the years were troubled and reforms slow. The President had little power to carry out any program. The Constitutionalists always controlled the Council, for one Councilor was chosen for each county. At first the Anti-Constitutionalists controlled the Legislature; but the opposition had a sufficient minority in 1783 and 1784 to block the measures most needed, simply by depriving the house of the quorum of two-thirds required, and the Legislature elected the fall of the latter year was heavily Constitutionalist again.

We would expect the Anti-Constitutionalists first to attack the unjust Test act, which so crippled their party.[31] Speaker George Gray estimated that the law deprived nearly one-half the freemen

[31] See such an attack, *Freeman's Journal*, Sept. 12, 1781.

of their civic rights, and the disfranchised men certainly owned more than half the taxable property. In some Pennsylvania communities, as in some of New York, the voters were not numerous enough to administer the local government. Thus in Byberry township, in Bucks County, only three men were free from disabilities. But the difficulties facing a repeal were heavy. A great petition to the Assembly in the spring of 1784 asked for abolition of the tests, and even George Bryan signed it, but nothing was done. The Legislature met again in midsummer, and found fresh petitions, including one from young Quakers and others who had reached the age of eighteen since the tests were instituted, and had religious scruples against them. As the session approached its close, and many Constitution-alists started home, the moderates mustered their greatest majority, until on September 28, 1784, they suddenly introduced a bill re-pealing the tests. The Assembly divided evenly, Speaker Grey cast his deciding vote for the bill, and in high dudgeon the opposition, nineteen in number, marched out and left the Assembly without a quorum. The session thus came to a summary end. The seceding members issued an address, recalling that the Constitution required all bills to be printed, and except upon a sudden necessity, to be held over for passage the succeeding session. This requirement had often been disregarded, but the Constitutionalists were right in adding that "no sudden necessity exists . . . ; on the contrary, in a few days a new Assembly will be convened. . . ."

The Constitutionalists objected that a repeal of the Test Act would let those who had done nothing in the Revolution enjoy its fruits, and held that so many men had opposed the war that in some counties they could elect candidates "who execrated the alliance be-tween the United States and his most Christian Majesty, and who still cherished a hope of reunion with Great Britain." They found confirmation of their fears in the talk in Philadelphia of a restora-tion of the College charter, and in the Penns' petition for a larger share of their old estates.[32] A bill for restoring the College charter and property to the former trustees was pressed just far enough in the summer of 1784 to elicit a tremendous uproar. Dr. Smith was much in evidence in the Assembly—"like a Prime Minister," his

---

[32] See *Freeman's Journal*, September 29, 1784. Apropos of the agitation over the Test Act, see an attack upon those who were "violent for the most unbounded for-bearance and moderation," in the *Freeman's Journal* of January 30, 1782. The author denies the Constitutionalist charges—the "frightful stories about the waste of public money, the embezzlement of forfeited estates, and the purchase of city lots."

enemies said. A typical newspaper attack on the College, signed "A Plebeian," recalled that the annulment of the Charter and seizure of the Proprietary's lands had been enacted on the same day in 1779, as the fruits of the same principle, adding: "It was always foreseen that they would be attacked from the same quarter. When one falls, the other must totter." The same withdrawal of the minority which defeated the Test Act revision also defeated the College trustees.

The fall election in 1784 was fought out upon the Test Act and College charter, constitutional revision receding into the background;[33] while an important part was played by the general economic depression, for which the Administration was blamed. The report of the majority of the Censors, then just issued, offered good ammunition against the Anti-Constitutionalist régime, and the radicals won so decisively that their Assembly strength was about three to one.[34] A public meeting in Bucks, typical of others elsewhere, denounced the tactics of the Anti-Constitutionalists in the former Assembly, and declared against the non-jurors.[35] When General Anthony Wayne led a new effort for a revision of the Test Act in the Legislature of 1784-85, a contemptuously adverse committee report was adopted 42 to 15.

To various disturbances of the public order during Dickinson's administration we need advert only briefly. The first was a riot by released troops of the Pennsylvania Line. These ill-paid veterans, like others in the national army, were offered furloughs in the spring of 1783, Congress wishing to dissolve the army and yet to hold large forces subject to recall if Great Britain did not sign the definitive treaty. It was impossible to pay the troops properly before they dispersed, and when members of the Pennsylvania Line at Lancaster learned this fact, their resentment broke down all dis-

[33] "Since the year 1777 the Constitution has gained *many* proselytes. Some have been seduced by offices; others have been misled by their attachment to the principles of the men who were in power. . . . Lastly, some have yielded to the Government through necessity, believing that no attempts to improve it would ever be revived." Pa. *Packet,* Feb. 2, 1779. Graydon says (Memoirs, 307-8): "To counteract the Constitutionalists, the disaffected to the Revolution were invited to fall into the Republican ranks; and there was an agreement, or at least an understanding, among the lawyers, who were generally on the Republican side, neither to practise or accept any office under the Constitution, which in that case, they would be bound, by an oath, to support. But the Constitutionalists had a Roland for their Oliver. They had prothonotaryships, attorney-generalships, chief justiceships, and what not to dispose of."

[34] Outrageous frauds were proved at the Lancaster election, which a writer in the *Freeman's Journal* (Oct. 20) sarcastically describes: "Did we not seal up the box after the close of the poll? Did we not put it into a closet, either with or without a lock, in Mr. Hubley's tavern? Did not numbers of us stay in the house with it from the most virtuous motives?"

[35] *Freeman's Journal,* Nov. 10, 1784.

cipline. Some fifty, about the middle of June, set out for Philadelphia to state their grievances to Congress. Arrived in the city, they were joined by five times as many discontented soldiers hanging about there, and all marched to the State House, where both Congress and the Executive Council were sitting. "I assure you it was a serious affair," wrote one Councillor, "for about one-half of them was drunk. They kept us about three hours, and we had no military force to suppress them." By the exertions of President Dickinson and General St. Clair, this outbreak was soon quieted, but meanwhile Congress had moved to Princeton in alarm. It showed a marked coolness for some time towards the Pennsylvania Government, which the Congressmen pronounced inefficient in coping with disorder.

The Wyoming troubles a year later illustrated the unreasonableness and selfishness of many legislators and most Councilors. When in the spring of 1784 a disastrous flood rolled down the Susquehanna and devastated the Connecticut settlement in the Wyoming Valley, President Dickinson urged the Legislature to send forward prompt relief. Instead, some members declaring that the pushing Yankees should have stayed in New England out of harm's way, the Assembly sent troops to take steps preparatory to the removal of the settlers, national arbiters having just decided that the valley belonged to Pennsylvania, not Connecticut. Guerrilla warfare ensued, and was intensified when a new force went to the scene under Colonel John Armstrong. The Pennsylvania claimants to the land improved by these industrious Connecticut folk were jubilant, and bragged in the press that the perpetual nuisance offered by this brawling crew of interlopers would be abated; while a large part of the State, including a majority of the Council, rejoiced with them. But early in July, when too ill to attend public gatherings, President Dickinson sent a warning and an appeal to the Council, pointing to the danger of open hostilities with Connecticut. On September 11 the Council of Censors also made an impressive remonstrance, lamenting the sufferings of the settlers, the opprobrium brought upon the State, the expense to the treasury, the prospect of a quarrel with a sister State, and the violation of the Articles of Confederation. Thus spurred to responsible action, the Legislature finally disavowed the injuries committed, and took steps to make reparation.

The Legislature of 1784-85, with its overwhelming Constitutionalist majority, surpassed any which had preceded it in the folly of its measures. Its chief action was the annullment of the charter of the Bank of North America. This bank, founded by Robert Morris and chartered in the spring of 1782 by the Anti-Constitutionalists, had proved of almost indispensable value to the State and nation. It had saved the Confederation's finances from ruin; in Pennsylvania it had brought specie into circulation again, and its own notes had as much value as silver. The demagogues among the Constitutionalists organized a characteristic campaign against it. They declared that it facilitated, but did not augment, circulation, and hence was enriching a small mercantile group at the expense of the many; that it was undermining public credit; that its hostility to other paper was causing a steady diminution in the circulating medium, whereas the need for more currency was a crying one; and that with its huge capital ($10,000,000) and small number of directors (twelve) it was a dangerous money machine, able to rule the State with a rod of iron. Could they have had a marked preponderance of power in 1783 or 1784 the Constitutionalists would have destroyed it. Now their opportunity—along with general economic discontent—arrived. They revoked the Bank's charter, overriding the arguments of thirteen members who drew up a paper demonstrating the value of its work, and who declared that corporations ought not to be annihilated on caprice, by a vote of 50 to 12. The bank's stock went below par, but it continued operation under a charter from Congress.[36]

A loan office was opened by the Legislature in the stead of the bank, and to issue more paper for depreciation. Two laws were then passed by a deal between representatives of the back-country settlers on the one hand and of certain city elements on the other. These were the funding measure by which Pennsylvania agreed to pay the Federal debt owed to its citizens, and a land law by which State lands were to be sold at a price, its opponents said, much below the market value. A new law regulating elections was also passed, alleged to be much in the interest of the Constitutionalists. One of its provisions, however, that abolishing plural voting, was thoroughly sound; it made it illegal for men to vote outside the township or precinct in which each resided, whereas citizens before had sometimes traveled long distances to cast a second ballot in the same election. The net effect of the bank-charter repeal, the loan office, funding, and land laws was highly disastrous to the Constitution-

[36] See minority protest against the repeal, Md. *Journal*, Oct. 11, 1785.

alists. The first measure in especial produced a reaction which, as Paine had warned his fellow radicals, overthrew the Pennsylvania Constitution and assured the ratification of the Federal Constitution.

As Dickinson's third term drew near its expiration in 1785, the eyes of Pennsylvanians turned unanimously toward Franklin as his successor. The resignation of the State's greatest son as American plenipotentiary to France was accepted by Congress March 7, 1785, and he had returned at once to Philadelphia, where he was received with every honor. In October he was unanimously elected President of the Executive Council. He also, in spite of his great age, was to serve three years, the first two with Charles Biddle as Vice-President, and the third with Peter Muhlenberg in that office. The State needed his calming hand. "It strikes me that you will find it somewhat difficult to manage the two parties in Pennsylvania," Jay wrote him. "It is much to be wished that union and harmony may be established there. . . . Unless you do it, I do not know who can." [37] Franklin's wisdom and dignity impressed everyone, and he exercised the greater control over both parties in that he agreed with the extremists of neither; his demeanor to both "was so truly oily and ingratiating," wrote Graydon, that it always remained doubtful to which he belonged. He had nominally been a Constitutionalist, holding the frame of government adopted in 1776 a good one, but the principal specific measures that he now supported were those of the Anti-Constitutionalists. In 1787 most Constitutionalists opposed the new Federal Constitution, and on that issue he was heartily with the Anti-Constitutionalists again. He had the further advantage that from the outset the two parties were so nearly balanced in the Assembly that an arbiter was acceptable.[38] "Neither is sure of carrying a point," wrote Francis Hopkinson in March, 1786. "This situation excites the orators and leading men of the House to the most vigorous exertions." Franklin's success in keeping factionalism within bounds surprised himself, though he modestly ascribed it to the innate talent of Americans for sane self-government.

[37] Jay's Works, III, 169-170.
[38] Said a correspondent of the N. Y. *Packet*, Oct. 24, 1785: ". . . but which side has a majority, this one thing is certain, that it will be so small, as not to form a quorum without the other. Thus will be prevented the decision of any of the momentous questions peculiarly obnoxious to either party. It has been said, that if the Constitutionalists had been able to command the same decided majority they had last year, they would impose such a tax on bank stock, as must necessarily involve a dissolution of the company; and, on the other hand, that the Republicans, if sufficiently strong, would proceed to a repeal, or at least a revisal, of the test laws, and also a repeal of the lately enacted law for annulling the charter of the bank."

V. Federalist Efforts in New York

While the years leading to the struggle over the Federal Constitution were thus less angry than before in Pennsylvania, political passions in New York showed no diminution. The fight over strengthening the national government opened there in 1784. Its inception is found in the legislative debates upon the great post-Revolutionary measures for adding to the powers of Congress.

Indeed, the contest in New York over the Congressional regulation of commerce, and the Congressional collection of an impost revenue, was as fierce as in any part of the Union. Clinton, like Hancock on ticklish questions, was loath to commit himself, but though he refrained from expressing open hostility to an extension of the national authority over ocean trade, his real sentiments were well known. He insisted upon State control of the great shipping business which centered in New York. Both of these questions were squarely posed in 1784, when Congress, stung by the British discriminations against our commerce, in April requested authority for the general regulation of trade. The New York Legislature had already taken a hostile attitude. It had just levied a tonnage tax and passed its first tariff act, which that fall was followed by a second. Under these statutes, one custom house was established at the port of New York (the radical General John Lamb was the first collector) and another at Sag Harbor, Long Island. Many articles were made dutiable: a sixpence was levied on every gallon of madeira, three-pence on other wines, two-pence on rum and other spirits, and graded amounts on vehicles, ironware, watches, certain agricultural implements, and so on. A double duty was to be paid upon all imports owned in part or wholly by British subjects, except when these vessels had been built within New York State.[39]

Schuyler in the Senate and Duer in the Assembly fought these measures. The second, more comprehensive, and more offensive was vetoed by the Council of Revision, which pointed out that every attempt by one State to regulate trade without the concurrence of the others must do only harm; that the discriminating duties must lead to countervailing duties; and that State legislation on the subject would interfere with the nation's commercial treaties. These facts were evident, but the bill was nevertheless repassed over the

[39] Laws of New York, 1777-1801, I, 585, 599 ff.; II, 7 ff.; see "Memorial History of New York City," III, 32-33.

veto. Thereupon Hamilton brought into play all possible instrumentalities for influencing the Legislature to grant Congress a general control over ocean commerce. It was easy for him to appeal to those in the lower part of the State who saw British selfishness crippling their trade—a mass-meeting was held in New York city, which adopted resolutions; circulars were prepared, and correspondence was opened with other States; and under the Chamber of Commerce, headed by John Alsop, the most influential merchants sent a memorial to the Legislature (March 14, 1785). As a result, at the end of the spring session in 1785 the Legislature passed an act authorizing Congress for fifteen years to prohibit the import or export of goods in vessels of nations "not in the treaty" with us, and to prevent the subjects of such nations from importing any goods except from their own countries. A proviso was attached, however, forbidding the United States to collect any duties within New York except by legislative consent.

This proviso brought up the related question of the impost amendment to the Articles of Confederation. In 1783 Congress had asked the States to permit it to levy and maintain a system of custom-house duties for twenty-five years, to pay the public debt. But a measure meeting the wishes of Congress failed in the Legislature in 1784, and when renewed in 1785, it was defeated in the Senate, which was under Clinton's close influence. The revenues collected at the port of New York were so large that legislators and executive officers were more and more unwilling to part with them. In further evidence of its anti-federalism, the Legislature in March changed the delegation in Congress. Of the four able New Yorkers sitting there, Jay, Walter Livingston, Lansing, and Egbert Benson, the first two were decidedly favorable to a strong national government, and when Jay was called from the floor (December 21, 1784) to be Secretary for Foreign Affairs to Congress, the Clintonians seized the opportunity to reinforce Lansing by appointing three new men, of whom John Haring and Melancthon Smith held State Rights views, and John Lawrence alone was a federalist.

Thinking men in New York explicitly recognized the broader implications of the impost question: that it was part of the battle to decide between a strong or a weak federal government. This recognition was shown in the newspaper skirmishing that accompanied the April elections for the Legislature in 1785. "Consideration" urged that the States should give Congress not only full commercial authority, but "all powers necessary for an active and firm Continental government." On the opposite side, "Rough Hewer, Jr." (Abraham Yates) declared that all history had demonstrated that republicanism could flourish only in small States, and that a powerful Continental Legislature would devour the rights of the thirteen commonwealths. If you put the sword and the purse into the same hand, however that hand might be constituted, ran the hackneyed argument of "Sydney," you render it absolute; "When this is compassed, adieu to Liberty!" Hamilton, looking beyond the impost amendment to a Constitutional Convention, knew that the struggle for the two could be waged together.

By various devices hostile factions got their candidates into the field. In the middle of April a meeting of the wealthier citizens, at Cape's Tavern, with Isaac Roosevelt in the chair, nominated James Duane for the Senate, and nine others for the Assembly, while a week later a committee of mechanics named Thomas Tredwell for the Senate, and its own list of nine for Assemblymen. Tredwell and eight of the mechanics' nominees for Assemblymen were chosen.[40] But Hamilton had played his cards so that the federalists could count on three trusty agents out of the Assembly delegation. One of these three, Robert Troup, relates that:

Hamilton had no idea that the Legislature could be prevailed upon to adopt the system as recommended by Congress, neither had he any partiality for a commercial convention, otherwise than as a stepping stone to a general convention to form a general Constitution. In pursuance of his plan, the late Mr. Duer, the late Colonel Malcolm, and myself, were sent to the State Legislature as part of the city delegation, and we were to make every possible effort to accomplish Hamilton's objects. Duer was a man of commanding eloquence. He went to the Legislature and pressed *totis viribus* the grant of the impost agreeably to the requisition of Congress. We failed in obtaining it. We bent all our strength in the appointment of commissioners to attend the commercial convention, in which we were successful. The commissioners were instructed to report their proceedings to the next Legislature. Hamilton was appointed one of them. Thus it was, that he was the principal agent to turn the State to a course of policy that saved our country from incalculable mischiefs. . . .

At the spring session in 1786, Malcolm, Troup, Duer, and other Assemblymen, with Schuyler in the Senate, put forth every exertion for the impost amendment. At the same time, public meetings were held in various towns. The Legislature was bombarded with petitions. The assent which other States had given to the amendment was so nearly unanimous that, although some of the measures carrying it required modification, the eyes of public-spirited men every-

[40] N. Y. *Packet*, April 18 and 25, May 2, 1785.

where were fastened upon New York: as it approved or disapproved, the amendment would carry or fail.

The first reverse came April 13, 1786, when John Lansing had the impost bill amended in the Assembly, 33 to 22, in such manner as to make the duties collectable by the State, not by national officers. This effectually mangled it. Two days later the bill reached its third reading. Duer made an heroic effort to restore it, proposing that since national uniformity in the collection of duties was desirable, the Legislature should agree that, whenever Congress should devise a uniform set of regulations, it would adopt them by law, but this compromise was defeated, 32 to 21. All the New York city and county members who voted stood by Duer, as did half the Albany members, and a group of Assemblymen from Long Island and Staten Island. Later in the month Schuyler in the Senate similarly tried to amend the bill so that it would grant the United States power to issue regulations for the collection, but was also beaten, 10 to 6. On May 4 the measure became law, in such form that New York retained the sole right to levy and receive duties, and was also to be allowed to pay over the revenue in State bills of credit, thus opening the way to confusion of accounts and evasion of the burden. Essentially, the long battle was lost, and Congress rebuffed, for some States had assented only upon condition that the United States should be allowed everywhere to collect the impost direct.[41]

An interesting satire upon the kind of appeal by which demagogues defeated the impost plan appeared in a New York paper early in April. An attempt to turn the sword of the State Rights men against themselves, it catches just the tone of a Clintonian stump-speaker playing upon ignorance, class-feeling, and pocket timidity: [42]

For Congress put Legislature, and then let a cunning clam-catcher, on the south side of Queens County, harangue his Rockaway neighbors, thus: Gemmen, I say we must be careful how we give power to *Legislature;* let us keep the staff in our own hands. Look to your chink, neighbors; keep the loaf under the arm; *the sword and the purse!* Odd zoogers, it makes one cold again! Let *Legislature* have a power to march us up to the Mohawk country to be scalped, and then pay our own charges out of our own pockets, into the bargain! Ha! No, no, none of that fun for me. I say let us give *Legislature* no power; or to cut the matter short, have none at all; we have no occasion for any; let every town do its own business. What business have we to raise money to defend the frontiers? Let the northern men take care of themselves; every hog eat his own apple, I say. Every county and every town stick to itself and mind its own business. *Legislature* wastes money like water. They have given, I hear, 500 good dollars to some lawyers, for nothing but to tub up old fusty books about a pack of trumpery that we have no use for. Can't we meet and make our own laws, to prevent undersized Rams running at large, and the Hogs from

[41] Legislative Journals, 1786.
[42] Quoted in Mass. *Centinel,* April 22, 1786.

digging up the clam flats? What the deuce do we want of any more? They have feathered their nests pretty well, faith; 500 hard dollars for nothing! It would take 800 as fat turkeys as ever catched grasshoppers on Hempstead Plain, to make up this swinging sum. Fine economy truly, just like Congress with their ambassadors to outlandish places! . . . The rich always hate the poor. There is not a fat farmer in all North Hempstead, that will give a poor Rockaway man a boiling of pork, until he has earned it by the sweat of his brow. I say let us be ourselves, and make our own town laws; then I would be for passing a law, that *dried clams should be received in full payment for all old debts;* but to make it good, so as to fetch the pork out of them overgrown fellows' cellars, I would pass a law to make *dried clams a tender in all cases whatsoever.*

In despair, Congress at once passed a resolution asking New York to reconsider its action, and amend the impost measure. This was in August, 1786, and the Legislature having adjourned, a special session would be necessary. Clinton refused to call it on the ground that the Constitution forbade him to do so except in an emergency, and that he saw none. A critic in the *Daily Advertiser* voiced the federalist view when he asked if it were not an emergency to have the life of the national government imperiled, and civil war impending.[43]

Had political factions been as well developed in New York by 1786 as in Pennsylvania or Massachusetts, the State election that year would have turned squarely upon the impost issue. But Governor Clinton, finishing his third triennial term, encountered virtually no opposition in his spring campaign for reëlection. The commercial men in the southern senatorial district, led by Hamilton, Troup, and Duer, would have liked to see Jay in the Governor's chair. Schuyler also wrote from Albany pressing Jay to run. The prospect for his success was by no means dark. Clinton's appointment of a host of incompetent political spoilsmen to office, his hostility to Congress, and the fact that he was not "safe" at a time when paper money folly was abroad, could all be used against him. It was also represented to Jay that no other candidate against Clinton was really available. In the counties east of the Hudson, Chancellor Livingston would have had the support of a considerable body of intelligent men, but the Livingston family had made such a lukewarm record in the Revolution that his chances elsewhere were hopeless. Schuyler might have been mentioned, but although he would have run well about Albany, and wherever else Burgoyne's invasion was vividly remembered, he would have failed utterly in the southern part of the State.[44] However, Jay flatly refused. The political condition of New York was not really desperate, he explained, and

[43] Aug. 31, 1786.
[44] See Hamilton, "Hist. Republic," III, 172-73.

until it was, he could not feel justified in deserting his supervision of the foreign affairs of the nation. Always modest, always deeply conscientious, he added that inasmuch as his post was more laborious than Governor Clinton's, paid less, and carried less honor, he would be accused of self-seeking if he dropped it to seize at the Governorship. Clinton was quietly reëlected.

In New York city, interest in the contest centered in the campaign of Hamilton for the Assembly. Though industriously opposed by the Clintonians, the gallant young lawyer was so well supported by the business vote that he took fourth place in the list of nine chosen. He had a number of fairly sturdy federalist supporters.[45]

The session of 1787, opening in January in New York city, was the scene of a series of defeats for the conservative Whigs at the hands of the radicals, but out of these defeats they plucked victory. Governor Clinton opened it with a non-committal speech informing the Legislature of the request of Congress with regard to the impost, and of his reasons for refusing a special session. The Assembly committee appointed to draft a reply was headed by Hamilton, and its polite rejoinder made no reference to this subject. But the Governor's defenders, led by Hamilton's friends Varick and Malcolm, forced a debate on the subject, did as much as they could to defend Clinton's excuse from Hamilton's attacks, and finally amended the reply to include a word of commendation for his constitutional scruples. Hamilton then succeeded in having the laws which contravened the treaty with England referred to another committee of which he was chairman, and reported a bill for their repeal, using the general formula which Congress had proposed to the States for this purpose. The Trespass Act, and an act relating to debts due to loyalists, were the chief measures against which the British had protested. He carried the bill to the Assembly (April 17), and aroused so much popular support for it that Jay wrote John Adams that New York was growing decidedly more humane towards the Tories. Then he had the mortification of seeing it fail in the Senate.

One gain for the loyalists and the neutrals of the war, however, was achieved. The Federalists under Hamilton and Schuyler were able to repeal the act which had disfranchised certain adherents of the Crown, and to secure them full rights at future elections. In this Malcolm supported Hamilton vigorously, and the measure was

[45] Leake, "Lamb," 301-2.

ready for approval by the Council of Revision on February 3. The temper of the State was indeed slowly changing, as Jay said; there was a tendency to let the harsh laws fall into disuse, and many exiles were now returning to meet, not coats of tar and feathers, but a hearty welcome.[46]

Meanwhile, there had been brought up the most important measure of the session, a bill for granting the impost in full and free measure. Hamilton made for it one of the greatest speeches of his life. He derided the idea that a powerful Congress would ever tyrannize over the States. Pointing to the frequent failure of the States to pay their quotas of the Congressional requisitions, and to the slenderness of the national revenue, he showed how this worthless financial system put an unfair burden upon New York, which had displayed great faithfulness in meeting its quotas. He recalled the hostility of Connecticut and New Jersey to New York, and the eagerness of foreign enemies to take advantage of disunion. He did not deny the fact on which Clinton and many others based their main objection, that the introduction of a set of national tax collectors within the State would impair its sovereignty. In fact, he admitted it with a directness which some Congressional politicians deplored; but he showed that its consequences would be salutary, not injurious. If New York insisted upon modifying the Congressional plan so as to place the collection of the impost in the hands of the State agents, he argued, the weary task of gaining State assent to it would have to begin again; in order to reassure one nervous State, ought eleven others to be compelled to alter their enactments or plans? Hamilton's speech, as Chancellor Kent wrote years later, received praise from all:

I well remember how much it was admired for the comprehensive views which it took of the state of the nation, the warm appeals which it made to the public patriotism, the imminent perils which it pointed out, and the absolute necessity which it showed of some such financial measure to rescue the nation from utter ruin and disgrace. [Kent's "Memoirs and Letters," 297.]

Many of the most distinguished men in the State and nation (the Congress then being in the city) were in the halls or galleries awaiting the Legislature's decision. The labor of the merchants, the New York City Assemblymen, the newspaper essayists, was in vain. On the final vote the Clintonians rallied 36 votes against 21 for the

[46] Legislative Journals. Hamilton three years earlier had lamented the forced exodus of many merchants, carrying eight or ten thousand guineas apiece, and had predicted that the State would feel the effects of the popular frenzy for twenty years. Livingston MSS.

impost plan. "It is whispered," the *Daily Advertiser* ironically said,[47] "that the Governor is in secret an anti-impost man." Clinton doubtless thought himself patriotic in his attitude, an attitude much like that of Samuel Adams, John Hancock, Patrick Henry, and other elder statesmen. More than one utterance of his might be quoted to show a real solicitude for the Union—in 1784, for example, he had favored giving Congress power to counteract the British commercial decrees; and an astonishingly large number of intelligent New Yorkers, including, we have seen, Hamilton's intimates Varick and Malcolm, shared his State Rights prejudices. But the stubbornness which Hamilton thought a reproach against his character made him in this instance blind to the truer patriotism.

Like the State Rights leaders of Rhode Island, those of New York made little effort to justify their acts, knowing they could not meet Hamilton's arguments. It was truthfully said that "the impost was strangled by a band of mutes." But against these dark clouds a bright rainbow was already being bent, as Chancellor Livingston perhaps saw when he sent Hamilton (March 5) his congratulations, not his condolences. It was clear that the only hope for a vigorous Union lay in the approaching Constitutional Convention, and in showing the impotence of the old governmental system, the anti-federalists solidified the federalists behind new demands. Clinton overreached himself. Hamilton had returned from the commercial convention at Annapolis the previous September exuberant with hope for a new national compact, and the Legislature's narrow and short-sighted action only turned men's gaze to the gathering at Philadelphia, now less than three months away.

The Continental Congress had met in New York city February 2, 1787, and had elected St. Clair its president. The honest Scotch soldier, though the chief representative of the majesty of the republic, held an empty office; while in the same building was Governor Clinton, busy performing many duties and dispensing a wide patronage. Clinton treated Congress with condescension, and some of his lieutenants regarded it as an intruder on the soil of the State. At the same time, the Governor privately declared that the Articles of Confederation were sufficient for the purposes of the nation, or at most required only slight amendment; and that the deputies to Annapolis should have been content with the announced object of their gathering. He

[47] March 3, 1787.

thought a Constitutional Convention likely to impress the people
with a sense of evils which did not exist, and to increase the public
confusion. Hamilton hospitably threw his house open to members
of Congress, where he argued at length for a more perfect Union
until he won over a number of wavering men; of Rufus King of
Massachusetts he observed, "I revolutionized his mind." Moreover,
his influence spread like a leaven throughout the State.

Hamilton evinced his political dexterity when he chose the day
after the impost vote to introduce in the Legislature a motion instructing the New York delegation in Congress to support a Constitutional Convention. This Convention, said the resolution, should
revise the Articles by such amendments as a majority might think
necessary. The motion passed the Assembly without difficulty, and
the Senate (where the Clintonians, led by Abraham Yates and John
Haring, tried to hamstring it) by a majority of one. The Legislature
of course struck out the grant of permission to a mere majority in
the Convention to change the Articles as they pleased; but Yates
failed to carry a stipulation that all changes must be consonant with
the New York Constitution. The Legislature then appointed three
delegates to the proposed Convention. Hamilton, the only federalist,
was elected with two dissenting votes; Justice Robert Yates, a popular Albany citizen, unanimously; and the unpopular John Lansing in
the face of heavy opposition. Perceiving the dangers in a delegation so decisively anti-federalist, Hamilton essayed to enlarge it by
two additional men, naming Jay, Duane, Egbert Benson, and Chancellor Livingston as a list from which the selection might be made.
Once more the Assembly was with him, but Clinton's influence in the
Senate defeated the proposal.[48]

We need not follow in detail New York's part in the making or
the acceptance of the Constitution. How Yates and Lansing quitted
the Federal Convention in the midst of its work, a step beyond doubt
approved by Governor Clinton; how Hamilton, strongly supported

[48] "It is currently reported and believed," says the N. Y. *Advertiser* of July 21,
1787, "that his excellency Governor Clinton has, in public company, without reserve,
reprobated the appointment of the Convention, and predicted a mischievous issue of
that measure. His observations are said to be to this effect:—that the present confederation is, in itself, equal to the purposes of the Union:—That the appointment of
a Convention is calculated to impress the people with an idea of evils which do not
exist:—therefore, that in all probability the result of their deliberations, whatever it
might be, would only serve to throw the community into confusion." The Pa. *Packet*
of Aug. 3 adds: "A gentleman from New York informs us that the anti-federal disposition of a great officer of that State has seriously alarmed the citizens, as every
appearance of opposition to the important measure upon which the people have
reposed their hopes creates a painful anticipation of anarchy and division."

in New York city, at once came into the open and attacked the
Governor; how while Yates and Lansing did all they could to discredit the proposed Constitution, Hamilton, Livingston, and Jay
organized a powerful phalanx of advocates; how an association of
radicals, headed by General John Lamb, was formed in defense of
State Rights; how Hamilton characteristically carried the war into
the enemy camp, conceiving the idea of "The Federalist" and during
the autumn and winter writing most of its papers—this is an old
story. It is also an old story how the State convention which met in
June, 1788, to debate ratification, contained at least two avowed
anti-federalists to every federalist; how Hamilton presented the
chief arguments to break down their opposition, was joined first by
one man and then another, and finally, in the conversion of
Melancthon Smith, the foremost anti-federalist debater, won the
victory. Clinton, who presided over the ratifying convention, expressed himself as plainly against the Constitution as political prudence allowed, refused to imitate Governor Hancock in compromis-
ing, and was beaten on a fair field. "The fact is," one observer wrote
of New York city, "that the sense and property here are universally
in favor." [48a] The Governor kept up the fight after all hope of
success was lost, and a few days after ratification, his supporters in
the Convention weakened the acceptance by proposing a second
Federal gathering for considering the amendments offered by the
various States. In the closing days of the year the Clintonians in
the Legislature also seized a final opportunity to strike at Hamilton
by refusing to include him among the delegates who were chosen to
sit in the Continental Congress till the new Constitution came into
effect. A short time thereafter he was in Washington's Cabinet, out
of reach of their malice.

VI. Federalist Efforts in Pennsylvania

In Pennsylvania, meanwhile, the three great achievements of
Franklin's Administration, the modification of the Test Act, the
restoration of the charter of the Bank of North America, and the
ratification of the Constitution, had been rapidly carried through.
This was done in a reaction against the outrageous acts of the radical
Constitutionalists in 1785, and especially against their attempted destruction of the Bank. For all three achievements President Frank-

[48a] Corr. and Journals of S. B. Webb, III, 89-90.

lin, though an octogenarian and half disabled by gallstones, exerted himself energetically, taking action for the first, indeed, as soon as elected. A great number of the non-jurors of Philadelphia placed a petition before the Executive Council on November 7, 1785, asking liberation from "that state of disgraceful slavery" in which they were held by the Test Act. The next day Franklin and the Council sent a message to the Legislature asking for a revision of the obnoxious legislation. At the commencement of March, 1786, the bill reached a third reading. Its progress had been accompanied by much agitation and suspense, and a great concourse of people crowded the legislative gallery and waited in the street outside. A number of petitions had been received in opposition, including several from outlying counties in such threatening language that they had been thrown under the table. The measure passed, 45 to 23, Robert Morris and George Clymer having the gratification of voting for it.[49] Though the old oath, obnoxious in demanding support of the Pennsylvania Constitution, was abolished, every voter might still be required to swear that he had abandoned allegiance to George III, that he gave complete loyalty to Pennsylvania, and that since the Declaration of Independence he had not aided the British forces.

During 1787 the bank was rechartered for fourteen years. Franklin was an earnest believer both in banking and in this particular institution, which was ably and prudently conducted. Since no man of sense could now deny the bank's merits, greater political feeling was aroused during the session by an effort of the Constitutionalists to transfer the State capital to Harrisburg, a bill being actually taken up to remove it to this more central site. Harrisburg, a hundred miles northwest of Philadelphia, was only a few years old, though the chief town of Dauphin County, and had less than a hundred houses. The chief advocate of removal was the rising Constitutionalist leader Findley, who had come to the Pennsylvania frontier from Ireland in 1763, and had grown up with the virtues and prejudices of the backwoods. Federalists were right in saying that one of Findley's motives was his desire to keep the Legislature away from the influence of Congress, which was reported about to return to Philadelphia. Harrisburg was a Constitutionalist center, and the Assembly there would be in contact with the rough fringes of civilization, not with the wealth, education, and con-

[49] Minutes Supreme Executive Council, XIV; N. Y. *Packet,* Dec. 1, 1785; Pa. *Packet,* March 6, 1786.

servatism of the American metropolis. It happened that Dauphin was one of the four counties in which the Germans were most numerous, the others being Lancaster, York, and Northampton, and the Germans, who usually had about one-fifth the membership of the Assembly, were not averse to the change. But Findley's shrewd move failed, and not for another generation did Harrisburg become the fixed capital.[50]

The same year witnessed the conversion of the Anti-Constitutionalist party of Dickinson, Morris, and Wayne into a party supporting the new Federal compact, and the Constitutionalist party of Bryan and Findley into a body opposing it. Old party lines were to a limited extent obliterated. Many men, Franklin among them, desired a Federal Constitution but no new State Constitution. A few perhaps wanted a new State Constitution and no Federal Constitution. But on the whole, the party opposing progress along the whole line was the Constitutionalists, who had always feared a new State instrument, the non-jurors, the College, and the Bank, and who now conjured up a host of fears regarding the Federal Convention.

On September 18, 1787, President Franklin feebly walked into the Assembly hall, and laid the Constitution before the legislators. On the morning of the 29th, the next to the last day of the session, Clymer moved to refer the Constitution to a State convention, and on behalf of the minority, Whitehill requested postponement of the question till afternoon. But when the afternoon came the minority members, nineteen in number, failed to attend, and refusing to heed an official summons, blocked a quorum. The friends of the Constitution in the Assembly and city were outraged by this trick. Accordingly, a party gathered at dawn the next day, seized two of the delinquents, just enough to make a quorum, at their lodgings, and dragged them into their seats. The State convention was then called, to the disgust of the seceding nineteen. Philadelphia, like New York city, was overwhelmingly for the Constitution, and even President Franklin, placed on the anti-federalist ticket for the Convention as a decoy, received less than one-fifth as many votes in the city as the highest federalist candidate—235 as against 1215. The number of members elected to the Convention was the same as the number of legislators. In four counties, Lancaster, Berks, Westmoreland, and Dauphin, the anti-federalists made gains over their

---

[50] N. Y. *Advertiser,* March 13, 1787; Md. *Journal,* March 13, 30.

showing in the Legislature, and in three, Northumberland, Washington, and Franklin, suffered losses.[51]

After a session of three weeks, the Pennsylvania Convention ratified the Constitution by a vote of 46 to 23, the second ratification it received. The news, announced on December 13, 1787, was greeted with joy by the federalists and with sullen anger by the anti-federalists. One reason for the joy was that it made a new State Constitution almost imperative, and that the Constitutionalists had lost their long fight. Under Judge Bryan, Findley, Whitehill, and Smillie, they salved their discomfiture by the immediate publication of an address to the people. They alleged that the secrecy in which the new Federal instrument had been drawn up made it suspicious; that the people and Legislature had been frightened into consenting to a State convention by unfounded talk about impending anarchy; that the election of this Convention, set for an absurdly early date, had called out only 13,000 of the 70,000 voters; and that the 46 members who had ratified the Constitution represented but 6800 freemen. In short, they used arguments against the Federal instrument amusingly similar to the arguments which Dickinson and his followers had employed against the new State instrument in 1776-77.

In preparation for the Congressional elections in the fall of 1788, the anti-federalists, responding to a circular letter sent out from Carlisle, met at Harrisburg at the beginning of September to frame a ticket and a plan of action. Thirty-three delegates attended from thirteen counties, including Judge Bryan, Assemblyman Whitehill, and Albert Gallatin, an ardent young Swiss who had taken a prominent anti-federalist part in the ratifying convention. Their ostensible purpose was to propose amendments to the Federal Constitution, and draft petitions to be circulated in support of them; but then narrower party aims were the more important. The course they decided upon was caution itself. They knew that popular sentiment was unfavorable to them. Some delegates first proposed that they bring forward a ticket with three federalist and five anti-federalist candidates for Congress, in the hope of splitting the federalist vote. Even this seemed risky, and a balance was struck between the two parties, four of each composing the ticket. Pains were taken, moreover, to see that two of the federalists thus induced to accept an anti-federalist Congressional nomination were of German blood—Daniel

[51] McMaster and Stone, Pa., and the Fed. Const., 1787-88; S. B. Harding, in Amer. Hist. Assn. Report, 1894, p. 370 ff.

Heister, who had been a brigadier of militia, and Peter Muhlenberg, the patriot parson who had told his congregation at the beginning of the Revolution that there was a time to fight as well as to pray, and had fought so well that he became a major-general. The federalists, on the other hand, named a straight party ticket. The result was decisive. When the polls closed in the last week of November, it was found that not one of the four anti-federalists had been elected. The balloting was not by districts, but by a general State election, and a Philadelphia paper thus summarized the result:[52]

> Six of the federalists in the federal ticket, and two German federalists in the anti-federal ticket, are the successful candidates. The two latter gentlemen were put high in the return by the general voice of the Germans, joined by some of the federalists; and it is a very remarkable proof of the strength of the federal interest, that the two unsuccessful candidates in the federal ticket, though thrown out by the two federal German competitors, were yet above all the remainder, both federal and anti-federal characters, in the opposition ticket.

The Legislature elected the fall of 1788 was strongly federalist and Anti-Constitutionalist. It at once chose two federalists as United States Senators—Robert Morris, and William Maclay, remembered as author of a famous political diary. Franklin's term having expired, it further emphasized the federalist character of Pennsylvania by electing Thomas Mifflin and George Ross as President and Vice-President of the State. Mifflin had attained the rank of major-general in the war, had later been president of the Continental Congress, and had sat in the Constitutional Convention. The Legislature then, early in 1789, turned its attention to new internal reforms. In March it took the first of the steps which gave Pennsylvania her Constitutional Convention of 1790. This action was accompanied by the long overdue, and now almost too late, revival of the College under its old charter. Provost Smith, who had labored indefatigably for this result, was in the city to receive what he always called "my college." But its old faculty and equiment, its traditions and spirit, were gone, and to build them up seemed a heart-breaking task.

As in Pennsylvania, so in New York the moderate or conservative Whigs in State affairs had become federalists in national affairs, and the radical Whigs had largely become anti-federalists. At the election of one-fourth the State Senate in 1788—a quarter of the upper

---

[52] Pa. *Journal*, Dec. 20, 1788; see also Pa. *Journal*, Nov. 29; Pa. *Packet*, Sept. 13, Oct. 2; and Md. *Journal*, Sept. 23, 1788.

chamber was renewed annually—the federalists were able to obtain a small but decisive preponderance in that body. In New York county the federalist candidates for the Assembly polled as many as 2375 votes, while the vote of the anti-federalists ranged from 1000 to 1500. But up-State the anti-federalists retained the advantage, electing their Assemblymen even in Albany and Montgomery Counties, where Schuyler had much influence.[53] The anti-federalist complexion of the Assembly was indicated by its December election of delegates to the last Continental Congress, when Hamilton received only 22 votes, and Abraham Yates 34. But it was an important achievement for the federalists to gain control of one legislative branch, as events soon proved.

Before the Legislature of 1789 met, Clinton's partisans were confident that they were strong enough in both chambers to elect two anti-federalists as United States Senators. Had the chambers sat jointly, they could have done so. But there was no rule as to the manner of election, and the federalists in the Senate insisted that it must be concurrent. They held to this position against all pleas and arguments, and the session ended with no choice. The same disagreement prevented the choice of any Presidential electors, so that New York did not vote for Washington. Much rancor arose from this deadlock, each side bitterly blaming the other. The federalists who comprised the wealth and culture of New York city knew that they risked losing the choice of their metropolis as the temporary seat of the national government, and Knox wrote Washington praising their "honorable firmness—hazarding the removal from New York rather than saddle the Government with two anti-federal Senators." Schuyler brought forward a sensible compromise, suggesting that each house should nominate two Senators, and if the nominations were different, the Senate should choose one of the men named by the House, and the House one of those named by the Senate; the same plan to apply to the choosing of electors. But the Clintonians wanted all or nothing.[54]

This drawn contest was in one light the opening skirmish in the State election of 1789 for Governor and other officers, as pitched a political battle as New York ever saw. Clinton approached the campaign for his fifth term with a confidence bred by his past victories, his popularity, and his well-marshaled army of appointees.

[53] N. Y. *Journal*, June 5, 1788.
[54] N. Y. *Advertiser*, April 7, 1789.

Hamilton, Schuyler, Jay, and Chancellor Livingston hoped to over-turn the State and seat a Governor friendly to federalism, but they did not underrate the difficulty of the task. Clinton was as forceful and genial as ever; though Hamilton could not remember a single useful measure since 1783 for which the State was indebted to him, most people thought him a good Governor; and he was a born fighter. It was true, as Schuyler said, that he had misused his patronage. But the important fact was that he had more of it than any other American official. Gouverneur Morris says that office-hunting, which disappeared during the war, became a raging disease at its end, and in every county, Clinton had grateful hench-men, civil and military. Whom should the federalists choose to meet him? Jay, Hamilton, and Schuyler all looked forward to Federal preferment. The New York city friends of Chief Justice Richard Morris proposed that deserving jurist and old-school gentleman. Up-State, the friends of Pierre Van Cortlandt pointed out that he had always been Lieutenant-Governor and deserved promotion.

But the chances of success were so slender that the federalists imitated their opponents in Pennsylvania, and resorted to stratagem. At Bardin's Tavern in New York city on February 11, 1789, a meet-ing of several hundred of the party, presided over by a merchant named Constable, with Hamilton, Troup, Duer, Aaron Burr, and other leaders present, resolved upon trying to divide the anti-federalist vote. That is, they decided upon Robert Yates as nominee. Yates had resigned from the Constitutional Convention and had opposed the Constitution at home, but he had since, in a charge to a jury which received wide publicity, delivered himself of a cordial exhortation to support it; and he hence seemed available. Pierre Van Cortlandt was unanimously endorsed for Lieutenant-Governor. A committee including the four young men just named was appointed to correspond with other counties for the promotion of these candi-dacies. Nine days later Hamilton published a newspaper appeal to the voters in behalf of Yates which is one of the shrewdest, most tactful productions of his pen.[55] It was necessary, he stated, that the next Governor should be free from any temptation to embarrass the national government, whether that temptation arose from a preference for smaller confederacies, from personal ambition, from an impatience of the restraints of national authority, from a fear of

[55] N. Y. *Advertiser,* Feb. 20, 1789.

Federal domination, or from mortification caused by political dis-appointments. A surly Governor might not only hamper the Federal Government, but bring down upon New York the ill-will of other States. It was desirable to find a Governor who would also moderate factional spirit, and heal the unhappy divisions of the past; since in addition to the old parties in New York the Constitutional Convention had given birth to two new and more extensive parties. Nothing was more essential, apart from the choice of a man who would keep nation and State in harmony, than to settle upon one who would mollify the existing resentments. Where could he be found? Very courteously, Hamilton referred to the eminent merits of Lieutenant-Governor Van Cortlandt and Chief Justice Morris, both federalists. But—

Had it been agreed to support either of them for the office of Governor there would have been reason to fear, that the measure would have been imputed to party, and not to a desire of relieving our country from the evils they experience from the heats of party. It appeared, therefore, most desirable to select some man of the opposite party, in whose integrity, patriotism, and temper, confidence might justly be placed; however little his political opinions on the question lately agitated, might be approved by those who were assembled. . . .

The federalists willingly followed Hamilton, Troup, and Duer. On February 23 a larger meeting was held in the city, with many important merchants present, and though its purpose was to nominate a man for Congress, its sense was taken upon the Governorship, with the result that only a dozen objected to Yates. At a third meeting a few days later the choice of Yates was again almost unanimously approved. Indeed, he was thoroughly qualified. Born in Schenectady and educated in New York city, he had been admitted to the bar fifteen years before the Revolution. His services in the war had been varied. He wrote patriotic essays, was a member of the Committee of Safety, for a time had charge of military operations under the Provincial Congress, helped block the Hudson against Howe's fleet, and assisted Schuyler in drawing plans for the defense of upper New York. Becoming a judge of the Supreme Court in 1777, he distinguished himself by his insistence on impartial justice for men accused of Toryism, and displayed a fine independence when he scorned the Legislature's threat of impeachment for this stand. He had also been one of the Council of Administration which governed southern New York for a short period after the British evacuation. If Clinton can be called the Hampden of the Revolution in New York, we are told, Yates was its Pym; and though both titles are inflated, Yates was an able, sturdy patriot, whose record was marred only by his greed for office.

At an early date, gatherings in various parts of the State had renominated Clinton and Van Cortlandt for the anti-federalists. By the end of February both parties had held many public rallies, and the attacks and counter-attacks were becoming intense. Marshaled behind Yates and his coalition were John Jay, not too busy with foreign affairs to lend active support; Chancellor Livingston, who in a few weeks would administer the oath of office to Washington; and James Duane, who had been made first Mayor of New York in 1784, and exerted nearly as much influence there as Livingston did east of the upper Hudson. Duer and Burr gave their assistance, and in Albany County, Schuyler, who hoped to be United States Senator. Behind Clinton was ranged a less distinguished but formidable group. Melancthon Smith, a fine debater and careful student of political history, who had for a time led the opposition to the Constitution in the Poughkeepsie Convention, was still with the Governor, and so were John Lansing and Gilbert Livingston.[56]

No weapon that could be used against Governor Clinton was left ungrasped. It was asserted that he had hoarded his "immense salary," and that his niggardliness had prevented him from assuming a decent dignity, or offering a decent hospitality, so that in his dozen years of service he had accumulated not less than £30,000. This was just the reverse of the argument that Massachusetts federalists used against Hancock. Hamilton declared he found fault, not that the Governor was frugal, but that he was penurious. When Clinton's overdue accounts were settled in 1782, the State had paid him more than £8000, and his subsequent salary had been £9000, of which, said Hamilton, his mode of living left no doubt that he had saved half; computing the interest for six years, the Governor's fortune could not be much short of £20,000. Recalling how during the sojourn of Congress in the city Clinton had done almost nothing to make its members welcome, Hamilton—himself the soul of hospitality, and careless of money to a fault—accused him of failure to discharge an important official duty. Indeed, Clinton had only once reached deep into his pocket, that once being when just after the British evacuation of New York he gave a dinner to Washington and

[56] See N. Y. *Journal* and *Advertiser,* February and March; Mass. *Centinel,* March 4, 1789.

other generals, Luzerne, the French envoy, and a crowd of other gentlemen. Unfortunately, some federalists exaggerated the charge.[57]

Clinton was also charged with domineering over the Council of Appointment and prostituting its powers for partisan objects. The Constitution did not state whether the Governor, who with four Senators composed the Council, was to have the sole, or merely a concurrent, power in nominating State officers; he had no vote save in case of a tie. Gouverneur Morris has praised Clinton for the position he took. "Soon after the peace, an attempt at nomination was made by members of the Council; to this the opposition of Clinton was characteristically firm; he had the honorable pride to defend the rights of his office, and hold his share of Constitutional responsibility." Hamilton blamed him: "he has constantly claimed the right of *previous nomination,* and we are greatly misinformed if he has not extensively practiced upon that pretension. The exercise of such a power places the choice essentially in the Governor." It almost did so, for he could repeat his nominations indefinitely. But Clinton was right, and had done both what was best for the State, and what Jay, in writing the Constitution, seems to have intended should be done. Where Clinton was really assailable was in the bad character of some nominations, and in his anti-federalism.

For their part, the Clintonians made the most of Yates's turncoat tactics, imputing to him a lack of principle. They stigmatized the federalists as an aristocratic party, and raised the cry of a conspiracy of propertied men to oppress the poor. "New York is a very important State," wrote "A Yeoman"; "and the high-flyers do not like to see so great a number of its citizens dissatisfied with any part of the new Constitution. They think, if they can once get Governor Clinton out of the way, we will forget that we have liberties to guard, and they may then go on without opposition to make their powers as strong as they please. What otherwise can be their reasons for joining all their powers against his? All he aims at is, to obtain the amendments which the whole country says we ought to have." [58] In the autumn of 1788, following the ratification of the Constitution, eight men, including Melancthon Smith, Marinus Willett, John Lamb, and Samuel Jones, met at Fraunces's Tavern and formed a society for the purpose of procuring a national revising convention. A considerable number of men, especially in the rural communities,

[57] Hamilton's Works, I, 560-62; N. Y. *Advertiser,* March 23, 25, April 1, 1789.
[58] N. Y. *Journal,* March 26.

hoped for such a revision, and they were kept reminded by a State committee of correspondence that their votes ought to go to Clinton.

The contest was close, and though the balloting was held at the end of April, the result was not fully known until the first of June. Yates carried five counties—that of New York, 833 to 385; those of Albany and Montgomery, the Schuyler strongholds, by 1577 to 1000, and 277 to 181, respectively; and Columbia and Dutchess by small margins. When in Columbia the Clintonians took steps to void the election in the town of Livingston, on a number of highly technical objections, one ardent federalist rode thirty-five miles in an afternoon to give his party leaders warning.[59] Clinton swept the eight other counties of the thirteen. In Orange he was given four votes to every one for Yates, in Clinton his vote was all but unanimous, and in Ulster he received the huge vote of 1039 to 206. But in all, of a poll of 12,353, Clinton had only 6393, or a bare majority of 429. He had won a victory so narrow that in moral effect it was Pyrrhic. He explained to a visiting Virginian, one of Patrick Henry's friends, that the combination against him had been almost overwhelming—that almost all the gentlemen, and all the merchants and mechanics, had united to strike him down forever.[60] But in the taverns, in newspaper offices, and on street corners, the political generalship of Hamilton was a theme for praise. This astute young man of thirty-two had taken full advantage of the tide toward federalism in New York, and had all but defeated the most popular man in the State, head of the most effective political machine in America.

To emphasize Hamilton's triumph, the Assembly was carried by the federalists, who now controlled both legislative branches, while three of the five members of Congress, chosen by districts, were of that faith. Egbert Benson, so long Attorney-General, and more recently one of the ablest of laborers for the Constitution, was one; another was John Lawrence, a city lawyer whom Hamilton had supported as a man of sense, eloquence, and early and decided attachment to the Constitution.

In short, though when the Federal Government came into full operation it found George Clinton still presiding over New York, with three years yet to govern, the outlook for federalism in the State was bright. Summoned in special session, the Legislature promptly

[59] Corr. and Journals of S. B. Webb, III, 130-31.
[60] Henry, "Henry," III, 389-95; for election results, see *Advertiser*, May 27 ff.

called Schuyler and King to be Senators; the latter being a Massachusetts man who, after long service in the Continental Congress, had removed to New York the previous year. At the same time, Washington's inauguration gave Hamilton a voice in suggesting the Federal appointments, and Hamilton was too shrewd to miss using them, so far as he conscientiously could, for federalist ends. He as Secretary of the Treasury, and Jay as Chief Justice, wielded greater influence in the State than ever; and three others of their party, Duane, Richard Harrison, and William S. Smith, became respectively judge of the district court, Federal Attorney, and Federal Marshal. Clinton appreciated the strength of the federalist position, and at once took steps to arm himself against it.

VII. Politics in New Jersey and Delaware

As in New York, so just across the Hudson in New Jersey during all this period the Governor's chair was occupied by one man. William Livingston was a member of the same rich landed family from which sprang Edward and Robert R. Livingston. Educated at Yale, he had gained a reputation there for originality, had come to the New York bar a quarter-century before anyone seriously proposed independence, and in the constant struggle between Whig and Tory, had kept up a fertile production of pamphlets and newspaper articles. Though a poor orator, he was a ready writer, publishing in 1747 a long poem in imitation of Pomfret, called "Philosophical Solitude," and constantly printing fugitive essays. As an editor, his reputation in the Colonies was considerable just before the Revolution. In 1772 he removed to "Liberty Hall" at Elizabeth, New Jersey, with the intention of retiring; but the busiest part of his life was before him. Retirement would in any event have been premature, for he was only fifty-three in 1776.

New Jersey, when the Revolution began, saw that he was one of her ablest residents, and was glad to utilize his services as Pennsylvania utilized those of a recent New Jerseyite, Reed, and Delaware utilized those of a former Pennsylvanian, Dickinson. Though Livingston hesitated to approve the Declaration of Independence, after once accepting it his determination never flagged. Soberly progressive in temper, quick-witted, cultured, he had also the tenacity of his Scotch stock. John Adams was pleased with his appearance, saying: "He is a plain man, tall, black, wears his hair; nothing elegant or genteel about him. They say he is no public speaker, but very sensible and learned." This onetime dabbler in verse and essays returned from the second Continental Congress to take a brigadiership of militia at Elizabeth, and was soon skirmishing with the enemy. The first Legislature under the new State Constitution met at Princeton August 27, 1776, and the two houses at once went into joint session to choose the Governor. One group wanted Livingston, and another Richard Stockton, a native of the State, long a law officer, and a signer of the Declaration. On the second day John Cleves Symmes transferred his decisive influence to Livingston—Stockton being consoled by the office of Chief Justice. The State had for Governor a man on whom Washington relied only less than on Trumbull of Connecticut—the purest type of patriot.[61]

New Jersey lay in an exposed situation, the enemy always within her limits, and at one time in possession of virtually the whole State. In guarding against attack, punishing partisans who plundered the people, adjusting the quarrels of the militia and regular troops, and trying to satisfy the demands for supplies from both, Governor Livingston was kept more than busy. "New Jersey, which almost touches the fortifications of New York, has displayed heroic constancy," a French officer exuberantly reported to his government. "Its militia assembles of its own accord at sight of a redcoat. Their Governor is a Roman. The republicans call him Brutus; the royalists an American Nero." When the British army pushed across the State in 1776, the well-equipped regulars in pursuit of Washington's ill-conditioned army, Livingston spared himself no exertion. He wrote personally to all State officers of the rank of Colonel or above, and scattered printed circulars to arouse the people.

The Legislature had to remove from Princeton to Burlington, then to Pittstown, then to Haddonfield; and finally, in the remotest corner of the State, with nowhere else to meet and almost no territory for which to pass laws, dissolved. Of the newly organized State government only a vestige was left, and all was gloom until the Christmas battle of Trenton. After Trenton and Princeton, more and more of the State was reconquered, but a British army always lay along the northern boundary, and Livingston had to govern a commonwealth never secure until 1782.

[61] Sedgwick's "Livingston"; *Mass. Hist. Soc. Proceedings*, LV, 225 ff.

Especially in the western section, the problem of utilizing all military resources without outraging the Quakers was difficult. Encouraged by Washington, Livingston urged upon the Legislature a law strengthening the militia, and obtained a partial measure in March, 1777. "The act is extremely deficient," he wrote Washington, "and it has cost me many an anxious hour to think how long it was procrastinated, and how ineffectual I had reason to suppose it would finally prove." At the same dangerous time, with Howe's strong army threatening Washington's weak force at Morristown, and Burgoyne ready to begin his march from the north, Livingston prevailed upon the Legislature to pass another act constituting the Governor and twelve members of the Legislature a Council of Safety, with extraordinary powers for six months to act against the enemy. Repeated but abortive attempts were made by Tory or British commands to capture Livingston, a reward of 2000 guineas having been offered for his person. The enemy appreciated the part which he played in strengthening Washington's levies in the spring of 1777, when the Americans finally pushed Howe back upon Staten Island.

All this time the Governor could not refrain from using his pen to defend the Revolution. In February, 1777, he published in the Philadelphia *Packet* an essay satirizing the mendacity of Rivington's Tory Paper, the *Gazette,* in New York. In December he published in the newly founded New Jersey *Gazette,* at Burlington, papers on the exchange of Burgoyne and the attempted conquest of America, and he brought out even a *jeu d'esprit* on the bulky petticoats of the Dutch women of Bergen County. During 1778 he made many contributions to the New Jersey *Gazette,* and prided himself upon the fact that the British would rather hang him for writing than for fighting. Rivington retorted by bestowing on the Governor such epithets as Don Quixote of the Jerseys, the Itinerant Dey of New Jersey, and the Knight of the Most Honorable Order of Starvation. Finally, the Assembly intimated that it thought the essays rather undignified for a Governor, and Livingston discontinued them.

Until after the Federal Constitution went into effect, Livingston remained Governor. There was frequently some opposition to his reëlection, but it never attained much strength. In the fall of 1778, when the British in Philadelphia and New York half encompassed the State, he received 31 votes to 7 in favor of General Philemon Dickinson, who had commanded the Jersey militia at the battle of

Monmouth. Two years later Livingston obtained 28 votes out of 36, David Brearly and General Dickinson dividing the rest. The election of the fall of 1781 was unanimous; we have no record of the vote in 1782; and in 1783 he received 33 votes out of 34. It is evident that as Governor and Chancellor he gave entire satisfaction, and that the State had few party quarrels. In 1784, when General Elias Dayton was nominated against him, he obtained 38 votes out of 43. The following summer he declined an appointment as Minister to Holland, in succession to John Adams. He was one of the delegates to the Constitutional Convention, and of course used his influence to obtain ratification of the Constitution; New Jersey, after only a week's debate, came under the "new roof." The feeling in the State at this time was generally federalist; there were only a few who, like Abraham Clark, a signer of the Declaration, preached a State Rights doctrine. As a small commonwealth lying unprotected between two great ones, New Jersey had much to gain from the new Federal Government. The Congressional election of 1789 was fiercely fought, but the line was drawn rather between the eastern and western sections than between the federalists and anti-federalists.

As New Jersey's politics at some points touched those of New York, so Delaware's at some points touched those of Pennsylvania. Had the conservatives remained in the saddle in Pennsylvania, the course of affairs in the two States might have run fairly parallel.

A spirit of caution and moderation dominated the three lower counties on the Delaware. Thomas McKean, who held Delaware office almost continuously from 1762 to the end of the Revolution, has told us that "a majority of this State were unquestionably against the independence of America." In Kent and Sussex, more than half the population were Episcopalians, and in both, but particularly Sussex, the ministers fostered Toryism by representing the Revolution to be designed in the interests of Presbyterians. Newcastle County, lying nearest to Pennsylvania, had a large Ulster Scotch population, and three-fifths of its people were Presbyterians, so that Whiggism was stronger here. The man who more than any other shaped the first State policies, George Read, held moderate views. A Marylander by birth, and a lawyer by profession, he had been Attorney-General from 1763 until he became a delegate to the Continental Congress in 1775. He was a patriot of the same stamp as Dickinson and Robert Morris, struggling to delay an assertion of independence and voting against the Declaration, but zealous to maintain it afterwards. The first Legislature chosen under the State Constitution recalled McKean and Rodney from Congress, the two delegates who had advocated independence there, but reëlected Read.

This Legislature chose a Council of Safety of fifteen members, and on February 12, 1777, it named John McKinley as the State's first President. He also was highly conservative, and his election angered the radicals as much as had the rebuke to McKean and Rodney. In September following, the British suddenly fell upon Wilmington, seized President McKinley from his bed at dead of night, and captured the little patriot vessels in which were kept the public records and moneys. George Read, as Vice-President, hurrying from Congress by a circuitous route to take the vacant chair, soon showed that McKinley's capture had done the patriot cause no harm. Read appreciated the fact that the die was cast, and was unremitting in his endeavors to arouse the three counties and to counteract the general disaffection.

Partly because Read's energy put a new spirit into the State, partly because the British capture of Philadelphia strengthened the radicals, at the election in March, 1778, the progressive element beat the conservatives. It was able to choose its old captain, Rodney, as President. In spite of ill health, Rodney was a man of ability and aggressiveness. Tall and thin, he made a strange impression upon all he met. "His face is not bigger than a large apple, yet there is sense and fiery spirit, wit and humor in his countenance," wrote Adams. He served throughout the war, and might have continued Governor after the expiration of his term in 1781 had it not been unconstitutional for him to succeed himself. The fourth chief executive was John Dickinson, who accepted the place very unwillingly. His moderation commended him, for by this time the conservatives had regained their dominance. Dickinson in the fall of 1782 was elected President of Pennsylvania, and held the two offices until he resigned in January, 1783, though he had previously turned his duties in Delaware over to John McCook. The terms of Nicholas Van Dyke (1783-6) and Thomas Collins (1786-89) followed.

Political currents flowed smoothly in Delaware after the Revolution. There was some persecution of loyalists and neutrals by volunteer local agencies in 1783 and 1784; in the spring of the former year, for example, the radicals of Sussex County held a convention, and agreed that if any Tories came back, the militia officers were to give them two days in which to get out.[62] But this amounted to little; indeed, the loyalists were so numerous that a widespread persecution would have been impossible except by turning the State upside down. There were no constitutional questions of importance, and Delaware early put her finances in good order. The Federal Constitution was received with such enthusiasm that Delaware gave the first ratification; and the Governor elected in 1789, Joshua Clayton, was a staunch federalist.

[62] See *Freeman's Journal*, June 4, 1783, for the vigorous resolutions by which the Sussex Whigs announced their intention of dealing roughly with returned Tories.

CHAPTER EIGHT

POLITICAL DEVELOPMENT: THE UPPER SOUTH

THE two upper States of the South were on the whole much better governed than the three lower. This was due in part to the fact that since Maryland and Virginia suffered less from the war than the Carolinas and Georgia, their recovery was simpler, and the temptation to deal harshly with their former enemies weaker. They had also an advantage in leadership, for they found abler men than either North Carolina or Georgia, while the superior character of the population, besides accounting for much of the better leadership, had much general influence upon the government. Annapolis was the wealthiest town of its size in America, and in the coastal parts of Maryland, divided for the most part into great plantations like those of Virginia, a considerable number of families gave their sons not only education and leisure, but a tradition of public service. The Virginia Tidewater boasted an aristocracy, rich, conservative, and well tinctured by culture, that with the lawyers of the inland country gave poise and foresight to the State's administration. Poise was just what was lacking in North Carolina during most of the period from 1776 to 1789; it was shockingly absent in Georgia throughout the Revolution; and it failed in South Carolina twice after peace. In Maryland the peculiarities of the Constitution went far towards assuring it.

I. POLITICAL HISTORY OF MARYLAND

Indeed, Maryland's political history was set apart by the consistency with which House and Senate clashed upon important questions. It was long a question with some whether the frame of government was not the worse for the care with which the two houses had been balanced against each other.[1] Had not mobility been too much sacrificed? When the Constitution was proclaimed, its provision for the indirect election of the Senate struck many as bizarre,

[1] B. W. Bond, "State Govt. in Md., 1777-81" (Johns Hopkins Studies, Series XXIII, Nos. 3 and 4.)

and awakened an opposition which for a time threatened a legislative deadlock like that of the same months in Pennsylvania. The electors of the Senate met in Annapolis a fortnight before Christmas, 1776, and chose the fifteen members of the upper house, while the House of Delegates was popularly elected a few days later. In their dislike of the new Constitution, several of the Senators planned to absent themselves from the Legislature, and thus prevent a quorum. They believed that the Constitution could then be proclaimed invalidated, and that the power of framing a new one would revert to the people. In the face of this danger, a special appeal was made to several wavering senators! Early in 1777 the legislature was successfully organized at Annapolis; and it there chose Thomas Johnson, one of the leaders in the pre-Revolutionary agitation, to be the first Governor.[2]

The Senate and Assembly soon justified those who had prophesied that they would come into sharp conflict. One of the first disagreements was upon the question whether local civil officers should be eligible to the Legislature, the Senate maintaining that they should not. The upper chamber, its members enjoying a tenure of five years, was conservative, while the House, made up of men who had to keep a constant eye upon the voters' good will, and who had less property, was a more changeable, radical body. In the fall of 1778 another quarrel arose over the pay of the legislators, the House maintaining that no gentleman could live in Baltimore on less than $8 a day, and the Senate, led by Charles Carroll of Carrollton, pointing to the danger of making money rather than a sense of public duty the incentive towards office-seeking. This dispute went so far that the house accused the Senate of unnecessarily prolonging the session, and of using "unbecoming sarcasm and irritating sneers." Meanwhile, one hot-headed Assemblyman, Samuel Chase, actually declared that Senator Samuel Wilson was a traitor, that Senator Thomas Jennings was suspiciously near a loyalist, and that Daniel of St. Thomas Jenifer was secretly advocating a reunion with Great Britain. No better illustration could be found of the difficulty which a radical felt in understanding a conservative during these years of war. A legislative inquiry quickly exploded the charges. In 1779 the House refused to accept any communications from the Senate regarding the annual appropriation bill, maintaining that it had

[2] Md. *Journal*, April 1, 1777.

exclusive jurisdiction over money acts; and the Senate vehemently protested.

A more serious quarrel arose over measures which the radicals brought forward at the spring session of 1777 for the restraint of Tories. The danger from disaffected elements seemed considerable. In January, the patriots of the lower eastern shore had excitably warned Congress that they feared a rebellion in two counties there, and troops were dispatched. The panic caused a wave of resentment against certain prominent Tories on both shores. An extensive program of regulations and penalties was drawn up to punish Toryism. As a loyalist observed, it was "rigid to a violent degree," and was so earnestly combated in the Senate that at length it passed only in a much modified form. Any person who affirmed the authority of Great Britain, or tried to induce anyone to return to British allegiance, was to be fined not more than £10,000 in current money, and imprisoned not more than five years, or banished; lesser offenses against the patriot government were to be punished by slighter penalties; and no one was to travel without a pass. Radical Whigs, considering this legislation too hard to execute and faulty in not applying to neutrals, demanded a Test Act. Twice one which they framed passed the House, and twice it failed in the Senate. The upper chamber would consent to a bill requiring all officeholders and voters to take an oath of allegiance, but it opposed one which would harshly punish all citizens who refused the test.[3]

However, in this instance the Senate yielded. At the October session in 1778, it consented to a law which made all non-jurors of eighteen or older subject to a treble tax, the loss of their civil rights, and debarment from trade or the learned professions; a most unjust and impolitic law. Quakers, Dunkers, Mennonites, and Methodists refused the oath for conscience's sake, and almost one-third the State's inhabitants remained non-jurors—"the far greater part of them ignorant, harmless, and inoffensive people."[4]

Beginning the autumn of 1779, much feeling was again aroused between the two houses by proposals for a general confiscation of loyalists' estates.[5] In the previous May, British forces had entered

[3] For discussions of the Test Act, see Md. *Journal*, July 22, 27, etc., 1777.
[4] Md. *Journal*, June 16, 1778.
[5] Some light is thrown on the temper of the time by an occurrence of July, 1779. One Wm. Goddard published in the Md. *Journal* of July 6 certain "queries political and military," which were thought to reflect upon Washington and the French. A party of citizens, led by Samuel Smith, three or four other officers, a negro drummer, a horse-shoer, and others, called upon Goddard and forced him to sign an apology.

Chesapeake Bay, taken possession of Portsmouth, and laid waste the shores for a long distance. The alarm had led to the hurried fortification of Baltimore, the mustering of all available militia, and the collection of stores for a siege. The State had already spent so much in raising Continental troops that its treasury, as Governor Johnson despondently wrote the delegates in Congress, was empty. This discouraging fiscal situation led the radicals to greet with alacrity the new proposal. Seizures of Tory property were the talk of the hour in New York and Pennsylvania. Many rich Marylanders had found refuge with the British and their property could be had for the taking. A confiscation bill was with all speed drawn up, and late in the fall jubilantly passed by the House. The Senate, however, led by Charles Carroll and other wealthy men, declared that "we are not convinced of the justice of the bill, less of its policy, and least of all of its necessity," and defeated it. The House in an indignant uproar then voted resolutions denouncing the obstructiveness of the upper chamber and requesting the voters to "express their sentiments upon the present differences between the two branches of the Legislature"—an appeal for an informal referendum.

During the winter the two newspapers of the State, the *Gazette* of Annapolis and the *Journal* of Baltimore, were crowded by essays for and against confiscation. There could be no question which side was taken by popular feeling, and when the Legislature met again, petitions from all sections for the bill covered the desks of the presiding officers. Members of the House affirmed that unless the property of Tories were sold, the State Treasury could not meet the obligations due in 1780; and the Senate began to waver. Before the close of the year an event decided it. Maryland before the Revolution had invested £27,000 in the stock of the Bank of England, and had been trying to obtain its repayment; but in the fall of 1780 Franklin, who had reached Paris upon his second mission, sent word of the Bank's flat refusal. In their anger, some Senators changed their stand, and early in 1781 the Confiscation Act, which by this time had been modified, was passed with slight opposition.

Later disputes between the two branches were frequent. Several occurred in January, 1783—a quarrel over the question whether the

In the Md. *Journal* of July 27, however, he renounced his apology, and attacked "the cowardly tyrants, into whose horrid fangs I was inhumanly betrayed by the infamous magistracy of this unhappily enslaved town."

Governor, Council, legislators, and higher judges should be exempted from militia duty, the Senate affirming that such men ought not to be made to shoulder a musket; a quarrel over the civil list, the Senate again maintaining that salaries should be moderate; and a quarrel over a bill for the naval defense of Chesapeake Bay. Always the Senate was more conservative and thoughtful, and invariably its objections were to the eventual benefit of the State. Each side prided itself upon the stilted and sarcastic papers it drew up for the other and the public. In these interchanges there is an echo of the Colonial quarrels between a privilege-loving, cautious Council, and a democratic, impetuous Assembly.

Maryland's first three Governors were able men. Rich Thomas Johnson had gained his election by a sweeping majority, forty votes against nine for Samuel Chase and a few scattering. A resident of Annapolis, long a legislator, and now nearing middle age, he had left the Continental Congress the summer of 1776 to serve in Maryland's Constitutional Convention, and thus, like Clinton, missed being a "signer"; later he became a brigadier-general of militia, and was in the field with Washington when chosen Governor. Having served the three successive terms the Constitution allowed, Johnson retired the fall of 1779, and Thomas Sim Lee, a member of the great family prominent in Virginia, was elected Governor over Colonel Edward Lloyd. Three years later came William Paca (the name is sometimes thought to indicate Bohemian origin), who was, with the exception of Charles Carroll of Carrollton, the most distinguished son of the State in the Revolution. He had been one of the many young Marylanders attracted to the college in Philadelphia, and he supplemented his training there by study in the Middle Temple, London. Into the years 1774-82 he crowded labors as an organizer of the Revolution in the Province, a signer of the Declaration, State Senator, Chief Justice, and chief judge of the court of admiralty and appeals. He also was twice reëlected.[6]

It is worth noting that none of the State's most radical chieftains was elected Governor. The principal of these was the vehement Samuel Chase, later the defendant in the most famous but one of the nation's impeachment trials. Born the son of an English minister, he had been liberally educated, was admitted to the bar just in time to share in the opposition to the Stamp Act, and early began

[6] Bond, 14 ff.

his long career in the Legislature. After 1770 he became so prominent in his Whiggism that he was made one of Maryland's first
delegates in the Continental Congress. With Franklin and Charles
Carroll of Carrollton, he went north in 1776 to win the Canadians to
participation in the Revolution, but returned betimes to play a leading rôle in persuading Maryland to consent to independence. In the
spring of 1776 two other delegates in Congress, Johnson and Goldsborough, had favored delaying the Declaration, while the Provincial
Convention itself regarded an assertion of national freedom as premature; but by organizing county meetings, and by incessant speaking, Chase and his associates brought Maryland into line. He was
one of those men who are enthusiastically followed without being
implicitly trusted, and whose following is greatest among the inexperienced and ignorant. Even John Adams, whose views as to
independence were precisely the same as Chase's, criticized him for
want of judgment, called him boisterous, and noted that in debate
he was tedious upon frivolous points. He was so indiscreet that in
the latter part of 1778 he brought himself under suspicion of having
speculated in flour upon the basis of his knowledge of a secret resolve
by Congress to purchase 20,000 barrels of that commodity. Charles
Carroll of Carrollton solemnly accused him of this breach of trust
in two newspaper essays of August, 1781; Chase published his defense the next month; and the Legislature which met soon afterwards, inquired into the matter, found the evidence poor, and
acquitted Chase.[7] But the hostility between him and various conservatives contributed much to the irritation between the two houses.

One of Chase's protégés was the equally noted Luther Martin,
who by Chase's influence was in 1778 appointed Attorney-General
of Maryland.[8] In that post he prosecuted the Tories with such
bitterness that he offended the State's better sense, and made many
enemies. After the war, in 1784-85, he sat in the Continental Congress. He had meanwhile, in 1783, married the daughter of the
Captain Michael Cresap whom Jefferson, in his "Notes on Virginia"
published the next year, accused of brutally murdering the family of
the friendly Indian chief Logan; an accusation that Martin never
forgave, one of his favorite comparisons being, "as great a scoundrel
as Tom Jefferson." Gifted with high talents and cursed with fatal

---

[7] Md. *Journal*, Aug. 23, 30, 1781; Sept. 24, 1782.
[8] See Goddard's "Luther Martin," Fund. Pubs. Md. Hist. Soc., 1887.

weaknesses, he was one of the most picturesque figures Maryland has produced. His eloquence, at its best, could even be compared with that of Patrick Henry; in later years he was called by Taney, who rose to be Chief Justice of the United States, "a profound lawyer"; and many illustrations are given of his sway over judges and juries, the rapidity with which he grasped a case, and the clearness with which he expounded it. His passion for drink only slowly impaired his prestige. He would be left fuddled by despairing colleagues a few hours before an important case, and amaze them by walking into the courtroom on time, alert and prepared. Reverdy Johnson has related how he abandoned Martin drunk one night at an inn when they were attending court, and went to bed, to be awakened a few hours later by Martin entering and sitting soberly down to read the prayer-book. Martin was author of the once-famous definition: "A man is drunk when after dinner he says or does that which he would not otherwise have said or done." In the decade 1780-90, when still young, he was building up his fine reputation at the bar, and as Chase's second was a political power.

The Revolution was followed in Maryland by factional quarrels of as much heat as those in most other States. The legislative session which opened November 1, 1784, and ended early in 1785, was especially prolific of them. No less than four subjects of controversy appeared—the College bill, the Duty bill, the Potomac bill, and the bill to relieve non-jurors of the penalties imposed upon them. The opponents of the legislation passed, and wise, progressive legislation it was, called this "the black session."

The College bill was a measure to give the western shore its own seminary of learning, a mate to that existing on the poorer, more sparsely settled eastern shore. In 1782 the Legislature had passed an act founding the latter, under the name of Washington College, at Chestertown, and granting it £1250 a year. Friends had subscribed a small endowment, distinguished Marylanders had accepted appointments as governors and visitors, and William Smith, the exiled provost of the college in Philadelphia, was made President. The school thrived. Why should not the western shore also have a college and a State appropriation? asked delegates for Baltimore and Annapolis. "I reflected," said one of them, "that Maryland was one of the few States of the Union which has no colleges, by which means she was tributary to Europe, Pennsylvania, Jersey, and Delaware, for the common rudiments of education—that immense sums of money were daily drawing out of the State, never again to be restored, for the purposes of education, which ought to be retained among us—in short, every possible exertion should be made to render Maryland respectable in science and literature." [9] The State had about 275,000 inhabitants, or enough to support two colleges in a day when colleges were little more than high schools. Quite properly, therefore, the Legislature chartered and appropriated £1750 a year to an institution called St. John's College, at Annapolis, which was to form, with Washington College, the University of Maryland.

Washington himself brought his influence to bear in behalf of the Potomac Bill, in which most legislators saw a useful internal improvement and a link with the West, but which a few regarded as likely to make Alexandria or Norfolk the rival of Baltimore, already the nation's fifth commercial city. The Legislature had in May, 1783, appointed men to examine the Potomac, and they reported in the autumn that two years' work and $92,000 would open it to the Great Falls. At Washington's suggestion, the Virginia Legislature in 1784 named three deputies, one of them himself, to confer in Annapolis with Maryland, representatives. Washington was therefore in the capital when, in December, the bill was brought up and passed. With a concurrent Virginia act, it chartered the Potomac Company to improve the river's navigation, and authorized a State subscription of £5000 worth of stock—the whole initial capital being only £50,000. Within a few months all the stock was subscribed.

The Duty Act was simply one of the various State tariff acts, levying duties not only upon imports but upon exports in foreign bottoms. As for the bill to relieve non-jurors, it unfortunately failed, after precipitating another quarrel between the House and Senate. This time the Senate, inveterately cautious, was ranged against the non-jurors, while the House had become their champion; on January 14, 1785, with Samuel Chase as its principal sponsor, the bill was carried in the House 34 to 9, but next day the upper chamber defeated it 9 to 1. Forthwith the House approved an indignant message which Chase had written, declaring that: [10]

To disfranchise a number of citizens by depriving them of the right to elect representatives, and to bind them by laws to which they are prohibited by law from giving any assent, is the highest exercise of legislative power, and ought only to be *exercised* in *extreme exigency,* for the safety of the State, and ought not to be con-

[9] David McMechen, Md. *Journal*, Sept. 23, 1785.
[10] Md. *Journal*, Sept. 12, 1788.

tinued after the necessity ceases. We believe there are thousands cut off from citizenship by the law which we propose to repeal, a law made amidst the tumult and rage of war. Amongst those proscribed are numbers of Quakers and Methodists. . . .

This message proposed as a compromise that non-jurors be allowed to vote, but be excluded from office. The Senators, who had been chosen when the war was at its bitterest crisis, refused even this, and the House, after asking whether lenity was not more likely to win support for a republican government than harshness, yielded.

In every section of Maryland, during the summer of 1785, demagogues appealed to the unthinking by attacks upon the men who stood for progress in education, internal improvements, and commercial independence of England. A pair of colleges would be too expensive, they said; and this grant of £3000 a year obliged the poor laborer to assist the wealthy planter in giving polish to his sons, while his own children remained ignorant. It was correctly replied that the Legislature in 1773 had set aside £16,000 for higher learning, and that this sum, diverted to war use upon a solemn promise of repayment, now amounted to more than £25,000. Moreover, a number of free schools for the poor had already been established; and how could teachers be provided, without seminaries to train them? Every tavern-keeper and tavern-haunter opposed the College Act because it included restrictions upon the sale of liquor by licensed retailers, and provided for raising money by a license tax upon all "ordinary keepers." To spend £5000 in clearing the Potomac was also called unforgivable, whether the improvement would accomplish nothing and waste money, or be successful and enrich Virginia at Maryland's expense. As for the duties, they would be a heavy tax on the poor and injure the Chesapeake trade.[11]

The State greatly needed a medium of trade—why, grumbled some, didn't the legislators issue paper? It needed improved roads, laws to govern the care of the poor, and a better system of courts, yet the lawmakers were indifferent. One appeal to the "neglected mechanics" pictured Liberty wringing her hands and asking: "If taxes are multiplied with the public distress [tariff duties], if economy is neglected in proportion as it becomes necessary [Potomac bill], and if the injustice of the Legislature adds to the convenience of the rich from the necessities of the poor [College Act], is it not

[11] For this controversy, see Md. *Journal*, Jan. 7, 1785; March 29, Aug. 23. In 1786 was published a pamphlet, "Several Acts of the Gen. Assembly Respecting St. John's College."

the exclusive privilege of my sons openly to complain?"[12] In Baltimore the two Delegates, David McMechen and John Sterret, were fiercely assailed, but were reëlected at the October polls.[13]

Yet Maryland's legislators managed to keep the State in the safe and liberal path. In the spring of 1782, after the usual dispute between Senate and House, they granted Congress power to levy the five per cent impost, and in June, 1783, they followed this with their consent to the revised impost amendment. At the close of 1786 the bill to relieve the non-jurors of their penalties was revived, and passed both houses—easily in the lower, by a close margin in the upper. Chase was, as before, its leading advocate. One argument lay in the fact that the discriminations against loyalists, Methodists, Quakers, and the German sects were actually driving many valuable inhabitants to the west, the emigration being described as a "rage."[14] Early this same year the Legislature wisely refused to transfer the capital from the ancient seat in Annapolis to Baltimore, quashing the agitation by a vote of two to one in the House.[15] Above all, the cry of misled farmers and mechanics for soft money was denied.

The struggle over the paper money question first became acute at the fall session of 1785, and it involved the angriest contest between the two houses in Maryland's history. It is sufficient here to say that the wisdom of those who devised Maryland's peculiar system of an indirectly chosen Senate was never better proved. In the fall of 1785 and the spring of 1786 the old Senate, its five-year term almost ended, stood like a stone wall against the paper emission which Chase and the House of Delegates were demanding. The new Senate, chosen by the electoral college in September, 1786, proved adamant in its opposition, and Maryland escaped a heavy financial blow.

Nor was Maryland less wise in national affairs. Everyone knows that the State led in the movement for divesting the larger States of their claims to extensive western areas, placing all such tracts at the disposal of Congress. Everyone knows that it was out of the conferences between Maryland and Virginia over the navigation of the Potomac and Chesapeake, and over uniform tariffs and currency, that there grew the Annapolis Convention of September, 1786. The

[12] Md. *Journal*, Sept. 30, Oct. 4, 1785.
[13] Md. *Journal*, Oct. 7, 1785.
[14] Md. *Journal*, Sept. 23, 1785; Sept. 12, 1788.
[15] Pa. *Packet*, Feb. 4, 1786; N. Y. *Packet*, Feb. 9.

prime movers for the Federal Convention were Washington, Madison, and Hamilton, but they owed much to the coöperation of Maryland leaders. It was Maryland's Legislature which, on November 22, 1785, proposed to bring Pennsylvania and Delaware into the Annapolis conference, and emboldened Madison to maneuver for the passage by the Virginia Legislature of a resolution inviting all the States to send delegates.

But ratification of the Constitution was not easily obtained in Maryland. When the Legislature met in November, 1787, it asked the delegates to the Federal Convention to report upon its proceedings. They were five in number, of whom three, Daniel Carroll, Daniel of St. Thomas Jenifer, and James McHenry, had signed the Constitution, while two, Luther Martin and John Francis Mercer, had quit the gathering in disgust before it ended. Martin laid before the Legislature a powerful paper opposing the Constitution—it is said that decades later Calhoun was wont to recur to Martin's arguments. With force of style, the Attorney-General argued that the government proposed was not really a federal government, but one tending towards the consolidation of all State governments; that the small States, like Maryland, were inadequately protected against encroachments; and that in a nation so extensive and imbued with such political traditions as America, liberty would be impossible when energetic State governments were destroyed. He objected to many specific provisions which seemed to impair the rights of the States, as that giving Congress the power to lay direct taxes, and he appealed to an old sentiment in Maryland when he pointed out that the national government would have no authority to erect a new western State out of the vast territory of Virginia, or Georgia, without the consent of those States. The arguments in favor of the Constitution were presented to the Legislature by Dr. McHenry, a man of less brilliance but solid parts. Born in Ireland, McHenry had studied medicine under Dr. Rush in Philadelphia, had become a soldier in the Continental army, and had been Lafayette's aid; he was a close friend of Washington. A call for a State convention to debate ratification was carried in the House by a majority of seven.

The campaign for seats in the State convention was the hottest political struggle Maryland had experienced since Samuel Chase's fight for independence in 1776. The opposition to the Constitution was led by Luther Martin, Samuel Chase, and Governor Smallwood, while William Paca declared that unless he were assured that certain amendments could be obtained, he would fight it as energetically as anyone. An equally influential array of names was mustered on the federalist side—Charles Carroll, Ex-Governor Thomas Johnson, McHenry, Daniel Carroll, George Plater, the Tilghman family, and A. C. Hanson. It told against the Constitution that two of its makers, Martin and Mercer, were so eager to denounce it. On the other hand, the reaction from the paper-money craze assisted the federalists, for it could not be forgotten that Chase, and the radicals and debtors who with him had clamored for bills of credit, were one in opposing the Constitution. "Honest, independent men," wrote a federalist, "should be alarmed in seeing them, the speculators and all the applicants to the Chancellor [i.e., bankrupts], laying their heads together in opposing the Government." [16]

Before the polls opened it was agreed that the federalists would easily elect a majority of the Convention. But the anti-federalists stuck to their guns, and in Annapolis and Baltimore especially the campaign was fought to the last minute.

In the latter city the people at first planned to send to the convention their two delegates in the House, McMechen and Sterret. But doubts arose as to their federalism, and a large meeting at Starck's Tavern just before the election put them a direct question: would they vote for ratification without first demanding amendments? They refused to answer, and on the second day of the balloting two rival candidates whose approval of the Constitution was unquestioned, McHenry and Dr. John Coulter, were hurriedly nominated.[17] The town gave them almost a thousand votes apiece, while McMechen and Sterret both fell well short of 400. The public rejoicings exceeded any since the close of the war. The shipbuilders, ship outfitters and provisioners, merchants, manufacturers, and several thousand citizens joined in a procession which wound through the different streets, preceded by the flag and a smartly decorated ship, supported on the shoulders of sailors; as this emblem of union passed, the crowd gave voice to "reiterated acclamations of joy." [18] The result was similar in aristocratic Annapolis, where the two federalists elected were A. C. Hanson and Nicholas Carroll. In the counties which contained these cities, however, anti-federalist dele-

[16] Md. *Journal*, March 14, 1788.
[17] *Idem*, Sept. 19, 1788.
[18] *Idem*, April 11, 1788.

gates were chosen. Two members of the influential Ridgely family had places on the anti-federalist ticket in Baltimore County. In Ann Arundel County, John Francis Mercer ran, and when an effort to make Governor Smallwood a candidate failed because of his absence, Samuel Chase, though now a resident of Baltimore, was impressed to take his place; they easily beat the federalist ticket, headed by Charles Carroll of Carrollton.

In some districts the anti-federalists were completely smothered. Thus in Washington County they polled only a score of votes, while the federalists had nearly 600, and could have mustered 1500. The final returns showed that only a handful of men would vote outright against the Constitution, while nearly two in every three would oppose amendments; more than half the counties, in fact, instructed their delegates to ratify without considering the amendments that Paca and others wished.[19]

The Convention, which met immediately after the election (April 21, 1788), afforded one of the early illustrations of a perfect "steam roller." It was not a deliberative assembly at all. The majority came to the hall with a definite program, and fearing some obstruction or stratagem on the part of the minority, pushed it through ruthlessly. The convention no sooner entered upon its business than it resolved that there should be no debate upon the amendment of the Constitution, but that after the instrument had been twice read, and debated as a whole, President Plater should put the question of ratification. When Paca tried to offer his amendments, the majority pointed out that they were instructed "to ratify the proposed Constitution, and that as speedily as possible, and to do no other act." The federalists did not deign even to speak in answer to their opponents, and carried the ratification 63 to 11. Afterwards Paca's twenty-eight amendments were submitted to a committee of both parties, which agreed to report the first dozen favorably, but this was never done, though Paca had the satisfaction of reading them to the Convention. In brief, the anti-federalist minority was excluded from a hearing, and, as it indignantly declared, the majority would not even let the yeas on the motion smothering the amendments be entered on the journal.

In Maryland, as in other States, men in the latter part of 1788 looked back regretfully to the time when party divisions had been

[19] Md. *Journal*, April 15, 18, 1788.

more local, more transient, and less angry. Each side blamed the other for the change. In Baltimore, a federalist writer insisted that Sterret's and McMechen's treachery to the federalist side "was the just cause of all our present disturbances. This introduced the distinction of federal and anti-federal in this town, scarcely known or felt before." That fall the campaign for seats in the House brought to the surface alarming party passions.[20]

The contest in Baltimore even produced rioting. When the federalists nominated Dr. McHenry and Dr. John Coulter, and the anti-federalists David McMechen and Samuel Chase, it was seen that the race would be close. Animosity began to a----when McHenry accused Chase of being unfriendly to the mechanics' interests; and much excitement was shown at a public meeting called by Robert Smith, one of the richest merchants, who denounced Chase bitterly for his opposition to a strong Federal government. A few days later, at a Chase-McMechen meeting in the Fell's Point or shipping district, the anti-federalist speakers were routed by heckling, groans, and drums. Several street affrays by grog-excited men followed. On September 15, Chase and McMechen held another meeting at the Court House, and as they were returning to the residential section, were attacked by a score of men with bludgeons; some of their party were knocked down, and the rioters smashed the windows of Chase's house. While the fever was at its height the four days of polling came on. Chase and McMechen received 502 and 494 votes respectively, against 635 for McHenry and 622 for Coulter, and though the anti-federalists, who won the county seats, raised the cry of fraud, the Legislature did not sustain the charge.

Immediately the attention of all politicians was turned to the choice of Congressmen and Presidential electors.[21] The State was allotted six Representatives, and the Legislature decided that they should be chosen on a general ticket, but that each must reside in the district for which he was nominated. A caucus of federalist leaders and legislators, in which both McHenry and Samuel Smith were prominent, was held at Annapolis late in 1788 to make ready

[20] For this election see files of Md. *Journal,* August, September, and October, 1788; Steiner's McHenry, 114 ff.
[21] See files of Md. *Journal,* January and February, 1789. The Federalist ticket for Representatives comprised Michael J. Stone, Joshua Seney, Benj. Contee, Wm. Smith, Geo. Gale, Daniel Carroll. The anti-federalists did not attack the Federal Government, but declared that their candidates "are jealous guardians of the rights of the people, and avowedly opposed to that aristocratical influence and spirit which are prevalent in the councils of this State."

for the contest. It agreed upon tickets for Congress and the electoral college which mass-meetings in various centers immediately endorsed, and a State committee was appointed to conduct the campaign. The anti-federalists, conscious of their weakness, resorted to the same tactics as in Pennsylvania—that is, they nominated a ticket made up in part of their own men, in part of federalists. This ticket, they said, represented an uncompromising enmity to "that aristocratical influence and spirit which are prevalent in the councils of this State, and dangerous to public liberty." They stood, they explained, only for amendments to the Constitution to secure the safety of the people and State, and their nominees were careful to promise a firm support of the new government. The federalists, on the other hand, insisted upon the dangers of launching the new system under the auspices of its enemies. Special efforts were put forth by both sides in Baltimore. William Smith, a man of wide commercial experience, was named there for Congress by the federalists, and Samuel Sterret, a capable lawyer, connected with influential county families, by the anti-federalists.

The result was the expected federalist victory. The party elected its six Congressmen by votes ranging from 7725 to 5154, as against votes for the anti-federalist nominees ranging from 2727 to 1829. The most prominent of those elected was Daniel Carroll, and of those defeated, John F. Mercer. The federalist majority for Presidential electors was even more emphatic. During the polling, the *Maryland Journal* reported great jubilation:

The Point displayed a spirit of federalism which does it the greatest honor. The little ship was brought forward, and several other emblems descriptive of the occasion. It would be injustice to the *friseurs* to omit mentioning, in a particular manner, their patriotism. They appeared at the polls with a figure representing the goddess of Federalism, and an excellent painting of General Washington, and conducted themselves throughout the election with becoming order and decorum.

Maryland's election of United States Senators had meanwhile taken place at the fall legislative session. The two houses agreed that the choice should be made on a joint ballot, but that no person was to be declared elected unless he received a majority of the attending members of each house. At this time the Senate consisted of fifteen men, and the House of eighty. On December 9, 1788, the joint session was held, and a resolution was passed that one Senator should represent each shore—a resolution that long fixed Maryland's policy. Charles Carroll of Carrollton and Uriah Forrest were nominated for the western shore, John Henry and George Gale for the eastern; and on the third ballot, Carroll and Henry, both federalists, were chosen. Maryland's members of Congress were thus all federalists.

The Governorship had passed into the hands of William Smallwood in 1785, and in 1788 into those of John Eager Howard, who was a personage of especial interest. His inherited estate comprised a large part of what is now the city of Baltimore, and he gave liberally from it for public purposes. The sites of the public market, the cathedral, the Washington Monument, and much of the park area were once all his. It was his gift of a residential block that was instrumental, in 1786, in bringing Samuel Chase from Annapolis. He had distinguished himself in the Revolution, especially at the Cowpens, and Washington esteemed him so much that he offered him the Secretaryship of War, just as he offered another former Maryland Governor, Johnson, the Secretaryship of State—both declining. At his fine mansion "Belvidere," which commanded a remarkable view of bay and town, he dispensed a hospitality which delighted the older generation. The early Maryland Governors, in fact, had an aristocratic quality, and Howard was the most aristocratic of all —a worthy contemporary of Hancock and Pinckney.[22]

II. Virginia Progressivism Under Jefferson

When we turn from Maryland to Virginia, we turn from a population of roughly a quarter million in 1780 to one of roughly 575,000, and from an area of fourteen thousand square miles to a vast region bounded on the west by the Mississippi. We turn from a State which furnished no national leaders to one which counted them in the army, the Congress, and the diplomatic service. Virginia was more exclusively rural than Maryland, for her largest city, Norfolk, had in 1789 less than half the inhabitants of Baltimore, and her second largest, Richmond, only about five hundred houses; but her extent, wealth, and array of talent made the occurrences within her borders far more interesting to Boston mechanics and Georgia planters than events in Maryland.

Nowhere did the struggle between progressives and conservatives have a broader meaning than in Virginia, nowhere were its lines more clearly drawn, and nowhere was it harder fought. The progressives

[22] Howard, "The Monumental City," 507-9.

advocated a wide program of social and political reforms. The lines were definite because the leaders would accept no compromise, and because the two sides were supported by two economic and in part by two sectional groups. The struggle was intense because, as in Pennsylvania, it meant the defeat or victory of the small privileged groups which had once dominated affairs; as in New York, it meant the downfall of influential and proud families; and above all, it meant the choice between the dignified tradition of colonial politics, and a new democracy which seemed dangerous and repulsive to lovers of the old order, fruitful and splendid to the young radicals.

The first progressive triumph in Virginia, the adoption of a liberal Constitution, was immediately followed by another in the election of Patrick Henry as Governor over John Page and Thomas Nelson. Henry accepted the post as a consolation for his lost military command. Just so had two great agitators of New England and the Middle Colonies, Hancock and Dickinson, been thwarted in their military ambitions. Nelson, who had been head of the upper house in the days of the Crown, and was a "harmony" candidate, received 45 votes, or fifteen less than Henry. The orator took his oath of office July 5, 1776, and settled down in the Williamsburg residence of the royal Governor—a poetic retribution for the way in which Lord Dunmore a few weeks previously had referred to "a certain Patrick Henry of Hanover County." Though Henry had theretofore been plain and unassuming, he now took on a dignity worthy of the successor of a long line of haughty Crown Governors; and with this new mien came a remarkable change of character.

The three years that Henry was Governor witnessed his transformation from a fiery zealot of change to a defender of old institutions. His military disappointments, the death of his wife, his failing health, his tendency toward indolence, and the grinding routine of his office, against which the impetuous orator chafed, all played a part in this alteration. But more important was the fact that to him the bounds which the Revolution attained with independence were sufficient; that while he longed for the freeing of Virginia from Great Britain, he had nothing of Jefferson's desire for egalitarian freedom. For Henry the Revolution reached its end in the Declaration; for Jefferson it reached its beginning. Whereas Jefferson had the faculty of absorbing new ideas and constantly expanding his ambitions, the political ideas of Henry were fixed. The leadership of the progressives passed at once from Patrick Henry to the young democrat from Albemarle, and his coadjutors Mason, Wythe, and Madison. They were social reformers, not merely political radicals.[23]

Jefferson, reëlected to Congress about a week before Henry was chosen Governor, refused to accept, alleging, with reference to his wife's ill-health, "private causes." But his chief motive was his desire to seize the progressive helm in Virginia. "When I left Congress in 1776," he wrote years later, "it was in the persuasion that our whole code must be reviewed and adapted to our republican form of government, and now that we had no negative of councils, governors, and kings, that it should be corrected in all its parts, with a single eye to reason and the good sense of those for whose government it was framed." Already he had plans for altering the whole social structure of Virginia; his scheme for a Constitution had reached the Convention too late, and he intended to be prompt in reaching the Assembly.[24] In October he took his seat, and a place on the chief committees. The "laboring oar" was in Virginia, he said, not Philadelphia. The State had an opportunity of showing the American people—to quote his Declaration—how "to institute new government, laying its foundations on such principles and organizing its powers in such forms, as to them shall seem most likely to effect their safety and happiness."

His ready-made program was partly that of a practical politician and partly that of a Utopian idealist; and although he had not Henry's forensic power and personal magnetism, he had indomitable persistence and much adroitness. On October 11, four days after the House sat, he obtained leave to introduce a bill for establishing courts of justice throughout Virginia. Next day he was authorized to bring in a measure to destroy the status of entail, and another for a revision of all the laws. Two days later he followed this with notice of a measure dealing more harshly with entail, and at the same time he and his aides began their agitation for the disestablishment of the Episcopal Church.[25]

The struggle thus initiated between conservatives and radicals lasted in one phase or another for years, though Jefferson achieved

---

[23] Eckenrode, 167 ff. For the increased stateliness of Patrick Henry's manners, see Henry, "Henry," I, 457-58; the Governor seldom appeared on the streets, and "never without a scarlet cloak, black clothes, and a dressed wig."
[24] Randall's "Jefferson," I, 196; "Writings," Memorial Ed., I, 53.
[25] Eckenrode, 169 ff.

some objects at the outset. It was mainly confined to the Assembly. Here Jefferson was supported in debate by a number of able colleagues. One of the chief was George Mason, a plain-spoken controversialist; "of expansive mind, profound judgment, cogent in argument," wrote Jefferson. Another was Wythe, who had been a personal friend of Fauquier, Botetourt, and other royal Governors, and who as professor of law in William and Mary had trained some of the House's best members. Though small in stature and frail of health, he was a pertinacious debater. Most effective of all Jefferson's supporters was the youngest, Madison, now twenty-five.

The opposition to the abolition of entail and the church establishment naturally enlisted almost the whole weight of the State's aristocracy. This was headed by Speaker Edmund Pendleton, who was Virginia's foremost legal scholar, taking precedence even of Wythe. Jefferson characterized him as cool, suave, resourceful, and so determined that "if he lost the main battle, he returned upon you, and regained so much of it as to make it seem a drawn one, by dexterous maneuvers, skirmishes in detail, and the recovery of small advantages." He knew his class, and could argue plausibly that as those most affected by the entail system approved it, it was not an abuse. Robert Carter Nicholas, a veteran attorney whose influence had been upon the side of conservatism in the Constitutional Convention, was his best second; and behind them stood Bland, now old and half blind, Carter Braxton, John Page, and others. A preponderance of sentiment, though largely inarticulate, was with Jefferson in his enmity to primogeniture and entail; while public feeling was more powerfully and articulately enlisted with him to destroy the "spiritual tyranny" of the Establishment.

The progressives at once scored two important victories. They outlawed entail, refusing to consent to Pendleton's proposal that it merely be made allowable for tenants in tail to abandon it if they liked. They also repealed all laws restricting men in their religious opinions, and exempted dissenters from contributions to the Episcopal Establishment; and though the government still had the right to levy taxes upon Episcopalians for the support of their own church, Jefferson succeeded in having these levies suspended until the next session. The connection between the government and church remained, but it was greatly weakened. Both progressives and conservatives for the most part united in a third reform, the redrafting of the legal code, and following the passage late in October, 1776, of his bill for the revision of the laws, Jefferson was made a member of a committee including Pendleton, Wythe, Mason, and Lee, to do the work. Upon one minor proposal only were the progressives defeated. They wished the seat of government removed from Williamsburg, where, as Jefferson argued, it would be easy for the British to land at night behind the town from either the York or James, and capture it before its papers, munitions, and perhaps even the government officers could be removed. But the conservatives knew that the eastern location of the capital, making it easy to reach from the Tidewater, hard to reach from the democratic West, was of political value to them. Moreover, there were weighty sentimental considerations in favor of keeping the seat of government where it had been located since the youth of the colony. Not until the session of May, 1779, was the removal to Richmond carried.[25a]

By his measures affecting estates and the church, Jefferson before Christmas, 1776, had so antagonized the landed aristocracy and the clergy of Virginia that he felt their enmity throughout his long career. But he had become unmistakably the leader of the forward-pressing faction of the Whigs, the great figure to which advanced opinion pinned its hopes for further reform; and outside the State his innovations attracted wide attention. The spring session of the Assembly in 1777 showed the majority solidly with him. For the speakership the conservatives nominated R. C. Nicholas and Benjamin Harrison, while the progressives put up George Wythe, whom Jefferson always implicitly trusted. Wythe was easily elected. Three-fifths of the population of the State already lay west of the Tidewater, the 50,000 able-bodied freemen of 16 to 50 years of age enumerated in 1780-81 including about 19,000 in the Tidewater counties and about 31,000 beyond. Representation in the House was according to counties, but the conservative Tidewater counties were only 36 in number, and those to the westward 39.

Indeed, Jefferson and his party easily maintained their ascendancy for more than two years. In 1778 he carried a bill to prohibit the importation of slaves, in accordance with a demand which had been strong before the war. In June, 1779, the conservatives tried to regain some of the lost ground by offering a measure for the reës-

---

[25a] Old Landon Carter in 1776 heard some legislators talk of transferring the capital "up to Hanover, to be called Henry-Town"; 5 Amer. Arch., II, 1305-06.

tablishment of religion on the basis of a general state support of all churches; and though Jefferson's great final bill for religious freedom failed at this session, so also did this conservative attempt at a retrieval. The net upshot of the debate on religious questions was a slight gain by the progressives, who obtained the final repeal of the act of 1748 providing state-guaranteed salaries for ministers of the Anglican church.

Both of the reëlections of Patrick Henry as Governor were unanimous, and the Legislature showed its trust by repeatedly granting him extraordinary powers to meet the exigencies of war. The first bestowal, in December, 1776, set afloat a rumor that the Assembly was the theater of a conspiracy to make Henry a dictator. It is said that the fiery Archibald Cary, hearing of this conspiracy, requested Henry's brother to tell the Governor that "the day of his appointment shall be the day of his death, for he shall feel my dagger in his heart before sunset"—evidence of the silly political nervousness of some Virginians. No one thought of vesting in Henry greater powers than Congress repeatedly vested in Washington, or than the Legislatures of South Carolina, Maryland, and Pennsylvania gave Rutledge, Johnson, and Reed, while actually, the executive authority of Virginia was exercised less by the Governor alone than by the Council. Administration by 1778 had worn its accustomed grooves. While Jefferson and his aides were concerting their social reforms, Henry and his Council were tied to the unescapable drudgery of making war, raising revenue, and disciplining Tories.

When the time came (1779) to choose Henry's successor, the conservatives held that Page ought to be promoted, while the progressives nominated Jefferson. There was no personal rivalry. Jefferson's supporters believed that as Governor he would be able to advance their cause irresistibly, and his opponents doubtless feared the same result, though a shrewd few may have seen that his election would rather bind and gag him. He was chosen in January and began his term June 1. From the latter date his decline as a leader began. "My great pain is lest my poor endeavors should fall short of the kind expectations of my country," he said in his speech of acceptance. His forebodings were justified to an extent which would have wrecked the career of any leader less versatile, buoyant, and resourceful. His Governorship lasted two years, one of them the blackest in his public life. He came to the helm when his power in

Virginia was at its greatest; he left it humiliated and stripped of most of his following.

One reason for Jefferson's discomfiture lay in certain real defects of capacity, amply illustrated when later he was President of the republic. A greater reason was that he became Governor at a disastrous moment, when the British turned from the north and launched their campaign to subjugate the South. The month before his election the enemy had seized Savannah, and before he had completed his first year in office, they captured Charleston. Washington, who was guarding the Hudson, hurried most of his Southern troops off to the new theater of war. Though Virginia had not yet been seriously invaded, it had borne its part in the struggle, and was keenly feeling the burden. The two State regiments originally raised for home defence had long ago been sent north to complete the Continental quota. Now it was bitterly complained by the Carolinas and Georgia that the other States were failing to send help, and Jefferson strained every nerve to contribute to the forces facing Cornwallis.

As throughout 1779 and 1780 the recruiting for service farther south went on, the Virginia militia became much depleted. Governor Jefferson wrote Washington to this effect on September 23 of the latter year. "The number of regulars and militia ordered from this State into the Southern service are about 7000," he stated. "I trust we may count that 5500 will actually proceed; but we have arms for 3000 only. . . . We are still more destitute of clothing, tents, and wagons for our troops." [26] A month later he wrote General Gates that Virginia could not outfit all her men—could not even give them shoes. Transport facilities and provisions could be had only when commandeered, and the Governor himself had lost a wagon, two horses, and two negroes by impressment. The treasury was empty, specie had disappeared, and paper money was growing more and more worthless. The State, in fact, found itself stripped of the means of defense just at the moment when the British were in the best position for invading it. Sensible Virginians did not blame Governor Jefferson for sending generous help to the stricken States to the southward, but they did blame him for not leaving Virginia even an effective emergency guard; he could have supplemented his aid to Virginia's neighbors, they argued, by devising a plan for rallying and arming short term home forces.

[26] "Writings," Memorial Ed., IV, 107.

In the first British assault the State got off rather easily. Late in October, 1780, the enemy moved a fleet of sixty sail into the James, and, repeating on a larger scale a stroke they had executed in the last months of Henry's Governorship, threw ashore 2500 men who did a little plundering in the region of Hampton Roads, lay in camp a month, and then returned to their ships. The chief effect of this raid was simply to make plain to everybody the State's unpreparedness. The Legislature, in its fall session at Richmond, was galvanized into action; it issued more paper money, called upon the counties to furnish clothing, military stores, and wagons, and ordered 3000 men drafted. Jefferson for three weeks tried to collect troops enough to fight the British invaders, and completely failed. Even General Nelson, the most popular soldier in Virginia, could not drum up a sufficient command to defend an important pass near the British base. What would be the future? Jefferson wrote Washington in great perturbation. complaining of an equal lack of weapons and of trained men.

But only a short breathing spell was offered. On December 31, 1780, came the news that a fleet of twenty-seven vessels of nationality unknown had just entered the Capes of Virginia; and this time the enemy moved with vigor. While Jefferson waited, doing nothing except sending General Nelson to the lower river counties with power to collect the militia, the fleet pressed up the James. On January 2 the Governor was assured beyond the possibility of doubt that the vessels were British, not French, and he hastily took the action he should have taken two days earlier—sent out an urgent call for the 4700 militia within reach of Richmond. In fact, Clinton had been spurred by Cornwallis's successes to send about 2000 men under Arnold to duplicate them in Virginia. Baron Steuben, who had been left behind by Greene and was at Richmond, thought that with the fighting men of Henrico, Hanover, New Kent, Goochland, Chesterfield, and other counties he could drive back the invaders. The Governor labored with desperate energy, spending days and nights in the saddle, and killing a blooded horse by galloping it about the country, but he could not get his troops together in time. Steuben kept south of the James, and Jefferson had to transport the State papers and some stores from Richmond across the river. The British on January 5 landed their forces at Westover, did what they liked in Richmond, and then dropped down in their ships to their old camp near Hampton Roads. They left behind a people convinced that, however great Jefferson was, he was not the man for Governor in such a perilous time.

The truth is that Jefferson was too much a believer in the voice of the people and in consultation with their representatives to make a good war Governor. While Virginia was financially helpless and without military defences, he had busied himself with detail, he had asked the Legislature's advice when he should have issued commands, and he had hesitated to take the brusque steps that would have made invasion dangerous. We can not blame him for his zeal in reinforcing the thin Continental armies. But it would have been possible in addition for a farsighted man, with more taste for action, to have raised troops, arms, and supplies for a mobile home force. After the loss of Charleston and the defeat at Camden these steps were imperative. The Legislature had been willing to support vigorous measures for it had authorized Jefferson to call 20,000 militia into the field in case of attack, to halt exports, and provide magazines. But the raw militia could not be mustered rapidly from the scattered farms and plantations, and were poor fighters when mustered. We may infer from Jefferson's utterances that he was restrained by a feeling that he must not press his authority too far. The act empowering a seizure of supplies having failed, he humbly apologized to the county magistrates in ordering further levies, saying that the Legislature would authorize them if in session, and that "substance and circumstance is to be regarded while we have so many foes in our bowels and environing us on every hand." He summoned the Legislature ahead of its time in 1780, and requested more laws, though laws were not what was wanted. When a former Continental officer, Alexander Spottswood, made a sensible suggestion for raising a legion of mixed infantry and cavalry, under Continental regulations, for State service, he replied that several parts of the proposal were "beyond the power of the executive to stipulate."

Arnold, before leaving Richmond, had offered to spare the town if he were allowed to carry off the tobacco, and when this was refused, had set the torch to it. When Governor Jefferson went back, he found that what could not be burnt had otherwise been destroyed—the merchants' rum had been staved in in the streets, and the salt emptied into the river. Plantations had been ravaged, for the British knew that tobacco paid much of the interest on the French

debt. Worst of all, Arnold and his array of British, Hessians, and
Tories had not departed, but in their fortified position at Portsmouth
were able at any moment to reascend the river. By January 18,
1781, the slow-gathering militia amounted to 3700 men, in three
widely separated encampments—one at Fredericksburg under
Weeden, one at Williamsburg under Nelson, and one at Cabin Point
under Steuben. In spite of the lamentable deficiency of muskets,
powder, and bayonets, Jefferson for a moment plucked up courage,
and even dreamed of some sudden, bold descent by picked frontiersmen into Arnold's camp, to drag the traitor to condign punishment.
He had better have been facing the grim realities. While he was
revolving this pleasing scheme, and while the Legislature, which
met in Richmond on March 1, was doing little more than order the
enlistment of the two legions for which Spottswood had submitted a
plan to Jefferson, the British were preparing their final stroke.

It proved a double blow, struck by Arnold from the seacoast and
by Cornwallis from the south. On April 18, when nearly all the
40,000 potential soldiers of the State were planting crops, the force
commanded by Arnold and Phillips again started from Portsmouth
up the James. It paid a flying visit to Williamsburg, proceeded to
City Point, and thence marched upon Petersburg, forcing Steuben's
small force to retire, and holding the town several days. This period
it spent in destroying contraband property in the surrounding country. Meanwhile Cornwallis, having beaten Greene at Guilford Court
House, had found the way open for an invasion of Virginia from the
south. On May 20 his worn army marched into Petersburg, effecting
a junction with Arnold; and at the head of this double force he
crossed the James in the direction of Richmond. The Legislature
had by now fled to a safer refuge. Lafayette, who had been hurriedly sent south by Washington, had only 3000 men. The British
were in overwhelming strength, and short of recklessly attacking
Lafayette, could do much as they pleased. They destroyed tobacco
by thousands of hogsheads, and ships, flour, ropewalks, hides, and
other property. In trying to cut Lafayette off from northern reinforcements, Cornwallis in the last days of May penetrated into
Hanover County, north and west of Richmond.

At the same time (May 28), a quorum of the Legislature assembled at Charlottesville, the Governor's home, within striking distance of the British. The opportunity was too good to lose. A swift

expedition under Tarleton was sent to bag the State officers, and only a speedy messenger saved Jefferson. The Assemblymen and Senators made an ignominious scurry, seven fell into the hands of the British, and the rest did not halt until they were safe over the mountains in Staunton. As he moved off down the James, Cornwallis laid waste many more estates, among them that of Governor Jefferson at Elk Hill, where he burned the barns, destroyed the growing crops, and cut the throats of horses. The total damage wrought by the British that summer was estimated at three million pounds sterling. With this last humiliation of the State, a new storm of abuse burst upon Jefferson.

Just before this mortifying chase of the government from Charlottesville, he wrote Washington that "a few days will bring to me that relief which the Constitution has prepared for those oppressed with the labors of my office, and a long-declared resolution of relinquishing it to abler hands, has prepared my way for retirement to a private station. . . ." [27] The second year of his Administration would end June 1, and he was in no mood to continue in office. He meant what he said of "abler hands." He saw that he lacked aptitude for energetic action; he had always believed that the powers of the Governor and chief military commander ought to be combined to ensure vigor in State defense, and now he knew his own deficiency in the qualities demanded by war. The Legislature, sitting at Staunton, took up the election of a new Governor on June 12. Some of Jefferson's friends naturally thought he ought to be given a third year, and his biographer Randall declares that he was obliged to dissuade them before another man could be chosen. But it is likely that his defeat would have been inevitable had he desired reëlection. Nor was his successor one of his followers. Thomas Nelson, of a wealthy and conservative Tidewater family, who was fitted for the post by his military experience, was made Governor, and began to assist in the campaign which ended in the capture of Cornwallis.

But Jefferson was not to escape with the humiliation merely implied by retirement. Though the fact that the Legislature was meeting in the extreme west, where the radicals could attend more easily than the lowland conservatives, was in his favor, a resolution was passed June 12, ordering "That at the next session of the Assembly an inquiry be made into the conduct of the executive of this State for the last twelve months." Its proposer was a young man of Jefferson's own county, of progressive leanings, later to be a devout follower of Jefferson, named George Nicholas. Three of the five charges made—charges that Jefferson had not promptly prepared the State for invasion, had not used all available means of defense, had discouraged others by his personal timidity when Arnold took Richmond, had ignominiously fled from Tarleton, and had abandoned the Governorship when it became a post of danger—were thoroughly unfair; and the next Legislature dropped the inquiry, giving Jefferson the thanks of the State for his able Administration. But Nicholas's resolution for the moment filled Jefferson with bitterness. When Edmund Randolph spoke to him of office that fall, he replied that "I have taken my final leave of everything of that nature. I have retired to my farm, my family and books, from which I think nothing will evermore separate me." [28] Dispirited, beaten, angry, he avoided state affairs, till he was sent by Congress as a special ambassador to France to help negotiate a treaty of commerce. From 1784 to 1789 he remained in Europe, and his considerable influence in Richmond was exerted by letters to friends.

When Jefferson had been elected Governor, the leadership in the House had passed to Patrick Henry and Richard Henry Lee, both one-time radicals who were now fast growing conservative. Jefferson bequeathed his unfinished program to Madison, Wythe, and Mason, and it made little further progress. From 1779 to the close of 1781, naturally, the Legislature was too much preoccupied by its fear of the British to undertake measures demanding long debate, and calculated to arouse internal antagonisms.

III. Virginia Conservatism Under Henry

After Jefferson's departure for Europe, the progressive party for several years became disorganized, though not completely impotent. The temporary discrediting of its great spokesman had injured it. Moreover, people by the end of 1781 were weary of war, turmoil, and change; their fervent wish was for a peace and prosperity like that of the years before the Revolution and they invested the old conservative régime with a tempting glamour. For a third reason, the conservatives had the better leaders, since in addition to Henry

[28] "Writings," IV, 187.

and Lee, the list included John Marshall, who—a lanky young lawyer of twenty-seven—was elected to the Legislature in the fall of 1782, John Tyler, Benjamin Harrison, and Henry Tazewell. These leaders could count upon a fairly solid group of Tidewater delegates. To ordinary observers the Legislature might have seemed a highly democratic body, inclined to radicalism. The velvet coats, knee breeches, silk stockings, and fine linen had largely disappeared when the Revolution ended. While the Tidewater representatives still dressed well, the majority wore homespun or coarse imported cloth, and the men from over the Blue Ridge appeared in buckskin leggings and hunting shirts. Debate became less formal, the contempt for deliberative dignity would have shocked stately pre-Revolutionary leaders like Peyton Randolph, banter and laughter enlivened the proceedings, and some members were palpably illiterate. But this rampant democracy in exterior traits did not carry with it an intelligent progressivism in legislation.

During the three years of reaction, 1782-4, Patrick Henry and R. H. Lee were personal but not party rivals in the House. Henry was the more powerful by far; his influence could be described only by the word Marshall used in 1783—"immense." In the legislative session of 1783, for example, Lee wished to be Speaker, but when Henry pointed to John Tyler, Tyler received the heavy majority of 41. At the session of 1784 Lee gracefully saved himself from another defeat by nominating Tyler. On many minor bills the two chieftains took opposite sides—so many that young Spencer Roane thought them "almost constantly opposed." Both were inclined towards those oratorical battles in which Virginians delighted and their forensic styles formed a striking contrast. Lee was quiet, graceful, correct in diction, and though somewhat monotonous usually pleasing; Henry, much more unequal in his efforts, could be much more striking and powerful, and if when uninspired he fell distinctly below his opponent, when aroused by the issue his passionate eloquence carried all before it. He was almost always victorious, says Roane. But if they seemed constant rivals upon small questions, on large questions and in general temper they harmonized, and when a real test arose in 1785 they joined hands against progressivism.

One evidence of the temporary conservative ascendancy lies in the character of the men who filled the Governor's chair after 1781.

Nelson, a warrior and not a statesman, who could train the cannon on his own Yorktown mansion but could not plan a tax-bill, served less than a year, resigning after the surrender of Cornwallis. He had been a better war Governor than Jefferson, for he saw just what the military situation demanded, and paid no excessive attention to Council or Legislature. The conservatives promptly elected Benjamin Harrison, a rich planter of Charles County on the lower James; and in the summer of 1784, Patrick Henry was chosen again, for the first of two successive terms.

But the best indication of the reaction is given by the bills passed and defeated.[29] The Assemblies both of 1782 and 1783 showed intense bitterness against the Tories, and in the latter year objectionable legislation was voted to prevent loyalist refugees from returning to Virginia. Instead of facing the financial problem manfully and courageously, the Legislature protected from distraint men whose taxes had fallen into arrears, while it clung to the objectionable system of payments in kind. Madison and others after the close of fighting proposed to reopen all accounts which had been paid in depreciated money, and have them settled by a legal scale of depreciation—a measure which promised tardy justice to cheated creditors. But Henry indignantly opposed this plan, and it was never pressed. At the spring session of 1783, moreover, though Jefferson himself visited Richmond to urge favorable action, the impost plan offered by Congress was rejected by a heavy majority. Its opponents used the familiar argument that the body which controlled the sword must not control the purse, and R. H. Lee was convinced that it would not only endanger public liberty, but strangle Virginia's commerce in the cradle, make the State pay more of the national burden than its share, and sacrifice the South to the North. The Virginians would go no further than to levy their own impost of five per cent., ultimately payable to a Congressional receiver.

At the spring session in 1784 conservatism reached its height, and the progressive and reactionary parties clashed on a wide front. Edmund Randolph, writing Jefferson three days after the Legislature met,[30] announced that the issues that would occupy the Assembly were "first, a general assessment; second, restitution of British property; third, payment of British debts; fourth, the introduction of a

---

[29] Journal, House of Delegates, *passim;* Lee's "Life of R. H. Lee," I, 235 ff.
[30] Conway's "Randolph," 55, 56; Eckenrode, "Church and State in Va.," 74 ff.; Journal, House of Delegates, First Session 1784, 70.

stamp act, under a less offensive name; fifth, the making of Norfolk the only port of entry and clearance." He might also have named the question of revising the State Constitution, and that of giving Congress the appropriations it asked. By a general assessment, of course, was meant a general tax for the support of religion, each taxpayer designating the church he wished to assist. "It has Henry for its patron in private," Randolph wrote, "but whether he will hazard himself in public cannot be yet ascertained." The progressives suffered three real defeats, but on the most important question, that of the religious assessment, they held their ground.

We may first note the defeats. The proposal to allow the recovery of British debts, then barred by law, had been made as soon as peace was declared. Virginia planters, in the easy-going days before the war, had been wont to order what they liked from London agents, pay by notes, and let their debts run up to ruinous sums. Many debts had become hereditary from father to son, so that, as Jefferson, himself a debtor, expressed it, "the planters were a species of property annexed to certain mercantile houses in London." [31] As ravaged Virginia was desperately poor, even partial payment in hundreds of instances would mean bankruptcy. The people and Legislatures were divided. Madison's proposal was to make the debt payable, with interest from the date of the definitive treaty, in two instalments, and if the British refused or delayed either the evacuation of the frontier posts, or the return of the slaves carried away from Virginia, to collect damages from the second installment. This was nothing more than public honor, under the treaty, demanded. R. H. Lee supported Madison, declaring that Americans would have done better to remain "the honest slaves of Great Britain, than to become dishonest freemen," but Henry defeated the bill. The attempt to revise the Constitution also met what Madison called "violent opposition" from Henry, and failed. Madison's plan to restrict Virginia's commerce to Alexandria and Norfolk was a desperate expedient for nourishing a rival to Baltimore and Philadelphia, but local jealousies made it necessary to add York, Tappahannock, and Bermuda Hundred to the list, and to render the act

[31] Jefferson computed the Virginia debts owed to the British at the close of the war at from $10,000,000 to $15,000,000, saying that her obligations were nearly as great as those of all the rest of America put together. The amount, he wrote in January, 1786, was twenty or thirty times as much as all the money in circulation in Virginia. "Writings," Memorial Ed., Vol. XVII, 107-23. See also Bemis, "Jay's Treaty," Appendix IV.

applicable only to foreign trade and ships. Despite earnest professions of a desire to support Congress, the Legislature broke up after making only a shabby excuse for meeting the latest Congressional requisition. In general, Madison thought that the session showed deplorable confusion and incompetence in Virginia's government.

But the final struggle over the religious question, precipitated at this session by the conservatives, resulted in their discomfiture. Recognizing the poverty into which the war had plunged the Anglican church, they brought forward two bills in its interest. One was for the incorporation of the Protestant Episcopal Church of Virginia, giving it legal title to the church buildings, glebes, and other property in its possession. The other, the general assessment bill, would simply place Virginia in the path then followed by the three New England States least liberal in religion. We shall later relate how that fall Madison, against great odds, had the general assessment measure deferred for another year; how he and his aides used the interim to conduct an impressive campaign of education; and how he finally, in the fall of 1785, killed the bill by showing that the majority in the State was thoroughly aroused against it. We also relate how, striking while the iron was hot, Madison brought forward Jefferson's old bill for religious freedom, and had it passed.

By mere chance another great reform failed at the close of 1785. The high sense of honor among Virginians made it impossible for many to think of giving up the struggle for an equitable settlement of the British debts. These men profited by the elevation of Henry from a seat in the Assembly to the Governorship, where he could no longer interfere, and by the fact that during the year 1785 Speaker John Tyler was half converted to their position. A bill was introduced providing for payment of the debts in seven annual installments, and it had the endorsement of a majority of the Legislature; some British merchants made an effort to have liquidation compelled in four instalments, but this concession the majority refused. The measure passed the House, where Madison championed it, but met with obstructions in the Senate which delayed it until past the usual time for adjournment—that is, until the beginning of January. Finally, the two chambers having agreed, the bill was voted by the upper chamber, and was ready for return to the lower, to be received, examined, and signed by the two Speakers. At that juncture occurred a *contretemps* which illustrated the uncertainty of travel in those days. Several legislators braved the wintry weather to cross the James River—as yet unbridged—from Richmond to Manchester for the evening, intending to return the next day. But a freezing night made it impossible to row back, and the Legislature could not find a quorum. It waited three days in the hope of moderate weather or a display of heroism by the absentees, and then disgustedly broke up.[32]

Nevertheless, the victory of Jefferson's bill for religious liberty showed that the reaction against reaction had now arrived, and the democratic impulse registered itself at new heights. In 1784, the year that Madison renewed the demand of interior Virginia for constitutional reform, Jefferson's "Notes on Virginia," containing an elaborate exposition of the constitutional abuses existent in the State, had been published in Paris in an edition of 200 copies for distribution among friends, chiefly in Virginia, and its influence soon began to be felt there. The next year the Methodists and Quakers presented petitions to the Legislature for the abolition of negro slavery, and a bill for the encouragement of manumission was actually passed. An attempt by the Tidewater to return the capital to Williamsburg, on the ground that its removal had been simply to meet the perils of the war, was defeated. Petitions were received in 1785 and the subsequent years for the repeal of the act incorporating the Episcopal Church and guaranteeing its property, and it ultimately was annulled.

Henceforth, the advanced ideas of democracy rooted themselves more and more firmly in Virginia. In the lowland region there was a steadfast cohort of conservatives, but changes occurred even there, for many families were impoverished by the war and moved away to give place to overseers or new settlers. The power of the planter oligarchy had been shaken ten years before the Revolution, it had been dealt heavy blows by the war, and now economic changes and movements of population were destroying it except as it was bulwarked by the Constitution and by its superior education.

Henry retired from the Governorship in November, 1786, and was succeeded by a native of Williamsburg, Edmund Randolph, who had been a member of the Continental Congress and Attorney-General. The Randolphs were one of the proudest of Virginia's families, tracing their lineage among the English gentry back to

[32] Madison's "Writings," II, 114-16; Henry, "Henry," III, 265-67; Hening, XI, 402 ff.

Plantagenet times. Already Edmund Randolph had had an eventful career, passing his childhood at Tazewell Hall, studying at William and Mary, and parting from his father in 1775 when the latter, a loyal King's Attorney, returned to England while the youth became an aide to Washington. His future career was to reach its climax in his appointment as Washington's Secretary of State, and his resignation under the disgrace of the Fauchet affair. He was not a man of forceful character, but his election was regarded by the radicals as a gain. It pleased Jefferson; it also pleased Washington, for Randolph believed in an energetic national government, and Washington wanted a Governor of such creed now that "our affairs seem to be drawing to an awful crisis." [33]   It displeased R. H. Lee and Colonel Theodorick Bland, who, as rival candidates for the conservative wing, were defeated for the office. Both these men a little later were consistent opponents of the Federal Constitution, while Randolph in his vacillating way first helped make it, then attacked it, and finally urged its ratification. He was succeeded in 1788 by Beverly Randolph, who had sat in the Assembly during the Revolution, had risen to be Lieutenant-Governor, and had thus reached the chair by simple promotion. Beverly Randolph had less ability than his relative, but he also leaned toward the progressive party in State affairs, and he gratified Madison by a qualified support of the Constitution.

Among the chief political questions in the three years 1785-88 were the repeal of the Incorporation Act; constitutional reform, bringing the east and west into direct conflict; internal improvements, accentuating this clash; and the State tariff, further intensifying it. The time was not ripe for alterations of the Constitution to do the West justice, and nothing could be accomplished except to register the marked grievance of the uplands and the Shenandoah Valley. As for internal improvements, however, the movement for them was in a vigorous infancy, and scored several successes.

The isolated settlers of the interior were desirous of having the Potomac and James made navigable above the fall line, and roads built over the Blue Ridge. At the autumn session of the Legislature in 1784 Washington appeared to use his influence for improvements in navigation, and helped establish that year the Potomac Company and the James River Company. The Legislature at once

[33] Conway's "Randolph," 59.

chartered both, and granted them a limited subsidy. Washington, Madison, and Jefferson saw in such improvements a means of linking the western settlements with the east, and thus binding the nation together, but the western settlers thought only of pocketbook considerations. Thousands had never seen a wagon, for the rude trails would admit only a horse and pack. Even around Richmond at the end of the Revolution there were no roads which would now be thought worthy of the name. It required two days to traverse the sixty-odd miles between that "filthy place," as R. H. Lee called it in 1783, and the old capital, Williamsburg, while as late as 1790 Jefferson wrote that the way from Richmond northward was so bad that he could never travel more than three miles an hour, and at night could go but one. To lift the tobacco of Augustus County, in the Shenandoah, to market, cost more than the crop would usually bring, for it required a fortnight to traverse one hundred miles with one of the clumsy four-horse or six-horse wagons, produce-laden, of the time.[34]

The Tidewater legislators, on the other hand, saw little benefit to their constituents in the opening of the upper reaches of the James and the Potomac. Ships of heavy burden could pass up the Potomac for nearly three hundred miles; on the James, vessels of 125 tons could ascend to within a mile of Richmond; the Rappahannock afforded two fathoms of water to Fredericksburg; and flatboats could navigate the Appomattox as far as Petersburg, the Pamunkey for seventy miles, and the Chickahominy for twenty-four miles. The population served by these waters shrank from the taxation involved in heavy subsidies to internal improvement companies. Its representatives held the public aid down to a subscription of $22,000 worth of the shares in the Potomac Company, $20,000 worth in the James Company, and a direct appropriation of $3333 for a road reaching inland from the upper Potomac. Moreover, they had to be placated by the inclusion in the program of the appointment of commissioners to investigate the problem of canal communication between Elizabeth River and North Carolina waters, with a view to augmenting Norfolk's trade. The modest scheme then passed, Madison wrote, with "precipitancy," the first step upon a path that was to prove long and troubled.

A greater bitterness was displayed in the Legislature over the

[34] See Beveridge's "Marshall," I, Ch. 7.

State tariff. The west, wishing to see large eastern cities built up to afford an urban market for its raw products, supported the law for restricting the number of ports of entry, whether for goods or immigrants, to five, and succeeded also in placing a duty upon all imports of wine, rum, cheese, beef, pork, iron, and hemp. To both measures the east, which wished prices upon all these commodities kept low, offered a stubborn resistance under George Mason and other of their old leaders, and it soon obtained the repeal of both. Madison in the fall of 1786 was half inclined to rejoice over the return of Mason to the Assembly, and half inclined to lament it, because the repeal of the Port Act would certainly be one condition "on which we are to receive his valuable assistance." The west also asked, much more than the east, for extensions of time in the payment of taxes, and for the right to compound for them in farm produce. Both the postponements and commutations were repeatedly granted, though leaders concerned for the State's financial stability combated them as far as circumstances allowed. Madison, the foremost of such leaders, had to admit after nearly four years of peace that "the trade of this country is in a deplorable condition," and "ruinous" to agriculturists, and in 1788 that "our specie has vanished," and "the people are again plunged in debt to the merchants." [35] Some concessions were unavoidable.

In all, a mixed political situation existed when the struggle for the Constitution began. The west desired internal improvements, and it furnished the driving power for most of the social reforms won, but its progressiveness was limited by the facts that it had a less educated intelligence than the east, that it harbored a warm feeling against sound money and sound treasury administration, and that it was inclined to be anti-federal. The lowlands were against State constitutional reform and for the most part against radical social changes, but they showed a general appreciation of the need for a strong national government. Leaders like Madison were unable to tell, in advance of actual debate on many of the issues, who would be against them and who for them. Thus it was that in trying to strengthen the national government, Madison joined hands with such past political opponents as Pendleton and such future opponents as Marshall, while he contended against such former allies as George Mason and such future allies as Monroe.

[35] "Writings," II, 151.

To understand the conflict between federalists and anti-federalists in 1787-88 we must go back to the years 1783-84, when federalist principles and plans began to meet their test. We have noted that Virginia's action upon the impost plan was unsatisfactory, but to Madison even Virginia's partial, suspended compliance was something to be thankful for. Other States in some instances did no better, and if all had done as well, the financial perplexities of the Confederation would have been much reduced. The Legislature in the fall of 1783, rather in hatred of the British than from any wish to invigorate the general government, also consented to the request of Congress for authority to enact commercial regulations in retaliation against Great Britain.

The most important victory in 1783, however, was Virginia's surrender of her claims to the Northwest Territory, accomplished at this same fall session after spirited debate and by the close vote of 53 to 41. The State's original offer to the nation on January 2, 1781, had been encumbered by seven main conditions—that Virginia be repaid for the cost of conquering the Illinois country, that Clark and his men be given a quantity of land there, that the promises of bounty lands for Virginians in the Continental Line be met, that friendly inhabitants be protected, that the unappropriated lands be used for the national good, that the region in due time be laid off into States, and that Virginia be guaranteed her Kentucky domain. A compromise was now arranged, Virginia giving up substantially everything but her demands for reimbursement and for the bounty lands. Madison was not in the Assembly when this great cession was made, but George Mason labored unceasingly for the settlement.[36] Much resentment was shown throughout the State, and several legislators who were accused of making a profit from the transfer—three great land companies had obtained tracts in the ceded region in contravention of the Virginia laws—were defeated by their constituents the following year.

In 1784 another notable victory was won for the national idea. The lawless frontiersmen at this time needed a sharp restraint from acts which were an infraction of the treaties of the United States with European nations or with Indian tribes. Mason wrote in the fall of 1784 that "we are every day threatened by the eagerness of our disorderly citizens for Spanish plunder and Spanish blood," and

[36] Rowland's "Mason," II, 64-65.

six weeks later that there was no concealing the danger "of our being speedily embroiled with the nations contiguous to the United States, particularly the Spaniards, by the licentious and predatory spirit of some of our Western people." Virginia pioneers hated any Spaniard, while many of them would murder an Indian in cold blood. The remedy, when European subjects were the victims, was a law providing that whenever a Power offered evidence that the perpetrator of a crime on its territory had fled to Virginia, Virginia should, at the instance of Congress, surrender him. The bill which Madison introduced provided this, and also that under certain circumstances Virginia should herself try any citizen who committed a crime on foreign soil against the people of a friendly nation or tribe.[37]

This measure was a bitter pill for the individualistic westerners, to whom extradition seemed an infraction of the basic right of trial by a jury of the vicinage; while Tyler and some other Tidewater legislators joined the frontier in its opposition. But Madison found an unexpected ally in Patrick Henry, who was concerned not for America's foreign relations but for the Indian. The orator was an unfaltering friend of the noble red man. One of his pet schemes was a fantastic plan, which he induced the Legislature to support this year by bounties, for promoting intermarriage between Indians and whites, and thus producing what he predicted would be a superior race. Only Henry's support carried the extradition bill, and then only by a majority of one vote. Henry's attitude toward Congress at this time was far friendlier than in 1788. In 1784 Madison thought him "strenuous for invigorating the Federal government, though without any precise plan," and this year he wrote a resolution and had it passed declaring that whenever any State persistently failed to meet the Congressional requisitions, Congress ought to have power to collect the money by distraint upon the property of the State or its citizens. He and George Clinton went through the same change of attitude.

The success of the impost plan, the extradition bill, the measure to permit regulation of commerce by Congress, and the cession of the Northwest Territory, thus showed that up to 1785 the dominant sentiment of Virginia was friendly to a vigorous central government. It will also be recalled that at the end of 1785 the bill to fulfill the peace treaty by arranging a settlement of the British debts came

[37] Madison's "Writings," II, 98-99; Hening, XI, 471.

within a hair's breadth of succeeding. What produced the reversal which made Virginia's ratification of the Constitution so doubtful? What made Patrick Henry and the men of the west firm opponents of the Constitution? The factors were several, but the most important was the question of American navigation of the Mississippi, which wrought all western Virginia and Kentucky to a high pitch of excitement and anger.

The Mississippi question was as simple as it was important. The preliminary treaty with Great Britain contained certain public articles, and one secret article, defining the boundaries of the United States on one side, and of Louisiana and the Floridas on the other, and declaring that the Mississippi should always be open to British and Americans alike. The secret article, which soon became known, was particularly offensive to Spain, for it provided for the possibility of England holding West Florida under the final treaty. Moreover, Spain deemed her authority over the mouth of the Mississippi absolute. In 1784 Madrid declared that until it was ready to admit that the boundaries between its possessions and the United States were truly described in the treaty, it would maintain its claim to the exclusive control of the Mississippi, and would under no circumstances permit American craft to pass up or down. This intelligence, communicated formally to Congress on November 19, produced the greatest indignation in the South and West. None felt more strongly than the people of western Virginia; and Patrick Henry caused the Legislature to resolve, at the end of 1784, "that it is essential to the prosperity and happiness of the western inhabitants of this commonwealth to enjoy the right to navigate the river Mississippi."

When in the summer of 1785 Don Diego Gardoqui arrived as a Spanish agent to draft a treaty of commerce and amity, Congress explicitly instructed Jay to insist in the firmest manner upon the free use of the river. It is unnecessary to follow these negotiations in detail, protracted and unsatisfactory as they were, or to describe the deep anxiety with which the South hung upon them. The people knew that Spain might refuse to conclude a liberal commercial treaty except on condition that the Mississippi was closed, and they knew also that New England prized the trade with Spain, and cared nothing for the western waters.

Month by month, as the parleys dragged on, migration was making the question more serious for the South. Settlers were pouring into the trans-Allegheny region of Virginia at a rate that by 1790 gave it a population of 100,000. Landless men and land-hungry small owners streamed out of the Piedmont region of Virginia and North Carolina; sons of Tidewater families sought fortune there; adventurers, hunters, and trappers "squatted" upon the great tracts unclaimed or owned by foreign and eastern capitalists; and European immigrants pushed direct down the Ohio, or came into the Shenandoah and were drawn westward by the glowing reports of rich land. The western reaches had begun to trade with the Spanish settlements as early as 1782, when one Jacob Yoder left Redstone, a village on the Monongahela, with a boatload of flour to be sold in New Orleans; took furs in New Orleans and sold them in Havana; and brought sugar from Havana to Philadelphia, thus blazing a long and perilous but profitable path.[38] All Virginia, but particularly the region inland from the "fall line," felt for the economic rights of the trans-Allegheny settlers, and nearly everyone foresaw the brilliant future of the Southwest.

There was hence the greatest indignation when early in 1786 indications began to appear that the closing of the Mississippi, with the consent of the North, was a dire possibility. Monroe, sitting in Congress at New York, wrote Madison on May 31 that he had no sooner arrived in the city the previous winter than he had learned that Jay wished to be relieved of his instructions to demand free navigation of the river, and that a strong party was supporting Jay. Confirmation of Monroe's disquieting reports soon came with the news, first, that a Kentucky flatboat, captained and loaded with goods by a certain Thomas Amis, had been seized June 6, 1786, by the Spaniards at Natchez; and second, that on August 3, 1786, Jay had, in presenting some tardy results of his negotiations, urged upon Congress that in view of the value of Spanish amity and of the ocean trade with Spain, the United States should surrender the navigation of the Mississippi for twenty-five or thirty years.

It seemed to most Virginians that the eight northern States were deliberately planning the mutilation and injury of the South to gain a few dollars, for they felt with Jefferson that the abandonment of the Mississippi "is an act of separation between the eastern and the western country." They were ready to believe that the North would even break up the Confederation before it would be balked of

[38] Hulbert, "Historic Highways," IX, 123-24.

its object. In transmitting to Governor Harrison a full account of the Jay-Gardoqui affair as he had seen it from his Congressional vantage-point, Monroe added that a secret plan was even then being considered by committees of northern members of Congress to partition the Union and set the South adrift.

Inevitably, a powerful party arose in Virginia, headed by Patrick Henry, which believed that the manifestation of sectional cross-interests and selfishness in this Mississippi question proved that a stronger Union was impracticable. Madison, who had fought for the Southern standpoint in Congress, saw with dark forebodings the result of Jay's proposal in his State. To Jefferson he wrote from Philadelphia of the postponement of the assertion of American rights on the Mississippi: "Passing by other States, figure to yourself the effect of such a stipulation on the Assembly of Virginia, already jealous of Northern politics, and which will be composed of about thirty members from the western waters, of a majority of others attached to the western country from interests of their own, of their friends or their constituents, and of many others who though indifferent to the Mississippi, will zealously play off the disgust of its friends against Federal measures. Figure to yourself its effect on the people at large on the western borders, who are impatiently waiting for a favorable result to the negotiations with Gardoqui, and who will consider themselves as sold by their Atlantic brethren. Will it be an unnatural consequence if they consider themselves absolved from every Federal tie, and court some protection for their absolved rights? This protection will appear more attainable from the maritime power of Great Britain than from any other quarter. . . ." [39] The justification for this view was writ large in the events that followed.

Governor Henry sent a warning to the people of Kentucky, and urged them to take steps to protect their rights. Meetings were held in the trans-Allegheny region, committees of correspondence were formed, and not only were measures adopted to stop the trade of all Spaniards on the upper Mississippi, but a hotheaded scheme was formed for an expedition under George Rogers Clark to drive them from its lower extent. When the autumn meeting of the Legislature in 1786 approached, there was no doubt that it would energetically assert the rights of the South and West. "Indeed," Madison

[39] Rives, "Madison," II, 119-20; for Monroe's communications, see his "Writings," I, 144 ff.

wrote Monroe, "the only danger is that too much resentment may be indulged by many against the Federal councils." The Kentucky members presented a memorial asking for assistance. On November 29 the House unanimously passed resolutions declaring the American right to use the Mississippi, characterizing its surrender as dishonorable, and stating of the nation that "a sacrifice of the rights of any one part to the supposed or real interests of another part would be a flagrant violation of justice," and a direct contravention of the end for which the Federal government was erected.

Some Virginians, to be sure, took the other side. Though R. H. Lee was with western Virginia in opposing a strongly centralized national government, he suddenly swung against it on the Mississippi question, thinking the commercial treaty with Spain too highly valuable; and he lost his seat in Congress because he actually voted with Jay's faction there.[40] Washington himself leaned toward Jay's view, believing the navigation of the Mississippi not important until the western country was more thickly populated. Moreover, the threatened treaty with Spain was never concluded, the wrath of the Virginians slowly cooled, and in time, though not for some years, it was allayed by vigorous and effective measures to give them the use of the Mississippi. But meanwhile the harm had been done: the indignation of many citizens had guaranteed their unbending opposition to all plans for a more perfect union, and had rendered others lukewarm. Madison had been declaring that the interests of all parts of the United States, including the West, would be better served if more power were granted to Congress, and here was flat evidence to the contrary. In Virginia's ratifying convention, no subject was adverted to oftener than the Mississippi. "This new government, I conceive," said Henry, with his most impressive tyranny-scenting manner, "will enable those States who have already discovered their inclination that way, to give away this river." Grayson said the same thing, adding: "This contest for the Mississippi involves the great national contest . . . whether one part of the continent shall govern the other."[41]

[40] Journal House of Delegates, 66-67. R. H. Lee at first spoke of the Atlantic fisheries and the navigation of the Mississippi as the two legs on which the republic must stand; but for evidence of his change of position with regard to the Mississippi—"if this navigation could be opened and the benefits be such as are chimerically supposed, it must in its consequences depopulate and ruin the Old States"—see "Letters," Ballagh Edition, II, 426-27. For the plot of Gen. James Wilkinson and others to separate Kentucky from the Union, see R. M. McElroy's "Kentucky in the Nation's History," Ch. 4.
[41] Elliot's "Debates," V, 151-52, 365.

IV. RATIFICATION IN VIRGINIA

The struggle over the Constitution produced a marked realignment of political forces. From the beginning of the movement for a Constitutional Convention, which had been first fairly launched in Virginia in 1786, Madison and Washington had influential Virginians with them. The most noteworthy of the young men were John Marshall, a son of the frontier—he had been reared in a valley of the Blue Ridge—who in the House and the Council of State had made a considerable public reputation; George Nicholas, already known as one of the State's ablest lawyers, and a man of influential family; and Harry Innes, who, though yet in his early thirties, had been legislator, judge, and in 1785 had become Attorney-General. Prominent among the older workers for a stronger national government were Edmund Pendleton, now nearly sixty-five, and "Light-Horse Harry" Lee, the veteran soldier, who in 1786 was sent to the Continental Congress. Madison's associates at the Annapolis Convention in September, 1786, were Edmund Randolph and St. George Tucker, of whom the former in especial was eager to see the Articles of Confederation amended.

By the time the Federal Convention met, it was possible to foresee how the different sections of Virginia would incline to regard its work. Broadly speaking, it was evident that the westerners, individualists to the core, and aroused by the Mississippi controversy, would oppose a closely centralized form of government; and that the Tidewater, which saw a hope of renewed political power in the change, would support it. It was known that Madison, so recently a bitter enemy of the Tidewater political school, would head that section in his fight for the Constitution, and that Henry, a few years before hand in glove with the lowland conservatives, would be chieftain of the irreconcilable democrats of the mountain and the trans-Allegheny districts. We must remember that it was only a month before the Annapolis meeting that Jay had made his weak-kneed proposal for an agreement with Gardoqui.

Five of Virginia's delegates to the Constitutional Convention—Washington, Mason, Edmund Randolph, Wythe, and James Blair—were Tidewater representatives; two, Madison and Henry, were not. A pointblank refusal came from Henry to serve in any body that purposed the strengthening of the Union at the expense of State powers, while both Governor Randolph and George Mason, though staying in the Convention to the end, refused to sign the Constitution. When the Convention broke up on September 17, 1787, therefore, three of the four delegates who returned to advocate ratification were Tidewater men, while Madison had been born within the Tidewater and now lived not far from it.

The contest was thus defined at an early date as one between the lowlands on the one hand, and the Piedmont and Kentucky on the other, each struggling to win the doubtful Shenandoah Valley and the northernmost part of the trans-Allegheny region, in what is now West Virginia. In some respects it was a simple continuation of the old struggle between the conservatives and the western radicals, though there were many complicating currents. If we turn from the geographical division to the division among occupational and economic interests, here also we can make qualified generalizations. The planters were for the Constitution; the lawyers and judges were for the most part in favor of it; and the old soldiers, from their predilection for strength and authority, largely supported it. The pioneers were almost to a man against it, and the great majority of small upland farmers were in the opposition. The debtor class, and especially the many debtors who owed money to the British, were alarmed by the fear that the Constitution would make payment of their obligations at face value unescapable, while thousands of settlers who had taken land confiscated by the State from Crown grantees were apprehensive that their titles would be endangered. Madison's father reported that most of the Baptists were hostile, and the Episcopalians friendly.

The election of delegates to the ratifying Convention occurred early in 1788, after prolonged public discussion. At the close of 1787 Charles M. Thurston, a legislator, wrote the mayor of Winchester concerning the Constitution: [42]

I will place at the head of those for it Judge Pendleton, who is looked up to as president of the Convention to be held in June, Nicholas, Wythe, Blair, the Pages, Johnson, Stuart, Hervie, Jones, Wood, and a multitude of others. Against it—first, as the leader of this party, Henry, Mason, Governor Randolph, Lawson, John Taylor, with most of the general court lawyers and many of the judges, the Nelsons, R. H. Lee (in many instances, father against son), and many others. In a word, the division of the multitude is great; but after all, it appears to me, the party in favor of the Constitution must prevail. The signature and approbation of our great Washington will give it a preponderancy to weigh down all opposition.

[42] Cf. Madison, "Writings," XI, 252; Grigsby, "Hist. of the Va. Fed. Conv.," I, 34 ff. Thurston's letter is in the Providence *Gazette*, Jan. 12, 1788.

Madison at the same time, writing to Jefferson, described "the body of the people" as favorable to the Constitution, though he feared some changes might be produced by the united influence of Henry, R. H. Lee, George Mason, and Governor Randolph. Washington in April told Lafayette that he thought the Convention would ratify. On the other hand, Henry believed that four-fifths of the Virginians opposed the Constitution, and that south of the James nine-tenths were against it. One shrewd merchant in Virginia was apprehensive of defeat for the instrument, pointing out to his patrons in Philadelphia that two groups were fighting it, men with power and unwilling to surrender it, and men without money who feared the Constitution would force them to pay their debts. The most careful estimate that has been made is that two-thirds of the State was actually hostile to the Constitution. The great majority of voters had never read it, nor heard an honest, able analysis of it, but instinctively they disliked anything that weakened the familiar State government, and invigorated a strange, distant power. Even some of the delegates to the Convention had not read the Constitution.

But the federalists made a better showing in the elections than anyone had expected. Henrico County, containing Richmond, was anti-federalist. Three candidates there stood for two seats—Governor Edmund Randolph, supposedly against the Constitution, the popular John Marshall, for it, and the unpopular William Foushee, bitterly opposed to it. Randolph had 373 votes, Marshall 198, and Foushee 187, the first two being elected; [43] and as Randolph finally switched to support the Constitution, the county was happily misrepresented. Madison, arriving home the day before the Orange County election, might have been defeated but for a happy chance by which he met and converted an influential Baptist minister. Best of all, in counties distinctly hostile some fair-minded men, not afraid in the end to defy their constituents, were chosen. Henry exerted himself feverishly, spreading such unfounded reports as that the acceptance of the Constitution would mean loss of the Mississippi and the restoration of the religious Establishment, but though his success made Madison nervous, others maintained their confidence. We have a letter from a Virginian to a Bostonian, declaring: [44]

[43] Md. *Journal*, March 11, 1788. See a Fredericksburg letter in the Md. *Journal*, April 11, 1788, predicting the success of the opponents of the Constitution in the approaching Convention.
[44] Md. *Journal*, April 8, 1788.

Our Governor has expressed quite different sentiments regarding the new Constitution, since its adoption by your state. Although the majority [in Massachusetts] was small, yet the speeches of some of the minority after its adoption [i.e., their acquiescence without party rancor] have gained more proselytes to federalism here than if the majority had been much larger, and the Convention had dissolved with any animosity. . . . Most of those now opposed to it, are persons whose estates are much involved, by owing large British debts, which they think must be paid when we have a Federal head. But as Governor Randolph now speaks in favor of it, and as he has much influence, I am confident that it will not only be adopted, but by a very respectable majority. North Carolina follows of course.

Madison wrote Jefferson a fortnight later, declaring that it seemed probable that "a majority of the members elect are friends of the Constitution." The region north of the Rappahannock, he said, had generally elected federalists, and so had the Shenandoah, while the counties south of the James had seated anti-federalists; the northern transmontane section was largely federalist, the territory between the James and Rappahannock was "much chequered," and Kentucky would probably divide. The contest in the Convention was exceedingly close, and the federalists triumphed not by force of numbers but by better tactics and stronger arguments. Madison, Wythe, Marshall, Nicholas, Pendleton and Blair led their forces with masterly skill, seizing with avidity on the opportunity Mason offered them of debating each clause of the Constitution in detail. Henry had eloquence, Monroe and Grayson had persistency, and Mason had dignity, but their party could offer no minds to match those of Madison and Marshall, and no influence to equal that exerted by the absent Washington. In the final vote, after three weeks and two days of deliberation, the 89 delegates who carried ratification were furnished by the lower Tidewater, the upper Tidewater, the Shenandoah, and a region which now embraces five West Virginia counties. The 79 opposing votes came in the main from the Piedmont and Kentucky. A number of the delegates voted for the Constitution in flat defiance of the wish of their counties. Mason and Monroe sadly agreed that the chief single factor in their defeat had been Washington's wishes. Even as it was, ratification might have been beaten had a letter which Governor Clinton sent to Virginia in behalf of the New York Convention been promptly laid before the delegates.[45]

Not even a brief lull followed the political strife which had attended the ratification of the Constitution. Though Henry had been worsted, he could still control the Legislature, and he intended to make trouble. The federalists had defeated by only eight votes a

[45] Conway's "Randolph," 110-12; Rowland's "Mason," II, 276 ff.; see Ambler, "Sectionalism in Virginia," 58, for map.

motion to make ratification conditional upon the previous amendment of the Constitution; and Henry and Mason, with bad grace, had declared that they could not actively support the Constitution in its existing form. Under their auspices an effort was made to induce the anti-federalist minority of delegates to sign a mischievous address to the people. It was Henry's hope that he could now, by employing all his energies, obtain a thorough revision of the instrument; and Madison wrote Jefferson that Henry's friends entered into his scheme "with great zeal."

They showed their zeal when the Legislature met for its autumn session in 1788. Henry's control of the House justified the adjective used by his enemies, "omnipotent." Washington's secretary, Tobias Lear, has accurately described this sway. "In one word, it is said that the edicts of Mr. H. are enregistered with less opposition in the Virginia Assembly than those of the Grand Monarch in his parliaments. He has only to say, Let this be law, and it is law." This unchecked control by Henry, it should be explained, arose largely from the fact that so many of his opponents were now out of his way. In midsummer he had acquiesced in the Assembly's election of Madison to the Continental Congress, partly because he did not care to stem the sentiment in Madison's favor, but chiefly because he wished that leader put where he would give no trouble. Both George Nicholas and John Marshall were busy practising law; Pendleton and Wythe had returned to the bench; and Henry Lee was in Congress, while Edmund Randolph was too vacillating and too slight in parliamentary stature to be of great assistance to the federalists. With Henry, moreover, were ranged a number of men of considerable ability and influence—as Monroe, Ex-Governor Benjamin Harrison, and William Grayson, who had received an education at Oxford and in London, had been one of Washington's aides, and had sat in the Continental Congress before he had opposed the Constitution in the State Convention. The federalist minority was led by inexperienced members and made only a weak fight.

Just what was Henry's program? On October 29, 1788, he declared his opposition to all measures for organizing the Federal Government unless they were accompanied by action looking towards amendment of the Constitution, an object which he thought required another national convention. He then procured the passage of resolutions asserting that "many of the great, essential rights of

freemen, if not cancelled, were rendered insecure under the Constitution," and stating that to reassure the public and prevent "those
disorders which must arise under a government not founded on the
confidence of the people," the new Congress should call a second
Federal Convention to make alterations. The federalists proposed
a sensible alternative. Before the State Convention had adjourned,
it had drawn up a bill of rights and a score of articles as amendments
to be urged upon the nation. Now a resolution was introduced calling
upon Congress simply to submit these extensive amendments for
ratification by the States. But it was beaten 85 to 39, and Henry's
program was carried without a division. It included the dispatch of
a circular to the other States, and an answer to Governor Clinton.

Henry also intended, in his battle for revision, to choose Congressmen obedient to his will. This had been evident before the Legislature met. Washington had predicted in September, 1788, that
Henry's party would try to elect "so many of their own junto under
the new government as, by the introduction of local and embarrassing
disputes, to impede or frustrate its operation"; and had shown no
little apprehension of the result. A divided delegation in Congress
seemed fair to the federalists, but they had little hope of obtaining
one of the Senatorships. Washington told visitors to Mount Vernon
early in the fall that he was especially alarmed by the prospect that
both Senators would be anti-federalists; the rumor being that Henry
and R. H. Lee would be chosen. When the time for a choice by
the Legislature came early in November, Henry nominated Lee and
Grayson, and voiced an emphatic objection to Madison, who had
been named by his friends rather against his own will. He even declared that Madison's election might produce civil war in the State,
referring to the temporary excitement caused by lying rumors that
Madison advocated the surrender of the Mississippi, and was opposed
to any Constitutional amendments. One of Madison's friends admitted a doubt whether he would obey legislative instructions touching a question of the Federal tax power. "See, gentlemen," exclaimed Henry, "the secret is out—it is doubted whether Mr. Madison will obey his instructions!" Yet the election was unexpectedly
close. Lee received 98 votes, Grayson 86, and Madison 77.[46]
Madison's friends asserted that the tide was turning, and that if

---

[46] There were 63 scattering votes. For testimony as to Henry's dominance of the
situation, see a Richmond letter in the Pa. *Journal*, Dec. 6, 1788.

the balloting had been delayed a few days, all Henry's efforts to defeat him would have been in vain. They were discouraged, but Madison himself took the reverse philosophically. He had originally meant to stand for the House, but the Virginia federalists, from Washington down to Edward Carrington, had insisted that he would be more useful in the Senate.

And now Henry undertook, by the first gerrymandering measure in the republic's history, to blight Madison's ambitions even for the House.[47] A legislative committee was appointed to divide Virginia into ten Congressional districts, and by Henry's wish the district in which Madison must stand was made up, as one man put it, "of counties most tainted by anti-federalism." Of the eight counties, five had sent anti-federal delegates to the recent Convention, and a sixth had divided its vote. Henry also had the Legislature decree that the choice of the people must be confined to a resident of their own district—an enactment that many believed unconstitutional, and that evoked from the federalists of other districts an offer to test it by nominating Madison.[48] It was understood that Monroe, already a popular politician, would be Madison's opponent. Having arranged all this, Henry followed his custom of hastening back to his beloved Leatherwood estate, though it was only the middle of November. "And after he had settled everything relative to the government wholly, I suppose, to his own satisfaction," wrote Tobias Lear, "he mounted his horse and rode home, leaving the business of the State to be done by anybody who chose to give themselves the trouble of attending to it." He was as much the boss of the Virginia Legislature as Hancock had ever been boss in Massachusetts, or Clinton in New York, but he was not to be spared the sight of some matters going agley.

However much Henry's party controlled the Legislature, it was not certain of the electorate. The popular trend was toward acceptance of the Constitution, especially as it was seen that Washington would head the new government and would have the help of the ablest men in the nation. The choice of Presidential electors in January, 1789, and of Representatives in Congress the next month,

---

[47] For a defense of this measure, see Rowland's "Mason," II, 309 ff.
[48] See letter of G. L. Turberville to Madison in the Lenox MSS., N. Y. Public Library, dated Nov. 13, 1788, in which Turberville says that when Henry brought in the gerrymandering measure, "without argument, or answering a single reason urged against it, [he] launched into a field of declamation, brought all the imaginary horrors of the new government upon us, and carried a decided and large majority with him."

was a heavy blow to the anti-federalists. Only three of the twelve electors turned out to be of their party, the Piedmont electing two and the Tidewater one. Only three of the ten Representatives, again, were theirs, coming also from the Piedmond and Tidewater.

The contest between Madison and Monroe was genuinely spectacular. Upon examining the ground, Madison's friends found a decided possibility of winning, declaring that the voters could be brought over to federalist views by a campaign in person. Monroe was no mean antagonist, for his insistence in Congress upon the right to navigate the Mississippi had won the gratitude of Virginians, and he had much personal attractiveness. Tall, rawboned, awkward, diffident, he nevertheless possessed rugged strength of character, kindliness, and democratic simplicity. He was in the field early, writing letters, making injurious allegations as to Madison's views, and electioneering actively. It was necessary for Madison to show equal energy, but he long held back. Inclination and his apparent duty both summoned him to the winter session of the Continental Congress. Canvassing for votes he always despised, and tried to shun. In 1777 he had failed of election to the Legislature partly because he would not canvass, partly because he would not stand treat with liquor. However, in the dead of December he came home over the frozen roads half an invalid, plunged into the battle in person, and thereafter spared no effort. He refused to dignify the misleading reports which were in circulation against him by a formal denial. But he wrote many letters explaining his position, made a speech-making tour of the district, with special attention to critical Culpepper County, and engaged in several joint debates with Monroe, who was palpably his inferior in logic and mental agility. There was never the slightest ill-will between the two, Monroe for his part professing to be reluctant to stand between Madison and Congress. Madison carried through later life a memento of one of his speaking trips, for while addressing a German audience in the snow outside a country church, his nose was frozen and permanently scarred.

When the votes were counted, Madison was found victorious by the large majority of approximately 300. By his election to the House instead of the Senate his party profited in a degree which neither he nor Patrick Henry realized for some time. During the first decade of Federal history, the Senate counted for little, and the House for nearly everything and while Virginia's Senators virtually disappeared from public view, Madison's abilities soon made him the leader of the House.

The result of the defeat of the anti-federalists in the Presidential and Congressional elections was to cripple them for years, and to force their chieftain into retirement. Henry was burdened by debts, and found it necessary to devote himself with unwonted diligence to the bar to store up a competence for old age, so that he practiced regularly, chiefly in Prince Edward County, for the next half dozen years. Much in demand, he was especially renowned for his power over juries in criminal cases; in civil cases he would seldom submit sufficiently to the drudgery of mastering complicated transactions. In 1794 he gave up all connection with either law or politics, and settled upon a fine estate overlooking the Staunton River to spend his last days in resting and supervising its cultivation.[49]

The Assembly remained anti-federalist, voting in 1790 almost two to one against a resolution approving the Federal assumption of State debts, electing Monroe in the same year to fill the vacancy in the United States Senate occasioned by Grayson's death, and in general showing a united front against the measures of Hamilton and Madison; but there was nevertheless a coherent, forcible federalist minority in its hall. Meanwhile, the amendments proposed by Madison had made the Constitution acceptable to the narrowest irreconcilables. The old divisions gave place to a resumption of still older cordialities in the State's politics. George Mason, before his death in 1792, made overtures to Madison through Jefferson, and received Jefferson's assurance of the young statesman's esteem. "I have heard him say," wrote Jefferson, "that though you and he appeared to be different in your systems, yet you were in truth nearer together than most persons who were classed under the same appellation"—which was quite true.

[49] See the picture of his retirement in Howe, "Va. Hist. Colls.," 221.

CHAPTER NINE

POLITICAL DEVELOPMENT: THE LOWER SOUTH

In their early political history no States offer a sharper contrast than North and South Carolina. From 1776 to 1780 they were governed in diametrically opposite spirit. The radicals of little property or wisdom obtained control in North Carolina, while in South Carolina the Constitution insured control by the patrician class of planters and merchants. It need not be said that North Carolina's government during and after the war was short-sighted and demagogic. The people of other States, who knew that North Carolinians were poor, ill-educated, and of varied origin, were not surprised by this; they expected so little from the commonwealth that when William Hooper made a powerful speech in the Continental Congress, other delegates showed amazement. Yet North Carolina had men who might have given her a sound administration—men like Hooper, Samuel Johnston, Caswell, Davie, and Iredell—while her population, with all its faults, was the very stuff of democracy. South Carolina's government was good but unprogressive. The Revolution did not throw it into the hands of the unfit but neither did the Revolution introduce half the healthy social and legal changes it introduced into Virginia. The State had no such exponent of a new order as Jefferson.

North Carolina's population was much the greater—at the first census her white inhabitants, almost 300,000, were approximately twice as numerous as those of South Carolina. The empty upland region of both States attracted settlers rapidly, but North Carolina's was the larger and was nearer the main sources of emigration. It is against the background of this new, unstable, poor population of Scotch-Irish, Scotch, Germans, and English in the western counties that we can best understand the character of North Carolina's government.

I. NORTH CAROLINA POLITICS TO 1780

Among the few groups of well-to-do conservatives, the chief place was taken by a set of leaders in the northeastern part of North

Carolina, just under the Virginia line. Edenton, founded in 1716, was the center here of a fertile region which lent itself to plantations of a Virginia type. Men called it the granary of the Province. It was bounded by swamps and the climate was humid, but among its streams and forests there was much good arable land. The oldest of the Edenton group, a planter, was Colonel John Harvey, long the Speaker, whose death in 1775 deprived the Whigs of their foremost leader. Another patriot who died early in the Revolution was Colonel Richard Buncombe, a rich gentleman of West Indian birth who was mortally wounded at Germantown. Thomas Jones, of Edenton, helped draft the Constitution of 1776, but was not thereafter prominent. Joseph Hewes, a signer of the Declaration of Independence, was a Quaker merchant who had come to Edenton as partner in a trading company which owned its special wharf there.

But the two men who made Edenton notable were Samuel Johnston and James Iredell. The former, born in Dundee, Scotland, in 1733, was a nephew of Governor Gabriel Johnston, the ablest of the Colony's executives. He was early brought to America, obtained an elementary education in Connecticut, studied law, and was made clerk of the Superior Court of North Carolina in 1767, holding also the position of Naval Officer. Three years later he entered the Legislature, and became a Whig leader. Having inherited wealth, which he increased, and being of an aristocratic and studious character, he lived at "Hayes" much as George Mason lived at "Gunston Hall," spending much time in the library of more than a thousand books which his uncle the Governor had begun.[1] Stern in appearance, lofty in manner, of a somewhat Puritanical rigidity, he was not popular, but he was respected. His protégé and the husband of his sister was the much younger James Iredell, sprung from the family of Henry Ireton, Cromwell's lieutenant, which altered its name at the Restoration. Iredell was born in Sussex a quarter-century before independence; at seventeen he obtained through court friends an appointment as controller of customs at Roanoke, and in 1768 arrived at Edenton. The youth was ambitious, and found time to study law when not keeping the custom house books or acting as deputy for his principal London patron, who owned large tracts of North Carolina land. It was natural for Johnston, Harvey, Buncombe, and Hooper, drawing plans for the first Provincial Congress,

[1] R. D. W. Connor, "Hist. N. C.," I, 206; 367 ff.

to interest Iredell in them, and thenceforth his talents were, as far as his slender purse allowed, at the service of the State.[2]

Edenton, in short, though a town of only 400 people in plain frame houses, was a political and social center not to be sneered at, and Iredell's letters and diary give us an interesting picture of its life just before the Revolution. Hornblow's Tavern was a convivial gathering place, where cards and billiards were played for stakes. The town gentry and planters entertained at dinners and tea-parties, with dancing and backgammon. Boating expeditions went up the creeks; an occasional sleight of hand performer delighted "the dregs of the town," and there was easy Southern preaching. The serious-minded men varied their legal and political studies by reading the ancient classics, the Spectator and other essays, Walpole's historical works, and the British magazines. Lovemaking—Sir Ned Dukinfield was Iredell's rival for the hand of Hannah Johnston—gave opportunity for the cultivation of Southern gallantry. This social life, as in many places in Colonial days, had a truly idyllic quality.

In the opposite or southeastern corner of the State, the Cape Fear region, was another community which furnished many Revolutionary leaders. Wilmington, younger than Edenton, at the outbreak of the Revolution was slightly larger, and contained 180 houses by 1790. Here lived Cornelius Harnett,[3] the Sam Adams of North Carolina— except that he was wealthy while Adams was poor—who served in the Continental Congress from 1775 until shortly before his death in 1781. The principal conservative leader was William Hooper, a native of Boston, who graduated from Harvard at the head of his class, and became a North Carolina citizen in 1764;[4] John Adams in the first Continental Congress named Hooper with Henry and R. H. Lee as the foremost in oratorical talent.[5] A partner of Hooper's in conservatism was Archibald Maclaine, a Scotch-born lawyer noted for his interest in science and letters, and for his hot temper. Hooper and Maclaine were in constant communication during and after the Revolution with Johnston and Iredell, each pair encouraging the other. Josiah Quincy, jr., after traveling from South Carolina into the Wilmington and Edenton districts in 1773, declared the northern Colony had more "men of genius, learning,

[2] McRee, "Life of Iredell," I, *passim.*
[3] R. D. W. Connor, "Cornelius Harnett."
[4] See James Murray, "Letters," 114.
[5] "Works," II, 396.

and true wit, humor, and mirth." [6] Outside the Cape Fear and Edenton groups, the only conservative who requires mention is Allen Jones, a planter of Halifax, at the fall line of the Roanoke River.

The radicals were many, and made up in numbers what they lacked in ability. One of them had been a ringleader among the Regulators—Thomas Person, of Granville County, whose farm was ravaged by Tryon's army, and who was excepted from the general amnesty declared in 1771.[7] He was a surveyor, and before he died became the owner of 60,000 acres, but his sympathies were with the poor border population. John Penn,[8] a Virginian, was related to the patrician John Taylor of Caroline, and had read law with a cousin, Edmund Pendleton; but when in 1774 he crossed the boundary into Granville County, Penn identified himself with former Regulators like Person. Timothy Bloodworth was born in poverty in the Cape Fear region, and throughout his life his meagre and ill-assorted information exposed him to ridicule. He was by turns a preacher, blacksmith, farmer, doctor, watchmaker, wheelwright, and politician, and he really had a great deal of native ability. One of the few radical leaders who was rich was Willie Jones, of Halifax, the brother and opponent of Allen Jones. The two were sons of an agent and attorney for Lord Granville, one of the proprietary lords of North Carolina, and were educated at Eton. Though Willie Jones was a thorough democrat in politics, in his social life he was an aristocrat, who dressed well, lived sumptuously, raced, hunted, played cards, and was proud of his wealth and position; General Greene wrote in 1783 that he prostituted excellent talents to sport and pleasure. Thomas Burke, another extremist, was an impetuous, quick-tempered Irishman, who emigrated to Virginia, studied medicine and law, and just before the war removed to Hillsborough.

It will be noted that most of North Carolina's leading men were born elsewhere. In fact, the whole population was new—in 1706, it had been less than 6000. It will also be noted that environment had much to do with political opinion, two lowland settlements fur-

---

[6] *Mass. Hist. Soc. Proceedings,* June, 1916, p. 462. "In Charlestown and so through the Southern province I saw much apparent hospitality, much of what is called good breeding and politeness, and great barbarity. In Brunswick, Wilmington, Newbern, Edenton, and so through the North province there is real hospitality, less of what is called politeness and good breeding, and less inhumanity. Property is much more equally diffused in one province than the other, and this may account for some, if not all, the differences of character of the inhabitants."

[7] Jones, "Defence Rev. Hist. N. C.," 136-37; N. C. Booklet, July, 1909, sketch of Person by S. B. Weeks.

[8] N. C. Booklet, September, 1904, sketch of Penn by T. M. Pittman.

nishing nearly all the conservative leaders. In most of the back country in 1775 the social characteristics were those of the frontier. The settlers paid little attention to inconvenient forms of law, and no more to tax-gatherers than they could help; educated men were rare; and no man acknowledged another's superiority. A majority of uplanders had absolutely no ties with England. They wanted a government which would directly represent them, and in which the Legislature would overshadow the Governor. Their constant demand, from which the evident need for schools, roads, and a better defense could not budge them, was economy and low taxes. Of the 70,000 free white males above sixteen years of age at the first census, less than 22,000 were in the three coastal districts of Edenton, New-bern, and Wilmington, while of the 54 counties, only 23 lay in these districts. The disproportion was not so great in 1776 and North Carolina was not a State in which it was easy to draw sectional lines, but the western radicals had an easy control.

The choice made for the first Governor was excellent. Richard Caswell, chosen by the Provincial Congress which framed North Carolina's Constitution (December 20, 1776) took possession after the Christmas holidays of the Governor's palace built at New-Bern a decade before and called his first Council meeting for the middle of January. Politically, he was one of a number of moderate leaders, like Alexander Martin and Abner Nash, who stood neither with the radicals nor conservatives. He had led a wing of Tryon's army at the Alamance, and when the Revolution—he had been made a popular hero by his victory over the Tories at Moore's Creek Bridge—began he was regarded as distinctly hostile to some leaders of the west; but as it continued, his tendency was towards the left. His popularity is proved by the fact that he was elected Governor seven times, oftener than any successor. Nathaniel Macon, no mean judge, called him "one of the most powerful men that ever lived in this or any other country," and his eminence in the Revolutionary period was deserved. Few men in the State had enjoyed so much political experience, for he had entered the Legislature in 1754; no one else had such sleepless ambition, both political and military.[9] The first State Legislature was elected in March, and began its session in April—thereafter, like Virginia's, to hold at least a spring and fall session every year till the Revolution closed.

[9] See R. D. W. Connor, "Makers of North Carolina," 116; Connor's "Hist. N. C.," I, 419-20; Ashe's "North Carolina," I, 564.

At once there occurred the inevitable clash between the conservative minority and the radical majority. Men had hoped there would be little party feeling,[10] but when the election of delegates to the next Congress began, harmony ended. The radical John Penn wished to succeed Hewes, who had served creditably at Philadelphia, had cast an almost decisive vote for independence, was a much older resident than Penn, and was a favorite of the conservative Edenton community. Penn attacked him with the outrageous charge that he had been too frequently absent from Congress, and that by accepting a place on the Marine Committee of Philadelphia, he had held two posts at once. The westerners came to Penn's support, and as a stinging rebuke to the conservatives, elected him to Hewes's seat.

Iredell, who had been appointed one of the commissioners to prepare bills for the first Legislature, thereupon wrote that he was sick of politics, that affairs were already in "a most melancholy train," and that the best cause in the world was being "grossly injured by many of its conductors." Samuel Johnston refused with asperity an election as one of the two State Treasurers. He wrote a friend that after seeing the new Legislature at work, he was as little pleased with it in practice as he had been in theory; and that he was more certain than ever that while a highly democratic government might suit a populous, educated, well-matured commonwealth, it was unsuited to North Carolina. He characterized many of the legislators as "fools and knaves, who by their low arts have worked themselves into the good graces of the populace," and he did not abstain from mentioning individuals. "I saw with indignation such men as Griffith Rutherford, Thomas Person, and your colleague, J. Penn . . . principal leaders in both houses; you will not expect anything good or great . . . from the counsels of men of such narrow, contracted principle, supported by the most contemptible abilities. Hewes was supplanted . . . in Congress by the most insidious arts and glaring falsehoods, and Hooper, though no competitor appeared to oppose him, lost a great number of votes." Hooper, in fact, alleging financial reasons, but sharing his friends' anger over the defeat of Hewes, refused to return to Philadelphia,

---

[10] Abner Nash, a member of the upper house, wrote ten days after the session opened that "We are all harmony, and a perfectly good agreement, as far as I can see, is likely to prevail in our houses of legislature." N. C. State Records, XI, 720. Nash was a moderate, who was made Speaker.

where he had been a useful link between the New England members, with whom he was intimate, and the South.[11]

The autumn session of the Legislature in 1777 passed an act establishing courts which was good because Iredell had drafted it, using earlier enactments as a model and receiving aid from Maclaine.[12] But two of its three appointments to the bench were wretched. It could not pass over Iredell, whose legal knowledge and experience, with his judicial mind, well fitted him for the office. But for his colleagues it chose two unfit radicals, Samuel Ashe and Samuel Spencer. Ashe was a member of a well-known family, who had read law with an uncle, but never gained a mastery of it, and who was swayed on the bench by his strong prejudices. Spencer was an even less respectable figure. He had little legal training. As a clerk of the Anson County court in colonial days, his extortionate fees had aroused mob violence and led to a popular address of remonstrance. The choice of these mediocre men excited derision, which the bar from year to year was at little pains to conceal; but they clung to office, so that Spencer was able to play an evil rôle in helping delay the ratification of the Constitution. The Legislature was a Legislature of the people, and it was showing that the popular majority was ignorant and politically inexperienced.

Throughout 1778-79, the legislators continued to enact many bad along with a few good laws. The able Caswell was twice reëlected Governor,[13] and the able Abner Nash continued speaker of the Senate, but the House was dominated by Person and Willie Jones. No adequate measures were taken for defense. The regiments for the Continental Line filled so slowly that in the spring of 1778 the Legislature tried to force the counties to raise 2400 men for them; but even then the outfitting of the recruits was left to the local militia companies. That spring a short-sighted measure was passed to prohibit the export of beef, pork, or maize, one founded on an alleged "scarcity of provisions in this State," but unjustifiable in the

[11] McRee's "Iredell," I, 358-59.
[12] N. C. State Records, XXIV, Introduction, and pp. 48 ff.
[13] Caswell saw that the conservatives were not wholly slighted. As S. A. Ashe says ("Hist. N. C.," I, 643): "Caswell and his council tendered appointments to Samuel Johnston and other conservatives, as well as to their democratic friends. Allen Jones was year by year honored by the Assembly [he was elected speaker of the Senate repeatedly], while his brother, Willie, received no particular mark of its confidence, although Jones County was named for him. Iredell was appointed to the bench, and when he retired Maclaine, certainly a conservative, was elected. He declined, recommending John Williams, who was in high favor with the Assembly. On Avery's resigning the office of attorney-general, Iredell was elected to that position."

blow it dealt the trade of North Carolina. Hundreds of wagons had yearly creaked over the rough roads to Charleston, and the State now badly needed the money and manufactures obtainable in return. In 1777 an act was passed for the full and final confiscation of Tory property, but it was found in the following year to be impracticable, and to require supplementary legislation.

The financial legislation of North Carolina was somewhat cruder than that of most States. Excessive issues of paper money were made, without provision for gradual amortization of the debt, while the redemption of the paper which had been authorized by the Provincial Congresses was postponed and repostponed. A general property tax for war purposes was early resorted to, but it was kept too low.[14] Thomas Person's characteristic legislative services were bids for popularity by proposals for lower tax-rates and for reducing Governor Caswell's salary.[15] In the spring of 1780 the State made a grant of $300 to each volunteer who responded to a call for 4000 troops;[16] in other words, with an ill-collected tax of three-pence in the pound to fill the Treasury, a little force of 1500 men might cost the State $450,000 in bounties alone, no small sum even in depreciated currency. Hooper wrote Caswell: "Are we to ascribe it to a dearth of genius, or to the restraint imposed upon the press, that no pen appears to lash the public and private vices of this licentious State?"

The purposes of the early confiscation legislation were carried out at the beginning of 1779 by a new law as faulty as it was drastic. Its deformities moved even Willie Jones to protest that "it involves such a complication of blunders and betrays such ignorance in legislation as would disgrace a set of hog-drovers." The conservatives, supported by Cornelius Harnett's strong influence, labored for suspending the confiscations, but as Iredell wrote, there was too much land in the opposite scale. The vengeful radicals wished to punish the Tories, they hoped to lighten their taxes by the sale of confiscated property, and some thought they could pick up the estates of former neighbors at a bargain. The House was actually milder than the Senate, which, wrote Iredell, "will not suffer any plan of moderation."

[14] N. C. State Records, XXIV, 6 ff.; spring session, 1777.
[15] About 1777 Caswell wrote his friend Burke, the future Governor, that Person was "more troublesome this Assembly, if possible, than formerly." N. C. Records, XI, 470-71; see also N. C. Booklet, Vol. IV, No. 5.
[16] State Records, XXIV, 339; these men were to serve only three months. A bounty of $500 was offered recruits for the Continental battalions, to serve three years or the war; *Idem*, 337-39.

Sold at auction, the property fetched only a tithe of its real value; but the chief counts against the law were its cruelty and injustice. The Legislature did not make sufficient provision for the impoverished dependents of the Tories, while the enactment was so badly drawn that many loyal citizens suffered along with the disloyal, and soon the Legislature had to halt its execution.[17]

At this juncture new and weightier problems fell upon the incompetent Legislature. A British fleet and army arrived before Savannah, Georgia, just before Christmas in 1778; in six days they captured the town; and in two weeks they had almost cleared Georgia of patriot forces. The news no sooner percolated to the back settlements of North Carolina than the Highlanders and other Tories assumed a threatening attitude. The skies had blackened with startling suddenness. During the early days of 1779 the Legislature of 1778 was hastily convened in a third session, and made a few preparations for defense. But it could do little, and would the new Legislature in the spring be more efficient?

At any rate, Governor Caswell could do nothing but wait for it to act. Harnett wrote him from Philadelphia upon the urgency of filling up the Continental battalions if North Carolina were not to remain a laggard. Reproach from this quarter was too much. "My good friend Mr. Harnett knows," Caswell retorted, "that by the Constitution of this State, nothing can be done by the Executive Power of itself, towards this most desirable purpose, and that [as] the General Assembly is not to meet until the month of April, of course ways and means must be fallen upon to accomplish what he hopes, in time to render that service to the common cause, he and I both wish, and I think that if there is any blame to be fixed on those who formed the Constitution a very considerable part he ought to take to himself for cramping so much the powers of the executive." [18] The impotence of his office, which did not even permit him to call the Legislature in emergency session, was almost intolerable to Caswell's energetic temper.

When the new Legislature met at Smithfield, "a rascally hole for such business," [19] the perils of the situation were plain. General Lincoln's forces in March suffered a defeat in Georgia, and immediately the British commenced their invasion of South Carolina. When

---

[17] McRee, "Iredell," I, 419 ff.
[18] State Records, XIII, 31-32.
[19] So Whitmel Hill; see his letter, State Records, XIV, 1-4.

Charleston falls, North Carolina "becomes a victim of easy conquest, merely for want of proper arms," wrote Whitmel Hill, a member of Congress, from Smithfield; "our men are numerous and willing, but their means of defense most deplorable." The Legislature had hardly convened when an alarm came from a new quarter—the British had landed at Portsmouth, Virginia, throwing Edenton into a panic. The militia were called out, and Hill went to see them. "My private sentiments were despair, from the miserable appearance of their arms," he lamented. When General Lincoln saw the ragged, weapon-less, ill-trained levies that crossed the border from North Carolina to his aid, he sent an angry expostulation. They are "very naked," he wrote Governor Caswell. "It is painful to see them in the ragged condition in which they appear." If the troops were not better armed, he pointed out, they would be of little service in battle; if not better clothed, they would fall sick when the hot season came on.[20]

Wherein previous Legislatures had been remiss was shown by William Bryan, a State brigadier, in a letter of April 27, 1779, in which he disgustedly resigned.[21] He minced no words. First, the militia establishment was weak, "as there is no law, sufficiently penal, to compel men when drafted to turn out and march, whereby seldom more than half the number ordered enters upon duty." Second, these half-filled companies totally lacked essential arms and other equipment; "nor is it possible the necessary supplies can be obtained when there is no Quartermaster-General or commander of military stores appointed to supply the militia with the numberless articles which come under those two departments." He complained that the field officers, whom the Legislature appointed, were in large part inexperienced or otherwise incompetent. In short, the State's troops "have but a faint resemblance to a military force."

Against its sea of difficulties the new Legislature did take some measures. It passed an act in May for raising 2000 regular troops before midsummer, if necessary by militia drafts, and it authorized Governor Caswell to send 2000 militia into Georgia or South Caro-lina for three months. No less than £500,000 in paper was voted, again without provision for its gradual redemption. In the fall Cas-well was empowered to send 3000 militia southward.[22] The State

[20] State Records, XIV, 61-62.
[21] *Idem.*
[22] State Records, XXIV, 254-62.

had reason to be thankful that the war dragged on so slowly that there was time not only for these measures but for others to follow them. In December, 1779, Governor Caswell's term expired, and the Constitution made his immediate reëlection impossible—made it necessary to change horses in the middle of the stream. In his stead Abner Nash was chosen. If Caswell had done little to invigorate the State government, Nash was able to do even less, for he did not enjoy Caswell's popular strength. Thus the crucial new year began, with the capture of Charleston only four months distant. North Carolina faced a gloomy outlook.

II. South Carolina Politics to 1780

Meanwhile, the government of South Carolina had proved itself much more efficient, for the reasons which often make an aristocracy more efficient than a democracy. South Carolinians also had an advantage in that their permanent government was organized early in 1776, many months before North Carolina's, and harmony was more easily attainable because the population was smaller and more homogeneous. But South Carolina's chief favoring circumstance was that her Constitution did not break sharply with the past, and made few innovations. Before the Revolution the government, so far as it was American, was in the hands of the planter-merchant aristocracy, and after the Revolution, it was in the same well-educated, well-practiced hands.

The sharp cleavage between the planters of the low country and the small farmers of the upper country was, as elsewhere, in the South, the result of geographical conditions. For about eighty miles from the sea the State is level, then comes a belt of sandy hills, and finally the traveler reaches an upland region of hillocks and plains, of grain, forests, and large herds. In the uplands in 1775 few negroes were employed, and even in the middle belt the farmers worked hard over their own indigo, tobacco, and grain. The bracing upland air as well as the Northern form of agriculture encouraged white labor. But for fully forty miles from the sea the cultivators were nearly all blacks laboring under the direction of overseers. Rice flourished in the river swamps fed by tidewater, and in inland swamps furnished with artificial reservoirs. Cotton and indigo grew best upon the coastal islands, but were profitably cultivated on the mainland also.

No white man on the lower coastal plain, or for a distance of perhaps a hundred miles up the main rivers, thought of settling a farm and improving it without a body of slaves. The income of the planters was sometimes prodigious. Just before the war Joseph Alston admitted a revenue of £5000 to £6000 a year sterling from his five plantations, and was reputed to receive much more, though he had begun life with but a half-dozen negroes.[23] The head of the Lowndes family had an income of £4000 a year.[24]

For spending much time in Charleston, a city of 12,000 whites and blacks, the planters had various reasons. Many had important commercial interests, for Charleston was the only great commercial city of the South, with so brisk a trade that 350 sail in the harbor were no unusual sight. The town was flat and low on the tongue of land at the confluence of the Ashley and Cooper Rivers, its water-supply was brackish, and the streets were too narrow for health, convenience, or safety from fire; but being well-drained, and cooled in summer by the sea-breezes, it was regarded as the most healthful residence short of the high hills, and was sought from even the West Indies. It offered a wide variety of amusements: a St. Cecilia's Society to give musical entertainments; bustling coffee-houses; horse-racing; a Monday-night Club; a dancing assembly, with bad music but good dancing and refreshments; and gaming. It had architectural attractions, for the State House was much admired, there were a number of fine churches, and some of the houses were imposing brick mansions, with tiled roofs. Miles Brewton's home, for example, was said to have cost £8000 sterling, and visitors marveled at his blue satin curtains, gilt wallpaper, elegant mirrors, heavy plate and fine wines. The proceedings of the Legislature were conducted with a dignity that befitted the aristocratic temper of the Province. The costly mace was laid before the Speaker, who sat in black robes and a wig, and the members kept their hats on, in imitation of Parliament. Of course Charleston was by no means exclusively peopled with planters, shippers, merchants, and professional men. But the small tradesmen, mechanics, and white laborers were, said a keen Yankee observer, quite different from the "middling order" of Boston—they were "odious characters."

If North Carolina's radicalism was evinced in her neglect of

---

[23] Journal Josiah Quincy, *Mass. Hist. Soc. Proceedings*, June, 1916, p. 453.
[24] See McCrady, "South Carolina Under the Royal Govt.," *passim;* Wallace's "Laurens," Ch. 2.

Johnston and Hooper, South Carolina's conservatism was written large in her choice of Rutledge and Laurens as her first President and Vice-President respectively. Gadsden might rally the "Liberty boys," the hot-spirited clerks and mechanics, but the wealthy, cautious, and one-time Anglophile men of weight easily overbore them.

Both men were of the second generation of respected Provincial families. Educated in England, John Rutledge evinced his ambition by a close attention upon Parliamentary debates, and by otherwise diligently training himself for the bar and the Legislature. As a young lawyer he zealously opposed the Stamp Act, and he was among the most energetic Whig leaders just before the Revolution; but in the Continental Congress he showed himself distinctly a representative of the business-minded lowland planters—it was on his motion that rice was exempted from the non-importation agreement. "A rapid speaker," John Adams noted of him. He was chairman of the committee which made the first draft of the State's first Constitution; he and Charles Pinckney had for a decade been regarded as the two foremost lawyers of the Colony; and everyone had expected his choice as first President. Vice-President Henry Laurens was a member of a rich Huguenot family. His father had established himself as one of the principal merchants of Charleston, and Henry, the eldest son, increased by his commission and importing business the fortune he had inherited. Buying large tracts of land, he became a planter also; indeed, he protested against his election upon the ground that at the moment he could not spare more time for public affairs from his many private concerns. But he had been in the Commons House almost uninterruptedly since 1757, and was not to be spared by his State till after peace came. He was less of a conservative than Rutledge, but still a conservative.[25]

When these men were elected, independence was more than three months away, and a large group in public life clung to the hope that the partition of the Empire could yet be averted. But after the first spring fighting in the Province, the views of the majority changed sharply. There soon began a thoroughly sound movement for displacing the temporary Constitution of March, 1776, by one which would recognize the independence of the State as permanent, give it a Governor instead of a President, and effect some of the social re-

[25] Wallace's "Laurens," *passim;* Letters of John Rutledge, *S. C. Hist. and Genealogical Mag.*, 1917.

forms which Jefferson was carrying through in Virginia. The radicals under W. H. Drayton and Gadsden furnished its driving power, but they steadily won men from the moderate ranks.

Gadsden by now was a veteran political warrior, fifty-four years old. By birth and environment he was a patrician—the son of an officer in the royal navy, the possessor of a good education gained in England, a successful merchant as well as planter, and a man whom the royal Governors had thought it worth while to befriend.[26] Lyttleton had been glad to take him as a fellow officer on an expedition against the Cherokees. He had many traits of inborn leadership, but his temperament was thoroughly democratic, and he was in his element when he was leading the violent shouters for change. In the Legislature and Continental Congress he spoke frequently and impetuously, with a hot, incorrect rush of language. Drayton, a gifted young lawyer, had lost none of the courage with which in 1775, when Gadsden was in Philadelphia, he had led the progressives to victory. The demand for a new Constitution slowly became overwhelming. Early in 1778 the Legislature seized a favorable moment for meeting it, and presented a new framework of government, in the form of a legislative enactment, to President Rutledge for his signature. This was done with unexpected suddenness. Rutledge had watched the measure without much concern, for, he says, "I really never imagined that this bill would have reached me."

It was to the consternation of many conservatives that President Rutledge vetoed the new Constitution and then resigned. He did not believe that a Legislature had any lawful power to write such a fundamental law, and Locke, Bolingbroke, and other authorities supported his opinion. He took a paternal pride in the original Constitution; to him it represented the happy day when hope of reconciliation with England was still tenable, and he perhaps disliked the grant of religious equality to all Protestants. Vice-President Laurens, at this time in the Continental Congress, condemned his act. It seemed to many alarmed planters that it gave Gadsden and Drayton an opportunity to put them in the wrong, and score a decided victory; but the moderates and conservatives were able to keep their hands on the tiller. They accepted Rutledge's resignation, voting him their thanks for his vigilant and faithful discharge of duty, and then they elected a successor to suit themselves, overriding the effort of

[26] Colls. "So. Ca. Hist. Soc.," IV (1887), F. A. Porcher on Gadsden.

the radicals to choose Gadsden as Governor—Arthur Middleton refused the place, and they gave it to Rawlins Lowndes.[27] Sprung from a West Indian family, Lowndes had been distinguished in judicial and legislative capacities for years. In 1786 he had moved to celebrate the repeal of the Stamp Act by erecting a statue of Pitt in the State House, and though a consistent Whig, he was almost as cautious as Rutledge himself, so that the extremists had dubbed him "the great procrastinator."

Had the conservatives consulted simple preference, they would have chosen some such man as Charles Pinckney for Lieutenant-Governor. Although fully identified with their party—only the previous year he had opposed the disestablishment of the Anglican Church—he had moved forward, like Laurens and Lowndes, to support the new Constitution. But they consulted political expediency; Gadsden's troublesomeness suggested that he should be honored—and shelved—by being given the place. This adroit trick they had played before, when they had tried to silence Drayton first by placing him in the chair at the Second Provincial Congress, and later by appointing him to the dignified but supposedly innocuous post of Chief Justice. Gadsden's indignation at being thus "got out of the way" was intense. From being an independent leader he was dragged into the entourage of a slow-moving Governor; moreover, the next Legislature would choose a full-term Governor, and he charged that his enemies had plotted to make him ineligible.

Yet Gadsden loyally supported Lowndes, and such support was needed. The more irresponsible radicals in Charleston were hard to control. Partly under pressure from them, partly in thoughtlessness, the Legislature on March 28, 1778, passed a drastic act obliging every free male inhabitant of mature years, under severe penalties, to give assurance of fidelity to the State. It was so sweeping that it could not possibly be enforced. When the time approached to punish those who had failed to obey it, Governor Lowndes was sick, and seeing the hopelessness of his predicament, wrote to Gadsden imploring assistance; whereupon the old warrior-politician hurried to Charleston, and on June 5, with the Council, issued a proclamation extending the time allowed by the act. But the "mob," as Gadsden frankly called his old followers, was excited and angry. The proclamation was hardly in the sheriff's hands, wrote Gadsden to a friend,

[27] McCrady, "S. Ca. in the Rev., 1775-1780," Ch. XI; Wallace's "Laurens," 223.

"before some myrmidons alarmed the town, we were setting up a proclamation against law going to ruin their Liberties and what not!" A deputation called upon Lowndes and Gadsden, hot words were exchanged, and Gadsden almost came to blows with its spokesman. He saw more clearly than ever before where the unchecked impulses of the ignorant extremists would lead the State, and wrote:[28]

"I am afraid we have too many amongst us (who) want again to be running upon every Fancy to the meetings of (the) liberty tree. Query whether there is not a danger amongst us far more dangerous than anything that can arise from the whole herd of contemptible, exportable Tories."

The first election of a Legislature under the second Constitution (November 30, 1778) showed how firm was the grip of the moderates upon the State. The long list of conservatives sent to the State House included four Pinckneys, three Rutledges, two Middletons, and two Laurenses. No new spirit had been infused into politics by the extension of the franchise and the transfer of the choice of the upper house to the people. The ruling families of the lowlands retained their supremacy. The most important of the members-elect was John Rutledge. His popularity had been diminished hardly a whit by his opposition to the Constitution, and public opinion designated him as the new Governor—a designation which the Legislature ratified as soon as it met in January, 1778. Thomas Bee, after some delay, became Lieutenant-Governor—another conservative.

Rutledge's election came almost at the same time that news of the capture of Savannah reached Charleston, serving notice that critical days lay immediately ahead. Shrewd men like Henry Laurens had seen from the beginning of the war that the British would try to cut off Georgia and the Carolinas. An attempt to capture Charleston was now a certainty. The Legislature that elected Rutledge assigned him and his Council power, before it adjourned, to "do everything that appeared to him and to them necessary for the public good." Indeed, the crisis arrived before it was expected. General Prevost, after taking Savannah, defeated General Lincoln at Briar Creek, Georgia, and then outmaneuvered him. By a forced march he suddenly appeared before Charleston early in May, 1779, and took post on the Neck which linked the city with the mainland. As Charleston was well fortified, with artillery mounted on the ramparts

[28] McCrady's "S. Ca. in the Rev., 1775-1780," 271.

and armed galleys plying in the rivers, a direct assault by the British would have been insane. Resorting to negotiation, Prevost sent an ultimatum to Governor Rutledge and the Council on May 12. The general nature of the response is known, but not its exact form. One reliable authority, Major-General William Moultrie, says that Governor Rutledge and his Council sent out a note.[29]

"To propose a neutrality during the war between Great Britain and America, and the question whether the State shall belong to Great Britain or remain one of the United States to be determined by the treaty of peace between those two Powers."

But John Laurens, who was as well acquainted with the facts, declares that the proposal to Prevost regarding the city was:[30]

"That he should be permitted to take possession of it provided the State and harbor should be considered as neutral during the war, the question whether it belonged to Great Britain or the United States to be waived until the conclusion of it, and that whenever that should happen, whatever was granted to the other States, that [South Carolina] should enjoy."

In other words, in offering to make South Carolina neutral, did Governor Rutledge regard her as eventually a passive pawn in the peace negotiations, or did he stipulate that when the war ended she should stand on the same footing as her sister States? Laurens' version is the more probable, for Rutledge never lacked courage. Whatever the proposal, Prevost would not accept it. While he negotiated, he heard that Lincoln was on his heels, and retired during the night so unexpectedly that Charleston could hardly realize its safety.

But the second attack met with complete success. The Assembly was in session when on March 29, 1780, the British crossed the Ashley and landed on Charleston Neck, beleaguering the city by land and sea. Most of the legislators fled at once. Before doing so, however, they again conferred such extensive authority upon Governor Rutledge that for decades he was spoken of as "the Dictator." They granted him and the Council, till ten days after the next session, "a power to do everything necessary for the public good except the taking away the life of a citizen without a legal trial." The legislators fortunately saw that it might be weary months before they met again, though they did not suspect that it would be weary years, during which Rutledge almost single-handed would have to maintain a semblance of effective government.

[29] "Memoirs," I, 433.
[30] McCrady, "S. Ca. in the Rev., 1775-1780," 367.

Rutledge at once issued a proclamation calling the militia and all the able-bodied men of Charleston to arms. The progress of the British siege was inexorable. Their ships immediately came over the bar before the outer harbor, and up to the city. It was on April 9 that Admiral Arbuthnot ran past Fort Moultrie and on April 12 Governor Rutledge and three Councilors seized the last opportunity, so tight was the cordon being drawn, of escaping from Charleston. Lieutenant-Governor Gadsden, for the old radical had succeeded Bee, with five of the Councilors, remained to encourage the defenders. It would have been wise for General Lincoln to have withdrawn the army from the city at the same time. His engineers advised against staying; so did the other officers, except Pinckney and Moultrie; and Washington, too distant to advise, thought that it was folly to remain. One factor in Lincoln's decision was the demand of Gadsden and the Councilors that the city be held to the last but Gadsden had no authority which the general was bound to obey. The British lines and parallels gradually grew closer till on May 12 Charleston was surrendered without much hard fighting.

Sir Henry Clinton jubilantly wrote three weeks later (June 4, 1780) from his headquarters in Charleston to Lord George Germain that all resistance below the North Carolina line was ended. "I may venture to assert that there are few men in South Carolina who are not either our prisoners or in arms with us," he said. British rule had in truth been almost completely reëstablished. Among the military prisoners were General William Moultrie, Colonel C. C. Pinckney, and Lieutenant-Colonel John Laurens, the son of the former Vice-President. As for the civil prisoners, they included Lieutenant-Governor Gadsden, Dr. Ramsay, and three signers of the Declaration of Independence, Edward Rutledge, Thomas Heyward, Jr. and Arthur Middleton. The British boasted much because Arthur Middleton, together with the aged patriot Gabriel Manigault, applied for British citizenship. Charles Pinckney and Daniel Huger, members of the Governor's Council who had left town with Rutledge, came in to camp and offered their paroles. Rawlins Lowndes and Henry Middleton retired to their plantations in frank acceptance of defeat.[31] A large number of the irreconcilables were sent to St. Augustine, and others were confined near at hand. But a surprising number of lowland citizens did not prove irreconcilable, as was

[31] McCrady, "S. Ca. in the Rev., 1775-1780," 533 ff.

shown when before the middle of September, 1780, 168 petitioned for British protection, and before the middle of July, 1781, another 213 had done so. Addresses of congratulation were presented to the British commanders after the capture of Charleston and the battle of Camden, and no less than 210 South Carolinians signed them. The disheartened Rutledge wrote from Charlotte, N. C., as the year 1780 ended, that the spirit of resistance had been almost stamped out. "The unfortunate affair near Camden, the want of any support ever since, and the little prospect of any, have affected the conduct of many, who were well-disposed, and whose hearts may, perhaps, still be with us." [32]

Had the British acted a politic part, they might have quenched the last embers of the rebellion in South Carolina. By bringing back William Bull and making him Governor, by giving the civil authorities full powers, by accepting the neutrality of men who would not fight for the King, they might have won the people. Instead, their sternness and cruelty left many no choice but to take up arms. In the discouraged letter just noted, Rutledge described this mistaken British policy. They had hanged many opponents, especially men charged with violating paroles, they had "burnt a prodigious number of houses, and turned a vast many women, formerly of affluent, or, easy, fortunes, with their children, almost naked, into the woods"; in short they seemed determined "to break every man's spirit, or, if they can't, to ruin him." But the spirit of South Carolinians was not to be broken. With surprising rapidity an effective partisan resistance was begun.

The fall of Charleston left the South Carolina militia so depressed that Rutledge despaired of their use. They would not serve at a distance from home, for they were apprehensive that the Tories would destroy their property and kill their families. Their embodiment in large units being impossible, the British pushed rapid columns into the upper country, and took strategic positions there. The patriots were nonplussed, till in July a smart victory by one of Sumter's detachments pointed the way to successful operations, and that month he was made a brigadier of State troops. On August 6 he defeated another mixed body, five hundred strong, at Hanging Rock, but a fortnight later was himself almost annihilated at Fishing-Creek by Tarleton. Francis Marion organized a troop of less than

[32] "Letters." *S. Ca. Hist. and Gen. Mag.*, January, 1917.

eighty men and did so much with it that Rutledge made him also a brigadier-general of militia. Andrew Pickens observed his parole faithfully until the British broke their pledges by plundering his plantation, when he entered the field; and after Cowpens he became the third brigadier. The aroused patriots gathered in small bands, often taking most of their arms and ammunition from the dead or from prisoners; and they waged an harassing warfare of surprise attacks, ambuscades, and assaults upon isolated posts.

It was under these circumstances that during 1780 the leadership of the State decisively changed. Except for Rutledge and a few others, the old patrician patriots who had marched in procession in honor of Wilkes and had dominated the Provincial Congresses were dead, imprisoned, paroled, or otherwise out of active affairs. A new set of chieftains was arising, as patriotic as the old, but of a different training and spirit, and manifesting no such conservatism. The ruthlessness of the British and the outrages of the Tories helped these men to break totally with the past. Sumter had been born in the upper country of Virginia and after his removal to South Carolina still belonged to the uplands. Pickens had been born in Pennsylvania, and had settled at the Waxhaws, also in the new back country. Marion sprang of a Huguenot family on the South Carolina coast, but he was not a Charlestonian, and he removed well into the interior, to Eutaw Springs. New men, as Isaac Motte and Francis Kinloch, appeared as delegates to the Continental Congress.

Thus the struggle was carried on until at the beginning of 1781 it assumed a much more hopeful look. Nathanael Greene took command of the Southern forces late in 1780, and most of his brilliant successes were won on South Carolina soil. When Cornwallis marched from North Carolina into Virginia, he showed his generalship by turning at once to reconquer South Carolina. By the end of June, 1781, he had forced the British back to the coastal country, where they were prodded and stung by his cavalry captains, "Lighthorse Harry" Lee and William Washington, and by Sumter, Pickens, and Marion. The battle of Eutaw Springs, in September, was indecisive, but the British lost so heavily that they retired into Charleston, and thenceforth they were kept penned there by Greene. Governor Rutledge saw to it that South Carolina's troops coöperated closely with Greene, and in the fall prepared to reorganize the government with a capital outside Charleston.

III. North Carolina Politics 1780-1787

Meanwhile, in the months that followed the capture of Charleston, North Carolina and her weak government had been tested as by fire. Intelligent men knew what the capture foreboded. Ten days after it occurred Iredell, travelling from town to town to attend the courts—he had been chosen Attorney-General by the Legislature in 1779—found people "everywhere flying from home," and Wilmington crowded with refugees. The State's Continental battalions, with a thousand militia, had been surrendered at Charleston, and it was difficult to raise and outfit new troops. Her work in supplying the Southern armies with provisions had already begun to impoverish the people, and the depreciation of the currency and deadened trade made recuperation difficult. Worst of all, few States contained so great a proportion of Tories as North Carolina, and they were eager to rise—too eager for Cornwallis, who wanted them to wait until the ripe crops would afford them sustenance. Bands sprang up as by magic in some sections, ravaging the farms of the patriots, while news came of the restiveness of many of the oldtime Regulators.

North Carolina's Legislature was sitting at New Bern when the siege of Charleston was closing, and could face the emergency. Several conservatives were there, notably Hooper and Maclaine—Johnston was sent to the Continental Congress this year—and they gave the session what wisdom it possessed. This was little in the opinion of Iredell, who wrote that the laws "are certainly the vilest collection of trash ever formed by a legislative body." Governor Nash was authorized to send 8000 troops to South Carolina, Congress having urgently demanded such a force; he would have liked to command it himself, but it had been arranged that ex-Governor Caswell should lead it. A law was passed for recruiting 3000 men for three years' service in the Continental line, each volunteer being granted $300 down and the promise of a rich western tract, while even the recruiting officers were allowed $250 for every man they found. For a thousand uses money was needed, and most of it came from the printers. Not only was an additional £1,240,000 in paper arranged for, but the Governor was authorized to emit more if an emergency occurred during the legislative recess, though officials were already distributing bills in a way that made them contemptible.[33]

[33] State Records, XXIV, 317-39.

One large body of the 8000 militia ordered out was collected in the eastern part of the State under Caswell, another in the western under Gen. Rutherford. Caswell united them early in August in upper South Carolina, and made them a part of Gates's army, the backbone of which had newly arrived from the North. As such, units belonging to them shared in the heavy defeat at Camden on August 15, 1780, when Gates lost nearly 2000 men, and was able to rally his militia only at Hillsborough, 180 miles away. Another staggering British blow, already alluded to, was delivered a few days later against Sumter at Fishing-Creek. For the moment North Carolina believed that the war was lost, and some Britons that it was won; but Caswell rallied several regiments which had been in the rear at Camden, and called the militia of three counties to meet them at Charlotte—being confident, he wrote Governor Nash, of a formidable camp in a few days.

The panicky Assembly, convening September 5, undertook several more foolish measures, the chief being one designed to thrust the Governor out of all contact with the war.[34] This action in part reflected the dislike which many radicals had for Nash's record as a moderate. Their procedure was to create a Board of War "for the more effectually and expeditiously calling forth the powers and resources of the State and disposing the same in such manner as to enable the generals and commanders . . . to act with vigor and precision"; a Board which took general charge of military affairs, being empowered to concert a plan of campaign with the ranking officer of the State, while the Governor twiddled his thumbs. As Davie, one of the most capable Southern commanders, said they were "Martin, a warrior of great fame; Penn, fit only to amuse children; and O. Davis, who knew nothing but the game of whist." [35] If only because it possessed the contempt of field officers, the Board was incompetent to direct the State's part in the war. Nash justly felt aggrieved at being pushed to one side under those circumstances which in other States led to the endowment of the Governor with unusual powers. Another statute called for the collection of specific provisions from each property owner; Samuel Johnston called it the most oppressive and least productive tax ever known in North Carolina.[36] A new act for receiving loans was passed, its preamble

[34] State Records, XXIV, 355.
[35] McRee, "Iredell"; see also F. M. Hubbard, "Life of Davie," 53 ff.
[36] The collectors were empowered to take a double tax if payment was not prompt. "Though intended to relieve the country from a more oppressive form of

admitting that the issue of more paper money "would have a tendency to increase the price of necessaries, and be greatly injurious to the public."

Fortunately, North Carolina had better soldiers than lawmakers. The far-reaching victory of King's Mountain in October, 1780, not only freed the upper country of North Carolina from the threat of the Tory force raised there but halted the British invasion of the State, Cornwallis retreating hastily to the South Carolina frontier. Most important of all, the battle checked the well-laid schemes of Cornwallis and the Tory leaders for a general uprising. The loyalists whom early in the summer the British had found difficult to restrain now could not be persuaded to move. "This Province is most exceedingly disaffected," Cornwallis wrote a fellow-officer. Greene's arrival diffused a new courage throughout the Carolinas. Finally, in January, 1781, occurred the American victory over Tarleton at the Cowpens, in western North Carolina, which in the words of Cornwallis's biographer was the most serious British defeat since Saratoga.

Yet when the Legislature met the day after Cowpens for its third session, it faced a situation very grave still. Cornwallis could renew his invasion at any time, and before the end of February had actually marched to Hillsborough, and invited all "loyal subjects to repair, without loss of time, with their arms and ten days' provisions, to the Royal Standard." The first task of the Legislature was to abolish the Board of War. Greene disliked this body, and the soldiers and people had a low opinion of it. As for Governor Nash, he charged the Legislature with having changed "our form of government; for by your acts you have effectually transferred the powers vested by the Constitution in the Governor into the hands of commissioners." He was not conscious, on the strictest self-examination, of having done anything except with a view to the State's good. When he entered office, he had been solemnly presented with the Constitution and the sword, and yet within four months the one had been violated, the other handed over to the Board of War. "In short, gentlemen," concluded Nash, "I hold at

exaction, this tax seems to have been paid with great reluctance. Much time was consumed in collecting it, especially in the thinly settled districts; and great difficulty was experienced in transporting the heavy articles, and driving the live-stock to the points, which were constantly changing as new movements of the troops were contemplated, where they would be needed. . . . The commissioners of the counties were under an imperfect responsibility. . . ." Hubbard's "Davie," 64-70.

present but an empty title, neither serviceable to the people nor honorable to myself"; and he threatened to resign the Governorship forthwith.[37]

The Legislature yielded to this ultimatum, and abolished the Board. It substituted a Council Extraordinary for it, which exercised some of its powers and was to advise with the Governor "in all cases whatsoever"; but this Council was to exist only till the next meeting of the Legislature, and was not so irritating. The energetic William Davie, now Quartermaster-General, was allotted a greater authority by the two houses, and the impressment of supplies was made less unjust in nature.[38] Bills were passed for strengthening the militia, and reorganizing the Continental battalions. Then the Legislature adjourned, having elected Ex-Governor Caswell, Alexander Martin, and one Bignal as members of the Council Extraordinary. Its exertions had again fallen short of pleasing the conservatives. Hooper, who was driven from his home in February by the advance of Cornwallis, wrote Iredell his testy impression of affairs: [39]

A country on the verge of ruin; a corrupt, or what is worse, an idiot Assembly; an indolent Executive; a treasury without money; a military without exertion; punctilios superseding duty—in a word, upon the true test of patriotism, the approach of the enemy, the vociferation of persecution and confiscation being resolved into silence or ineffectual efforts in order to promote doubts and disputation, show what we have to expect from the opposition in this State.

Despite military perils, the Legislature for 1781 was duly elected and met in June in Wake County, a corner of the well-settled portion of the State still safe from British surprise. It was high time, for the Council Extraordinary had taken extraordinary steps. In March it and Governor Nash had issued an order requiring every inhabitant to give up one-fifth of his provisions for the army—an order obviously impracticable. Another order, equally fatuous, required every man who had abandoned his post in the recent battle of Guilford Court House, where Cornwallis had defeated Greene, to enrol in the Continental army for a year. The State was rankling under the disgrace inflicted upon it by the raw, ill-armed militia, who on that close field had fled precipitately; but the placing of cowards in the Continental Line was not calculated to strengthen the

[37] State Records, XV, 225-29.
[38] Davie called impressment legal robbery, and in December, 1781, he wrote Gen. Greene: "The specific levies of government are quite inadequate." Hubbard's "Davie," 69, 70.
[39] McRee's "Iredell," I, 486-88.

latter. The Legislature voted a variety of military and fiscal measures, but its most important act was the election of Dr. Thomas Burke, an honest, hot-headed Irish physician and lawyer, to be Governor.

Nash might have been reëlected, but declined to serve any longer now that "the executive power had been so divided that it was impossible to govern with any advantage to the people." Burke was wise enough to take office only on condition that this division of authority cease. The Legislature let the Council Extraordinary die, but provided that the Governor must share the supreme military command with the Council of State (the executive council). But he would have none of this; the office had sought him, he declared; he would take it as the Constitution created it, or not at all. The Legislature knew that Burke was a born fighter. As a member of the Continental Congress in 1777, he had seized a musket when Philadelphia was threatened, and fought at the Brandywine. He had never brooked a slight, and could speak and write effectively. Moreover, the radical legislators hardly dared quarrel with one of their own wing, whom they had elected in opposition to the conservative nominee, Samuel Johnston. They yielded, and the Governor in his military capacity ignored the Council of State.[40]

The people hoped much from the new Governor, believing that with energy and capacity he might partly relieve them of their heavy taxation and the forcible levies. The governmental and economic life of North Carolina was at the lowest ebb. Under Nash, the Board of War, and the military leaders, as Nash wrote Burke, "men, not knowing whom to obey, obeyed nobody." "The resources of the State," Davie told Greene,[41] "whether from a blunder in our polity or want of address in the executive, are of no more service than if they were really exhausted; . . . neither our money nor our credit is any longer a medium." Every farm in some sections had been half stripped of live stock and stored grain to furnish the armies. The impressments were deeply resented by merchants who thereby lost their little stores of cloth, ammunition, rum, coffee, and sugar. Burke bent hard to his problems, and a message he sent the Council on July 26, 1781, urging the strengthening of the State's finances and the restoration of order, showed that he had no illusions: [42]

[40] See sketch of Burke, "North Carolina Booklet," October, 1906.
[41] Hubbard's "Davie," 70-71.
[42] State Records, XIX, 855 ff.

The country is everywhere unprepared for defence, without arms, without discipline, without arrangements; even the habits of civil order and obedience to laws changed into a licentious contempt of authority and a disorderly indulgence of violent propensities. Industry is intermitted, agriculture much decayed, and commerce struggling feebly with almost insuperable difficulties. The public money is unaccounted for, the taxes uncollected or unproductive . . . and the treasury totally unable to make payment.

Burke made a stand against the excesses of the forage-masters and impressment officers, who had committed intolerable outrages. He halted Governor Nash's ruinous policy of impressing all imported articles upon the moment of their arrival, which had so discouraged trade that North Carolina had not fifty bushels of salt for her troops, and as little for the general public. He travelled about the State trying in person to restore confidence, until his activities were suddenly cut short. In September, he and a number of other State officers were unsuspectingly transacting business at the village capital, Hillsborough. The noted Tory leader, David Fanning, a young South Carolinian, swooped down upon the place, and after some fighting made more than 200 prisoners. Among them, Fanning reported, were "the Governor and his Council, a party of Continental colonels, captains, subalterns and seventy-one Continental soldiers taken out of a church." This was a month before Cornwallis's surrender.

Governor Burke was taken to Charleston, whence, as a prisoner of state, not subject to exchange, he was paroled to James's Island, in the harbor opposite Fort Moultrie. The British were inconsiderate in their treatment of him. James's Island was a shelter for ruffians of the back country who were so brutal that the Charleston Tories would have nothing to do with them, and though Governor Burke repeatedly petitioned for protection, he did not receive it. "After I had been there some considerable time," Burke relates, "a number of refugees were sent on who became immediately contentious, and I perceived they committed every species of offence, even murder, with impunity, their persons were unknown; their dress was all alike, that is literally dirty rags; their outrages were committed in strong parties, and as they always retreated in security to their encampment, it was impossible to detect them; they were under no control or discipline, and they were desperate with want, rage, and disappointment." [43] Burke redoubled his importunities for a guard, but in vain. He knew that the North Carolina Tories especially

[43] State Records, XVI. 14.

wanted his life. At length, a party of the refugees fired on a small group at his quarters, and killed a man standing on one side of him, and wounded another on his other hand; while their violence would have gone farther but for the interference of a British officer. Burke concluded that he was justified in breaking his parole, and on a chill January night, when the guards were under cover, he escaped. He wrote back to Gen. Leslie offering to return a man of equivalent rank, or to surrender himself again on condition that he would be treated like other Continental officers, but the British commander could not consider these proposals. Thereupon he resumed his duties as Governor, his term being near its end.

When the Legislature met early in 1782, Burke refused to stand for reëlection, probably because he knew defeat would be certain. He had shown energy and ability, but his absence from the State in the crisis of the war, and the circumstances of his return—for many agreed with Greene that it was dishonorable—counted against him. His merits were no recommendation to a Legislature which did not want an independent-minded Governor. Discerning men knew, as Hooper wrote (April 8) that careful measures had to be taken to save "this wretched State from its present anarchy and gloomy expectations." But the Legislature could not deal properly with even the remaining war problems. Forces had to be kept under arms at the South, where Charleston was still in British hands. The best means of supplying them had been found to be the new State commissariat and quartermaster's departments; but on the ground that unlawful impressments, and misapplications of public stores, had been committed by men masquerading as State commissaries, these departments were now abolished, and the clumsy system of county commissaries was restored. On returning home, some Assemblymen even drove off their cattle which had been collected by commissary officers, and urged their constituents to do the same.[44]

More disheartening was the wrong mood in which the Legislature approached the problems of peace. This was signally evinced by its election of Alexander—familiarly called "Paddy"—Martin, a noted radical, to be Governor, for he was a rancorous hater of the British, and represented a policy of repression and persecution for all Tories. Burke had pursued a just and moderate policy toward the loyalists. When others wished them hanged in scores, he had planned to dis-

[44] Hubbard's "Davie," 75-76.

pose of them advantageously and humanely by exchanging them as prisoners of war for the Americans who languished in Charleston. "The checking of the furious resentment that prevails among the people, and produces tragical effects," he wrote Governor Mathews of South Carolina, "and the preventing the number of judicial convictions for treason which involved the government in the dilemma of suffering numbers to be executed *summa jure,* or by interposing pardons weaken the due authority of the laws, were with me strong motives for adopting those measures by removing the objects." [45] The conservatives united upon Samuel Johnston, who would of course have been even a milder Governor than Burke. For some days they counted upon the assistance of Caswell, who was a moderate and a resident of the eastern part of the State, in electing Johnston; but Caswell dashed this expectation by suddenly throwing his great influence on Martin's side.

Besides electing Martin, the Legislature of 1782 passed a measure renewing the sale of confiscated property, and naming some seventy men or companies specifically whose possessions were forfeited. A vindictive clamor arose for executions. No Southern State had suffered more than North Carolina from the strife between Tory and patriot. The followers of Fanning and similar Tory leaders were half soldiers, half desperadoes, and even Tarleton, a gallant and efficient British officer, had not only committed houses to the flames and destroyed the food of whole countrysides, but had let murder and rape go unpunished. Men who had lost their all, whose sisters or daughters had been assaulted, who had seen a brother or son with his throat cut in a pool of blood, demanded vengeance. Though many Tories fled within the British lines, the criminal dockets were crowded with indictments for treason. Only the exertions of the soberest citizens, including Attorney-General Iredell, and the refusal of many soldiers of the Continental Line to see a disarmed enemy hurt, saved the State from a large number of executions.

The Legislature of 1783 was not superior to its predecessor. It was prevailed upon to pass an act of pardon and oblivion for treason, misprision of treason, felony, or misdemeanor committed since July 4, 1776. But this act excepted all who had served as officers under the King, all named in the confiscation acts, all who, having attached themselves to the British, remained outside the State more than a

[45] State Papers, XVI, 217-18.

year after the passage of the law, and any person guilty of murder, robbery, rape, or houseburning. The clamor of debtors caused the Legislature to pass a foolish measure for a suspension of suits. Sufficient protection would have been afforded the poor if the State had halted the execution of court judgments for a time. The Legislature reëlected Governor Martin, the ambitious Caswell being the chief opposition candidate. Caswell hoped for the solid eastern support he had denied Johnston the previous year, but the conservatives, nursing their grudge and led by the quick-tempered Maclaine, strained every nerve to defeat him. Crestfallen, Caswell wrote his son: "The Edenton and Halifax men with a very few exceptions voted for Governor Martin, saying I had crammed him down their throats last year and they were determined to keep him there."

James Hogg, a member of this Legislature, wrote Iredell in condemnation of its qualities just as Johnston, Maclaine, Hooper, and Davie had written of the Assemblies in previous years: [46]

I will not venture to describe to you the temper of the Assembly—my style is too feeble for such a subject. I think you, and Mr. Hooper, and Mr. Johnston, would have been of great service in this Assembly to the country, nor am I satisfied with your apologies;—if such men do not stand forth in this critical period, and lend their aid, this country won't be worth living in. A set of unprincipled men, who sacrifice everything to their popularity and private views, seem to have acquired too much influence in all our Assemblies.

It was true that the best men in North Carolina were often unwilling to make the surrender of money and time involved in public service. In the very letter of 1782 in which he spoke of the State's anarchic condition, Hooper added that he had "resolved to make no sacrifice of my private interests to the public concerns." He had just suffered much from the British occupation of Wilmington, losing slaves, furniture, silver, and "above 100 valuable volumes," one of his greatest joys in life; but he could have afforded attendance upon the Assembly. Iredell's service as Attorney-General was too brief, for he resigned in 1782, and if his principal motive in stepping out was his distaste for the prosecution of Tories, he was affected also by the consideration that he could make more money at private practice. Johnston stood too much on his dignity in refusing to give parliamentary battle to "unprincipled men."

When the election of the Legislature of 1784 occurred, public attention was centred chiefly upon the treaty of peace. The conservatives hoped that it might be used in the Legislature to obtain

[46] McRee's "Iredell," II, 45-46.

justice for the loyalists. "Without it, I despair of doing anything of immediate consequence," wrote Iredell. "Should it be laid before us, it will then be seen whether we will suffer anger and resentment so far to get the better of reason and sound policy, as to render us infamous over all Europe." The question whether its provisions should be enforced elicited a surprising number of pamphleteers. Johnston and Iredell called a public meeting on August 1, 1783, at which they had a set of resolutions and one of instructions to the Edenton legislators voted. These two documents show clearly the objects sought by the conservative low-country leaders. The resolutions declared that the terms of peace ought to be "sacredly fulfilled"; and called for the payment of interest on the State debt, with the gradual reduction of the principal. The instructions demanded support of the impost amendment asked by Congress, reprobated any new issues of paper money, advocated a systematization of the State finances, pointed out the expediency of permanent and liberal salaries for judges, and asked for the encouragement of trade and manufacturing. The conservative leaders made an unusually energetic bid for office. Johnston was elected Senator for Chowan County by twice as many votes as his nearest competitor; Hooper was sent to the House for Orange County by a heavy majority, Maclaine for Wilmington, and Allen Jones for Halifax.[47]

But it was soon evident that the Legislature would oppose a strict observance of the treaty. The final days of April, 1784, it devoted to debate. The conservatives exhausted all their arguments, but the resolutions they introduced were, so far as they assented to the recommendations of Congress for liberal treatment of all loyalists and British residents, rejected in the Commons by a vote of three to one. "Imps of hell," General Rutherford called the Tories, and Nash was almost as vehement. Furthermore, the Legislature flatly violated the treaty in its action upon the payment of British debts, declining to remove the obstacles which prevented British subjects from suing for the payment of obligations, and voting to sell some British debts that were part of the assets of confiscated estates. The petitions of various loyalists for the restitution of property—they included two of Iredell's friends and two men whose claims had received the express recommendation of Dr. Franklin—were spurned. Hooper was left dejected: "There is not a frenzy of misguided political zeal—

---

[47] McRee's "Iredell," II, 94 ff.

avarice clothed in the cover of patriotism—of private passion and prejudice, under the pretence of revenging the wrongs of the country . . . that can give me the least surprise hereafter"; and Iredell repented of having had anything to do with the House.

In other respects the Legislature was delinquent in its discharge of Federal obligations. During the war the State paid so little upon the Congressional requisitions that at its close it owed the Continental Treasury $18,230,000. Upon three new requisitions early in 1784 North Carolina paid not a cent. Moreover, after 1780 the State was grossly negligent in maintaining a representation in Congress. The Legislature would not appropriate money to pay the full expenses of the delegates, the journey was painful, and they received no public appreciation. From July 21 to September 21, 1781, William Sharpe alone sat for North Carolina; then till early in October the State was unrepresented; and later Benjamin Hawkins was the sole delegate until March 19, 1782, when he went home and left no one in Congress until July 19. The radical Thomas Person, elected in 1784, did not stir a step towards Philadelphia.[48]

Again, North Carolina—against the protest of thirty-seven legislators—ceded her transmontane lands to the nation by a conditional act of April, 1784, a praiseworthy step. But it was self-interested. A national movement was at that time on foot for levying a Continental land tax, and another for the apportionment of Continental requisitions strictly according to population, so that North Carolinians felt that it might be prudent to detach the wide Tennessee country, steadily filling up with poor inhabitants. The settlers beyond the mountains were not loved, anyway. "The offscourings of the earth, fugitives from justice," one legislator described them; "we will be rid of them at any rate." Yet after all, the grant was withdrawn that fall.[49] It is to the credit of the State that she early assented to the request of Congress for power to levy a five per cent duty on imports, and for the right to control trade with foreign nations;[50] but it must be remembered that North Carolina had good reason for doing so. A greater Congressional authority over commerce meant a clear gain, for North Carolina had little direct commerce, and so paid tribute to her two great neighbors.

From 1784 to 1787 the Legislature refused to carry out the peace

[48] R. D. W. Connor, "N. Ca.," I, Ch. 27.
[49] W. K. Boyd, Ch. 1; State Records XXIV, 561-63; 678-79.
[50] Thomas Person protested against the impost grant; State Records, XVII, 944; XXIV, 561.

treaty in its entirety. After its hostile action in the former year, Johnston, Hooper, and Maclaine consulted with one another upon their proper course as lawyers. They agreed that suits brought for British debts, and suits by persons who lay under disabilities during the war, might—in spite of the attitude of the Legislature—now be maintained. One judge would certainly be against them, and they feared all three would be so, but they wished to try.[51] As Maclaine apprehended, the judiciary was unfriendly. Not until the Federal Constitution had received its first State ratifications was the treaty swallowed: on December 22, 1787, the legislators formally voted that it was part of the law of the State.

IV. South Carolina Politics 1780-1787

Meanwhile, in South Carolina an even greater outburst of violence and passion had followed the restoration of the State to the patriots. It found one expression in harsh legislation against the supposed Tories and turncoats who had accepted the authority of the British when they overran the State, and another outlet in riots, tarring and feathering, and murder. But responsible men gradually brought it under control, its final phases merging with the malevolence shown by the unpropertied radicals for the aristocratic governing body of planters. From these disturbances the State plunged into a period of economic troubles, matching those of the North at the time of Shays's Rebellion.

In November, 1781, the British forces having been withdrawn to the vicinity of Charleston, Governor Rutledge issued writs for an election to the Legislature to be held December 17-18.[52] He originally planned to hold the session at Camden during the first week in January, but it actually began at Jacksonborough on the 18th. This was the only lowland town available—a mere hamlet of sixty houses, a courthouse, a jail, and large rice warehouses, on the Edisto 35 miles from Charleston. One reason why the patriots selected it was that it would signalize their recovery of the State, General Greene remarking that it would humiliate the British to know that

---

[51] State Records, XVII, 148-51.
[52] "Cassius" (Aedanus Burke?) in his pamphlet, "Address to the Freemen of the State of South Carolina" (1783) condemned the mode of holding this election as arbitrary. "The writs of election were accompanied with *printed instructions* to the returning officers, not to admit any person to vote, but such as obeyed his extraordinary proclamation [of September 27, 1781]. The returning officers had also further orders from the Governor to choose particular men whom he named, and according to such nomination they were chosen."

the Legislature was sitting within sound of their reveille.[53] The best men in the State had been elected by the two houses and though a quorum was barely made in each, they were an embodiment of South Carolina's ability and experience. Three signers of the Declaration of Independence, Heyward, Rutledge, and Middleton, had been chosen; the most important military figures, Generals Sumter, Marion, Pickens, Henderson, Huger, and Moultrie, and Colonels John Laurens and C. C. Pinckney were there; and a number of other distinguished men, as Gadsden, Hugh Rutledge, and the annalist, Dr. David Ramsay. The low country was dominant, but for the first time the up-country was influentially represented. Sumter, Pickens, and the Hamptons were among those who attended from above the fall line of the rivers.

As Governor Rutledge and others expected, the session was brief. The laws which had rendered paper currency a legal tender for debt were repealed, but at the same time poor men were protected by a prohibition of suits for the recovery of debts until ten days after the next General Assembly should meet. The State's consent was granted to the Continental impost. The Legislature elected a new Governor without factional quarrels, first tendering the place to Gadsden, who declined it because of his age and physical infirmities, and then choosing John Mathews, who had been in Congress since 1778, and had been recalled to attend the Jacksonborough sittings. Mathews had distinguished himself in combating the intrigue of the French Ambassador, by which the Carolinas and Georgia might possibly have lost their independence to procure that of the other States.

But what made the Jacksonborough Legislature famous was its law of confiscation, banishment, and amercement, passed against the protest of some of the ablest members. South Carolina's treatment of the Tories had been much milder than that of many sister States, but it was too much to expect a Legislature meeting in such circumstances to be magnanimous. Rutledge in opening the session spoke of the propriety of action with regard to the traitorous citizens who had congratulated the British commanders on their victories, had borne arms for the King, or had otherwise "endeavored to subvert our Constitution": [54]

[53] Greene's "Life of Nathanael Greene," III, 429 ff.
[54] Ramsay, "Rev. of S. C.," II, 234 ff.; for a view of the attitude a typical colonel took toward the Tory "villains that perpetrated this wanton, horrid murder, burning, and plundering," see R. W. Gibbes, "Doc. Hist. of the Amer. Rev., 1776-1782," 207-09.

The extraordinary lenity of this State has been remarkably conspicuous. Other States have thought it just and expedient to appropriate the property of British subjects to the public use, but we have forborne to take even the profits of the estates of our most implacable enemies. It is with you to determine, whether the forfeiture and appropriation of their property should now take place. If such shall be your determination, though many of our firmest friends have been reduced for their inflexible attachment to the cause of their country, from opulence to inconceivable distress, yet . . . it will redound to the reputation of this State, to provide a becoming support for the families of those whom you may deprive of their property.

These words fell upon the ears of many men who had lost most of their property, of some who had been cruelly imprisoned, and of some whose families had suffered from Tory ruthlessness; and the result was legislation applying to two great bodies, each member of which was specified by name. The first body was in part banished, and the property of its members was vested in State commissioners who were directed to sell it at auction within five years. It included British subjects, never citizens of South Carolina; all men who had served with the enemy and had not obeyed a proclamation issued by Governor Rutledge in 1779 to surrender themselves; some of those who had congratulated Clinton, Cornwallis, and Admiral Arbuthnot; holders of British commissions; and those who had not only avowed allegiance to the King, but had proved themselves inveterate enemies of the State. The second body included men who had accepted British protection, and had failed to surrender themselves in accordance with the proclamation of Governor Rutledge issued just before Yorktown,[55] or who had supplied the British with money. They were amerced 12 per cent. upon the actual value of their property.

It is worth noting the names of some of the men who were wise and humane enough to oppose this legislation. Gadsden attacked the confiscations as "an auto da fé," while Marion is reported on the authority of the fabulist-historian Weems to have offered a toast at Governor Mathews's table, "Damnation to the Confiscation Act!" Though General Greene did not wish to interfere in the State's internal affairs, he did not long conceal his opinion of the law. "Where is the justice or wisdom," he asked, "in punishing these men, who can no longer injure us, for having always continued to think as we all thought ten years ago?" The preamble to the legislation made

[55] "Cassius" rightly said that Rutledge's proclamation of September 27, 1781, was the fountain-head of all the persecution, for it assumed that all who had taken British protection had committed treason, and forfeited their lives and property. "Our inhabitants did nothing more than their duty in taking protection; and if they thought they could secure better treatment, or alleviate their calamity by congratulations, they had an undoubted right to do it."

an unfortunate impression, setting forth as the cnief reason for passing it the propriety of retaliating upon the Tories for the damage they had done to Whig property, and making no mention of the urgent necessity of finding money for defensive purposes; although two regiments had to be raised for the Continental Line, and Marion wrote that the confiscations and amercements would provide a fund of at least a million sterling.

Critics of the legislation not only condemned it as being *ex post facto,* but declared that the lists of men to whom it applied had been drawn up with gross partiality, and that the evidence on which the alleged Tories or turncoats were convicted might be mere gossip, or the fabrication of individuals who cherished a grudge. Moreover, they said, allegiance and protection are reciprocal, and the citizen was excused from offering the first when the State ceased to offer the second. "Cassius," thought to be that hot, impetuous, kindly Irish judge, Aedanus Burke, reminded the people at the beginning of 1783 that "the State soon after the reduction of Charleston may be strictly said to have been conquered. Not only the capital, but every post throughout the country was in the hands of the enemy. The Governor, who represented the sovereignty of the State, had provided for his safety by flight, and all the Continental troops in South Carolina were either killed, taken, or routed."

It was asserted that the "crimes" for which amercement was provided were especially venial, since the acceptance of British protection had been unavoidable for many. A number of the members of the Jacksonborough Legislature had asked for such protection. Gen. Moultrie had advised several Charleston friends to do so. When the tide began to turn in favor of the Americans, some men were able to escape to the American forces, or hire a military substitute, as the Governor's proclamation just before Cornwallis's surrender required, while some equally patriotic men were not. It could not be denied that the lists of estates to be confiscated or amerced were compiled either with shocking carelessness or a flagrant disregard for justice. "Cassius" wrote that one legislator would have suffered banishment and the loss of his estate had not a fellow member secreted the slip of paper on which his name was written. Some men of influence or family dignity were let off lightly or scot free. Colonel Thomas Pinckney, an old man tottering to his grave, was named in the lists. But Henry Middleton, Rawlins Lowndes, and

Daniel Huger, who had taken comfortable refuge under the British flag, and stayed there, suffered no penalty. The upper country had swarmed with Tories, yet only ten estates were confiscated there.

General Alexander Leslie wrote from the British headquarters in Charleston denouncing the confiscations, which he contrasted with the British policy of merely sequestrating Whig property; and he made a raid toward the Santee in retaliation, carrying off some negroes to present to injured Tories. Governor Mathews in reply described the British sequestrations in their true confiscatory light, and warned the enemy against further raids. If any occurred, he pointed out, the Legislature might be provoked into declaring null and void all the debts due to British creditors from South Carolinians; however, in significant words he added that his ambition would be to execute all laws "with lenity." Lenity indeed distinctly marked the enforcement of the confiscation and amercement legislation. Moultrie tells us in his "Memoirs" how much it manifested itself the very next year, 1783: [56]

. . . for the honor of the Jacksonborough Assembly, the most of these very men were members at the first meeting of the General Assembly which met in Charleston after the evacuation. When they had got possession of the country again, and peace was restored, they were softened with pity, and had compassion for their fellow sufferers, and listened with cheerfulness to the prayer of their petitions. I had the honor of being appointed chairman of a large committee from the Senate, to meet a very large committee from the House of Representatives, to hear . . . the several petitions; and after sitting several weeks, and giving everyone a fair and impartial hearing, a report was made to the separate houses in favor of a great majority; and a great part of those names which were upon the confiscation, banishment, and amercement lists were struck off; and after a few years, on their presenting their petitions year by year, almost the whole of them had their estates restored to them, and themselves, restored as fellow citizens.

Under the modification of the Confiscation Act allowed in 1783, seventy-seven banished persons were allowed to return conditionally, and the sale of their estates was halted. Succeeding legislatures took action in similar spirit, till in 1787 even Lieutenant-Governor Bull was allowed to return, having petitioned that he might rest his aged bones in South Carolina's soil. By these recessions from a vindictive measure, South Carolina in some measure redeemed her reputation for a generous chivalry.

Charleston's, the first of the two great evacuations with which the Revolution closed, was not less dramatic than that of New York, and the emotion evoked was as great. The date was December 14, 1782. By prearrangement General Leslie moved his troops

[56] Moultrie, "Memoirs," II, 325-26.

from his advanced works and barracks slowly down to Gadsden's Wharf and more slowly disembarked them. General Wayne's men followed at 200 yards, the British often shouting to them to halt, for they were too close. Some loyalists stayed in spite of their evident peril, but the great majority had taken a painful farewell of old neighbors. It required four hours for the American forces to advance three miles, but just an hour before noon Wayne's men drew up in column before the State House. The enemy fleet, no less than 300 sail, lay a vast curved line and a magnificent sight as it moved out of the harbor. At three o'clock "Light Horse Harry" Lee's cavalry rode down the guarded streets, forming an escort for Generals Greene and Moultrie, Governor Mathews, the Council, and a group of other officers and citizens. "The great joy that was felt on this day by the citizens and soldiers, was inexpressible," Moultrie writes. "I cannot forget that happy day when we marched into Charleston with the American troops; it was a proud day to me, and I felt myself much elated, at seeing the balconies, the doors, and windows crowded with the patriotic fair, the aged citizens and others, congratulating us on our return home, saying 'God bless you, gentlemen, you are welcome home, gentlemen!' Both citizens and soldiers shed mutual tears of joy."

To no other State except Georgia did evacuation mean so much, for no other State had been so nearly submerged by the British tide. Uplands and lowlands in wide sections had been laid waste— crops, fences, and outbuildings destroyed, furniture carried off, and slaves killed or driven away. A Briton named James Simpson wrote Sir Harry Clinton two months after the capture of Charleston that nothing but his own observation would have made him believe that one-half the distress he witnessed could have been produced so rapidly in so rich and flourishing a country. Many families which four years before had enjoyed every luxury were without food, clothing, or money. He instanced the losses of Rawlins Lowndes, whose country estate had brought him £3700 a year before the war, but during the struggle had not fetched £40 a year, whose houses were ruined, and who had lost more than 80 good slaves. Joseph Johnson,[57] one of the few Carolinians who has left his personal recollections of that dreary time, says that "the whole country was

---

[57] "Traditions and Reminiscences," 387-88; for Simpson's words, see Amer. MSS., Royal Institution of Great Britain, Vol. XIX, No. 10.

impoverished, and to an extent scarcely credible." Taken as a youngster across the State in 1783, he rested with his father at a respectable wayside farmhouse. One of its children, gossiping with him, exultantly declared: "Ah, boy, I've got a new shirt, and it's made out of daddy's old one, and daddy's got a new shirt made out of mammy's old shift, and mammy's got a new shift, made out of the old sheet." To Moultrie we can again turn for a view of the country-side in 1783: [58]

I remained at Winyaw till late in September, at which time I paid a visit to Gen. Greene. It was the most dull, melancholy, dreary ride that anyone could possibly take, of about one hundred miles through the woods of that country, which I had been accustomed to see abound with livestock and wild fowl of every kind, and was now destitute of all. It had been so completely chequered by the different parties, that not one part of it had been left unexplored; consequently, not the vestige of horses, cattle, hogs, or deer, etc., was to be found. The squirrels and birds of every kind were totally destroyed. The dragoons told me, that on their scouts, no living creature was to be seen, except now and then a few camp scavengers [the buzzards], picking the bones of some unfortunate fellows, who had been shot or cut down, and left in the woods above ground. . . .

My plantation I found to be a desolate place; stock of every kind taken off; the furniture carried away, and my estate had been under sequestration.

South Carolinians themselves were not surprised that the three or four years beginning with 1783 were years of turmoil. Reviewing the State's history in 1789, Edward Rutledge wrote Jay that two causes had chiefly contributed to this. One was that people had grown used to military activity, and unused to any settled, peaceful authority. Moreover, the importance which a considerable number of individuals assumed for the services they had rendered during the war made it difficult to restrain them, for there were too many military and naval commanders who did not wish to fall back into the ranks. Rutledge here referred to such men as Commodore Alexander Gillon, leader for some time of the most turbulent party. In a notable charge to a grand jury in 1783, Aedanus Burke agreed that much of the violence was the war's aftermath: our citizens, he said, from putting their enemies to death, have reconciled themselves to slaying one another. The other cause of political strife mentioned by Rutledge was the immense debt the people owed, a debt they could not repudiate, and which weighed like a millstone about their necks, until it drove the Legislatures and the people into impolitic acts.[59]

The Legislature which opened in Charleston near the end of

[58] "Memoirs," II, 354-56.
[59] S. Ca. *Gazette,* June 10, 1783; Jay's "Works," III, 367-68.

January, 1783, acted in many ways generously and wisely; but it showed a poorer spirit when it made a qualified repeal of the law of 1782 granting Congress the right to impose the five per cent. impost. The controversy over this question gave rise to a strange episode in General Greene's interference. Greene, now commanding the Southern department, had his headquarters in Charleston, where he was in close contact with the conservative gentlemen— such as the Rutledges and Pinckneys—who later espoused Federalism so warmly, and were at this time in favor of the impost. His relations with some other South Carolinians had been unhappy. He had shown a constant dislike of General Sumter, for example. His hostility to the Confiscation Act had offended the extremists. In the later skirmishing of the war, his subordinate, Kosciusko, had captured some valuable horses in a raid. Law and army usage demanded that they be sold at auction for the benefit of the Continental Army; but some citizens identified the horses as their own, and—horses being invaluable in that stripped country—Governor Mathews supported their claim with vigor. The dispute was submitted to the Continental Congress, which decided in favor of the State, but it left a good deal of ill-feeling. At the British evacuation, it was noticed that no State military officer of high rank had been invited to ride into the city with the victorious troops of Greene and Lee, although Marion was within easy call.[60]

In short, though the Legislature had voiced its warm thanks to Greene for his services, and had voted him a valuable and well-equipped estate called Boone's Barony, south of the Edisto, many South Carolinians, especially of the radical upland party, disliked the brave Yankee Quaker. He now made a grave misstep. When the Legislature was on the point of repealing the impost grant, he sent a protest to the Governor, requesting that it be laid before the Legislature. He called attention to the dangers that surrounded the weak national government and that might affect the States. He was one, he said, who believed that independence could be a blessing only under Congressional influence, and who feared above everything the tendency to sacrifice national interests to local and State desires. In closing, he spoke of the risk of a military mutiny, and declared that if the war recommenced under these circumstances, "your ruin is inevitable."

[60] Greene's "Life of Greene," III, 468 ff.

When the Governor transmitted the letter, the lower house was the scene of a violent outburst. "A Cromwell! A dictator!" shouted the more excitable members. It was plain that Greene had injured the cause that he meant to help. "Hampden" through the press denounced both Greene's action and the impost, speaking of the latter in a way that showed a deep antagonism to a powerful central government. However, the Legislature qualified its repeal of the impost grant by levying a duty of five per cent under State authority, the proceeds to be used solely for Continental purposes.[61]

Resisting Greene's attempted interference, the Legislature no less spiritedly refused to yield to the turbulent mob of Tory-baiters. The planters and merchants, the fine old families, still dominated the two houses, though a prominent part in the proceedings was taken by the uplanders. Soon after meeting, it had elected one of the patricians, Speaker Benjamin Guerard, as Governor—a dignified, mediocre man, who, as one of the Charlestonians confined in a prison-ship in the harbor, and later exiled to Philadelphia, had given liberally of his wealth to help his fellow-unfortunates. As we have noted, nearly eighty banished persons were allowed by this legislative session to return conditionally to the State. Governor Guerard was a friend to such generous measures, and publicly declared later that one means of making America a great nation lay in "forgiving and pitying our enemies." The arguments of "Cassius" for a general amnesty made many converts among thoughtful people. British merchants in Charleston were already being tolerated and traded with. In the city's reviving social diversions many signs of conciliation could be observed. But all this was wormwood and gall to a set of men who could not put aside the passions of the war.

Who were these irrepressibles? In Charleston they were the "Liberty Boys" of a few years before, with an additional rabble which had followed the Americans back into the city. The first men to join hands under the Liberty Tree in Charleston in 1766 had included two carpenters, a retailer, a boat-builder, a painter and glazier, an upholsterer, a bookkeeper, three coach-makers, a blacksmith, a butcher, a factor, a schoolmaster, an upholsterer, and a joiner who was described as the oldest and most influential mechanic of the city.[62] These laboring men who had played a useful part with

---

[61] McCrady, "S. Ca. in the Rev.," 1780-83, p. 689-90.
[62] Johnson, "Traditions and Reminiscences," Ch. I.

their political turbulence early in the Revolution, now played an evil rôle. Their chief leader in their useful days had been Gadsden; their chief leader now was Commodore Gillon. The future commodore, when the war began, was a merchant and shipper, with an extensive European connection, and was noted for his wealth and profuse style of living. He was not of the born Charleston aristocracy, but had begun life a poor boy in Rotterdam, and had come to the city as the master of a brigantine. Active and pushing, he first made himself useful in the war as an importer of munitions for Congress and the State; with two small vessels in 1778 he captured a pair of British blockading privateers, and drove off a third; and later he commanded the frigate *South Carolina,* a French vessel which he obtained in Amsterdam.[63]

Gillon had early been appointed naval commander for South Carolina, and after some time was sent to Europe to try to purchase three frigates for the State. This mission did not succeed, partly because of what Henry Laurens called Gillon's "fervor for accomplishing everything by the force of his own powers." However, some of his achievements abroad were of value, and he generously contributed to the Revolution from his own pocket. During the British occupation of Charleston his estate was sequestrated, his wife was expelled, and his son was sent a prisoner to St. Augustine, injuries which Gillon never forgot. A rash, heady, outspoken man, he easily mingled with and led the "mob." Thanks to his youth in Europe and later sojourns there, he could speak seven languages and write five, but he had no sympathy for refinements in education. When one day in the Legislature Charles Pinckney used a sounding Latin quotation, Gillon contemptuously capped it with one in German.

Gillon and his followers were indignant over the softening of the Confiscation Act. They could hardly restrain themselves when the exempted men took up their residence in Charleston. The news of the preliminary treaty of peace, with its clauses favorable to British and Tory residents, reached America in March, 1783, and added fuel to their anger. The result appeared in rioting. In general, the mob was satisfied with ducking its victims or tarring and feathering them, but by midsummer four men had been murdered in Charleston,

[63] For a life of Gillon, see S. C. *Hist. and Gen. Mag.,* IX; see also Johnson, "Traditions and Reminiscences," 127 ff.

and one outbreak there reached serious proportions. We wished, said one radical,[64] to see the laws of the Jacksonborough Legislature enforced against the abandoned parricides who tried to destroy our liberties. We do not mind if the net offered by the legislation is evaded by the small flies, the farmers and shopkeepers, but we hate the wasps and hornets, the influential aristocrats, who are breaking it. These nabobs, he pursued, accepted British protection and engaged in the rum trade, or fled to the interior with their negroes and left Charleston to be defended against Clinton by the honest workmen. They suffered no penalty, and should now be punished.

The street rioting, thus flimsily excused, excited the indignation of all moderates and conservatives. Governor Guerard, with the leading gentlemen behind him, promptly interfered. The planters published a warning that they would ride into Charleston by thousands if needed. We have little reward for the sacrifices of eight years of war, they declared in the *Gazette of the State,* if we are to be governed by the passions of individuals, and not by laws. To be sure, the planters and merchants, many of them deeply in debt to the British, were themselves far from cordial to their late enemies. At a great public meeting in Charleston on July 21, attended by many of the upper as well as the lower classes, it was unanimously resolved that the Legislature be petitioned to prevent the return of Tories who had borne arms with the British; and that it also be requested not to do more for the adherents of Great Britain in the war than was guaranteed them by the preliminary articles of peace. But South Carolinians of the dominant lowland ranks were not only shocked by the disorders, but felt a threat against their supremacy in the talk of "nabobs." [65]

---

[64] Brutus, in S. Ca. *Gazette,* August 6, 27, 1783.

[65] S. Ca. *Gazette,* July 22, 1783; Pa. *Gazette,* August 20; McRee's "Iredell," II, 67. What the Tories were suffering at this time is made plain by a June letter in the Providence *Gazette,* July 19, 1783: "On the 16th came on at Charleston the sales of the property of the loyalists, which I am told amounted to £120,000 sterling, though I should think it more. This week the sales at Camden and Ninety-Six are to begin. The terms of the sales were, five years credit, with interest from possession, at 7 per cent, and on account of the credit most lots went off at three times their value. It was but a short time I stayed at the sales—the scene was too affecting to be looked on with composure. The loyalists' ladies, in number from twenty to thirty, attended the sales themselves, in hope, as it is the *all* they and their children had to depend on, humanity and compassion might operate on the minds of the crowd, and that none would bid against them. Full of this idea, they were attended by General Greene, Colonel Washington, and Colonel Hustis; but they were unfortunately mistaken.—A Mrs. Inglis claimed property as her own, not her husband's, and referred to proofs: However, the sale went on; the house was put up at £1500, and was raised upon her to £2620. A Mr. Burns' property sold for about £12,000. This gentleman died about ten years ago in Britain; his son, the heir, a young boy at his education in Scotland, and, I believe, never was in America. May the Lord reward our ministers according to their works!"

Gillon and his aides formed two ultra-democratic societies. One was termed the Marine Anti-Britannic Society, had no members outside of Charleston or the near vicinity, and existed ostensibly to nurture an interest in naval affairs and to care for the dependents of old sailors, but actually to breathe fire against Tories and "the natural enemy," England. It celebrated the first anniversary of Evacuation Day at the City Tavern. An elegant dinner was served in the Long Room, with a peal from the bells of St. Michael's at the beginning, and military music between the courses. There were thirteen toasts, all expressing hostility for "the yet inexorable foe to American greatness, the haughty recusant of reciprocity, and the votary of monopoly," and for the "Tory caitiffs." But the more important society was the Whig Club of Six Hundred, partly a secret organization, which tried to extend its political influence throughout the State. Both were angered by the definitive treaty, published in the *Gazette of the State* of December 18, 1783. They were more angry when Governor Guerard's message early the next spring asked the Legislature to remit the penalties provided for those who had only taken British protection.[66]

New outbursts of violence in both city and country marked the early months of 1784. When a dozen Tory farmers failed to leave their Fishing Creek plantations as soon as their old neighbors demanded, eight were slain and the other four escaped to the coast penniless. Other Tories were given "the juice of the hickory" on their bare backs to within an inch of their lives.[67] In Charleston the storehouses on the wharf filled with confiscated property were fired in April. "It must distress and alarm every good citizen," declared a writer in the *Gazette of the State,* "to see the many insults on government so frequently happening . . . at the corner of almost every street. Where can this end? . . . Are we henceforth to look upon ourselves as under an orderly established government or a set of *self-created* upstart bullying censors? No man that is not wilfully blind, but must have seen from whence sprang the shameful riot of last year; which it is well known greatly injured the Trade and Credit of this country." [68]

The enmity of the democrats for the "nabobs" had some amusing aspects. Many radicals petitioned Governor Guerard on April 14,

[66] S. Ca. *Gazette,* December 18, 1783.
[67] *Ibid.,* April 29, 1784; Md. *Journal,* July 13, 1784.
[68] S. Ca. *Gazette,* May 6, 1784.

1784, to forbid any more dancing assemblies in the State House. The growth of luxury, and dissipation, they said, was alarming to men who had seen aristocracy decline during the Revolution and hoped it would never rear its head again. Being a tactful aristocrat, Governor Guerard asked the Legislature to take the requested action, pointing to the danger that the animosity and partisan hatreds kindling in the city might be made uncontrollable by some trifle; but the Senate refused to act, and the dances continued. The imbroglio that spring between stiff old Ex-Governor Rutledge and William Thompson, keeper of the City Tavern, was serious.

On St. Patrick's Day a negro wench belonging to Rutledge obtained his permission to ask Thompson if she might go upstairs in the tavern to watch the City Artillery firing. Thompson refused, and Rutledge called him to his mansion to explain the supposed affront. The two men already detested each other. Thompson's tavern and the streets near it were a resort for the rioters who had been tarring and feathering Tories, while he had insulted several gentlemen on their way to the dancing assemblies. Disorders by his friends had been expected on the very night of St. Patrick's Day. The interview developed into a heated quarrel; Thompson was shown the door; and he had the effrontery to challenge Rutledge. As a member of the Legislature, Rutledge called this challenge to the attention of the House, and Thompson soon found himself in the city jail. Though several of his friends sat in the House, it was unanimous in confining him—Thomas Bee wanted him banished. But once in prison he had a host of applauders; the Marine Anti-Britannic Society published its congratulations upon his manly resistance to aristocratic principles, and when he was released he and his friends concocted a venomous address. The people must oppose, he said, "the nabobs of this State, their servile toad-eaters, the bobs, and the servilely servile tools and lickspittles of power to both, the bobbetts." [69]

The political contest reached a climax in the city election of September 13, 1784, in which an intendant—corresponding to Mayor—was chosen by popular vote from the city wardens. By election day intelligent citizens were keenly aware that the disorders were ruining the trade and public credit of the State. They believed that if they could have three or four years of prosperous trade with

[69] See S. Ca. *Gazette,* April 15, 22, 29.

Europe and the West Indies they would be on solid ground again. Should they imperil this for a mean gratification of the feeling of revenge? They knew also that every outburst in Charleston disgusted the planters. In a letter published two days before the election Gadsden warned "the public in general, and Commodore Gillon in particular," that a wedge was being driven between the rural and urban interests. The State would see through the selfishness and demagoguery of the reckless Charleston agitators, he said, and might even be provoked to take away the city charter. The extremists answered with more abuse of the "nabobs," and especially of the legislators. "I know the generality of the citizens despise the generality of the members," wrote Gillon; "as is evident from the publications condemning the measures they pursue." Most of the publications, however, were actually upon the other side, for the conservatives wielded the best pens, and the *Gazette* was glad to enjoy the State printing. When the polls opened, the radicals supported Gillon, and the conservatives the incumbent, Richard Hutson. The latter was reëlected by the decisive vote of 387 to 260. Where, asked the *Gazette,* were the Six Hundred—in the country for their health? " 'Tis matter for great triumph—Law and Liberty trampling on Anarchy and Tyranny," it said. Thenceforth the disorders subsided.[70]

A sensation followed the election, however, when on September 16, 1784, the South Carolina *Gazette* published a secret letter which the corresponding committee of the Whig Club of Six Hundred had sent throughout the State in advance of the fall elections for the Assembly. It stated that the Club depended upon the citizens to see that the Legislature was radical. No man ought to be chosen who would not bind himself to act as his constituents directed; and the voters should assert, two months before the election, their determination to support no one but a "Democratic Whig." Liberty in the State hung upon this vigilance:

For we tell you, that most of the *wealthy* families of this commonwealth, equally in the country as in the city and its vicinage, yet retain their former principles of monopolizing power, and all the honorary and lucrative offices of the State to themselves, their families and dependents; [they hope] by destroying the republican equality of citizenship, for which they generally neither toiled nor spun, and for which the middling and the poor had shed their blood in profusion, to introduce family influences into the government, and thereby establish in their own hands an odious aristocracy over their betters.

[70] S. Ca. *Gazette, passim,* especially September 11, 14, 1784.

This direct indictment of the Charleston and low-country oligarchy, in which there was much force, was calculated to appeal to up-country farmers as well as to Charleston mechanics and shopkeepers. The letter adroitly mingled an appeal to the prejudice against Tories with an appeal to the prejudice against the wealthy, privileged aristocracy, and asked for the establishment of new Whig Clubs in various localities all over the State, to be bound together by active correspondence. "Elect no wealthy candidate, who is a . . . *supplicant for your votes* from this city, where, if he had been a good man, he would have been undoubtedly chosen; and elect no man who is not a *permanent* resident of the parish or district he is set up for." It was true that many legislators sat for districts in which they owned lands but seldom or never resided. In conclusion, the letter abused the lawyers, "that double-tongued race of men, who are bred up in chicanery and deceit," for their defense of the loyalists.

This statement of the radical position angered all conservatives, rich or poor—and many were now very poor. They avowed that they had no doubt the letter was written by Commodore Gillon. They denied that any offices were monopolized. Who were the members of this idle aristocracy, supposed to be engrossing them? They were the men who had fought to the last under Lincoln, and who had been exiled to St. Augustine, or detained as prisoners at Haddrel's Point, or immured in Charleston dungeons, and whose names the British had enrolled in the black and dismaying catalogue of confiscation or sequestration. Meanwhile, the factious Gillon had been safe abroad, gloating over his ability to win large sums of prize money by easy raids upon commerce. But the radicals, their opponents rejoiced, had been prostrated by the city election, and now the opportunity was at hand in the legislative election to destroy their faction utterly.[71]

It was plain at the outset of 1785 that new political questions were taking the place of the old quarrels over loyalists and nabobs, for governmental realism demanded attention to economic and sectional issues. The spring session of the Legislature showed the conservatives as well entrenched as ever. They gave the Governorship to General William Moultrie, a patrician who had made a brilliant Revolutionary record; he had been the first American officer to hoist a distinctive battle-flag, the hero of the attack upon Sullivan's

[71] S. Ca. *Gazette*, September 25, 1784.

Island, and the most courageous leader in the defense of Charleston. All over the State men were growing more ready to forget the rancors of war and to frown upon attacks against the Tories. Aedanus Burke wrote from Ninety-Six that, although the people there had just lynched a Tory murderer named Love, they were eager for tranquillity and would harm no loyalist soldier except those guilty of wanton barbarity in the war.[72] Many plunderers and other mischievous loyalists had returned, and were not molested, nor did resentment exist against fighters under the British flag who had killed patriots of the Ninety-Six region in open action. Governor Moultrie tried to remove the principal cause of outbreaks when he warned all offenders still under decree of banishment from South Carolina or any other commonwealth to leave the State.[73]

A clash between the upland and lowland sections had been evident as soon as the war ended. In 1784 the question of a Constitutional Convention arose in the Legislature, the upper country wanting a revision and a larger representation. We have seen that the Senate defeated the proposal. Next year a reapportionment of the Legislature took place, as stipulated by the Constitution, but without materially affecting the strength of the sections. When the houses met in the spring of 1786, circumstances presented the question of removing the capital to a more central location, and the back country urged it forcibly. The State House had burned, and the Legislature had to sit in the Custom House in Charleston, fitted up with plain benches and unpainted desks. All the members from above the fall line agreed that the next session must be held in their section, but a quarrel occurred as to the exact place. Sumter owned large tracts on the Wateree River, the northern of the two streams which unite to form the great central river of the State, the Santee. In anticipation of the capital's removal, soon after the war he had commenced building a village there called Stateburg. However, Colonel Wade Hampton, Colonel T. Taylor, Commodore Gillon, and others of influence owned land on the Congaree, or southern of the two streams, and insisted upon its advantage. The head of navigation on the Congaree was duly selected, and a site laid out for the future city of Columbia.

The financial crisis which overtook South Carolina in 1785, and the necessity for laws to relieve debtors, introduced sinister elements

[72] N. Y. *Packet*, July 25, 1785.
[73] N. Y. *Packet*, April 11, 1785; Md. *Journal*, April 19, 1785.

into State politics. The notorious Pine Barren Act, authorizing the tender of lands to satisfy a debt, expired in the spring of 1786. But during the latter year the diarist Timothy Ford declared the government still uncertain and capricious. A variety of factions were to be distinguished in the Legislature, but the debtor interest was predominant; and too many laws, thought Ford, were enacted not because they were right, but because they satisfied a clamor. Edward Rutledge wrote his friend Jay in the fall of 1786 that several of the ablest South Carolinians had grown so disgusted with "the artifices of some unworthy characters" that they had resolved to retire from public life. Henry Laurens, back from his diplomatic service in Europe, for example, did so, dividing his time after 1785 between his plantation on the Cooper and his house in the city of Charleston.[74]

Though during two years the suffering was acute, South Carolina rode out the financial storm.[75] By 1788, as in other States, prosperity was returning. As it came, the undesirable element in the Legislature weakened, and conservative and federalist influences gained strength. In the spring of 1787 General Moultrie was succeeded as Governor by Thomas Pinckney a representative of one of the principal Charleston families. Pinckney had been educated in England; he was the son of the wealthy agent whom South Carolina had kept in the mother country before the Revolution, and a cousin of the Charles Pinckney who died disgraced by his surrender to British authority; and he was destined, like his brother C. C. Pinckney, to be a leading advocate of the Federal Constitution. His election by 163 votes out of 170 was an evidence that the sane, well-educated, aristocratic element in the Legislature was quite too powerful to oppose. It was followed by even more reassuring evidence: the four delegates sent by South Carolina to the Constitutional Convention—John Rutledge, Charles and C. C. Pinckney, and Pierce Butler—were all men of the low country, and all believers in a stronger federal government.

[74] S. Ca. *Hist. and Gen. Mag.*, XIII, 181 ff.; Jay's "Works," III, 216-19; Wallace's "Laurens."

[75] South Carolina's financial measures are treated in another chapter; but Dr. Ramsay's account of conditions is worth noting here ("Hist. S. C.," II, 428-29). He tells us that the clamor for stay laws became irresistible when the depression was at its height, "for property, when brought to sale under execution, sold at so low a price as frequently ruined the debtor without paying the creditor. . . . Assemblies were called oftener and earlier than the Constitution or laws required" to give relief. Stay laws and an emission of paper money did so. But the former "destroyed public credit and confidence between man and man, injured the morals of the people, and in many instances ensured and aggravated the final ruin of the unfortunate debtors."

V. Ratification in the Carolinas

In North Carolina a conservative was elected Governor in the same year that Pinckney took his seat in Charleston. In the spring of 1787 the Legislature made Samuel Johnston the fifth executive of the State; a recognition of ability long overdue, but not a sign of any greatly increased strength on the part of the conservative party. The radicals still held North Carolina in their hands as the old issues passed away, and the new issue of a strong or a weak national government became the center of attention. The conservatives of course became federalists. They had been reinforced before 1787 by several new men of ability, most notably by Davie, who had settled at Halifax and appeared regularly in the Legislature; Richard Dobbs Spaight, who like Davie was British-born and had won distinction in the war; and Hugh Williamson, who had joined the Edenton group, and who varied his service in the Continental Congress with terms in the Commons House. Williamson was by origin a highly educated Pennsylvania physician and teacher, who at one time had been intimately associated with Franklin. But the radicals, though they had no better leaders than Person, Timothy Bloodworth, Judge Spencer, and Willie Jones, had the votes and the loyalty of the great majority of the people. They wanted no interference with the government from outside the State; low taxes; and a genuinely democratic administration—i.e., one in which the Legislature should continue dominant, and in which no irksome property qualification should be required of voters.[76]

The North Carolina Legislature sent a delegation to the Constitutional Convention only after much pressure had been exerted upon it by Johnston, Iredell, and others. Caswell and Willie Jones refused to attend, and the five who went to Philadelphia were Martin, Davie, Hugh Williamson, Spaight and William Blount. Martin alone was opposed to the drafting of a new Constitution. But this delegation misrepresented the State, for most North Carolinians regarded even a revision of the Articles of Confederation with distrust. Some, like Willie Jones, disliked the proposed Constitution because they disliked the idea of a Federal judiciary. Most of them, like Thomas

[76] H. G. Connor, "The Convention of 1788-89," N. Ca. Booklet, Vol. IV, No. 4; Amer. Hist. Assn. Report, 1895, I, 101 ff.; C. L. Raper, "Why North Carolina At First Refused to Ratify."

Person with his tens of thousands of acres, disliked it because they feared the Federal tax-gatherer. Specie was almost unknown in most rural districts, the paper medium was worth hardly half its face value, and the people found it hard enough to pay their State taxes alone. Agriculture was imperfectly developed, and trade, which would have fostered a sentiment of federalism, was not developed at all. The western regions had little conception of what the benefits of the "new roof" might be. Finally, an intense individualism had stamped the North Carolinians, and they believed the proposed instrument a threat to State Rights.

In the upland part of South Carolina much of the population was homogeneous with that across the border, and it also disliked the idea of a distant government sending its revenue agents and marshals into every county. But in South Carolina, it was the men corresponding to Johnston, Iredell, Williamson, and Davie who controlled the government throughout.

Preceding South Carolina's ratifying convention there occurred (January, 1788) an illuminating debate in the Legislature.[77] The opposition to the Constitution was led by Rawlins Lowndes, only a few up-country men—among them Patrick Calhoun of Ninety-Six, father of John C. Calhoun—sustaining him. Lowndes had been too conservative to approve at first of the Declaration of Independence, and now was too conservative to approve of a competent national government. He argued that the Confederation amply met the nation's needs; that South Carolina ought not to be limited to two decades in the importation of negroes, a commerce that "can be justified on the principles of religion and humanity"; that the Constitution would give New England a monopoly of the carrying trade; and that it did not sufficiently embody the principle of checks and balances. He even argued that the States should have the power to issue their own paper money. The principal refutation of his objections was undertaken by John Rutledge, C. C. Pinckney, and Pierce Butler, who had signed the Constitution, but they had capable helpers. The whole tendency of the State's history since 1783 had been federalist. In the spring of 1784 the Legislature, after flaring out at Greene, had repassed the bill giving Congress power to levy a five per cent. impost, the vote being three to one. The next year Congress had been granted authority to regulate the State's trade,

[77] Elliot's "Debates," IV, 253 ff.

though most men believed that such regulation would injure South Carolina by lessening the vessels available to carry her products.

The ratifying convention in Charleston was held before the similar body in North Carolina met (May 13, 1788). Sumter captained the back-country anti-federalists, including Wade Hampton of Saxe-Gotha, Aedanus Burke of the Lower District, and William Hill.[78] Governor Pinckney presided, and although a very inadequate report of the proceedings exists, there is evidence that C. C. Pinckney spoke more effectively on the Federalist side than anyone else. After but eleven days, the Constitution was approved by a vote of 140 to 73, with only 21 of the noes coming from the Tidewater region. Much may be said against an apportionment which in the Legislature and Convention gave the lowlands their excessive strength; but much may also be said in praise of the results.

A different story must be told of North Carolina. When her convention met in a church at Hillsborough (July 21, 1788), out of 284 members the anti-federalists had a majority of one hundred. A half dozen of the best conservatives, including Hooper, General Martin, William Blount, and Allen Jones, had been defeated for seats.[79] The majority was fully responsive to the leadership of Willie Jones, Person, and Bloodworth. The chief federalists present—Governor Johnston, Iredell, Maclaine, and Spaight—saw insuperable difficulties before them. For a few hours it seemed uncertain whether there would be any debate at all, for Willie Jones suggested that, to save expense, the delegates vote at once upon ratification, and adjourn. But when Iredell declared that he was amazed by this proposal to decide without deliberation perhaps the greatest question ever submitted in North Carolina, the anti-federalists assented.

The arguments of the opponents of ratification were simple. It was courting tyranny, they asserted, to give Congress the power to levy and collect taxes. They pointed out that Congress had the right to fix the time and place for the election of its members, and that this would help create a central legislature virtually independent of the people. They contended that the Federal courts would over-

---

[78] McCrady, "S. C. in the Rev.," 1780-83, pp. 731-32.
[79] Hooper wrote Iredell of the Constitutution: "The Western country in general is decidedly opposed to it. Mr. Moore and myself essayed in vain for a seat in the Convention. Our sentiments had transpired before the election." N. C. Booklet, IV, No. 4. In fact, Hooper had a fist-fight with an opponent, and "came off second best, with his eyes blacked."

ride all others, and would destroy a citizen's right to justice in the courts of his own State. A different kind of attack was made by one of the ablest delegates, the Rev. David Caldwell. Caldwell, as a poor Pennsylvania farmer, had been seized at twenty-five with a burning desire to preach, had persevered against many hardships until at thirty-six Princeton gave him a degree and at thirty-eight he was licensed a minister, and, removing to North Carolina, speedily became known for his earnestness and eloquence throughout the uplands.[80] At Hillsborough Caldwell expounded the compact theory of government, and demanded that the Constitution be tested by it. But the plainer objections appealed to the plain delegates. Willie Jones soon outlined his plan for obtaining changes.

> . . . I beg leave to mention the authority of Mr. Jefferson, whose abilities and respectability are well known. When the Convention sat in Richmond, Virginia, Mr. Madison received a letter from him. In that letter he said he wished nine States would adopt it [the Constitution], not because it deserved ratification, but to preserve the Union. But he wished the other four States would reject it, that there might be a certainty of obtaining amendments.

Admitting that it would take eighteen months to frame amendments, Jones declared that "for my part, I would rather be eighteen years out of the Union than adopt it in its present defective form." It soon became clear that the Convention would not ratify even conditionally. Some delegates were incredibly bitter and narrow. Person is said to have remarked that "Washington was a damned rascal and traitor to his country for putting his hand to such an infamous paper" as the new Constitution. On August 1 the committee of the whole presented a resolution calling for a declaration of rights and for amendments to "the most ambiguous and exceptionable" parts of the Constitution, and next day it was adopted, 184 to 84. North Carolina was now an independent nation outside the Union.[81]

Iredell had expressed a fear that if his State once broke the bonds of the Union, it would remain outside permanently. But this was idle; the example of the sister States and the logic of events brought it inside the circle within a little more than a year. Even at the fall session of the Legislature in 1788 the anti-federalist majority showed signs of weakening, for it called a new convention to be held

---

[80] Foote, "Sketches of N. C.," Ch. 17.

[81] Elkanah Watson ("Memoirs," 262-65) gives an amusing instance of the way ignorant North Carolinians misrepresented the Constitution. He heard a country preacher explain to the voters what the Federal District, ten miles square, was for. "This, my friends," said he, "will be walled in or fortified. Here an army of 50,000, or perhaps 100,000 men, will be finally embodied, and will sally forth, and enslave the people, who will be gradually disarmed."

at Fayetteville in November, 1789. Long before this date arrived it was known that the Constitution would be amended by the addition of a bill of rights. In the elections for the convention Willie Jones failed of being returned for his county, a heavy blow to the anti-federalists; and when it met, Governor Johnston, Davie, and Hugh Williamson so easily overbore the remaining opposition that the Constitution was ratified 195 to 77. Another important victory for the federalists followed that same month when the Legislature voted upon a long list of nominees for United States Senator, and defeating Person, Bloodworth, and other nominees, chose Johnston and Benjamin Hawkins—the latter a friend of Washington's and for some years a delegate in the Continental Congress. The South Carolina Legislature of course also elected two federalist Senators, Pierce Butler and Ralph Izard, both lowlanders. But in South Carolina as in North Carolina some of the district elections for Federal Representatives went in favor of the opposition. From the former State were chosen General Sumter and Aedanus Burke as well as federalists like Daniel Huger; from the latter there appeared John B. Ashe and Timothy Bloodworth as well as federalists like Hugh Williamson.[82]

VI. Georgia Politics, 1775-1789

When we turn to the history of Georgia we turn to a State in which the vicissitudes of government were even greater than in the Carolinas. It was a younger, weaker State. Not only did the British drive the patriot authorities from village to village, and make the Province their own; the disputes between the two patriot factions became so angry that in the darkest hours of the war two sets of officials were struggling with one another.

Archibald Bulloch was President of Georgia when it adopted the Constitution of 1777: the foremost patriot leader, who as head of the temporary government had called together the Convention which framed the Constitution. Born in Charleston, he was well educated, he had practiced law along with his activities as a planter, and in a political career that dated from his entrance to the House in 1768, he had evinced some of the administrative grasp and decision shown

[82] For matter on politics in 1789 in North and South Carolina, see McRee's "Iredell," II, 170-72; files of S. C. *Gazette;* Jervey's "Hayne and His Times," Introduction. At the same time that Pinckney was reëlected Governor in January, 1789, by a majority of 179, Gillon received 82 votes for Lieutenant-Governor, and was finally elected.

long after by a descendant of his, Theodore Roosevelt. The Legislature displayed its confidence in him when in February, 1777, fighting having begun along the coast and river near Savannah it requested him to assume extraordinary powers during the emergency. But immediately thereafter he died, and with him died all hope of preventing a split between the radical and conservative Whigs. The latter, after laboring so effectively during 1775 to delay Georgia's participation in the Revolution, were now hopelessly outnumbered. The Council of Safety elevated Button Gwinnett, one of the most hot-tempered radicals, to Bulloch's place until such time as a Governor could be regularly chosen under the Constitution. Gwinnett was a native of Bristol, England, who had stocked an island plantation with slaves and grown wealthy. When the Legislature met in May he expected to be chosen the first Governor. But by adroit maneuvering, the conservatives saw that the place went instead to John Adam Treutlen, a representative of the wing of the Salzburger Germans which had taken the patriot side. Gwinnett had already been on bad terms with Lachlan McIntosh, a conservative who had been appointed brigadier-general in preference to him, and now was enraged to hear that McIntosh gloated over the election. They fought a duel at twelve paces and Gwinnett was killed.

Henceforth the conservatives waged a losing war with the radicals, who dominated the Legislature. Lachlan McIntosh had to seek military service in another part of the Union. The chief remaining conservative leaders were Joseph Habersham, the son of a teacher who, coming to Georgia with Whitefield, had risen to become the most influential man in the Colony; William Few; and John Wereat. They denounced the activities of the popular Liberty Society in Savannah, and complained that the measures of the Legislature were concerted by a caucus of the radical leaders at night meetings in a Savannah tavern.[83] Wereat called Joseph Wood, whom the radical majority elected to the Continental Congress in 1777, a demagogue and scoundrel, who had never done an honest deed in his life. The radicals were accused, with reason, of having allowed the Constitution to be flagrantly violated when it was first put into operation. Savannah and Sunbury had not been allowed separate elections to choose their members of the Legislature, as the Constitution intended, but the counties in which they lay had chosen the representatives in

[83] Frank Moore, "Materials for History," 39 ff.

a general county election. Several representatives had been elected for counties in which they did not reside and one man after a residence of only three months in the State, though the Constitution demanded a year. But the year 1777 passed without marked political disturbance. The year 1778 opened with the extremists still in control of the Legislature, and they elected John Houstoun, one of the most ardent of the patriots, the second Governor.

Thus far the only military operations of note had been two abortive attacks by the patriots upon the British post at St. Augustine, in 1776 and 1777 respectively; but with the spring of 1778 the Georgians saw that they would soon be on the defensive in a desperate struggle. In April the Executive Council, saying that it was impressed by the "calamitous situation" of the State, temporarily surrendered all its powers into Governor Houstoun's hands. The fall of Savannah in December, after a siege of less than a week, threw the whole State open to the British. Within a few weeks it was entirely overrun. Taken on two sides, for the forces which captured Savannah, under Lieutenant-Colonel Campbell, were assisted by a column which General Prevost led overland from East Florida, the Georgians were completely overmastered. The popular Governor of Colonial days, James Wright, was replaced in his chair in Savannah, the confiscation acts of the Whigs were turned against their own property, and many citizens accepted British protection.

The most precarious and uncertain existence was led by the patriot government after the fall of Savannah. Governor Houstoun and his Council, fleeing from the coast, summoned the Legislature to meet in Augusta to elect a new Governor, but Augusta was at once captured. No legislative session was possible anywhere, and after Houstoun's term expired, the Council continued to exercise the Governor's authority. This being the only course possible, no one was troubled because it was extra-constitutional. In midsummer of 1779, the British having abandoned Augusta, frantic efforts were made to bring the Legislature together there, but so nearly extinguished was the patriot cause that no quorum could be obtained. Finally, the conservatives resolved to take matters into their own hands. They constituted a majority of the twenty-five men whom it was possible to get together at Augusta. This rump body organized, and on July 24 appointed nine men, including Wereat, Habersham, John Dooly, and Seth John Cuthbert, to be a new Executive

Council; instructing them to use every power necessary for the safety of the State, but to keep to the spirit of the Constitution. The Council on August 6 chose its most prominent member, Wereat, to be President, making him virtual Governor.[84]

This coup was received with indignation by the radicals. Seizing upon the excuse that the rump Legislature had acted without constitutional warrant, they at once repudiated the authority of Wereat and his Council. Their leader was George Walton, who had been captured at Savannah and later exchanged, and who with his associates now asserted that the Council was in part made up of Tories, and condemned the whole body as illegal, unconstitutional, and dangerous. Their obvious course was to organize a rival government. Walton, Richard Howley, George Wells, and others called upon the people to choose a new Legislature, to meet at Augusta in November, and these new legislators, duly assembling on November 4, elected Walton Governor for the brief remainder of the year, also appointing a Council. There were thus two Governors and two Executive Councils for the last seven weeks of the year. Neither Governor was regular nor constitutional, neither would have aught to do with the other, and the affairs of the State were in the utmost confusion. The combined effort of General Lincoln and Admiral D'Estaing to recover Savannah from the British by assault having been bloodily repulsed in October, the State—which for a moment had hoped for freedom—again passed almost completely under British domination. Yet the bitterness between the two patriot factions was intense. One of Walton's first acts (November 30) was to forge a letter to Congress, purporting to be signed by Speaker William Glascock, assuring it that all Georgians were hostile to the appointment of General McIntosh to command in the State, and asking it to keep him in some distant field. This ugly quarrel, paralyzing resistance to the enemy, was even more disgraceful than that which rent Pennsylvania when Howe first menaced the latter State.

One regular government soon took the place of the two bickering Whig bodies, but the quarrels of faction continued. Both the radicals and moderates participated in an election for a new Legislature which was held at the close of 1779, in response to a proclamation issued by Wereat. The radicals were certain to win, for the rich southern counties in which the conservatives were strongest were

[84] Jones's "Georgia," II, 365 ff.; Knight's "Georgia and the Georgians," I, 292 ff.

held by the British; and when the Assembly met in Augusta early in 1780, Walton and his associates completely controlled it. They saw to it that it elected Howley Governor, and Wells President of the Council, and lost no opportunity to throw odium upon Wereat's emergency administration. One of their first acts was to declare that Wereat's group had exercised powers subversive of the Constitution, and that it had possessed no legal standing whatever. Wereat and his friends replied in March, denouncing Walton's irregular Legislature the preceding fall as a manifest breach of the Constitution. It had been composed of only twenty-odd men, they recited, yet they had called themselves the House of Assembly, and had actually wielded both the law-making and executive powers. Many citizens believed, they added, that this bobtail Assembly was contrived simply to further the political interests of Walton and his crew. In such manner did the two parties continue squabbling when almost the whole State was lost.

In the spring of 1780 a series of disasters actually brought the revolutionary government to the point of extinction. Governor Howley set out for the Continental Congress, and President Wells died, throwing the executive reins to a totally new hand. When this successor and a handful of Councilmen tried to make Augusta the seat of their authority, they were chased out by the British. As the enemy's advance spread over the whole lower South in 1780, the republicans held in Georgia only two remote upland counties, Richmond and Wilkes; they had been driven back against the frontiers, where, in a few settlements to which the British had not penetrated, they were menaced by hostile Indians. They had to make their capital at an inaccessible hamlet called Heard's Fort. Many of the ablest, most patriotic Whigs had been driven into exile in other States. Even Heard's Fort became so dangerous a post that in May, Governor Howley, who had resumed his executive duties, was warned by the Council to remove to the Carolinas, lest he be captured. He took this advice, and again the government lapsed into the hands of the Council and its president; the president in turn fled to North Carolina, and another took his place. Many Georgians felt that it mattered little whether there was a government or not, there was so little of the State left to govern.

As in South Carolina, during 1780 the American flag was carried by no armed forces save small bands which, ranging the country rapidly and hiding amid swamps and forests, struck at the enemy whenever opportunity offered. Tory bands retaliated, and moved through Georgia robbing, burning, and murdering. A loyalist account rightly asserts that these skirmishes, with now one side and now the other victorious, did nothing but depopulate and ruin the country. The Fanning of Georgia was one Thomas Brown, a Tory from the beginning, who early in the Revolution had been seized on his farm near Augusta, tarred, feathered, and hauled about the streets behind a mule. He swore he would have vengeance, and when the British gained the upper hand, he took it. As a Colonel in the British forces, he was placed in command at Augusta; and with the Tories and Indians behind him, he drove the patriots out of the surrounding district, confiscated property, and sent even women and children into exile in North Carolina. One blazing September day in 1780, Brown was attacked by the Whigs under General Elijah Clarke, who shut him up in a blockhouse he had built at Augusta, wounded him and many of his garrison, and seemed on the point of capturing them all. But amid the groans of his thirst-tortured wounded, Brown held out. At the last minute he was relieved by the approach of a mixed force of Indians and Tories, and he took a fearful revenge, hanging all the disabled fighters whom Clarke had left behind.

But finally, in the spring of 1781, the main British forces marched north into Virginia, and it became possible to free part of Georgia. Augusta was captured by Henry Lee on June 5, 1781, and was at once used as a capital by the men who sprang forward to revive the State government. Elections for the Legislature were held, and in August the Assembly was able to meet again and to choose the first regular Governor since Howland's term had expired at the beginning of the year. Governor Nathan Brownson held office for only a few months, for in the first days of 1782 another Legislature chose John Martin in his stead. Greene and the American troops steadily drove the British back, until when they had been shut up in Savannah, Martin and his Council were able to move down to Ebenezer, and reëstablish the patriot administration near the coast. On May 21 the British were defeated in a smart skirmish near Savannah, and on June 11 evacuated the city and State.

Under Governor Martin, in 1782 a semblance of peaceful administration was fast obtained. When he called the Legislature in special session that spring, he was able to announce that three departments of government were in full operation. The business transacted at this session included a definition of the State boundaries, provision for raising the quota of Continental troops, and the establishment of a court of claims. Preliminary steps were taken by the Governor to stop the border warfare between Whigs and Tories along the Florida line, and to check the depredations by the Indians in the upper part of Georgia. He had to call attention to the fact that many people of the State, "for want of common sustenance, are now reduced to a perishing condition"; indeed, the British had so thoroughly devastated Georgia in their slow withdrawal that General Wayne's troops had been obliged to depend upon provisions from the Carolinas. The first section to rally was that along the coast, and the conservative leader John Wereat set an example of generosity by loading his flatboats with rice, and having them poled up the Savannah to be distributed among the needy. With the harvesting of the autumn crops, however, the country was relieved of its greatest distress. Under Governor Lyman Hall, who was elected in 1783 by another energetic Legislature, the recuperation of the State—assisted by a steady inflow of settlers—continued.

In its main outlines Georgia's later history closely resembled South Carolina's. She also had her Jacksonborough Legislature when, immediately after the war ended, the question arose of the treatment of the Tories and those who had accepted British protection. "Whereas it is absolutely necessary a fund should be raised for defraying the contingent and necessary expenses of this State," declared an act of January, 1782, seizure would be made of the estates of all "persons who shall now be, or may have been within the British lines, as British subjects, and who are not included in the act of confiscation passed March 1, 1778, or in the act for burying in oblivion certain high crimes and misdemeanors, passed August 12, 1781. . . ." This act of oblivion had pardoned those forced to accept British protection during the war, but who had joined the American forces before October 1, 1781, and had not been guilty of murder or plundering. Naturally, many men who were really innocent of any voluntary disloyalty to the United States, in or near Savannah, had been unable to take advantage of it, and now were to suffer. Moreover, additional harsh legislation followed. On May 4 an act was passed confiscating the property of additional persons by name; and in August, after Savannah was regained, an act amercing a considerable list of estates 8 per cent., and others 12 per cent., was voted.[85]

A natural reaction, as in South Carolina, followed. The Legislature of 1783 contained men who had given the subject sober thought, while eloquent intercession before it was made in favor of the scores of worthy Georgians who were being punished far beyond their deserts. The result was the passage of legislation to relieve certain groups from the decree of banishment, and to transfer the names of specified persons from the confiscation lists to the amercement lists. When the Tories and loyalists first began to return, unfortunately, the same ebullitions of popular violence occurred as in South Carolina. Governor Hall, the Attorney-General, and a majority of the Council, moreover, after the Legislature adjourned, refused to abide by its decision, and proclaimed their opinion that the enactment readmitting the banished loyalists was not law. The Assembly was angry for a while, but its indignation cooled.[86] It had all the advantages which time could give it, and in 1784 it dropped Hall, electing John Houstoun, who had been Governor early in the Revolution. This year, and in every subsequent year until after the ratification of the Federal Constitution, some further relaxation of the harsh enactments of 1782 was voted.

Like other Southern States, Georgia had a sectional issue which became increasingly prominent after 1783. Population pressed at an amazing rate into the inland section. We find Chief Justice George Walton, in a charge to the grand jury of Liberty County in 1784, declaring that "the late amazing augmentation in the number of our inhabitants in the Western District will soon give a new feature to our political affairs—a consideration which ought to command the earliest attention to our elder citizens."[87] The first Constitution had provided for eight counties, five in the so-called lower district along the coast, two in the middle district half-way up the Savannah River, and one in the western or upper district, not far from the head of the Savannah. The second Constitution, in 1789, provided representation for eleven counties, one being added in the middle district and two in the upper. The population of the upper district in 1791 was 37,946; that of the middle district, 25,336; and that of the seacoast district, despite its marked pre-

[85] Marbury and Crawford's "Digest of Laws," 62-90.
[86] *Freeman's Journal*, December 31, 1783.
[87] Jones, "Delegates from Georgia to the Continental Congress," 187-88.

ponderancy of slaves, only 21,536. Uplanders were naturally inclined to complain that new counties were not created fast enough.

Slowly but steadily, however, the west won concessions for itself.
It was early provided that, beginning in 1783, for three months each
summer the executive departments should be transferred from
Savannah to Augusta, and their work there carried on for the convenience of the up-country people. In 1784 was passed the first
legislation for the University of Georgia, and when this institution
was opened a short time later it was at Athens, far beyond Augusta
in the western part of the State. Lowland Georgia was increasingly
jealous of the upper country, but it could not hold its advantageous
position so securely as lowland South Carolina.

Governor Houstoun, who had the satisfaction of laying before the
Council the announcement of the definite treaty of peace, was succeeded by Samuel Ebert, who had been Lieutenant-Colonel of the
State's first battalion. Ebert gave way to a rich and shrewd Scotch
merchant of Savannah, Edward Telfair; and Telfair to a man of
sharply contrasting character, General George Mathews, a Scotch-
Irishman of Virginia origin, energetic, impetuous, and—though
able—unlettered. Mathews himself illustrated the land-hunger of
the time. A keen speculator, he bought at a bargain a large area
of land on Broad River, called the Goose Pond Tract, and was
responsible for its colonization. The Governorship was offered in
1788 to General James Jackson, who had received the formal surrender of Savannah, and whose youth—he was but thirty—was forgotten in the distinction with which he had served in the field and
at the bar, but he declined on the ground of inexperience. In his
place was chosen George Handly, also English-born.

The feeling of national patriotism was strong in Georgia. In
1786, when the Legislature delayed granting the national government
the revenue powers it desired, the protest was instant. The grand
jury of Wilkes County, in the upper part of the State, presented
"as a great and dangerous grievance, the refusal of this State to
grant powers to Congress to lay an impost of five per cent. on all
foreign articles of commerce imported into this State." In the lowlands the grand jury of Liberty County was equally emphatic: "We
present as a great grievance that Congress have not power sufficient
to carry into effect the regulation of our trade." [88] Some of the

[88] N. Y. *Advertiser*, January 18, 1786.

considerations that had made Georiga so loyal to the Crown now operated to make her loyal to the idea of a strong Union. She was the weakest of the States. Her whole population was still less in 1788 than that on the bleak hills of Vermont, she was exposed to attack by the Indians, the British, and the Spaniards, and her great area and rich resources were a tempting prize. Feeling that she needed the protection of the rest of the Union, Georgia therefore coöperated warmly in the movement which gave the country the Federal Constitution. To Philadelphia she sent William Few and Abraham Baldwin. The President of the State Convention which ratified the Constitution was John Wereat, and the ratification was by unanimous vote.

CHAPTER TEN

PROGRESS IN LIBERALISM AND HUMANITY

An impressive revolution in the character of social institutions accompanied the Revolution which we regard as primarily political. A number of important changes in the laws and practices concerning religion, land-tenure, penal affairs, charities, and education proceeded from the establishment of independence, and almost all these changes were salutary. In many ways the colonists had been hindered by England from taking progressive action. Even if innovation did no injury to British interests, it was likely to be inharmonious with British traditions, and seemed to broaden the gap between the two lands. But all too frequently British interests were involved, as in the maintenance of the slave trade, of the Episcopal establishment, and of fairly uniform sets of laws in the home and daughter countries. Even during the years of fighting the State legislators were busy with the overthrow of the Establishment and the guaranty of religious liberty; the annulment of laws of entail and primogeniture in favor of a democratic system of inheritance; and the opening up, with the new political prospects, of new vistas of humanitarianism also.

I. Progress Towards Religious Freedom

The establishment of church equality and freedom of conscience had always been an ambition of the most liberal colonial leaders, and one that in several Colonies had been thwarted by the popular majority, not by British authority. Roughly speaking, in New England outside Rhode Island the Congregational church was favored by the State, though British authority had no predilection for it. In the Middle Colonies the Church of England and the Friends divided a place of slight advantage over other sects; the Anglicans having certain special statutory privileges in a part of New York and in Maryland, and the Quakers enjoying real though not nominal privilege in Pennsylvania and Delaware. In the South the Church of England was bulwarked by the state, but it met a rising opposition from the increase of dissenters. Nowhere in British America were the Catholics wholly immune from religious disadvantages. It is not strange that New England, considering the circumstances of its settlement, should have refused to give all Protestant sects absolute equality; and complete tolerance was a much more difficult goal in Massachusetts than in Virginia. In the march toward modern religious liberalism, those States were most laggard in which one church had obtained a marked ascendancy, whether it was the Episcopal or Congregational; those were most progressive in which no sect could count a majority, or in which, as in New York and North Carolina, the Episcopalians had the support of the colonial government, but were otherwise so weak that their pretensions to special favor must collapse with it. But whether conditions were auspicious or inauspicious, religious freedom marched steadily on.

In Massachusetts in 1776 the old Puritan Congregational Church was the established church. In every town the support of at least one place of worship in that Church was compulsory, and was maintained by public taxation of all estates and polls, special exceptions under certain conditions being made for Baptists, Quakers, and Episcopalians. The ministers were nominated by the church for each town or parish, and confirmed by the local political division. Those who were communicants of a minor sect which had not yet been given the privileges of the Baptists, Episcopalians, or Friends, had to support the Establishment. Catholic priests were liable to imprisonment for life; and the tithing men could arrest Sabbath breakers and hale truants off to church. The commonwealth was nothing if not religious. The Abbé Robin says in his "New Travels" that Sunday was observed with such strictness that Boston was a mere desert, all business being "totally at a stand, and the most innocent recreations and pleasures prohibited"; while he tells how in 1781 a Frenchman who lodged with him in Boston and indiscreetly played his flute on Sunday, was almost mobbed. The first warm agitation in favor of religious liberty, after independence, took place in the Constitutional Convention of 1780, where it was the chief topic of debate.

Yet the article on religion in the new Constitution seemed at first a step backwards.[1] It was drawn up by Samuel Adams, Caleb Strong, and Robert Treat Paine, three devout and narrow Calvinists, with the assistance of Timothy Danielson of western Massachusetts, and two ministers. Its intention was undoubtedly liberal. It declared that "no subordination of any one sect or denomination to another shall ever be established by law"; and its provision that the towns should always have "the exclusive right of electing their public teachers [ministers] and of contracting with them for their support and maintenance," had in the end such happy results that grim Puritans compared it with a cockatrice's egg. But it instructed the Legislature to require the several towns to make suitable provision by taxes for the support of religious instruction; and instead of following the old plan of giving members of certain dissenting sects an exemption from religious taxation as wide as the commonwealth, it simply empowered them to obtain from each town a remission of taxes, to be used for the support of their own ministers. Town treasurers found it easy to invent pretexts for refusing to give these dissenting pastors their share of the moneys collected. The inexact phrasing of the article as regarded exempted sects also made trouble. The courts, acting upon the general principle that all property and polls were liable to taxation for the local Congregational church, construed the exemptions so narrowly as to cause great hardship.[2] Every denomination that invaded the State after 1780, the chief being the Methodists and Universalists, had to carry on a long, costly suit to obtain exemption.[3]

The truth is that the article was loosely drawn: it was possible for narrow-minded town officers and judges to interpret it narrowly, but it was possible for others to interpret it liberally, and as the State grew more enlightened in religion, it proved a serviceable foundation of freedom. That liberalism was spreading already is shown by the fact that the Boston delegates in the Constitutional

[1] For one of the many thoughtful town protests against the article, see that of Gorham published in the Boston *Gazette,* June 12, 1780. "Why, in the name of wonder," Gorham asked, "is a man's estate to be given to a teacher of the parish, where he cannot in conscience attend upon his teaching?" For the early history of the movement for greater religious freedom in Massachusetts, see Susan M. Reed, "Church and State in Massachusetts, 1691-1740."

[2] Thus, in the Boston *Gazette* of February 19, 1781, the reformer Isaac Backus complained that a Haverhill gentleman received a certificate of membership in the local Baptist church, signed by the minister and three principal members; yet the case was turned against them by the court, only for want of the words "belonging thereto." He instanced another defeat of justice by a technicality. See the Providence *Gazette,* March 2, 1782, for the abuse of the Baptists of Attleborough.

[3] See Amory's "Sullivan," I, 181-86, for an account of the interesting test case of the Universalists, brought by an army chaplain.

Convention were at one time instructed to ask for an alteration in the instrument that would give perfect toleration.[4] But for years, criticism of the article and of State legislation was very bitter. The Baptists complained that those who wished to change from the Congregational to the Baptist or other church had to obtain a special license; and that the article limited the resources of small congregations to a pittance. In 1800 a law was passed more favorable to religious liberty, and in 1811 another, but the Congregationalists still held peculiar privileges.[5]

In New Hampshire the relation of the government to the churches when the Revolution began was similar to that in Massachusetts, and the Constitution of 1784 was not an iota more progressive than the Bay State's. Governor Benning Wentworth had reserved land, in every township he granted, for the support of the Church of England; but Episcopalians were few, and next to the Congregational Church the Presbyterian, introduced by Scotch-Irish immigrants from Londonderry, had the most communicants. It was the law in 1775 that all should attend church regularly, but it was not enforced as it once had been. During the colonial period all citizens were required to pay taxes to support the Congregational church except the Presbyterians, Quakers, and in late years the Baptists. The Constitution of 1784 placed religious affairs in the same posture as in Massachusetts. The Legislature was "empowered" to "authorize" the towns to lay taxes for the support of ministers, the clause as first interpreted being really one which instructed the Legislature to compel the towns to lay such taxes. It was made as difficult as in Massachusetts for new sects to obtain exemption; for dissenting ministers to obtain their due share of taxes; and for converts to transfer their allegiance from Congregationalism. It was almost impossible for an agnostic belonging to no sect at all to escape religious taxes. The dissenting denominations felt a keen discontent, but the progress of reform was even slower than in Massachusetts. In both States liberalizing tendencies were stubbornly fought by the rural populations, which were dogmatic in

[4] Brissot de Warville wrote from Boston in 1788 ("New Travels," edit. 1792, 100) that all sects openly professed their opinions: "The ministers of different sects live in such harmony, that they supply each other's places when anyone is detained from his pulpit."
[5] One clause of the Massachusetts Constitution required officeholders to affirm their belief in the Christian religion. It so offended the principles of Joseph Hawley, a devout Christian, that he refused to take a seat in the State Senate based on this requirement. Journals, Constitutional Convention of 1820, 1st ed., 85.

their religious beliefs and fearful that the removal of state support from the church would undermine the morals of the land.[6]

But it was in Connecticut that religious intolerance showed its harshest aspect. The land of Jonathan Edwards, the greatest of colonial preachers and philosophers; of Benjamin Trumbull, who in the sixty years of his New Haven ministry wrote more than 4000 sermons; of Joseph Bellamy, founder of the first Sunday-School in America—this land was not one to look with kind eyes upon another than its ancient faith. Dissenters were long scarcely tolerated at all, though the Baptists obtained a footing in 1705, the Episcopalians had by 1750 about twenty-five congregations, and a more diversified immigration, as the eighteenth century wore on, increased the strength of the dissenting sects. All citizens were long compelled to attend church regularly, and to pay taxes for the support of the Congregational ministry. The history of Connecticut's emergence from her illiberal position is a long and interesting one. The process began with the rise of the Episcopalians, Baptist, and other churches; it reached its second stage after the "Great Awakening" of 1740-42, which produced a schism between the old Established Church and the "new light" churches of the Congregationalists; and its third stage began soon after the close of the Revolution. Even at the third stage Connecticut was very far from true tolerance.[7]

Naturally the Episcopalians, with the advantage of their British connection, led the van in the march toward religious freedom. In 1727 they obtained a law exempting them, if they consistently attended an Episcopal church and supported its minister, from taxes for the Congregational church; the taxes being taken up by the town officials, but turned into the treasury of the local Anglican congregation. Two years later the Quakers and Baptists obtained the same privilege. It remained impossible, however, for members of these sects who lived near no church of their faith to escape the taxes laid for the Established Church; and in a number of ways adherents of weak dissenting congregations were discriminated against by tyrannous local officials. The schism in the Congregational Church following the "Great Awakening" brought about a new struggle for toleration. At first the members of the separatist congregations were taxed for the support of the old congregations from

[6] See Salem *Mercury*, March 4, 1788, for the bigotry shown in the New Hampshire convention ratifying the Federal Constitution.
[7] Clark's "Connecticut," 277; Purcell, "Conn. in Transition," 92 ff.

which they had seceded, and were even prosecuted for non-attendance there; and in 1745 feeling ran so high in New Haven that a father refused to attend the funeral of his separatist son. But the "new light" churches began a brave battle. In 1755 twenty congregations, of a thousand members, formally complained to the Assembly that their goods had been distrained to meet assessments for the benefit of the Establishment, and that some of them had been imprisoned. When their petition for relief brought no answer, they sent a committee to protest to the English government. In 1770 the Legislature granted the separatists formal permission to worship in what edifices and congregations they pleased, and exempted the estates of their ministers from taxation; but the onerous requirement that the laity pay taxes to the Establishment remained.

A year after the Declaration of Independence the long-pressed demand of the "new light" dissenters was granted by the Legislature. It exempted "those persons in this State commonly called Separates" from taxes for the support of the Establishment, upon condition that each of them annually lodge with the clerk of the local established church a certificate vouching for his or her attendance upon the "new light" services, signed by the minister, elder, or deacon of the separatist congregation. When in 1784 the first edition of the laws and acts of the State of Connecticut—the State code—was published, this right of escaping taxation for the Establishment by offering a certificate was confirmed. In addition, all religious bodies recognized by law were permitted to manage their temporal affairs as freely as did the Establishment, and to sell pews and establish funds as they liked. Immigrants into the State, minors, and widows were allowed a fair period in which to choose a sect.[8]

Yet all who were not Congregationalists belonging to the Establishment were still, and with good reason, dissatisfied. It was galling to a dissenter's pride to have to offer a certificate of his church allegiance, and narrow-minded town clerks could refuse to recognize a certificate when any technicality assisted. Everyone not a member of a recognized congregation of dissenters, whether he was irreligious, or his sect was too weak to form a local church, was still taxed for the Establishment. The Baptists pressed the fight for a fuller religious liberty, and they were assisted by other denominations that gained in strength. The Episcopalians were hard hit by the Revolu-

[8] For an admirable outline of this progress see M. Louise Greene, "Development of Religious Liberty in Connecticut."

tion, but recovered fast, and their first American bishop, Samuel Seabury, who was consecrated in Great Britain in 1784, took up his residence at once in Connecticut. Methodist missionaries entered the State in 1789,[9] made converts in spite of fines and imprisonment, and were soon able to organize flourishing churches. The irritation of these denominations had much to feed upon, for the Congregationalists made use of their control over the State government to obtain many special privileges. Thus in 1785-86 the Legislature, arranging for the sale of the Western Reserve lands, and the division of the proceeds among the various Protestant sects, also enacted that there should be reserved in each township sold 500 acres for the gospel, 500 for the schools, and 240 acres "to be granted in fee simple to the first gospel minister who shall settle in such town." The wealthy Congregationalists, carrying out on a large scale the planting of missions in the West, naturally received the most benefit.

Beyond the western boundary of Connecticut we pass into a territory of much greater religious freedom, though the Catholic disabilities in the middle Colonies were drastic. In New York the Anglican Church enjoyed little beyond a nominal establishment. The Dutch and English Calvinists were the most numerous sects, and just before the Revolution they and the other dissenting bodies were estimated by a contemporary historian to outnumber the Anglicans fifteen to one. "Hence partly arises the general discontent on account of the ministry acts; not so much that the provision made by them is engrossed by the minor sect as because the body of the people are for an equal universal toleration of Protestants, and utterly averse to any kind of ecclesiastical establishment." It was in New York City that the Episcopalians were strongest; and there, at the middle of the eighteenth century, there were two Episcopalian churches, two Dutch Calvinist, two German Lutheran, and one each of the English Calvinist, Baptist, French Huguenot, Moravian, and Quaker sects— besides a Jewish synagogue. In such a cosmopolitan Province religious toleration, like other kinds of toleration, could not help flourishing. The Anglican ministers were chosen by their congregations, and maintained, with a little help from the government, in the main by voluntary contributions. At the time of the Revolution, the Establishment was limited to four counties, and taxation to support it was not onerous—it is hard to find evidence of the collection of

[9] Beardsley, "Life and Corr. of the Rt. Rev. Samuel Seabury," *passim.*

tithes; but in 1773 petitions from some Long Island towns protested against the favored position of the Anglicans, and a constant election cry was "No Bishops."

As soon as the allegiance of New York to the Crown was cast off, all the old connection between church and state was automatically dissolved. No one knew just how close, in law, this connection had been. In the last years of British rule the Anglicans had offered detailed legal arguments to prove that their church was upon an establishment as sound and durable as that it occupied in England; while the dissenters brought forward equally detailed arguments to show that it was not. But everyone knew that the connection had not been popularly approved. Formal expression was given to the severance in the Constitution of 1777. It declared that all such parts of the common or statutory law "as may be constructed to establish or maintain any particular denomination of Christians or their ministers," were "abrogated or rejected." The Episcopal Church could make no objection; it was barely able to maintain its vitality under the losses it suffered from the persecution of the loyalists. Thenceforth all faiths in New York were on a perfectly equal footing.

In New Jersey the equality of the different Protestant faiths was quite clear, there being no statute for an Establishment. As in New York, the dissenters far outnumbered the Episcopalians. Samuel Smith, writing from his own knowledge in 1765, tells us there were then about 160 churches in the Colony, representing a dozen different denominations. About one-third were Presbyterian; one-fourth were Dutch Calvinist; about one-fifth were Quaker, and the Baptist and Episcopal churches were each less than one-eighth of the whole. About 1730 an Episcopalian had admitted, speaking of Pennsylvania and New Jersey, that there were "such a prodigious number of sectaries that the Church of England is like a small twig growing under the spreading boughs of a mighty tree." Moreover, the Anglican clergy, as in New York, lived too freely, and spent too much money on wine and too little on books, to be much respected. Most dissenting ministers, on the other hand, were active and influential, and to the Presbyterians and Dutch Calvinists the Province owed most of its educational facilities. The assumption of independence confirmed religious freedom, for the Constitution of 1776 provided that no man should be required to support or attend a church against his will, and that there should be no establishment of one sect over another.[10]

In Pennsylvania and Delaware, as in Rhode Island, religious freedom was as full and real as anywhere in the wide world; the only exception to the universal toleration lying in a sporadic and occasional tendency to deal harshly with Catholics. The Constitutional basis of government laid for the two Colonies in 1682 guaranteed a wide charity for all forms of belief, and non-interference by the government in matters of conscience. The Anglican Church had little vitality in the Quaker Colonies; the Calvinist Churches had much; and the Province was renowned in the Old World as well as new for the variety of its small religious groups, the German immigration alone furnishing a half dozen distinct and eccentric sects. The immigration tended slowly but steadily to reduce the dominant strength of the Quakers. The Scotch, Scotch-Irish, and many of the Welsh supported the Calvinist churches, the Germans maintained the Lutheran congregations or the small societies like the Dunkards, Mennonites, and Ridge Hermits, and the Baptists and Anabaptists were numerous. There were certain religious tests for office, which many of these sects strongly supported. The Irish and German Catholics, strengthened by the Acadians, formed a small but growing body by the outbreak of the Revolution.

But if the state had nothing to with the church in Pennsylvania, the church often had much to do with the state. By their numerical superiority and great wealth, their energy and intellectual ability, the Quakers during most of the eighteenth century previous to the Revolution controlled the Assembly. When Provost William Smith was rising to prominence as a leader of the "proprietary party," at the beginning of the French and Indian War, he accused the Quakers of mismanaging the Colony, and represented the meetings of the Quaker Church as political cabals; with the result that the Assembly voted his letters libelous, and ordered his arrest. There is no doubt that in their votes relating to military preparations against the French and Indians, and to relations with England, the Quaker Assemblymen were swayed largely by their religious convictions. The policy of the government was in many ways a Quaker policy, and as such was abominated by the hot Scotch-Irish borderers, who were political realists in their dealings with the

[10] Cf Elmer, "Reminiscences of New Jersey," 33.

Indians, and by the Episcopalians, who were warmly loyal to England.

In the fifties the revolt against Quaker influence in the government became pronounced, in the sixties it began to succeed, and in the seventies it completely won its object. The conservative Quakers at the beginning of the Revolution were forced out of touch with affairs, and the reins passed to men of progressive stamp, some of them being Friends, but the great majority belonging to other churches. Subject, as conscientious objectors to military service, to special assessments, which were often collected in an extortionate way, many Quakers complained during the war of independence that they were grievously persecuted.[11]

In Maryland, Virginia, and the Carolinas the Church of England enjoyed a recognized supremacy as the state church, its establishment in all four Colonies being explicitly fixed by law. In Maryland general taxes were levied in support of the Church, and as its communicants were in a minority in the Province, it became much disliked by a large part of the population. Only one fact enabled the sects of dissenting Protestants to reconcile themselves to the Establishment—their dread of the numerous, able, and wealthy Catholics. About fifty years before American independence, we find Maryland clergy complaining to the Bishop of London of the "vast numbers of Jesuits who by their sophistry and cunning make proselytes daily throughout the whole government," and who were grown so impudent as to "disperse their Popish books through all quarters of the country."

Every Anglican clergyman in Maryland had his house and glebe, or farm; he was guaranteed a tax, settled by law and collected by the sheriffs; and he had various fees, as those for performing marriages. Secure in his emoluments, and, since he was appointed by the Proprietary or Governor, virtually free from fear of dismissal, the ordinary cleric was no model of virtue. The term "a Maryland parson" was a byword farther north. In 1753 Dr. Chandler, a

---

[11] The sufferings of the "Virginia exiles" were long remembered. Brissot de Warville ("New Travels," 416-17) sympathetically describes the later vexations to which the sect was subjected. "Each citizen is obliged by law to serve in the militia, or to pay a fine. The Quakers will not serve nor pay the fine. The collector, whose duty it is to levy it, enters their houses, takes their furniture, and sells it; and the Quakers peaceably submit. This method gives great encouragement to knavery. Collectors have been known to take goods to the amount of six times the fine, to sell for a shilling what was worth a pound, never to return the surplus, nor even to pay the State, but afterwards to become bankrupts. Their successors would then come and demand the fine already paid; but the Quakers have complained of these abuses, and an act is passed suspending these collections till September, 1789."

frank American minister, wrote home that "the general character
of the clergy is wretchedly bad," and that it would "make the ears
of a sober heathen tingle to hear the stories" told of some of them.
A contemporary tells us that a current couplet ran:

> Who is a minister of the first renown?
> A lettered sot, a drunkard in a gown.

There was no proper disciplinary authority, and favoritism entered
into the appointments; so that the majority of the ministers had the
brains, education, and moral elevation of Parson Trulliber. Yet
the people were taxed heavily, as taxes went in America, for this
clerical crew. The quarrel between the Legislature and Governor
Eden which came to a head in 1770 involved, among other factors,
the question whether every poll should pay thirty or forty pounds
of tobacco to the Church, the Governor insisting on the latter
amount. Since the price of tobacco was high, and they had other
sources of income, the Maryland clergy were rated the best-paid
in America. In 1767 one parish was worth about £500 a year. The
people also had to pay special taxes for church-building, for fencing
graveyards, and other purposes, and even in wartime beneficed
clergymen were exempt from the general taxes. "I am as averse to
having a religion crammed down my throat," wrote Charles Carroll
of Carrollton on July 1, 1773, "as to a proclamation"—Governor
Eden having usurped certain legislative rights by proclamation. The
burdens under which the Calvinists, Catholics, and Quakers lay were
one of the real if minor causes of the Revolutionary spirit.

When the Revolution began, the Anglican Church was destitute
of influence over the Provincial Congresses; the very vices of the
clergy, encouraging skepticism and dissent, had assisted in the
development of a spirit of religious tolerance. The bill of rights
adopted in 1776 forever ended the Establishment in Maryland. All
further assessment by vestries for the support of the ministers was
forbidden, and it was declared that no one should be compelled to
attend any worship but that of his choice. The Episcopal Church
was treated generously in that it was secured in all its glebes,
churches, chapels, and other property, and provision was made for
continuing the repair of churches in progress under earlier laws.
Finally, the bill of rights empowered the Legislature at any time to
levy a common, equal tax for the support of Christianity in general,

on condition that each person might either pay to his own denomination, or have the money devoted to the poor.

It is evidence of the sentiment against any connection between church and state in Maryland that but one serious effort was made to give effect to this power. After the peace, petitions began to come from certain vestries lamenting a decline in piety and morals; and the legislature early in 1785 laid a bill providing for a general church tax before the people. A huge uproar arose against the measure, which was denounced by some as a preliminary step towards a new Establishment. Great numbers, it was said, would scruple in conscience to pay it; the tax might be raised from four shillings to twenty-four.[12] That fall it was decisively beaten.[13]

The struggle for disestablishment in Virginia was as interesting as the later one in Connecticut, and much more momentous in its influence. The Anglican Church at the beginning of Virginia history had firmly entrenched itself through the immigration of the Cavaliers. The leading statesmen—Washington, Jefferson, Madison, Mason, Pendleton, the Lees, the Randolphs—of the Revolution were of families which had supported the Church ever since their forbears had come from the mother land. However, the unquestioned supremacy of the Establishment had been somewhat shaken in pre-Revolutionary days by two factors: the disrepute into which many of the horse-racing, fox-hunting, wine-drinking clergy fell, and the fact that the immigration of Presbyterians, Quakers, Lutherans, and above all, Baptists, had reduced its communicants to a minority of the Colony's church-members.[14] The newer denominations grew especially strong west of the Blue Ridge, and about 1765 their moral position was improved by the persecutions to which the Episcopalian party tried to subject them. A familiar anecdote tells how in 1768, when three Baptist ministers were being tried in Spottsylvania County, the deep voice of Patrick Henry, who had come for miles on horseback, was heard lifted from the rear of the room in

---

[12] That is, in the hundred pounds. See Maryland *Journal*, February 4, 8, 18, 1785.
[13] A movement in behalf of a bill to establish religious freedom was at once begun in earnest. See Maryland *Journal*, June 7, 1785.
[14] Edmund Randolph draws this striking contrast: "The Presbyterian clergy were indefatigable. Not depending upon the dead letter of written sermons, they understood the mechanism of haranguing, and have often been whetted in dispute on religious liberty, as nearly allied to civil. Those of the Church of England were planted on glebes, with comfortable houses, decent salaries, some perquisites, and a species of rank which was not wholly destitute of unction. To him who acquitted himself of parochial functions these comforts were secure, whether he ever converted a deist, or softened the heart of a sinner. He never asked himself whether he was felt by his audience. To this charge of lukewarmness there were some shining exceptions." M. D. Conway, "Life of Randolph," Ch. 17.

protest. "May it please your lordships," he interrupted, "What did I hear read? Did I hear an expression that these men, whom your worships are about to try for misdemeanor, are charged with preaching the gospel of the Son of God?"

In Virginia, as in Maryland, tithes were levied upon all citizens for the support of the Established Church, while the whole public was also responsible for the upkeep of the church buildings. The salary of ministers had been fixed in 1696 at 16,000 pounds of tobacco for each, a stipend largely increased by the legal fees for marriages, funerals, and christenings. Like Maryland, Virginia had a hot and rather discreditable dispute about salaries just before the Revolution—"the parsons' cause." Every minister was entitled to his parsonage, and his glebe of two hundred acres, and most of them cultivated their land like other planters. Shocking stories are told of their gambling, profanity, and drunkenness, but the Establishment was infinitely stronger in the allegiance of the dominant lowland public than in Maryland.

Towards the close of 1774 the Baptists began to cherish hopes not only of obtaining liberty of conscience, but of wholly overturning the Establishment, and petitions for this purpose were circulated industriously. Baptist spokesmen appeared before the Provincial Convention of July, 1775, and obtained various minor concessions, as that dissenting ministers should be on an equality with the Established clergy in the army. A year later, in June, 1776, the Declaration of Rights of George Mason was reported, embodying the assertion that "all men should enjoy the fullest toleration in the exercise of religion, according to the dictates of conscience, unpunished and unrestrained by the magistrates. . . ." This was cast aside upon the initiative of Madison, who had been trained in the dissenting college at Princeton; and a broader, briefer section was substituted, its essential portion reading that "All men are equally entitled to the free exercise of religion." Madison believed that the word "toleration" was objectionable, for it implied a system in which the free exercise of religion was permissive, instead of an unquestioned natural right; and he objected also to a clause in Mason's section which empowered the courts to punish a man when in exercising his religion he was found to disturb the peace, happiness, or safety of society. The section as finally adopted was a compromise, which declared the persecution of dissenters unjust, but did not rule out the existence of a state church. The reformers hence had at once to begin their fight against the laws supporting the Episcopal ministry.

The general battle, which closed victoriously ten years later, began with the first session of the Legislature in October, 1776. This Assembly received petitions both for and against the Establishment, the Baptists, Lutherans, and Presbyterians praying to be relieved of any further support of the Episcopal Church, and some Methodists, strangely enough, protesting that "very bad consequences" might arise from abolishing the Establishment. The petitions brought on what Jefferson described years later as "the severest contests in which I have ever been engaged." [15] Though most Virginians were dissenters, a majority of the legislators were Churchmen, and it was possible to win ground only at those points where the justice of the liberal cause was indisputable. By earnest effort the progressives, against the opposition of Pendleton and R. C. Nicholas as leaders of the Episcopal party, succeeded in repealing the laws which made it criminal to maintain certain proscribed opinions or exercise proscribed forms in religion. They also obtained the passage of a bill relieving dissenters of the burden of taxes and contributions for the Establishment, and they persuaded the Legislature to suspend the ecclesiastical taxes upon even church members for one year. These were marked gains, and afforded much encouragement to Jefferson, Madison, and Mason. For their part, the conservatives carried resolutions declaring that religious assemblies ought to be regulated, that provision should be made for continuing the succession of the clergy and superintending its conduct, and that the question of a general tax-levy for all churches should be reserved.

Thereafter, not a year passed in which the Legislature was not bombarded with petitions and memorials upon the abolition of the Establishment. Pressing the issue, Jefferson and Madison had little trouble in obtaining a suspension from year to year of the ecclesiastical tax upon church members. The Baptists and Presbyterians were active in marshalling public opinion. Anglicanism had been thrown under a cloud by the Revolution, many of the clergy being loyalists, and now was the time to strike. In 1779, as part of his revised code for Virginia, Jefferson drew up a bill for establishing religious freedom, which would completely have divorced church and

[15] "Writings," Memorial Ed., I, 57.

government, and it was reported in June, just after he was elected Governor. It failed. But there did pass a bill by Mason which forever relieved citizens from the payment of taxes for the Episcopal Church. The clergy still had their rich glebes, and the greater part of all the marriage fees, but they lost their tithes, and became dependent largely upon voluntary contributions. It may seem strange that if this measure, which practically ended the Establishment, passed, Jefferson's could not; but this was because his radical proposal seemed irreligious to many, and because a compromise plan had found favor with the Presbyterians, and an eloquent advocate in Patrick Henry. Briefly, it proposed that the State should establish all Christian denominations, make them equally state religions, and support them by regular taxation; it was pressed vigorously in the next few years by many outside as well as inside the Episcopal Church.

Henceforth the "general assessment" was the chief religious question before the Legislature. Our available evidence shows that by the end of 1783 the plan of taxing everyone for the support of all Christian ministers had gained wide favor, and was approved by a majority of Episcopalians, Methodists, and perhaps Presbyterians; but it was opposed by the Baptists and many in all other denominations who agreed with Jefferson that any link whatever between church and state was an evil.[16] In 1784 the advocates of the plan seemed on the eve of victory. On November 17 the Legislature voted that incorporation ought to be granted to all Christian churches that applied for it; the vote, 62 to 23, showed Madison leading the minority, supported by W. C. Nicholas, John Taylor of Caroline, and John Breckenridge. Patrick Henry instantly moved to commit the Legislature to the general assessment, introducing a resolution that "the people of the commonwealth . . . ought to pay a moderate tax or contribution for the support of the Christian religion, or of some Christian church, or denomination, or communion of Christians." It passed 47 to 23, and a committee was appointed under Henry to draw up a bill. A number of petitions favorable to it came in, including one from the clergy of the whole Presbyterian church; while only one memorial was listed against it. A majority

[16] War had brought, it appears, an increase of crime in Virginia, and this was attributed by many to a decline in religion. Among those who believed in legislative support of all the churches to check this decline were not only Henry and R. H. Lee, but Washington and John Marshall. Rives' "Madison," I, 602; Rowland's "Mason," II, 90.

both of the Legislature and the people appeared to believe that unless the obligation to support religion were made unescapable, stinginess and indifference would let many churches die; and Henry showed with his convincing oratory how nations had declined when religion decayed. Madison made an elaborate argument against the bill, one of the best of his life, but his opposition seemed in vain.[17]

Yet the measure was beaten. Madison's twenty-odd followers fought it at every step. During the session a bill was reintroduced to incorporate the Episcopal Church; a bill which had once been objectionable, but was now shorn of harmful features. Madison backed it on strategic grounds, writing Jefferson that its rejection "would have doubled the eagerness and pretexts for a much greater evil—a general assessment—which there is good ground to believe was parried by this partial gratification of its warmest votaries."[18] The ballot was 47 to 38. But the principal reason for the failure of the assessment plan was that Patrick Henry, according to his inveterate easy-going practise, rode away near the close of November to his home in the west, leaving it without its most skilful sponsor. His retirement was "very inauspicious to his offspring," rejoiced Madison; the bill's "friends are much disheartened by the loss of Mr. Henry." The measure had passed its third reading; but now it was proposed that it be postponed, printed, and distributed, and the people invited to signify their opinion respecting its adoption at the next session of the Legislature.[19] This seemed reasonable, and the proponents of the bill were the more ready to accede to it because they believed that the popular reply was certain to be favorable. It was at the same time that a similar measure was laid by the Episcopalians and others before the people of Maryland, and supported by an active campaign.

With the breaking up of the Legislature, Virginia witnessed a campaign of education that most effectively compassed its purpose. It was planned, not by Madison, but by George and Wilson Cary Nicholas, who believed that while a majority of the counties were in favor of the bill, a majority of the people were opposed, and that the fact could be shown so conclusively that no legislature would have the effrontery to pass the measure. Madison drew up a

---

[17] C. F. James, "Doc. Hist. of Struggle for Relig. Liberty in Va.," 140. The notes of Madison's speech are given in his "Writings," Hunt Ed., II, 88-89; it is summarized in Hunt's "Madison," 81-83.
[18] "Writings," Hunt. Ed., II, 113.
[19] Journal of the House of Delegates.

memorial of remonstrance, at the instance of George Nicholas;[20] it was printed as a broadside by the Phoenix Press in Alexandria, and copies were sent throughout the State for the reception of signatures; and by September 24, 1785, Edmund Randolph was announcing to R. H. Lee that "the Presbyterians will have a sufficient force to prevent the general assessment, possibly to repeal the act of incorporation." When the Legislature assembled in October, Henry had dropped his membership to become Governor, Mason and Madison were ready for battle, and the number of signed remonstrances was enough to bury the assessment bill out of sight. It was one of those mischievous measures which carry a plausible face, but are easily stripped to their true worthlessness by a penetrating argument; and this argument Madison had furnished. The measure was lost by a small majority in committee of the whole, and relinquished forever.[21]

Seeing his favorable opportunity, Madison now brought forward Jefferson's bill for establishing religious freedom, which had lain on the table since 1779. He made an able speech, it was adopted in the House 67 to 20, and became law in January, 1786.[22] The measure, which declared that there must be no interference whatever by the government in church affairs or matters of conscience, nor any disabilities for religious opinion, was truly epoch-making. Viewed by large numbers as completely subversive of religious interests, it proved the cornerstone of religious freedom for many a State outside Virginia, and was pointed to abroad as a model of advanced legislation on the subject. It was translated into French and Italian. Jefferson regarded the law as one of his three greatest achievements; after his death the request was found among his papers that on his tombstone he be identified as the author of the Declaration of Independence, the statute for religious freedom, and the University of Virginia. There remained but one vestige of the Establishment—the continued Episcopal tenure of the glebes.[23]

It was impossible for the Established Church or any church to wax strong in poor, sparsely populated, and isolated North Carolina. William Byrd, in his history of the dividing line, drew a strik-

[20] "Writings," Hunt Ed., II, 183.
[21] The most thorough account of the struggle for religious freedom in Virginia is H. J. Eckenrode, "Separation of Church and State in Va."; Bishop Wm. Meade's "Old Churches, Ministers, and Families of Va.," is also valuable.
[22] Hening's "Statutes at Large," XII, 84.
[23] James, "Doc. Hist. of the Struggles for Religious Liberty in Va.," 140 ff.

ing picture of the neglected spiritual condition of the people. Many communities paid tribute neither to Caesar nor to God; the chaplain with Byrd's party was clamorously importuned to perform baptisms; and in many places marriages were celebrated either by justices of the peace or not at all. In 1715 the Province was mapped into nine parishes, and the first royal Governor, Burrington, was ordered to see that every church had a minister, an endowment, and a glebe. Futile efforts were made to legislate vigor into the Establishment. In 1757 Governor Dobbs complained to the Assembly that some of the parishes systematically evaded the laws compelling them to make suitable provision for the minister, and proposed that the church rate be levied, not parish by parish, but upon the Province as a whole; but the Assembly refused. Not until 1766 could Presbyterian ministers perform the marriage ceremony, and even then the Episcopal clergyman had to be given the fee; the other dissenting ministers, Quakers excepted, could not perform it until 1776. The Schism Act was enforced, to the great detriment of education, long after it was forgotten in England. Yet at the outbreak of the Revolution there were only six Episcopal ministers in the whole Colony. One recent investigator believes that in a half century the North Carolinians had hardly paid sufficient taxes to the Establishment to support two clergymen for a year.[24]

While the Anglican Church was at a standstill, the dissenting denominations grew steadily. The immigration into the back counties was made up largely of Calvinists, Quakers, and German sects. When the Episcopalians had six resident ministers, the Presbyterians and Moravians had each as many, while there were a number of itinerant dissenting missionaries. In 1765 the Baptists of Virginia and North Carolina between the James and Neuse formed the Kehukee Association. The Regulators' troubles which began three years later were participated in chiefly by Baptists and Presbyterians, together with a few Quakers like the fiery Herman Husbands.

The Anglican Church of North Carolina was wrecked in the Revolution. Most of the ministers remained loyal to the Crown, were deprived of their cures, and returned home; and as a majority of the communicants were also Tory, the disappearance of the Estab-

[24] S. B. Weeks, "Church and State in North Carolina," Johns Hopkins University Studies, Series XI, Nos. 5-6.

lishment meant almost the disappearance of Episcopalianism. The Constitution and Bill of Rights adopted by the fifth Provincial Convention in the fall of 1776 ensured perfect religious freedom, providing that "there shall be no establishment of any one religious church or denomination in this State in preference to any other," and that no one should be compelled to attend any church or pay for its maintenance. It was a simple matter to bring the laws of the State into conformity with these provisions. All ministers alike were shortly given the right to perform the marriage ceremony, and the existing restrictions upon the Quakers and other sects were removed. The Episcopal churches were generously confirmed in their right to their glebes and other property. In one respect the Constitution failed, for at the behest of an able and aggressive back-country dissenter, the Rev. David Caldwell, it prohibited any person who denied the existence of God or the truth of the Protestant religion from holding civil office. The discussion of this prohibition, wrote the indignant Samuel Johnston to his friend Mrs. Iredell, "blew up such a flame" that it almost halted the Convention's work.[25] The liberal-minded Hooper was so angered by the test that he broke off abruptly a cherished friendship with its advocate Thomas Jones.[26]

In South Carolina the Episcopal Church was in comparatively prosperous circumstances, its condition being the best in America. Just before the Revolution there were twenty parishes; the ministers were remarkably well educated, talented, and upright; and the rich planters and merchants, so English in all their characteristics, had every reason to regard the Establishment with pride and devotion. The immigration of northern colonials, and of the Scotch-Irish and Highlanders from overseas, built up several scores of dissenting churches, principally in the upland country. The dissenters were not tithed for the Establishment, but were taxed indirectly, since some provision was made for the Church from the custom duties. They complained of this; they complained that their congregations could not hold property as corporations, but only through trustees; and they complained that their fashionable members were tempted to desert them for the aristocratic Anglican church. Yet there was remarkably little ill feeling between the denominations when the Revolution began. Nor did the war itself deepen it, for the clergy

[25] McRee's "Iredell," I, Ch. 9.
[26] Jones, "Defence of Rev. Hist. of N. Ca.," 317-18.

and communicants of the Establishment in South Carolina supported the patriot cause almost as loyally as did the Presbyterians and Baptists of Charleston and the interior.[27]

Shrewd churchmen doubtless knew that disestablishment would come; but it did not come with the suddenness with which it was effected in North Carolina. In 1776 the Rev. Mr. William Tennent, a Congregationalist from Connecticut, was already agitating the question; but the dominant lowland planters, being nearly all church-men and used to a social and civil fabric of which the Church was an integral part, were not ready for the step. The Constitution of 1776, which discarded the King, did not discard the Establishment. The Congregationalists or "White Meetners" kept up their demand for it; a memorial drawn up by Tennent received many thousands of signatures, especially in the up-country; and when the Assembly debated the subject in 1777, Tennent, a member, made a powerful plea for disestablishment. The weight of the argument was all with him. He was able to show that in the decade preceding 1776 the Treasury had paid very nearly £165,000 for the support of the Church, and asserted that of this perhaps half had come out of the pockets of the dissenters; he could point out that while the Episcopal congregations numbered twenty, the dissenting congregations numbered seventy-nine. The Episcopalians, he said, should be content with their superb churches and parsonages, their numerous glebes and other church estates. Let it be a fundamental article of the Constitution that no religious sect should be established in preference to another, he demanded.

But sentiment was still stronger than reason. It was argued that the poor-relief and the management of elections were interwoven with the old law for the Establishment, and such influential leaders as Lowndes and Charles Pinckney stood bravely by the church. In the end it was agreed that the bill for disestablishment should be circulated through the State for discussion, preparatory to the next session of the Legislature.[28]

The next legislature decided for disestablishment. With the new and better Constitution which it adopted early in 1778, the progressives won the day. This instrument declared that all Protestant

[27] McCrady, "S. Ca. in the Rev., 1775-1780," 205-06; but note Ramsay, "Hist. S. Ca.," II, 21: "The Episcopalians since the Revolution labored under peculiar disadvantages"—the chief of these being the lack of bishops, and the consequent impossibility for a dozen years of ordaining ministers.
[28] See Ramsay, II, 17 ff., for a contemporary view of these changes.

sects, demeaning themselves peaceably and faithfully, should enjoy equal religious and civil privileges, and that any church-society might be incorporated. The Episcopal churches, however, were confirmed by the Constitution in the property they already held.

Georgia fell in with the whole Southern movement. The Established Church there was weak, for it was comparatively young. The first permanent missionary had entered upon his duties in 1733; and it will be remembered that John Wesley arrived in 1736, labored diligently as an Episcopalian, and returned to England in consequence of an unfortunate love affair. Under the royal government all dissenters were given complete toleration, and they quite outnumbered the Anglicans. A certain Puritan element entered into the legislation of the Colony, for all persons were compelled to attend church, work and play on Sunday were forbidden, and the constables patrolled the streets, as in New England, to see that the taverns were closed and that all were at service. At the time of the Revolution there were only a few Anglican clergymen settled in the Province. Several of them took the part of the mother land, and left America; and as their places were not supplied, their denomination languished. The dissenters took advantage of their opportunity to overturn the Establishment. By the Constitution adopted in February, 1777, it was declared that all persons should have the free exercise of their religion, provided that it was not repugnant to the peace and safety of the State—this being the clause in George Mason's proposed article to which Madison objected—and should be required to support no teachers except those of their own faith.

How urgent the necessity for constitutional guarantees of religious freedom appeared to many people in the young American republic was shown when the Federal Constitution was given to the States for ratification. The lack of any safeguards for liberty of faith at once struck critics in all sections. The Virginia Convention proposed an amendment guaranteeing freedom of conscience. North Carolina's Convention seconded the proposal, adopting the same language. New Hampshire proposed an amendment in different words. New York's Convention devoted one of sundry recommendations and principles to the subject. The dissenting minority of the Pennsylvania Convention laid emphasis upon it; and Rhode Island in finally ratifying suggested the need for a special guarantee. In the first Congress attention was directed to the oversight by James Madison, and the required guarantee was made the first Constitutional amendment proposed to the nation.[29]

II. Primogeniture and Entail Decay

Only less important than the laws for a Church Establishment, as a pillar of aristocracy and privilege, were the laws of primogeniture, entail, and manorial interest. As the fight against the Establishment was most prominent in the South, so the fight against these undemocratic institutions had chiefly to be waged there.

In Virginia most of the aristocracy was deeply attached to entail and primogeniture. The founders of the great families had obtained wide estates, and wishing to ensure the perpetuation of their name and influence, had settled them upon their descendants in fee tail. Such families, as Jefferson says, "were thus formed into a patrician order, distinguished by the splendor and luxury of their establishments"; from them the King selected the colonial councilors, and they were often deeply attached to the Crown. The people so disliked some of them that for a generation after the Revolution it was difficult for certain men—a Burwell, a Randolph, or a Carter—to carry an election. For this reason, and because entail smacked so much of the British land system, Jefferson's action in attacking it as soon as the Revolution began was not so bold as it seemed. It succeeded with a rapidity, however, which amazed even him. On Oct. 7, 1776, he took his seat in the House of Delegates; on Oct. 12 he obtained leave to bring in a bill to enable tenants in tail to convey entailed property in fee simple; and on October 14 he reported a measure to do away with the whole scheme of entail by repealing the existing law. The Assembly contained many representatives of the landed aristocracy, bound by ties with each other and by self-interest to protect the existing order; as matters stood, the great landholders were bulwarked against even creditors who wanted the entailed land to satisfy debts. Yet the bill passed promptly, as if on the flood-tide of democracy. Jefferson tells us that the conservative Pendleon, "who, taken all in all, was the ablest man in debate I ever met with," fought for the entail system to the last; when he

---

[29] Elliot's Debates, II, 118 ff., 148 ff.; IV, 242-44. Philip Schaff's "Church and State in the United States," 22 ff. should be consulted. It is true, of course, that many Americans criticized the Constitution for not recognizing the Christian religion, or imposing religious tests for office.

found that he could not preserve it, he tried to obtain a compromise, but by a few votes he was beaten.[30]

The cognate principle of primogeniture Virginians did not sweep away until 1785. When Jefferson, Wythe, and Pendleton set themselves in 1777, under legislative authorization, to revise the State's laws, Jefferson proposed the abolition of the statute of primogeniture, making real estate, like personal property, descendible to the next of kin by the statute of distribution. Pendleton wished to preserve it; and when he saw that this was out of the question, suggested that on the Hebrew principle the eldest son should have a double share. No, answered Jefferson, not unless he could eat a double allowance of food and do a double allowance of work. Jefferson carried his point; and his alteration in the law was taken up by the Legislature two years after the final peace, and approved by it. The effect of these reforms was succinctly described by Washington when he told Brissot de Warville at Mount Vernon in 1788 that "the distinction of classes begins to disappear." [31] It was pictured at greater length years later in Congress by Henry Clay:

In whose hands now are the once proud seats of Westover, Cerles, Maycocks, Shirly, and others on the James and in lower Virginia? They have passed into other and stranger hands. Some of the descendants of illustrious parentage have gone to the far West, while others lingering behind have contrasted their present condition with that of their venerated ancestors. They behold themselves excluded from their fathers' houses, now in the hands of those who were once their fathers' overseers, or sinking into decay.[32]

The democratic State of Georgia hastened, unconsciously or consciously, to follow the lead of Virginia. The Constitution adopted early in 1777 declared that estates should not be entailed, and that when a person died without a will, his or her estate should be divided equally among the children, the widow taking a child's share, or her dower. In North Carolina the reform was a little tardier. In 1784 the Assembly, resolving that entails gave wealthy families an undue influence in a republic, and were a source of great private injustice, made them illegal; and at the same time provided for a more general and equal distribution of the real property of persons dying without a will.[33] In South Carolina action against entail had been taken just before the Revolution, but the old rule of primogeniture re-

[30] "Writings," Memorial Ed., I, 54, 55.
[31] Washington also spoke of a general improvement in manners. Horse-racing was disappearing; so were tavern parties and heavy drinking in homes; while court sessions were "no longer the theaters of gambling, inebriation, and blood." Brissot de Warville's "New Travels," Ed. 1792, 434.
[32] Cong. Debates, VIII, Part I, 290.
[33] State Records N. C., XXIV, 572-77.

mained in force until the Federal Government had been well established. When the Constitution of 1790 was drawn up, the young Governor, Charles Pinckney, suggested a section instructing the Legislature to abolish the rights of primogeniture, and it was written in. The very next year the Legislature acted upon it.[34] As for Maryland, it had passed legislation in colonial days making it possible for the heirs of entailed estates to alienate them by a rather difficult process, and broader legislation followed in 1783. Three years later, moreover, an act was passed abolishing primogeniture.[35] Before the end of Washington's first Administration, therefore, the last vestiges of the Colonial imitation of British aristocracy in land inheritance had been abolished at the South.

In New York, at the time of the Declaration of Independence, the eldest son had the same rights as in the South; and in New Jersey,[36] Pennsylvania, Delaware, and the four New England States, he took a double share of the landed inheritance. By one act after another most such rules were swept into oblivion. The New York Legislature of 1786 abolished entails, and divided the realty left by the intestate into equal parts among the lawful issue. A year later this principle of division was extended to personal property.[37] In Pennsylvania, as Franklin once happened to tell a dinner-party at Passy, the unreasonableness of giving the eldest son a double portion had often been argued. When he was clerk of the Assembly, some members proposed that instead the youngest son should get the favored treatment, inasmuch as he was the more likely to be left—by his father's death—without an education; but the law was not altered. However, such measures now tended to lapse.[38] Massachusetts in the spring of 1784 directed that the estates of those who died leaving no will should descend equally to the children, save that the eldest son should have a double share.[39]

The destruction of the rights of the great Proprietaries, and the confiscation of many large estates of Tories for distribution by sale, also lent an impulse to democracy. In Maryland the Legislature

[34] Statutes at large, S. Ca., V, 162; Jervey, "Robert Y. Hayne," Introduction.
[35] S. A. Harrison, "Life of Bozman," Md. Hist. Society, Fund Pub. No. 26; Laws of Md., Maxcy's Ed., I, 468; II, 16.
[36] New Jersey passed an act in 1784 to do away with the entailment of real estate; Acts of Gen. Assembly, 1783-84, pp. 97, 98.
[37] J. C. Hamilton, "Hist. of Rep.," III, 214; Laws of N. Y., 1777-1801, II, 191.
[38] Franklin's "Works," Bigelow Ed., VIII, 421. The Pennsylvania Constitution of 1776 ordered that the Legislature should "regulate entails in such a manner as to prevent perpetuities," but this had actually been done by the Colonial Legislature long before; cf. Pa. *Gazette*, October 23, 1776.
[39] Acts and Laws, 1784, p. 65. Entail is still legal in Massachusetts.

of 1780 confiscated the property of all British subjects, save that only of ex-Governor Sharpe. By its law the great landed domains of Henry Harford, the Proprietary, were sequestrated to the State; the quit-rents being afterwards abolished, and not taken by the State, the original freeholds became the unrestricted property of those in whose hands they lay. Harford later received £10,000 from the State when it cleared up its business dealings with the Bank of England, and he was paid £90,000 indemnity by the British Treasury. Pennsylvania similarly took over the holdings of the Penns, and abolished the quit-rents; and it granted the family, "in remembrance of the enterprising spirit of the founder," £130,000. Virginia did away with quit-rents in the fall of 1777.

In New York the lordships and manorial privileges of the great estate-holders or patroons were relegated to oblivion. Before the Revolution Stephen Van Rensselaer, had he been of age, would have been acknowledged by the English as the sixth lord of the manor of Rensselaer, and by the Dutch as the eighth patroon. Now he was simply Mr. Van Rensselaer, though by courtesy he was always called patroon.[40] The abolition of manorial privileges, however, made no difference in the terms of the leases governing the rented lands, and they were often, as on Livingston Manor, oppressive in their terms. A real gain for social and political equality, nevertheless, resulted from the sale of wide tracts of land confiscated from aristocratic families like the De Lanceys, Skeenes, Jessups, Beverly Robinson, and John T. Kempe. James De Lancey's lands went to about 275 different persons; Roger Morris's 50,000 acres in Putnam County to nearly 250; and the tracts in the central and northern parts of the State were divided into farms of 100 to 500 acres and sold to poor tillers.[41]

In all parts of the country the Revolution meant the emergence of men from obscure and poor social ranks into positions of power. We think of this as natural enough in South Carolina and Virginia, where a heavy crust of aristocracy was shattered by the upheaval. But it was true even in such a comparatively democratic State as Massachusetts. Many of the best families of Boston and Cambridge

[40] B. W. Bond, "State Govt. in Md. 1777-81," 15; Browne's Md., 285; Laws of Md., Maxcy's Ed., I, 391; Hening, IX, 359; G. W. Schuyler, "Colonial New York," I, 227-31. In New York there was left one bit of property which even yet is held in entail by the direct descendants of the grantee—Gardiner's Island, at the tip of Long Island.
[41] Van Tyne, "Loyalists," 279-80; see B. W. Bond, "The Quit-Rent System."

were Tory—even one of the Quincys was so—and were compelled to remove, leaving their estates behind. New men came in to buy their property at a bargain, and take their places in commerce and the professions; and many of them came from the country squirearchy and small town gentry. Among these country migrants to Boston were the Adamses and Fisher Ames from Norfolk County; the Prescotts from Middlesex; and from Essex the Cabots, Lowells, Parsonses, Lees, Jacksons, Pickerings, and Elbridge Gerry. They took and long held an ascendancy in Massachusetts politics.[42]

III. ATTACKS UPON SLAVERY

The separation of the Colonies from Great Britain made possible the first concerted and effective attacks upon slavery in them. The official attitude of the British Government toward slavery and the slave trade had not been as liberal as that prevalent even in many parts of the South. The Crown, for example, had in 1769 vetoed the measure by which the Virginia Assembly sought to make the further importation of slaves illegal. In Massachusetts efforts in 1771 and 1774 to abolish the slave trade, strongly supported by Puritan opinion, had been defeated by the royal authorities.[43] Similar attempts in New Jersey and Delaware just before the Revolution failed in the same way. Only in the self-governing Colonies of Rhode Island and Connecticut, and in Pennsylvania, which laid a prohibitive duty, was the importation of slaves halted.[44] By the Treaty of Utrecht in 1714 England had agreed to furnish the Spanish Colonies with negroes for thirty years; and a trade had been built up the perpetuation of which was valuable to powerful British interests, like the Royal African Company. Many liberal Englishmen, of course, reprobated the slave trade emphatically—Burke called slavery itself a permanent curse upon the New World; but the British Government merited the denunciation which Jefferson included in his first draft of the Declaration of Independence. George III, he declared, had "waged cruel war against liberty itself, violating its most sacred rights of life and liberty in the persons of a distant population [Africans] who never offended him, capturing and carrying them into slavery in another hemisphere, or to incur miserable

[42] Lodge, "Boston," 167-68.
[43] Wilson, "Rise and Fall of Slave Power," I, 3 ff.
[44] Mary S. Locke, "Anti-Slavery in America," 71.

death in the transportation thither." This he struck out because South Carolina and Georgia wished the slave trade maintained, and many Northern citizens had engaged in it.

British America in 1776 had about a half million negroes, nearly all of whom were slaves. In New England, Pennsylvania, and New Jersey, slaves were seldom met, and their ordinary treatment did not differ greatly from that accorded to white laborers or indentured servants. In New York the negroes were numerous, and were much more harshly treated; their position was more degraded, and they were felt to be a potential menace. It is probably a fact that for a long period in the eighteenth century the New Yorkers showed more fear of their slaves and more brutality to them than the South Carolinians, but this was not true by the time of the Revolution.[45] In the great slaveholding communities of the lowland South the negroes were ignorant, dirty, and heathenish; they were subject to the most repressive measures, enacted by legislators who dreaded nothing so much as a servile insurrection; and they were always carelessly and often cruelly used. Nevertheless, all the infant States except the two southernmost were in the main opposed to the slave trade, and in all there were men who believed in early abolition.[46]

In their new freedom the States first and most decisively dealt with the importation of negroes. The Quaker movement against slavery in the Middle Colonies had long been strong, John Woolman and others of talent having labored devotedly in it; and Delaware was the first to take action. Her Constitution of 1776 forbade the importation of slaves for either sale or labor. In Virginia Jefferson brought in a bill in 1778 to cut off the slave trade, which passed without opposition. Almost all educated men in the Old Dominion believed, as they had repeatedly protested to the Crown authorities, that the trade was one of great inhumanity, and gravely injurious to their well-being, since it discouraged the settlement of more useful inhabitants. The Pennsylvania Legislature followed suit in 1780; that of Maryland did so in 1783; and the New Hampshire Constitution of the latter year stopped all importation of slaves. Connecticut and Rhode Island renewed their laws against importation in 1784, and New York passed one in 1785. By this time

[45] Doyle, "English Colonies in America," V, Ch. 6, deals admirably with the colonists in relation to the inferior races.
[46] As an example of the constant agitation over slavery, note the publication in the Pa. *Mercury*, May 13-20, 1788, of the "Thoughts Upon the African Slave Trade" written by John Newton, the poet Cowper's friend.

petitions were pouring in upon the New Jersey Legislature, and in response the State first, in 1786, imposed a heavy fine for bringing in a slave—£50 if the negro had come from Africa since 1776, £20 if before [47]—and in 1788 made the law much more severe, while also forbidding the exportation of any slave resident for a year or more in the State, except with his own or his parents' consent.[48]   In North Carolina the slave trade was discouraged in 1786 by a tax of £5 a head.   In South Carolina the able and energetic Edward Rutledge, who had been foremost in the abolition of primogeniture, opposed it; in 1785 he championed an unsuccessful proposal to have the importation of negroes forbidden for three years,[49] and in 1787 and 1788 acts for a temporary prohibition actually passed.

Thus within little more than a decade after the Declaration of Independence, a wave of State legislation against the importation of negroes swept the Union, prohibiting the traffic everywhere except in South Carolina and Georgia, and temporarily stopping it even in South Carolina.   In a number of States negroes were automatically made free when imported.   Rhode Island, where the owners of slave-ships had been numerous, in 1787 made participation in the slave trade between even Africa and the West Indies punishable by a heavy fine.

The emancipation of slaves was much more difficult to effect, yet the movement made steady headway at the North.   A popular repugnance to slavery had always been marked in the Congregational as well as the Quaker Colonies.   The "Body of Liberties" or code of Massachusetts Bay in 1641, for example, had declared that there should never be any slavery except of captives taken in just war, or of those who were willingly sold.   Rhode Island in 1652 enacted that "no black mankind or white" should serve in slavery for more than ten years, or after the age of twenty-four—this being the most humane legislation regarding slavery put into effect in the seventeenth century in any part of the world.   The Revolution was a struggle for human freedom, and the slowest intelligence was aware of the gap between slavery and the ideals professed by the rebellious colonists.   Many blacks who fought in the Revolution were thought thereby to have earned their freedom.   Massachusetts granted some slaves who enlisted for three years their liberty;

[47] See N. Y. *Packet*, March 9, 1786, for comment.
[48] H. S. Cooley, "Slavery in N. J.," Johns Hopkins University Studies, Series 14, Nos. 9, 10.
[49] Rutledge was beaten 65 to 48; cf. Pa. *Mercury*, December 16, 1785.

Rhode Island raised a regiment of negroes under Colonel Christopher Greene, and Connecticut a company under Col. David Humphreys. In the South, Colonel John Laurens labored to have suitable slaves emancipated and enrolled in the army, and Virginia in the year of peace freed all negroes who had served honorably.

Vermont, not a member of the Union, led the van; for she adopted a Constitution in 1777 which declared against slavery forever. She was quickly followed by Massachusetts. In that State, a bill to forbid slavery had been reported by a committee in 1777, and had been allowed to die following an unsuccessful attempt to learn from Congress whether it would have a tendency to injure the Union. However, the Bill of Rights of the Constitution of 1780, declaring all men born free and equal, and endowed with the inalienable right of enjoying their lives and liberties, effected the desired object. The Supreme Court, passing upon cases argued in behalf of the slaves by men of such note as Levi Lincoln, Caleb Strong, and Theodore Sedgwick, construed this declaration to require the total manumission of negroes previously held in bondage. The New Hampshire Constitution of 1784 contained in its Bill of Rights a statement of the same purport, which also was held to set all slaves free.[50] These three States constituted the only free soil of the country at the time the Federal Constitution was adopted.

However, other Northern States during these years began making themselves free soil by a process of gradual emancipation. In 1780 the Pennsylvania Legislature passed the first act for this purpose, reflecting the deep dislike of slavery felt by not only the Friends but the Mennonites and other sects. Much of the credit for it is due to George Bryan,[51] and an indefatigable abolitionist, Anthony Benezet, is said to have interviewed every member of the Legislature. In the same year a measure for gradual abolition passed the Connecticut House, was continued till the next session, and was then set aside; but it became law in an improved form in 1784.[52] Under it no negro or mulatto born after March 1, 1784, could be held as a slave after reaching the age of twenty-five. Rhode Island in the same year passed a similar law. New York and New Jersey

[50] Cf. Mass. Hist. Soc. Colls., Series V, Vol. 3, 375 ff., letters to Jeremy Belknap on New England slavery in 1788.
[51] Papers of the Pa. Governors, III, 675 ff.; Pennsylvania had an abolition society, founded in 1774, of which in 1787 Franklin was president, and Dr. Rush and Tench Coxe were secretaries. The act is in Laws of Pennsylvania, 1810 Ed., Ch. 870.
[52] B. C. Steiner, "Slavery in Conn.," Johns Hopkins University Studies, Series XI, Nos. 9, 10.

took no such action until some years after the Federal Constitution went into effect. The former State, however, had an active Society for Promoting the Manumission of Slaves,[53] of which in 1787 Jay was president, and Egbert Benson and Melancthon Smith were prominent members. In Maryland an energetic movement was on foot in 1788 for piecemeal abolition. "Othello" argued in the *Maryland Journal* that slavery "is inconsistent with the *declared* principles of the American Revolution," and that either the Americans should at once free all their slaves and colonize them in the West, or arrange for their gradual liberation, "so that it may become a known and fixed point, that *ultimately,* universal liberty, in these United States, shall triumph. . . ." This plea he reinforced by a picture of the miseries and cruelties of slavery in parts of the South. Nevertheless, in 1789 a bill to encourage manumission, eloquently supported by William Pinkney, was defeated by a close margin in the House.[54]

At the South only a minority wished with Washington for some plan by which slavery could be abolished by law, though the minority included in Virginia such men as Jefferson, R. H. Lee, Henry, and Madison. The economic development of this section bound greater and greater interests up with slavery. Several Southern States repealed the Colonial statutes which forbade emancipation except for meritorious service, and considerable numbers of liberal-minded gentlemen made their slaves free. But Washington wrote Lafayette in 1785 that petitions for the abolition of slavery presented to the Virginia Legislature could scarcely obtain a hearing, and within a decade after the removal of the old restraints upon manumission, in Virginia they were again imposed.[55] In the Carolinas and Georgia opposition to all abolitionist doctrines was intense, for if the negroes were profitable on the Virginia tobacco plantations, they were indispensable on the rice and indigo areas farther south; while the half-savage, sullen blacks of many districts could not be freed with safety to the whites.[56] A few months before

---

[53] In the New York Constitutional Convention of 1777 Gouverneur Morris, supported by Jay, labored vainly in behalf of an article calling upon future Legislatures to abolish domestic slavery as soon as possible. Sparks, Morris, I, 125. See N. Y. *Packet*, April 14, 1785, for the continuance of the agitation.

[54] It was difficult to protect manumitted blacks in their liberty. See the Charleston, S. C. City *Gazette*, September 26, 1789, for a report of the kidnaping of free negroes by a gang which sold them farther south. Pinckney's noble speech in the Maryland House was reprinted in pamphlet form.

[55] W. W. Henry, "Henry," III, 303-04, shows Gov. Henry intervening to save a free black woman and her child from being reduced to slavery again. Manumission was authorized in 1782; Hening, XI, 39 ff.

[56] John Laurens spoke of the hopelessness of crusading against slavery in the lower South; Wallace's "Laurens," 474-75. Elkanah Watson, traveling in the South

Washington was inaugurated a negro near Charleston was sentenced to be burned to death for murdering his master, and the sentence was executed in the presence of his fellow-bondsmen. An ordinance of South Carolina for regulating the conduct of slaves and free negroes in Charleston, passed in 1789, indicates the apprehensions that were never lulled there. Not more than seven male slaves were ever to be allowed to assemble together, except for a funeral; no negro gathering was to last later than ten at night in summer, and nine in winter; no negro could on his own account buy, sell, or barter, licensed fishermen excepted; and no negro was to engage in any mechanic or handicraft trade for himself. In 1786 and again in 1787 the Georgia militia and minute-men waged petty wars against camps of desperate refugee slaves in the wilderness, dislodging them from their lairs on the Savannah with grape-shot.[57]

But this Southern opposition to the progress of emancipation only threw Northern approval into greater prominence. Immediately after the Revolution the Pennsylvania Abolition Society was revived, and its work inspired the formation of similar bodies in other States, the first national convention being held in 1794.

The debate upon the slave trade in the Constitutional Convention showed how widespread an hostility to it had developed. The majority sentiment was of a kind to justify Lincoln's fundamental contention of many decades later, that the fathers of the republic had designed to place slavery in the path to ultimate extinction. We can note only that the discussion showed a cleavage between the various Southern States on the question, and a lesser cleavage between Northerners; there was no hard and fast sectional division as yet. Luther Martin, of Maryland, argued for suppressing the slave trade as "inconsistent to the principles of the Revolution and dishonorable to the American character." Charles Pinckney, on the other side, was positive that South Carolina would not accept the Constitution if it prohibited the slave trade, although he admitted that his State might "by degrees, do of herself what . . . Virginia and Maryland have already done."[58] Mason, of Virginia, spared no adjectives in assailing "this infernal traffic" and its evil

in 1777, recorded his horror and disgust at certain scenes of slavery; in his "Memoirs," Ch. 3, he describes "a heart-rending spectacle; the sale of a negro family, under the sheriff's hammer."

[57] New York *Advertiser*, May 23, 1787; N. Y. *Packet*, May 25, 1787; *Freeman's Journal* (Phila.), November 15, 1786.

[58] Elliot's "Debates," V, 456 ff.

effects—the discouragement of arts and manufactures, the degradation of labor, the prevention of the immigration of a needed white population, the creation of an aristocracy with arbitrary manners— and observed that although the upper South forbade the importation of slaves, all this would be in vain so long as Georgia and South Carolina imported them unchecked. Baldwin, of Georgia, was emphatic in regarding the importation of slaves as a local, not a national, matter; "Georgia was decided on this point. . . . If left to herself she may probably put a stop to this evil." Rutledge of South Carolina also insisted on the right of importation.

Of the Northern delegates, Gouverneur Morris vied with Mason in denouncing both slavery—"a nefarious institution," "the curse of heaven on the States where it prevailed"—and the trade which fed it. Like others, he regarded the counting of a certain proportion of the slaves in apportioning Federal representation as an incentive to importation. But Roger Sherman and Oliver Ellsworth were for leaving importation to the States. The former did not regard the admission of negroes as open to "such insuperable objections"; the latter felt sure that abolition was making steady headway, and that "the good sense of the several States would probably by degrees complete it." Gerry, of Massachusetts, concurred. It will be observed that the strongest opposition to the slave trade came from Maryland and Virginia—and there were not lacking men to point out that these were the chief slave-breeding States; and that while the strongest defence came from the three Southernmost States, several New England delegates were quite willing to see the States allowed to prohibit or permit the trade as they liked. But it should also be noted that Pinckney and Baldwin, of the two States most attached to the importation of blacks, believed that public sentiment there might soon put an end to it. The compromise that resulted is well known. The importation of slaves was not to be forbidden by Congress prior to 1808, but a small tax was to be allowed.

IV. PENAL CODES AND PRISONS

While passing legislation for more humane treatment of the black race, the Legislatures did not forget an increased humanity toward erring freemen. The cruelty of the criminal law throughout British America in 1775 was a direct reflection of the cruelty of the English penal code. In her system of justice the mother country was, in some respects, far in advance of most parts of Continental Europe. But just as little distinction of punishment was made by law between him who broke a pane to steal a loaf and him who murdered to get a purse, between a poacher and a parricide, as in some of the darkest Continental lands. In Blackstone's time the number of crimes punishable with death was no less than one hundred and sixty, and this long list was later increased. In practise, this severity was mitigated by rigid insistence upon a close technical adherence to the rules of correct pleading and proof, and acquittal when there was any error in prosecution; by the rule as to benefit of clergy; by the disposition of juries to acquit criminals threatened with undue punishment; and by the pardoning power of the Crown. Nevertheless, about the time of the Revolution a poor London girl in her teens, the mother of two babies, whose husband had been impressed into the navy and who in consequence was thrown into the streets, was executed for stealing a bit of linen to put bread into her children's mouths.[59] During the Revolution efforts at reform were made in England, and soon after it Jeremy Bentham riddled the Draconian laws through and through, showing that in the repression of crime a sure punishment was more effective than a severe one.

The Colonies adopted in general the civil and criminal laws of the parent nation, having as little disposition as liberty to do otherwise. In some Provinces, to be sure, the spirit of freedom which animated the settlers or founders produced changes. William Penn drew up for Pennsylvania, in advance of its actual settlement, a body of concessions which was the foundation of a criminal code of great liberality. None might be deprived of life, liberty, or estate except by a jury of twelve; the right of challenging jurors was secured to the utmost; imprisonment for debt was hedged about by careful safeguards; and theft, by an adaptation of Mosaic law, was to be punished by a two-fold restitution. Assent to the Colony's equitable foundation-code was refused by the Crown, but it was nevertheless kept in force by the colonial Legislature for thirty-five years. In the end the Colony exchanged its penal laws for those which obtained in the mother land, though the predilection towards a more humane system persisted and was easily revived after 1776. Georgia and North Carolina were for a long time safe refuges for insolvent

[59] Marks, "England and America," 1763-83, Ch. 55.

debtors, though before the Revolution their laws, like those of other Royal Provinces, had been brought into harmony with Great Britain's; and the Massachusetts Body of Liberties (1641) had humane features.

Taking the United States as a whole, its penal codes in 1776 presented a sorry spectacle. In New York, for example, then and for two full decades later, sixteen crimes were punishable by death on the first offence—among them robbery, burglary, house-breaking, arson, and forgery; and as many felonies were punishable with death on the second offence. In Delaware any of twenty crimes might cost a man his life. Jefferson gives a good account of the specific instances in which the criminal law of Virginia differed from England's in his "Notes on Virginia"; but these variations concerned only debtors, the care of the poor, the treatment of slaves, marriages, and minor matters.[60] The laws of Connecticut still made fifteen crimes punishable with death, though in part these laws were now dead letters. Rhode Island was entitled to claim the fairest record. By her early laws the crimes of treason, murder, manslaughter, burglary, robbery, witchcraft, rape, and offences against nature were all subject to capital punishment, but arson was removed from this list; burglary was always treated leniently when committed by a minor or a person made desperate by want, and no execution for it occurred after 1766; and in 1768 witchcraft was formally dropped from the roster of capital offences.[61]

In the reform of the criminal code, as in so many other fields, Virginia led the way. When Jefferson left Congress in 1776 to sit in the Virginia Assembly he felt persuaded, he said later, that the code must be adapted to a republican form of government, and everywhere corrected "with a single eye to reason and the good of those for whose government it was framed." In the autumn its revision was authorized, and he, Pendleton, Wythe, George Mason, and Thomas L. Lee were appointed to execute the task. Mason and Lee, avowing their lack of legal knowledge, resigned, and in the division of the task Jefferson assumed that portion relating to the criminal law. It was agreed by him and his associates that the punishment of death should be abolished except for treason and murder, and that for other felonies the penalty should be hard labor on the

[60] "Writings," Memorial Ed., II. 182 ff.
[61] See Field's "Rhode Island," III, Ch. V.

public works, and, in some instances, application of the *lex talionis*. "How this last revolting principle came to obtain our approbation," he says, "I do not remember." The revised criminal code was laid by till the end of the war. Brought up in 1785 by Madison, who was laboring with general success to have the other revisions of the State laws approved, it was defeated in the House by a majority of one—this because of the prevailing rage against horse-thieves. Fortunately, Governor Patrick Henry this year refused to allow men guilty of no extreme crime to be executed, and pardoned them upon the understanding that the mayor of Richmond would provide against their escape while they were kept at hard labor.[62] But in 1788 men were hanged in Richmond for mere robbery.[63] It was not until Jefferson by his own exertions in 1796 carried his penal revision that the State was safe against these barbarities.

Though the movement for ameliorating the criminal code was begun later in Pennsylvania, it succeeded earlier. The Constitution of 1776 commanded a revision. Just a decade later the legislators abolished the death penalty for robbery, burglary, and unnatural crimes, and lightened the penalty for certain offences not capital before.[64] This act was regarded as an experiment, and next year there were Assemblymen who swore that it had caused the greatest dissatisfaction among the people, and an immense increase of rogues and vagabonds.[65] Nevertheless, the humane principles of the innovation were preserved and broadened in acts of 1790 and 1791. Finally, in 1794 an entire revolution was effected in the criminal code, and death was reserved for the punishment of deliberate homicide. This sweeping reform was of powerful influence all over the

[62] Rives's "Madison," II, 155-56. The old punishment for horse-thievery was death. Jefferson proposed three years' hard labor, with pecuniary reparation. There was a great increase in horse-stealing all over America during the confusion of the war. In Pennsylvania a movement to make the crime punishable by death was defeated only by Judge Bryan. In New Jersey this punishment was actually provided, and thenceforth New Jersey had more horse-thieves than Pennsylvania. Wm. Bradford, "An Inquiry How Far the Punishment of Death is Necessary," 1793. In South Carolina, a Revolutionary veteran writes, after the war "highway robbery was a common occurrence, and horse-stealing so frequent that the Legislature made it a crime punishable with death, in order to protect the poor farmer who, at the very season for ploughing his crops, might be reduced to the want of food by his only horse having been stolen from him." Joseph Johnson, "Traditions and Reminiscences," 400. By a law of 1780 Pennsylvania did go so far as to prescribe that on the second offence horse-thieves should be branded H T on the forehead. Laws, 1810 Ed., Ch. 579.

[63] Pennsylvania *Packet*, June 19, 1788. One was "Edward Watkins, from Caroline, for breaking into and robbing the dwelling house of Mr. Sutton of sundry wearing apparel"; the other was one William Armstrong who had entered a country store.

[64] R. Vaux, "Sketch of the Origin and History of the State Penitentiary of Pa.," 8.

[65] Pa. *Packet*, November 10, 1787. Since eighteen crimes had been nominally punishable with death on the first offence, there was still room for reform. But the barbarous old punishments of branding, ear-cropping, ear-nailing, and heavy flogging were abolished. Laws, 1810 Ed., Ch. 236, Ch. 1231.

Union. The man chiefly responsible for it was William Bradford, a careful student of liberal writings on the subject by British and Continental authors. He was ably seconded by Dr. Benjamin Rush [66] and Judge Bryan. How much the reform was needed will appear from the fact that in the years 1779-1789 inclusive, twenty-six persons were put to death in Pennsylvania, the land of Quaker moderation, for burglary; twenty-three for robbery; four for rape; and one each for counterfeiting, arson, and a crime against nature. This was in spite of the frequency of pardons for those convicted. Bradford tells us that soon after the amendment of the laws, two men were convicted of robbery and burglary respectively, and were told that they could accept the new punishment in place of the old death penalty; they refused, hoping for a pardon, which one received, while the other poor fellow was executed.[67]

Maryland's record unfortunately stands for that of most States in this matter. A proposal in 1778 by the House for a complete revision of the criminal law failed, the Senate being willing only to investigate the question; and in the heat of the war the subject was then forgotten. Even in New England it took time for enlightened ideas to gain ground, and there was one notable instance of reaction. Massachusetts in 1785 passed a series of harsh criminal laws. Robbery, rape, burglary, and sodomy were punished by death, arson by life imprisonment, and manslaughter by prison and branding.

If little was actually accomplished in reforming the penal law in other States, everywhere discontent was being expressed. Educated Americans were as well aware of the efforts of Beccaria to improve the condition of the criminal laws in Europe as they later were of the efforts of Howard to remodel the prisons of that continent. We know from Jefferson's autobiography that he was early familiar with Beccaria, who had an English translator in 1768; before the Revolution Charles Carroll of Carrollton ordered his book from abroad; and it was used as basis for newspaper articles ardently demanding that the United States make itself a model for the Old World by requiring blood only for blood. It is noteworthy, how-

[66] See Dr. Rush's fine argument against public punishments, American Museum, II, 151 ff. (August, 1787); and his argument against capital punishments, Amer. Museum, IV, 78 ff. (July, 1788)—equally forcible and well written.

[67] Wm. Bradford, "An Inquiry How Far the Punishment of Death is Necessary." The total number convicted of robbery was 93; of burglary, 100; Cf. John R. Tyson, "Annual Discourse Before the Hist. Soc. of Pa., 1831." It should here be noted that soon after the penal code of Pennsylvania was reformed, a movement began in that State to reform the civil code. The subject, at Albert Gallatin's recommendation, was referred to a commission headed by Judge James Wilson; Wilson being an aged man, it did nothing. Adams's "Gallatin," 84 ff.

ever, that when in 1790 the Federal Government passed an act for punishing crimes against the United States, it fixed the death penalty, after heated discussion, for the forgery of the securities of the nation.[68]

"In England," wrote Voltaire, "if a poor fellow cannot readily pay a little money when his hands are at liberty, the better to enable him to do it, they load him with handcuffs." So they did in the United States. Much progress was made before 1789 in the reform of the laws upon imprisonment for debt, but much was left for later decades. New York before this date had passed an act by which any debtor, who should get creditors representing three-fourths of his debts to petition for his release, might be freed after he had surrendered all his property; but this was only a partial advance. Pennsylvania legislated for the relief of debtors at the same time, and Massachusetts in 1787 came to the rescue of debtors who could not support themselves in jail.[69]

When the Assembly rose in New York city in 1787, Lansing asked for the attention of the members while he read a list of the prisoners confined for debt hard by. There were ten men whose debts collectively reached £24, he said, languishing without hope of release; and at his suggestion the members unanimously made a gift of one day's pay to relieve them.[70] We have it on good evidence that at this time there was one worthy prisoner, among two dozen

[68] The newspapers of the time abound in revolting reports of the administration of harsh State laws. In Philadelphia in 1783 five men were about to be put to death for one robbery, and the press commented on the fact that the sole plea for mercy came from the widowed and destitute mother of one. Two veterans of Burgoyne's army, men in want, committed a robbery without violence and were executed for it in 1784 in Cambridge, Mass. In Essex County, N. J., in 1786, people were horrified that a young man sentenced to hang for burglary showed bravado, not contrition. In Maryland in the summer of 1786 two men were put to death for burglary and two more for horse-thieving. In the summer of 1785 the whole country was interested in the execution of a man in Philadelphia for assaulting a servant girl. In the fall of 1787 two men, one protesting innocence, were executed for counterfeiting in Charleston. Some of the lesser sentences are only less horrifying. In Rhode Island in the fall of 1783 a man who stole a horse was given 117 stripes at the cart-tail, his estate was confiscated, and he was banished; while as he had set fire to his cell, he had the letter A branded on both cheeks. In Springfield, Mass., two years later, a wight named Wheeler, for coining fifty base dollars, was set in the pillory, drawn to the gallows and kept there an hour with his rope about his neck, given twenty stripes, his left arm was cut off, and he was sent to hard labor for three years. Pennsylvania and New York in 1787 each let a counterfeiter off with branding and hard labor for life. In many States women were publicly whipped on the bare back for larceny, receiving as much as 39 lashes with a cat-o'-nine-tails. In Connecticut a man was actually punished for perjury under the famous law of 1784; he was branded on the forehead, and sentenced to wear a halter for the remainder of his life.

For American acquaintance with Beccaria, see Rowland's "Carroll"; and Md. *Journal*, December 13, 1785. An Englishman, Rack, author of "The Inequality of Our Penal Laws," was read in America; Pa. *Mercury*, April 28, 1786.

[69] N. Y. *Packet*, May 1, 1786; N. J. *Journal*, April 10, 1788; "Laws of New York, 1777-1801," I, 649, II, 242 ff.; "Mass. Acts and Laws, 1787," p. 650; "Laws of Pennsylvania," 1810 Ed., Chs. 1110, 1137.

[70] N. Y. *Packet*, March 27, 1787.

in all, who had been in jail more than a year for a single debt which he might have discharged in less than that time if free; his creditor was a man in the same business who wished to escape competition.[71] The Society for the Relief of Distressed Debtors during 1788 furnished food to more than a hundred imprisoned persons, for many never knew where their next meal would come from, brought blankets and fuel, and procured the discharge of twenty-six.[72] Maryland in 1787 passed a law, limited to one year, enabling an insolvent debtor to pass through bankruptcy proceedings to freedom, but the effort to extend it in 1788 failed.[73] In both Boston and Philadelphia a good deal of futile agitation was at different times set on foot for imprisoned debtors.[74] Readers of the Pennsylvania *Packet* could see such advertisements as the following from time to time:

Old Gaol, Feb. 28 [1783].

Now confined for debts, about £40, one who can make over, on security, a house which rents for £20 per annum, exclusive of ground rent. Whoever will be so humane as to lend the above sum, will not only relieve me from a cold gaol and unmerciful creditors' cost of suits (as I paid last summer near £4, now have the same sum to pay for the same debt) but likewise save my property, and enable me to follow my trade, to help support myself in my old age, being now sixty-three.[75]

In still another field reform was slow. Conditions in the prisons almost everywhere at this date would be unbelievable had there not persisted down to our own time prison abuses which show how much a ruder, rougher age might tolerate. Too often the State and larger city prisons were identical, the State not spending the money for

[71] N. Y. *Packet*, March 6, 1787.
[72] N. Y. *Journal*, February 19, 1789.
[73] There is no need here to recite all the various stay laws and laws temporarily protecting the bodies of debtors passed in the paper-money agitation of 1785-86, though their influence was salutary. How little the humane purpose of Maryland's law was appreciated may be gathered from the appeal of "A Real Federalist" before the election of delegates to the State ratifying convention in 1788: "Elect no man who supported the law allowing insolvent debtors to discharge their persons from perpetual imprisonment, by *honestly* delivering up *all* their property to the use of their creditors. The Legislature have no *right* to interfere with *private* contracts, and debtors might safely trust to the humanity and clemency of their creditors, who will not keep them in gaol all their lives unless they deserve it." Md. *Journal*, March 21, 1788. See Md. *Journal*, June 1 and July 11, 1787, for the workings of the law. The vote on its rejection in 1788 was 39 to 12; Md. *Journal*, June 3, 1788.
[74] See A. B.'s article, Boston *Independent Chronicle*, January 22, 1784: "The perusal of a late piece in the *Independent Chronicle*, soliciting charity for those unhappy men confined for debt in this town must excite the ardent wish of every man of benevolence, that some method might be adopted to relieve those distrest sufferers. . . ." The keeper of the Philadelphia jail in 1785 certified that of 151 persons there confined, about one-half were debtors, of whom not more than fifteen could support themselves; the other 60 being so miserably poor that they must perish with hunger and cold unless fed and clothed by charitable people. Most of them were confined for small debts, and were yet hopeless of ever paying them. A grand jury which visited the Philadelphia jail in 1786 "found many unhappy creatures, confined for insignificant debts by the cruelty of hard-hearted creditors. Among these were five men and two women, making in all seven persons, whose collective debts amounted to not quite so many pounds." The jury contributed its wages to relieve them. *American Museum*, IV, 37-38 (July, 1788); Pa. *Packet*, September 25, 1786.
[75] March 1, 1783.

separate incarceration. It was usual to herd the convicted, of all ages and both sexes, together inside the prison structure; in New York, Philadelphia, and other cities the males were employed in a body upon the streets—as "wheelbarrow men"—working, with a distinguishing dress, a ball and chain, and an armed guard, where the idle and malevolent could insult them.[76] In many prisons the inmates were suffered to go in filthy rags, and their beds were dirty and verminous. They had inadequate facilities for washing, and the men could seldom shave. The night rooms were swept and washed at infrequent intervals. Diseases, including the "jail fever" whose ravages Howard found so terrible in England, were common. The cells were freezing cold in winter, and the food served was a veritable starvation ration. The world-wide practise of garnish or chummage, by which the jailor or the other inmates compelled a newcomer to part with all his money or to strip, was firmly planted in American jails, while the jailers were frequently brutish fellows, caring nothing for the woes of those they supervised, willing to see them perish in swarms from typhus, and not only extorting special fees, but making an enormous profit out of the sale of food and drink.[77]

Bad as the physical conditions were, the social and moral evils were the worst. Respectable debtors, including women, and many others completely innocent of real wrong-doing, were compelled to mingle with the brutally depraved. The Grand Jury of Philadelphia County in 1787 complained that the prison was "open, as to a general intercourse between the criminals of the different sexes; and that there is not even the appearance of decency (from what they can learn) with respect to the scenes of debauchery that naturally result from such a situation, insomuch . . . that the gaol has become a desirable place for the more wicked and polluted of both sexes." They added that the jailer sold liquor to all.[78] A year previous the

[76] Sometimes there was an iron collar around the neck. Passers-by would furnish the wheelbarrow men with charity, and sometimes plied them with rum; riots among them were not uncommon; Pa. *Packet*, August 25, 1787; N. Y. *Packet*, May 25, June 29, 1787; Pa. *Mercury*, Oct. 16, 1788; N. Y. *Advertiser*, January 16, 1788.

[77] See Pa. *Packet*, October 12, 1789, for opinions of public regarding Reynolds, keeper of the Philadelphia jail.

[78] They further complained "that the common hall, originally intended for the accommodation of debtors only, is become a place of resort for the criminals and debtors indiscriminately. It is with considerable concern that the jury mentions that . . . many worthy characters who have been so unfortunate as to be confined there for debt, who have once seen better days, and have been reduced by misfortune, should not have the liberty of a place to receive the air, without being interrupted by wretches who are a disgrace to human nature; together with the horrid noise of chains, and disorder of every kind. . . ." Pa. *Gazette*, September 26, 1787.

grand jury had reported that with some of the women herded into the jail they had found "their innocent though imprisoned children, from two to ten years of age; what can be expected from those whose infancy is passed in such a nursery as this?" [79] A writer of the post-Revolutionary generation described the Philadelphia prison of these years with horror:

No separation was made of the most flagrant offender and convict, from the prisoner who might, perhaps, be falsely suspected of some trifling misdemeanor; none of the old, hardened culprits from the youthful, trembling novice in crime; none even of the fraudulent swindler from the unfortunate and possibly the most estimable debtor; and . . . intermingled with all these, in one corrupt and corrupting assemblage, were to be found the disgusting object of popular contempt, besmeared with filth from the pillory; the unhappy victim of the lash, streaming with blood from the whipping post; the half naked vagrant; the loathsome drunkard; the sick, suffering with various bodily pains, and too often the unaneled malefactor, whose precious hours of probation had been numbered by his earthly judge.[80]

Young and impressionable youths became familiar, when cast into these jails, with the names, trades, and abodes of counterfeiters, pick-pockets, and thieves, learned the locations and attractions of all the dens of vice in town, and were drawn into partnerships in villainy. Older men of character found their self-respect hard to preserve. It required a strong will to resist the temptation to neglect one's physical condition—to let the hair grow, the teeth decay, the skin crack for want of washing, the nails become long. Women suffered most from the lack of separation, and instances are recorded in which ladies of the highest character were confined with scoundrels whose victims they became.[81]

The beginnings of reform we find in Pennsylvania. Here in 1776 was founded the Philadelphia Society for Assisting Distressed Prisoners, this being the year before the publication of Howard's epoch-making work on "The State of Prisons in England." The members were few, and the body was dissolved when the British entered the city; but in 1787, just after the first improvement of the criminal code, some philanthropic men established the Philadelphia Society for Alleviating the Miseries of Public Prisons, the early members including Tench Coxe and Benjamin Rush. Their pity was aroused, the founders stated, at sight of "the miseries which penury, hunger, cold, unnecessary severity, unwholesome apartments, and guilt (the usual attendants of prisons) involve"; and their principal objects were

---

[79] Pa. *Packet*, September 25, 1786; cf. Pa. *Mercury*, July 22, 1785.
[80] "Notice of the Discipline of the Prison at Philadelphia," Roberts Vaux, 1826.
[81] See first report of the Prison Discipline Society, 1826. Intoxication and fighting seem to have been common in the New York jail. See Providence *Gazette*, November 21, 1789.

to have all the prisons visited weekly, to report abuses, to investigate the effects of the punishments prescribed, and to suggest improvements in discipline and penal method.[82] The president for the first forty years was Bishop William White of the Episcopal Church.

How dire was the need for such an organization may be inferred from the petition of prisoners in the Philadelphia jail to charitable citizens, published in January, 1785. They recited that two men had just died there of starvation; that the allowance of food by the authorities, half of a fourpenny loaf each day, was totally insufficient; and that many more would inevitably have died of cold and hunger, had it not been for the gifts of some good people, and the assistance they received when working as a wheelbarrow gang in the streets. More than sixty poor wretches, however, the petition added, were allowed to work on the barrow only thrice a week, and were in great need.[83]

Within a short time the Society memorialized the Legislature for the substitution of private or solitary labor by the prisoners for public labor, and for the separation of the sexes. As the Philadelphia prison, used also by the State, was only a small two-story building, with underground cells for convicts sentenced to death, there were physical obstacles to the institution of any decent penal system. In 1788, in response to a request from the Supreme Executive Council for information, the Society prepared a detailed report upon the existing abuses. Liquor, it showed, was introduced in quantities as great as twenty gallons a day, and sold at exorbitant prices to inmates—principally the debtors—who were allowed to get it nowhere else. The forcible stripping from prisoners of their clothes or money was common. The Society pointed out "three great evils which call for attention, viz.: the mixture of the sexes, the use of spiritous liquors, and the indiscriminate confinement of debtors and persons committed for criminal offences." There were others only less great, as the oppression connected with the jail fees.

Two years previously, for example, one man, acquitted in court and ordered released, had been held in jail for weeks because he

<hr />

[82] An account of the founding of this society appears in the Pa. *Mercury*, May 25, 1787. An accompanying editorial quotes Burke upon prison reform, and declares of the members: "they will have before their eyes as their model the great Mr. Howard, the *friend of mankind* (whose name has become illustrious throughout Europe, and is just rising in deserved estimation among us), in their hands his book."
[83] Pa. *Packet*, January 31, 1785.

could not pay fees of four shillings sixpence demanded by the jailer.[84] It had frequently been demanded that jailers be granted a fixed salary, so that they would not have to wring their support from the wretched people in their care. It was time, too, that heat was provided in winter. In 1789 the Society devised a plan for the permanent improvement of prison discipline, while the Legislature passed a law requiring the keeper to prevent all communication between men and women felons, keep liquor out of the jail; and stop the extortion of perquisites. In 1790 the reformers had the satisfaction of seeing their general plan placed upon the statute books.

The Act of April, 1790, effected a radical change in prison discipline, influential over the whole nation. It instituted a basis of classification, for it enumerated various types of prisoners of each sex, and ordered them separated as much as possible. Prisoners at hard labor were to be kept outside the public view, and their communication with one another was to be greatly restricted. Drink was strictly prohibited, and jail fees and the practise of garnish were abolished. Suitable clothing was provided, and religious instruction arranged. But even after new cells had been constructed in the yard, the jail was too small for fairly testing this system of improvements. The separate confinement of classified groups of prisoners and the prevention of excessive communication was possible only when the number of prisoners was for some reason or another at a minimum. The Society therefore continued to petition for a large new penitentiary, and to point out that it would be more than ever required when the much-needed revision of the penal code was effected.[85]

The feature of the Pennsylvania Act of 1790 which excited the most interest was the plan of punishing the more hardened offenders by placing each in a separate cell for the performance of his tasks. The Act called for the erection in the jail yard of a number of tiny cells, each isolated from the common yard by a wall which would "prevent all external communication." This experiment was watched with interest by States which had witnessed the failure of humiliating public labor. It was thought to succeed, and in due time was taken up elsewhere. In Virginia during the later years of the

[84] Pa. *Packet,* September 25, 1786.
[85] Tyson, "Annual Discourse before the Hist. Soc. of Pa., 1831."

Confederation the ground was being paved for it. Jefferson and his co-workers in revising the laws had provided for hard labor on the roads, canals, and other public works as a penalty for serious crimes. The plan of course failed of adoption when the new code failed, in 1786. But Jefferson meanwhile, in Europe, had been struck with the success of a trial in England of solitary labor, had also heard the idea suggested in France, and from a Lyons architect had obtained the copy of a prison-plan for separately confined inmates. This he sent to the elder Latrobe, the architect of a proposed State prison at Richmond, about 1787; and the general building plan was ultimately adopted, though Virginia did not pass a law for solitary labor until after the adoption of the Federal Constitution. As we now know, solitary confinement is inhuman, but the movement showed that men were awaking to the existing abuses.

The most striking example of what a place of detention should not be was to be found in Connecticut. Here shortly before the Revolution there was selected as a general prison an old copper-mine at Newgate, in Granby township, on the western slope of a high hill fourteen miles north of Hartford. In the fall of 1773 a legislative committee reported that it had prepared "a well-finished room" of twelve by fifteen feet and placed over the shaft an iron door; and an act was passed constituting "the subterraneous caverns and buildings" a jail for burglars, horse-thieves, and counterfeiters. To thrifty-minded Assemblymen, and Connecticut legislators never lacked thrift, the paramount advantage of this ready-made prison was its cheapness; but it was also chosen because escape would be difficult, and the prospect of confinement underground would probably strike terror to criminals. Three parallel galleries ran toward the heart of the hill, extending some eight hundred feet, and connecting by many cross-passages. The greatest depth reached was three hundred feet. The galleries were low and narrow, being cut through solid rock, but they expanded to a considerable height in a central chamber which was fitted up with sleeping accommodations for the convicts. Their floors were covered with slime, and in some places during rainy seasons with shallow pools, fed by an unceasing drip from the roofs. The darkness was of course intense. Happily, the mine was warm in winter, and fairly cool in summer.

Connecticut committed her first prisoners to Newgate at the end of 1773. Two years later she began to remit thither her political prisoners—Tories, suspected spies, and stray Britons, many of them men of education, character, and means. They naturally raised a great outcry over the cruelty of such underground incarceration. In 1781 twenty-eight prisoners rose against their keepers and escaped. After the war repairs were made, and a harsher discipline was instituted. Many of the prisoners were chained to a beam overhead while working at nailmaking or cooperage. In the basement of the guardhouse was a comparatively comfortable room in which those guilty of the less serious crimes were disposed—the "jug"; the others were kept in the dirty central cavern at night, huddled in an indiscriminate body in wooden bunks under a wet roof, and against damp walls. Their clothes mouldering on their backs from the dampness, racked by tuberculosis and rheumatism, and tormented by vermin and rats, the prisoners must have suffered greatly. Yet the more abandoned used to volunteer for the remotest dungeons, as places of night confinement, it being explained that they could there "curse and swear and fight, and do other unutterable abominations," unmolested. Probably, stated the Prison Discipline Society many years after this period, "there has never been on earth a stronger emblem of the pit than the sleeping rooms of that prison, so filthy, so crowded, so inclined to evil, so unrestrained." There was no classification, and as Timothy Dwight remarked, "the young adventurer in villainy was in effect put to school to the adept." [86]

In other New England States the penal conditions till long after 1789 were such as to belie the reputation of the section for enlightenment and humanity. Neither New Hampshire nor Vermont built state penitentiaries till early in the next century, for crime was so rare that the expense seemed unnecessary. The former had possessed an old Provincial jail at Portsmouth, but its wretched state, which had excited frequent comment, made it necessary to rely upon local places of detention. Massachusetts was awakened in 1785 by the exploits of certain notorious thieves, such as Stephen Burroughs, who broke from county jail after county jail with ease, setting the laws at naught, to the necessity of providing a secure State prison. In March of that year the General Court provided for a jail on Castle Island, in Boston Harbor, for all persons sentenced to confinement at hard labor. Four years later the Legislature ac-

[86] For matter upon the Newgate prison see C. B. Todd, "In Olde Connecticut," Ch. 12; Kendall's "Travels"; Dwight, "Travels," I, Letter 27; "Report of Prison Discipline Society," 1826.

cepted the principle that disgraceful punishments in public should give way to confinement at hard indoor labor, and thereby made the need for increased prison facilities a pressing one. But the Castle Island prison did not meet it. There were no solitary cells, and visitors described the place as having "the air of a school for sin and infamy." [87] In Rhode Island the Newport jail had been used by the Provincial authorities for Provincial malefactors; and when after the Revolution it was seen that a change was urgent, the Providence jail, which had been built many years before at a cost of only £2000, and was wholly unsuitable, was utilized. Yet during the troubled period of the Confederation there was not even an agitation for a decent prison.

County or municipal jails were employed by New York for State prisoners until near the end of the century. Conditions were worse in the Bridewell in New York city than among the State convicts, but this was only because the Bridewell was the more crowded; the administrative system was equally bad in both instances. In New Jersey also the State relied upon the county prisons.[88] Maryland kept her stocks, pillory, and whipping post during the period of the Confederation. She had no State jail; the principal prison was that of Baltimore County, which had been built together with the county courthouse under an act of Assembly passed in 1768.[89] The pillory and whipping post stood under the courthouse. Many convicts were sent to work upon the public roads, being employed as were prisoners in some Southern States for a half-century after the Civil War; that is, in gangs, chained together at the ankle and sometimes also at the waist, and guarded by armed overseers. At night they were crowded into "blockhouses" along the line of work. But even at this early day the more humane portion of the public frequently expressed its disapprobation of the gang-work and the inevitable accompanying brutality.

Tourists who travelled through the South would have inquired equally in vain for State penitentiaries. Virginia in 1776 threw Tories into a Williamsburg jail in which they suffered so terribly that their complaints brought on a legislative investigation. The committee of inquiry informed the Provincial Convention that the prison was overcrowded; that despite the heat, there was no fit ven-

[87] S. Ca. *State Gazette.* Boston correspondence, February 25, 1795.
[88] Barnes, "Hist. of the Penal, Reformatory, and Corrective Institutions of N. Jersey."
[89] Scharf's "Maryland," II, 43.

tilation; that some of the rooms were kept clean, but others abounded in filth; and that even in the clean rooms there was a smell so offensive that it would injure men of the most robust health. They added that one old man was in a fever, proceeding probably from his "peevishness" under his chain.[90] We know little about the Carolina or Georgia prisons, but that little is not reassuring. Thus we find a Charleston grand jury in 1795, for example, presenting as a grievance "the horrid situation of the gaol." [91]

V.   Changes in Education

As new social and political conditions were evolved during and after the Revolution, there came changes in education to correspond with them. The organization of the schools and the means of fostering them varied greatly in different States in 1776. It is a familiar fact that in Europe wherever Calvinism, Lutheranism, and Puritanism prevailed, universal education was likely to be cherished by the people, and there alone. Hence wherever in America the influence of Puritanism, Scotch Presbyterianism, or the Dutch Reformed Church was strong, a sturdy growth of free public schools presently appeared; while in Colonies where the Anglicans had a dominant social or governmental position, a more aristocratic ideal had a repressing effect upon democratic education. In the New England Colonies outside of Rhode Island there was a generous and far-sighted government activity in education up to the Revolution. In New York and the Middle Colonies generally the parochial system had been early planted by the Quaker, Lutheran, Mennonite, and other churches; these church schools were supplemented by charitable schools, and the idea grew up that the only government interference necessary was in assisting the maintenance of pauper tuition. In Virginia, the Carolinas, and Georgia most children of the well-to-do were taught by tutors or in private schools; and while there were some church schools, they were few compared with those of the Middle Colonies.

Several decades before the Revolution there appeared evidences that north of the Potomac, and especially in New England, European educational ideas and procedure were being modified, and that American schools were being differentiated into a type of their own.

[90] Eckenrode, "Rev. in Va.," 153-54.
[91] S. Ca. *Gazette,* January 26, 1795.

By 1750 the common schools of New England were being recognized as town schools, not church schools—a recognition impossible a century before, when town and church-society had in many ways been identical. As population flowed westward in New England, the towns ceased to be compact communities, but spread over dozens of square miles of hill, plain, and forest, with small settlements dotted here and there. The people in the half-inaccessible outskirts of these sprawling towns needed and demanded schools of their own, so that before 1760 the district school system—unfortunate but inevitable—began to take firm root. Improved texts competed with such crude and narrowly religious books as the New England Primer, which had first appeared in 1690, and had rapidly spread to the borders of Maryland. A decline began to be evident in the Latin grammar schools—at the famous Boston Latin School, founded in 1634, had been educated Franklin, Hancock, Cushing, Bowdoin, Robert Treat Paine, Sr., and Samuel Adams [92]—because they were not sufficiently practical and democratic; and the distinctively American academy began to rise in its place. Two new urban colleges, Pennsylvania and King's, both founded only a few years before George III mounted the throne, aligned themselves with this practical tendency, the former becoming noted for scientific and medical instruction. In obedience to the democratic movement Yale in 1767 and Harvard in the year of the Boston tea-party, ceased to list their students according to the social rank of their parents. Education on this continent was ceasing to be English, and growing American.[93]

The Revolution afforded a new basis for this movement. At first, to be sure, it seemed that its influence was negative, not positive. The war struck a disastrous blow at education all over the Union. Teachers enlisted, funds were appropriated to military purposes, and interest in cultural affairs flagged. Charity schools were usually the first to close, but private and even town schools soon followed them. In New York city the schools almost went out of existence when the British took possession. In New Hampshire scarcely a vestige of grammar school education was left in 1781.[94] Moreover, when the

---

[92] S. A. Drake, "Old Landmarks and Historic Personages of Boston," 57.
[93] See the histories of education in Massachusetts and Connecticut by G. H. Martin and B. C Steiner respectively.
[94] Dartmouth College, which Governor John Wentworth did so much to found and which was opened in 1770, sturdily survived the war. Phillips Exeter Academy began instruction in 1778, and exerted a wide influence, causing other academies soon

several States began to take action to regulate education, it was sometimes retrogression, not progress. But good or bad, in the sum it showed that Americans were going to develop their own educational institutions to fit their own needs, and that in the end they would move forward rapidly. It showed that the whole basis of education had changed and improved. That basis had been, for British America as a whole, primarily religious. The Revolution made the primary basis political. It made the citizenship self-governing, and vastly enlarged the bounds of that citizenship; and it was recognized that the men who cast the ballots and ran for offices should be educated men.

Scarcely had the Revolution ended before leading statesmen were expressing this idea that in an independent America, the government must support education, or thoughtfulness and knowledge would cease to be pillars of the state. While the British still held New York city, Jan. 27, 1782, Governor Clinton urged on the legislature the promotion and encouragement of learning. Besides the general advantages, he said, they would find that "it is the peculiar duty of the government of a free State where the highest employments are open to citizens of every rank to endeavor by the establishment of schools and seminaries to diffuse that degree of literature which is necessary to the establishment of public trusts." Jefferson wrote Madison in 1787, just after a number of States had shown what confusion could be wrought in financial affairs by an ignorant electorate, in the same vein: "Above all things, I hope the education of the common people will be attended to; convinced that on this good sense we may rely with the most security for the preservation of a due degree of liberty." John Adams, in his "Defence of the Constitutions," written in 1786-87, remarked that the instruction of the people, in the practise of their moral duties "and of their political and civil duties, as members of society and freemen, ought to be the care of the public, and of all who have any share in the conduct of its affairs, in a manner that never yet has been practised in any age or nation." Jay and Madison might be quoted to the same effect, and Washington's injunction in his Farewell Address.[95]

to be founded. Washington sent two of his nephews to be educated there. Sanborn, "N. H.," 242.

[95] Cf. Academicus, addressing the convention which drew up the Virginia Constitution in 1776; Va. *Gazette,* May 31, 1776. He exhorted the members to remember "that it is *learning* alone which can give any lasting stability to your structure; for will a soul, grovelling in ignorance, perceive the value of that Constitution which you now design to frame?" He asked for aid to William and Mary College.

In seven among the original thirteen States, the first Constitutions said nothing upon schools or education—in Virginia and South Carolina, in all of the Middle States except Pennsylvania, and in New Hampshire. Two States made no Constitutions, leaving four which treated the subject in their fundamental law. Yet John Adams, in his "Thoughts on Government" addressed to Wythe early in 1776, writing of the new Constitutions, had stated that "Laws for the liberal education of youth, especially of the lower class of people, are so extremely wise and useful, that, to a humane and generous mind, no expense for this purpose would be thought extravagant." Of the four State Constitutions which mentioned education, that of Georgia simply directed the establishment of schools in each county, to be supported at State expense; that of North Carolina ordered the State to maintain a school or schools for youth, and that of Pennsylvania a school in each county, "at low prices," while in both States learning was to be promoted in one or more universities; and that of Massachusetts contained an admirably full section, declaring it the duty of the legislatures and magistrates to cherish learning in all its seminaries, especially at Harvard, in the public schools, and the town grammar schools. In her second Constitution, New Hampshire copied the Massachusetts provision. Delaware, in her second Constitution, briefly ordered the Legislature to establish schools. The first Constitution of Vermont, that of 1777, directed the towns to maintain schools at low prices, a grammar school in each county, and a university for the State—an admirable section.

Until 1789, there was almost no legislation in the States affecting the status of the common schools. Recovering from the shock of the war, the country felt too poor to undertake new responsibilities in this field. A committee of the regents of the University of the State of New York, including Hamilton, Jay, and Duane, recommended in February, 1787, the public promotion of schools, but none was established for several years. Pennsylvania similarly lagged. Jefferson in 1779 brought forward in Virginia an admirably comprehensive plan for a State system of general elementary education and higher training, but his bills received no legislative approval until 1796. In North Carolina the constitutional injunction that the Legislature establish a school or schools for inexpensive education was disregarded. Vermont, at one extremity of the nation, and Georgia at the other, were alone in taking constructive action. The former in 1782 authorized the division of towns into districts, provided for the supervision of district schools, and arranged for their maintenance partly by a rate-bill upon parents and partly by taxes and subscriptions; while State aid was also granted. In Georgia Governor Lyman Hall, a native of Connecticut and a graduate of Yale, furnished the impulse for educational legislation. In 1783 he urged upon the Legislature "an early foundation for seminaries of learning," and it at once granted a thousand acres to each county for the support of schools, this proving especially useful in encouraging academies. New York, Pennsylvania, Maryland, and South Carolina all took notable steps for the endowment of higher education, but even in this field progress was for some years to be very slow.

Much might be said of the effect of liberty upon the States in awakening a new interest in internal improvements—there was a burst of proposals for waterways and roads after the peace. The Revolution meant a great deal to the press, freeing it from a governmental scrutiny of the political utterances of books and periodicals which in many Colonies had been close, and had resulted in a number of famous legal battles. Mason's Bill of Rights declared that the "freedom of the press is one of the great bulwarks of liberty and can never be restrained but by despotic governments." Declarations of the same purport were made in the early Constitutions of all the other Southern States, the New England States, and Pennsylvania. Much might be said upon other of the results of independence upon State affairs. But it is sufficient to repeat that the political revolution constituted only half of the history of the American people written between Lexington and Yorktown; that a social and an intellectual revolution also occurred.

CHAPTER ELEVEN

THE STATES AND THEIR MONEY AFFAIRS

THE republic had to begin its history with the worst of financial expedients, an emission of paper money. To the second Continental Congress a committee of the New York Provincial Congress, headed by Gouverneur Morris, presented a report upon the possible methods of raising money for the nation's needs. It believed that an issue of bills would be the soundest measure if they were given immediate and general circulation, and if means were provided for redeeming them. If this were done, it added, the paper "will be a new bond of union to the associated Colonies, and every inhabitant thereof will be bound in interest to endeavor that ways and means be fallen upon for sinking of it." [1] Three modes of procedure were available. Each Colony might print for itself the sum apportioned by Congress; or Congress might print the whole, and each Colony become responsible for redeeming its proportionate share; or Congress might print the whole, and apportion the several shares to the different Colonies, but require that if one Province defaulted, its sister Provinces must pay its debt. The committee favored the third plan, and Congress adopted it. On June 22, 1775, it decided to issue bills of credit, not bearing interest; and £3,000,000 was duly emitted.

This emission, earnestly opposed by Franklin and others who wished to obtain money by floating popular loans, was divided among the States on the basis of their supposed population, including negroes. It was not a strictly fair basis, but nearly enough so, for wealth bore a roughly direct ratio to population. Virginia's allotment was the highest, $496,278, and Delaware's the lowest, $37,219.60. There was of course much Congressional guesswork in the estimates of population.[2] According to the program of Congress, each Colony was to sink its quota in four equal payments, a

[1] 4 American Archives, II, 1262.
[2] Congress early asked for State censuses. A Congressional committee in the spring of 1783 made the following computation: New Hampshire, 82,200 white inhabitants; Rhode Island, 50,400; Massachusetts, 350,000; Connecticut, 206,000; New York, 200,000; New Jersey, 130,000; Pennsylvania, 320,000; Delaware, 35,000; Maryland,

year apart, beginning November 30, 1779. For this end they were to levy special taxes, and send the proceeds to Philadelphia in Continental bills, Colony bills, or gold and silver. But as it became plain that the difficulties with England would be long-continued, three millions was seen to be a totally inadequate sum, and before the end of 1775 another issue of the same amount, against the renewed protest of Dr. Franklin, was voted.

Congress continued issuing paper in ever-heavier quantities until the spring of 1780, and the bills depreciated faster and faster. There were thirty-seven emissions in all. Their steadily increasing size was necessitated by the more and more appalling drop of the paper in value, and it became clear that if the pace were kept up, the printing presses would soon be turning out money by the billion. The rake's progress had to be stopped. Congress tried to reassure the public in the summer of 1779 by pointing out that if the national debt at the end of the war reached $300,000,000, this would be only a hundred dollars for every inhabitant, an amount trifling if its payment were spread over twenty years. But at the end of the year it was plain that redemption of the paper at face value, or anything like it, would be impossible. On March 18, 1780, Congress therefore took the momentous step of a qualified repudiation of the Continental bills.

In face value these squarish bits of yellow paper with which the country had been snowed under were worth well over $240,000,000, but Congress agreed that it would be liberal to estimate their actual specie worth at $5,000,000. The States were therefore asked to send Congress $15,000,000 a month for thirteen months in these old bills, and Congress promised to repay the States with a new issue, at the rate of one dollar of the new for forty of the old. The old Continental bills were of course to be destroyed as they came in. To keep the new issue sound and valuable, it was to be redeemable in specie in six years, was to bear interest at five per cent., and was to be receivable in payment of taxes. If any State failed to redeem its share, the United States was to be responsible. It was agreed that the new issue should have not more than one-twentieth the face value of the old, which meant not more than ten millions, and that three-fifths of the bills should be paid to the States, and the rest kept in

220,700; Virginia, 400,000; North Carolina, 170,000; South Carolina, 150,000; and Georgia, 25,000, making a total of 2,339,300. N. H. Prov., State, and Town Papers, VIII, 976.

the national treasury. As a matter of fact, less than $4,500,000 worth of the new replacement bills were actually struck off.

Thus terminated the great adventure of Congress with large-scale emissions of paper money. In the end almost $120,000,000 worth of the Continentals was paid into the Congressional treasury, and the holders received $3,000,000 therefor. Of course the virtual repudiation of this immense mass of paper was a heavy blow to thousands of holders. They had parted with valuable property for the nation's promise to pay, and many public-spirited men were ruined.[3]

I. Congressional Demands on the States

Congress had meanwhile tried a variety of expedients to add to the more and more precarious income derived from paper money issues. In 1776 it turned to the plan of Franklin for floating a loan among the people, and asked patriotic Americans to lend five million Continental dollars, to be repaid with interest at four per cent. Such loans were not at this period a common practice among nations. Upon such uncertain security as the American cause offered, and with so low an interest rate, the response was feeble, though not an utter failure. Congress in the same year resorted to a lottery. In January of 1777 it took a long step forward—one which it would certainly have taken long before had it only possessed more faith in the willingness of the State governments to assist it. It called upon the thirteen Legislatures to raise by taxation during 1777 as much money as the wealth of the inhabitants justified, and send it to the Continental treasury. No quotas being fixed, the returns were disappointing, though they also were not a complete failure. Printing press, popular loans, a lottery, and a requisition upon the States had now all been resorted to.[4]

As the issue of paper became more and more plainly a failure, Congress more and more depended upon requisitions, until they became its sole reliance. After the Articles of Confederation had

[3] A Pennsylvania farmer is quoted in the Pa. *Packet*, May 9, 1780: "I am near seventy years of age, I have a large family of children to provide for, a great part of my property has been sold long since for Continental money, which I have kept by me in confidence it would have been redeemed at the value I received it, but I am disappointed and ruined. My loss is very heavy, and it greatly afflicts me; . . . but I will never forsake the cause of liberty and die Tory."
[4] Journals Cont. Cong., VII, 36; A. S. Bolles, "Financial Hist. U. S.," I, 51. As Franklin said, borrowing was not an efficient resource, "because no interest can tempt men to lend paper now, which, paid together with that interest a year hence will not probably be worth half as much as the principal sum is at present."

been sent out for ratification, and Congress saw before it a prospect of definite powers, it was encouraged to make firmer requests of the States, specifying the exact amounts to be raised. At the beginning of 1778 the Legislatures were informed that it would be necessary that year to raise five millions by State taxation. A somewhat arbitrary apportionment was adopted, which took cognizance of such facts as that New York city and its vicinity were occupied by the British and could not pay. It was unnecessary to be scrupulously fair in the appointment, for the sums were regarded as loans, to be repaid with interest. The States were requested that fall to refrain from issuing any more bills of credit upon their own account, and were asked to call in previous issues when possible; it being suggested that they henceforth "provide for the exigencies of war and the support of government by taxes levied within the year, or such other expedient as may produce a competent supply."

One requisition in 1778 and 1779 followed another; and as they were payable in the Continental bills that the printing presses were furiously turning out, they aggregated sums that were nominally huge—those of May and October, 1779, aggregating a total of $60,000,000. The whole amount yielded by the requisitions before Congress called in the depreciated Continentals was $54,667,000 in Continental and State paper, which was equivalent in specie—accepting the scale of depreciation that was used by Congress at the time the various State payments were made—to $1,856,000. After the recall of the Continental bills at 40 to 1, the requisitions were of course for nominally smaller sums, that of January, 1781, when the plight of the nation seemed truly desperate, being for only $890,000. The response of the States was not more vigorous, and the money received from these later requisitions up to the time of the surrender of Cornwallis in October, 1781, was only $1,592,000 in specie. In brief, all the money requisitions from the beginning of the resort to them by Congress in 1777 until the close of active fighting produced the pitiful total of $2,448,000.

Late in 1779 Congress asked the States for grants of specific supplies, or as they were called, "specifics," and ordered its agents to commandeer needed goods.[5] Near the close of the year the States were called upon to forward corn, wheat, and flour in specified

---

[5] The States had been recommended on October 2, 1778, to authorize commissioners to seize goods for the armies. See Bolles, I, 67-68; 89; 93.

amounts to places designated by the Commissary-General, Virginia, for example, being requested to contribute 20,000 barrels of corn. A few days later a general call for supplies was sent out, each State being left free to furnish what it could, and all being assured that as the supplies came in, the States would be credited for them at their money value. These levies "in kind" were a wasteful and otherwise unsatisfactory substitute for the levying of money taxes.

One objection lay in the unevenness of the burden placed upon the States, the South in the closing campaigns bearing more than its share. Another was that the cost of transporting supplies to the troops often exceeded the cost of the same commodities in the vicinity of the army encampments. "It is too precarious a dependence," wrote Hamilton in September, 1780, "because the States will never be sufficiently impressed with our necessities. Each will make its own ease a primary object, the supply of the army a secondary one. The variety of channels through which the business is transacted will multiply the number of persons employed, and the opportunities of embezzling public money. . . . Very little of the money raised in the several States will go into the Continental treasury, on pretense that it is all exhausted in providing the quotas of supplies, and the public will be without funds for the other demands of government." Like all Hamilton's writings on financial subjects, this expressed a shrewd grasp of realities. The actual value of the provisions and other supplies furnished by the States for Congress, from beginning to end, is put by Hamilton's report of 1790 at $881,000.

The year 1781 was notable in the country's history not for the surrender of Cornwallis alone, for it was the year that Robert Morris took charge of national finances. Hamilton had suggested in the spring of 1780, in writing to Morris, that Congress should appoint a minister of finance, and that he would be glad to hear it say to Morris, "Thou art the man." [6] Peletiah Webster in February of the same year urged the appointment of a single officer in place of the Treasury Board, and in September Hamilton declared that "Mr. Robert Morris would have many things in his favor for the department of finance." On February 9, 1781, Congress created the office of Superintendent of Finance, and defined with praiseworthy exactness his duties. Morris entered upon them in the middle of May. A successful Philadelphia merchant, who by twenty years of labor and

[6] See "Works," I, 215-228, 253; III, 61 ff.

enterprise had won the right to live at some ease, he regarded his new burdens with misgiving; for, as he wrote Jay, he knew that the reason for his appointment lay in "the derangement of our money affairs, the enormity of our public expenditures, the confusion in all our departments, the languor of our general system, the complexity and consequent inefficacy of our operations."

Morris saw clearly what ought to be done, but to do it was a different matter. The old resort to one makeshift after another, the timid requests, the dependence upon the good will of the States, the reliance upon such uneconomical and irritating expedients as the calls for specific supplies, must be swept away. In their place taxes ought to be laid in specie, and as far as possible to be imposed and collected by the national government. It was impossible at the time for the government to lay or collect a cent, and while this remained true, it was important that the State payment of national requisitions should somehow be made more regular and certain. Morris wrote with exasperation to Jay in July, 1781: "The various requisitions of Congress to the several States, none of them entirely complied with, create a considerable balance in favor of the United States, and the claiming this balance is delivered over to me as revenue; while on the other hand the dangerous practice of taking articles for the public service, and giving certificates to the people, has created a very general and very heavy debt. . . . If the certificates were not in my way, there is still an infinite difference between the demand of a balance from the States and an effectual revenue."

Morris promptly made a firm gesture. On May 21, 1781, the national treasurer was directed to draw upon the States at thirty days' notice for their unpaid quotas of the requisition of August, 1780, and to give notice that he would call for other quotas as they came due. The States had responded very unevenly to the requisitions, the New England group doing by far the best, and it was hoped that the laggards could somehow be prodded forward. All State payments were of course regarded as loans, to be repaid by the national government with interest. But though theoretically no State lost by paying the government more than its due share of the war-costs, it was plain that actually it ran a great risk of doing so. What if the government never repaid, or paid only in part? Hence the constant State jealousies over money matters, and the complaints of Massachusetts and others that they bore an undue part of the burden; hence the indisposition of many to do more than they could avoid. On July 25 Morris made an appeal to the thirteen State executives. "It gives me great pain to learn that there is a pernicious idea prevalent among some of the States that their accounts are not to be adjusted with the continent," he wrote. "Such ideas cannot fail to spread listless languor over all our operations." But the States proved as recalcitrant in their dealings with the earnest financier as they had been with the careless Treasury Board. "It is like preaching to the dead," Morris said of his appeals. On October 19 he prefaced another Congressional request for funds, $8,000,000 this time, with a new circular explaining that it was impossible to obtain money abroad when none was forthcoming at home, and that the public creditors simply could not be paid until the States awakened to their plain duty.

Once more the response of the States was feeble and uneven, and so it remained. The demand for eight millions for 1782 was followed by one of two millions for the services of 1783. But the whole tax-income of Congress for these two years was computed by Morris at only $1,466,000, and the heavy deficit had to be made up by contracting new debts at home and abroad. In disgust and discouragement, early in 1784 Morris gave notice of his resignation, and there being no person competent or willing to take his place, Congress placed the treasury under three commissioners.[7]

The remaining requisitions up to the year 1789, and the fruit they bore, may be briefly summarized. In the spring of 1784 Congress called for the payment of a total of $2,670,000, partly in specie and partly in "indents"; and it added the liberal provision that all receipts would be credited upon previous unmet requisitions. Even had this sum been paid in full, it would not have discharged all the arrears upon old requisitions; and the next year Congress demanded the whole balance of $3,000,000 due. In each of the three following years there came new requisitions. Hamilton's report and the Report of 1790 disagree in their estimate of the returns, but the differences can be reconciled, showing that the receipts were $1,017,595 in

---

[7] See Oberholtzer's "Robert Morris," Ch. 4. A committee of Congress after conferring with Morris, reported in May, 1782, that further circulars to the States would be useless, but that it was imperative that the most effective means be used to obtain a response to the requisitions. Congress therefore resolved to send John Rutledge and George Clymer southward, and Joseph Montgomery and Jesse Root north and east, to exhort the laggard States to act. They came back discouraged. Some States, they found, had even raised money to meet their quotas, and then had begun applying it to their own uses. Journals Cont. Cong., XXII, 289 ff.

specie, $1,541,631 in "indents," and $27,730 in supplies. After the adoption of the Constitution, in straightening out the accounts with the States, Hamilton credited them with additional receipts to the value of $947,326. The grand total paid by the States to Congress, from the beginning of 1784 to the end of the Confederation, may therefore be placed at $4,434,282.

In the fifteen years 1775-1789 the entire amount obtained from the State governments after vast effort, under the system of requisitions, was about ten and a quarter million dollars; and this though the States represented a sturdy population which, despite the losses from the war, grew markedly in wealth during the period. Of course the national government obtained large sums from the people through its emissions of paper, and considerable sums through the loan offices. The distractions of war, especially in invaded sections, the losses from British devastation, the stoppage of most of our commerce, and the stringency of coin, multiplied the difficulties of the State tax-collectors. But Morris repeatedly expressed his conviction that the States were amply able to pay if they would, and he was quite right. But for Rhode Island's stubbornness at one critical moment, and New York's later, Congress would have won the right to levy a five per cent. duty on imports, thus in a measure making it independent of the States. While it was dependent, their selfishness, their jealousy of one another, and their want of respect for the government of the Confederation, made a reliable national revenue impossible.

The unevenness with which the States shared the national burden was of course great. It is difficult to exhibit it, because, in the first place, no full and correct statement of what the several States paid and failed to pay Congress was ever made out; and in the second, because of the many complicating factors involved, some States suffering more from invasion than others, and some expending much more on their own troops and warships than their neighbors. But we know that during the years 1779-81 inclusive the payments of the States in valid drafts upon their treasuries, as received by Congress, were as follows: Massachusetts, $447,000; Connecticut, $375,000; Virginia, $278,000; Pennsylvania, $188,000; New Hampshire, $123,000; and Maryland, $116,000. New York had furnished $98,000 and North Carolina $73,000, the other five States paying smaller sums. Connecticut was certainly doing much more nearly her full part than Pennsylvania. Hamilton in May, 1790, gave the nation a "general abstract of the sums of money, including indents and paper money of every kind, reduced to specie value, which have been received by, or paid to, the several States by Congress, from the commencement of the Revolution to the present period:"

State	Paid to State	Received from State
New Hampshire	$ 440,974.29	$ 466,544.60
Massachusetts	1,245,737.25	3,167,020.32
Rhode Island	1,028,511.33	310,395.21
Connecticut	1,016,273.15	1,607,259.31
New York	822,803.60	1,545,889.45
New Jersey	366,729.63	512,916.23
Pennsylvania	2,087,276.00	2,629,410.41
Delaware	63,817.60	208,878.68
Maryland	609,617.60	945,537.39
Virginia	482,881.58	1,963,811.71
North Carolina	788,031.12	219,835.79
South Carolina	1,014,808.25	499,325.22
Georgia	679,412.49	122,744.52

These statistics do not tell the whole story.[8] Hamilton admitted that the figures for moneys received from the States did not show "the actual specie value," that being in some instances impossible to ascertain. The South contributed heavily in provisions and other "specifics," not included in the table. But after all allowances have been made, it is evident that the burden was unfairly divided.

II. State Reliance on Paper Money

So much for the direct contributions of the States to the national treasury; what were the expenditures of the States for themselves, and what were the indirect expenditures for the nation? The States had to raise troops and put them into the field; they had to take emergency measures to prevent invasion, to meet it, or to repair its ravages; they had to maintain their own governments. They issued their own paper money, and they had their own difficulties in improvising tax systems, in borrowing abroad, and in obtaining a revenue from commerce. All contracted great debts. Jefferson, in writing of Hamilton's assumption plan, said that "nobody knew what those debts were, what their amount, or what their proofs. . . . We do not know how much is to be reimbursed to one State and how much to another." He hardly exaggerated the confusion and doubt which overlay the accounts of the States like a heavy cloud, and will

[8] Some illuminating supplementary tables may be found in Pitkin, "Hist. U. S.," II, 538. Of course, some States were quite unwilling to accept Hamilton's computation as just. Hamilton's table is printed in American State Papers, "Finances," I, 53.

always overlie them. A complete, detailed record of the finances of all thirteen would be a maze of figures and estimates hardly penetrable and quite profitless.

But a summary view of State finances in the years 1775-1789 is readily obtainable, and it shows that certain generalizations can be made applicable to the financial history of the States as a group. The problem in 1775 of raising enormous sums of money for immediate war purposes was not novel, for the French and Indian wars had presented it, but the conditions were novel—much of the population opposed the war, and the motherland could not, as before, be counted on for ultimate help in wiping out the debts by her reimbursements. The first recourse on any large scale was to paper issues. Then, when the danger of these emissions was discovered, taxation was earnestly attempted, accompanied in most States by a lull in the printing of paper money. In the closing years of the war, 1780-81, the poverty of many communities and their protests against the heavy tax burden forced a sporadic return to bills of credit, but by no means on the former scale. After the war, a gallant effort was made to restore financial stability. Paper was repudiated, or redeemed at a depreciated rate; taxes were levied with new vigor; several States profited largely, and all but a few to some extent (1781-85) by renewed confiscations of Tory property; some States borrowed abroad; lands were sold; and in the commercial States duties returned large sums. In 1785-86 a fresh demand for paper money, inspired by the prevailing hard times, swept the country, but was conquered before it had done great damage.

Nearly all the Colonies had issued much paper money in the eighteenth century, with results so bad that after 1740, when a pound in the New England currency was worth one-fifth, in South Carolina currency one-eighth, and in North Carolina currency one-fourteenth a specie pound, Parliament had tried to check the emissions. Thoughtful colonists were as much opposed as thoughtful Englishmen to excessive issues; and in 1764 Parliament forbade legal tender emissions altogether. Yet paper money of various kinds remained common. In 1774 some $12,000,000 was estimated to be current. The issues were of two main kinds, and Pennsylvania had exemplified the best method. This was to print a certain sum to circulate a

⁹ Amer. State Papers, "Finance," I, 71. See Doyle, "English Colonies in Amer.," London ed. 1907, V, 124 ff; Beer, "British Colonial Policy, 1754-1765," p. 179 ff.

certain period, say ten years; to issue the bills as interest-bearing loans to individuals, amply secured by lands; to repay annually a certain fraction of each loan, one-tenth if redemption was provided for in a decade; and meanwhile to give the treasury the benefit of the interest. This paper, a legal tender, usually passed at face value. Pownall wrote enthusiastically that it provided "the true Pactolian stream, which converts all into gold that is washed by it." [10] The older plan, more widely followed and more easily carried out, was to issue bills simply to pay governmental obligations, pledging certain taxes to redeem them. The paper of one Colony circulated little in any other, so that in 1775 the Massachusetts authorities had to give special orders to secure the acceptance of Connecticut and Rhode Island money.

When the Colonies turned after Lexington to paper issues, they expected the disagreement with the mother land to be temporary, and hoped that the short contest would not prove expensive. The contemporary writer Belknap attributes to this much of the colonists' want of wisdom. "Bills of credit were emitted with no other fund for their redemption than taxation, and that deferred to distant periods. It was imagined that the justice of our cause, and the united ardor and patriotism of the people, would preserve the value of these bills during the contest which we were very sanguine would be short." [11] No one, as another annalist of the time, Ramsay, states, believed at the outset but that the bills would be redeemed promptly and at full value. [12] The machinery for raising adequate sums by taxation existed in no Colony. Governor George Clinton told the legislators at Kingston in September, 1777, that "The want of an organized government has hitherto rendered it impossible to make any provision for sinking the money which the war has obliged us to issue," and other executives could make the same complaint. Had the machinery existed, it would have been crippled in some States by the British or Tories, and if it had existed uncrippled, the people would have been unwilling to make effective use of it. The rattle of musketry near Boston was quickly followed by the rattle of printing presses from New Hampshire to South Carolina. The hard fact is that, under the circumstances, bills offered the only practicable means of financing the war. The first paper emission authorized by a

[10] "Admin. of the Colonies," 4th ed., 186.
[11] Farmer's Edition, 378.
[12] "Hist. of S. Ca.," II, 172-73.

revolutionary authority was ordered by the Provincial Congress of Massachusetts on May 20, 1775, amounting to £26,000.

In many States it is difficult to arrive at the total of emissions of paper. Issues of bills of credit would sometimes be authorized, but not fully made; a new issue would often replace an old one; confusing distinctions were drawn between bills of credit and treasury notes; government promises to pay, as certificates issued in return for loans, for commandeered property, and in lieu of army pay, passed like paper money and were substantially identical with it. It must again be remembered that the States had no uniform currency. "The ideas annexed to a pound, a shilling, and pence are almost as various as the States themselves," said Robert Morris. The Spanish dollar in Georgia meant five shillings, in Virginia and New England six, in North Carolina and New York eight, in South Carolina thirty-two and a half, and elsewhere, seven and a half.[13] To compare the financial dealings of one State with those of another is a vexatiously complicated task.

The specie value of the currency issued by the States during the Revolution was estimated by Jefferson in 1786 at $36,000,000, or just as much as the specie value of the Continental currency. The debts contracted by the States he placed at $25,000,000, as against $43,000,000 contracted by the national government—his estimate of the whole cost of winning our independence being $140,000,000. Hildreth, writing a generation after Jefferson, placed the total cost of the Revolution much higher—$170,000,000—but the share of the States markedly lower. The States, he computed, raised $30,000,000 through taxes and repudiated paper, and contracted $26,000,000 in debts. Hamilton, the best authority, ventured no estimate of the amounts of State paper issued and repudiated, but placed the State debt in 1789 at $21,000,000.[14] Though some States have a fairly good record as regards paper issues, and some a record of gross folly, it is not easy in view of their different situations to apportion praise or blame. Connecticut suffered little from British invasion, Pennsylvania much; Massachusetts was populous, rich, and free from the enemy after the first few months, while North Carolina was poor, of mixed population, and for the last years of the war heavily overrun by the British.

---

[13] Amer. State Papers, "Finance," I, 101 ff.
[14] Bullock, C. J., "Finances of the U. S.," 174-75.

Nearly all the States—North Carolina was an outstanding exception—made their most indiscreet issues in the first two and a half years of the war, before the close of 1777. Most of them then tried to check their emissions, and a number were able to do so completely. The sad teachings of experience were reinforced by urgings from responsible sources. In the last days of 1776 representatives of the four New England States met at Providence to debate fiscal questions. They resolved, in the words of the endorsement voted by the Rhode Island House, "that no further emissions of paper bills be made, but that the several treasuries be supplied by taxes, or by borrowing the necessary sums, to be repaid in three years or sooner . . ." In an emergency, they would approve the striking off of bills for three years or less, supported by taxes. In midsummer of the next year another convention of New England commissioners was held at Springfield, Mass., and again exerted its influence to check the flood of paper.[15] Meanwhile, on February 15, 1777, Congress recommended that the States stop printing bills, recall those already circulating, and rely for a paper medium wholly on the supply authorized by Congress, and this wise demand—it was hardly less—was several times repeated, as on November 22, 1777. Under the latter date, Congress again called for the withdrawal of State issues of paper, and counselled the States to "provide for the exigencies of war and the support of government by taxes levied within the year," or other expedients.[16]

New England turned toward the safe path first of all. Connecticut made her first emission of paper money in April, 1775, when the Assembly voted £50,000 in bills of credit for two years without interest. The next month £50,000 more was voted for three years, and in July, together with a third emission of the same size, the legislators were wise enough to levy a tax for its redemption. Other votes of paper money followed, until by June, 1776, the total authorized was £260,000, and with this the State stopped short; it was high time, for the bills had depreciated so fast that they were now being refused. Resort was had to force laws, the Legislature in October, 1776, making both Continental and Connecticut bills legal tender, and ordering that anyone who tried to depreciate them should forfeit the full value of the money he received and the prop-

[15] N. Y. representatives were present at the second meeting; Records State R. I., VIII, 48; 97-98; 236.
[16] Journals Cont. Cong., VII, 125; IX, 953 ff.; Bolles, I, 148.

erty he offered for sale. This legislation was accompanied by laws setting the prices of various commodities, and was of course a total failure. But the State wisely refused to put forth any more paper money until in 1780 it became possible to do so in lieu of the new Continental bills to which it was entitled. Provision had been made for the redemption of all paper by taxes, and after February 1, 1778, it was called in as fast as possible in order to give a clear field, as Congress requested, to Continental currency.

Even little Rhode Island, whose course later was all that it should not have been, almost ceased the issue of paper money early in 1777. The State suffered greatly from invasion. Newport, the metropolis and seat of wealth and commerce, was in British hands from December, 1776, till October, 1779, and the whole coast was under British guns or open to British marauding parties. In Providence during 1777 the destitute refugees mounted from scores into hundreds, and that year Rhode and Block Islands, and Conanicut, were exempted from taxes on all personal property except cattle. In the two years 1775-76 no less than £152,000 in paper was issued, though the State's population did not exceed 50,000. The first bills, all too generously, carried two and a half per cent interest, and were redeemable by taxes at the end of two and five year periods. As it was learned that other States were striking off paper that bore no interest, provision was made for their hurried recall, and later emissions carried no interest. In December, 1776, the legislature mustered up courage to vote a tax of £40,000, and thenceforth, with one minor exception the following May, it stood by its resolve to print no more bills of credit during the war. It repeatedly borrowed upon treasury notes, usually in anticipation of taxes, but it committed no grosser errors. The borrowings, the taxes, the ravages of the British, and the steady depreciation of State and Continental paper, left Rhode Island financially prostrate in 1781, and in the fall of that year State paper ceased to be legal tender.

Massachusetts and New Hampshire also have a fairly creditable record, for after the initial years of war both ceased to debase their currency and began taxing their people energetically, though both also resorted to heavy borrowings. The Bay State during 1776 made six emissions of bills of credit, totalling £370,042, and then ceased, while New Hampshire made her last regular emission of bills in the spring of 1778. Both issued some of the 40 to 1 paper in 1780, and that was all. But Massachusetts continued till the end of the war to float heavy and constant loans by means of treasury notes. That is, the treasurer received larger and larger sums of paper money in exchange for notes bearing six per cent. interest, and secured by special tax levies. These levies made the nominal burden on the taxpayers heavier and heavier, until in 1780 no less than £11,200,000 was demanded from them; but the actual weight, because of the steady depreciation of money and the growing difficulty of collecting taxes, never became crushing. Immediately after Yorktown an excise act was passed to assure the payment of interest on the State securities. The New Hampshire legislature was forced to abandon paper by the same causes which operated elsewhere. By the end of the second year of the war it had issued £113,600 in bills, while a flood of counterfeits had appeared, so that the money was fast becoming worthless. A legislative committee promptly drew up an improved plan for taxation, and that same year (1777) £40,000 was levied.[17]

In the Middle States we find the same general record. Heavy emissions of paper in 1775-76, extending in some instances to a later date, were followed by a sharp check and a recourse to taxation, which was by no means as heavy as it should have been, and which was accompanied by borrowing.

Pennsylvania had the advantage of wealth, but the disadvantages of a radical government and a population largely disaffected. The first issue of paper money was in June, 1775, and was known as resolve money. Before the year ended no less than £137,000 had been voted, more followed in 1776, and in March, 1777, another £200,000 was struck off. Then emissions were wisely stopped until the spring of 1780. Depreciation was of course rapid. In a little over twenty months, nearly half a million pounds had been issued, in addition to a mass of old provincial money still circulating, and the torrent of Continental bills. As elsewhere, the State paper was a legal tender for debts, and dishonest men seized with avidity upon the temporary opportunity it offered of discharging them cheaply. The prostration of trade in 1779 evoked an inquiry by special city committees, which found that the unwillingness of farmers and merchants to exchange goods for rag money was crippling

---

[17] Massachusetts Acts and Laws, 1775-80, 61, 64, 71, 74, 84, 96, 99, 101, 126, et passim; New Hampshire Province, State, and Town Papers, VIII, 520, 588, 722, 779, 823. Lotteries were repeatedly used by Massachusetts to raise money.

the supply of the army. Though less effectively than in Connecticut or Massachusetts, the authorities turned to high taxation.

New York also threw much paper into circulation in 1775-76, so that by the time the State Government was well established the load of obligations was alarming. Governor Clinton in September, 1777, told the Legislature that its failure to provide a sinking fund had burdened the people with debt and was striking at the very root of the currency. Attempts at price regulation merely aggravated the evil. "The only effectual remedy is that of reducing the quantity of circulating medium by taxation," he said, recommending laws to this end. The legislators were willing to stop the emissions, but they viewed a reduction of the early issues by taxation with reluctance. There were no paper issues after 1777 until the 40 to 1 bills appeared, and in 1778 an act was passed for cancelling all bills having a face value of a dollar or less. The Governor's message of 1779 once more referred to the falling value of the paper currency, and the necessity of supplying a cure. A joint legislative committee thereupon reported that "frequent and heavy taxes equally laid on all real and personal property, and such voluntary loans as might be granted to the United States," would prevent the further issue of paper and restore its credit. Tardily and half-heartedly, New York took the proper road. This year the tax-bill called for $2,500,000, and the Senate tried unsuccessfully to make it $3,500,000; while in 1780 provision was made for the collection within nine months of $7,500,000 in the depreciated currency of the time. Maryland's financial history was substantially similar.[18]

The South witnessed the greatest abuses of State credit, and had the least success in the imposition and collection of taxes. The economic shock of the war was especially grave in the section which depended upon the export of tobacco and other bulky agricultural products. Moreover, just as the thirteen States were turning

---

[18] For Pennsylvania's paper money record see Laws of Pennsylvania, 1918 ed., I, chapters 741, 896, etc.; for the report of the city committee on trade in 1779 see the *Pa. Packet*, Sept. 25, 1779. New York's fiscal measures are contained in Laws 1777-1801, ed. 1886-87, I; consult the index. For Maryland's paper money laws see Scharf's "Maryland," II, 476-480, and the published laws for each year. The statute relating to the 40-to-1 bills is Chapter 7, June session, Laws of 1780. Maryland's revolutionary government at first raised funds by subscription from the various counties, and by taxes. Then repeated emissions of paper were made, until by the close of 1777 no less than $1,077,000 in bills was outstanding; and the issues were halted. When Congress called in the Continental bills at the 40-to-1 rate, Maryland provided that all State money should similarly be redeemed by a new emission at the same rate; and amply secured it by real property.

towards improved financial measures, the South became the seat of the active fighting.

Virginia's policy was to authorize enormous issues of treasury notes, virtually identical with bills of credit, and secured by no real provision for redemption by taxes. The authorizations soon became huge. As early as the spring of 1777 we find one for a million dollars; between the fall of 1780 and the spring of 1781 they aggregated £45,000,000. Just what quantity of State notes went into circulation it is impossible to say, but the sum was very great, and it was swollen by counterfeiting. The inevitable consequence ensued—the obligations became almost valueless. Just after the surrender of Cornwallis, this fact was recognized by a sweeping measure of repudiation, which annulled all the State's fine promises to pay in full, and impoverished the Virginians who were patriotic enough to have exchanged valuable property for treasury notes. All holders were bade to bring their paper in within a specified time, and receive a loan office certificate for one dollar in return for every $1,000 surrendered. A millionaire in paper money, in other words, would get $1,000! We may contrast this step with Maryland's redemption of all her State money at the 40 to 1 rate used by Congress, and with Connecticut's scrupulous honoring of all obligations.

North Carolina's financial history bears much the same appearance of recklessness, though we must remember that in the last years of the war she and Virginia, trampled by contending armies, were in an unfortunate position. The Provincial Congress threw $125,000 into circulation in the fall of 1775, and in April, 1776, added $250,000 more, the total amounting to £150,000. The State government made a brave effort throughout 1777 to support the war by the proceeds of taxes and loan offices, but circumstances proved too strong for the legislators. In August, 1778, they placed £830,000 in circulation, of which £630,000 was to be used in redeeming issues by the Colony and the Provincial Congress. One emission followed another until the total for the years 1775-80 inclusive was no less than $6,500,000. In the last stages of the war the distribution of certificates for various treasury purposes became prodigious, and in the single year 1781 the sum of $26,250,000 was authorized in bounties to volunteers. North Carolina's whole population did not exceed 260,000, and it was a poor population, so that when all allowance is made for depreciation, these amounts remain shocking.[19]

We know that the people of South Carolina were unfortunately circumstanced for five years before the Revolution. Heavy importations of slaves and luxuries—3,000 to 5,000 negroes annually just before the war—had drained away the specie, and little gold or silver circulated beyond the immediate vicinity of Charleston; while no emission of paper had taken place since 1746, save a very small one in 1770. Barter was necessarily substituted for trade with money in many places. Just before the war two expedients were hit upon to lessen the inconvenience which this entailed in business. The Assembly clerk in 1774 gave certificates to the public creditors stating that their demands had been recognized as valid, and so sound was the government's credit that the certificates passed as money. Again, five men of wealth, Henry Middleton, Roger Smith, Miles Brewton, Benjamin Huger, and Thomas Lynch, in April, 1775, issued joint and several notes of hand in convenient denominations payable to the bearer, and these readily went into circulation at face value.

The first patriot emission of paper money in South Carolina took place in June, 1775, and the last during the active conflict was made four years later, in the spring of 1779. Within this period the issue of more than £10,000,000 was authorized, but much of it was conditional upon the failure of appeals for loans, and Ramsay tells us that only £7,817,553 in ostensible face value really went into circulation.[20] We should bear in mind that the pound in South Carolina was worth less than one-fourth as much as the same denomination in North Carolina and New York, and about one-seventh as much as the pound sterling; and when we make allowance also for the rapid depreciation, the real value of the emissions at the time they appeared was about £480,000 sterling in specie. This sum, however, was itself large for a State of small population and an empty treasury. During nearly two years, or until April, 1777, the paper sustained its value, but then fell rapidly, and with it declined credit, financial stability, and the vigor with which the war was being prosecuted. After the beginning of 1778, the Continental bills became more and more common, and as in other sections, accelerated the drop of the State bills. Legislation was enacted

---

[19] For Virginia see Hening's Statutes, IX, 61, 286, 456; Z, 31, 241, 279, 321, 399, 456. A wealth of material on all phases of North Carolina's financial history is to be found in the N. C. State Records, XXIV, covering 1777-1788 inclusive.

[20] Ramsay's "South Carolina," II, 171.

to control the price of goods, and the paper was still held to be a legal tender, but nothing could check its decline.

After the legislators in Charleston stopped the emission of paper early in 1779, taxation and the floating of popular loans were relied upon until the British conquered most of the State. Then all financial provision necessarily lapsed save the commandeering of army supplies. Where the British flag waved, the royal money circulated, and elsewhere little need for money existed, buying and selling having almost ceased. "Those who had the necessaries of life freely divided with those who were destitute. Luxuries or even comforts were not contemplated. To make out to live was the ultimate aim of most." [21]   South Carolina's paper by the final year of fighting was almost worthless, and it became necessary for Governor Rutledge, under the extraordinary powers given him by the legislature, to suspend the laws making it a legal tender.

In all sections of America, indeed, the steady depreciation of paper money took place. In Boston butter at one time sold for $12 a pound, and a barrel of flour for $1,575, while frugal Samuel Adams paid $2,000 for a suit of clothes.[22]   In Philadelphia one trader declared in the *Packet* that having bought a hogshead of sugar and sold it for more than it cost him, the proceeds would buy only a tierce. The people of Fairfax County and the town of Alexandria, Virginia, in 1777 protested to the legislature against the terrific price of commodities. R. H. Lee wrote Patrick Henry a year later that already the continental issues exceeded seven-fold the sum necessary for a medium of trade, that the State emissions had greatly increased the evil, and that the counterfeiting was still more injurious. In June, 1779, John Tazewell believed that "the amazing depreciation of our paper currency seems to threaten us with speedy ruin." [23]   Early in 1781 North Carolina officers had to pay $250 in their currency for a day's labor and $12,000 for a single horse, while the Assembly formally recognized a depreciation of the currency to one-ninth its face value.

In a number of States south of New England which ceased issuing paper in 1777 or 1778, the crisis of the war in 1780-81 forced a second marked resort to it. The demands of Congress were greater and greater; the population, denied an overseas market for crops,

[21] Ramsay's "South Carolina," II, 182-183. For South Carolina's paper emissions see Statutes at Large, Cooper Ed., IV, 360, 361, 393, 461, 508.
[22] Cf. Sumner, "Hist. Am. Currency," 46, 47.
[23] Henry, "Henry," II, 10-13; N. Ca. State Papers, XIV, 309-10.

grew rebellious in the face of taxation; sources of loans had been largely exhausted; and much of the South was devastated. Government after government saw no other way of obtaining funds.

This fact was evident before Congress adopted the plan in 1780 of dividing part of a new issue of $10,000,000 among the States. Connecticut issued £190,000 in bills of credit, but this, pursuant to Roger Sherman's advice,[24] was in lieu of the State's share of the new Continental bills. Moreover, the issue was promptly redeemed. The New England States showed continued caution in dealing with paper money. Thus Rhode Island, the most indiscreet in later years, which was entitled to £130,000 of the new "forty to one" money, took only a part of it. Rhode Islanders saw that the state was not only responsible for the redemption of the issue, but that it would have to pay interest to the holders. Massachusetts likewise shrewdly refused a part of her quota. But elsewhere in the Union, the only recourse seemed to be to the printing press.

Pennsylvania's resort to paper money in 1781 was a picturesque and instructive episode. The amazing depreciation of older emissions had forced the Legislature, in the spring of 1781, to establish an official scale to show what constituted a just satisfaction for debts. But not all its former blind faith in paper money was knocked out of that body. In March, 1780, the Assembly had authorized the issue of £100,000 upon the security of lands in Philadelphia and of Province Island, all belonging to the State—the security causing the bills to be called "island money." Just a year later, against the earnest protests of Robert Morris, General Mifflin, and sixteen other influential citizens, an additional £500,000 was authorized; of which £100,000 was to be redeemed annually for five years. Anyone who refused to accept these bills in payment of debt or for salable goods, was subject to rigid penalties. The conservative Anti-Constitutionalists stood fast in opposition to the measure, and published an eloquent denunciation of it; and the sequel soon justified their attitude.[25]

An effort was made to float the first part of the huge emission in a way to inspire confidence in it. On May 11 the Executive Council issued a proclamation stating that one-third of the last £500,000 had already been printed, and taken by State troops, that goods had

---

[24] Trumbull Papers, Mass. Hist. Soc. Library, March 23, 1780, *et seq.;* Cf. Trumbull's "Trumbull." 243-44.

[25] This Legislature also forbade for six months suits to collect large debts contracted before 1777. For paper money issues, see Laws of Pa., 1810 Ed., I, Chs. 896, 928; II, Ch. 934.

been sold for the bills to the public commissioners, and that any reduction in the value of the paper would be a public calamity. It asked the people to accept the money and promised that no more would be issued until the Legislature again met. The Constitutionalists held a mass-meeting which voted its approbation of this request. The principal business men of Philadelphia, however, simply agreed at a general meeting that they would take the new paper at the rates prevailing on May 1—which they did not long do. The Council kept its promise to issue no more than the £166,666 already in circulation; and when the Assembly met again, the sound-money party labored energetically to obtain some guarantee of the ultimate redemption of the outstanding paper. The earlier March issue of £100,000 of "island money" rose to par when the city lots belonging to the Penn family, with Province Island, were sold to provide a redemption fund, and those who had bought it at a specie ratio of eight to one made a handsome profit, for in due time they were paid.

But the later and larger issue depreciated rapidly and irremediably. The severe penalties prescribed by law for refusal to accept the money at par had no effect. It fell steadily until it required anywhere from $250 to $300 to buy one dollar in gold—this depreciation being less than that which had overtaken the Continental bills, but sufficient to make the money worthless for trade. The Council finally recognized its failure by ordering that the paper be received in payment of debts to the State at 175 to 1. In the early fall of 1781, the bills disappeared, and gold and silver amazingly took their place. President Reed wrote the State's loan agent in Europe that the rag money had found "an honorable, and what you will perhaps think more extraordinary, a peaceful exit." A timely trade with the West Indies in flour, springing up immediately, gave the farmers a market and brought large quantities of hard money into the State.

Maryland's experience paralleled Pennsylvania's. In 1781, finding resources for the war and a sufficient circulating medium alike wanting, the Legislature voted £200,000 in bills of credit, redeemable within four years. This act was not wholly culpable, for it was possible to pledge large amounts of confiscated British property for the discharge of the debt, and much of it was sold by auction at once, while additional means were found to bolster the State's credit. Most Assemblymen pledged themselves to take the bills, at least in stated quantities, at par; subscription papers, supported by public meetings and local committees, were circulated throughout the State, and it was understood that a subscriber's property was pledged for his subscription. But Americans everywhere had lost confidence in such emissions.

"It was impossible for it to succeed; opinion was wanted," said the Maryland *Gazette* succinctly. "Notwithstanding every position they had made, it scarcely passed as specie at all between individuals. Some few creditors, indeed, who could not violate so recent and solemn an engagement, received it with reluctance. A few merchants, of more than common public spirit, sold goods for it at the old price; others . . . raised the price . . .; and the farmers and planters generally would not sell their commodities at all." [26] Three months after the bills went into circulation, they had enormously depreciated. They were by law a legal tender, and the creditors who had to receive them suffered greatly. "Cheating became, as it were, a reputable business, being practised by the representatives of the people and authorized by law." An enactment to limit the price of goods, and restrictions upon exportation, increased the feeling of conservative men that they were being ruled by "blockheads and knaves," and by laws "which mark their framers for cheats or ignorant statesmen, and which stamp indelible disgrace upon a whole community." [27] This was precisely the feeling of the conservative business men of the Anti-Constitutionalist party in Pennsylvania.

New Jersey in the spring of 1780 authorized the issue of £225,000 of the new forty-to-one bills; besides this, later in the year the legislature ordered a new emission of £30,000 in bills of credit. Prudent Virginians regretted toward the end of 1780 that "our only resource is the wretched one of more paper money." [28] In 1781, when the theatre of the final scenes of war, the State authorized what would seem incredible emissions if we did not remember the extreme depreciation—first an issue of £15,000,000, and later one for £20,000,-000. Though this money was not a legal tender for debt, it was receivable in payment of taxes, and proved later very embarrassing to the State. North Carolina threw no paper money proper into circulation in 1781 and 1782, contenting herself with issuing certifi-

[26] December 2, 1784; see also Pa. *Mercury*, December 24, 1784. This paper was emitted on security of double the value in lands. Laws of 1781, May session, Ch. 23.
[27] Md. *Journal*, in a denunciatory sketch of the whole paper money history of the State, September 17, 1782.
[28] Rives, "Madison," I, 278-79.

cates. But in the spring of 1783 the Legislature voted £100,000 in
bills for redeeming old money, paying the Continental line, and defraying the costs of government; to support this issue, confiscated
property was set aside.   Other States participated in this general
but temporary reversion toward paper money near the end of the
war.

III.   Taxation and Other Revenues

When the States in 1777-78 first abandoned or reduced their reckless paper issues, they had to turn, however reluctantly, to such
direct levies as the people had never felt.   Congress in its message
to the State governments upon finances in November, 1777, urged
that property-owners be heavily assessed.   "Hitherto spared from
taxes, let them now with a cheerful heart contribute according to
their circumstances."   In the following May it reiterated the advice.   "Is there a country upon earth which has such resources for
the payment of her debts as America?   Such an extensive territory?
So fertile, so blessed in climate and production?   Surely there is
none."   Why, then, the disastrous depreciation of paper money?
"Because no taxes have been imposed to carry on the war."

Taxation is now such an inevitable accompaniment of civilized
government, and in most lands high taxation, that it is hard for us
to place ourselves in the idyllic age when leaders were exhorting the
yeomen, shopkeepers, and shippers to submit to the tax-gatherer.
When John Adams declared that "taxation as deep as possible is
the only radical cure," and Roger Sherman that he saw no means
of supporting the patriot cause and its currency "but by taxing to
the full amount of our expenditures after having emitted a sufficient
sum for a medium of trade," there were few who agreed with them
that adequate taxation would be the cheapest way out.   The annalist
Ramsay was one, saying that in South Carolina "a great deal might
have been done at an early period to support the [paper] money."
Here and there an enlightened community responded with cordiality
to the proposals of the statesmen, but only here and there.   George
Mason, versed in political economy as well as political science, induced his neighbors of Fairfax County to call upon the Virginia Legislature in the fall of 1777 for vigorous taxation, and to declare that
the people would readily submit to it.   Already New England had
led the way, Massachusetts in the previous spring having ordered

taxes laid to bring £455,000 lawful money into the treasury. Some wise Bay State towns in 1777 objected to the policy of calling in bills of credit on loans, and asked to have them sunk by taxes; so that a law was enacted allowing any town to lessen its proportion of the public debt by taxing itself if it chose.[29]

Taxes had been low in the Colonies, and in some they had been almost unfelt. Most of the provincial governments had cost little— Rhode Island's about £2,000 a year just before the war. In the governmental disorganization at the beginning of the Revolution, the taxpayers found it easy to evade their obligations. In Connecticut at the close of the year of independence, the *Courant* remarked that taxes had been "none, or next to none, for some time," and were only beginning "in a low degree to take place." Near the end of the war the New York legislators apologized for the heaviness of the money burdens they were laying on the people, but pointed out that the taxes were lower than might be expected, and that the war had been carried through several campaigns at great expense before any taxes were collected.[30]   At first taxes were hard to obtain because men were unused to them; later because of the ravages of war and the effect of paper-depreciation upon credit and trade; and always in some degree because the States had no sound machinery for tax-collection.

But money was hard to raise for another reason also; throughout the Revolution nothing grieved statesmen like the inferior sensitiveness of the patriotic nerve when compared with the pocket nerve. In Pennsylvania, during the darkest days of the British conquest of the South, a certain meeting of the Legislature was expected to show that a fine spirit of self-sacrifice was abroad. Thomas Paine uttered a cry of indignation over what it really showed. "What particularly added to the affliction was that so many of the members, instead of spiriting up their constituents to the most nervous exertions, came to the Assembly furnished with petitions to be ex-

[29] See Ramsay's "South Carolina," II, 178. The long, interesting, and important call by Fairfax County for direct taxation is in the Md. *Gazette,* October 28, 1777. Other States took admiring notice of the action of Massachusetts; see Md. *Journal,* November 18, 1777. The law of 1777 is in Mass. Acts and Resolves, 1775-80, p. 150.
[30] Cf. Governor Clinton's call for taxation in September, 1778; Messages from the Governors, II, 52. New Jersey began heavy taxation in the fall of 1778; Mulford, "Hist. N. J.," 457 ff. In South Carolina taxation, apart from a levy on polls, had been practically unknown. For the apology of the New York Legislature mentioned above, see Assembly Journal, 1871, 63 ff. Dr. Franklin, examined by a committee of the House of Commons in 1766, and asked if the Americans paid considerable taxes, replied, "Certainly many, and very heavy taxes." But this was when the burden of the Seven Years' War was still great. "Examination of Dr. B. Franklin," Phila., 1766.

empt from paying taxes. How the public measures were to be carried on, the country defended, and the army recruited . . . when the only resource, and that not half sufficient, that of taxes, should be relaxed to almost nothing, was a matter too gloomy to look at." [31]   President Reed wrote Washington that the rich and not the poor were shrinking from the burden of the war. Many wealthy men concealed part of their property, or refused to declare it, or declared it and then evaded payment. Outside the path of the armies, he said, the country was richer than when the first shots were fired at Lexington, but the selfishness of Whigs and the opposition of Tories, conjoined with the long disuse of taxes and the quarrels of party, had half paralyzed the amassing of public funds.[32]

Jefferson estimated the taxable property of Virginia at a hundred million dollars, and declared at the end of the Revolution that a tax of one per cent. upon it would, in comparison with anything yet laid, be deemed almost crushing. Yet in the dark spring of 1781 the various burdens of the war led to outbreaks of violence in the Old Dominion. In Hampshire County there was rioting by those who wished, in the words of one State agent, "to be clear of taxes and draughts." On the Eastern Shore efforts to collect tax-arrears and enlist reluctant drafted men caused disturbances that continued intermittently for months and required militia interference.

To outline in detail the tax laws of all thirteen States is a task that happily we need not undertake. It is sufficient to lay down certain salient facts in the history of State taxation during the war period. The first is that the initial levies, which in most States were made during 1777, but in a few were deferred till 1778, were timid. In South Carolina, for example, where nothing but the poll tax had been really felt, less than one-third of a dollar was asked in 1777 for each negro and each one hundred acres. "A fear of alarming the people, and too sanguine hopes of a speedy peace," as Ramsay says, "induced the legislature to begin moderately; more with a view of making an experiment than of raising adequate supplies." [33]   The second outstanding fact is that the principal reliance of the States was placed upon the general property tax and poll tax, with excise and income taxes in a decidedly secondary position. Virginia, it should be noted, had long depended mainly

[31] "Writings," II, 150.
[32] Bolles, "Pennsylvania," II, 72.
[33] Ramsay's "South Carolina," II, 182.

on import taxes, and the general property tax was one of the war's gifts to her.[34] A third fact is that in passing wartime tax laws the States found it almost impossible to keep pace with the depreciation of money; before the revenue had reached the treasury, it had dwindled to an inadequate value. Finally, we discover a marked tendency to broaden the field of taxation—to place a special levy on articles of luxury like carriages, to get at income, and to place duties on commerce. State taxation before 1783 was not a success in any proper meaning of the word; it did not meet State needs. But the thirteen governments learned valuable lessons from their varied experience.

Some of the States began with much simpler laws than others. Pennsylvania in the spring of 1777 was content with a tax of five shillings in the hundred pounds on all estates real and personal, a poll tax, and certain excise and license taxes. New York distinguished between real estate and personal estate, laying in the spring of 1778 a tax of threepence in the pound on the former and one and a half pence on the latter. South Carolina's first tax was ten shillings for every slave or hundred acres, five shillings for every hundred pounds in town realty, and five shillings for every hundred pounds at interest, in tradesman's stock, and in profits of professional men or tradesmen. The principal item in Maryland's tax law of the spring of 1777 was a general property levy of ten shillings in the hundred pounds. But Virginia that fall enacted a more complex measure. The Richmond legislators levied a general property tax of ten shillings in the hundred pounds, and a like tax on cash capital; a tax of two shillings in the pound on annuities or income from money at interest; a tax of ten shillings in the hundred pounds on salaried income; a poll tax of five shillings on every tithable, with certain exceptions, above twenty-one; fourpence a head on all neat cattle; an export tax of ten shillings on every hogshead of tobacco; and excise and license taxes. This remarkably comprehensive measure, later broadened to include taxes on luxuries and on more livestock, was the basis on which Virginia kept her finances till she had to turn to taxes in kind.[35]

A few instances will show how all the States, from Massachusetts to Georgia, were compelled to increase the tax rate to enormous

[34] Cf. Richmond College Hist. Papers, II, No. 1, 72.
[35] Laws of Pa., 1810 ed., I; New York Laws, 1777-1801, I, 37 ff. (March 28, 1778); S. Ca. Statutes at Large, Cooper Ed., IV, 365 (Jan. 16, 1777); Laws of Maryland, 1777, Feb. session, Chs. 21 and 22; Hening, IX, 349 ff. (October, 1777).

amounts in an effort to keep abreast of the depreciation of paper. Maryland's ten shilling tax of 1777 became twenty-five shillings in the hunred pounds the following year, £13 in 1779, and £25 in 1780, when taxes in kind were introduced. South Carolina made three levies between the Declaration of Independence and the fall of Charleston four years later. We have said that the first was almost a third of a dollar for every slave and hundred-acre land-unit. The next, in 1778, was nominally ten times and actually twice as heavy; and the third, in 1779, was a tax of $20 in paper or about $1 in specie for every slave and hundred acres. In the fall of 1778 the Virginia legislature had practically to treble the tax laid the previous autumn, and the next spring the poll tax on slaves rose to £5. Everywhere assessors tended to value property in pre-war money and collect taxes in war money. Unfortunately for tax-payers, they did not invariably follow this rule, and gross inequalities resulted. The Virginia legislature in 1779 complained that some officers had valued lands at the price they would fetch in gold and silver, others in paper bills; some had paid no attention to the rise in land values since 1771, others had allowed for it; and some had valued land at what it would bring if a whole county were sold at once, others at the price given in small sales. The injustice was glaring.[36]

In every section the difficulty of obtaining a true revenue in money, as paper became worthless and specie was hoarded, led to the collection of taxes in products of the soil or home manufactures. This development was most pronounced in the South after the British threat began to be pushed home, and it is interesting to trace it in some detail in North Carolina and Virginia.

The North Carolina legislators in the spring of 1777 levied a general assessment of a half-pence in the pound on lands, lots, houses, slaves, money, stock in trade, horses, and cattle. Free adults who were worth less than a hundred pounds were ordered to pay four shillings as a special poll tax. The tax rate was steadily raised until in the spring 1780 it reached sixpence in the pound, and later that year, a few weeks after the crushing disaster at Camden, a specific provision tax was laid. Every hundred pounds' worth of property was to pay a peck of maize, or a half peck of

[36] Laws of Maryland, 1778, March session, ch. 7, Oct. session, ch. 7; 1779, March session, ch. 11, July session, ch. 5, November session, ch. 35; 1780, March session, ch. 25, June session, ch. 7. S. Ca. Statutes at Large, Cooper ed., IV, 365, 487, 497, 528. Hening, Statutes, IX, 547, X, 9.

wheat, or five pounds of flour, or a peck of rough rice, or three pounds of pork, or four and a half pounds of beef. At the June session in 1781, when the war was at its most critical stage, with Cornwallis in Virginia, a combined money and specific provision tax was levied. Every pound of taxable property was to pay, in the debased currency of the time, four shillings tax, and every pound in money to pay fourpence. All single freemen having less than a thousand pounds' worth of property were to pay £150 in currency. The supplementary provision tax was substantially as before, a slight reduction in the quantity of meat being allowed. In 1782 a more nearly normal tax was levied, but in consideration of the scarcity of specie, the payers were allowed to offer three fourths of it in tobacco, hemp, deerskins, beeswax, tallow, indigo, flour, rice, pork, or linen. These commodities were carefully valued in the law—for example, Indian-dressed deerskins were to be worth three shillings a pound, pork seventy-five shillings a barrel, and indigo six shillings a pound.

Virginia had turned earlier to taxation in kind, and had a terrible struggle to free her financial system from it. As early as the spring of 1779 every man and every able-bodied woman slave above sixteen was required, beginning the next year, to pay an annual tax of a bushel of wheat, or two bushels of corn, rye, or barley, or ten pecks of oats, or fifteen pounds' of hemp, or twenty-eight pounds of tobacco. Similar levies followed. When in the late autumn of 1781 Patrick Henry fathered a new tax law, which levied a pound on every hundred pounds' worth of land, two shillings on every horse and mule, threepence on neat cattle, five shillings on carriage wheels, and fifty pounds on the billiard tables when found in taverns, specie was quite unavailable. All the levy was made payable in tobacco, hemp, or flour, except the tax on land, of which half could be paid in tobacco or hemp and one tenth in Continentals of the new emission. The following spring deerskins, for the benefit of the West, were added to the list.[37]

Once having won this privilege, Virginia taxpayers refused to surrender it. A party arose, after the fighting ended, which tried to effect the permanent transfer of taxes to a specie basis, but it

[37] For North Carolina's laws, see State Papers, XXIV; for the difficulties and waste attending the collection of "specifics" there, see F. M. Hubbard, "Life of W. R. Davie," 64 ff. For Virginia's laws, see Hening, IX, 369, X, 79, 233, 241, 338, 490, 501, X, 66. In October, 1780, Virginia called upon the counties for fixed quotas of clothes, provisions, and wagons, while the previous spring army impressments in any amount had been authorized.

waged an uphill fight. In the spring of 1783 the right of commutation was repealed, but a vociferous clamor led to its revival that fall. It was then voted to drop the taxes in kind early in 1784, but circumstances forbade that desirable step. In the autumn most of the counties west of the Blue Ridge had to be allowed to pay in hemp, and the people of the whole State had to be relieved of one-half the tax of 1785. Their poverty and the scarcity of specie seemed to make this imperative. In 1786, again when a paper-money agitation was with difficulty stifled, the legislature was determined at least to provide some easy "facility." The whole tax of the current year was made dischargeable, by a heavy majority, in tobacco at a fixed valuation. Madison wrote Washington that he had sadly acquiesced, "as a prudential compliance with the clamor within doors and without, as a probable means of obviating more hurtful experiments." But the reform forces resumed the struggle with better prospects as economic conditions improved. In 1787 tobacco was receivable for only certain taxes, and the following year all taxes were required in the form of specie and warrants, a reduction in the levy being conceded as a reward. Virginia was out of the woods at last.[38]

Other sections had a similar experience. At the northern extremity of the nation, New Hampshire in 1782 voted a tax of £110,000 upon polls and estates, to be paid in State certificates, or in rum, beef cattle, leather shoes (valued at six shillings apiece), yarn hose, cloth, felt hats, blankets, or wheat flour. Massachusetts four years later allowed the payment of arrears of taxes assessed previous to 1784 in a long list of commodities, including potash, pearlash, tow cloth, cod oil, dried fish, and whalebone. The discontent that was producing Shays's Rebellion required these emollients. New York in the spring of 1781 laid a tax payable in wheat. We find that Maryland took the plunge at about the same time as Virginia and North Carolina. By successive laws in 1780 she required the payment the following year of a special provision levy of a bushel of wheat or twenty-five pounds of tobacco for every hundred pounds' worth of property, and permitted meat, breadstuffs, and tobacco to

[38] Hening, XI, 289, 299, 540; XII, 258, 456; Henry, "Henry," II, 169-172; H. B. Grigsby, "The Va. Fed. Conv.," II, 204. An excellent sketch of Virginia's financial history is to be found in the *Va. Hist. Mag.*, X, by W. F. Dodd. There is no doubt that the collection of any part of the taxes in specie greatly stimulated emigration to the south and west. Even the rich counties of Cumberland and Buckingham presented petitions in the fall of 1789 stating that specie was too scarce, and the price of produce too low, to make possible the payment of taxes in hard money. See Rives, "Madison," II, 78-79.

be offered also for the regular 1781 tax. At one time in Maryland the civil officers were allowed to draw their salaries in wheat, the Governor being allowed 4,500 bushels a year; and Virginia was compelled to pay her militia in tobacco, brigadier-generals receiving 125 pounds a day and privates 7½ pounds.[39]

Naturally, the States incurred great losses upon these taxes in kind. In Pennsylvania the farmers often insisted upon excessive valuations for their goods, or presented kinds of produce for which the State had little use. North Carolina found that much time was lost in collecting the "specifics," especially in thinly-settled districts; and that it was difficult to transport the heavy articles and drive the livestock to points of collection that shifted with the army camps. Governor Burke complained after the fighting stopped that there was not a sufficient variety in the supplies, and that there was no system in the administration. In Virginia the loss from accidents and depreciation was lamented, as was the fact that collectors often speculated with the supplies, while the scarcity of money operated against the ready sale of provisions, so that they spoiled unused. There were districts in which the collectors, after covering fields with lowing herds and raising hillocks of flour, could not pay bills of a few pounds sterling in cash. As for Maryland, the sheriffs and collectors were there accused in 1780 of some curious frauds. They bought up certificates for provisions, acceptable in paying taxes, at a discount, and turned them into the treasury instead of the money received from the people, which they pocketed. They also bought up tobacco of bad quality to pay the tobacco assessments of citizens who had fallen into arrears; and then they exacted exorbitant sums from these poor people to reimburse themselves.[40]

Having to build their tax system largely from the foundation up, amid the hurry and stress of war, the States found them wretchedly

[39] N. H. Prov., State, and Town Papers, VIII, 927; Mass. Acts and Laws, 1786, 604 (Nov. 8, 1786); Laws of N. Y. 1777-1801, I, March 27, 1781; Laws of Maryland, by years; Scharf's "Maryland," II, 476-480; Hening, X, 223. Payment in "specifics" was not always allowed in Maryland after 1783.
[40] Calendar Va. State Papers, III, 214, 323. See the matter indexed under Col. Davies in this volume for a vivid insight into the difficulty of collecting anything whatever of value from many Virginia counties in 1782-83. The Governor said in April, 1782, that there were but four shillings in the treasury, and no means of getting more; p. 133. Note the complaint of a writer in the Providence, R. I., *Gazette*, March 23, 1782: "The people at large have paid in taxes to the utmost extent of their abilities; and yet it is an indisputable fact that the army was indifferently fed, badly clothed, and worse paid. Are the citizens in a better condition to contribute to the support of the war than they have been? Ask the farmer, whose stock has been sold by the collector for half its value—ask the hard laborer, and industrious mechanic, whose wives and children have suffered for want of bread—ask these, and then determine whether the war can be supported by mere taxation."

imperfect. In not one was the plan for raising money either thorough or equitable; from all we catch complaints of injustice and discrimination. At the close of the period of the Confederation a writer in the Providence *Gazette* soundly observed:

In a number of instances the manner of State taxation is oppressive to those citizens who have small property. Repeated attempts have been made, in most of the States, to amend their respective systems; but with little success. . . . The present manner of taxation is favorable to a number of opulent members in every legislature, who, though they may not be a majority, can impede any essential alteration; and this is a serious reason for a transferal of the State debt to the United States, who, in the arrangement of a new system, may avoid the oppressive points of State taxation.[41]

One primary injustice lay in the poll tax, which fell upon the poor at least as heavily as the rich. It was particularly burdensome in New England, where the writer just quoted declared that it furnished considerably more than a fourth of the total revenue of Connecticut, and he believed not a smaller part of that of Massachusetts; "art cannot contrive a more oppressive mode of drawing money from a people." As a matter of fact, just after the war the poll tax gave Massachusetts at least a third of her revenue. No families were larger than those of the poor, and fathers had to pay the tax of their older sons. It also discouraged manufacturing, in that it checked the employment of apprentices. In Virginia on the eve of the Revolution the tax system had been broadened because the legislators declared that certain other levies were easier to the people than the poll-tax. Another salient injustice lay in the taxation of both cultivated farms and wild lands at precisely the same rate for every hundred acres. Still another, finally, lay in the sheer disregard of many potential sources of tax-income.

Efforts at reform frequently met that selfish opposition of which the Providence writer speaks. In New England the mercantile and maritime classes controlled the Senate, and the Senate was a rock in the path of healthy changes. Fairness counselled abolition of the poll-tax and the imposition of stiff duties; but even when a tariff was enacted in 1782, the rates were low and smuggling was scandalously prevalent. In New York, on the other hand, rural interests held the advantage and pressed it against the traders of the metropolis. For decades before the war they had manifested a stubborn determination to place the burden of taxation on commerce rather than on land; and in opposition to them had risen a

[41] Quoted in *American Mercury*, Dec. 12, 1789.

defensive combination of New York county, Westchester, and the three special jurisdictions or pocket boroughs, Schenectady, Rensselaerwyck, and Livingston Manor. The interior of the Province was over-represented, and even this combination could not always resist it. After the Revolution, when a large part of the population of New York and Westchester was disfranchised because it had accepted British rule, the up-State element was irresistibly powerful. The metropolis had no sooner been evacuated than a special tax of £100,000 was assessed upon it and the surrounding country, on the ground that the occupied region had paid no taxes during the war. Then came two tariff acts in close succession, burdening trade heavily.

During the war New York at first relied upon a blanket levy; as we have seen, the tax law of 1778 carried threepence in the pound on lands, and half that amount on personal property. But it was soon found that assessments had been partially and unequally made, and that some county treasurers had practised shameful frauds. Late in 1779 New York therefore abandoned the plan of State-wide assessments. Instead, a fixed sum was levied on each county, with the promise that if the apportionment was later found to be unfair, the State would repay deficiencies or collect overcharges, with six per cent. interest. No longer could one county undervalue its lands or neglect its collections to throw an undue burden on its neighbors. The first apportionment ranged from $999,593 for Albany to $30,661 each for Orange and Westchester. A spirited debate raged around these quotas. First an Albany member moved that his county pay only $833,000 of the $2,500,000 to be raised, but the motion was negatived by the solid vote of all the other counties; and on the initiative of a Dutchess member, Albany's quota was fixed at the sum already named. In revenge, the Albany Assemblyman thereupon proposed that Dutchess be required to pay $800,000, but was once more overruled, and the figure was fixed at $703,189. Nobody pretended that the quotas were scientifically fixed.

After the war this hit-or-miss method of distributing taxes continued. Governor Clinton in a message to the legislature in the fall of 1784 deplored its failure to provide for a proper estimate of the value of taxable property throughout the State. Nobody could know how much of a burden the State could endure, he said, and he deplored the constant animosities aroused between counties regarding the quotas.[42] But there were powerful interests arrayed against a really equitable tax system.

At the South the people of the lowlands tyrannized over those of the uplands. In North Carolina in 1785, for example, a sharp debate arose over taxation. Several members of the House energetically attacked a Senate bill taxing salt, saying that it fell too harshly on the poor. When the regular tax measure for the year was introduced, Waightstill Avery, Thomas Person, and nine others from the western reaches dissented. They had three main objections. First, many poor people, settled on thin lands "from which it requires the utmost industry and frugality to procure a scanty supply of the mere necessaries of life," ought not to be compelled to pay a tax rate equal to that "imposed on the richest lands equally near to places of exportation." Second, much of the value of produce was lost in transportation over long distances, and it was hence oppressive to tax lands near and lands distant from market, of equal fertility, at the same valuation. Third, they objected that a moderate tax on lands according to their real value, which Avery said varied from £10 an acre to £10 a hundred acres, would produce a much larger revenue, so that the existing plan of taxation starved the treasury.[43] These first protests were unavailing, and in 1786 the tax was still five shillings on every hundred acres without regard to location. In the following year, however, the reforms won a victory; each hundred acres west of the Cumberland mountains was made to pay a tax of one shilling, each hundred acres between the

---

[42] Robert Morris, contemplating a Federal poll tax in 1782, offered some very imperfect reasoning in defense of the plan. The objections, he said, were drawn principally from foreign lands. "In some parts of Europe, where nine-tenths of the people are exhausted by continual labor to procure bad clothing and worse food, this tax would be extremely oppressive; but in America, where three days of labor produce sustenance for a week, it is not unreasonable to ask two days out of a year as a contribution to the payment of public debts." Only laborers would really feel the poll tax, he said, and "labor is in such demand with us, that that tax will fall on the consumer." Journals Cont. Cong. XXII, 441. For a good account of the rural vs. urban struggle to avoid tax burdens in provincial New York, see *Political Science Quarterly*, Vol. XXX, No. 3, p. 397, essay by C. W. Spencer. A queer episode of New York history in 1778 should be noticed. Under the impression that the war profiteers ought to be penalized, the two houses instructed the assessors to levy an additional tax, varying in amount according to their own judgment (!), upon men believed to have amassed large sums out of the necessities of the country. Happily, the Council of Revision was able to kill this oppressive bit of folly. Assembly Journal, 1778, 41-43; 1779, 51 ff. The legislature, unfortunately did not in this period realize its ambition to distribute tax burdens equitably. In 1784 the Senate told Gov. Clinton that it deplored "the want of fixed principles for equal taxation," and would again try to ascertain and define them; Senate Journal, Oct. 21, 1784. Hamilton wrote in 1782: "The whole system (if it may be so called) of taxation in this State is radically vicious, burthensome to the people, and unproductive to the government." Works, VIII, 55.

[43] N. C. State Records, XVII, 409-12; Pa. *Packet*, February 4, 1786.

Cumberlands and Appalachians two shillings, and each hundred acres east of the Appalachians three.

Complaints of equal vehemence arose in Virginia. The Provincial Convention in the summer of 1776 laid a tax of one shilling and threepence on every tithable person, and one shilling on every hundred acres. The rich planter of Prince George or King William counties hence in many instances paid a smaller land tax than the poor farmer whose barren acres covered a large tract of Henrico or Gooch. When in the next year a comprehensive system of taxation was adopted, this inequality remained. Tithes for the established church had to be paid by each poll, and this was an additional grievance of the poor; but as female slaves as well as male freemen were tithable, and such slaves were held principally by the tidewater aristocrats, the injustice was less than it might seem. In 1783 the year's receipts were estimated by Thomson Mason as £90,000 from the land tax and £50,000 from the poll tax on whites, both of which fell on rich and poor alike; but the slave tax yielded almost as much—£120,000. Under the comprehensive tax system of 1777, broadened and improved in the revision of 1781, the taxes upon carriages, money, property, cattle, and income fell more heavily on the rich than the poor, on the lowlands than the uplands. But the principal reform was not wrought until the fall of 1782, when Virginia was divided into four great regions for land valuation. They corresponded roughly to the four natural divisions, the Tidewater, Piedmont, Valley, and Trans-Allegheny sections. An acreage taxed ten shillings in the first was to be taxed seven shillings six pence in the second, five shillings sixpence in the third, and three shillings in the extreme west. Five years later the poll tax was happily also abandoned as an evident evil.[44]

In South Carolina taxes were laid from the beginning on land and negroes, and the former, being at a uniform rate for each acre, were highly inequitable. Three such levies were made between the Declaration of Independence and the fall of Charleston four years later. The first, in 1777, was almost a third of a dollar for each negro and each hundred acres. After fighting ceased, annual

---

[44] Washington complained in 1781 that the steward of his Virginia estate could not pay the taxes upon it, and that he had to sell negroes for this purpose; "the taxes being the most unequal (I am told) in the world—some persons paying for things of equal value, four times, nay ten times, the rate that others do." Writings, IX. 182-84. For abandonment of the poll tax, see W. F. Dodd, *Va. Hist. Mag.*, X. For land tax, see Hening, X, 140; Richmond College Hist. Papers, II, No. 1.

taxes were laid in the same unfair fashion, so that a quarter-section of pine-barren, almost worthless, paid as much as a quarter-section of the best indigo or rice lands. But the upland population won its first real voice in legislative affairs in 1783, was clamorous for a reform, and soon gained its point. In 1784, crowning an effort intermittently maintained for thirty years, it carried a law for the ad valorem taxation of land, which was hailed as "a manifest public testimonial" that henceforth every citizen would "bear his part of the public burden, according to his strength, more or less, and no further." [45] All lands were now rated at something like their real value, but none was assessed at more than $26 an acre, and none at less than twenty cents. [46]

Finally, the same clamor for reform arose in Georgia. There was at first no adequate taxation at all, and after Cornwallis's surrender the Council had a hard struggle to induce the House to levy even what it did. In 1783 the legislators taxed every negro or other slave, every town lot, and every hundred acres a quarter of a dollar, or just half what the Council had recommended; together with $1 on every free negro and $2 on every white idler. Two years later the demand for more comprehensive taxes and for classification had borne fruit. Lands were listed as tide swamp, pine barren, inland swamp, salt marsh, high river swamp, oak and hickory land, sea islands, and so forth, and in some instances as of first, second, and third quality each, while the range of other taxes was wide, covering real estate in town, wharves, carriages, stock in trade, and doctors and lawyers. But Georgia still cleaved to the inequitable poll tax, every white freeman this year being required to pay four shillings and eightpence, and every slave half as much. [47]

Apart from taxation, the States relied largely upon borrowings from their people, and when this failed, upon requisitions or forced loans. The first effort in Massachusetts to raise money for the war was by a loan. On May 3, 1775, the Provincial Congress authorized the borrowing of a hundred thousand pounds, lawful money, at six

---

[45] S. C. *Gazette,* July 17. 1784.

[46] Ramsay, "S. C.," II, 190-91. We find the tax act of 1785 listing lands in nine classes, some with several subdivisions; they ranged in value from £6 to 1s. sterling an acre. On all lands there was a one per cent. ad valorem tax, as on all other property. It is clear that the classification was an enormous gain for equity. Statutes at Large, Cooper's Ed., IV, 689.

[47] Marbury and Crawford, "Digest of Laws," 452-58 *et passim;* Hollander, "Studies in State Taxation," Johns Hopkins Univ. Studies, XVIII, 220-21. In July, 1783, the Council protested to the House against the slenderness of the tax bill, saying with perfect truth that it was "inadequate to the great and pressing exigencies of the State."

per cent, with the promise of repayment June 1, 1777. Though many attempts were made to push the loan, it failed. Other States passed through the same experience. Maryland raised her first funds by assessing (December 12, 1774), a total of £10,000 on the counties, according to population, a measure half-way between a tax and a forced requisition. Congress advised the States in 1777 to open loan offices in every district and town, with officers empowered to issue certificates for loans as low as $200. It was often difficult, in practise, to distinguish between the certificates and paper money, for they were passed from hand to hand like bills of credit. As money fell in value, the sums which it was attempted to borrow became nominally greater and greater: North Carolina's legislature in 1779 ordered that £1,000,000 be obtained on loan.

There were a few striking examples of widespread self-sacrifice in loaning or giving the States money. The Pennsylvania Legislature in the spring of 1780 received from Washington a letter which painted in vivid colors the desperate condition of the republic—the army's distress, the danger of mutiny, the lack of money. A despairing silence was broken by one member who had been a hopeful patriot: if Washington's letter was accurate, he said, "it appears to me in vain to contend the matter any longer. We may as well give up first as last." But the clerk, Thomas Paine, and others, believed that private credit could come to the rescue. Paine sent a friend $500, and begged him to open a subscription list among his friends; Robert Morris stepped forward with a large gift; and soon no less than £300,000 in Pennsylvania currency was raised. When the Maryland Legislature in the same gloomy spring called on the citizens to take up a loan by advancing specie, paper, or tobacco, members of the Legislature at once made up a subscription list, Daniel of St. Thomas Jenifer giving $2,000 in paper and five hogsheads of tobacco, and Charles Carroll of Carrollton ten hogsheads of tobacco. Subscriptions were set on foot in all sections, and large sums obtained.[48] But such manifestations of patriotism were rare. The returns from State loan offices finally dwindled to a mere trickle. High interest rates did not prove a bait, and when South Carolina, on ceasing to issue paper money, offered three per cent. more than the interest paid by individuals, the result was discouraging.

[48] Scharf, "Md.," II, 375; Laws of 1780, June session, Ch. 2.

In Rhode Island during 1779, the subscriptions to a loan for Continental purposes having been few, the Assembly ordered the assessors to apportion $100,000 of the loan among those able to pay, and gave them power to enforce payment—a virtual conscription of wealth. The usual State course was simply to empower the proper officers to seize supplies and to pay in certificates. Virginia in 1779 and the succeeding years obtained army supplies by merely taking them and giving receipts, which were made receivable for taxes. In 1780 there were many seizures, in addition to heavy taxes in kind, the latter including such items as 3,000 suits of clothes and 74 wagons and teams. In 1781, with the tide of war rolling up from the South, the Virginia Treasurer was empowered to borrow not only money but tobacco, hemp, and flour, at six per cent. interest. In North Carolina two years earlier each county had been required to supply a certain number of hats, shoes, stockings, and yards of cloth. North Carolina's impressments in the final struggle with Cornwallis and Tarleton became so harsh, indeed, that Davie called them "legal robbery qualified by a promissory note." Two months after Cornwallis had been bagged he wrote that the promissory notes "are called 'State tricks,' and will be no longer received; so that I have been obliged to procure the necessary supplies by impressment and contribution."

Several States also tried to borrow money abroad, and met with even less success. Difficult as it was for the nation to obtain funds in Holland, France, and Spain, it was much more difficult for an individual State to do so. Maryland sent a commissioner abroad, one Matthew Ridley, who in 1781-82 negotiated in Holland a loan for 300,000 guilders; but the Legislature thought the terms disadvantageous, and ordered Ridley to repay the money already in his hands. Later another loan, to be repaid by annual tobacco shipments, was floated with the Dutch.[49] The Virginia Legislature in the fall of 1778 authorized the Governor to negotiate a foreign loan for £1,000,000 in money and military stores. Governor Henry tried to effect the loan through Dr. William Lee, the State's agent in Europe, and a special agent, one Captain Lemaire. Lee's ill-temper defeated his own efforts, but Lemaire in the spring of 1779 obtained a shipment of artillery and munitions by the French Gov-

---

[49] McSherry, "Md.," 310. Samuel Chase soon after the peace recovered Maryland's investment of Colonial days in the stock of the Bank of England, amounting to $650,000.

ernment amounting to £256,633. In Lee's stead Mazzei and others were later employed with success, and procured loans of a considerable amount.[50]   South Carolina in 1784 was offered a foreign loan to help lift her from the bog in which she had been left by British devastation, and accepted it, her debt five years later being still nearly £100,000.[51]   Pennsylvania was not so fortunate.   In the spring of 1780 the Legislature authorized the borrowing of £200,000 abroad, to be repaid on the State's faith after ten years.   James Searles, who had been in the Continental Congress, went to France and Holland, but found it impracticable to carry any negotiation through.   Governor Trumbull's son also vainly tried in 1781 to obtain a Dutch loan of £200,000.

The most interesting source of State income was of course the general confiscation of Tory estates.   One of the first proposals of this stroke was made by Paine in his enormously popular "Common Sense," brought out a half-year before independence; and the idea of waging the war with the American property of their opponents naturally appealed to many patriots.   It satisfied a lust for vengeance that had expressed itself in rioting, and it was profitable. Vandalism against Tory property was stopped, and some States began their confiscations even before Congress, on November 27, 1777, recommended that they all seize the possessions of men who had forfeited "the right to protection," and invest the proceeds in Continental loan certificates.   South Carolina alone failed to pass a confiscation act before the surrender of Cornwallis.

It has been plausibly estimated that hardly less than a third of the citizens of the Colonies were either actively Tory in their sympathies, or so neutral that they had no sympathy for the patriot cause; and in every Province the Tories included some of the richest —as also some of the most intelligent and respected—men.   They were now, with exceptions all too rare, stripped of what they owned in patriot-controlled territory.   In some States they were given the privilege of appealing for jury trial; in some a peremptory process of attainder allowed of no appeal whatever.[52]   In certain States

<hr/>

[50] Henry, "Henry," II, 13-16.
[51] The French Government grew urgent in pressing for the repayment of this debt; see Mass. *Centinel,* January 24, 1789; *American Museum,* V, 416.
[52] Double or treble taxation for non-jurors, including many neutrals and many who by religious conviction were averse to taking oaths, was common.   Where the patriot armies were in control, the soldiery sometimes plundered the estates of the hostile or neutral mercilessly; and when Washington forbade his troops to molest any Tory, it was said by one Tory that his words were like Venetian succor—too late.   Van Tyne, "Loyalists," 276-77.

the sheriffs and other regular officers of the law saw to the eviction of the old property holders and the installation of the new; in others, special commissioners were selected to supervise the seizure and sale, or trustees were chosen by the probate authorities to take charge of loyalist property. Almost everywhere the method of disposing of the seized property was laid down by law; but in several States irregularities occurred, and the downright corruption attending the confiscations became a public scandal. Even when the letter of the law was obeyed, rascals could line their pockets. Governor Livingston, of New Jersey, for example, complained that some commissioners of confiscated estates bought land immediately with the proceeds of their sales, and then, much later, paid the proceeds to the State in money that had meanwhile depreciated.

The richest fruits of the policy of confiscation were not reaped until the Revolution was in its last stages, and in a number of States till active fighting had ceased. Not until 1780 was confiscation really lucrative in Pennsylvania. It reached a broad scale in Maryland the same year, and in the next an issue of £200,000 of paper was based upon it. North Carolina passed her first confiscation act in 1777, but not until 1779 did she carry it into real effect, and then only in the face of a fierce opposition roused by its unduly severe terms. The British occupation in New York and South Carolina made it necessary for those States to withhold their most ambitious confiscatory measures until after the evacuations. Rhode Island's act of confiscation was passed in the fall of 1779, and could not be fully enforced till 1780. Virginia enacted a law of forfeiture in the spring of 1779, not long before the British invasions, while Maryland delayed until the fall of 1780, and even then incorporated generous exceptions in her statutes.[53]

It is indubitable that the States profited greatly by their seizures. Several found little upon which to lay their hands because Tories were few, as in Connecticut and New Hampshire. The latter State seized the pretentious manorial holdings of Governor John Wentworth, but they did not even cover the debts outstanding against them until his father, Mark Wentworth, generously waived his own large claims till the other creditors were satisfied. South Carolina realized little because her initially stern measures were followed by

---

[53] For Livingston's complaints, see Sedgwick's "Livingston," 392-93; for Virginia's interesting acts on British property, Hening, IX, 377; X, 66; XI, 81; for Maryland's act, Laws, Maxcy's Ed., I, 403, 413.

measures of exemption and even restitution. But New York alone obtained more than $3,600,000 in specie from the sale of the loyalists' property. The commissioners who sold confiscated property in Maryland realized a total of £454,181, and the Intendant, or State Treasurer, an additional sum. In Georgia one estate alone, that of Sir James Wright, was worth £34,000, or $160,000.[54] When the British Government opened an avenue for the submission to it of loyalist claims for compensation, more than 5,000 loyalists came forward, while this was a number much short of those who had suffered direct losses. For demands based upon any of the three allowable grounds, loss of property, of office, or of definite professional income, the British commissioners made awards totalling £3,292,492, and this was less than half of what the Tories had asked.[55] There were various actual losses by confiscation, as of land bought or improvements made during the war, or of uncultivated ground, or of property of defective title, for which the claimants were given no compensation, no matter how convincing their evidence.

Among the other sources of income, the two chief were the sale of lands and the laying of import duties and tonnage dues. Pennsylvania, during the spring before Yorktown, opened a land office which at once became one of her important means of revenue, and contributed much toward her prompt self-extrication from debt. The holders of State certificates in many instances laid them out in the land office. The Massachusetts Legislature in 1788 sold the State's western lands for £300,000 in State notes and £10,000 in specie.[56] Two years earlier, in a statement issued to set at rest the discontent which had led to Shays's rebellion, the General Court had shown that no less than £34,650 in notes for pay to soldiers had been redeemed by the sale of lands; and that additional notes for which tracts in Maine had been sold, but which had not yet been paid into the Treasury, amounted to £30,693. When at the beginning of 1784 Governor Clinton urged the establishment of a fund for discharging New York's debt, he enumerated among the means not only direct taxation, but the sale of public lands, the laying of

[54] For the sum realized in Maryland, where Daniel of St. Thomas Jenifer accused the commissioners of outrageous grafting, see Md. *Journal*, January 19. 1787.. For Wright's estate, see Stevens's "Georgia," II, 344 ff. New Hampshire took twenty-eight estates; Prov., State, and Town Papers, VIII, 803. By 1786, post-war sales amounting to £221,374 were reported in North Carolina, and a new confiscation law was passed as late as 1787. See Boyd's "North Carolina," 9.

[55] Sabine. I, 112.

[56] This "will put their public debt on a respectable footing," said the N. Y. *Journal*, April 10, 1788.

internal duties and excises, marine passes, and a tax on auctions; and that spring the legislature passed an act for the settlement of waste and unappropriated lands. Virginia in the spring of 1779 established a land office and offered unlimited areas at £40 for 100 acres.[57] All the Southern States discharged much of their obligation to the soldiers with land, and all of them also sold land for cash or certificates.

The income of the States from tariffs or tonnage dues was greater than would be supposed. It was generally largest in Pennsylvania, Virginia, and New York, but it formed an important part of State revenues elsewhere. The total dutiable imports of the nation during this period averaged, we may safely estimate, more than fifteen million dollars a year. A committee of Congress in 1783 computed that the goods shipped from Europe, exclusive of tea, brandy, and wine, were worth £3,500,000 sterling, or $15,555,554. In 1790 the imports paying *ad valorem* duties to the Federal treasury came to $15,388,409.[58] It was evident that a moderate tariff would yield three quarters of a million annually, and that the chief commercial States would find the impost a means of reducing their direct taxes. Manufacturing tradesmen who wanted protection and rural taxpayers who wanted relief, gladly joined hands to pass the tariff laws.

Not until after the treaty of peace were tariffs for protection and a high revenue introduced, though low tariffs had been well known before. Pennsylvania in 1780 had passed an act which levied special duties on certain tropical products and liquor, and one per cent. *ad valorem* on other goods. Virginia in 1782 also levied duties on liquor, sugar, and coffee, and a tariff of one per cent. on all other imposts. These were typical of the modest beginnings. We find South Carolina in 1782 imposing a somewhat higher rate—some special levies, and two and a half per cent. *ad valorem* on all else. Then came tariffs which really counted, political hostility for Great Britain reinforcing the other motives for their enactment. New York's first tariff act the spring of 1785 was followed by a much more severe one that fall. Every coach or chariot paid £20, every gold watch £1 6d., every gallon of madeira or malt liquor, sixpence; while a long list of imports was taxed five per cent. and another

[57] See Ambler, "Sectionalism in Virginia," 44 ff., for an account of the unfortunate results of Virginia's liberality in granting her lands, large tracts going to speculators for a mere song.
[58] Journals of Congress, Ed. 1823, IV, 201; Bemis, "Jay's Treaty," 33.

list two and a half per cent. Pennsylvania and Rhode Island enacted high tariffs in 1785. Virginia in September did the same, emphasizing a protective purpose. Massachusetts, influenced by her powerful commercial community, was reluctant. But her tariff act the summer of this year greatly increased the list of dutiable goods, while in the autumn of 1786, under the dangerous pressure of the rebellious west, the legislature laid duties of from one to fifteen per cent. on a long roster of commodities, and hit luxuries—against which there was now a nation-wide clamor— especially hard.[59]

Just how large were the sums thus raised by the States? In 1785 the Pennsylvania committee of ways and means estimated that the revenue would be, one year with another, £82,232 annually. Virginia, trying hard to pay off her enormous debt, found that in a little less than a year, 1786-87, her customs receipts, including the export duties on tobacco, were almost £87,000. In 1788 the New York collector of customs paid into the treasury no less than £70,-298 as the proceeds of the tariff. The statement of the Massachusetts legislature after Shays's rebellion declared that the whole sum received during the years 1781-85 inclusive from the tariff and excise was £154,378, or more than one-tenth the whole amount of taxes levied in that period. This was little enough, but as we have seen, the tariff had just been increased. In South Carolina the tariff was sufficient to pay the whole civil list of the State. North Carolina, in spite of her small commerce, collected in 1787 from the impost by water and the British tonnage dues no less than £17,165.[60] It is interesting to note how Elbridge Gerry ranked the commerce of the several States when in 1789 he reported to the national House an estimate of the probable net proceeds from the Federal tariff and tonnage dues, drawn from the latest data available. It was a rough computation, for the revenue laws were diverse and the modes of keeping the accounts varied greatly. The estimated tariff collections in Pennsylvania were $376,841; in New York, $245,165; in Maryland, $223,620; and in Massachusetts, $216,366. Virginia fell into fifth place, with estimated collections of $176,185, and

[59] Laws of Pa., 1810 ed., I, chapters 914, 987, 1177; Hening's "Statutes," X, 165, 501; Laws of Maryland, 1780, June session, Ch. 7; Acts and Laws of Mass., 1781, p. 94; 1782, p. 166; 1785, p. 300; 1786, p. 526; Laws of New York, 1777-1801, I, 585, 599, II, 7, 11.
[60] *Amer. Museum*, V, 252; Grigsby, "Va. Fed. Conv.," II, 172 ff.; Rowland's Mason, II, 60-62; N. Y. *Packet*, Jan. 23, 1789; report by North Carolina legislative sub-committee, published in S. Ca. *State Gazette*, Feb. 17, 1789.

South Carolina into sixth, with $137,887. No other State was expected to return more than $80,000.[61]

A salient feature of State finance during and after the Revolution was the way in which large arrears of taxes were allowed to accumulate, and a few instances will show eloquently how the treasuries suffered from this fact. The arrears in Massachusetts in the years 1781-86 inclusive amounted to no less than £279,437, or nearly one-fourth the whole taxes levied in that time. The total of unpaid back-taxes in New Hampshire was estimated at £120,000 in 1785. Pennsylvania in the five years preceding March 21, 1783, had passed acts for raising the enormous sum of £20,996,995 in Continental bills, £367,381 in State money, and £745,297 in specie. The failure to pay in some sections was so marked that the Legislature resolved that the counties "have hitherto contributed towards the public expenses in very unequal proportions," contrary to the bill of rights, and that a remedy must be found. In the years 1782-83, the State laid taxes for £645,000, but the amount actually paid was £202,367—less than a third.

In New York in the midsummer of 1782 special legislation went into effect to compel the payment of back-taxes. As for Maryland, the total tax arrears for 1784-85 were £97,000, and the House estimated in the spring of 1787 that those for 1786 would be about £100,000. In Virginia the difficulties of collection early became insuperable. We have mentioned the armed resistance to tax collectors during the war. In 1781 half a dozen counties paid nothing at all, and many others furnished no revenue except the license taxes, which amounted to a mere pittance. Only about half the counties paid anything under the general assessments. All this indicates a hopeless disorganization of Virginia's revenue system. Indeed, the State government, headed by the stern soldier Thomas Nelson, Jr., encouraged the troops to collect supplies from the countryside as they were needed. This "seizing scheme" caused great restiveness, but it was unavoidable. After 1781 the tax system should have been reinvigorated. Yet we find that one of the standing grievances of men like Madison was the tendency of the House to postpone the date on which taxes fell due, on such excuses as that the people must be given the benefit of an approaching market. Legislation to make distraint for unpaid taxes was also delayed or defeated. Arrears

[61] American State Papers, Finance, I, 14.

reached such a volume that in 1787 the treasurer received more than £33,000 ($110,000) on their account, or nearly one-fourth the year's receipts in current taxes. In North Carolina the Treasurer collected for the year ending November 1, 1788, the sum of £35,862 on account of taxes for that year, and as arrearages for previous years no less than £54,131, or half again as much.[62]

No complaints of government at that period were commoner than expressions of dissatisfaction with the mechanism for collecting State moneys, and none were better based. Why doesn't the Legislature demand the immediate payment of outstanding taxes? asked a writer in the *New Hampshire Mercury* in 1785.[63] Here the State is paying interest for borrowed moneys, taxes are rising, and those who do pay them are shouldering a double burden. It would be only right if those who have heretofore made punctual payment would refuse to contribute any more until the arrears were collected. I have seen several Legislatures, wrote Governor Livingston of New Jersey, economize by paring the salaries of officials to the bone. But I have not yet seen one calling to serious account the sheriffs who have defrauded the State of hundreds of pounds apiece, or the commissioners who have plundered us of thousands.[64] Governor Burke of North Carolina in 1781 complained that the numberless men employed in collecting revenue exhausted much of it, while by neglecting to settle with the county courts, they prevented the clearing up of the accounts and the due collection of outstanding taxes.[65] Two years later Samuel Johnston made the same complaint, saying that the scattering of the State's money through many hands was

[62] Arrears in New York reached such a sum that at the fall session in 1781, Governor Clinton recommended stern measures to collect them, and the following June again referred to them in his address to the Legislature. For the arrears in Massachusetts, see "Address of the General Court to the People," 1786; for those in Maryland, see "The present State of Maryland, by Delegates of the People," 1787. The Maryland *Gazette* of April 1, 1785, put the arrears of the previous year at £132,818. Thomas Johnson wrote Washington in 1787 that the State was "so embarrassed with a diversity of paper money and paper securities, a sparing imposition and an infamous collection and payment (or rather non-payment) of taxes," that he could not say when there would be money in hand to meet a debt of £300! Sparks, "Letters to Washington," IV, 195. For arrears in Virginia, see Calendar of State Papers, 1781, 128, 134, 239, *et passim;* Richmond College Hist. Papers, II, No. 1.

[63] June 21, 1785.

[64] Sedgwick's "Livingston," 392-93. For "An Act to compel the officers of the State to pay forward the same species of monies and obligations by them received in trust for the State" (it being common for them to pay forward in money that had greatly depreciated) see Acts of N. J. Gen. Ass. of 1783-84, p. 114.

[65] In 1782 it was necessary to send special agents to almost every county commissioner, as Governor Burke said, "either to interest him in his duty," or "to urge him to a more precise execution"; this was "expensive and laborious," but absolutely necessary. Burke declared that the collectors were bound by no law then in force either to make returns of their collections, or to account for their expenditures, save perhaps to a Legislature too busy to inquire into such matters. N. C. State Records, XV, 497-98; XVI, 5-19.

annually costing thousands. Legislation to give more vigor to the collection of taxes became familiar in all parts of the United States. In North Carolina, for example, an act was passed at the October session in 1779 to compel sheriffs and collectors to account for taxes, one at the spring session in 1780 for more effectual tax-gathering, and later laws for the same purposes in 1781, 1784, 1785, and 1787— a half dozen in all! [66]

One State after another resorted to the appointment of a special officer to assist the Treasurer and to scrutinize the general fiscal administration, laying statements of the public finances before the Legislature. He was usually called the Comptroller. The lead in this reform was taken by Pennsylvania, in which the financial confusion at the close of the Revolution was extreme. In March, 1781, a committee composed of Reed, Bayard, and Rittenhouse reported to the legislature on the reasons for the steady accumulation of uncollected taxes. One cause was the dearth of competent tax-gatherers, for suitable men would not undertake the disagreeable duty for the low compensation offered; another was the authorization of payments in kind; and a third was the fact that farmers frequently regarded the Continental or State certificates as receipts for the payment of their face value in taxes. The unwise removal of excise officers, just beginning to understand their duties, at every fresh overturn in politics, kept the excise department in constant chaos. Finally, prosecutions for the non-payment of taxes were seldom attempted. The movement for reform in Pennsylvania led to the establishment of the position of Comptroller-General, filled first by John Nicholson. He was to collect arrears, settle accounts, and prepare an annual abstract of financial operations for the Assembly; and at once he began saving his modest salary many times over. "All accounts and demands are liquidated with a diligence and an ability that is of the most important advantage to the State," commented the *Freeman's Journal*.[67] "A chaos of old papers have been waded through with immence patience, and many errors of former auditors and committees of Assembly discovered." [68]

[66] See Reed's "Reed," for many letters describing the waste of Pennsylvania money during the war; and Bolles's "Pennsylvania," II, 65 ff. In North Carolina gross frauds in the forging of war claims were connived at by public officers; see Boyd's "North Carolina," p. 3.

[67] December 31, 1783. Nicholson had authority to fix the specie sums due to soldiers, and to issue interest-bearing certificates for them. A mechanism for adjudicating appeals from this authority was constructed in 1785. See Laws of Pa., 1810 Ed., II, Chs. 959, 1147.

[68] Similar offices were created in North Carolina and New Hampshire. "The disorder of the public accounts calls loudly for a remedy to distinguish what should be

It is interesting to note that the admirable work of Robert Morris for the nation led to suggestions that the all-powerful Legislatures appoint similar officers for the States. The finances of Massachusetts and New York were as well-ordered as those of any State save Connecticut and Delaware. But "Consideration" nevertheless protested in the Massachusetts *Centinel* in 1786 against "the loose mode of doing this business by committees" of the Legislature, a mode which meant that no one was responsible for the success or failure of financial policies. "Witness," he argued, "the loss of Tory estates—the old money—the public securities refused, which were offered by the officers of the late army, for Eastern lands: and those lands now in danger of being totally lost to the public." Why not appoint the Treasurer to superintend all financial affairs as a Financier?[69] Later in the year another correspondent suggested that Gen. Lincoln be made Commissioner of Finance, and empowered to draft a comprehensive financial program. During November the office of Comptroller-General was duly established. In New York a year later a writer in the *Advertiser* called for a superintendent of finance who would bring all disbursing officers to strict account, see that taxes were collected, and lay exact fiscal statements before the Legislature. In 1789 a House committee in South Carolina reported that it was essential that there be one or a few persons empowered to "control and superintend the finances of the State," but the Senate disagreed.[70]

IV. PAPER MONEY MOVEMENT OF 1785-86

It remains to record the most interesting episode of State financial history under the Confederation—the great paper money agitation of 1785-86; and the antecedent circumstances must be kept clearly in mind. In these two years the country felt itself full in the trough of the economic depression that had swept over it like a wave in since 1781. Actually, it was already in the slope of the

charges against the United States," Governor Burke told the Legislature in April, 1782; N. C. State Records, XVI, 5-19. In South Carolina the Legislature made many efforts to take direct supervision of the fiscal department through committees. "Nevertheless," wrote Ramsay (II, 192), "many frauds were committed without detection, and much was lost from neglect and mismanagement. No man in or out of office could tell with any precision the amount of the debts and credits of the State." For the Connecticut controllership, see New Haven *Gazette*, June 22, 1786; for the New Hampshire office, N. H. State Papers, XXI, 407. Virginia in 1780 appointed a solicitor-general to help collect arrears and bills; Hening, X, 358.

[69] February 28, 1786.
[70] N. Y. *Advertiser*, March 17, 1787; S. C. *State Gazette*, February 17, 1789; Mass. *Centinel*, September 30, 1786; Mass. Acts and Laws, 1786, p. 511.

succeeding wave of prosperity, but it could not know that. The skies seemed darker and darker. In 1783 the States, the towns, the counties, were heavily oppressed by debt; the public had suffered from the total loss of perhaps two hundred million dollars in repudiated paper, and from increasing taxation; and large areas had been laid waste. From an exhausting war recovery was naturally slow and hard, and it was made harder by European trade restrictions. The British regulations regarding the West Indies alone cost American merchants a trade worth $3,500,000 annually. Because there was no national coinage of specie, and a steady purchase of goods from overseas was maintained, the business and agricultural depression was accompanied by a stringency of hard money.

All over the nation after Cornwallis's surrender shrewd statesmen called for a pay-as-you-go policy and for taxation to reduce debts. The State debt of Massachusetts was about $7,100,000, and there not a few urged repudiation, though this would mean a sore loss to many patriotic creditors, and even destitution to many returned soldiers. Governor Hancock in 1783 took a wiser view. He urged the Legislature, in view of the dire need of many veterans who were being forced to sell their wage certificates at one-eighth their face value, and of other considerations, to take vigorous measures to raise money. An additional tax of $470,000 was voted for the soldiers, and in 1784 the tax screws were still further tightened. Roger Sherman was a prominent advocate in Connecticut of heavy taxation. Governor Clinton opened the year 1784 in New York by urging "productive funds for the discharge of the interest and sinking, as soon as may be practicable, the principal of the public debts." Madison in Virginia preached the same doctrine. Governor Guerard of South Carolina in 1783 called for retrenchment, a bank, and a sinking fund, "that so, we may accomplish the full and honorable discharge of all our debts." [71]

These exhortations fell at the moment that most men were hoping for relaxation and ease; and complaints that it was impossible to pay more taxes became nation-wide. They were sometimes justified, but more often baseless. Governor Rutledge admitted in South Carolina at the commencement of 1782 that "in the present scarcity

---

[71] S. C. *Gazette*, February 19, 1784. Governor Rutledge had preceded Guerard by saying, at the beginning of 1782, that "all unsettled demands should be liquidated, and satisfactory assurances of payment given the public creditors." R. W. Gibbes, "Doc. Hist. Am. Rev., 1781-82," 237.

of specie it would be difficult, if not impossible, to levy a tax to any considerable amount, towards sinking the public debt. . . .," and R. H. Lee in similar vein wrote Madison, near the close of 1784, expostulating against the latter's views. Daily accounts were being received, he said, of the powerful migrations from Virginia to the southward and southwestward, caused by land hunger and the hatred of heavy taxes. Virginia's tax rate Lee thought to be probably the heaviest in the world, and he proposed cutting it down, and doing no more than pay the interest and a very small part of the principal of the State debt yearly.[72]

In New York just after Cornwallis's surrender the Legislature protested that it believed it impossible, in the exhausted condition of the State, to comply with any of the Congressional requisitions. A New England correspondent of a London journal sent it in 1784 an account of the aversion of the Massachusetts legislators to taxes. "They are not chosen for any particular abilities, but are sent with express direction to oppose all taxes. The cry is, don't tell us of the necessity of the times, but let us have no taxes." He pictured their dull, lifeless sessions. "If in the midst of a drowsy harangue, the word *taxes* should be mentioned, the sound electrifies them in an instant, like sleeping geese; when alarmed, every head is elevated, every eye is opened; all is bustle and attention; and no sooner has the speaker sat down, but twenty of these no-tax men will rise together, to let fly a volley of objections."[73]

Answers to all these complaints were easily made. When Connecticut excused herself from paying a Continental requisition, Morris wrote Governor Trumbull (July 31, 1782) that the people were talking nonsense. In all countries it was constantly being complained that times were hard, money was scarce, taxes were heavy, and the like. But the very universality of the complaint, he declared, showed that it was usually unfounded. The simple fact was that the ordinary man would always find use for all the money he could get hold of, and more, and that the taxgatherer would therefore always be an unwelcome visitant.[74] He wrote more testily to Virginia. The inhabitants there, he said, wouldn't pay money in taxes because they wanted it "to purchase foreign superfluities and administer to luxurious indolence." A New Jersey writer in the spring

[72] Letters, II, 300.
[73] Republished S. C. *Gazette*, December 16, 1784.
[74] Oberholtzer, "Morris," 147.

of 1782 argued that there was not another three million people on the face of the earth so prosperous as Americans. The income of an industrious common laborer, he declared, was equal to that of a tradesman in England.[75] In Virginia there appeared an ironical essay on "Proofs of the Scarcity of Money." This scarcity so hampered racing, the essayist said, that at ten turfs within the State a total of only £2,610 was paid yearly to winning horses. Great crowds of poverty stricken people in fine clothes, betting money, thronged the turfs. There were now only five times as many four-wheeled carriages as there had been two decades before; while many families had given up a chair worth £15 or £20 for a chariot worth many times as much. When the "American Comedians" had appeared in Richmond and Petersburg in the last two years, the audience of penniless men eager to forget their money troubles crowded the theatre to suffocation. In cock-fighting the spring had passed, and only £355 had been paid to owners of winning cocks. But all such answers, sarcastic or denunciatory, were in vain.[76]

Two States escaped the paper money agitation almost wholly, Connecticut and Delaware; in three more the paper money party could not gain control of the Legislatures; and in several others no extensive harm was wrought. We must remember that the paper money doctrine was endemic, and that what happened in 1785 was that it simply became epidemic and virulent. North Carolina in 1783 made an emission for the relief of the soldiery, which Samuel Johnston's conservative party hailed with alarm.[77] In the same year in Virginia the demand led Fairfax County to instruct its representatives to oppose all future emissions. In Maryland in 1784 a definite proposal was formulated—that £100,000 in paper be loaned at six per cent. During 1785-86 the wave of economic discouragement reached its crest in all the States; depression and pessimism were converted in many communities into desperation; and like an irresistible swell the demand arose everywhere for help— for stay laws, for paper money, and for a postponement of taxes. It was strong in many towns, and overwhelming in many country districts.

"Pennsylvania and North Carolina," Madison wrote Jefferson in

[75] N. J. *Gazette*, April 17, 1782. More wealth was lost by indolent agriculture in the years 1776-78, he said, than all the Federal levies amounted to.
[76] N. Haven *Gazette*, October 5, 1786.
[77] For its protest against paper money and the law suspending suits, see McRee's Iredell, II, 63-64.

1786, "took the lead in this folly." It was no accident that the two States which were worst governed during the Revolution did so, and that they suffered far more than any others from their emissions.

The second distinctive paper money episode in Pennsylvania history is one of great interest. When the war ended the State had made an earnest, intelligent effort to abolish its financial difficulties. In order to take care of its share of the "forty-to-one" bills of 1780, the Legislature passed an act for levying $93,640 in taxes annually for six years. In June, 1784, the first tax-levy in specie was made, for a sum no less than £200,000—before the war the government's yearly income had not exceeded £40,000. Payments were still short of the expected mark, for well-to-do men, including many Quakers, concealed part of their property after the war as well as during it, and when it could not be concealed, delayed paying their assessments. But steadily the burden was brought closer home to those who ought to bear it. By the end of 1784 the accounts had been fairly set in order, and the whole indebtedness ascertained. It was known that the interest upon the debt to the general government amounted to about £125,000; that the Penns would have to be recompensed for their lands; and that provision must be made for the debt owed to citizens of the State. Had Pennsylvania possessed a double-chambered Legislature, it might have kept on in the path it had wisely taken in liquidating its liabilities.

But at this juncture, in December, 1784, the single house proposed that the State should assume all debts of the United States to citizens of Pennsylvania, in cancellation of an equal amount of the State's debt to the general government; and that it should establish a perpetual fund for paying six per cent on these debts. Such a fund would be costly, and the Legislature had to admit that even the existing taxes were so heavy that the arrearages had been enormous. It therefore resolved that "to enable the good people of this State to pay the arrearages of taxes with greater ease and facility, bills of credit to the amount of . . . £183,232 be prepared." President Dickinson, in a message of February 1, 1785, protested against this with his usual conservative wisdom. The assumption, he said, would be needless, costly, and a blow to the nation's credit, for it would make it appear that the State distrusted the ability of the national government to pay the Pennsylvania creditors. And he especially objected to the paper emission. Already, he pointed out, the State had more than £160,000 in circulation, which had depreciated so that it required $2.50 in it to buy one dollar in specie, and which, though it might be used at face value in buying State lands, was still falling.[78]

The President had earnest supporters. The legislators in the spring of 1785 found before them a petition from the "middle counties" declaring that the funding and paper money plan meant the ruin of the State. The Continental certificates of debt owed to Pennsylvanians would, under the plan, be good for the purchase of Pennsylvania lands. The result, the petitioners alleged, would be that a few of the speculators in these certificates would obtain great areas, set up manors, and hold the tenant population in vassalage. The poor would not be benefited by the plan, for very few of them "have certificates in their possession; these are chiefly in the hands of those who have taken advantage of the vices, the ignorance, or the necessities of the men who fought and bled for our defence, so as legally to rob them of seven parts in eight of their dearly earned wages." The certificate holders who did not want to buy land would be paid interest on their holdings. "A tribe of speculators have haunted the poor soldiers at every place where they were called to settle their accounts, and have, by every artifice in their power, seduced them to part with their certificates at one-eighth or one-tenth their value; then, in order to relieve these poor sufferers, their widows and children, etc., very few of whom have no certificate in possession, and in order to preserve the public faith, justice, and credit, it becomes necessary to make every certificate bear interest!"[79] At least, the petitioners asked, discriminate between the original holders of certificates, and those who bought them at a fraction of their face value. From the mercantile interests of Philadelphia came a protest against the paper money feature, presented after a public meeting at the City Tavern that was fifty to one against the emission.[80]

But two groups zealously pushed the plan: the public creditors, and the many paper-money enthusiasts. The former had long petitioned the Legislature to relieve their sufferings in consequence of the failure of Congress either to pay its debts to them, or to allow

[78] Pa. Archives, Series IV, Vol. 3, 991 ff.
[79] Pa. *Packet,* March 12, 1785.
[80] Pa. *Packet,* Feb. 24, 1785.

them interest. It was an act of essential justice, demanded by State honor, they argued. In newspaper essays and vehement public meetings, they recalled how during the war the holders of certificates had loaned money, furnished supplies, and bled in the field, and how scurvily they had since been treated. Many veterans were represented to be languishing in debtors' cells. As for paper money, a noisy party everywhere outside of Philadelphia held that the lack of a circulating medium was palpable. In the end, the two groups won, though not simultaneously. The funding bill was not enacted until the next year, 1786. It need be said only that it allowed the exchange of certificates, issued to Pennsylvanians by Congress, for State certificates, and that it made of the latter—the "new loan certificates"—the foundation of the State's funded debt. The authors of the law were to the last angrily accused of jobbery, and there is no doubt that some pretty fortunes were made as by the waving of a wand.[81]

The paper money measure, however, was passed immediately—that is, on March 16, 1785. It provided for emitting £150,000, of which £100,000 was to be a fund for paying public creditors, and £50,000 was to be loaned at six per cent upon real estate security. To preserve the value of the bills, they were made receivable for all taxes, imposts, or debts due the State; while it was stipulated that funds for redemption, besides the interest on £50,000, should be set aside from the ordinary revenues in sums sufficient to redeem £20,000 a year.

Dickinson was right in saying there was no good reason for this issue of Pennsylvania paper. Peletiah Webster published an essay early in the year declaring and proving that there was a full circulating medium, and that labor and produce alike found a ready cash market. It was indeed hard to borrow money, and public securities of all kinds sold very low, but that was because the public, with

[81] These two groups largely united in pushing a third measure, the annulment of the charter of the Bank of North America; see Pa. *Packet,* March 9, 1785. The files of the *Packet* contain much upon the soft money movement; e.g., issues of March 5, 8, and 18th. Some of the many complex financial and economic results of the funding law are evident from a complaint in the Pa. *Gazette* of February 3, 1790. This writer states that the funding law checked private loans of all kinds, for no one would lend money for 6 per cent. when the State gave 24 or 30 per cent, "according as the certificates were sold for 4s. or 5s. in the pound, which was their current price for several years after they were funded." It let creditors loose upon their debtors, in order to purchase certificates with the money, and many farmers were ruined. It checked trade and manufacturing, for men employed ready capital in buying certificates. The weight of taxes required to carry out the law drove many families to the West and South. It took from realty the value that was given the certificates; and it restrained the sale of the State lands.

good reason, distrusted all ordinary "security." Inasmuch as the paper issued was not made a legal tender in payment of private debts, it created no profound disturbance; but the State had ample reason to rue it.

For only a few months the bills passed on a par with specie. By midsummer of 1786, the depreciation had reached 12 per cent. In July of 1787, by concerted action, the banks and markets of Philadelphia ceased to accept them. By the summer of 1788 the money had fallen so low that it had ceased altogether to be a medium, and was simply an article, of commerce. The public creditors were then petitioning that it be given currency again by making it receivable for local taxes as well as State taxes, but this was out of the question.[82] Since the State government accepted the bills at face value, they were in constant demand for discharging taxes and duties. The State thus lost in receiving them, and paying them out again at a discount; the officers of government lost by receiving them for salaries; and public creditors lost by receiving them as interest. Taxpayers who hoped that they would fall still further in value delayed paying their taxes so that they might take advantage of the fall. Since they could not be bought in outlying sections as readily as in Philadelphia, the people of remote rural districts had practically to pay a higher tax rate. Moreover, tax collectors were faced by the constant temptation to keep whatever specie came in, and substitute bills of credit for it at a neat profit. In all, despite the fact that up to September 10, 1788, no less than £87,000 of the bills had been redeemed and destroyed by the State, leaving only about £63,000 outstanding, they were a thorn in the side of the government. In the latter part of this year a subscription was set on foot for their purchase and destruction by public-spirited men, whom the State, of course, would be bound to repay.

Why did New Jersey have recourse to paper money?—so Brissot de Warville asked Governor Livingston's son in 1788. The State ships products to New York and Philadelphia, and thus draws money constantly from those cities. She is a creditor, and why does she

[82] The petitioners alleged that its depreciation was such as to cause "very great distress and loss to individuals; and, by giving hopes of further depreciation, to tempt great numbers of people to delay the payment of the debts, taxes, and customs due to the State." It circulated only in Philadelphia, and very slowly there; and they thought that making it payable for local taxes would remedy this. For the slow depreciation of the bills, see Md. *Journal,* August 9, 1785, which says some advertisements give them a preference over specie, and the Pa. *Packet* of July 17 and 18, 1787. The text of the paper money act is in Laws of Pa., 1810 Ed., II, Ch. 1526.

use the resource of a miserable debtor? The reason is simple, replied young Mr. Livingston. "At the close of the ruinous war that
we have experienced, the greater part of our citizens were burdened
with debts. They saw, in this paper money, the means of extricating themselves; and they had influence enough with their representatives to enable them to create it." The clamorers for paper
bills in the spring of 1786 threatened the courts with violence if they
tried to collect debts, and some communities refused to elect any
assessors in order to delay tax-collection. On May 26, 1786, a bill
passed emitting £100,000. It was to be loaned on realty mortgages
at six per cent. for twelve years, no one person receiving more than
£100 or less than £25. The security was to be at least double the
loan, and from the eighth to the twelfth years inclusive one-fifth of
the principal was to be repaid annually; while the emission was
made a legal tender for all private and public debts. This paper
immediately depreciated; specie disappeared; and it became impossible to borrow money on the best security, the lender fearing repayment in the bills.[83]

"In North Carolina," wrote Madison apropos of Pennsylvania's
experience, "the sum issued at different times has been of greater
amount, and it has constantly been a tender." North Carolina really
fared worse than the Keystone State. We have noted that in 1783
an emission of £100,000 was authorized. In November, 1785,
another issue of the same amount was ordered, with the simple result
that for several years the public and private finances in the State
were staggered. In the House eight members, led by Maclaine and
Hugh Williamson, signed a vigorous paper in opposition.[84] They
pointed to the depreciation of the issue of 1783, a sure omen of the
fate of the new money. Such a currency, to be a legal tender for
all purposes, they said, strikes us with alarm for the honor of the
State, the security of trade, and the safety of all honest men. They
described the dangers with which it was fraught for civil servants,
merchants, creditors, and for commerce, which was already much
depressed. But the dominant radicals in the Legislature would not
be denied; and when ordinary methods of putting the money into

---

[83] New Jersey also issued an irregular kind of paper currency, called "revenue
money," which had twenty-four years to circulate, and fell quickly. Brissot de
Warville, "New Travels" (1788), Letter 6; N. Y. *Packet*, May 25, 1786; Acts of
Gen. Ass. of N. J., 1785-86, 293-313; Pa. *Packet*, January 17, 1786. See an essay
on New Jersey paper money by "Silver-Money" in the Pa. *Gazette*, October 14, 1788.
[84] N. C. State Records, XVII, 410-11.

circulation proved slow, large purchases of tobacco were made by the State and paid for in paper at an excessive valuation. The result was what had been prophesied. Many men who had been doing an interstate or overseas business left for other parts. By November, 1786, hard money was at a premium of fifty per cent. Nevertheless, one citizen wrote, "the wretched creditor is obliged to receive this paper trash for sterling debts, nay, frequently happy to receive it as the only liquidation he can get of accounts that have been standing for years." [85]

Georgia was the fourth and last State whose experiment with paper money can be called unfortunate, though it was neither an extensive experiment nor one with alarming results. During the summer of 1786 the Legislature authorized the issue of £50,000, part of which was to be used if an apprehended war with the Creeks occurred, and the remainder to pay the arrears due the State's soldiers. Chatham County, in which lies Savannah, opposed the emission, but the planters and farmers carried it by a heavy majority. Loaded with debt, unable to obtain credit, with no specie available in whole communities, their distress was great.[86] An effort was made to support the issue by patriotic appeals; one captain bid for some of the first bills printed at the rate of nearly twenty-two shillings a pound; but the mechanics were rebellious. A meeting of sixty-six of them in Savannah, nearly the whole body in that town, resolved not to take the money, declaring that it had no better security than the paper already issued, which the State had called in at the rate of one silver dollar for one thousand paper dollars. Actually—hostilities with the Indians being postponed—only about £30,000 was printed. Thanks to this fact, and to the pledge of the large tract called the New Cession for its security, the bills, after some damaging fluctuations, were finally redeemed.[87]

In two States the emission of paper can be called, if not a success,

[85] A traveler reported in the Md. *Gazette* of July 29, 1785, that importation had so fallen off in North Carolina that men everywhere dressed in jeans and cotton stripes, women in cottons, of their own manufacture. See also a letter from North Carolina in the Mass. *Centinel,* November 25, 1786; and for the depreciation of the issue of 1783, S. C. *Gazette,* July 15, 1784. Its accompaniment of sheer grafting made, this issue of 1785 famous throughout America. The sum of £36,000 was reserved for the purchase of tobacco, which was to be sold for the reduction of the State's share of the Continental debt. After great delays, blundering, and corruption, over £37,500 was spent exclusive of fees, storage, and carriage, and the amount sold was less than the amount purchased. Boyd, "N. Ca.," Ch. I.

[86] Pa. *Packet,* January 9, 1786.

[87] Marbury and Crawford, "Digest of Laws," 379-80; Pa. *Packet,* January 9, 1786; N. Hampshire *Mercury,* October 25, 1786; N. Haven *Gazette,* September 14, 1786. Governor Telfair opposed this issue; Stevens, "Georgia," II, 374.

at least quite harmless—South Carolina and New York. Both took precautions to see that the paper was kept at or near its face value; and in the former especially it could be pleaded that the issue was absolutely unavoidable. The South Carolinians had excellent reason for seizing at any straw that promised economic and financial relief. The conditions among them in the fall of 1785 were described by one witness as constituting "anarchy":

> The produce of this country has borne no proportion to their enormous imports since the peace. Many of the inhabitants . . . being obliged to leave the country while the English had the ascendancy . . . returned home in a destitute, forlorn condition; and to supply their wants took up goods and other articles, wherever they could procure credit. These were charged about 100 per cent. more than the ready money price. Their mode of living, perhaps more profuse and luxurious than in any other part of the Continent, increased the evil. The day of payment arrives, arrests and imprisonment alarm the community, and every man becomes tremblingly alive all over for the misfortunes of his neighbors, expecting his own turn next. Thus the magnitude of the evil suggests a desperate remedy; they stop the course of the law, so that throughout this wealthy State, except in Charleston, the seat of government, a sheriff does not serve a writ, or levy an execution.

Credit was absolutely dead in South Carolina in 1785. Stay laws passed in 1782 and subsequent years suspended suits for all debts antedating the spring of 1782, until 1786, when one-fourth became payable. To illustrate the lack of money, it was stated that one man who owned four negroes had taken a fifth on his note, payable in three years, and that when the term expired in 1786, an execution was levied upon his estate, and all five negroes were sold for less than the original price of one.[88] Henry Laurens wrote in the spring of 1786 that he frequently had less than a dollar in cash, and during the same season the negroes on one of Edward Rutledge's plantations were in danger of starvation. A succession of bad crops and desolating freshets had conspired with the reduction of the export trade to make it impossible for planters or farmers to recover from the destruction of the war, or to pay for the goods that they had ordered on credit; and the merchants were as badly off as the agriculturists.[89]

One utterly indefensible measure of the Legislature was the so-called Pine Barren Act of October 12, 1785. It authorized a debtor who was under prosecution to tender any kind of lands at two-

[88] Pa. *Mercury,* June 2, 1786.
[89] A good account of the financial prostration of South Carolina may be found in Wallace, Laurens, 428-30. Timothy Ford says in his Diary of the time (S. C. Hist. and Genealog. Mag., XIII), that a number of British merchants after the Revolution imported large cargoes of slaves from Africa, which the planters bought, paying only one-half or one-fourth down; thus a large part of the State fell deeply in debt. The merchants in 1784 began to insist rigidly upon payment, and "an universal alarm took place." In some localities the sheriffs were defied, and one fiery planter, served with a writ, obliged the officer to eat it on the spot. What Ford says is fully confirmed by a writer in the Md. *Journal,* October 14, 1785.

thirds their value, their worth to be fixed by three independent arbiters; if the property so tendered exceeded the debt, the creditor was to give his bond for this excess, payable in six months. Unprincipled men took advantage of the act to offer lands lying at such a distance that the expense of viewing and appraising them would nearly equal the debt; and a creditor frequently preferred relinquishing his claim to sending good money after bad. In the same way, men might tender personal possessions, and they sometimes assembled hay, corn, pigs, fodder, and so on far up-country, and called upon the Charleston merchant nearly two hundred miles away to transport the property to the sea. Two merchants advertising for a settlement of accounts due, early in 1786, stated in the press that all debts now had to be regarded as "nearly upon the same footing as debts of honor." Laurens a few months later sighed for the time when everyone would be "out of debt and become honest again." The Pine Barren Act was good only until the next meeting of the Legislature, and by it was allowed to become extinct.[90]

Much less objectionable, however, was the act of the autumn of 1785 for issuing £100,000, this money going into circulation early the next year. More than 130 Charleston merchants, traders, and other men of substance pledged themselves to receive it as gold or silver. The bills were issued as loans to individuals, bearing interest to the State, and were not legal tender for private debts. The merchants loyally carried out their agreement. A slight depreciation soon set in from two causes: specie was in almost exclusive demand for foreign trade and travel, since the paper was not known outside the State; while the planters began demanding a higher payment for grain or indigo in paper than in specie, and thus lowered faith in it. But a mass-meeting of planters and merchants at the State House in the summer of 1786 checked the depreciation by a new agreement to regard the paper and specie as on an exact parity, and to coöperate better in maintaining that parity. The famous Hint Club was organized, to call upon those who gave a preference to specie with an emphatic hint to mend their ways. These expedients met with marked success. The paper held its value, was of great utility

[90] Ford's Diary; Pa. *Packet*, June 10, 1786; N. Y. *Packet*, November 28, 1785. The two merchants here spoken of (N. Y. *Packet*, May 4, 1786) were forced thus to plead for payment because many of the duties and other payments to the State were demanded, by law, in specie. "We are willing to pay the treasurers," they said, "but unable." The law is in S. C. Statutes at Large, Cooper Ed., IV, 710. From 1784 to 1788 inclusive the annual tax bills were accompanied by the issue of indents, varying from £64,000 to £125,000 annually, to facilitate tax payments.

to the hard-pressed planters, and returned a steady revenue to the State. Such was its success that in 1789, when specie dollars were pouring into Charleston, it was preferred as being more convenient to use.[91]

In New York there was a much stronger but quite futile opposition to paper money. The two parties met with in all States, one for and one against an emission, began forming in 1784, and were squarely aligned against each other by the end of 1785. The advocates of a paper issue were in the main a country party, and the opponents a city party. Naturally, the men with capital—creditors, importers, wholesale merchants, and professional men—were against any measure which would depreciate their holdings and cut their investments in two. The pinched farmers and retail merchants, the small manufacturers, the laboring men, debtors everywhere, could point to a hundred symptoms of need for paper money. Every other goodman on the street or the country highway was in debt, and could not find the money to pay his obligations. Money lenders charged double interest, demanded double security, and insisted upon collecting their loans on the day they fell due. Lands and houses, put in the market by poor devils who had not a ready sixpence, brought only half their real worth. Why should honest citizens not be given an opportunity to borrow money from the State, paying a reasonable rate of interest, and thus tide themselves over till better times? Thomas Paine published a pamphlet attacking the fallacies of the paper money craze, and the ever watchful and sagacious Chamber of Commerce of New York, whose history is filled with so many acts of wisdom, published a petition of protest (February 13, 1786); but all efforts to stem the tide were in vain.[92]

Not that the sound money party failed to check the tide at first. In 1784 the Senate refused to pass a bill for emitting bills of credit (sums of £100,000 and £150,000 were proposed), and in 1785 it halted a bill for £100,000 which the House passed 22 to 18. In 1786 the upper chamber still viewed an emission with reluctance,

[91] Md. *Journal*, Jan. 15, 1789. A new demand for an emission of paper, at least £300,000, found expression in the Legislature of the spring of 1789, its supporters coming from the interior. They said that the emission of 1785 had benefited the rich, and that now the poor should have a turn. When a bold editor of the *State Gazette* poked fun at the scheme, the Legislature haled him before its bar and extorted an apology. *Gazette*, March 16, 1789. The paper money of 1785 was loaned on security of lands worth twice the value, or gold or silver plate worth twice as much; and was to be repaid in five years. Statutes at Large, IV, 712.

[92] N. Y. *Packet*, February 16, 1786. The Chamber proposed that if the Legislature did issue paper, it should not be a legal tender, so that it would not be to the interest of borrowers to see it depreciated.

though it formally admitted that "from the scarcity of money in this State, the property of debtors is daily sold on executions for a very inconsiderable part of its value, to the total ruin of such debtors and their families." The House voted to issue £200,000, and the Senate amended the measure to make the sum £150,000, and to obliterate the clause which made the bills of credit a legal tender in certain circumstances. The Assembly refused to accept the amendments, however, and the sum of £200,000, equivalent to $500,000 Spanish-milled dollars, stood.

It was loaned only upon excellent security, and was made a legal tender for private debt only in case of suits. When the first bills came from the press, the public was reluctant to take them, and a few men of wealth set an ostentatious example by going about to crowded inns and barrooms, demanding the bills in place of the more cumbersome specie. By the end of the year even the opponents of the paper issue had to admit that the credit of the bills was good. They fluctuated in value, and at times were at a discount of as much as ten per cent., but they remained a valid circulating medium. In midsummer of 1787 it was boasted that they were "universally received upon a par with gold or silver, in large or small quantities." [93]

And what of the Southern and Middle States which resisted the paper-money movement of 1785-86? In all it was strongly felt, but two commonwealths it passed over harmlessly and without long-continued excitement: Virginia and Delaware. In the old Dominion the legislative session which terminated in January, 1786, showed— as Madison reported—a "considerable itch" for paper money, though no bill for it was introduced. "The partisans of the measure, among whom Mr. Meriwether Smith may be considered as the most zealous, flatter themselves, and, I fear, upon too good ground, that it will be among the measures of the next session." Gold and silver were seldom seen. Had Virginians not evaded their debts to British creditors, great numbers would have been bankrupts. But the Legislature contented itself with delaying and weakening the tax payments—this alone being a bit of folly which Madison thought the wisdom of seven sessions could not repair. [94]

[93] See Legislative journals, Clinton's papers, and the press. The N. Y. *Advertiser*, February 24, 1787, recounts much of the history of this paper money issue. The Pa. *Packet*, January 31, February 2, June 23, 1787, testifies to the good credit of the issue.

[94] Rives, "Madison," II, 78, 79; 143-48. Madison expected George Mason to lead the fight against paper money, and when Mason did not appear, he himself came

In the Delaware Legislature in May, 1786, the paper money
question was hotly debated. It was proposed to issue £21,000, and
in the House the measure passed by a vote of 12 to 6. The Council,
however, rejected the bill by a large majority.[95] Little Delaware's
financial policy, under the initial guidance of Dickinson, had been
wise. In 1781, instead of issuing any "forty to one" money to its
people, the State had sunk the whole quota of it by taxes paid into
the Continental treasury, with a considerable surplus. It thus got
rid of paper money altogether, and at the spring session of 1782,
declared gold and silver the lawful money of the State.[96]

The State below New England in which the paper money struggle
was fiercest and most protracted was Maryland. The debate on a
proposed emission there was in full swing early in 1785. There
was some specie in Baltimore, the soft money enthusiasts admitted,
but there was almost none in the country towns. The rural districts,
they argued, were producing much wealth which they found it impossible to market. Flour and wheat were frequently stored to grow
mouldy, and were more frequently sold by barter. Lumber, tar,
pitch, and turpentine were almost altogether bartered, for no one
could offer cash for them.[97] A Bostonian wrote[98] after a visit to
Baltimore that "The state of affairs there is truly distressing—
money vastly more scarce than here—credit sunk—and hardly any
business doing. People seemed pretty unanimously to wish for a
paper currency, which though it might not be a radical cure would
at least prove a temporary succedaneum, until some effectual steps
could be taken to turn the balance of trade in favor of America."
Baltimore felt her depression the more because she had been ex-
periencing a boom.

The opposition, however, was alert. One "Philadelphus" argued
in June that the emission would injure the poor, and benefit only
foreign traders and domestic speculators. The former would sell
their merchandise easily and at high prices in Maryland, money

forward with a powerful speech, the brief for which has been preserved ("Writings,"
II, 279 ff.). By votes of 85 to 17 the Legislature both rejected the paper money
proposal, and declared that an emission would be "unjust, impolitic, and destructive
of public and private confidence, and of that virtue which is the basis of republican
government." The bill to make tobacco a "facility" for tax arrears was passed
72 to 33. Madison himself, as he wrote his father ("Writings," II, 289) acquiesced
in it to obviate more hurtful measures.
[95] Wilmington letter in N. Hampshire *Mercury*, August 9, 1785.
[96] Dickinson in the Pa. *Packet*, January 16, 1783. Dickinson claimed also for
Delaware the honor of being the first to arrange for the equitable adjustment of
debts on a scale of depreciation, and to stop all tender laws.
[97] Md. *Journal*, August 12, 1785.
[98] N. H. *Mercury*, August 9, 1785.

being plentiful. The latter would take care to make heavy purchases, as of land, in advance of the emission, giving notes payable at a date well in the future; and would thus double their own fortunes on the ruin of the sellers.[99] "Current Money" argued that the planters needed not money, but sense and prudence. Many had mortgaged their land to buy slaves and to clear away timber, with the result that the Baltimore market had been flooded with produce and prices had been depressed much below the Philadelphia rates. Moreover, idleness had grown since the peace. "Many of the land-holders themselves, who till then were very laborious farmers and planters, have since that time hardly ever worked a single day, but strut about their farms and plantations like gentlemen, some of them with guns in their hands and dogs at their heels." [100]

When the Legislature met in November, 1785, it was almost inundated with appeals for and against paper money. From Balti-more County came a petition in behalf of an emission signed by 910 respectable names.[101] But the proposal failed and went over until 1786. The stone wall of opposition lay in the Senate, which, elected for five years, passed out of office within a few months. In the summer there came on the choice of electors for the Senate, and the electoral college named comprised many of the State's ablest men— Matthew Tilghman, Thomas Sim Lee, George Plater, Samuel Chase, John Eager Howard, and others. It met in September, and—interest in the new Senate turning chiefly on the question whether it would be for or against paper money—chose the men who for the next half decade were to constitute the upper house. Never had the wisdom of those who devised Maryland's peculiar plan of an indirectly elected Senate been better vindicated. The body as reconstituted was one of marked ability, including Stone, the two Carrolls, Thomas Johnson, Paca, Plater, George Gale, and Richard Ridgely. Most important of all, it was known to be, at least in the main, opposed to an issue of bills of credit.[102]

At the session of the autumn of 1786, the old question at once arose. On December 1 leave was granted in the House, 41 to 21, for bringing in a bill to emit paper money on loan, and the next fortnight was devoted to debate.[103] The views of the House majority

[99] Md. *Journal*, June 25, 1785.
[100] *Idem*, December 20, 1785.
[101] N. Y. *Packet*, January 2, 1786.
[102] Md. *Journal*, September 15, 22, 1786.
[103] N. Y. *Advertiser*, December 19, 1786.

were completely fixed, and were later briefly described by it in an address to the people:

The result of our opinions on this inquiry was, that you could not discharge your *private* and your *public* engagements; and that you must neglect your *private* obligations or your *public* duty. . . . Your honor, welfare, and safety required that every exertion should be made to support the Union. We thought it imprudent and useless to levy on you *further* taxes, unless some expedient could be devised to assist you in the payment of them, and also in the discharge of your private debts.—In every State there ought to be as much circulating money as will represent all the property and labor bought and sold for cash; and the current money of every country ought always to be in proportion to its trade, industry, alienations, and taxes. . . . We are convinced that there is not a sufficient quantity of circulating specie in this State to answer the purposes of commerce alone because the chief produce of the country, tobacco and wheat, cannot command a proper and reasonable price; because lands, houses, and negroes will not sell for one half their actual value; and because specie cannot be borrowed unless at an exorbitant premium (from 20 to 30 per cent.) to carry on trade and manufacturing, or to cultivate or improve our lands.[104]

The State's debts were heavy, declared the House, and the arrears of taxes alarmingly great. Marylanders owed the British about £400,000 sterling, or two-thirds as much as before the war, while it required £116,000 in specie annually to carry on the State government, and the State's debt to the Dutch bankers must be reduced.[105]

The bill which the House majority prepared to meet these conditions was carefully drawn. It provided for the printing of paper to the amount of £350,000 current money, and for the circulation of £250,000 of it on loan at 6 per cent., secured by landed property of more than twice the value. Not more than £200,000 was to be in circulation at one time, unless the Governor and Council agreed that more would not depreciate the money. Each borrower was required to pay his interest and one-twentieth of his debt annually, and half of the interest and all of the accumulating twentieths were to be used to sink the emission. The paper was not to continue unredeemed more than ten years. It was to be received for all taxes and duties due since March, 1784, and for all civil salaries; but it

[104] This address was published in the Md. *Journal*, February 2, 1787.
[105] The House estimated that Maryland's share of the Continental expenditure for 1786 exceeded £100,000 in specie, and that the annual expenses of government in Maryland were about £16,000 in specie. Most of the State debt, except the sum of £45,700 due to the Messrs. Vanstaphorst, was supposed to be funded by bonds for confiscated British property, and interest on it need not be allowed for. But could the State raise £116,000 in specie in one year? The assessed valuation for all its property was only about ten million pounds in currency, and a tax of no less than one pound, eight shillings, fourpence, including the county tax of five shillings, would be required on every one hundred pounds. This would have to be imposed at a time when the annual imports were £600,000 in current money, and the exports of tobacco, wheat, corn, and lumber were about £538,333. "The great number of suits in the general courts, and in the several county courts, by British and domestic creditors, for the recovery of very large sums of money, convinced us of the inability of many of you to satisfy these creditors; and we know that above eight hundred executions were issued against the State debtors in the last general court, to compel the payment of the interest then due to the State." The Present State of Maryland, by the Delegates of the People, 1787.

was not to be a tender for any debt, unless the contracting parties so agreed. The House intended, it said, to suspend the collection of tax arrears until £100,000 of the emission was in circulation.

After a full debate, which converted some advocates of paper to the opposition, the bill passed the House, 37 to 25. It was accompanied by a measure which suspended executions against the body of the debtor and compelled the creditor to take substantial property for his debt at its actual worth; the courts had been crowded with suits, and this supplementary enactment carried by the smashing majority of 40 to 14.[106]

But when the paper money bill came up in the Senate, that body showed an entirely different spirit. Its debate, also exhaustive, resulted in the unanimous rejection of the measure. Then ensued an angry quarrel between the two branches. Look at New York, the House declared: there paper was emitted as we propose, on loan with landed security, and it passes at par with gold and silver unless for the purchase of these metals for export, when the difference is two and a half per cent. Look at Pennsylvania, where the paper also passes at par, except for the purchase of specie, when the difference is from five to ten per cent. Your bill, rejoined the Senate, appears to us "utterly incompetent to afford relief." After eight weeks, the House adjourned, though the Senate protested that the chief business of the session was unfinished—that delegates had not even been appointed to the impending Federal Convention. The House rejoined that the Senate alone was to blame, and the war of arguments and accusations was carried to the public.

Annapolis was the center of the opposition to paper. Senators Stone and Charles Carroll of Carrollton drew up resolutions condemning the emission bill, which were adopted at a meeting at Mann's Tavern there. Judge Hanson framed instructions to the Annapolis Assemblymen to oppose the bill, and these also were adopted. Besides the three men named, Daniel, Carroll, Thomas Johnson, Plater, Ridgely, and the rich, battle-scarred John Eager Howard were prominent in the fight against paper. The advocates of soft money realized that Charles Carroll was the center of the opposition, and attacked him fiercely. Naturally, they alleged that his wealth in-

---

[106] The Senate saw that its worst features were not passed into law. For the rancor it aroused, see the Md. *Journal*, March 21, 1788: "It is downright *robbery* in a debtor to give his creditor land or negroes in payment of a debt contracted in gold or silver."

spired his attitude—he could loan money at outrageous rates, they said; he annually received £12,000 to £15,000 in interest; and he did not want his usurious business spoiled.[107] The dissensions rose to an alarming pitch, so that the courts in some counties were suspended, and here and there the two sides began to form military bodies.

But though the question colored the elections for the Assembly in 1787, it was so clear that the Senate would stand firm—and that the Assembly minority would encourage it to do so—that the question gradually passed out of men's minds. There was an echo of it in the Federal Convention when Luther Martin, a disciple of Chase's and always excitable, objected to the section of the Constitution which prohibited any State from emitting bills of credit. He believed that some States had received great benefit from paper issues, and that they might again at critical times be very advantageous, and even absolutely necessary. He also believed that States might sometimes have to protect debtors from rapacious lenders, by passing laws partially to stop recovery in the courts, or to allow payment by the debtor in instalments, or by tender of property. Thus tenaciously did a considerable number of men hold to pernicious economic theories.[108]

New England stood apart in this paper money agitation. It was one section where violence actually broke out, and yet it was the section where the movement did the least harm, little Rhode Island alone yielding to it. Connecticut almost wholly escaped the infection, the land of steady habits having the guidance of men who were just as shrewd as old Governor Trumbull had been. On May 30, 1787, a debate took place in the House on a motion by a good Colchester farmer to grant leave for bringing in a tender law, and it was beaten 142 to 22. "Many a sarcastic sneer arose," said a contemporary, and "the disdain of honest men struck the spirit of paper money with terror and dismay." [109]

The paper money crises in New Hampshire and Massachusetts occurred at the same time and took the same direction. The rural populations here felt the prevalent distress as keenly as the farmers of New York, or the planters of Georgia, and the petty merchants

107 Md. *Journal*, March 2, 1787.
108 Elliot's "Debates." I, 344-89.
109 Pa. *Packet*, June 21, 1787; N. Y. *Advertiser*, July 18, 1787; cf. N. Haven Colony Hist. Soc., I.

were as great sufferers. In New England, as in the Middle States, there was no crop failure to play the rôle it played in parts of the South. The harvests in 1785 and 1786 were good, but the farmers asserted, with much truth, that no market could be found. Apples and pears rotted on the trees, wheat and maize could not be disposed of in the towns, meat and flaxseed could only be bartered in small quantities for the articles the farmer needed. To obtain cash to pay debts and taxes was almost impossible, and yet the creditors and tax-collectors were insistent.[110] The balance is lost between property and money, wrote one New Hampshire man; "insomuch, that an estate which formerly would have sold for £1000 and is allowed not to have depreciated in real use and utility, will not, at this day, command £300; and that money, which formerly could have been hired at six per cent., cannot be procured at three times that premium; nay, it cannot possibly be had at any rate, or any security." European creditors pressed the Boston and Portsmouth merchants, the latter pressed the rural dealers, and the dealers began to sue the farmers and seize their property.

The grumbling over taxes in Massachusetts was especially great, and yet the financial position of the State was not desperate.[111] Its domestic debt amounted to £1,326,446 s.16 d.2; its share of the Continental foreign debt to £353,925 s.7; and its share of the Continental domestic debt to £1,162,200. However, against the last-named item there were large offsetting claims for money spent and service done. Considerable sums were expected from land sales in Maine and in the West. Shrewd statesmen in Massachusetts were therefore not staggered by the total of the figures given, about £2,850,000. When men spoke of repudiation, these leaders hastened to condemn the suggestion. "Can we be willing that the history of the American Revolution shall be blackened with the tale, that we refused to redeem the securities we had given to effect it, and shall our posterity hear of the event, because the perfidy of their ancestors exceeded their glory?" Some grumblers declared that the people were ignorant of what became of their taxes. But this was

[110] In one year after the war closed the population of 140,000 was asked to pay $1,000,000 in taxes. To encourage the inflow of specie, the Legislature exempted from practically all duties and port charges every vessel which brought in enough gold and silver to pay for its outward bound cargo; and from one-half of the duties if it paid in cash for half its cargo of exports. Stackpole, II, 240 ff.
[111] Legislative Address to the People, 1786, 5-17; Minot, "Hist. of the Insurrection," 1 ff.; Sears's Hancock, Ch. 17; Holland, "Western Mass.," I, 233; Mass. Acts and Laws, 1786, p. 368.

a mistake, it was answered, for no expenditures were concealed. The stipends of State officers were lower than in Provincial days. In the black year 1786 the legislature laid taxes aggregating only £466,225. But the hard fact was that, owing to the unjust tax system, the poor paid most of it.

At the spring session of the legislature in 1786 a bill was presented to satisfy the clamor against lawyers as a set of bloodsuckers and trouble-makers—a clamor that had been raised in almost every State, but had been especially vehement in Massachusetts. This bill threw the courts open to all reputable persons, fixed the charges of attorneys, and tried to set strict safeguards against champerty. The Senate refused even to consider it. A bill to make real and personal estate a legal tender was defeated in the House, 89 to 35. No paper-money bill was initiated, the only test of strength on the paper-money question being an imperfect one afforded by a foolish proposal to emit money and arrange for its depreciation at fixed periods and fixed rates. This brilliant plan was thrown aside by a vote of 99 to 19. In all, the session was reassuring to the champions of honesty and wisdom in finance, and it infinitely chagrined the malcontents and radicals. It brought on immediately the riotings and disturbances of which Shays's Rebellion was the chief episode.

These disorders were preceded, as a great signal gun, by the convention of delegates from fifty towns in Hampshire County which met at Hatfield on August 22, 1786. The western part of the State was especially aflame with the demand for cheap and easy money. Though this convention was intended primarily to issue a vigorous call for paper money, it drew up resolutions specifying nine other distinct grievances. One was the existence of the Senate, which it regarded not as a representative body, but an undue check on the representative body; one was the existing mode of representation; one the fact that officers of government were not annually dependent on the General Court for the amount of their salaries; one the existence of the unnecessary courts of Common Pleas and General Sessions; one the fact that the principal civil officers were not all annually elected by the General Court; one the excessive fees allowed judges; and three had to do with the use made of the impost and taxes, which the radical members of the convention held were misapplied when any parts of them were employed to pay Continental requisitions or to redeem the promises made to Revolutionary soldiers. In short, the paper money enthusiasts wished to give Massachusetts an ultra-democratic government like Pennsylvania's, or worse, and to run it on the strictest pennypinching principles. The spirit that produced this gathering was also brewing violence. Late in August a mob prevented the session of the Court of Common Pleas in Hampshire County, and early the next month another forced the adjournment of the same court for Worcester County. Then Shays emerged, and everyone is familiar with what followed.

The vigor with which Shays's Rebellion was suppressed was a powerful argument in favor of State Constitutions which vested ample power in the executive. Governor Bowdoin displayed equal energy and sagacity. A proclamation which he issued on September 2 showed his early comprehension of the situation, and encouraged all public officers in the performance of their duty. Five days later he called all the judges, councilors, and legislators into conference upon the measures to be adopted, and thereafter he never hesitated.

Some men believed it illegal for the Governor to call out the militia until the Legislature had declared a state of rebellion, while others doubted whether the militia could be trusted. But Bowdoin kept the sheriffs in close touch with him, and placed armed forces in readiness at points where outbreaks were feared. In November the arrest of the first ringleaders was ordered, and before the middle of the month Bowdoin had reviewed 2000 militia and a number of volunteers at Cambridge. So alarmed was Congress that under a pretence of raising troops against the Indians, it voted to enlist 1300 men to save Massachusetts, but this was unnecessary. At the height of the crisis, as the year 1787 opened, Bowdoin ordered a general muster of 4400 men, while he obtained private loans totalling more than £5000; and the suppression of the revolt quickly followed.

Although this outbreak is often spoken of as utterly reprehensible, there was much to excuse it. The tax burden was most unfairly distributed, not only because of the poll tax and the failure to levy upon trade, but because the assessments in the western counties were too high. The town of Greenwich computed that during each of the five years preceding 1786 the farmers had paid in taxes the entire rental value of their land. Many farms were being sold at one third their value to satisfy debts and tax-liens. Immigration into Massachusetts fell off, while emigration to upper New York and other favored States increased steadily. The scarcity of specie had caused the passage of a tender act in 1782, by which cattle and other commodities could be used to satisfy debts, but the sales of this property usually fetched little. In saying that the State government favored the vested interests, the malcontents brought a charge which contained much truth. In the end, Shays's Rebellion accomplished three results. It not only did much to frighten Americans into approving the Federal Constitution, and to increase the prestige of a well-centralized form of State government, but it brought about a number of healthful reforms in Massachusetts. The most notable, which we describe elsewhere, was the overhauling of the whole tax system.[112]

The reaction against Shays's Rebellion was of great benefit in calming the paper money fever all over the nation. By an early date in February, 1787, complete quiet had been restored in the State. The Legislature had already published a popular address, in which it showed how far the State's financial condition was from being alarming, and rebutted the current argument that there was too little circulating medium. "Immense sums have been expended for what is of no value," said the General Court, "for the gewgaws imported from Europe and the more pernicious produce of the West Indies; and the dread of a paper currency impedes the circulation of what remains." "At the close of the war we greedily adopted the luxurious modes of foreign nations. Altho' our country abounds with all the necessaries of life, the importations from abroad, for our own consumption, have been almost beyond calculation."

The discontent in New Hampshire in 1785-86 was of a piece with that in Massachusetts. In the autumn of the former year a tender law was passed to save poor debtors from jail or from utter penury. By its terms the debtor might offer his creditor, whenever an execution for debt was attempted, either real or personal property in satisfaction of his obligation. If the creditor did not wish to take it, he could refuse, and at the expiration of a year levy upon any property of the debtor which he could find. The result might have been foretold. Persons known to have a large property, one correspondent informed the outside world, in many instances await the sheriff with a broad grin. They have nothing to turn out except a few articles of no possible value to the money-lender. Their live stock, furniture, and implements have been in part hidden and in

[112] Mass. Acts and Laws, 1786, pp. 368, 504, 511, 513, 526.

part, together with their acres, made over to a third person; "so that a creditor had better relinquish his demand than be at the expense of a suit." And as another writer observed, money grew scarcer than ever; "for as far as goods and real property were substituted as a medium in commerce, so far specie, of course, ceased to circulate; and credit being thus injured, the moneylenders turned their keys on that cash which might otherwise have been loaned to the needy." [113] But in spite of the cheats, many creditors chose to press their suits, until the courts were jammed.

The Legislature which met on September 13, 1786, was distinctly impressed by the discontent and suffering[114] which its members saw in many communities, and prepared in detail a plan for a paper issue, which it laid before the towns. It was proposed to emit £50,000 in bills of credit, of which £10,000 should be used for Government expenses, and the remaining £40,000 be loaned on landed security of value double the loan, and at six per cent. interest. No one person should be loaned more than £150, or less than £50, and payments of principal should be so arranged that the whole loan would be repaid in six years. Taxes should be levied to sink in four annual payments, 1789-92, the £10,000 appropriated for State expenses. The money was not to be a tender for private debts. It will be seen that this was a moderate and reasonable plan for a paper issue, evincing a sound caution learned in the Revolutionary disasters. But it was more cautious to make no emission at all, and the soundest part of the State insisted upon the fact. Meetings in Portsmouth and other towns promptly resolved that the paper money plan was unwise. The resolutions of Exeter present the case for the opposition in representative terms. They declare that the emission would drive gold and silver out of circulation; that the guarantees against depreciation were insufficient, inasmuch as the certificates issued to soldiers in evidence of the State's debt, though equipped with an even better security for redemption, had fallen much below face value; and that the fate of the "new emission" of 1780, worth one-third as much as specie, was a plain warning. Finally, Exeter questioned the motives of the paper money leaders. Many of them, said the resolutions, were eager to obtain depreciated paper "to answer their fraudulent ends" by paying off their debts cheap; they

---

[113] Letter from N. H. in *Pa. Mercury*, June 2, 1786; N. Hampshire *Mercury*, September 27, 1786, which gives an excellent account of the disorders.
[114] See *N. H. Mercury*, Sept. 6, 1786.

would never rest till they had made it a tender for all obligations.

In the latter part of September there was a certain amount of quite bloodless rioting in and near Exeter, easily checked by Governor Sullivan. In the first days of 1787 the returns from all the towns upon the paper money proposal were counted, and a heavy majority was found against it. Action taken at the next session of the Legislature emphasized the victory of the conservatives. It was voted that the government had no right to make paper money a legal tender for debts already contracted, and that no new issue of bills of credit should be made.

Rhode Island alone yielded to the paper money mania. A good old divine, Dr. McSparran, once remarked that Rhode Islanders were the only people on earth who had hit on the art of enriching themselves by running in debt.[115] The debt of the little State in 1783 was estimated at $700,000, or about $13 for every man, woman, and child.[116] The British occupation of Newport had cost $400,000, for half a thousand houses had been destroyed and whole villages driven to take refuge on the mainland.[117] The thriving commerce of that town, Bristol, and Providence had been almost swept from the seas; and the country people did not know how to pay their taxes or mortgages. It was only natural for this population, more illiterate than that of the other New England States, to conclude that its salvation lay in the means to which Dr. McSparran referred. In January, 1785, the paper money advocates petitioned the Legislature for an issue of bills, but were rebuffed. Irritated but not discouraged, they perfected their organization, and set to work with such energy that they completely dominated the Legislature of 1786.

That spring an emission of £100,000 was authorized, and soon began to appear from the presses. It was to be given to borrowers who would pledge double the value of the loan for its repayment, pay four per cent. interest for seven years, and agree to reimburse the State within fourteen years. The farmers and other debtors hastened to obtain their share of the money, and the rest of the community hastened with equal alacrity to declare their unwillingness to accept it at face value. By August, recorded one hater of rag money, the bills had ceased to have any real currency; "only the unprincipled, who are involved, and a few small traders or brokers for

[115] Updike, "Narragansett Church," 515.   [116] Field, III, 226.
[117] Bates, "R. I. and the Formation of the Union," 115.   The forests on the island had been felled, the farm lands laid waste, and 2000 persons forced to flee as refugees.

them, negotiating it in order to tender for legal debts." When so negotiated, it was worth from one-half to one-fourth as much as specie. Men who held provisions, clothing, or other commodities would part with them only for hard money.

The struggle that ensued between supporters of the bills of credit, and those who resolutely refused to take them, moulded the politics of the State during four years. Forcing acts were passed to punish those who refused to sustain the credit of the new money; when the Supreme Court declared the second of these acts unconstitutional, four of the judges were dismissed; and a new forcing act was framed, embodying a test oath and depriving recalcitrant citizens of their civil and many other rights. This impossibly drastic piece of legislation, however, was overwhelmingly defeated by the Legislature in November, 1786. Meanwhile, the debtors of Rhode Island hastened to take advantage of the situation by laying the paper before their creditors. The newspapers by September were full of advertisements by the justices of courts, certifying that bills of credit had been lodged with them to pay bonds, mortgages, and notes. One single newspaper issue contained advertisements in which more than £783,[118] lawful money, due on thirteen obligatory notes, was tendered. The form in which these advertisements were couched gave the Rhode Islanders a nickname which clung to them for years—the name of "Know Ye" men. "To all whom it may concern," the notices began, "know ye, that Wm. Doe, of Providence, in the county of Providence, merchant, on the 31st day of August last, lodged with me the sum of £491 lawful money, due to Richard Roe, of Providence aforesaid. . . ."

The stoppage of business and the public excitement were gradually mitigated, but the opposition to the paper as a legal tender increased.

A town meeting in Providence in the early part of 1789 denounced the employment of it to pay debts at face value as "abominably wicked and unjust," and renewed the instructions which had bound the representatives of that little city to fight for "a repeal or alteration." The paper money had by that time depreciated, in trade, to one-twelfth its face value, while the two neighboring States had made it impossible for Rhode Islanders to collect debts from their citizens. Finally, in the autumn of 1789, the Legislature repealed the law making the bills a legal tender at par, and fixed the

[118] Pa. *Packet*, September 23, 1786.

value at which it should be received by creditors, in satisfaction of awards in lawsuits, at one-fifteenth the value of specie.[119]

But in early State finances the darkest hour was just before the dawn. Even while the States were gripped by the paper money spasm, evidences of returning prosperity began to be discernible. In August, 1786, just before Shays's rebellion, when every rascally South Carolina debtor had taken advantage of the Pine Barren Act, when the angry battle of the two Maryland houses was beginning, Washington wrote Luzerne: "The people at large (as far as I can learn), are more industrious than they were before the war. Economy begins, partly from necessity and partly from choice and habit, to prevail. The seeds of population are scattered over an immense tract of western country. In the old States, which were the theatres of hostility, it is wonderful to see how soon the ravages of war are repaired. Houses are rebuilt, fields enclosed, stocks of cattle, which were destroyed, are replaced, and many a desolated territory assumes again the cheerful appearance of cultivation. In many places the vestiges of conflagration and ruin are hardly to be traced." [120] This was true. Shrewd State leaders were able to take advantage of the fact in adjusting taxes and tax collections. After 1786 we hear less of huge arrears and of wholesale evasions. Tench Coxe was able to write in 1794 that the public debt was smaller in proportion to wealth and population than that of any other civilized land, and that "the United States (including the operations of the individual States) have sunk a much greater proportion of their public debt in the last ten years than any other nation in the world." [121]

When the new Federal Government went into effect, in no State was the debt appallingly high, and in some it was already low. In September, 1789, the national House asked the States to transmit memoranda of their public debts, and six did so, bearing dates between January 1, 1789, and April 1, 1789. The highest debt reported was South Carolina's, which amounted to $5,386,232.05. Next came

---

[119] Tardy justice was done the State's creditors in 1791, though at no cost to the State. The Legislature ordered that payment of the State debt, made in depreciated paper, should be reduced to specie; the difference between the original value of the debt and the sum paid upon it in paper money then to be covered by a note. This note was then, under the Assumption Act of Congress, transferred to the Federal Government to be discharged by it. Field, III, 228.

[120] "Writings," XI, 48-50.

[121] "A View of the United States," Ch. 16. It must be remembered that the heavy depreciation of State paper made it easy to amortize the debt which it represented. New Hampshire, for example, early bought up its State bills at the rate of one hundred to one, and in 1794 paid five shillings on the pound for bills of the "new emission of 1780." Barstow's "N. Hampshire," 302-03.

Massachusetts, whose debt was $5,226,801.29. The debt of Virginia was third, being $3,680,743.02, and Connecticut was hard on her heels, with a debt of $1,951,173, while New York had a debt of $1,167,575. New Jersey alone reported a burden of less than a million—$788,680. No accounts were received from the other States, but Hamilton found data for estimating the loads borne by three— he placed Pennsylvania's at $2,200,000, exclusive of the Continental debt she had assumed, Maryland's at about $800,000, and New Hampshire's at about $300,000.[122] We can easily add authoritative figures for the three other important States. A legislative sub-committee in North Carolina placed the total State debt at $3,480,000;[123] the debt of Rhode Island in 1787 was roughly $510,000; [124] and that of Georgia in midsummer of 1786, as Governor Telfair informed the Legislature, fell a little short of a million dollars.

South Carolina's debt, so much the greatest in the Union, was after all only about $22 for every resident of the State, black or white. That of North Carolina was less than $9 per capita, Virginia's almost exactly $5, and New York's below $3.50. It will be seen that the three great Southern States had the heaviest aggregate debts, that the two chief New England States came next, and that the two greatest Middle States formed the third group. The size of the State obligations was very fairly proportioned to the ability of the several States to pay—for at this time the population of the South much exceeded that of the North.

That by 1789 the States did not feel oppressed by their financial burdens there is ample evidence. The Virginia Legislature in the fall of 1787 had provided a safety fund for the gradual extinction of the public debt. In 1790, protesting against assumption, it declared that a large part of the Old Dominion's liabilities had already been discharged, and that measures had been taken to afford the most certain prospect of extinguishing the whole at a period not far distant.[125] When Maryland in 1784 was debating a bill to

---

[122] Am. State Papers, "Finance," I, 28-29.
[123] Report in S. C. *Gazette*, February 17, 1789; see also N. C. State Records, XXI, 1059 ff.
[124] Field, III, 227.
[125] Amer. State Papers, "Finance," I, 90. The whole Virginia revenue system was revised in 1787, and the State strained every nerve to pay off its debt. Its gross receipts in 1787 were £305,244. The "regular disbursements" were much greater than the ordinary expenses, showing that the interest-bearing debt was rapidly being paid; while by the special certificate tax the floating debt was fast reduced, £328,693 being discharged in 1785-90. It is not strange that the Legislature protested so vigorously against assumption. W. E. Dodd, in *Va. Hist. Mag.*, X.

establish funds for paying the State debt within six years, Charles Carroll of Carrollton protested that, if the buyers of confiscated British property were made to hand over the ·purchase money promptly, the State debt might be wiped off the ledgers sooner. The Massachusetts Legislature in 1786 was hopeful of extricating the Bay State from debt within a few years. New York's financial position improved rapidly: addressing the Legislature in January, 1787, Governor Clinton declared that "very considerable reductions" had lately been made in the sums owed to citizens of the State, and that it was evident that the measures adopted to clear away the whole obligation, "when carried fully into execution, will be found to answer the expectations which were formed of them."

Thus the States were able to begin their careers under the Federal Constitution, in advance of Hamilton's assumption measure, with a genuinely hopeful financial outlook.

CHAPTER TWELVE

STATE QUARRELS AND STATE FRIENDSHIPS

WHEN the Revolution ended, the States were united, in Washington's words, by a rope of sand. Not only were the Articles of Confederation a makeshift plan of union, but the very spirit of union seemed wanting. The States had fought beside each other without any notable disharmony. But they were far from being a closely-bound, affectionate family, and in the first years of peace they were to exhibit much petty jealousy and not a little actual quarrelsomeness. Each State and section had its own interests; their political and economic differences seemed to be growing; and in 1783 the general feeling was that any hope of close union was rather sentimental than practical. The drafting of even the weak Articles of Confederation was, as Congress declared, "attended by uncommon embarrassments and delay." It stated that "to form a permanent union, accommodated to the opinions and wishes of so many States, differing in habits, produce, commerce, and internal police, was found to be a task which nothing but time and reflection, conspiring with a disposition to conciliate, could mature and produce."

There were certain general rather than particular factors making against a firm union—the memory of colonial quarrels, the sectional prejudices which have some existence in nearly all countries at nearly all times, and the influence of a political philosophy which did not believe that large confederations were practicable. The first was by no means unimportant. Till a few years before the Revolution, no real sense of American nationality existed among the colonists. They often called themselves Englishmen or British subjects; they were Carolinians, Pennsylvanians, or New Englanders; but they felt little need for a term applicable to all the colonists, and the colonists alone. The New Englanders regarded themselves as a fairly homogenous, united body, Rhode Island alone falling outside the sisterhood. A more tenuous bond of sectional feeling was manifest in the Middle Colonies, and another in the South. But there was no genuine community of sentiment between the Boston merchant and Virginia planter, the Georgia drover and Pennsylvania farmer. Their regard for one another was comparable to the regard of the present-day Australian for the Canadian or South African.

This disjunction struck the later European travelers forcibly. Kalm, the Swede, noted in 1749-50 that the Colonies did not always help each other in their wars. Frequently, "while some Provinces have been suffering from their enemies, the neighboring ones were quiet and inactive, and as if it did not in the least concern them." There were instances, he added, "of Provinces who were not only neuter in these circumstances, but who even carried on a great trade with the Power which at that very time was attacking and laying waste some other Provinces." Burnaby, who traveled a decade after Kalm, thought that fire and water were not more antagonistic than some of the different Colonies. Nothing could exceed their mutual jealousy. "In short, such is the difference of character, of manners, of religion, of interest of the various Colonies, that I think, if I am not wholly ignorant of the human mind, were they left to themselves, there would soon be civil war from one end of the continent to the other." It would be easy to multiply expressions of the same view by colonists themselves. Otis, in his answer to the Halifax Libel of 1765, prayed that the Provinces might never prove undutiful to mother England. Such a day would usher in "a terrible scene. Were these Colonies left to themselves to-morrow, America would be a mere shambles of blood and confusion before little petty States could be settled." [1]

A favorite Tory argument in the opening days of the Revolution was that civil war among the Colonies, if they became independent, was inevitable. Galloway argued in the first Continental Congress that the danger was always present of open hostilities. "They are at this moment only suppressed by the authority of the parent state; and should that authority be weakened or annulled, many subjects of unsettled disputes, and which in that case can only be settled by an appeal to the sword, must involve us in all the horrors of civil war." [2] In Maryland, the Tories declared that "Our independency may produce endless wars among ourselves, and with them, a certain

---

[1] For Kalm's view, see Pinkerton's "Voyages," III, 460 ff.; for Burnaby's *Idem*, 52; for Otis's, "Answer to the Halifax Libel," 16.
[2] See Journals Cont. Cong., Sept. 28, 1774.

loss of liberty is to be sustained from our foreign foes." [3]   In Virginia they asserted, as a patriot remarked, that the destruction of "the finest constitution in the world" would bring "a dreadful train of domestic convulsions in each republic; of jealousies, dissensions, wars, and all their attendant miseries, in the neighboring republics; in which forms of government they seem to imagine that Nature breeds:

> All monstrous, all prodigious things. . . .
> Gorgons, and hydras, and chimeras dire." [4]

In justice to these Tories, it must be remembered that a few years after peace sober patriots were echoing their words. Knox wrote Washington early in 1785 that "The different States have not only different views of the same subject, but some of them have views that sooner or later must involve the country in all the horrors of civil war." [5]   Gerry, refusing to sign the Constitution, declared that he feared a civil war among the States.[6]   Others, signing it, went home to utter sentiments identical with that long attributed to Washington when the Convention rose—that if this instrument was rejected, probably another would never be made in peace; "the next will be drawn in blood."   Before the Federal Convention met, the Connecticut *Courant* said that if the Union were dissolved, "It is by no means an improbable supposition that real and imaginary injuries would occasion mutual complaints and accusations among the States; that they would become more and more unfriendly; that animosities would begin, and rise higher and higher; that fresh provocations would embitter the minds of the people in one State against those in another; that . . . they would have recourse to arms; that the war becoming more fierce, one side, in danger of being conquered, would call a foreign nation to its aid; that the foreigners would be victorious, subdue those States which were hostile to them, and oppress those whom they came to assist." [7]   One Maryland politician set a date to his prediction.   Without a stronger union, he averred, civil war would ensue "in less than ten years." [8]

[3] Md. *Journal*, July 22, 1777.
[4] Va. *Gazette*, April 12, 1776.
[5] Drake, "Knox," 145-46.
[6] See Austin's "Gerry," II, 44.
[7] Quoted in N. Y. *Journal*, March 29, 1787.
[8] George Lux, quoted in Md. *Journal*, April 4, 1788. See R. D. W. Connor, "Cornelius Harnett," 186, for Harnett's view during the Revolution of the possibility of civil war after it closed. See the "Life and Works of Fisher Ames," II, 370, for Ames's opinion.   Young Hamilton warned readers (*Continentalist*, No. 3, August 9, 1781) that the consequences of unrestrained rivalry among the greater States might be bloodshed.   "A schism once introduced, competitions of boundary and rivalships

I. General Causes of State Friction

The subjects of dispute between the different Colonies make up a varied list. Trade was one. The first Penn had to complain that goods exported to his Province by ships which touched at Maryland ports were compelled by agents of the Calverts to pay a duty of ten per cent. there. At about the same time the Proprietaries of East New Jersey made a similar complaint regarding New York. Governor Spottswood of Virginia registered a protest with the home authorities when traders from his Province passing through South Carolina were made subject to special charges imposed there.

Another theme of bickering between almost every pair of adjacent Provinces was the boundary lines. Connecticut, for example, quarreled with every one of her neighbors over territorial questions. The Massachusetts line had originally been run by two "mathematicians" employed by the Bay Colony. These ingenious gentlemen first fixed a starting point for the line near the southernmost point of the Charles River, and then, preferring a boat trip to a tramp through woods infested with Indians and wolves, sailed around Cape Cod and up the Connecticut River to a point which they thought opposite that of their commencement—erring on the safe side for Massachusetts, which they gave an eight-mile strip of Connecticut land. The resultant dispute endured for a century and a half, or till well after the Revolution.[9] As for the Rhode Island line, its dizzy uncertainties gave rise to Rufus Choate's witty remark: "The commissioners might as well have decided that it was bounded on the north by a bramble bush, on the south by a blue-jay, on the west by a hive of bees at swarming time, and on the east by five hundred foxes with firebrands tied to their tails." Frequently the quarrels were important, involving valuable lands and taxation rights, and they sometimes became ugly; at the very outbreak of the Revolution one between Virginia and Pennsylvania was ready to cause bloodshed.

In the old French wars, intercolonial quarrels and heartburnings were numerous. At their worst, they inspired accusations by one Colony that citizens of another aided the foe. At their mildest they

of commerce will early afford pretexts for war"; and European nations would interfere. "Unitas," in the N. Y. *Packet*, March 14, 1785, used the same argument. "Should this chain ever be broken—good God, what issues of death and misery lurk under the dreadful event!"

[9] Clark's "Conn.," 175 ff.

involved nothing more than the reproaches cast by the northern Provinces upon the Southern in the Seven Years' War for the comparative slenderness of the effort put forth by the latter; or disputes like that of Virginia and Pennsylvania over the route to be taken by Forbes against Fort Duquesne. Again, there was material cause for colonial ill-feeling in questions of religion. The Quakers of Pennsylvania and Catholics of Maryland could not regard unruffled the maltreatment of their co-religionists elsewhere. Other disputes arose from mere prejudice. Thus in 1760 Lewis Morris, father of Gouverneur Morris, declared in his will that he wished his son given the best education available in England or America, outside Connecticut; the boy must be kept from that Province lest he imbibe the "low craft and cunning so incident to the people of that country." [10]

How deeply provincial and sectional jealousies, based on differences of society and manners, cut, was shown as soon as Washington took command. Southern soldiers stood as a clan apart; the troops of the Middle Provinces regarded each other with a cordiality not felt for slaveholders or for frostbitten Yankees; and the New Englanders, whom Admiral Warren had found in the last French War the quickest to assert their rights as Englishmen, showed a coldness to other breeds. Complaint was soon heard among the Massachusetts and Connecticut regiments that the men of other sections habitually called them "damned Yankees." [11] An able North Carolina surgeon stationed at Fishkill early in the war wrote a member of Congress that he found the manners of the New York fighters "abhorrent," thought the whole people a "damned generation," and longed to get clear of them. [12] However, North Carolina soldiers themselves were in low esteem in some other States. At Valley Forge their indolence made them the last soldiers to shelter themselves with good huts, and even fellow Southerners reproached them. [13] When the transfer of the war to the Middle States led officers from all parts of the country into Pennsylvania, much indignation was

---

[10] Channing's "United States," III, 468.
[11] "And thank God I am not a Yankey. . . . For God's sake keep our troops together and keep them out of this damned country if possible." Letter of Colonel Wm. Thompson of Pennsylvania, before Boston, January 25, 1776; Pa. Mag. Hist., XXXV, 305. Letters of General Persifor Frazer of Pennsylvania characterize the Yankees as "a set of low, dirty, griping, cowardly, lying rascals," and show that many Pennsylvanians had a sneaking fear that after beating the British, the New England troops would try to "conquer the other Provinces." *Idem*, XXXI, 133-37.
[12] N. C. State Records, XIV, 49-50.
[13] Army Correspondence of John Laurens, 100.

voiced at the supineness there displayed. The Yankees may not all be heroes, wrote a Connecticut officer from Bucks County late in 1776; but he believed they "will not behave in the damned cowardly, rascally manner the people of this country have." [14]

Washington was thoroughly self-contained, but there is evidence that he found it a profound shock to be set down suddenly as commander in a camp made up almost wholly of New Englanders. He wrote to Lund Washington that "they are an exceedingly dirty and nasty people." He thought that the Massachusetts troops in especial had gained at Concord and Bunker Hill a reputation they did not deserve, and he rated their officers as indifferent or bad. The men might fight well if properly led, but at Bunker Hill they had failed to gain a complete success because they were poorly captained and imperfectly supported. He accused the Yankees of trying to monopolize the commissions in the army beleaguering Boston, and he went on—all this privately, of course—to denounce other vices. Within three months he had found it necessary to break one colonel and five captains for cowardice or theft. [15]

On the whole, the troops of the Middle and Southern States tended to draw together in a common unfriendliness toward the New Englanders. These sections had certain aristocratic traits and institutions in common, and resented both the leveling democracy and the moral narrowness of many New Englanders. Among the Yankee troops the officers were elected by the privates, and few belonged to the class of "gentlemen." Below the Connecticut line, officers were appointed in the ordinary British fashion, and according to British traditions prided themselves on their gentility. Old Israel Putnam, whose heroism and ability none doubted, excited disrespect among the Southerners when he rode about at the siege of Boston in much the same dress he had worn when he left his furrow at the news of Lexington. With an old hat, no coat, rolled-up sleeves, and a short sword hanging from a strap around his broad shoulders, he shocked young officers who had bought resplendent uniforms in Philadelphia or Baltimore. [16] Washington exerted himself to have the rules for selecting officers altered by Congress to make a wider field of choice

[14] Corr. and Journals of S. B. Webb, I, 174-75.
[15] Washington's letter is in the Corr. and Journals of S. B. Webb, I, 92-97. Graydon accused the Yankee officers of being shockingly mercenary, and Washington wrote that "the Massachusetts people suffer nothing to go by them that they can lay their hands upon."
[16] Trevelyan's "American Revolution," Pt. II, Vol. I, 198.

possible, and he expressed a wish that commissions should go as far as possible to "gentlemen." However, Yankee views also had to be humored, and General Schuyler, a rich and stiff patroon, lost the command against Burgoyne because he was disliked by the New England men.[17] Their militia would not fight under him, for they remembered him from the Seven Years War; and Congress, in alarm, gave the command to Gates. Graydon has told us that Schuyler's haughtiness was indeed plain:

> That he should have been displeasing to the Yankees, I am not at all surprised; he certainly was at no pains to conceal the extreme contempt he felt for a set of officers who were both a disgrace to their stations and the cause in which they acted.[18]

A New England captain visited Schuyler's headquarters at Lake George while the general was at dinner with a mixed company. Schuyler did not ask him to sit nor to have a glass of wine, and dismissed him peevishly, as if "a low and vexatious intruder." Stung by his demotion, Schuyler averred that his offense lay in his aversion to New England principles, and that he would never cease to hate them.

Graydon himself, a keen Pennsylvanian, regarded many New England officers with contempt, and says that far from aiming at a dignity which would promote discipline, they tried "by humility to preserve the existing blessing of equality." He sneered at a Connecticut colonel who carried his meat home in his own hands. Only one regiment, Glover's of Marblehead, seemed to him well-trained. Early in the war a court-martial, principally Southern, acquitted with alacrity a Maryland lieutenant who had shown insufficient respect for a Northern brigadier. John Adams, writing his friend Hawley in the fall of 1775, took a view of these prejudices flattering to his own sectional pride; it was natural, he reflected, for people outside New England to desire a wide gulf between privates and officers, since there men of sense and education were much fewer than in New England. But he was genuinely alarmed, nevertheless, declaring that "without the utmost caution on both sides, and the most delicate forbearance," these feelings "will certainly be fatal."

When Yankee troops failed in battle, the other regiments pointed

[17] John Adams, "Works," III, 47. Gates had become well acquainted in the camp at Cambridge, and was much liked. Adams notes the far-reaching consequences of the quarrel—it had much to do with the overturn of the Federalists in New York in 1800. New Jersey joined in Congress with New England against Schuyler, out of jealousy of her larger neighbor. Livingston Mss., Duer to R. R. Livingston, May 28, 1777.

[18] Graydon's "Memoirs," 127 ff.; Scharf's "Maryland," III, 341-42.

to the fact as a natural result of the leveling principles of their officers. In the action in which the Americans were driven from Kip's
Bay to Harlem Heights, the Connecticut militia broke and ran.
Washington, who reported the affair to Congress as "disgraceful and
dastardly," dismissed part of the militiamen—many had deserted—
as worse than useless. The New England troops for a short time
became, as Hooper of North Carolina, then in Congress, says, "a
byword among the nations—'Eastern prowess,' 'nation poorly,' 'camp
difficulty,' are standing terms of reproach and dishonor." [19] Rumors
and letters flooded upon Congress, John Adams says, representing
the Yankees as "cowards running away perpetually, and the Southern
troops as standing bravely." In the army camps bitter feeling was
aroused. Connecticut men, remembering Colonel Knowlton's brave
stand on the day after the rout, and the martyrdom of Nathan Hale,
would not patiently hear themselves called poltroons. A brigadier-
general wrote that "the Pennsylvania and New England troops
would as soon fight each other" as the British,[20] and this was no
great exaggeration.

Stalwart John Adams had made the speech in Congress nominating Washington to be commander-in-chief, thereby mortally
offending his associate Hancock, who till the last moment hoped the
choice would fall upon himself.[21] But he now attacked Washington,
on the ground that in his official letters "he often mentions things
to the disadvantage of some part of New England, but seldom anything of the kind about any other part of the continent." Adams also
noted that all three of Washington's aides came from the southward, that they were egotisical young men, and that they did not
respect either New England or Congress as they should have done.[22]
There was a fear in New England that the commander kept too
many Southerners near him, for it was not then understood how
little Washington allowed his aides to mould his opinions. The
Yankees were set apart in Congress much as in the armies. At the
first session, some of the Congressmen from the Middle and Southern Provinces made up a separate table. When Chastellux visited

[19] Jones's "Defense of Rev. Hist. N. C.," 321-26. Hooper accused the Yankees of
plundering friend and foe without discrimination.
[20] Gordon, "Hist. Ind.," II, 127 (N. Y. ed., 1789); Mrs. Grant's "Memoirs of an
American Lady," Ch. XX; S. G. Fisher, "Struggle for Amer. Ind.," I, 519; Reed,
"Reed," I, 239.
[21] Adams, "Works," II, 417-18. Adams was in part prompted by the fact that
there was "a Southern party against a Northern, and a jealousy against a New
England army under the command of a New England general."
[22] "Works," III, 87; I, 255-56.

Philadelphia in 1780, he found the New England delegates dining apart from the others, and took a meal with them.

Virginia and New England had much to applaud in each other in 1775-76, when they were together leading the rest of the nation to independence. They had every reason afterward to increase their mutual esteem. Yet how persistent were their sectional jealousies was shown by two incidents just before the Constitution was adopted. In Connecticut, during a debate on the judiciary early in 1787, Col. Wadsworth offered the practise of the Southern States in support of his argument. At once there was a stir. A Mr. Hopkins arose and warmly rebuked him for daring to mention these States, which "retain their former ideas of kingly government and partake too much of despotism." [23] In Virginia, R. H. Lee was often accused of partiality for New England. One such charge was made in 1777, and was indignantly and eloquently answered.[24] It was repeated after the peace, when the navigation of the Mississippi was an anxious question, for Lee inclined toward the Northern point of view. But these charges came to a climax in 1788, when in the Virginia Convention Patrick Henry rebuked Lee for his record. Lee replied indignantly, and James Innes spoke even more forcibly. "I observe, with regret," he said, "that there is a general spirit of jealousy with respect to our *northern brethren.* . . . We are told that the New Englanders mean to take our trade from us, and make us hewers of wood and carriers of water; and, the next moment, that they will emancipate our slaves!" [25]

As the final unfavorable factor of a general nature, there were the prevailing political ideas of the time. Upon this subject of extensive national unions, all European thought was bounded by a narrow horizon. Free institutions were thought to have operated successfully only in small countries. There were no single great republican states, and except for Rome there never had been any, while Rome's expansion had been accompanied by the death of republicanism. There were no great or successful republican confederacies. When Madison outlined for his own use a set of notes on "Ancient and Modern Confederacies," on which he later based three essays of

[23] *Conn. Magazine,* June 7, 1787.
[24] Randall's "Jefferson," I, 210-11; Henry, "Henry," III, 75; I, 530. Feeling in Congress was much as in the armies. Adams writes ("Works," I, 175-76): "When we first came together, I found a strong jealousy of us from New England." See also his reference (III, 44 ff., 65) to the "anti-New England spirit which haunted Congress" in the second session.
[25] See Henry Lee's words, H. B. Grigsby, "Va. Conv. of 1788," I, 160.

the Federalist (18 to 20 inclusive), he could make use only of the remote and unimpressive examples of the Achæan and Lycian Leagues of Greek history; of the "Germanic Empire," loose, awkward, and so poorly functioning that it repelled rather than attracted; and of the Swiss Confederacy and the United Netherlands, neither really successful as a federation.

The only well-known writer who had spoken in praise of the plan of confederating separate states was Montesquieu, and he only in a few short paragraphs and the most general terms; eulogizing, as Hamilton pointed out in the ninth essay of the Federalist, the confederated republic as a means of uniting the external advantages of large monarchies with the internal advantages of small republics. Any attempt to place large populations under a republican sovereignty was generally distrusted by political theorists, partly because no one really understood at that time the principle of indirect representation as it has since been applied. Lord Kames in his "Sketches" (1774) predicted the ultimate independence of the Colonies, and their choice of republican forms of government, based on their provincial systems. The Swiss cantons united, he said, for protection against the House of Austria; the Dutch states for protection against the King of Spain. "But our Colonies will never join in such a union; because they have no potent neighbor, and because they have an aversion to each other." [26]

Moreover, as the State governments took form, their functions seemed to many Americans to include all the really important powers affecting individuals and local communities. To the unthinking in especial there appeared so little need for a broad Federal sovereignty that its possible nature and powers, its potential usefulness, were neither studied nor comprehended. Communication between different sections was intolerably slow, Europe was in another world, and the political outlook was naturally a limited one.

Yet all three of the general obstacles to union, forbidding as they seemed, were easily pushed aside. The memory of old provincial quarrels was short-lived. It mattered naught to North Carolinians after the terror of Camden and the exultation of King's Mountain that their fathers had quarreled with South Carolina over the slice of territory that Governor Martin insisted upon handing over to the

[26] This was a familiar prophecy, often quoted—see Md. *Journal,* October 17, 1783, and *Conn. Magazine,* March 22, 1787.

latter Province. It mattered nothing to the Middle and New England Colonies after Saratoga that in the French and Indian War they had sometimes pursued different objects. The narrow Quakers who tried publicly to rebuke Cushing and Adams in Philadelphia for the supposed ill-treatment of the Friends in Massachusetts were early thrown out of power in Pennsylvania. As for the hostility of current political ideas to Continental union, the colonists were little swayed by political theorizing, and that part of the population most opposed to a strong union would in any event have been the last part to use legalistic and philosophical arguments. Everyone admitted that some form of political connection was needed, and the sole question was what the form should be. During the years 1781-87 the people were learning by hard experience that the State governments would not suffice for their needs.

The sectional animosities were not easily uprooted. But it is clear that among the troops the chief manifestations of them were ended by 1777. "Who, that was not a witness," asked Washington in bidding farewell to the army, "could imagine, that the most violent local prejudices would cease so soon; and that men, who came from different parts of the continent, strongly disposed by the habits of education to despise and quarrel with one another, would instantly become but one patriotic band of brothers?" [27] Prejudice is the creature of ignorance, and a much stronger antipathy than that between Northerner and Southerner, the antipathy between the French and the Anglo-Saxon was soon conquered by association. The esteem of the North for Washington, and of the South for Greene, was symbolic in 1781 of the esteem each section had gained for the private soldiers of the other. The comradeship of men from different sections was cemented by a considerable amount of interstate settlement after the war. Veterans who had marked an attractive locality in their campaigns returned to it, while marriages followed the quartering of every detachment in settled communities. The army officers tried to keep alive their acquaintanceship through the Society of the Cincinnati.

A similar cordiality was fostered among the political leaders of the States as they mingled in Congress. It is hard now to realize how little the principal men of one Colony knew of those of another in 1774. Boston and New York were only four days' journey apart;

[27] Washington's "Works," X, 330 ff.

yet when John Adams passed through the latter town to Congress, he learned for the first time the exact constitution of parties there, identified the various political captains, and shook hands with those of his own views. Adams had never met Roger Sherman nor Silas Deane, and had never heard of Charles Carroll of Carrollton or of the Tilghmans till they were introduced to him in Philadelphia. It is clear from his diary and from the letters of other members of Congress that in their social hours at the first two sessions the delegates spent much time discussing differences of government in the various Colonies, and that many of them were profoundly ignorant of the polity of distant Provinces.[28]

II. Specific Causes of State Friction

The particular, as distinguished from the general, causes of State division, were numerous. "Broils among the States," wrote Jefferson, "may happen in the following ways: First, a State may be embroiled with the other twelve by not complying with the lawful requisitions of Congress. Second, two States may differ about their boundaries. But the method of settling these is fixed by the Confederation [the Articles of Confederation], and most of the States which have any differences of this kind are submitting them to this mode of determination. . . . Third, other contestations may arise between two States, such as pecuniary demands, affrays between their citizens, and whatever else may arrive between two nations." [29] He did not mention quarrels over commerce and commercial restrictions; over questions of currency; over comparative military and financial burdens; over the western lands; or over foreign relations. There was indeed no end of pretexts which State pettiness might seize upon as an excuse for wrangling. And pettiness was met everywhere; Washington in 1784, writing Gov. Harrison of Virginia, named the "unreasonable jealousy" the States showed of each other as one of the causes which threatened "our downfall as a nation."

Disputes over trade were the most constant and discreditable of all. It was from one such dispute that there grew the meeting of

---

[28] Adams, "Works," II, 423. Adams, meeting Bulloch of Georgia, showed his total ignorance of that Colony by asking whether it had a Charter, with many other questions. The hottest personal quarrels in Congress, as that between Dickinson and Adams, had no sectional implications.
[29] "Writings," Ford Edition, IV, 146-47.

commissioners in the Annapolis Convention, the forerunner of the Constitutional Convention. Three years earlier the commercial wrangling had resulted in an effort, led by Massachusetts, to bring about the comprehensive Congressional regulation of trade. It divided the States among themselves, and weakened them in the commercial warfare it was then necessary to carry on against unfair foreign Powers. Hamilton pointed out in the Federalist that it had prevented the conclusion of helpful trade agreements with other lands. No nation would be foolish enough to enter into an economic treaty with the weak central government, conceding privileges of importance, when it did not know at what moment the engagements of the Union would be violated by its members; especially as all nations knew they could obtain frequent advantages in our markets without making returns. As for the unneighborly regulations of the States, Hamilton feared in the light of the past that they would become more and more "serious sources of animosity and discord."

Of this group of disputes, those hinging upon State tariffs were paramount in importance. The imports of the lower South were made largely through Charleston; of the upper South, through Baltimore and Philadelphia; of the Middle States and New England through Philadelphia, New York, Providence, and Boston. The passage of tariffs in Maryland, Pennsylvania, New York, and Massachusetts laid heavy burdens upon States to which transshipments were made. "The king of New York levied imposts upon New Jersey and Connecticut," later wrote Fisher Ames, "and the nobles of Virginia bore with impatience their tributary dependence upon Baltimore and Philadelphia. Our discontents were fermenting into civil war." Three general phases may be traced in the history of State imposts. During the Revolution Virginia alone levied duties upon a broad scale. In the first three years after the cessation of hostilities, all the States save New Jersey placed duties upon imports, but for revenue only, and not for protection. By 1785, New England and most of the Middle States had developed promising home industries, and sought to protect them by raising tariff walls against foreign imports. The Southern States had no such industries, and depended in many ways upon imported wares; so that except for Virginia, they abstained from making their tariffs protective. When the States had passed from the second to the third of these phases, the feeling between some of them became bitter, and at times almost savage. As rates were elevated and self-interest was openly avowed as the motive, it grew plain that certain States cared nothing how they injured their neighbors so long as they protected themselves.

The reasons why imposts were little known during the years of warfare are obvious. There was virtually no trade with England or her possessions, and much less than usual with other lands. In the years 1776-1779 inclusive, 570 American vessels were captured by the British. Moreover, the colonists felt they were fighting for economic as well as political freedom, and wished to set up nothing analogous to the hateful British restrictions upon trade. Till the close of the Revolution, their sentiment was for full freedom of commercial intercourse, and the free trade doctrines of Adam Smith and certain French economists were received with marked favor—many of the leaders, including Franklin, Jefferson, and John Adams, subscribed to the principles of Adam Smith. Virginia alone was in a position to tax commerce with advantage during the five years of war, and alone did so. She maintained a considerable exportation of tobacco, and with the resulting revenue drove a brisk import trade in liquor and other commodities. The opportunity to fill her treasury with a tariff was too good to be lost. Her neighbor Maryland began to resort to import duties after 1779.

With the energetic revival of foreign trade after the treaty of peace, there began the period of tariff for revenue only. The States had enjoyed a fair internal prosperity throughout the war, and were in better economic condition than would have been thought possible at its beginning. The merchant class was filled with the optimism and exuberant enterprise that usually come in the wake of a long and successful conflict; it longed for an opportunity to exert its unexercised strength, and was eager in buying. The States a few years later rang with the charge that an unwonted trade in "luxuries" was debilitating the nation. Meanwhile, home industries expanded with the same confidence. The people had a relatively large supply of hard money when the struggle ended, for they had received a great deal of specie which England had shipped for the supply of her forces; and this helped make British shippers eager for the American trade. The desire to restrict commerce as little as possible was still strong in the United States. "Why," asked Patrick Henry as the war closed, "why should we fetter commerce? Fetter not commerce, sir; let her be as free as the air—she will range the whole creation, and return on the wings of the four winds of heaven to bless the land with plenty." Generally speaking, till 1785 the States imposed duties only to lighten taxes; New Jersey and Delaware imposed virtually none for any purpose.

It soon became evident, however, that the infant industries of the States were in no position to withstand European competition. Moreover, since these importations deprived the country of its ready specie, and Congress had no authority to provide a substitute by establishing a uniform, well-based coinage, the money-stringency became distressing. When the States sought to relieve the depression which followed by issuing, in 1785-87, great quantities of paper money, home industry began to suffer from the rapid fall of prices in coin. Merchants who had bought goods too freely upon credit became unable to pay their debts abroad, and went into bankruptcy. One result of all this was to reduce State revenues rapidly at just the time when State needs, under the pressure of Revolutionary debts and rising administrative expenses, were greater than ever; and leaders turned to higher duties to fill the deficiency. They saw at the same time that the increased duties would bolster home industry against foreign goods, and would check the pernicious flow of coin to foreign lands. A further reason for resorting to protective duties of a markedly higher rate lay in the fact that it had become desirable to retaliate against European commercial restrictions.

Hence the four New England States, New York, and Pennsylvania, or almost the whole northern half of the Confederation, by 1786 decided upon markedly increasing their duties to make them protective. In 1782 Massachusetts, for example, had laid duties upon only a small number of imports, the rate never exceeding 5 per cent. In 1784, when the policy began to alter, the ad valorem rates on several articles were made 7.5 per cent., and on others, including vehicles, leather goods, and plated ware, 12.5 per cent. In 1785 a new tariff law gave still more prominence to protection by increasing the specific duties, and by making the ad valorem rates on some articles as high as 25 per cent. In 1786 another step was taken in a law which forbade any importation whatever of 58 articles. Some of these the legislators deemed luxuries which the people should not have; some were articles which could be manufactured at home. The laws of 1785-86 were avowedly, to quote the preamble to the former, "to

encourage agriculture, the improvement of raw materials and manufactures, a spirit of industry, frugality, and economy, and at the
same time to discourage luxury and extravagance of every kind."
Pennsylvania turned to a full protective tariff in 1785, with the passage of an act "to encourage and protect the manufactures of this
State by laying additional duties on certain manufactures which
interfere with them." Many articles were subjected to a specific
duty, an ad valorem rate of 19 per cent. was levied on others, and
special protection was offered makers of refined iron, shipbuilders,
and joiners. This act was the model followed in part by Congress
in framing the first Federal tariff act, that of 1789.[30]

Of the States south of New York and Pennsylvania, Virginia alone
levied duties of a really protective character. New Jersey and
Delaware dispensed with duties of any kind. Virginia's protective
duties were moderate, and laid on a short list of articles, including
salt, hemp, cordage, cheese, snuff, and some liquors.[31] Maryland
and the other Southern States had few industries to be aided by
tariffs, they profited by a large export trade, and they wished the
returning imports to be low-priced. All the import duties imposed
by the various States applied to interstate commerce just as to foreign commerce, unless specific provision were made to the contrary.
The levy of export duties was confined to three of the Southern
States, Maryland, Virginia, and Georgia. In early colonial times
they had been commoner, but the desirability of encouraging foreign
commerce had by 1765 led to their abolition almost everywhere.
Virginia confined her duty to tobacco; Georgia contented herself
with one on raw hides; and Maryland at one time or another taxed
the export of tobacco, wheat, flour, and pig-iron. In these export
duties there was little to cause ill-feeling among the States; and
the same may be said of the tonnage taxes which some States levied,
both to help pay for lighthouses, buoys, and other aids to navigation, and to assist American shipping by discriminations against
foreign vessels.

It was in the smaller States of the North that resentment against

[30] The friction between Massachusetts and New Hampshire at times was marked.
In 1777 they adopted reciprocally unfriendly laws. Massachusetts prohibited the
export of rum, molasses, textiles, leather, etc., and the New Hampshire Legislature,
declaring that this "prohibition will be very detrimental to this State, unless a
similar measure is passed here," retaliated. N. H. Hist. Soc. Colls., VII, 80;
Weeden, "Ec. Hist. N. Eng.," II, 783; A. S. Batchellor, "Brief View of the Adoption
of the Const of the U. S.," 16 ff.
[31] In 1786 Virginia punished evasions of the duty with excessive severity. For
Northern comment, see N. Y. *Packet*, March 2, 1786.

the tariff exactions of selfish neighbors was greatest. New York's duties came to be regarded with indignation by all the surrounding commonwealths. An impartial observer, Dr. Hugh Williamson, declared in 1788 that "half the goods consumed in Connecticut, or rather three-fourths of them; the goods consumed in New Jersey, or three-fourths of them; all the goods consumed in Vermont, and no small part of those consumed in the western part of Massachusetts, are bought in New York, and pay an impost of five per cent. for the use of this State." [32] Some of these estimates were exaggerated, but the truth was grave enough. Oliver Ellsworth said in the same year that it was incontrovertible that Connecticut annually paid more than $50,000 into New York's treasury. A recent historian has computed that one-third the Empire State's expenses were defrayed by this indirect tribute from the land of steady habits.[33]

In New Jersey "Candidus" professed in 1784 a serious fear that the people "will have to divide ourselves between the two great States that overshadow us with their present consequence, and will finally eclipse every ray of significance by their future splendor." But Jerseymen disliked New York more than Pennsylvania. Immediately after the conclusion of peace the inhabitants turned to the possibility of making their own great seaports, and on Oct. 1, 1784, enacted that Perth Amboy and Burlington should be free ports for twenty-five years.[34] All foreigners, whether mariners, manufacturers, or mechanics, who settled in these towns and for one month plied their usual calling, were then to become freemen and citizens. All goods, except slaves, could be imported without payment of State duties, unless an evident public necessity should sometime dictate the passage of a State tariff act upon goods which were discouraging home manufactures. Merchants, moreover, were to be exempt from taxes upon their stock or ships. While the Articles of Confederation were still unaccepted, in 1778, New Jersey had complained emphatically that they left the regulation of trade to the several States, and that justice and harmony both demanded that Congress

[32] McRee's "Iredell," II, 227.
[33] Johnston's "Connecticut," 316. "When we see the landholder and merchant seduced with a false idea that their real interests are different, it is not to be wondered at (though it must be lamented) that one State should suppose it can derive advantage or may escape danger, from circumstances of injury or oppression to another."—Appeal of a New York committee in behalf of the impost amendment, September 30, 1785; N. Y. *Packet*, November 10, 1785.
[34] Pa. *Packet*, June 5, 1783.

have this function. After the peace she protested to Congress against New York's duties. In 1785 New York, which laid certain discriminating duties against British-shipped goods, passed an act by which foreign goods brought into her limits from neighboring States were to pay these duties, unless the owner could clearly prove that they had not come to America in a British vessel, and of course it was hard to furnish such proof. Late in the year New Jersey decided to take more vigorous action in defence of her rights.

The national government had asked for about $165,000 as New Jersey's share of an annual Continental quota of three millions, and on Oct. 20, 1785, the Legislature voted that it would pay none of this requisition until all the States had accepted the impost plan. In support of its stand the State offered various arguments; but the chief were that the quota was excessive, and that New Jersey could not support a Congress which had proved unable or unwilling to remedy the commercial grievances she had against New York. The first objection was baseless, and Congress treated the second as irrelevant. It held that it was the business of New Jersey, not of the Confederation, to deal with New York in this particular, and that New Jersey should try to help herself by retaliatory measures, not by breaking up the Union. A Congressional committee appeared before the Legislature at Trenton in March, 1786. Pinckney, its spokesman, pointed out that New Jersey's action was making it impossible for the States to present a bold front to the Indians, then threatening frontier wars, and to the Europeans and Moors, then restricting American commerce. So far as New Jersey hoped to injure New York by this course, he added, her policy was mistaken; for it would only turn the animosity of other States from Clinton, and direct it against her. On the very day that he spoke, the Legislature rescinded its resolution.[35]

One pin-prick by New York was especially irritating to her neighbors. In the spring of 1787 the Legislature, not content with increasing the duties on foreign goods, extended the entrance and clearance fees to all vessels bound from or to Connecticut and New Jersey. For vessels under twenty tons burden, the fee was two shillings if they carried American goods, and eight shillings if they had any dutiable goods. This threw into the State treasury a share of the profits of the many boatmen who plied down the Sound and

[35] Lee's "New Jersey," II, 373; Bancroft, "Hist. of Const.," one-volume ed., 187.

from eastern New Jersey with firewood and foodstuffs, while it was troublesome as well as expensive for every shallop and sailboat to clear at the customhouse just as if it had been a full-sized English or French ship. The New Jersey Legislature took the only retaliatory action possible. The city of New York had purchased four acres at Sandy Hook for the purpose of "maintaining a lighthouse, public inn, and a kitchen garden thereon," and the Assembly promptly taxed the lighthouse £30 a month.[36] The Connecticut Legislature did nothing; but the merchants of New London signed a paper which pledged each to forfeit £50 if within the year he sent any goods whatever into the State of New York.

Delaware followed the example of New Jersey in an effort to escape the exactions of Pennsylvania—she passed an act making Wilmington and Newcastle free ports.[37] Not only this, but she exempted merchants in these cities from taxes on their stock in trade, and from all duties on either imports or exports for a quarter century. This struck a correspondent of the chief commercial newspaper of Pennsylvania, the *Packet,* with alarm.[38] We import and export for all Delaware, he wrote, as if it were a part of our State. But if we do not cease to tax Delaware's trade, this defensive measure will certainly attract foreign vessels to their two ports, and make them vigorous rivals to Philadelphia. The harvest of the Quaker City was reaped far southward. Madison estimated in 1783 that Philadelphia and Baltimore merchants made not less than thirty or forty per cent. on Virginia's imports and exports, and that the profits were "a tribute which, if paid into the treasury of this State, would yield a surplus above all its wants," his estimate of these profits being arrived at by a comparison of European and Virginian prices. From his convictions upon this subject sprang his bill to restrict imports and exports by foreign vessels to Norfolk and Alexandria.

Even the low tariffs of South Carolina were felt to be burdensome by her neighbors. The year after the formal conclusion of peace Hugh Williamson drew a melancholy picture of the sufferings of North Carolina between two richer and more commercial States. Virginia and South Carolina, he predicted, would impose tariffs of

---

[36] Pa. *Packet,* July 19, 1787.
[37] It is clear that these laws for free ports, like Connecticut's laws to encourage direct importation from abroad, conflicted with the efforts then being made to arrange for State coöperation in retaliation against Great Britain. Madison lamented this in a letter to Jefferson, March, 1786, "Works," II, 227 ff.
[38] March 6, 1786.

considerable weight.   North Carolina might do the same, but what would be the result?   Nearly half the goods that North Carolinians used were imported by land from the neighboring States, and as the sea-trade was carried on principally by small coasters, nearly half the remainder could be smuggled through the numerous inlets.   The goods coming by land would pay a tariff of five per cent. or more for the benefit of the treasuries at Richmond and Charleston, but they would hardly pay a tenth of that to North Carolina, for it would be impossible to guard two boundaries of 150 miles each. Goods brought by water would in general pay a duty in some Northern State from which they were transshipped, but the smugglers would see to it that any wares on which the North Carolina tariff was high paid no second duty.[39]   Georgia so resented the indirect toll levied upon her by the South Carolinians that, in 1785, pressure was brought to bear upon the Legislature to induce it to tax all goods imported into the upper part of the State from across the border.   Returns for 1784 showed that the region around Augusta had imported goods worth £35,000 sterling, and some legislators thought it would be proper to injure the Carolina merchants by discriminating in favor of the direct trade to Savannah, for they believed that Charleston was bleeding them.[40]

Thus in all sections of the republic was borne out the prediction made by the Pennsylvania Legislature in December, 1783, that "the local exercise within the States of the power of regulating and controlling trade can result only in discordant systems productive of internal jealousies and competitions, and illy calculated to oppose or counteract foreign measures, which are the effect of a unity of councils." [41]   The last part of this prediction points to another type of commercial dissension—dissensions over retaliatory measures against Europe.   After the conclusion of peace Spain closed many of her ports to our vessels.   France in 1783 for the most part excluded American ships from her West Indian possessions, and though in 1784 she adopted a more liberal policy, still refused them many privileges.   Great Britain admitted non-manufactured goods from

[39] N. C. State Records, XVII, 94-105.   North Carolina had another grievance against Virginia, relating to the trade with the Indians.   Colonel A. Campbell wrote of North Carolina, July 10, 1782: "I observe a jealousy of Virginia in assuming the whole agency with the Indians, and a monopoly of the trade.   Perhaps this is such a national concern that it may be best accommodated by regulations of commerce.   For I doubt whether Carolina would be competent to the task were it relinquished in their favor." Cal. Va. State Papers, III, 213.
[40] Pa. Packet, March 12, 1785.
[41] Bancroft, "Hist. Const.," two-volume ed., I, 334.

America to British ports free of duty, even in American bottoms, but she closed her West Indian islands absolutely against the United States, save that American lumber and breadstuffs could be entered in British vessels.

No foreign government perceived better than London the advantages it could gain from the commercial autonomy of the States. In 1786 it was planning to send consuls to the principal commercial centres, to have them approach the various States with offers of trade agreements, and thus avoid all need of negotiating with the national government.[42] The most striking conflict over retaliation was that between Massachusetts and Connecticut in 1785. While Congress was pleading for the grant of power to regulate all American trade, Connecticut passed a law which gave foreign merchants and manufacturers an advantage over Americans of the adjoining States. Governor Bowdoin, at the request of the Legislature, protested, declaring that this act was "the more exceptionable, inasmuch as for the sake of cementing the Union, which is the true policy of the confederated commonwealth, our laws exact no duties on the manufactures of the United States, and in regard to commerce, their citizens respectively stand upon a footing with our own."[43] Both Massachusetts and New Hampshire thereupon enacted commercial laws in direct retaliation against British trade restrictions, and Bowdoin sent a circular letter to all the Governors, appealing for support and urging their concurrence in vesting Congress with the powers it desired.[44]

But all other commercial disputes faded into insignificance beside that over the maintenance of American claims to the navigation of the Mississippi. These claims brought the United States into conflict with Spain, and in two different ways at two different times such a clash was extremely undesirable. The question first gained prominence two years before the Revolution ended. Virginia, by her charter and her conquests under Clark, claimed the Illinois and Kentucky country reaching to the banks of the Mississippi, and in November, 1779, her Legislature instructed her delegates in Congress to press for the free navigation of the river to the sea. Other

---

[42] Dip. Corr. of the U. S., 1783-89, Ed. 1837, II, 180 ff., shows us John Adams's mingled vexation and amusement, while in London, over the "idea of thirteen plenipotentiaries meeting together in a congress at every court in Europe, each with a full power and distinct instructions from his State."
[43] Hamilton, "Hist. of the Republic," III, 136-37.
[44] See Adams' commendation of these laws, Dip. Corr. of the U. S., 1783-89, I, 176.

Southern States supported this demand. Congress at this time was holding out to Spain the prospect that if it entered into an American alliance it would be able to regain the Floridas from England, yet it agreed unanimously that any alliance must be conditional upon "the free navigation of the river Mississippi into and from the sea." Jay, our envoy to Spain, thereupon reported from Madrid that such a condition was fatal to the chances of an alliance. Though Congress was at first immovable, and sent Jay instructions to argue stubbornly with the Spanish Government, the dark months of 1780, when the whole South was being overrun, the Armed Neutrality under Catherine of Russia was threatening to press for peace, and the French Government was frankly worried as to the outcome of the struggle, shook its determination. A demand arose within and without Congress for a conclusion of the Spanish alliance at all costs. The Georgia and South Carolina delegates united in the closing days of 1780 in moving a reconsideration of the instructions to Jay, and one of Virginia's two members, Theodoric Bland, came over to their side. Congress rescinded its instructions Jan. 2, 1781. However, Jay decided not to alter his attitude, no alliance was formed, and Cornwallis's surrender shelved the question.

But after the conclusion of peace the commercial interests of America wanted a treaty of commerce with Spain. Gardoqui arrived as Spanish Minister in 1785, and Jay, who was now Secretary for Foreign Affairs, was directed by Congress to negotiate an agreement with him. His instructions, like those of five years previous, were explicit in demanding the opening of the Mississippi; while Gardoqui, like the Madrid Government in 1780, emphatically declared that the river would be closed to American vessels. Once more it seemed to many Americans that the only escape from the predicament was for the South temporarily to yield. Jay thought so. His negotiations with Gardoqui took as their starting point the possibility that the United States would consent to the closing of the river for twenty-five years or slightly longer, and in August, 1786, he laid a plan of this character before Congress.

This proposal to surrender the navigation of the Mississippi for almost a generation in return for commercial privileges proved a great wedge between the northern and southern States. Most of the northern delegates in Congress heartily approved Jay's course. To their merchants, shippers, and farmers it was highly important that the Spanish ports receive our export trade, so that our raw materials might be exchanged for Spanish coin and European manufactures. They believed that trade with Spain might largely take the place occupied in the political economy of the Colonies by commerce with Great Britain; for there was not an American product that Spain did not want. A commercial treaty with such a Power would increase American prestige all over Europe, making us friends wherever its news penetrated. Moreover, they said, the right of navigating a river a thousand miles to the west, surrounded by vast tracts of wilderness, with only scattered and feeble American settlements in the country it drained, need surely not be insisted upon for two or three decades to come. But to the South and Southwest this attitude was a piece of monstrous sectional selfishness. These two sections viewed the Mississippi as the key to the possession of a great empire, while they argued that upon its navigation already hung valuable economic interests, which were increasing as with every year a new wave of migration rolled over the Appalachians. The day was coming when the sons of the South would carve out of the Southwest a territory richer and more flourishing than the whole United States as it existed in 1785. A free access to the ocean was indispensable to this territory, and if its future population could obtain it in no other way, it would break from the United States and perhaps even go over to Spain.

Jay reported his plan for the Spanish treaty in August, 1786; the Northern majority in Congress prepared a motion for the repeal of the old instructions limiting his powers of negotiation; and this repeal was carried by a vote of seven Northern against five Southern States. Intense anger was at once manifested in Virginia and the Ohio Valley. Some Southern statesmen attributed to the North the most despicable motives. The Yankee object, wrote Monroe to Governor Henry, "is to break up the settlements on the western waters . . . so as to throw the weight of population eastward and keep it there to appreciate the vacant lands in New York and Massachusetts." He cast equally bitter reflections upon individual members of Congress. King, he commented, had married a rich New York lady, "so that if he secures a market for fish and turns the commerce of the western country down this river [the Hudson], he attains his objects." He was convinced that Jay was dishonest.

An observer wrote from Louisville in December that the people on the western waters were absolutely thunderstruck when they heard of the treaty-plan. What, they cried, should they be sold as vassals to the cruel Spaniards? Should they be their bondsmen, as the Israelites were to the Egyptians? The Parliamentary tyranny that had caused the Revolution was less impudent and intolerable than this. They were already making preparations to assert their rights against the Spanish at New Orleans and Natchez; and if Congress did not support them, they would throw off their allegiance to the United States, and apply to some other Power, preferably Great Britain, to receive and sustain them.[45] Ominous rumblings came from western Pennsylvania. The brilliant young H. H. Brackenridge of that section ran for the Legislature in October on a platform demanding Pennsylvania's opposition to the suggested treaty.[46]

Would Jay proceed with the treaty, knowing that his support lay with one section, and that it was doubtful if public sentiment in two or three states of that section supported the course he was taking? Monroe in deep excitement wrote Madison that he believed Jay would hesitate until he had obtained a knowledge of the feeling of the real leaders of Pennsylvania and New Jersey, but that the Secretary was too far committed to mark time long. "I consider the party, especially Jay and the principal advocates, as having gone too far to retreat. They must either carry the measure or be disgraced . . . and sooner than suffer this they will labor to break the Union." Indeed, pursued Monroe, he had strong reason to believe that they were already intriguing with Northern leaders to split the nation. "They have even sought a dismemberment to the Potomac, and those of the party here have been sounding those in office thus far." [47] Monroe counselled secret measures to obtain the adhesion of Pennsylvania and Maryland to the South, in the event that a national division really occurred. Pennsylvania was especially important—"if a dismemberment takes place that State must not be added to the eastern scale." When such words could be written, the situation had plainly become serious.

But this dark cloud rolled swiftly away. Jay had no desire to

---

[45] Published in the Pa. *Packet*, July 7, 1787. The writer vividly describes the Spanish abuses at New Orleans. "Large quantities of flour, meat, etc., have been taken there the summer past, and mostly confiscated. Those who had permits from their Governor were obliged to sell at a price he was pleased to state, or subject themselves to lose the whole. Men of large property are already ruined by their policy."

[46] Pa. *Packet*, October 7, 1786.

[47] Monroe's "Writings," I, 160 ff. (September 3, 1786); Rives, "Madison," II, Ch. 24.

injure the South, and he was the last man in the United States to consent to a breaking up of the Union. If he was diligent in drafting a treaty with Gardoqui which consented to the closing of the Mississippi, it was because he sincerely believed that unless the United States yielded to Spain, war could not long be averted. The clashes already occurring in the West between the settlers and the Spaniards had given him great anxiety. However, as events showed, there really was no imminent danger of a Spanish war, and a majority of Congressmen never believed that there was. It was easier for the North to yield than the South, and during 1787 it began to do so. The Pennsylvania Legislature elected in the fall of 1786 was a body which realized that part of the State lay in the Mississippi Valley, and it gave its new Congressional delegation positive instructions to oppose the treaty, while Rhode Island also came over to the Southern view, and New Jersey's delegation became doubtful. When Madison offered a test question bearing upon the treaty, the delegates of five of the eight States present voted under his leadership upon the Southern side, and the delegates of the other three under Rufus King's leadership upon the Northern side. But only two of the five were Southern States, and had all the Southern States had delegations present, their vote would have decided the issue—seven States, a majority of the thirteen, being requisite. The treaty was not adopted; and the whole question had lost much though by no means all of its importance when the Federal Convention met.

III. Friction Over Commerce and Finance

The want of a uniform currency created financial and commercial difficulties that were prolific of ill-feeling among citizens of the different States. The nation had four general currency systems, each complicated by a score of petty local variations. The pound was 1547 grains of fine silver in Georgia; 1289 grains in Virginia and New England; 1031¼ grains in Maryland, Delaware, Pennsylvania, and New Jersey; and 966¾ grains in North Carolina and New York. The English guinea was worth about two shillings more in New York than in the other Middle States, while the Pennsylvania merchant who carried a guinea into New England found it there worth seven shillings less than at home. In other words, the shilling had values varying from one eighth of a dollar to its full sterling rate of about a quarter dollar.[48]   Jefferson suggested the adoption of the Spanish silver dollar as the national unit of currency, pointing out that it was known in every State, was in more common use than the pound or shilling, and had been employed by Congress for its computations.   This was true; but so long as the value of the dollar varied in different States with reference to that of the pound and shilling, and so long as other coins, doubloons, moidores, carolines, pistoles, and ducats, played a part in trade, no end of misunderstandings arose in business intercourse.

These difficulties were accentuated by the total unreliability of the paper currencies.   It was hard for even well-informed citizens to understand what value to attach to a handful of bills, and the tables of exchange between States would have filled a fat volume. With every new legislative session, newspapers bristled with schedules of depreciation.   The difficulty of making money transactions was further accentuated by the prevalence of counterfeiting and clipping.   The counterfeiters paid their chief attention to small coins, as in washing coppers with silver to make them sixpences, and sous with gold to make them moidores; a little caution was sufficient guard against them.   But clipping went to such lengths that at last all coin passed by weight and not by face value.   The United States Government in 1782 actually had Timothy Pickering clip a quantity of French guineas which had come over as a loan and which contained an unnecessary weight of metal.   If the Government paid them out as they were, the first takers would clip them and reap a snug profit; so the Treasury sent out for anvil, punches, and the information as to how goldsmiths put in their plugs—"a shameful business," said Pickering.   Unless a uniform national coinage were adopted and counterfeiting and clipping halted, Washington remarked, the Irish bull about making a dollar into five quarters would be an everyday reality, and every man would have to travel with scales to weight his specie.

Governor Livingston, of New Jersey, who lived in Elizabethtown and naturally did much business in New York city, found it so impossible to use Jersey money "at the unconscionable discount which your brokers and merchants exact" that he collected what New York money was due him and saved it to employ across the

---

[48] Jefferson's "Autobiography," Appendix F; Bancroft, "Hist. Const.," one-volume ed., 167.

Hudson.[49]　Jefferson kept careful account of his expenditures on his travels to Congress, and his memoranda disclose the vexations to which any traveller was subject.　A man could not be sure that what was sound money in one county would pass when he had crossed an imaginary line, nor that if his bills did pass, he would not be charged a ruinous discount.　When Georgia sold her confiscated property, the Legislature ordered that no currency of other States be accepted.　"This is done in order as they say," commented a correspondent of Governor Caswell, of North Carolina, "to humble the pride of the North Carolinians, who refuse to take their money, but at an under rate." [50]　The richest and strongest States, little affected by the paper money movement, sometimes refused to have anything to do with the bills of weaker neighbors.　Thus New Jersey's last important measure for emitting paper, the law for printing £100,000 which Governor Livingston and his Council were not brave enough to veto twice, was rendered largely nugatory by the adjoining States.　New York city and Philadelphia treated the new money with contempt, and it depreciated with breakneck speed.

But the worst State disputes connected with currency arose from the enactment of measures impairing the obligation of contracts. Madison classified these measures under four heads.[51]　They were the making of depreciated paper a legal tender for debts; the substitution of property for money as a tender for debts; laws for the payment of debts by instalments; and the closing of the courts of justice.　When such laws followed the flooding of a state with depreciated paper, any man who had loaned money in that State, or had exchanged a commodity for a future payment of money, was exposed to the complete or partial loss of his loan or commodity. Nothing did more to bring about the adoption of the Constitution than the recognition by business interests that they needed a safeguard against this invasion of justice and right.

Rhode Island was the chief offender under the first head of Madison's classification.　Madison had her in mind when he spoke of paper money as causing "the same warfare and retaliation among the States" as commercial restrictions.　Because of her conduct,

---

[49] Jay's "Works," III, 373-74.
[50] N. C. State Records, XIII, 68-69.
[51] "Among the numerous ills with which this practice is pregnant," Madison wrote of paper money issues, "one I find is that it is producing the same warfare and retaliation among the States as were produced by the State regulations of commerce." "Works," II, 261-62.

Massachusetts and Connecticut, when he wrote, had passed laws enabling their citizens to pay all debts owed to people of a paper-tender State in just the same manner as the latter paid their debts to the citizens of Massachusetts and Connecticut. That is, Rhode Island creditors were virtually outlawed in the neighboring States, and could no more collect a note at face value than a Boston creditor could collect a note in full in Providence. Connecticut in 1787 prepared a protest to Congress against the Rhode Island laws as violations of the Articles of Confederation. The opprobrium visited on the littlest State was unprecedented. No petty community of Greece, wrote General Knox, ever showed more turpitude than she, plundering the orphan and widow by her laws,[52] while the same language was used of Rhode Island by the *Connecticut Magazine:*

> There prowls the rascal clothed with legal power
> To snare the orphan and the poor devour;
> The crafty knave his creditor besets,
> And advertising paper, pays his debts.
> Bankrupts their creditors with rage pursue,
> No stop—no mercy from the debtor crew.[53]

Some men talked of keeping her out of the new Federal Union for her sins. The Rhode Island delegates in the Continental Congress complained of the insults to which they were exposed. We need not inform you, they wrote home, how it wounds our feelings "to hear and see the proceedings of our Legislature burlesqued and ridiculed, and to find that Congress and all men of sober reflection reprobate in the strongest terms the principles which actuate our administration of government." [53a]

The stay laws, under which debtors were allowed extensions of time upon their obligations—virtual moratoriums—took their most reprehensible form in Virginia and South Carolina. In North Carolina the closing of the courts to suits for debt was opposed by the best leaders because it meant loss to any creditor whose evidence was destroyed by the lapse of time. Of the laws for settling obligations by the tender of land or other property, South Carolina's "pine barren act" was the most famous, and injured a few citizens of other States. The action of some States in redeeming their paper money at an arbitrary scale of depreciation produced hardship for the holders of that paper in other States. Still another source of ill

[52] Drake, "Knox," 99.
[53] "The Anarchiad," given in full in Providence *Gazette,* April 14, 1787.
[53a] Staples, "R. I. and the Cont. Cong.," 566.

feeling was the fact that debts for military supplies furnished from one State to another were in some instances, as in North Carolina, treated as payable in depreciated paper.[54]

Sometimes State issues of paper money had quite unforeseen results upon commercial relations with a neighboring State. In Pennsylvania the bills of credit struck off early in the Revolution depreciated faster at home than in Maryland, where sanguine merchants trusted more than the Philadelphians did in their ultimate redemption. Already the trade of York and Cumberland counties in Pennsylvania had begun to turn to Baltimore because of that city's proximity, and of the enterprise of its importers; and since more could be purchased in Baltimore with the Pennsylvania bills, the York and Cumberland farmers now began trading there exclusively, a fact discussed with indignation in the Pennsylvania *Gazette*.[55] It was believed at a later date that jealous Baltimoreans encouraged the radical Constitutionalists who in Pennsylvania in 1784-85 were bent upon destroying the Bank of North America; these merchants saw with envy the benefits the Bank afforded to Philadelphia business. But for their meddling, wrote one angry Philadelphian, there would be no opposition to the Bank except that born from narrow partisanship.[56]

A long list this of irritations over tariffs, clearance regulations, Spanish trade, confused currencies, and legal tender laws—a list that might be extended. But it is a symbolic fact that out of one commercial dispute, that between Maryland and Virginia, grew the movement for a stronger Union. The Potomac lay between these two States, and Virginia, which in her Constitution of 1776 admitted that the southern shore was the boundary, feared that this admission might be interpreted as a total relinquishment of jurisdiction over the river, leaving Maryland free to impose whatever regulations she pleased on vessels plying to Virginia's Potomac ports. Out of the desire for an understanding grew the Annapolis and then the Federal Convention. Just so, out of interstate conflicts in the years after 1781 came some of the strongest bonds of union.

Before the Revolution the thirteen Colonies were so overwhelmingly agricultural that the interchange of their products did little to link them together; merchants and shippers looked with predominant concern upon the overseas trade. The Southern growers of

[54] Madison's "Works," II, 259.
[55] November 8, 1780.
[56] Bolles, "Pennsylvania," II, 232.

cotton, indigo, and tobacco found his chief market abroad, not at the North; the Northern Colonies imported almost all the manufactured articles they required. But during the Revolution the country had to be largely self-sufficing, and after it, European trade regulations encouraged Americans to do as much as possible for themselves. The war gave birth to foundries at Springfield, East Bridgewater, Easton, and elsewhere in Massachusetts, at Lancaster, Pa., at Trenton, and at Principio, Md. New Jersey in 1780 had over forty fulling mills for finishing cloth. After 1780 the industrial progress was remarkable. Textile mills began to rise in New England. Rhode Island and Pennsylvania became distinguished for their iron and steel manufacturing. By 1790 paper and powder, farm implements, vehicles, and furniture were made in quantities almost sufficient for the home market; and some articles, like nails, were better made in America than in Europe. Tench Coxe, addressing in 1787 the Friends of the American Manufactures in Philadelphia, spoke of the vast variety of goods produced at or near that city:

Meal of all kinds, ships and boats, malt liquors, potash, gunpowder, cordage, loaf-sugar, pasteboard, cards and paper of every kind, books in various languages, snuff, tobacco, starch, cannon, muskets, anchors, nails, and very many other articles of iron, bricks, tiles, potter's ware, millstones and other stonework, cabinet work, trunks and windsor chairs, carriages and harness of all kinds, corn fans, ploughs and many other instruments of husbandry, saddlery and whips, shoes and boots, leather of various kinds, hosiery, hats and gloves, wearing apparel, coarse linens and woolens, and some cotton goods, linseed and fish oil, wares of gold, silver, tin, pewter, brass, and copper, clocks and watches, wool and cotton cards, printing type, glass and stone ware, candles, soap, and several other valuable articles.

As the back country began to fill up, a brisk Western trade developed in the exchange of these manufactured articles for raw commodities. The Genesee, the Kentucky, the Tennessee, and the Ohio settlements furnished an eager market for the products of the coast. The Middle States drove a flourishing trade with the South in exchanging their flour and beef, their iron, wooden, and leather manufactures for the natural products of the warmer climate; and in this New England participated. A competent observer during the period of the Confederation says that Pennsylvania "actually became to a considerable extent the same resource for the furnishing trade to the Southern States that England had been before." As transportation improved, this interstate trade swelled in volume. It slowly became evident that the North required the agricultural products of the South, and the South the manufactures of the North, the two sections complementing one another. Business relations of all kinds increased, there was more travel, and the understanding of one State and section by another became far better than before.

IV. Jealousy Over War Burdens

As Jefferson suggested in saying that a State might be embroiled with the others for non-compliance with Congressional requisitions, the varying zeal of the States in their support of the union was a constant source of friction. A demagogue could appeal more easily to a State by suggesting that its yokefellows were shirking than in any other way. States which granted the requests of Congress for authority to lay impost duties and regulate trade resented the delays and refusals of other States. But their resentment was much stronger when it came to the refusal of requisitions which Congress had every right to make. Such refusals became familiar to the nation early in the Revolution. The evil, wrote Madison in 1787, had been so fully experienced both during the war and after it, resulted so naturally from the independent authority of the States, and was so common in other confederacies, that it might be regarded as a defect inherent in the existing system.[57] In 1780 the New York Assembly unanimously instructed its delegates in Congress to propose that whenever a State was deficient in furnishing money, supplies, or men, Congress should order Washington at once to send armed forces into that State, and compel it to do its part; it and Governor Clinton thought civil war preferable to the inanition and stubbornness some States were showing.[58]

Comparisons between States as to their respective military efforts were odious but inevitable. As one section after another was invaded, its citizens clamored that their sufferings were not properly understood, and that they were being neglected.

As a matter of fact, each section was at times remiss in military activity, as Washington's letters alone suffice to show. New England equipped and maintained more than half of the 231,950 regulars enlisted in the Continental Army; but New England militia were as prone as those of other sections to go home when their time expired, no matter what the crisis, and Washington protested to one

[57] Madison's "Works," II, 361.
[58] Journal N. Y. Assembly, Session beginning September 7 (date, October 10), 1780.

New England State against the raising of troops for State duty only. Early in Burgoyne's invasion he lamented that so few Yankee troops had appeared and that they had behaved so badly in the field. Later Washington contrasted the feebleness of Pennsylvania's efforts when invaded with the final vigor New England showed in helping crush Burgoyne. It astonished every part of the continent, he wrote President Wharton, that at the moment Philadelphia was threatened with capture, this most opulent and populous State had placed but 1200 militia in line against Howe. Just before he went into winter quarters at Valley Forge, he roundly remonstrated with the Pennsylvania Legislature for failing to provide the clothing and munitions, as well as men, it should have furnished. During the final stages of the war, he repeatedly complained of the South's failure to raise, drill, and equip troops as it ought.[59] In the South alone did indignation over supposed military neglect by other sections become serious. It was loudly voiced as soon as Cornwallis and Tarleton entered North Carolina. On Dec. 2, 1780, the Virginia Legislature dispatched Speaker Benjamin Harrison to lay the desperate situation of the South before Congress. At the same time it was proposed to remonstrate to Congress upon the indifference of that body and of the Northern States to the region, and one member actually drew up a violently reproachful paper.[60]

Meanwhile, in the lower South the ugliest rumors were afloat in the spring of 1780. "It is currently reported, and believed here," President John Rutledge wrote just after the surrender of Charleston, "that Great Britain will offer America the independence of all the States except North and South Carolina and Georgia—and perhaps even of North Carolina—and that such a proposition will be accepted." Aedanus Burke later said that many members of Congress believed that it would be necessary to make this territorial sacrifice, and there is the best of evidence that the possibility was seriously discussed. According to John Mathews, then in Congress for South Carolina, the French Minister earnestly suggested that it might be well to conclude peace on this basis, he won some to his side, and it was necessary for Mathews to denounce the proposal openly in the national legislature.[61]

[59] See Washington, "Writings," VI, 8 ff.; 117 ff.; Henry, "Henry," III, 120-22.
[60] Rives, "Madison," I, 275-80.
[61] Upon this interesting topic see S. C. Hist. and Genealog. Mag., October, 1916; McCrady's "S. Carolina 1775-1780," 538-43; Washington's "Writings," VIII, 438 ff.; Cassius's Address to the Freemen of the State of S. C., January, 1783.

Congress felt the necessity of reassuring the South. After hearing Benjamin Harrison's representations, it ordered that the Southern army should comprise all the regulars from Pennsylvania to Georgia inclusive, directed the Pennsylvania Line to join the forces in Virginia without loss of time, and took steps to furnish transportation and supplies of all kinds. Virginia's dissatisfaction was abated, and the remonstrance which had been drafted was never presented. To reassure the Carolinas and Georgia, Congress sent a circular to all the States on June 1, 1781, calling upon them to put every ounce of strength into the war, and declaring that if this was done, the prospect was good for driving the British from the country or at least confining them to the coast, "in order to give as little room as possible to the enemy's claim of *uti possidetis:* which will undoubtedly be most strenuously insisted on by them in the course of the negotiation—a claim totally inadmissible on our part." For emphasis, Congress added that it would "accept of peace upon no other terms than the independence of the thirteen United States of America in all its parts." Two of the five authors of this appeal were Southerners. When the Northern troops marched south to assist in the capture of Cornwallis, many of the men went reluctantly. They showed great discontent as they passed through Philadelphia, and Washington urged the Superintendent of Finance to seize the moment to advance them a month's pay in specie. But their appearance in Virginia, coupled with the emphatic pronouncement of Congress, set all Southern apprehensions at rest.[62]

After peace it was easy for a State to persuade itself that it was carrying an undue share of the financial burden. No part of the Articles of Confederation was so disputed as that which provided a basis for the apportionment of money-requisitions. It was first suggested that a State's quota be fixed according to the number of its inhabitants, exclusive of untaxed Indians, this being also the basis proposed for representation in Congress; but Virginia alone sup-

[62] See Journals Cont. Cong., XX, 585 ff.; Sparks's "Washington," Ch. 13. Some Southerners showed considerable jealousy of neighboring Southern States, and reluctance to give them military assistance. Thus General Allen Jones, a sober man, wrote Governor Caswell, on October 21, 1778, that he thought North Carolina by no means bound to send troops to help South Carolina, and that "were the Assembly sitting, I am sure a single man would not march to the South. We have always been haughtily treated by South Carolina, till they wanted our assistance, and then we are sisters, but as soon as their turn is served, all relationship ceases." N. C. State Records, XIII, 245-46. Hooper, the conservative, wrote in precisely the same bitter terms of South Carolina two months later; McRee, "Iredell," I, 404-06. Many of the Virginia militia objected to marching to the aid of the Carolinas; N. C. State Records, XIV, 75-76.

ported this plan. The Northern States wished freemen to have the exclusive right of representation, and the Southern States did not wish negroes taxed. Finally Congress and the States agreed that the valuation of land and the improvements thereon should be the measure for taxation, though they knew that it was a faulty one. In the spring of 1783 a Congressional committee attempted a reform, recommending that the whole number of free inhabitants, and three-fifths all other inhabitants except untaxed Indians, be taken as the basis. The proposal failed by a vote in which no section was clearly defined. Immediately afterwards, Hamilton suggested a new basis—the whole number of free inhabitants, including white persons bound to labor for a term of years, and three-fifths of all others except untaxed Indians, a census to be taken triennially; and his motion prevailed by a vote of all the states except Massachusetts and Rhode Island.

Massachusetts vehemently objected to the Congressional requisition of February, 1780, for specific supplies from all the States. Gerry offered its protest at Philadelphia; the commonwealth, he said, had contributed freely of its resources, but now it was tired of the attempts of the other members of the Confederation to load it with an unreasonable weight. A long and bitter discussion in Congress followed, and led to the resignation of Gerry, which the General Court of Massachusetts approved by formal resolution.[63] Though finally the active opposition of the Bay State died away, so late as 1785 Gerry blamed unfair taxation for the depressed value of Massachusetts lands,[64] and in the Massachusetts convention for ratifying the Constitution, Rufus King reproached other States for doing less than their share.

In the New York convention Alexander Hamilton voiced similar reproaches. Amid all its distresses, he said, New York State had fully complied with the national requisitions, and could not all the others have paid at least in part? Yet New Hampshire, which had suffered nothing from invasion in the Revolution, had paid not a cent since the peace, and North Carolina had been equally delinquent. One State alone, he declared, the State of Pennsylvania, had borne New York company in perfectly discharging its duty to the Union.[65] But in North Carolina a different story was heard. Hugh

[63] Austin's "Gerry," I, 319; Bolles, "Financial Hist. U. S.," I, 93-94.
[64] Lands in adjoining States, he said, paid not over two-thirds the taxes on Massachusetts lands; King, "Life and Corr.," I, 89-90.
[65] Elliot's "Debates," II, 56, 232.

Williamson, a member of Congress, in 1784 opposed the cession of the transmontane country to the nation because, in his opinion, North Carolina had not been given financial credit for her military assistance to Virginia and South Carolina, and for expeditions against the Indians, while other States had been recompensed for similar effort.[66] In Virginia keen apprehension was long expressed by some legislators lest the Union cheat it out of what it had spent on the George Rogers Clark campaign.

Many harsh speeches could be quoted attacking the alleged unevenness of State burdens. Richard Dobbs Spaight, of North Carolina, wrote in reference to the New England States the year after the signing of peace that ever since he entered Congress they had tried to weaken the power of the Union, and sacrifice the strength and dignity of the nation to their self-importance. They had attempted, he said, to dispute the powers expressly granted Congress by the Articles of Confederation. The obstinate refusal of Rhode Island in 1782 to accede to the first proposal for a Federal impost was, as Madison put it, a theme for the most pointed recriminations in other States. New York's refusal to consent to the second impost plan produced a like wave of resentment among both the public creditors and the friends of a firm national government. Other States saw her conduct for what it was, a selfish effort to hold to her revenues from commerce and thus line her purse while increasing the burdens of the rest of the nation. But hard speeches did little harm. The indignation which one State felt over the evasion of financial duty by another State led many citizens to think not of further relaxing the national authority, but of increasing it.

V. TERRITORIAL DISPUTES

Territorial differences, the second group in the list Jefferson furnished his French correspondent, caused several spectacular quarrels among the States, but they were not dangerous to the Union. The importance of the two chief disputes has been exaggerated because they involved actual bloodshed. These are the bickering of three Northern States over Vermont, and the sharp dispute between citizens of Connecticut and of Pennsylvania over the Wyoming Valley: both acute less as they had to do with the mere sovereignty of

[66] Boyd's "N. Carolina," 13, 14.

rival States over the disputed area than with the actual ownership of the land by rival sets of farmers; both producing more smoke than fire; and both settled, in their main aspects, by Congress. Other territorial disputes occurred over boundaries, but resulted in little ill feeling, while it must be remembered that the settlement of one complicated land controversy by the relinquishment of the Northwest Territory to the nation strengthened the Union in a signal degree.

Actual though petty civil war accompanied the clash of New York, New Hampshire, and Massachusetts over the district which a majority of the people of the Green Mountains declared to constitute the independent commonwealth of Vermont. The origins of the disagreement antedated the Revolution by a generation. For many years after the appointment of Benning Wentworth as Governor of New Hampshire in 1741, the Green Mountain territory was in dispute between that Colony and New York. Pending the decision of the Crown, Wentworth granted many charters for towns west of the Connecticut River, issuing no less than 118 between 1760 and 1764. New York, while making no grants, warned settlers against accepting those from New Hampshire. On July 20, 1764, the King in Council declared in favor of New York's claim, and ordered that the west bank of the Connecticut should be the dividing line between the two Provinces.

Populated in large part by men from Massachusetts and Connecticut, and remote from the capitals of New Hampshire and New York, the Vermont towns had developed a purely democratic government which made them so many little republics. They were attached to their town-meeting autonomy, which they would lose under New York; and as Yankees they disliked New York manners and modes of thought. Nor were these objections all. New York, asserting that the Order in Council issued in 1764 was retroactive, and had invalidated the Vermonters' title to their farms, tried systematically to evict large groups of settlers. The Vermonters had been ready to defend these farms in the French and Indian War, and were ready now. Particularly on the west side of the Green Mountains, their indignation rose high; and when the Revolution began, armed bands were ready to take the field against their fellow-provincials of New York.

With the opening of the war, the people of the New Hampshire

Grants seized the opportunity to throw off the British yoke and the New York yoke together. The town committees of safety declared themselves as emphatically against the latter as the former; on April 11, 1775, a convention of committeemen met in Westminster, and voted that the Grants must "wholly renounce and resist the administration of the government of New York." In the early part of the next year a convention from the towns remonstrated to Congress against the necessity of owning allegiance to New York; and although Congress recommended submission until the struggle with the mother country was ended, the movement for declaring a new State grew apace. It came to a head when on January 15, 1777, a convention representing all sections of the Grants met at Westminster, proclaimed the region a free and independent State, named it New Connecticut, and appointed delegates to petition Congress for representation—that is, to demand admission to the Union. This same convention, in an adjourned session, appointed a committee to draft a Constitution, and called a convention at Windsor for July 2, 1777, to act upon it. This, of course, was the summer of Burgoyne's invasion and defeat.

So much for the action of the Vermonters against New York; but how were New Hampshire and Massachusetts embroiled? While the new State was being formed, a certain discontent in the towns east of the Connecticut River, within the plain limits of New Hampshire, had been increasing. They were so remote from Portsmouth that the New Hampshire government over them had been little more than a name, and they did not want it to be anything else. Like their neighbors west of the Connecticut, they believed in almost universal manhood suffrage and the simplest form of town-meeting administration. Disliking Portsmouth for fear of its interference, they also disliked it because they had no sufficient legislative voice. First Hanover and its neighbors, where Dartmouth College had been founded in 1769, and where President Eleazer Wheelock was proving himself a gifted public leader, protested to the Provincial Congress concerning the under-representation of the region. Then groups of other towns did the same. Most of those who supported these protests were actuated by high principles, believing that it was hypocrisy to revolt against English tyranny, and at the same time to permit domestic tyranny and injustice; but as the movement tended toward a denial of the governmental power of New Hampshire, baser motives appeared, for some men were willing to use it to escape the taxes and troop-levies called for from Portsmouth.

Gradually there grew up the so-called Hanover Party, comprising towns both north and south of Hanover, and both east and west of the Connecticut River, but near it. Its activities were directed by a self-perpetuating body which had met in the college town in the month of the national declaration of independence, and which called itself the United Committees of the New Hampshire Grants. It leaned more and more to the side of the New Connecticut—also termed the Bennington or Vermont—government, with which it had almost everything in common. During July of 1777, at the same time that Vermont adopted her Constitution, the towns in the Hanover party declared that their people had no political connection with New Hampshire and were in "a state of nature." Six months later, when the government of Vermont was in full operation, with the rough but able Thomas Chittenden in the Governor's chair, the Hanover Party applied for a union with the new State. The Vermont Assembly wisely displayed some reluctance in thus provoking the hostility of New Hampshire, and referred the question to the Green Mountain people at large, who voted emphatically for the admission of the additional settlements. Some sixteen towns east of the Connecticut were therefore authorized to elect representatives to the Vermont Assembly, which soon proclaimed its determination "to maintain and support entire the State as it now stands."

The result was what might have been expected. New Hampshire, under President Weare, had no intention of letting a large part of the western side of the State be torn from it, and appealed to the Continental Congress for help. Vermont sent the shrewd Ethan Allen to Philadelphia to learn what the national authorities were likely to do, and Allen reported that while Congress was indisposed to support New York's claims to the Green Mountain region, it certainly was not going to allow the incorporation of the sixteen New Hampshire towns in Vermont. He believed that unless the sixteen towns were relinquished, "the whole power of the Confederacy . . . will join to annihilate the State of Vermont and to vindicate the right of New Hampshire to maintain, inviolate, the articles of confederation which guarantee to each State their privileges and immunities." This was clearly probable; a strong minority in the sixteen towns was opposed to the union; and Vermont hastily retreated. In February, 1779, the connection with the Hanover group was completely severed, and Vermont was restored to its original modest boundaries. The little State had troubles enough on the west without inviting more on the east, for a sporadic partisan warfare had broken out along the New York border.

By surrendering her thin claims to the Hanover towns, Vermont purchased the support of New Hampshire in her stubborn struggle against New York. Perhaps Ethan Allen at Philadelphia made a bargain to this effect with the New Hampshire delegates in Congress; perhaps there was no bargain at all. At any rate, New Hampshire was nervous lest the Vermont region should fall into the maw of New York, and earnestly debated the best means of preventing such a disaster to New England. The legislators, after hearing some Vermont representatives, finally decided (June 24, 1779) that New Hampshire should claim the whole of the territory, just as if the Crown had never made its decision of 1764 in favor of New York; but that if Congress should allow the Grants to become a separate State, then New Hampshire should acquiesce. In other words, New Hampshire's claim was to be maintained only until New York was defeated. With this decision, the tavern-keeper Governor, Chittenden, and Ethan and Ira Allen, were well satisfied. In the same month Massachusetts came to the aid of Vermont in the same fashion, her Legislature entering a claim to the territory on the basis of the cloudy terms of the old Plymouth Charter. The Crown had ruled against this claim, also, but it was a sufficient basis for the Massachusetts legislators in their wish to defeat New York's pretensions.

Had the Green Mountain boys been left alone to contend against New York, the issue would certainly have gone against them. The little mountain commonwealth would have had no choice but to submit, or to go over to the British side under the promise of being made a full Province. But with New England actively behind her, for Connecticut was warmly interested in the State her sons had done so much to settle, the case was different. The question was thrown into Congress, where it would be settled not in a narrow legalistic way, but with full attention to the principle of self-determination. New England wanted the additional sectional votes in Congress, and every small State in the Union objected to a further increase of New York's extensive territory. On September 24, 1779, Congress took a step which was in itself a victory for the Vermonters. It requested New York, New Hampshire, and Massachusetts to confer upon it the authority to adjudicate the whole controversy, and invited all three, with Vermont, to send representatives to Philadelphia on February 1, 1780, when it promised to make a final decision. The three States accepted the invitation, but Vermont, asserting that it was independent of the Confederation, declined to do so. The other accredited agents appeared at Philadelphia on the date named, among them a spokesman for the Hanover group of towns; Congress, since not enough disinterested States were represented in its membership at the moment, had to postpone the decision, but it was believed by all the parties that the postponement would be brief.[67]

The subsequent history of the Vermont question, though interesting, is too complicated for detailed rehearsal. After much maneuvering and counter-maneuvering, Congress on August 20, 1781, adopted a resolve that an indispensable condition of the admission of Vermont would be its relinquishment of all its claims to territory in New York west of the Massachusetts line as extended northward, and to territory east of the Connecticut in New Hampshire. This resolution in effect meant that Vermont's ultimate admission was certain. Six months later it acceded to the conditions laid down by Congress, and its entrance into the Union might have followed at once. For nine years such entrance was prevented by New York's maintenance of her claim, which was not withdrawn until 1790; but no one took New York's pretensions seriously, while Vermont's position, free from any share in the Continental debt or burdens, was a happy one. The whole dispute never seriously affected the good relations of any two States, and the calming and healing manner in which Congress treated it increased the slender prestige of that body.

All danger, if any existed, of a breach between two States over the Vermont territory was at an end soon after the war with England ended. The clash of Connecticut and Pennsylvania settlers over the Wyoming Valley, however, occurred in 1784, when the wartime bonds of the Union had been decidedly relaxed. If the dispute had been between the two States, instead of between irresponsible militiamen and land-speculators of Pennsylvania and a

---

[67] On the Vermont question see Stackpole, "Hist. N. H.," II, *passim;* Ira Allen; B. H. Hall; Hiland Hall; Vermont Historical Society Collections, I and II.

mere land company of Connecticut, its consequences might have been grave; but the governments were not brought into conflict.

This controversy also had its roots in colonial times. The beautiful Wyoming Valley, twenty-one miles long and three wide, lies beyond the Blue Ridge, with the Susquehanna rolling placidly through it. Within it now stands the city of Wilkes-Barre. When looked upon by the New Englanders who spied it out in 1750, it was a beautifully variegated tract of woodland and meadow, of level plain and rolling hills. There were mountain ranges on every side, with gaps through which the sparkling river entered and left the valley; and the size of the groves of sycamore, pine, laurel, and oak was alone enough to show the fertility of the soil, the bed of a prehistoric lake. The Delawares, Shawnees, and Nanticokes held the sides of the valley, which abounded in game. Connecticut claimed that by her royal charter of 1662, which extended her domain westward to the Pacific, she was entitled to the whole northern portion of the region now the State of Pennsylvania. This charter contained a proviso excepting the lands of New York, but not any other territory, while the charter to Penn which overlapped this grant was not issued until 1681, and was hence in the eyes of Connecticut men subordinate to their earlier assignment of a great continental strip. Interest in the western lands awoke in Connecticut about the middle of the eighteenth century, and in 1753 the Susquehanna Company was formed to develop these wilderness possessions.

The Connecticut citizens composing the company purchased the Wyoming Valley from the Six Nations in 1754, although the Penn family, Isaac Norris, and Dr. Franklin stoutly resisted the purchase on behalf of Pennsylvania. Both the Penns and the Connecticut government submitted their claims to British lawyers, and they obtained conflicting legal opinions as to the validity of their titles. For a time neither side made any determined effort to settle the disputed region. Then in 1762 two hundred Yankee farmers, with their families, entered it, but were promptly expelled by an Indian raid. Six years later the Penns made an effort to gain prior possession, persuading the Six Nations to denounce their deed to the Connecticut company and re-deed the valley to Pennsylvania; and they stationed henchmen in the district, with orders to hold it against all comers. The result, when in 1769 a fresh body of Connecticut settlers arrived, was the so-called first Pennamite War, a summer of desultory fighting between Penn's guards and the Susquehanna Company's colonists, which ended with the eviction, in August, 1771, of the Penns' agents. Happily, it was a private rather than public conflict: the peace-loving Pennsylvanians assumed that they had nothing to do with the Proprietary's quarrel, and Connecticut did not directly support the Susquehanna company.

At the outbreak of the Revolution occurred the Second Pennamite War, a much more serious episode. A considerable number of Pennsylvanians who had acquired a pecuniary interest in the Valley now supported the Penn claim; while the region, filling fast with Connecticut settlers, had been regularly organized under the Connecticut government—it was the town of Westmoreland, a part of Litchfield County, and it annually elected members to the Connecticut Legislature. Though Congress tried to stop the quarrel, it ended only when a strong Pennsylvania column had been thrown back by the Yankee defence; and then it ended only temporarily.[68] The able-bodied settlers went into the Continental army, forming the 24th Connecticut regiment. In 1776 Connecticut erected the Valley into Westmoreland County, and Connecticut taxes were levied, Connecticut laws were enforced, and Connecticut courts held full sway. But Pennsylvanians deplored the thought of having their State divided by a broad band of Connecticut territory, they knew that the acres involved were yearly growing more valuable, and they resented the presence of the Yankees in their midst, a people with strange manners and ideas. The two States would have continued to quarrel during the Revolution had Congress not asked them to let the issue lie dormant until the close of the struggle with the Crown. Within fifteen days after the surrender of Cornwallis, Pennsylvania petitioned Congress for a hearing of the case under that clause of the Articles of Confederation which provided a means of settling boundary disputes. Indeed, it was high time that the long controversy was set at rest.

Connecticut wished for a delay until it could bring certain papers

---

[68] See Silas Deane's notes upon the Second Pennamite War, Corr. and Journals of S. B. Webb, I, 107-10. Deane (October 15, 1775) says that the richest men in Philadelphia had become interested in the Wyoming lands, and had raised money for an armed force to drive off the Yankees. But he also blames the Connecticut settlers, who "have conducted in a most shocking manner." The excitement in Philadelphia was so great that "the very union of the Colonies" was thrown into a "critical situation." But consultations in Congress led to an agreement permitting the settlers to remain peaceably on the land during the war with England.

from England, but Congress ruled against this; and the two States agreeing upon a court of five commissioners—Wm. Whipple, Welcome Arnold, Daniel Brearly, Cyrus Griffin, and W. C. Houston —it opened its sessions in November, 1782, at Trenton. Upon strictly legal grounds Connecticut had an excellent case, as had New York in the Vermont controversy. But the question was one of expediency and equity, of national and State policy, rather than of mere law; and it has been thought that the leaders in Congress gave the court a strong hint that its decision should be in favor of Pennsylvania. At any rate, as far-sighted men the commissioners could hardly have decided except against Connecticut. If Connecticut were to use a careless, antiquated royal grant to split a State into two fragments, and to leap over New York to a New Connecticut on the west, other States could do the same. Massachusetts claimed a large section of western New York, and if the claim were allowed, it would cut New York entirely off from Lake Erie. It was clearly for the best interests of the nation that each State should be compact and well unified; it was also for the best interests of the States—Connecticut would have difficulty in governing a New Connecticut far to the westward. Already the small seaboard States without western grants were agitating for the relinquishment of such claims by their neighbors. On December 30 the court unanimously decided that the jurisdiction and preëmption of the land lay with Pennsylvania.

This decree, the first by which a serious collision between two States was averted under the Articles of Confederation, was quietly accepted by Connecticut. Now the Articles provided that in all boundary disputes a tribunal distinct from that which decided political boundaries might pass upon questions of private title to the lands; and the Trenton Court wrote the Supreme Executive Council of Pennsylvania urging that the Connecticut settlers be left undisturbed on their farms and in Wilkes-Barre until this tribunal could be selected. Connecticut and the Susquehanna Company had every reason to believe that the Wyoming settlers would be left virtually undisturbed. They had come to Wyoming with full faith in their land-titles, had conquered a virgin wilderness, and had displayed great heroism in defending the whole northern border of Pennsylvania from the Indians. Moreover, it had become customary in boundary disputes to allow the private holders of the soil to continue unharmed by changes in political jurisdiction. They had been thus left untouched in boundary disputes between Connecticut and all three of her neighbors, and between Massachusetts and New Hampshire. In the boundary disputes of Pennsylvania herself with Maryland and Virginia the original settlers had remained in possession of their farms.

It is unnecessary to recall in detail how completely Pennsylvania disappointed the hope that she would deal generously with the Wyoming Yankees. Her government, quite properly, remodeled the civil administration of the Valley, organizing two Pennsylvania townships there; but it did not stop with this. It suppressed the letter of the Court of Commissioners recommending a judicial adjustment of the land titles, and the Legislature, moved by a powerful lobby of land-claimants and by a selfish view of State interest, merely appointed commissioners to report a plan for accommodating the rival claimants. As was expected, the commissioners went to the Valley under the influence of the land-jobbers, made no real effort to arrange a compromise, and drew up a plan for ousting the Connecticut settlers—most of them to go within the year, the widows of men killed in the Revolution or the Indian massacre within two years. The Legislature approved it, satirically promised "a reasonable compensation" in raw State land to the families it was depriving of their well-established homes, and sent the commissioners back, with two companies of soldiers to support them. A bloody civil war, the history of which is familiar, at once broke out.

Had this guerrilla conflict continued long, a dangerous bitterness might have been generated between Connecticut and Pennsylvania. But sober men in the latter State quickly called a halt upon the evictions, burnings, and murderings. It was in May that the Pennsylvania troops drove the unoffending Yankee families eastward to the Delaware. When the State authorities heard of this, they dispatched the Northumberland sheriff to call the settlers back, dismissed the commander, and sent word to the Circuit Court judges to bring the aggressors to sharp account. When in July renewed fighting impelled the Executive Council to order militia to the scene, an unwise step, President Dickinson sent the Council a vigorous protest from his sickbed, deprecating the use of force. He pointed out that the settlers would regard the arrival of the militia "as the commencement of a war against them, and perhaps others, whose sentiments are of vastly more importance, may be of the same opinion." Moreover, in June the Council of Censors had begun its second session and it promptly remonstrated. Everyone knew what the Continental Congress felt regarding such occurrences. Above all, even the legislators directly under the influence of the lobby saw now that their arbitrary course was impracticable, and that the settlers simply would not submit to be ousted. At the close of summer they passed a new law to restore the dispossessed settlers to their home, pending an investigation to determine their rights under the Trenton decision, and on September 9 they appointed four commissioners to carry out this law. The Connecticut farmers were allowed peacefully to harvest their crops, and they celebrated Thanksgiving with a sense of returning security.[69]

There had been some excitement in Connecticut when the news of the painful flight of the evicted colonists to the Delaware reached New Haven and Hartford, but it was not marked. The people in general had never taken a keen interest in the Connecticut claims. Some of their leaders had harshly criticized the belligerent conduct of the Connecticut settlers in the second Pennamite War, Silas Deane, then in the Continental Congress, saying that they had "conducted in a most shocking manner"; and a little distrust had survived from that year. It has been supposed that the Trenton decision was arrived at with the possible help of a secret understanding between Connecticut and Congress, since Connecticut immediately afterwards ceded the nation all her western lands save the Reserve; at any rate, the State had resolved without heartburning to have done with the Pennsylvania lands. The Connecticut Legislature in the autumn of 1784 contented itself with sending a protest to the Continental Congress, and soon learned that there was no cause for real alarm.

In its later phases the dispute can be looked at in almost a humorous light, for as in Vermont, it called forth a good deal of mere bluster. The Susquehanna Company during 1785, without encouragement from Connecticut, took militant steps to meet the possibility of another attempt to evict its settlers. In midsummer it held a meeting at Hartford, at which it offered any 400 men who would go within the next few months to the Wyoming Valley, and

---

[69] See Pa. Archives, Series IV, Vol. III, 973 ff. It must be recalled that the Pennsylvania Legislature and Supreme Executive Council were in the hands of the radical Constitutionalist party, who were amenable to the influence of the land lobby; while President Dickinson and a majority of the Council of Censors were men of principle and responsibility, who took the other side. The exertions of Dickinson and the Censors, supported by a revulson in public sentiment, caused the State to

agree to reside there for three years, a half-share apiece in the company. Thus, in the Company's cant phrase, "Connecticut would man her rights." A militia force was organized in the Valley, which by the spring of 1786 enrolled nearly 600 men, ready to fight at the first appearance of a new armed force. Ethan Allen was induced, by a generous land-grant, to visit the region and engage to serve in the event of hostilities. Some of the Connecticut settlers in the Green Mountains, having won the one struggle, enlisted in the other by coming to the Pennsylvania lands. In all, by the summer of 1786 about 250 new families were in the district, enough to assist the Company materially in its claim to a sort of squatter sovereignty.

But the Company was not content with merely protecting the settlers in their Valley farms. Its members hoped to hold to their entire purchase from the Indians, and were hence unwilling to abide by the Trenton decision. Partly by members of the Company in Connecticut, partly by resolute Wyoming leaders like John Franklin, an old scheme was revived for establishing a new State in the region. Franklin traveled to Connecticut and urged it energetically; Oliver Wolcott outlined a Constitution; and it was suggested that William Judd, who in Jefferson's day came to be known as a Republican leader, should be the first Governor. This scheme was of course preposterous, and though it obtained support even in New York, where some men liked the idea of cutting Pennsylvania in two, few regarded it seriously.[70]

Like the Vermont question, the Wyoming Valley quarrel was not fully settled until after the framing of the Constitution, but it was virtually settled long before and had passed out of most men's minds. The Pennsylvania Government, after its first selfish blunders, acted with commendable moderation. It happened that Timothy Pickering, of Puritan blood, born in Salem, educated at Harvard, the head of a Massachusetts regiment in the war, was residing in Philadelphia in 1786, and had resolved to find a home in some new frontier or wilderness settlement. He was persuaded to visit

retrace the harsh and unjustifiable steps it had taken under the lead of hotheaded men. Benjamin Rush, an Anti-Constitutionalist, was among those disgusted by the affair, and wrote Pickering apropos of it: "All will *end well.* The new Federal Government, like a new Continental wagon, will overset our State dung-cart, with all its dirty contents (reverend and irreverend), and thereby restore order and happiness to Pennsylvania." (Upham's "Pickering," II, 301.)

[70] Some light is thrown upon this by the local histories of the Wyoming Valley, Luzerne County, and Wilkes-Barre; and a great deal by the Fairfield County Hist. Soc. Reports, 1896-97.

the turbulent Wyoming region, which he first inspected in August, 1786, and in which he prepared to take up his residence in January, 1787. He called meetings in the villages; he announced the erection of a new county, Luzerne, the Legislature having evoked its former organization of the Valley; and he assured the people that the original settlers would probably be quieted in the possession of their land by the next Legislature. New outbreaks occurred among the wilder Connecticut element that fall, and on October 2 Pickering was actually driven from his home by a lawless crew headed by John Franklin. But these disturbances were merely a brief final spasm, and an adjustment satisfactory to the majority on both sides was soon reached. Its cornerstone was a law of 1787 by which those settlers who had been in the Valley at the time of the Trenton decision were confirmed in the possession of the lands they had obtained from the Susquehanna Company, while the Pennsylvania claimants of the same land were awarded compensation in another district.[71]

Beside the Vermont and Wyoming disputes, all the mere boundary controversies were unimportant. The former genuinely alarmed lovers of State concord for a time; the latter were mere irritations, not one of which in itself threatened serious consequences. Their danger was cumulative. National leaders feared the psychological effect of a succession of petty altercations all over America, from the Merrimac to the Savannah. Thus Jay wrote Livingston at the end of 1782 that "The boundaries between the States should be immediately settled and all cause of dispute between them removed." Eight months later he counselled Gouverneur Morris: "Settle your boundaries without delay. It is better that some improper boundaries be fixed, than any left in dispute. In a word, everything conducive to union and constitutional energy of government should be cultivated. . . ." Not all the boundaries were actually fixed before 1789—some not for decades; but the disagreement caused no lasting nor extensive warmth.

Georgia and South Carolina petitioned Congress in 1786 to determine their disputed western boundaries, and the Congress duly

---

[71] Upham's "Pickering," II, Ch. 7. Pickering found about 250 families of old Connecticut settlers in the Wyoming Valley, and as many more of the new settlers which the Susquehanna Company had sent out with a grant of a half-share each. The former were satisfied to be secured in the title to their homes; the latter claimed for the company the great tract of land included in the original purchase from the Indians. Pickering helped to frame the legislation of 1787.

constituted a court of commissioners. Before it could act, however, the two States came to a satisfactory decision by direct negotiation,[72] which Congress duly ratified.[73] North Carolina had but one boundary quarrel of importance, that old one with Virginia to which William Byrd has given literary immortality in his "History of the Dividing Line." An effort in 1778 to carry the line between the States westward to the Tennessee River failed when the commissioners surveying it quarreled, and a strip was left to be a theme of controversy for many years.[74] Virginia's boundary dispute with Maryland[75] remained unsettled even when Washington became President, but that with Pennsylvania,[76] involving the curious knob which, as part of West Virginia, still projects northward between Ohio and Pennsylvania, and is called "the Panhandle," was ended by a joint commission in 1779.[77] Pennsylvania easily fixed her northern line in agreement with New York, and it was marked out by David Rittenhouse in 1785-87. Her charter boundary barely enabled her to touch Lake Erie, but the break in the western extremity of the long border with New York, which gave her a satisfactory lake frontage, with the port of Erie, was obtained later by purchase. This "Erie triangle," which had been jointly claimed by New York and Massachusetts, was ceded by them to the United States, and the nation permitted Pennsylvania to purchase it in 1792 for the modest sum of $151,640. New York and Massachusetts settled their territorial difficulties after the war by a meeting of agents at Hartford, Conn., where it was agreed that Massachusetts should have the preëmptive rights to two large tracts within New York's bounds, totalling about five million acres. New York of course retained all the governmental rights. One tract, of only 230,000 acres, was near the center of the State; the other lay farther west, in the Genesee Valley and along Lake Erie. Massachusetts soon (1787 and 1791) sold these New York lands for sums aggregating $1,100,000.

[72] See note in Pa. *Mercury*, June 1, 1787.
[73] In 1777 some ambitious South Carolinians proposed the consolidation of South Carolina and Georgia, or rather the absorption of Georgia by South Carolina. This so irritated the Georgia Government that a reward of £100 was offered for the arrest of W. H. Drayton, chief sponsor for the scheme. Knight, "Georgia's Landmarks, Memorials, and Legends."
[74] For disputes over the N. C.-Ga. boundary, see N. C. Booklet, III, paper by D. Goodloe.
[75] Va. and Md. acted most amicably during the war; on this boundary problem, see Fund Pubs., Md. Hist. Soc., No. 29.
[76] Some Virginians even claimed Niagara after the war, and wished to garrison it after the British evacuation; Public Papers of Geo. Clinton, VIII, 249-50.
[77] Amer. Archives, Series IV, Vol. II, 684. Four commissioners marked the boundary in 1785; see Md. *Journal*, November 22, 1785.

VI. The Western Lands An Issue

So far as strengthening the Union went, the settlement of the various boundaries had merely a negative effect; it removed causes of disagreement. The settlement of the greatest question of all, that of the western lands, operated directly to invigorate the Union, and it gave the national government a domain to administer for the common good. There existed two dangers to State harmony in the unfixed status of the great Northwestern and Southwestern wilderness in 1781. One lay in the conflicting claims of a half dozen rival States for parts of these regions. New York, Connecticut, and Massachusetts could all assert a title to some of the lands northwest of the Ohio, and Virginia believed that the whole great region was hers. South Carolina and Georgia were in dispute as to part of the territory now included in Alabama and Mississippi. But this friction was in no wise so threatening as the apprehension and irritation which the collective claims bred among the half-dozen States which had no pretense to western lands at all.

Maryland enjoys the credit of being the first to express this natural apprehension that she would be overshadowed by mighty neighbors expanding over great untouched reaches, and to press for the wise solution of the problem ultimately adopted. Her Provincial Convention on October 30, 1776, resolved that "the very extensive claims of the State of Virginia to the back lands hath no foundation in justice, and if the same or any like claim is admitted, the freedom of the smaller States and the liberties of America may be greatly endangered, this convention being firmly persuaded that, if the dominion over these lands should be established by the blood and treasure of the United States, such lands ought to be considered common stock to be parcelled out at any time into convenient, free, and independent governments." This early action shows remarkable alertness and far-sightedness.

It is unnecessary to rehearse the steps by which the claimant States surrendered the Northwest Territory into the nation's keeping. Curiously enough, for some time after Maryland had proposed that the Articles of Confederation should give Congress jurisdiction over the west, with power to lay it out from time to time in new members of the Union, the other small States failed to rally to her side. New Jersey and Rhode Island were unwilling to see the West gobbled by a few dominant commonwealths, and brought forward amendments to the proposed Articles of Confederation; but they were ready to leave the jurisdiction of the claimant States over the wilderness undisturbed, asking only that the revenues from the sale of the lands be reserved to the nation. Maryland, however, stood her ground, with ever-increasing support from other parts of the Union. Wm. Sharpe, a North Carolina member of Congress, writing Governor Caswell in 1779 on the prospects for a durable confederation, referred to the "great jealousies" respecting the Western claims, and declared that the representatives of some States wished Maryland to refuse to ratify the Articles, and to keep the threat of disunion over the head of Virginia and other claimants, until they gave up their pretensions.[78] Maryland ratified before they completed this surrender, but she had maintained her stubborn position until her victory was certain, even without an explicit guarantee of it in an amendment. New York had on February 19, 1780, authorized her Congressional delegates to make either a partial or complete cession; Connecticut offered a conditional surrender of some of her rights on October 10; and on January 2, 1781, Virginia voted to give up her lands northwest of the Ohio upon eight conditions. When all this had been done, and not before, Maryland entered the Union.[79]

Maryland's threat to obstruct a Confederation until her demands were met has its resemblance, of course, to Vermont's threat to join the British if her separate existence were not recognized, and the Wyoming settlers' threat to form a new State if they were not left alone in their homes. A good deal of resentment was engendered while the western lands were under discussion. The larger States repeatedly assailed the motives of their lesser neighbors, even the cool-headed Madison doing so. Rhode Island was influenced, Madison wrote, by "first, a lucrative desire of sharing in the vacant territory as a fund of revenue; secondly, by the envy and jealousy naturally excited by superior resources and importance." New Jersey, Pennsylvania, Delaware, and Maryland were actuated partly by the same reasons, he added, "but principally by the intrigues of their citizens, who are interested in the land companies. The decisive influence of this last consideration is manifest from the

---

[78] N. C. State Records, XIV, 216-17.
[79] The best treatment of Maryland's struggle is in H. B. Adams, "Md.'s Influence Upon Land Cessions to the U. S.," supplemented by B. W. Bond, "State Government in Md.," Ch. II. For documents, see Hening's Statutes, X, 547-567.

peculiar and persevering opposition made against Virginia, within whose limits those claims lie." [80]

On the other side, the small States could accuse the western claimants of egregious selfishness. Maryland in 1777-78 made it plain that she did not regard the Confederation as necessarily permanent, but as a temporary union brought about by circumstances, and in which, when these circumstances ceased to operate, "the States which have thus acceded to the Confederation will consider it no longer binding, and will eagerly embrace the first occasion of asserting their just rights and securing their independence." Would the States which had obtained great western areas then use the wealth and power derived from these territories in moderation? Maryland feared not:

Suppose, for instance, Virginia indisputably possessed of the extensive and fertile country to which she has set up a claim, what would be the probable consequences to Maryland? Virginia, by selling on the most moderate terms a small proportion of the lands in question, would draw into her treasury vast sums of money and . . . would be enabled to lessen her taxes: lands comparatively cheap and taxes comparatively low, with the lands and taxes of an adjacent State, would quickly drain the State thus disadvantageously circumstanced of its most useful inhabitants, its wealth; and its consequence, in the scale of the confederated States, would sink, of course. A claim so injurious to more than one-half, if not the whole of the United States, ought to be supported by the clearest evidences of the right. Yet what evidences of that right have been produced? . . . We are convinced, policy and justice require that a country unsettled at the commencement of this war, claimed by the British crown, and ceded to it by the treaty of Paris, should be considered as a common property, subject to be parcelled out by Congress into . . . independent governments. . . .

Quotations might be adduced from a dozen sources to show the jealous soreness which the non-claimant States felt. In 1779 a champion for them expressed the wish in the Pennsylvania *Packet,* the chief commercial journal of the country, that they could strike a bargain with Massachusetts and the other States eager to gain fishing rights in Canadian waters. They could offer to assist in obtaining these rights if the fishing interests would in turn help procure a surrender of the western claims. It was a palpable injustice for the non-claimant States to be "deprived of any share of these lands for which they have drawn their swords as well as others and which are the joint possessions of the whole." Any weapon was justified "against the most iniquitous article of the Confederation which cedes the just rights of the whole to aggrandize a few." [81] New Jersey in 1784 made an earnest effort to attract the loyalist merchants who were being so disgracefully mistreated in

[80] Rives, "Madison," I, 456-58.
[81] Pa. *Packet,* August 14, 1779.

New York city. One reason offered, by those who circulated a paper promising to secure peaceful settlement and trade to all the loyalists, was the commercial poverty of New Jersey; another was that "the other States have not considered us in the Confederation, but have reserved to themselves a vast tract of unlocated land to defray their quota of the expenses of the war, which expense must be collected from the sweat of our brow, though we have undergone more than our share of the severities" of the fighting.[82]

A Congressional committee did not exaggerate when it reported (September 6, 1780) that a surrender of the territorial claims, at least in part, must be vigorously urged, "since they cannot be preserved entire without endangering the stability of the general confederacy." The report went on to remind the States "how indispensably necessary it is to establish the federal union on a fixed and permanent basis, and on principles acceptable to all its respective members." The appeal which it embodied was agreed to without a roll-call. Unfortunately, even in Congress animosities upon the subject were manifest long after 1781, especially as its consideration became involved in the sectional intriguing that went on. The question had its influence upon the Vermont controversy, for at one time Virginia and other Southern States opposed the admission of Vermont partly because of their fear that the new member would throw in her lot with that of the other small States in fighting the western claims. The South also felt that New York's partnership with it in the western claims helped to keep Clinton's State outside the Yankee circle. "If this cession should be accepted," wrote Madison after New York's offer of February, 1780, to give up her lands, "and the affair of Vermont terminated, as these are the only ties which unite her with the Southern States, she will immediately connect her policy with that of the Eastern States; so far, at least, as the remains of her former prejudices will permit." The machinations of private land interests, like the Indiana or Vandalia Companies, whose titles depended upon New York's claims, played a part in Congress. North Carolina made her cession of western lands in the spring of 1784 conditional upon the action of other States and Congress in totally unrelated matters. She revoked it that autumn, explaining that she had voted it "in full confidence that the whole expense of Indian expeditions and militia aids to the

States of South Carolina and Georgia should pass to account in our quota of the continental expenses incurred by the late war; and also that the other States holding western territory would make similar cessions, and that all the States would unanimously grant imposts of five per cent. as a common fund . . ."; and that this confidence had been betrayed.[83]

One by one the early State cessions of claims to the northwestern territory were stripped of all embarrassing and unallowable conditions. Virginia by an act of October 20, 1783, finally put her grant in acceptable form, with only minor restrictions; Massachusetts followed her example on November 13, 1784; and Connecticut did the same (withholding only the Western Reserve of 3,250,000 acres) on May 11, 1786. Congress now controlled almost the whole vast territory. It should be noted that the national government was so loose that it was not possible fully to nationalize the lands; the Articles of Confederation gave Congress only such resources as came from the States, and the Northwest could not be vested in any single sovereignty. The deeds executed by the various States provided that the lands thus ceded should be divided among, or their proceeds divided among, the whole sisterhood of States.

One of the blessings that flowed from the cession, however, was that it led Congress to exceed the restrictions placed upon its powers. As early as March 1, 1784, a committee of which Jefferson was a leading member reported an ordinance, to be the organic law for the region. This ordinance was not adopted. But it was of great importance simply because it was drafted in spite of the fact that Congress, acting alone, had no written authority whatever to organize such a government. Presumably this could be done only in some manner agreed upon by the States, for the Articles of Confederation had not dealt with the contingency. Yet it was not intended that this ordinance should be referred to the States. It was called a "charter of compact" among the States to be created and the thirteen original States, and its provisions were to stand as "fundamental constitutions" without ratification. In this manner did a Congressional committee take the first step towards giving Congress an exertion of national sovereignty in the field of eminent domain. Already the western territory, as a common responsibility and

---

[83] N. C. State Records, XXIV, 678-79. The North Carolina Legislature ceded the western lands again at the fall session in 1789; State Records, XXV, 4-6.

promise of future greatness, was binding the people together and strengthening the central government.

The Ordinance of 1787 gave final expression to this new and far-reaching assumption of national sovereignty by Congress. Passed on July 13, 1787, while the Federal Convention was sitting at Philadelphia, its full title was "An Ordinance for the Government of the Territory of the United States, northwest of the river Ohio." It also was "a compact between the original States, and the people and States in the said territory"; and it became effective immediately, without submission to the various Legislatures or other formality. The territorial administration it provided, under Governor, Secretary, and three judges; the provision it made for a system of law; the terms in which it forever prohibited slavery; the encouragement it gave to learning; and the method it prescribed for the admission of new States to the Union, are familiar. It need only be emphasized that the Ordinance looked to a perpetual union of the States, indicated astutely the lines along which population and property would increase, and provided for the future of that ever richer, more populous West as part of the nation.

No one in the country could now avoid turning his eyes often to the west, and whenever he fixed them there, he could not help but catch a national as opposed to a particularistic vision. This would have been true had the United States been of a different geographical shape than it was; but it is seldom realized how much the peculiar configuration of the republic in its first years had to do with the sectional disagreements and resulting predictions of disunion. It was a long belt of settlement, from the snows of Maine to the palmettos of Georgia, so narrow that it could be called a ribbon of population. General Benjamin Lincoln shrewdly noted that from its narrowness and length, lying across different zones, the nation was likely to break in two. "Did the United States extend from east to west . . . ," he wrote, "instead of their extending, as they do now, from north to south, their union would, probably, be much more permanent, and they would be easier governed by the same legislative body than in their present situation." He pointed to the "evils, which are consequent on the extent of the United States, their different climates, their different productions, and the different views of the people in consequence thereof," adding: "I cannot believe that these States ever will, or ever can, be governed, and all

enjoy equal advantages, by laws which have a general operation."
He thought it inevitable that Americans must accept "a division,
which might be formed upon such principles as would secure our
public creditors, and thereby our public faith, and our after peace
and safety by a firm alliance between the divisions." But the
growth of the new west, with the colonization of southern Illinois
and Kentucky by Virginians, and the steady flow of the Pennsylvania
Scotch-Irish and other Northerners into the southwest, gave the
nation a new physical appearance and a new outlook.[84]

The inequality in the size and strength of the States was marked
even after the cession of the western claims. In 1788 Georgia ruled
over about 153,000 square miles; Virginia over about 103,000; and
North Carolina over about 84,000—a total of 340,000 for three
States. The other ten had an aggregate of only 167,000 square
miles, and Rhode Island had only 1360. But the disparity between
the great and small States could be used more effectively as an
argument for a stronger union than as one for distrust and aloofness.
Hamilton in 1781 suggested that without the stronger union, the
vanity and ambition of great States might lead them to try to place
themselves at the head of little independent confederations.[85] So
Oliver Ellsworth in the Connecticut ratifying convention seven years
later contended that if his State did not have a powerful Union to
protect her, she would fall a prey to "the ambition and rapacity of
New York" and Massachusetts.[86] Men with a federalist bent always
denied that the great States felt any natural solidarity as against
the smaller members of the nation. Thus James Wilson in Congress
defied any man to name any policy on earth which would be for
the interests of Virginia, Pennsylvania, and Massachusetts, and
would not also be for the interests of lesser States.[87]

VII. Forces Making for Harmony

In reviewing the disputes of the States over trade matters, their
disputes over war burdens, and their disputes relating to territory,
it must not be forgotten that there is also another story; a story of

---

[84] Lincoln to Rufus King, 1786; King, "Life and Corr.," I, 156-60.
[85] Madison said in 1787: "The weaker you make your confederation, the greater
the danger to the lesser States. They can only be protected by a strong Federal
Government." Yates's "Notes of Secret Debates," 181.
[86] Van Santvoord, "Lives Chief Justices," 232 ff.; Elliot, "Debates," II, 186.
[87] Journals Cont. Cong., VI, 1105-06.

forces and events making strongly toward harmony. Some of these were slight. Such, for example, was the pride the States felt in maintaining a creditable character before the world, and showing they were ready for sober self-government.[88] Washington thought it worth while in 1784 to mention to Governor Clinton the fact that internal dissensions had a tendency to lessen the national character and importance in the eyes of European powers. Much more important was the impulse toward union and harmony given by foreign enmities—those of the Indians, Spanish, and British. It is also to be remarked that from 1776 to 1789 there was going on a steady erasure of institutional differences and of social dissimilarities, making harmony more natural.

While the war with England was formally halted in 1783, the war with the Indians never ended. It is true that in 1783-84 there was a brief truce along the whole border, for the Indians were intimidated by the peace and the withdrawal of their former allies; but it was only brief. Irresponsible frontiersmen usually disliked the national government, which interfered with their freedom of action. The more sober inhabitants of exposed regions, however, welcomed its efforts to conclude treaties of peace with the Indians, to bring lawless Indian-baiters under control, and to intimidate the tribes. Despite the agreements which Congressional commissioners made with a number of Indian nations in 1785 and 1786, outlying settlements suffered more and more after the former year. The northwestern tribes, and especially the Shawnees, Wabash, and Miamis, were spoiling for a fight, and roving bands, bringing in scalps and plunder, excited the ambitions of the younger warriors. It became harder and harder to restrain the frontiersmen from provoked or unprovoked aggressions. Even such a prominent man as George Rogers Clark was involved in schemes to lay hands upon Indian lands in the northwest, and both the Confederation and Virginia had to take action to restrain the adventurers. Farther South the Carolinians and Georgians, the Creeks and Cherokees, were enacting the same drama—treaties violated upon both sides, invasions of Indian territory by white settlers, and bloody Indian expeditions against peaceful settlements.

---

[88] "We are known in no part of Europe by any other idea than that of the United States; and considered abstractedly from the Confederation, our credit would be trivial compared with what we most assuredly might command, if our character as a confederated republic was fully established." N. Y. *Packet,* July 28, 1785.

This sporadic warfare grew in intensity until it came to a head in the year of the ratification of the Constitution. Had it been a more active warfare—had the authority of Congress and the strength of the Congressional border forces been more urgently needed—the impulse it gave to solidarity among the States would have been greater. Benjamin Logan and Simon Kenton, in the north, and John Sevier and Joseph Martin in the south, were fast adding to their laurels as Indian-fighters. By 1788 the struggle in the Southwest was almost unremitting, the Cherokees, Creeks, and Chickamaugas all being in arms against the whites; and terrible are the tales of cold-blooded massacre on both sides. In truth, the irresistible westward tide of civilization made a conflict unavoidable, and shrewd statesmen recognized it. The State governments wished to postpone till the last moment the open recognition of war on the border. But they knew that it was coming; they knew that it would be well to be united against that day; and they knew that it would be easier to bring the struggle to a quick and successful conclusion if they submitted to Federal direction.

Behind the aggression of the Indians stood always the threat of British hostility, for British agents and Tories moved constantly among the tribes. The British held the three great lake forts of Niagara, Detroit, and Michilimackinac, with the smaller lake posts of the region, on the excuse that the Americans had not fulfilled their engagements under the treaty of peace. Till they were evacuated, the northern States regarded them nervously. British officers continued to administer the civil and military affairs of the Indian communities of which these forts and posts were the center, and they received the Indian chiefs as active allies. They and the great Indian confederacies of the Northwest were one in hating and fearing the march of the settler. There could be no open hostilities between British and Americans, but the powerful and inflammable feudatories of the former made covert hostilities all too easy.

More serious still, and more powerful in holding the States together, were the British discriminations against American commerce. In September, 1785, a New York city committee circularized all parts of the country in behalf of the impost amendment. "You cannot but perceive, that although the late treaty with Britain has given the name of peace, yet we in fact are called on to wage a variegated war," they wrote. "As the enmity is less open, so the enemies are more numerous." This fact they used in arguing for fraternal concord: "a happy but severe experience past [has shown], and we apprehend a future less happy and more severe will evince, that *our union is the basis of our grandeur and power*." [89] It was not the impost amendment, but another amendment granting Congress the power of regulating commerce for fifteen years, that was needed. Once given this power, Congress expected to forbid the importation of merchandise unless it came either in American ships, or the ships of nations which had made satisfactory commercial treaties with us. A number of Northern States after 1784 struck at Great Britain through their tariff laws, which were unfortunately a jumble of incongruities. By the end of 1785 ten States had in some fashion approved the amendment drafted to give Congress the desired authority, though not with a proper uniformity in the terms used. Delaware, Georgia, and South Carolina long failed to approve it at all. The effort to unite the States completely against British economic aggression thus broke down. But in 1787 it was evident that month by month more men and more influential interests were coming to Monroe's conclusion: "I am perfectly satisfied that the more fully the subject is investigated, and the better the interests of the States severally are understood, the more obvious will appear the necessity of committing to the United States permanently the power of regulating their trade."

In the Southwest the Spaniards played the same part as the British in the Northwest in secretly encouraging Indian attacks; the Gardoqui manuscripts show decisively that in 1786, when that minister was pretending the greatest friendliness toward the United States, the Spanish were supplying the Creeks with arms and ammunition. The Madrid Government was enraged when it learned of the secret clause in the Treaty of Paris by which America and England arranged that if the latter recovered West Florida from Spain, the boundary between it and the United States should then be reshifted to the north. The Spanish closure of the Mississippi equally enraged the South and Southwest. When the unexcitable Jay believed that a war with Spain was inevitable if the United States pursued the course determined upon, it is evident that the possibility of such a conflict had some weight in the scales against careless disunion. No such war could be won if the States quarreled among themselves.

[89] N. Y. *Packet,* November 10, 1785.

Year by year the social and political improvements wrought in the different States softened the differences among them. Carter Braxton, one of the most determined conservatives of the South, speaking of the people of New England in the Virginia Convention before independence, remarked: "I abhor their manners—I abhor their laws—I abhor their governments—I abhor their religion." [90] But when Jefferson and Madison had carried out most of their economic program, when primogeniture and entail were gone, when the church establishment had been destroyed, when a State Constitution had expressed doctrines of almost a "levelling" spirit, the Virginians found fewer dissimilarities between themselves and the Yankees. The upland inhabitants would have admitted that they and the farmers of Massachusetts had nearly everything in common. The revision of the State Constitutions made towards the same goal, for it tended to give all Americans much the same local government. Dr. Benjamin Rush in Congress in the summer of 1776 said that the United States was a true nation—"Our trade, language, customs, manners, don't differ more than they do in Great Britain." [91] This was indisputable, and the States grew more, not less, alike. It was because of the obliteration of small social and institutional differences that a New York correspondent of the Pennsylvania *Packet* was able to write in November, 1789:

A happy revolution of sentiment is observed to have taken place throughout the United States—local views and narrow prejudices are universally reprobated. A generous, national spirit pervades the whole Union. Formerly we used to call ourselves Englishmen, Germans, Irishmen, Scotchmen, etc., according to the country from whence we respectively originated—but *now* even the distinctions of States are scarcely heard—and like other great nations, who have risen to fame and empire, we are proud to be distinguished by the name of the country we inhabit, Americans.[92]

Predictions of total disunion, warnings of anarchy, were common from 1776 to 1788. Sometimes they were used to frighten men into greater cordiality towards proposals for strengthening the powers of Congress—thus Hamilton used them in his third Continentalist essay in 1781. Sometimes their authors were quite sincere. Early in the war General Knox repeatedly wrote that the Union was upon the verge of dissolution. Richard Henry Lee meant every word when he wrote in 1777: "I am persuaded as I am of my existence, that had it not been for Virginia and Jersey, with Georgia sometimes, our union would ere now have been by this means [local jealousies]

---

[90] MS. "Notes of Benj. Rush," Ridgeway Branch Library Co. of Philadelphia.
[91] Journals Cont. Cong., VI, 1081. See, to the same effect, "Army Corr. of John Laurens," 89-90.
[92] November 2, 1789.

broken, like a potter's vessel dashed against a rock." He ventured only to hope that this supreme evil might not take place before peace was established. Governor Edmund Randolph of Virginia told Washington in 1786 that the Legislature feared for the breaking up of the nation—"What our enemies have foretold, seems to be hastening to its accomplishment."

But especially after 1781, nine out of ten of those who expressed a fear of disunion did not fear the shattering of the republic into its thirteen original parts; they feared its splitting into two, or possibly three or four, sections. It was not total disunion, but sectional disintegration, that threatened. Richard D. Spaight, informing Governor Martin of North Carolina in 1784 that in his view the New England States had tried to weaken the Union to increase their own importance, said that they were pressing so hard upon the national framework that "I imagine it will break before they are well aware of it." A dissolution, he felt, would be to New England's disadvantage. The farm products of the Middle and Southern States, these States clinging in a new Union, would command the friendship of Europe, while the manufactures and commerce of the Yankee nation would excite foreign jealousy.[93] Rufus King thought in 1785 that the eight Northern States might quarrel decisively with the five Southern States over the Congressional regulation of trade; they could form, "and in the event must form, a sub-confederation remedied of all their present embarrassment."[94] General Lincoln, already quoted, looked toward a division between North and South on a line which he did not indicate. It was with such prophecies in mind that the Pennsylvania *Packet* in 1786, when South Carolina gave Congress the power to regulate trade, rejoiced that the "likelihood of disunion arising from the great diversity of interests between the Northern and Southern States . . . is now entirely annihilated."

During 1787, the year the stronger union was conceived, these proposals for new sectional republics were put forward most seriously. Madison, serving in Congress, found that a fellow member, Bingham of Pennsylvania, thought it would be best to divide the country into "several distinct federacies—its great extent and various interests being incompatible with a single government."[95] One Boston paper

---

[93] N. C. State Records, XVII, 172-75. Spaight pointed to the Wyoming and Vt. disputes as having "sown the seeds of dissension which I think will not end without a civil war."
[94] King, "Life and Corr.," I, 112-13.
[95] Rives, "Madison," II. 187.

early this year suggested that the Bay State refuse any longer to let the jealousy of New York or Pennsylvania keep it bound to the wretched measures that had so long made America the contempt of Europe. Massachusetts had exerted itself to give strength to the national government, but to no avail. The five New England States, united, could have nothing to fear. Let the General Court recall its delegates from the shadowy Congress at Philadelphia, send its neighbors proposals for a new Congress speaking for New England, "and leave the rest of the Continent to pursue their own imbecile and disjointed plans." [96] In Southern papers at the same time appeared a suggestion for the erection of four new nations upon the ruins of the Confederation. One should comprise the New England, one the Middle, one the Southern, and one the trans-Allegheny States. "The religion, manners, customs, imports, exports, and general interests of each, being then the same, no opposition arising from differences in these (as at present) would any longer divide their councils—unanimity would render us secure at home, and respected abroad, and promote agriculture, manufacture, and commerce." [97]

But these suggestions and warnings of sectional division did not go beyond mere words, and the words were soon forgotten by those who uttered them. It is significant that men in the New England States seldom or never thought of parting from the South unless they had the Middle States still firmly linked with them; while the South in turn never thought of setting up for itself unless it had the greater portion of the Middle States with it. Curiously, in the politics of Congress there was at one time an approach to a coalition between the New England members and the Southern members in opposition to those of the Middle States. When Yankee votes helped the South to obtain a decision that the nation should have its permanent capital on the Potomac, not the Delaware, Stephen Higginson of Massachusetts was much pleased. "It has long been my wish to see the Southern and Eastern States united," he wrote Bland of Virginia (January, 1784). "Their common safety and interest must be increased by that decision; for the Middle States have certainly laid such plans, and acquired such an influence, as would have given them the entire direction of the national concerns. Penn-

[96] Quoted in N. Y. *Advertiser*, February 23, 1787.
[97] Quoted in Mass. *Centinel*, April 18, 1787. This was the year in which the translator of Chastellux's "Travels," predicted an early division of the Union into two parts; footnote to page 107, ed. 1826.

sylvania, or rather a junta of ambitious individuals in it, had conceived the idea of lording it over the other States. . . . They always exerted themselves to keep up a high degree of jealousy between the Southern and Eastern States." [98]   R. H. Lee was always a fast friend of New England, so friendly that he was repeatedly assailed at home for neglecting Virginia's interests.   The fact that disunion was more seriously talked about in 1787 than before reflects not an increased desire for it in itself, but as an alternative to the evils the land was laboring under.   People were so sick of the impotency of Congress and the misbehavior of factions that they were ready to think of energetic little sectional republics as an alternative.   But a far better solution was at hand.

Not a statesman of importance in America wanted disunion—not even Hancock, certainly not even George Clinton, who has sometimes been accused of the desire.   The great mass of Americans in 1781 had been educated against it.   There were men a half dozen years later who not merely wanted the Constitution defeated, but believed that it might be best if the nation broke up—Jay knew some in the New York ratifying convention; but they were few. "The union of America is the foundation stone of our independence; the rock on which it is built; and it is something so sacred in her constitution that we ought to watch every word we speak, and every thought we think, that we injure it not, even by mistakes"—these are the words, not of one of the national leaders, not of the press in one of the commercial cities, but of the New Jersey *Gazette* of April 17, 1782.   They might be paralleled every year thereafter from every part of the Union.   After all, every great imponderable force was on the side of a close connection.   The inhabitants had the same language; were mainly of British blood; their laws, customs, and mental habits were much the same; and they had a common history that was not brief.   John Jay thought it worth while to remark when Rufus King married a daughter of the wealthy Alsop family in New York in 1786: "I am pleased with these intermarriages; they tend to assimilate the States, and to promote one of the first wishes of my heart, viz., to see the people of America become one nation in every respect."   Some small, some great, so many natural forces were at work that in the aggregate they were quite unconquerable.

[98] Rives, "Madison," I, 489-90.

CHAPTER THIRTEEN

THE RELATIONS OF THE STATES WITH CONGRESS

Upon the Continental Congress fell the responsibility for directing and leading the Revolution. It had to determine just the degree of activity to be given the struggle in its early phases. It alone decided upon the restriction of trade to injure England. It gave the signal in May, 1776, for the final overthrow of the old Provincial governments wherever they still stood. With a number of States yet reluctant, it declared our independence. Besides this guidance of policy, there fell upon it an immense burden of business detail, military, diplomatic, and administrative, for it had to raise troops, equip them, pay them, and reinforce them, through the States; to call upon the States for taxes to support itself, its agents abroad, and the departments it created; to obtain from them the munitions of war; and to pledge their credit for foreign loans. The second Continental Congress felt in especial a crushing responsibility. Yet when it was called to order at Philadelphia on May 10, 1775, at the moment when the cordon of militia was tightening about Boston, it hardly knew what were its powers.

The first Continental Congress had been a consulting body, and something more. The Colonies were exchanging advice. They wished to do nothing besides showing the Ministry that the essential rights of the colonists would be unitedly upheld, and searching for a reconciliation. The directions of Pennsylvania to her delegates, the most comprehensive of all, instructed them "to consult together . . . and to form and adopt a plan for the purpose of obtaining redress of American grievances, ascertaining American rights upon the most solid and constitutional principles, and for establishing that union and harmony between Great Britain and the Colonies which is indispensably necessary to the welfare and happiness of both." Several sets of instructions spoke exclusively of the restoration of harmony within the Empire, several exclusively of the maintenance of American rights, and several simply of consultation for the public good. South Carolina empowered her delegates not only to approve, but to "effectually prosecute" legal measures for a redress of grievances, while North Carolina explicitly bound her inhabitants to accept "any acts done by them." There was little danger that this Congress would go beyond the wishes of the patriot majority in America. "Fifty gentlemen meeting together, all strangers, are not acquainted with each others' language, ideas, views, designs," wrote John Adams. "They are, therefore, jealous of each other, fearful, timid, skittish." But besides the passage of spirited resolutions, an agreement for non-importation and non-exportation was voted. Although only North Carolina had agreed in advance to obey every Congressional measure approved by her delegation, the Congress unanimously resolved that its constituents were bound to adhere to the "association." [1]

The second Continental Congress wielded a fuller authority. North Carolina renewed her declaration that acts agreed to by her delegates would be obligatory, in honor, upon her people. Maryland also bound herself to execute all resolutions which Congress might adopt, while Georgia declared herself "heartily disposed zealously to enter into every measure" agreed upon. New Jersey, not at first, but on February 14, 1776, also agreed to abide by the resolutions of Congress. South Carolina again gave her delegates full authority to "effectually prosecute" the measures of Congress, and Rhode Island and New Hampshire authorized their members to adopt, "in behalf of this Colony," what the former called "all reasonable lawful and proper measures," and the latter simply "all measures." Doubtless all the other Colonies more or less felt an obligation to do whatever Congress directed.[2]

I. EARLY POWERS OF CONGRESS

When Congress met, the fear that New York would be attacked was uppermost in every mind. On May 15 it recommended—not

---

[1] See *Amer. Hist. Rev.*, XII, 529ff, C. H. Van Tyne, "Sovereignty in the American Revolution," for a full discussion of the powers of Congress and those of the States. The Journals of the Cont. Congress, I, 13-24, give the instructions of the States to their delegates. It should be remembered that the New York Legislature refused to approve the measures of the first Continental Congress, or to send delegates to the second; Journals Cont. Cong., II, 16. Though Congress bound its constituents to the Association (I, 75ff), it issued an argumentative plea to the States to respect it and all its other measures (I, 62).

[2] In the first New Hampshire Constitution, it was provided that the Continental Congress might, by "instructions or directions," prevent the execution of its provisions for the regular election of the upper house. In the first South Carolina Constitution, it was declared that "the resolutions of the Continental Congress, now of force in this Colony, shall so continue until altered or revoked by them." Thorpe, "Consts. and Charters," 2452, 3247. Under Georgia's first rough Constitution, all resolves of the Continental Congress were to have the force of law in the State.

ordered—a defensive and passive policy on the part of the patriot authorities in that city if the Crown forces arrived. After a long period of hesitation—"our determinations are very slow," wrote John Adams—it began taking the vigorous action meet for the times. Committees were appointed to deal with the fortification of New York, the collection of ammunition, the raising of money, and the drafting of a set of army regulations, and both Franklin and Adams have told us how they toiled far into the night at committee meetings. The Provincial Convention of Massachusetts opened the gate to the most important step of Congress when it intimated that, since the troops at Boston represented several colonies and were defending the rights of all America, Congress should undertake their supervision. On June 15 Congress appointed Washington commander-in-chief, and provided for filling the places of two major-generals, eight brigadiers, an adjutant-general, and several subordinate officers—the skeleton of a national army organization. On the preceding day it had voted to raise ten companies of riflemen in Pennsylvania, Maryland, and Virginia. Before the next month ended it had taken two important steps in civil government—it provided for commissioners to superintend Indian affairs, and created a postoffice department under Franklin; while late in June it authorized the first issue of bills of credit. In short, Congress showed itself disposed to use a large part of the powers which some States explicitly, and others tacitly, had conferred upon it. Just how far in its undefined field would it venture to go? [3]

John Adams thought that, without any opposition of consequence from the revolutionary authorities in the Colonies, it might have acted much more vigorously and rapidly. "We ought to have had in our hands, a month ago, the whole legislative, executive, and judicial of the whole continent, and have completely modelled a constitution; to have arrested every friend of government on the continent, and held them as hostages for the poor victims in Boston; and then opened the door as wide as possible for peace and reconciliation." This counsel was impractical, for public sentiment simply would not have consented to such defiance. But with autumn, and the receipt of the King's letter (November 1, 1775), refusing to accept the olive branch offered by Congress, and fulminating against the "open and avowed rebellion" of America, more determined meas-

[3] Journals Cont. Cong., II, 86, 89, 91, 175, 207, 208-09, etc.; American Archives, Series IV, Vol. II, 1819-1904 *et passim.*

ures were possible. Samuel Ward, of Rhode Island, truthfully predicted that American action would henceworth be spirited, clear, and decisive. Washington had already submitted a plan for raising twenty-six regiments, pledged to a year's service, and had stated that he wished to be able to count upon at least 20,000 men. On November 4, Congress, sanctioning his scheme, fixed the strength of the Continental Army at 20,372 officers and men, and asked the New England States—it did not feel able to command—to allow him to impress supplies after fair payment; [4] while measures to pay and arm the troops were taken the same day. On November 25, warships and privateers were permitted to capture British ships.

All these steps meant the abandonment of that defensive warfare with which Congress had declared the previous spring it would content itself. "We have hitherto conducted half a war," wrote John Adams in March, 1776; ". . . for the future, we are likely to wage three quarters of a war." But to go on to unrestricted warfare would require independence, and here Congress paused to await a fairly explicit assurance of the consent of the States.

At the opening of 1776 Massachusetts had given her delegates to understand that she was ready for independence, and it was known that the other New England Colonies supported this position. North Carolina on April 12 conferred upon her delegates the power to vote for independence and foreign alliances, and on May 15 the Provincial Convention of Virginia unanimously directed her delegates to propose independence in Congress. The Congressional resolution of May 10, recommending the establishment of new State governments, and the political revolution which followed in Pennsylvania ten days later, brought the greatest Middle Colony into line. New York, New Jersey, and Maryland, however, had instructed their delegates to oppose independence, and a revocation of these instructions had to be obtained; Samuel Chase in Maryland, and Jonathan D. Sergeant in New Jersey, with assistance from others, succeeded in this, though New Jersey acquiesced only at the last moment. The only Colonies which by July 4th had not assented to independence, or given evidence that they were ready for it, were New York and Delaware. Feeling in the former Province was so uncertain that the delegates simply withdrew from the

---

[4] For John Adams's opinions, see "Works," II, 411; for the action of Congress, Journals, IV, 320 ff. See Hamilton upon Congress's early powers, "Works," I, 204.

acts leading up to the drafting of the Declaration; in the latter, as the time came for the final vote, Caesar Rodney was known to be laboring successfully.[5]

Congress, it will thus be seen, used its powers in advancing the revolt from stage to stage so cautiously that no Colony could object to its acts. The Provincial instructions were in general so loose or liberal that, short of a premature declaration of independence, they allowed Congress entire freedom of action. Thus Massachusetts, instructing her delegation for the critical year 1776, declared it "fully empowered, with the delegates from the other American Colonies, to concert, direct, and order such further measures as shall to them appear best calculated for the establishment of right and liberty to the American Colonies upon a basis permanent and secure, against the power and art of the British administration." The real curbs upon Congress were the natural caution and responsibility of the delegates, and their knowledge that if they went too fast for the people, they would defeat their own ends. The country was like a squadron of thirteen ships, wrote John Adams; "the fleetest sailors must wait for the dullest and slowest." It has been said that if no States objected to any important act of Congress, at least seven—Virginia, New York, Pennsylvania, Maryland, New Jersey, Connecticut, and Rhode Island—tried to show their independent authority by passing resolutions to ratify the Declaration, but they may have done this simply for emphasis. Hamilton in 1784 wrote that New York's resolution was a non-essential affirmation, which did not pretend to authenticate the act.

The only protests against any early measures of Congress relate to trifling matters. The history of Maryland offers the most prominent examples. When Congress wished in 1776 to arrest the royal Governor, Eden, by its direct agents, Maryland's authorities showed resentment, and the Council of Safety refused to let him be seized. In the same year her Provincial Congress transmitted a demand to the Continental Congress that it pass an ordinance cutting off its

---

[5] For preliminaries to the Declaration, see Elliot, Debates, I, 42ff. It was said during the Congressional discussion of independence that "if the delegates of any particular Colony had no power to declare such Colony independent, certain they were the others could not declare it for them, the Colonies being as yet perfectly independent of each other." If independence were declared before the Middle Colonies authorized it, such Colonies "might secede from the Union." (Journals Cont. Cong., VI, 1088.) For the letter of the New York delegates dated July 2, asking the Provincial Congress "whether we are to consider our Colony bound by the vote of the majority in favor of independency," see Journal N. Y. Prov. Cong., II, 236; Burnett, "Letters of Members of the Continental Congress," I, 524.

members from other office. This was aimed primarily at John Adams, who had accepted the position of chief justice of the new superior court of Massachusetts, and it was an unworthy aspersion upon the motives of the advocates of independence. Later, in April, 1777, the Council of Safety sharply reprimanded Captain Nicholson of the Continental frigate *Virginia* for impressing Maryland citizens into the naval service, and ordered their immediate release. Nicholson was rash enough to pen a defiant reply, saying that Congress would support him, and he cared naught for "the threats of any council of Maryland." An emphatic remonstrance was thereupon forwarded to Congress by the Maryland authorities, who pointed out that Nicholson's acts were in violation of the State Constitution, and could not be tolerated. Congress of course disclaimed the acts of the captain, and suspended him from his command until he offered the humble apology which the Governor of Maryland demanded. In 1778 Maryland's Legislature again asserted itself in opposition to a Congressional measure. When "Light-Horse Harry" Lee, in pursuit of instructions from the Board of War, began seizing horses for his dragoons in Maryland, although he paid for them upon a generous appraisal, the Assembly forbade all such levies, and sent its order, together with a copy of Lee's instructions, to Congress.[6]

In trying to give strength to the army, and to make it a truly national force, Congress was always battling with the ignorance and jealousy of the States. Not only did the latter, proud of their separate militias, wish them maintained, but narrow-minded leaders feared that State liberties would be trenched upon if Congress obtained control of a large, well-drilled force bound to serve for a long term. A large part of the population preferred the light yoke of the States in military service to the strict discipline which the Continental generals would impose. If we were to take from Washington's writings those letters in which he complains of the evil results of the compromises between Congress and the States in military affairs, we should reduce his correspondence during the Revolution by almost a fourth; and beyond doubt, if he had pos-

---

[6] B. W. Bond, "State Govt. in Md.," Ch. II. There was also a slight clash regarding police powers with the State of Delaware in 1778. Congress ordered the military to secure and send to a safe place several Tories, and this offended the Delaware authorities, who granted a habeas corpus for their discharge. In answer, Congress stated that it had been told that a majority of the people of Kent and Sussex Counties, and some of those of Newcastle, were disaffected, and that its duty was to take precautions for the general welfare, and that it had therefore exercised similar powers in other States.

sessed a Continental Line of 20,000 men, well-trained, well-officered, and serving for the whole conflict, the war would have ended years before it did.

The enrollment of the Continental army of 20,000 authorized in the fall of 1775 proceeded slowly and discouragingly. Washington was disgusted: "Such dearth of public spirit and such want of virtue; such stockjobbing and fertility in all the low arts to obtain advantages of one kind or another in this great change of military arrangements, I never saw before, and I pray God's mercy that I may never see it again." By the beginning of December hardly more than 4,000 had enlisted, and when the year ended the total was only 9,650, of whom many were not in camp. The States had to be called upon to fill the gap, and Washington asked Massachusetts and New Hampshire to furnish 5,000 militia for temporary service. In the course of the spring the depleted army filled up, as it always did throughout the war when the winter snows melted away, till in March, 1776, it had become 15,000 strong; but the temporary service of some New England militia had to be requested that month for the attack on Dorchester Heights.

During the summer of 1776 the exigencies of the conflict, and the lack of any soldiers pledged for even a full year, caused Congress to accede to Washington's view of the desirability of longer terms of enlistment. On September 16 it resolved to enlist eighty-eight battalions, comprising 66,000 men, for the duration of the conflict. Each State was required to furnish a certain quota of troops, Massachusetts and Virginia leading with fifteen battalions apiece, and each was to furnish its men with arms and ammunition, but the pay and support of the soldiers in the field was to be a Continental charge. Land grants were promised the recruits who thus enlisted for the war. It was high time that something was being done. When Howe arrived off New York in the week that independence was declared, Washington's army numbered only 9,000 men, of whom 2,000 carried no arms, and more than 3,000 had weapons scarcely fit for use. Although during the next three months strenuous efforts were made to bring militiamen and others into the ranks, when at the end of August the American forces attained their greatest strength under a single commander in the whole war, the troops fit for duty numbered only about 14,000. Some 6,000 more were sick or otherwise incapacitated.

Washington's losses were heavy in the battles of the late summer about New York, nearly 3,000 men being captured at Fort Washington alone, while New Jersey, Pennsylvania, and Delaware sent only half the 5,000 reinforcements expected. During his retreat upon Philadelphia his army dwindled to less than 5,000, and had Howe shown due enterprise, this small force could have been scattered to the winds. Congress, in desperation, made another effort. On December 27, it authorized the increase of Washington's army by 12,000 infantry, 3,000 light horse, three regiments of artillery, and a corps of engineers, and required all enlistments for the Continental Line to be for three years or during the war. Above all, it gave Washington practically dictatorial powers over the Continental army for the next six months, authorizing him to displace any officer of lower rank than a brigadier, to fill vacancies, and to commandeer supplies at will.[7] But even after the victories of Trenton and Princeton, recruiting for the Continental forces continued very slow.

The years 1776 and 1777 thus witnessed, on the part of responsible men, a steady loss of confidence in the State militias; a steadily increasing conviction that the nation's main reliance must be upon a long-term Continental force; and an increasing perplexity as to the means of procuring it. During 1777 Congress continued exhorting the States, through its resolutions, to forward their due quotas of men for the Continental army, but without much effect; and following a conference between a Congressional committee and Washington, conscription was finally resorted to. That is, a resolution was passed requesting the States "forthwith to fill up by drafts, from their militia or in any other way that shall be effectual, their respective battalions of Continental troops."[8] But Congress had of course no power to enforce this demand, and despite the repeated exhortations of Washington, despite the wave of hope that followed Saratoga, and despite the French alliance, the response was weaker than Congress hoped it would be. Just after the news of the French alliance, in the late spring of 1778, Washington's army outside Philadelphia consisted of only 13,000 men. At the same date in 1779, the whole American force north of the Potomac aggregated but 16,000, part of which was in New England, part in the Highlands,

[7] Journals Cont. Cong., VI, 1045; Washington in 1779 wrote that America had never at one time had 26,000 men in the field. "Writings," VI, 161. But see John Marshall's "Washington," II, 469.
[8] *Idem*, X, 200.

and part lower down on the Hudson. Had Massachusetts and Virginia each furnished the fifteen battalions assigned them under the quota of the year of independence, and had no other State sent forward a man, the army would have numbered 22,500.

Thenceforth to the end of the war, military affairs continued upon this wretched basis. Every man of sense saw that the Continental dependence upon State activity or inactivity was a deplorable makeshift. Congress had its own recruiting officers, and in 1779 it offered the States a $200 bounty for each recruit; but the one power indispensable to it, that of drafting men into the Continental ranks, instead of merely recommending State drafts, it did not have. Washington wrote a year before Yorktown, in intense bitterness, that if he had possessed a permanent, responsible, and truly national army from the outset, "we should not have been for the greater part of the war inferior to the enemy, indebted for our safety to their inactivity, enduring frequently the mortification of seeing inviting opportunities to ruin them pass unimproved for want of a force which the country was completely able to afford, and of seeing the country ravaged, our towns burnt, the inhabitants plundered, abused, murdered, from the same cause." The militia to the end were totally undependable. On rare occasions they fought well, but usually very ill. They hurried to Gates's standard when Burgoyne invaded from the north, and they almost crushed Washington's spirit when, fighting at Brandywine and Germantown to save Philadelphia, he found them refusing to come to his aid. They would pack their effects, including ammunition and supplies badly needed by the army, and leave for home on the least excuse—to see to their crops, to visit their families, or to escape the rigors of winter. To them it was a kind of sacrilege to let nature's bounty in grain or fruit go ungarnered while they were wasting their time in the army. Washington gave the militia credit for some usefulness, as in light parties for forest skirmishing, but he solemnly declared that he was never "witness to a single instance that can countenance an opinion of militia or raw troops being fit for the real business of fighting." Their disgraceful conduct at Camden, where they fled on the first fire, was perhaps the sharpest proof of the truth of Washington's opinion.[9]

Washington placed his finger upon the salient need of the army when he wrote that "every matter which relates to it should be

[9] Writings, VIII, 502ff.

under the immediate direction and providence of Congress." He did not know sometimes, he said, whether he was commanding one army, or thirteen armies allied for the common defense.[10] While one State yielded full obedience to Congressional requests, another gave partial and grudging consent, and a third flatly refused, military affairs could not prosper. "The willing States are almost ruined by their exertions; distrust and jealousy succeeds to it. Hence proceed neglect and ill-timed compliances, one State waiting to see what another will do."[11] Many of the States were almost inert until threatened with invasion, when their populations would respond with a spasmodic and short-lived effort, and then return to inertia. Not only military weakness and defeat, but much of the derangement of the national finances, sprang from this condition. Two sets of men had to be paid and fed, the new levies coming in and the old levies going out; many raw troops had to employed where a comparatively few seasoned veterans would have sufficed; the cost of bounties and recruiting constantly rose; and the mere prolongation of the war spelt possible ruin. The commander also suffered much from incompetent officers. "Besides the inequality of provision already mentioned," he hence complained, "all the confusion we have experienced by irregular appointments and promotions has chiefly originated" in the division of authority.[12]

Had Congress at the outset refused to recognize the State militia or other State troops, and tried to institute a Continental draft to force men into the Continental army, we may be sure that it would have met the angriest and most stubborn opposition. The State authorities were too jealous of the means of self-defense to surrender them into Continental hands, and too confident of their own abilities in war to see any propriety in doing so. But Congress never even thought of such an attempt. Many of its members, feeling no sympathy with Washington's efforts to destroy all State distinctions in the army and make it Continental and nothing else, were willing to send out one futile requisition after another to the States, but any hint of more determined measures aroused their resentment. In the fall of 1780, when a Congressional committee returned to Philadelphia strongly impressed with Washington's views, the committeemen found themselves unpopular in certain Congressional

[10] *Writings*, IX, 63ff.
[11] *Idem*, IX, 173ff.
[12] *Idem*, VIII, 386ff.

circles. They were charged with being "too strongly tinctured with the *army principles*," and Washington felt constrained to write a letter to a Congressman deploring the distrust thus exhibited. The commander at this time wished a peremptory draft, but it was impossible to get it. He noted in his diary the following May, not six months before Yorktown, that scarcely a single State had one eighth of its quota in the field.[13]

Dependence upon the States was even more complete as regarded supplies. Shipments of food were constantly required for the State troops and Continental Line, and the correspondence between Congressional agents, especially the Commissary-General, and the States, would fill volumes. Governor Trumbull, of Connecticut, came to the assistance of the army larder at several critical moments, and in the terrible midwinter of Valley Forge, Governor Henry of Virginia, solicited by a Congressional committee under Francis Lightfoot Lee, took immediate measures to forward beef, pork, salt, and clothing.[14] Yet Congress at this time could not prevent the Pennsylvania farmers from carrying their provisions into Philadelphia for British gold, so much more valuable than Continental paper. Upon one excuse or another—and the mere difficulties of transportation were sometimes a good excuse—the States were always becoming delinquent in their provision of supplies. Washington and Congress were assiduous in requesting them to set aside stores of salt meat particularly, yet there was never a period of three months in which the command did not have to complain of the shortage of provisions. Repeatedly Washington had not more than a day's provender in camp, and once he had to draw from West Point some of the stores kept there to enable it to withstand a siege.[15]

[13] Nathanael Greene wrote July 4, 1780, that Congress was dreaming as usual, the majority of members being occupied with penny-hapenny politics. The Congressional committee on coöperation with the army command, consisting of Schuyler, Peabody, and Mathews, "have almost all got sick; and we are almost sick of them all, except Schuyler. The other two dare not do what they know to be right. Popularity is the bane of American liberty, and if a different policy is not pursued hereafter, ten to one it proves our ruin." Corr. and Journals of S. B. Webb, II, 268-69; Washington, "Writings," VIII, 461-64.

[14] Governor Henry bitterly reproached Congress for its neglect, saying that if national officers had exerted themselves, they might have had "a great abundance of provisions" from Virginia. Henry, "Henry," I, Ch. 22.

[15] Hamilton wrote Duane, September 3, 1780, that the States ought to have nothing to do with the army, the entire mustering and disposition of which should belong to Congress. The army was the cement of the Union, he said, and it should be the policy of Congress to destroy all State attachments in it. To this end, Congress ought to make all appointments and promotions. Yet at that time some parts of the army, Hamilton thought, would obey their States in opposition to Congress. The influence of Washington alone, if anything, could prevent this. To supply the army by State purchases was in two ways a bad plan. Each State would make its own ease a primary object, the supply of the army a secondary one; while much waste and embezzlement would occur. "Works," I, 203ff.

The interest of Congress in the cost of supplies led inevitably to its encouragement of the State regulation of prices. At first the States embarked independently upon this treacherous field. New England delegates, at a conference held in Providence from Christmas Day, 1776, to January 2, 1777, to discuss defense, paper money, and prices, agreed upon a plan for regulating by law the charges for produce, manufactures, imported goods, and labor.[16] Though the merchants raised a clamor of protest, the New England Legislatures, supported by public sentiment, duly enacted the plan. During the second month of 1777 the proceedings of the Providence conference were submitted to Congress, which not only approved the scheme, but advised that the Middle and Southern States each hold conventions for drawing up similar plans. The lower South did not heed the injunction, but delegates from the Middle States, with Virginia, met at Yorktown on March 26, 1777, and formulated a scale of prices. Sagacious men of course knew that this was folly, and the event soon proved it so. The price-fixing laws passed in the various States not only failed utterly, but increased the evil they were meant to diminish. Wherever they were partly enforced by local committees or constables, they caused great distress among shippers and retailers, to the ultimate injury of the consumers; but they were seldom enforced. Men continued to sell, whether covertly or overtly, at prices in excess of those legalized, and charged an additional profit as insurance to cover the risk they ran.[17]

When at the close of July, 1777, another convention was held at Springfield, including representatives of New York as well as of New England, it was determined to recommend the repeal of all price-fixing laws, and the substitution of statutes against forestalling and engrossing—that is, against speculative hoarding. John Adams set it down as his earnest opinion in September, 1777, that the Massachusetts law for controlling prices, if not repealed, would ruin the State and introduce civil war. Congress, taking up the subject in November, indicated a certain lingering confidence in price-fixing, for it proposed that three more conventions should meet early in 1778, and arrange new scales of prices for legalization by the State Legislatures.[18] One convention, at New Haven, was to

[16] Journals Cont. Cong., VII, 124.
[17] Lecky, "Amer. Rev." (Woodburn ed.), 290; Bolles, "Financial Hist. U. S.," I, 158-73.
[18] Journals Cont. Cong., IX, 956-57.

represent the eight northern States, one at Fredericksburg was to represent Maryland, Virginia, and North Carolina, and one in Charleston the two remaining members of the Union. Congress revealed one motive for this touching confidence when it asked the States to authorize the Continental commissary-officers to seize the goods of hoarders and speculators at the legalized prices.

A little later, in the last days of 1777, the army's need of clothing was so dire that it compelled Congress to pursue this last recommendation a good deal further. The States were asked to seize all the suitable woolens, stockings, blankets, hats, shoes, and other apparel in the hands of the merchants, giving receipts at the fixed prices for them and punishing all who tried to resist; while they were requested, as before, to grant the Commissary Department authority to take over foodstuffs collected by speculators. A Congressional agent in Boston, attempting to conclude a heavy purchase of clothing, had a little earlier been not only asked a price ten to eighteen times the normal valuation of the goods, but made to accept insults to the Congressional credit. Congress was well aware of the failure of State efforts to enforce price-fixing laws, and it recommended that to give them greater force, the number of retailers be limited, and each retailer be licensed under a bond to obey the regulatory legislation; making these drastic proposals, however, only reluctantly. "Unhappy the case of America!" exclaimed Congress; "laws unworthy the character of infant republics are become necessary to supply the defect of public virtue, and to correct the vices of some of her sons. . . ." [19]

One of the three sectional price-fixing conventions recommended by Congress actually met at New Haven in January, 1778, and agreed upon a scale of remuneration to be allowed by agents of the Commissary Department for food and clothing seized by the army. Several States tried to make these prices standard for the general public by law, but such efforts were as completely abortive as all which had preceded them. In the other sections no heed was paid to the Congressional requests. The price of commodities continued to advance sharply, and Congress indignantly passed a resolve on November 19, 1779, that this was in large part due to the arts of unprincipled and disaffected loyalists. Setting forth the injustice of profiteering, and the difficulties which it threw in the way of an

[19] Journals Cont. Cong., IX, 1043-47.

accurate drafting of fiscal estimates, Congress recommended that the States refuse to permit any charges "for articles of domestic produce, farming and common labor, the wages of tradesmen and mechanics, water and land carriage," which exceeded twentyfold the prices current throughout the year 1774. Imported commodities were to be rated in due proportion, but military stores were to be exempted from the price-fixing laws. Another meeting of northern representatives had meanwhile been held in October, and Congress approved its proposed measures of economic regulation.

One instrument for State control of the cost of living lay in the passage of internal embargo laws,[20] by which a commonwealth possessing a large supply of the essentials of life sought to keep them for itself. Such laws proved a sore embarrassment to useful commerce, and frequently wrought hardship to large populations.

Congress was told early in 1779 that the people of Massachusetts and Rhode Island were in distress for lack of foodstuffs, for example; the Assembly of the latter State reporting that "especially those who have come off from the island of Rhode Island [in consequence of the British seizure of Newport] must inevitably perish unless they are speedily supplied with the necessities of life." The Assembly asked Congress to request of New York and Connecticut a relaxation of their embargoes on provisions "so far as respected the supply of Rhode Islanders by land," which Congress did. But Congress also learned that no full relief could be obtained by the two States unless they also obtained shipments from Maryland, Virginia, and the Carolinas. Deeming that a private trade between the citizens of New England and of the South might be ineffective or injurious, it therefore requested the Governors of Maryland, Virginia, and South Carolina to permit the Governors of Massachusetts and Rhode Island to purchase and export, under proper regulation, such quantities of grain and flour as they might agree to be expedient. In April, Massachusetts having entrusted the purchase of the needed provisions to her Board of War, Congress asked the Middle States and Virginia to permit the free passage over their respective boundaries of whatever stores the Board acquired. In October, 1780, it became necessary for Congress to facilitate the movement of food the other way: it asked Maryland to let as much

[20] The New York Council of Revision pointed out the perils of this kind of legislation in the spring of 1781; it objected that it would provoke retaliatory embargoes, and encourage smugglers. Assembly Journals, March 10, 1781.

bread, flour, and wheat be exported to Virginia as the latter State needed for its public supply.[21]

It is hard for Americans today to comprehend the situation which thus existed when the national government had only the rudiments of a national army, and was compelled to cajole and exhort thirteen State governments controlling thirteen independent armies. It is hard for them to appreciate the situation when the national government had to plead with the States to limit the prices of the stores which its commissaries were purchasing in open market for the army. But it is hardest of all to conceive of the national government compelled thus to deal with domestic commerce. A simple matter of interstate trade had to be arranged as if it were intercourse among wholly independent nations.

Some States laid embargoes of their own volition—Massachusetts, for example, did so, and led New Hampshire, in a retaliatory mood, to follow suit. But for most States the embargo acts were initiated by Congress. It incorrectly believed that the embargoes were an absolute necessity, for it traced the poverty of the army to exports, when it was really due to imperfect transportation and interrupted trade. It also knew that the British captured some food ships and thus supplied themselves. Quite correctly, it believed that if an embargo was to be laid at all, it should be laid by Congressional mandate. This was because of "the distance of many States from Congress; the different periods of assembling their Legislatures; their remoteness in some instances from information; the possibility of one or a few States not seeing, or being unwilling to yield to the necessities of restraint, however obvious to the General Council; and the danger that, without the cooperation of all, the good end of the embargo might be totally frustrated."

Congress thus took one of its boldest steps in dealing with the States when on June 8, 1778, it passed a resolution forbidding the shipment from any State, between June 10 and November 15, of certain enumerated articles.[22] This measure met general State approbation, and the Continental legislators admitted that it was well enforced. From time to time the national legislature renewed the embargo. In August, 1779, it recommended that the States which had acts enforcing the embargo should continue them until January 1, 1780, and that they should extend all partial embargo acts to cover

[21] Journals Cont. Cong., XV, 1137.
[22] *Idem*, XI, 569, 578 ff.

every kind of foodstuff.[23] Later it called for a further extension of the time of the embargo. It was made plain in 1779 that Congress wished every State to confiscate articles imported into it in defiance of the laws of the State of origin; and it wished that whenever it became necessary to modify an embargo law with respect to commodities needed by another State, then the purchase of such commodities should be placed in the hands of Continental rather than State officers.

Enforcement was not easy, for even where the States tried loyally to maintain the embargo, smuggling occurred. At one time Congress found it necessary to take sharp action to prevent a violation of what it considered the implicit agreement among the States. In the autumn of 1779 it was learned that several vessels lay off the Delaware shore in the Delaware River, loaded with provisions for shipment. This was although the need for a full domestic supply of food was believed urgent, although Washington had declared that the army was hungry and that storehouses should be filled while the roads remained good, and although Delaware had poorly complied with the pending requisitions for State supplies. The Executive Council of Pennsylvania complained of the unfairness of letting Delaware evade the embargo, especially since much of the cargoes came originally from Pennsylvania; and the Governor of Maryland angrily asserted that if the Delaware were opened for exportation, he would open the Chesapeake also. Congress was aroused.[24] Three measures were hurriedly laid before it: one to order the Board of Admiralty to seize all vessels lying in the Delaware ready to violate the embargo, one to call on Delaware to maintain the embargo herself, and one requesting Congress to let the embargo in all the States be lifted as soon as possible.

II. THE ARTICLES OF CONFEDERATION

So long as the nation had no written organic law, the undefined powers of Congress might be regarded as very broad. As the supreme revolutionary body, whose authority the patriots accepted without question early in the struggle, it might exercise many attributes of sovereignty which any definite federative constitution

---

[23] *Idem*, XIV, 986-87.
[24] See Rives, "Madison," I, 304, for Madison's letter to Jefferson treating this as evidence of the necessity of "arming Congress with *coercive* powers."

would be certain to take from it.[25]   There were hence friends of a strong Continental government who were reluctant to bind the Continental Congress by hard and fast constitutional rules, thinking them in part unnecessary and in part an evil.   They could plead the fact that the British had no written Constitution, being governed by precedent and statutory law.   Samuel Chase wrote R. H. Lee just after the Declaration that "we do not all see the importance, nay, the necessity, of a Confederacy." [26]   But the education of the American people had made them unwilling to assent to this view.   They had grown used to written organic laws guaranteeing, defining, and limiting the powers of their colonial governments, and had hastened to write State Constitutions.   Long before independence, some of the American leaders were proposing an instrument to make explicit the governance of America within the Empire.

Jefferson implied a rough plan for the future in his "Summary View," which he wrote for the Provincial Convention at Williamsburg in August, 1774, and which was extensively circulated in both England and America.   The Colonies, under the British ægis, were to form an association of practically self-governing commonwealths, united to each other through the Crown, and this executive, there being no general Congress or legislature, was to veto any laws which would bring one Colony into friction with another.   Galloway laid before the first Continental Congress a much more detailed plan.[27]   He wished to see a British-American Legislature established, to consist of a President-General, appointed by the King, and a Grand Council, chosen by the Provincial Legislatures once every three years.   The Grand Council was to meet annually, elect its own Speaker, and to have all the privileges in America that the House of Commons had in England.   The President-General was to possess an absolute veto, and, with the advice and consent of the Grand Council, was to exercise all the administrative powers touching more than one Province.   Continental laws, as distinguished from Provincial laws, might originate in the British Parliament, and must in any event be approved by it.   This plan found some advocates, but was finally erased from the minutes of the Continental Congress.

---

[25] Thus Congress recommended the erection of independent State governments, when Duane and others protested it had no such power; and later it called upon the State Legislatures to give their Governors extraordinary emergency powers.

[26] Amer. Archives, Series V, Vol. I, 672. But Chase himself ardently believed in one.   Without it, he said, "we shall remain weak, distracted, and divided in our councils; our strength will decrease. . . ."

[27] Journals, I, 49ff.

With the probability of independence in his mind, Franklin also offered a detailed plan for a Continental Constitution to Congress in July, 1775,[28] but did not press it against the opposition of Dickinson and other conservatives. He proposed that the Colonies, each retaining internal independence, should form a close league or association of friendship for the conduct of their external relations. There should be a Congress, elected annually by the Colonies according to the able-bodied males—the adult polls—of each, which should defend the Colonies, send ambassadors, enter into alliances, settle all disputes between Colonies, plant new Colonies, control the general commerce of the nation, direct the army, and regulate the monetary affairs and the postoffice. The executive authority was to be vested in a Council of twelve, elected by Congress for terms of three years, one-third the membership changing annually. This Council was to prepare business for the consideration of Congress, and in the Congressional recesses was to execute its orders and fill all vacant offices *pro tempore*. Ireland, Canada, the West Indies, Bermuda, Nova Scotia, and Florida were to be invited to join the American confederacy; and the union was to endure until the British had ceased their oppressions and had made reparation to the colonies. Though this plan was referred to a committee, Congress never acted upon it. Roger Sherman made an effort to draft a scheme for a confederation at about the same time.[29]

It is true that Congress had less power after the drafting of the Articles of Confederation than before. But it is certain that its powers would have dwindled anyway as the war dragged on, and as the first flush of enthusiasm passed away. When there was no authority that it could confidently claim, there were always men who would question its right to almost any authority. After the second Congress the instructions to delegates show that the States no longer felt generally bound to obey every act to which their delegates assented. The notes of debate made by Burke of North Carolina early in 1777 show how flatly Congressional powers were denied:

Maryland and Pennsylvania were very solicitous to procure a vote of Congress, approving a meeting lately held by committees appointed by the four New England governments, to the end that this approbation might imply a right to disapprove. It occasioned very long and interesting debates. At length the general opinion was that Congress had necessarily a right to inquire into the cause of any meeting, and to require to know what was transacted at any such meetings, and also to require an explanation of anything that was dubious, and satisfaction for anything that was

[28] *Idem,* II, 195.
[29] Adams, "Works," III, 220.

alarming to the whole, or any one of the States; that this right necessarily existed in their power to take care each for his respective State that no injury happened to her from without. But that Congress had no right to prohibit meetings, or censure them if the transactions in them were not injurious to others. The delegate of North Carolina refused to say what his State could not do, declaring he thought she could do everything which she had not precluded herself from by plain and express declaration. . . . The question put, the approbation was denied, many voting against it lest its ambiguity should create further disputes; of this number was North Carolina.[30]

The Articles were highly essential, for, as Marshall said later, the Confederation preserved the idea of union until national wisdom adopted a more efficient system.[31] He believed that if a permanent union had not been agreed upon before peace was made, it was likely that the different parts would have fallen asunder after 1781. The pity was that the Articles were not better—that a vigorous national government such as Franklin sketched in 1775 was not pushed through immediately after the Declaration. Then, and then only, was State individualism sufficiently melted in the fire of national patriotism to yield to it. It is possible that under a shrewd and energetic leadership, Congress before the end of 1776 might have set up a government that would have shortened the war, and prevented many of the evils that followed it; but Congress was too little a national body, and too much a mere assemblage of ambassadors from States that regarded themselves almost as sovereign nations, to do this. The leadership was lacking also. Even John Adams seems to have had no early or consistent conviction of the need for a powerful Continental authority. He wrote in January, 1776, that "We have heard much of a continental constitution; I see no occasion for any but a Congress. Let that be made an equal and fair representation of the Colonies; and let its authority be confined to three cases,—war, trade, and controversies between colony and colony."[32] Yet no one deplored more than John Adams the weakness of the Articles, and he made a curious prophecy that within ten years the Confederation would be found inadequate, and would dissolve.

The chief issues which arose in debating and drafting the Articles of Confederation— this process extended from June 11, 1776, to November 15, 1777, when the Articles were sent to the States for ratification—may be briefly summarized. The first important dispute arose over the drafting committee's plan to apportion taxes

[30] N. C. Col. Records, 389; Journals Cont. Cong., VII, 112.
[31] Marshall's "Washington," I, second ed., 1836, 429-30.
[32] Adams wrote Gates that each Colony should establish its own government, and then a league should be formed between all; "Works," I, 207.

according to the gross number of inhabitants, the Southern States declaiming against the enumeration of slaves in rating the State quotas. Chase asserted that slaves were property, not population. Lynch of South Carolina also compared them with land, or dumb animals. But John Adams argued that slaves, like freemen, produced wealth, and should be reckoned when preparing an index of the wealth of the country, while Wilson wished to tax slaves in order to discourage slavery. A second disagreement arose over the proposal to grant each State one vote, and one only, in Congress. Franklin shared Adams's indignation over this proposal, but men from the small States feared that the great ones would overawe and oppress them. Other delegates from the lesser commonwealths agreed with him in emphasizing the fact that the union was to be federal, not an organic union like that of England and Scotland, and that it was therefore right for each State to have just one vote. It is impossible to read the debates without realizing how much the mutual jealousies of the States contributed to render them jealous of a powerful central authority.

This realization becomes even clearer in studying the debates upon two other questions. The proposal to give Congress the power of regulating Indian affairs and trade was passionately opposed by South Carolina. Georgia pointed out that if the Indian trade were not carefully administered, friction and warfare always arose, and that her long stretch of unprotected frontier would suffer the most. But South Carolina, sheltered behind Georgia and North Carolina, found the unfettered trade highly profitable, and Rutledge and Lynch voiced a demand that Indian affairs be let alone. It was evident that State weakness and rivalry constituted the chief cause of the general uncertainty of Indian affairs; if they had a united nation to deal with, neither the Indians nor the lawless frontiersmen would be eager to precipitate hostilities. But South Carolina stood out as long as possible, and when the desired clause was inserted, it was with a proviso that the legislative right of any State within its own limits be not infringed or violated. The discussion of the power which Congress ought to have over State boundaries, again, brought forth an alignment between those States which had claims to western lands, and those which had none.

The Articles which thus became the law of the land on March 1, 1781, have been the target of great abuse, and long before they were fully ratified shrewd men saw their inadequacy; but it was the general view that they made a sound constitution. A union for common defense and general welfare was provided. Each State remained sovereign and independent, and retained every right not expressly ceded by the Articles to the general government—thus establishing a principle of the first importance. The States were annually to appoint from two to seven delegates to Congress, and each State was to have one vote. Charges for government and defense were to be defrayed from a common treasury, to which the States were to contribute in proportion to the value of their surveyed land and improvements. To Congress was confided the management of foreign affairs, of war, of the postal service, the regulation of the value of coin and the standard of weights and measures, and the control of Indian affairs. The States were to live in amity, they were to extend full rights to one another's citizens, they were to deliver up fugitives of justice to each other, and when two or more of them fell out, any one State involved could submit the dispute to Congress. The assent of nine States was required for the passage of the most important Congressional measures.

The failure of the attempts by Congress to make the Articles really workable is an old story. These attempts consisted chiefly in requests to the States for money which was never paid, calls for additions to the army which filled no ranks, and petitions for special powers which the States never unanimously granted. Two months after Maryland gave the last ratification, Washington commenced a diary, to which he prefixed a biting description of the nation's empty magazines, ill-supplied warehouses, and lack of transport. He added that "instead of having the regiments completed to the new establishment, which ought to have been done agreeably to the requisitions of Congress, scarce any State in the Union has at this hour an eighth part of its quota in the field, and little prospect that I can see of ever getting more than half; in a word, instead of having everything in readiness to take the field, we have nothing. . . ." [33] The commander had shaped his measures early this year to attack Clinton in New York city, but he was forced reluctantly

[33] "Writings," IX, 236ff. At the close of the previous summer, Washington had reported that he was under the necessity either of dismissing part of the militia then gathering, or letting them starve when they came forward. He grimly added that his difficulties in supplying his forces would be lessened when the year 1781 began, for half the army would dissolve. Disaster loomed ahead: "If either the temper or the resources of the country will not admit of an alteration, we may expect soon to be reduced to the humiliating condition of seeing the cause of America, in America, upheld by foreign arms." "Writings," VIII, 386ff.

to decide against this, in part because his ranks were too thin and his force was too ill supplied. Congress in this dark hour before the dawn wrote, in desperation, a circular for transmission to the States, which, though never approved nor transmitted, remains to show into what straits the nation had been brought. The country was sinking deeper and deeper into debt, with no visible means of repayment; it was becoming harder and harder to raise money at home or abroad; and the troops were growing more and more disheartened. "The inattention in the States," ran its reproachful words, "has almost endangered our very existence as a people." [34]

While the Articles were still before the States for ratification, as their defects were slowly realized, much thought was given to the possibility of amending them. New Jersey was insistent in urging one important change. Her delegates said (1778) that she wished the sole and exclusive power of regulating trade with foreign nations to be vested in Congress, and the revenue of a national tariff used for the general benefit; arguing that any other course might involve many difficulties and embarrassments, and be attended with injustice to some States in the Union. She was induced to relinquish her proposed amendments, but once more before the Articles were fully ratified, her delegates evinced their dissatisfaction by a milder proposal. On February 3, 1780, Witherspoon laid a legislative resolution before Congress, stating the opinion of New Jersey that it was absolutely necessary for Congress to have authority, whenever nine States consented, to superintend the commercial regulations of every State, and to lay duties on all imports. Of course it was impracticable to add any such article. [35]

Five days after the Maryland delegates signed the Articles, Varnum of Rhode Island moved that a committee be appointed to digest such additions to the fundamental law as seemed necessary during the crisis of the war; these additions to lapse and become void when

---

[34] Cf. S. B. Webb, December 9, 1779: ". . . money depreciating, public virtue totally damned—morals of good men affected—public men and public measures like the money, [and] in short everything is as nothing should be—no steps taken for reinforcing our army against another campaign—members of Congress and their puppies throwing the whole country in a state of stupidity—with an idea our salvation is to be worked out in Europe this winter." "Corr. and Journals," II, 224-26.

[35] For Hamilton's plan of an alternative to the Articles (September, 1780), see his "Works," I, 203-28. Hamilton's conviction that the country needed "a solid coercive union" was Washington's conviction. The latter wrote: "If we mean to continue our struggles, . . . we must do it upon an entirely new plan . . . ample power must be lodged in Congress, as the head of the Federal Union, adequate to all the purposes of war." And again: "There can be no radical cure till Congress is vested by the States with full and ample powers to enact laws for general purposes." "Writings," IX, 13; 125. Hamilton even wrote of a revolutionary assumption of powers.

the conflict was won. His motion was the fruit of a movement in Congress awakened and given impetus chiefly by Madison, who was effectively seconded by Duane. The committee, consisting of Madison, Duane, and Varnum, was actually appointed, with instructions "to prepare a plan to invest the United States in Congress assembled with full and explicit powers for effectually carrying into execution in the several States all acts or resolutions passed agreeably to the Articles of Confederation." It worked rapidly, and on May 3 reported a scheme for really putting teeth into the Articles. Madison and his associates pointed out their chief defect—the fact that they gave Congress no power to enforce its measures—and to meet it suggested an additional article. It provided that whenever one or more States refused to abide by the decisions of Congress, or to observe all the Articles of Confederation, Congress was then "fully authorized to employ the force of the United States as well by sea as by land to compel such States to fulfill their Federal engagements," and particularly was authorized to make distraint on the property of the State or its citizens, and to cut off its trade with the rest of the United States and the world.[36]

Now began a series of delays. The proposed article, which greatly alarmed several delegates, Madison thought should become a part of the basic law when ratified by all the States not in the hands of the enemy. It was at once referred to a grand committee. Not even this much consideration was given to a motion by Mathews, of South Carolina, that during the rest of the war Congress should regard itself as empowered to execute any ordinances which it thought necessary for victory. And when the grand committee upon Madison's, Duane's, and Varnum's additional article made its report on July 20, 1781, it was seen that it also had been shelved. The committee brought in a neat plan of its own, falling into three divisions. It proposed that the States be requested to grant Congress the power to lay an embargo in time of war, the power to demand quotas of money, and the power to collect this money through its agents. Congress having refused to act directly upon

---

[36] At Richmond, in the middle of May, 1784, Patrick Henry met Madison and two other members in a coffee-house, and, expressing regret over the slow progress of the impost plan, suggested that Madison and one other legislator sketch a plan for giving Congress greater powers. The resolutions which the Legislature soon after adopted urged, among other things, that Congress speedily settle its accounts with the various States, and that the balances due to Congress "ought to be enforced, if necessary, by such distress on the property of the defaulting States or their citizens as the United States, in Congress assembled, deem adequate and most eligible." Bancroft, "Hist. of the Const.," two volume ed., I, 162.

even this substitute, another committee of three—Randolph, Varnum, and Ellsworth—was created to consider it in turn.

This third committee was bolder than the second, but not as bold as Madison wished. On August 22, 1781, it brought in a report which included an exposition of the Articles, a plan for their execution, and certain supplementary articles comprehending seven new powers. They allowed Congress to lay embargoes during the continuance of the war; to draft rules for the seizure of private property for war purposes; to control the collection of taxes imposed for meeting the requisitions of Congress; to admit as a new State any part of an old one, with the consent of the latter; to agree with any other nations as to the opening of American consulates abroad; within certain limitations, to alter the rules which regulated the mode of voting upon different measures in Congress; and—this was highly important—to distrain the property of any State which fell behind in its contributions in money or men. Though the report constituted one of the most earnest and careful efforts yet made for patching up the Articles, it proved as abortive as those which had preceded it. Action was postponed, and the subject was allowed to drop.

But the desperate fight to improve the national Constitution was still maintained. On October 3, 1781, the day Cornwallis wrote Clinton that the Americans were encamped about two miles from Yorktown, a fourth effort was made in Congress for at least a temporary increase of Congressional powers. A committee under Robert R. Livingston presented three resolves. One requested the Legislatures to vest in Congress the power "to call forth men and provisions and carriages whenever they shall deem them necessary for the common defense, and to assist their officers in collecting the same"— the boldness of the proposal lying in the latter clause. A second was designed to obviate, for the moment, the necessity of appealing to the Legislatures for men and supplies. Since many assemblies were not in session, and the military crisis would probably pass before they could be called, the committee suggested a resolution "that Congress, by the authority which the nature of the trust imposed in them vests them with, will immediately take measures to procure the supplies of men, provisions, and carriages necessary to give vigor and success in the operations of the present campaign." The final resolve simply asked the Governors for every possible assistance during the emergency. However, the surrender of Cornwallis a fortnight later removed the critical necessities which had prompted these measures.

The fact that the war was now ending impressed many statesmen with the urgency of strengthening the powers of Congress over the States before, to use Washington's word, the interest of the people in the national government was "relaxed" by happier times. For a while the hope persisted that by a simple process of amendment the Articles might be made over into a serviceable national Constitution. The creation of executive departments had begun in the first months of 1781. In January, Congress had created a Department of Foreign Affairs, and in February it agreed to a scheme for a Superintendent of Finance, a Secretary of War, and a Secretary of the Marine, while a committee of Congress recommended on February 16 the establishment of an Attorney-Generalship, and a Federal court to try offenders against the United States. By an ordinance for the trial of piracy cases, the first Federal tribunal was established on April 5. This elaboration of Federal machinery increased the powers exercised by Congress, and dignified the general government. But the legislators of New York, inspired by Hamilton and Duane, believed that something more than a mere piecemeal tinkering of the Articles was required, and on July 21, 1781, the Assembly voted a proposal for a general convention of the States to make the Confederation into a new instrument.

III. The Impost and the States

For the first four years after the Declaration of Independence the requests of the general government for men, funds, or provisions were of a conservative and hand-to-mouth character. Congress never looked far ahead, nor tried to arrange for a consistent supply of money or munitions, while it soon lost hope of obtaining an adequate national army bound to serve throughout the war. But in the early part of 1781 Congress moved to a more important step. The States were first asked to levy an import duty of five per cent. on all foreign goods, and to hand over the funds to Congressional agents; a few days later they were asked to allow Congress itself to levy the impost. No time limit was set, so that this revenue would automatically flow in indefinitely. The request furnished a sharp immediate test of State willingness to make a sacrifice for strengthening the general government.

The first State to assent was Connecticut, on March 8, 1781— Trumbull's government was always promptly loyal. New York followed closely, and in April New Hampshire and Pennsylvania voted their acquiescence. Virginia ratified in May, stipulating only that her grant was not to be effective until August; North Carolina and Delaware fell into line that autumn, and South Carolina and Maryland early in 1782; while Massachusetts acceded in 1782, but reserved to herself the right to appoint the collectors. Only Georgia and Rhode Island remained unresponsive, while the former offered evidence that her attitude was not unfavorable. Rhode Island's best known delegate in Philadelphia, Varnum, was earnestly in favor of increasing the powers of Congress, and had written home to Governor Greene that while "prudent caution" was no doubt requisite for the preservation of republican institutions, when it was pushed too far it defeated its proper ends. In August, 1781, his fellow-delegate, Mowry, joined him in assuring Governor Greene that they were at a loss to conjecture the rumors which had induced the State of Rhode Island to delay complying with the requisition of Congress.

Beyond scattered reports of a State Rights opposition there to the impost plan, the first notice to Congress that Rhode Island had assumed an unfavorable attitude was the displacement of Ellery, Varnum, and Mowry as delegates in 1782 by John Collins, Ezekiel Cornell, Jonathan Arnold, and above all, David Howell, who had compared the impost with the Stamp Act. When Howell appeared before a committee which Congress appointed in 1782 to learn why neither Georgia nor Rhode Island had acquiesced in the levy, he stated four reasons. First, the State depended almost wholly upon commerce for its prosperity, and had to bring in overland from Connecticut and Massachusetts a very large part of the agricultural commodities it needed. The merchants did not believe that they would be able to add the import duty to the price of goods they sold outside the State; or, if they could, they feared a retaliatory addition to the price of the farm products they ordered in return. Second, it seemed unfair to select for a national toll that one source of wealth which was most important to Rhode Island, and of little importance to many States. It would obviously be more profitable to the State to levy its own five per cent. duty, use part of the proceeds to pay its quota of the national expense as ordinarily determined, and keep the margin. Third, Rhode Island shared the anxiety of Maryland and other small States regarding the Western lands; if the trade that might enrich her was to be specially taxed, so should be the land sales that would enrich Virginia and Connecticut. Finally, Rhode Island strongly objected to yielding any authority over the State's domestic affairs to outsiders.[37] Not one of these arguments had real validity.

Congress could ill brook a delay. In May, 1782, a committee had conferred with Morris upon the financial situation of the country, and had reported that matters were going from bad to worse. Some States had passed no laws whatever for raising their quota of the moneys required by Congress for the year; some had passed laws for raising only a part; some had passed laws for raising the whole, but at a distant period; and a number of laws were in one respect or another defective. The committee, headed by Madison, placed no more trust in circular appeals; but, recognizing that some action was imperative, it recommended the dispatch of two missions, one north and one south, to try to persuade the States to take prompt action. During the summer both set out, and they returned with the most discouraging reports. In some instances they found it impossible to obtain more than fair words from a few members of the adjourned legislatures; in some they found an evasive attitude on the part of influential men; in some they even found that the States had raised money to meet their quotas, but were applying it to their own needs.

All this precipitated a resolution of October 10, 1782, calling upon Georgia and Rhode Island for a definite response to the impost question. Georgia indicated that in good time she would swing into line, but Rhode Island, urged thereto by her delegates, Howell and Arnold, definitely chose the opposite course. Howell wrote home that "This is but an entering wedge, others will follow, a land tax, a poll tax, and an excise"; and he and Arnold dwelt upon the argument that Rhode Island had as much right to her duties as other States had to their Western claims. The Assembly voted unanimously on November 1 against the impost, and Speaker

---

[37] The objections of Howell are summarized in Bates, p. 78; and a comprehensive letter which Robert Morris wrote to Governor Greene in answer to Howell is described on p. 79.

Bradford reported the result to Congress, with a statement of reasons which Madison and Hamilton crushingly answered.

As soon as an unofficial report reached Congress in December, 1782, of the Assembly's action, it was resolved to send a deputation to urge upon Rhode Island the desperate nature of the case. Throughout the country, the reception given to the news from Rhode Island, though generally unfavorable, was not unmixed. Many men were pleased. Word coming in that Maryland was on the point of revoking her grant, the Congressional deputation delayed its departure till three days before Christmas; it had not gone a half day's journey from Philadelphia before the news arrived that Virginia had repealed her grant, and, turning about, it was promptly excused from its errand. The bitterness in Congress among those who had looked with joy upon the proposed measure, as a long step towards a permanent strengthening of the national government, was great. Correspondingly great was the jubilation of Howell, Arnold, and a few others who had regarded with open distrust all the implications of the impost. There was some hope that Virginia, which had been induced to take its backward step by Richard Henry Lee at a moment when, the session just closing, the Assembly was very thin, would again step forward, but no such hope existed as to Rhode Island. The influence of Howell, who declared that her resistance to British tyranny was not more glorious than her stand against the impost, was evidently predominant in the little State.[38]

Partly as a punishment for Howell's opposition to its will, and partly to weaken his influence at home, Congress now turned to an investigation of certain newspaper dicta which it had noticed, and which it feared might injure "as well the national character of the United States and the honor of Congress as the finances of the said State . . ."; it being well known that he was the author. A Congressional committee fell upon one statement in particular. It was a communication in the Boston *Gazette* of November 10, 1782, from Philadelphia, alleging that letters to Congress from Adams, who had been in Holland, showed that the credit of the nation abroad was excellent, and that loans were readily procurable. This, said the committee, was an unfounded and untruthful assertion. The Secretary of Foreign Affairs was thereupon requested to obtain from the Governor of Rhode Island information as to the author of the

[38] Providence *Gazette*, April 12, 1782; Bates, 83.

communication. Nobody doubted his identity, but as Madison put it, it was believed that a formal detection would humiliate and discredit him in his own State. The result signally disappointed this expectation. Howell admitted that he had written the communication, but defended it as substantially true, and insisted that Congress had no authority over his correspondence with the State executive. Arnold seconded him, and the Assembly voted its approval of the whole course of its delegates.

Congress, as 1783 opened, had other troubles than the defeat of the impost plan. During the previous year even the current pay of the army had fallen greatly behind. The army was growing dissatisfied with its long wait for arrears, as a memorial from the officers showed, and some feared that the clamors of the rank and file would end in a revolt. Washington himself was worried over the probable consequences of discharging troops without a penny, with a burden of debt, and with the reflection that their reward for years of hardship and peril was misery and want. "You may rely upon it," he wrote the Secretary of War in October, 1782, "the patriotism and long-suffering of this army are almost exhausted, and that there never was so great a spirit of discontent as at this instant. While in the field I think it may be kept from breaking into acts of outrage; but when we retire into winter quarters, unless the storm is previously dissipated, I cannot be at ease respecting the consequences."

The officers felt their ill-treatment as keenly as the privates. At the beginning of the Revolution the commissioned men had been promised half pay for seven years if they fought to its end, and in 1780 this promise had been increased to half pay for life. When early in 1781 the question of commuting this life-pension to a cash payment was raised in Congress, it produced a marked stir inside and outside that body. Within Congress, it raised in a new form the issue between the partisans of a strong national government, and those of State rights. It was Hamilton's wish, and to a certain extent Madison's, that the whole public debt, including the money owed the army, be funded, and that Continental certificates be given the creditors. Both the officers and the creditors would then feel better assured of fair, uniform, and prompt attention, while both would be attached by strong ties of self-interest to the national government. On the other hand, the State Rights party wished all public obligations, including the payment of the Continental officers from the various States, left to the several commonwealths.

The army awaited the deliberations of Congress with rising impatience. In March, 1783, an incitation to violence was offered the Continental camp at Newburgh by a meeting of officers, but was stingingly rebuked by Washington. Immediately afterwards, upon his warm representations, Congress agreed to meet the troops' demands. The promise of half-pay for life was commuted to five years' full pay in one gross sum, for which certificates bearing six per cent. interest were issued.

Five years' pay seemed a large grant indeed to the impoverished States, and was bitterly resented by some, as a symptom of "extravagance" and as supporting the suspicion that Congress wished to hold both the sword and the purse. The results were especially serious in New England. In Massachusetts the General Court voiced its indignation vigorously. It informed Congress that the extraordinary concessions to the civil and military officers were producing "effects of a threatening aspect" throughout the State. The commutation of half-pay to officers was in especial, it thought, "a grant of more than an adequate reward for their services, and inconsistent with that equality which ought to subsist among citizens of free and republican States; . . . such a measure appeared to be calculated to raise and exalt some citizens in wealth and grandeur, to the injury and oppression of others." [39] In Connecticut the same sentiments were expressed. Trumbull resigned in the fall of 1783, and spoke in his final message of the necessity of strengthening the powers of Congress. The Legislature refused to express approval of his message as usual, disliking its tenor; "so exceedingly jealous is the spirit of this State at present respecting the powers and engagements of Congress," Trumbull explained to Washington, "arising principally from their aversion to the half-pay and commutation granted to the army." [40] These State objections led to the appointment of a Congressional committee, which sustained the grant as sound in policy and completely constitutional. But such were the reflections of State jealousy within Congress that, in the debate on its report, the declaration of the constitutional power of Congress was stricken out. The delegates of Massachusetts declined to vote on the final question.

[39] Hamilton, "Hist. Republic," II, Ch. 35.
[40] Washington, "Writings," X, 341-42.

The acceptance of these new burdens by Congress made it more urgent than ever to find a permanent and reliable revenue; the national leaders simply could not afford to regard the defeat of the impost plan as final. If the national debt were not gradually reduced, the Union would eventually break up under the strain, yet it was almost impossible to meet even the interest. Nothing but a general fund under Congressional control would obviate the State and sectional quarrels over financial burdens. Washington, in his address from Newburgh to the State Governors on disbanding the army, put the situation bluntly. He insisted:

That, unless the States will suffer Congress to exercise those prerogatives they are undoubtedly vested with by the Constitution, everything must very rapidly tend to anarchy and confusion. That it is indispensable to the happiness of the individual States, that there should be lodged somewhere a supreme power to regulate and govern the general concerns of the confederated republic, without which the Union cannot be of long duration. That there must be a faithful and pointed compliance, on the part of every State, with the late proposals and demands of Congress, or the most fatal consequences will ensue. That whatever measures have a tendency to dissolve the Union, or contribute to violate or lessen the sovereign authority, ought to be considered as hostile to the liberty and independency of America, and the authors of them treated accordingly.[41]

Madison, now the leader in Congress, moved quickly. Some thought that Virginia's repeal of her consent to the impost had tied his hands. The Legislature had said that "The permitting any power other than the General Assembly of this Commonwealth to levy duties or taxes upon the citizens of this State within the same is injurious to our sovereignty, may prove destructive of the rights and liberties of the people, and so far as Congress might exercise the same, is contravening the spirit of the Confederation in the eighth article thereof." It was commonly held that delegates in Congress were not free agents, but ambassadors of the State, bound to carry out its legislative wishes absolutely. But the very day after Bland laid Virginia's resolutions before Congress, on January 27, 1783, Madison offered a motion stating that Congress believed the establishment of permanent and adequate funds, supported evenly throughout the country, for the national government, to be indispensable. Both Hamilton and Madison spoke for the resolution, the latter the more effectively; for Hamilton contended that all collectors of Federal revenue should be appointed and paid by Congress, inasmuch as they would then feel an interest in supporting the Federal authority. To extreme State Rights men, erecting the Federal power into a bogie, this seemed a frank unmasking of the

[41] Washington, "Writings," X, 254ff.

sinister object of the advocates of a Federal impost. Madison glossed over Hamilton's indiscretion, showed the irrefragable reasons supporting the plan, and asked why there was so much distrust of Congress, which had long controlled the nation's purse.

On March 7, 1783, the Congressional committee upon revenue reported in favor of renewing the proposal for the five per cent. import duty, ad valorem, upon nearly all foreign goods, and asked for a similar duty upon all prizes condemned in courts of admiralty, and for a specific tax upon wines and other liquors, sugars and salts, pepper, cocoa, molasses, coffee, and tea, as they were imported. These duties were to run just a quarter-century after all the States had consented, and the revenue was to be applied exclusively to the payment of the interest on the national debt. It was to be collected by men appointed by the States, but acting under the orders of Congress.

This was, in all, an excellent plan. Hamilton, after earnestly supporting Madison's resolution, had suggested a much less sagacious scheme; he wished the taxes laid for the national benefit to be direct taxes upon property in the States, and he believed that they should be collected by appointees of Congress. It would have been impossible to obtain State consent to this scheme, even if their delegations in Congress had approved it. But Madison's plan was thought much more palatable than the old proposals, for the limitation of the taxes to a quarter-century, and the new arrangement for their collection, were designed expressly to meet objections that had been encountered in the States. With the revised impost plan was coupled an appeal for supplementary funds to provide for the current expenses of government; each State being asked to establish a substantial and sufficient revenue for the payment of its quota. The whole body of requests was approved by Congress on April 18, 1783, with only the Rhode Island delegates, Hamilton, and Higginson of Massachusetts voting in the negative. It was sent out with an explanatory address, written by Madison, and with a refutation, from Hamilton's pen, of Rhode Island's objections to the first impost plan.[42]

An account of the attitude of the various States has been left us by Madison, who was in a position to analyze shrewdly the

---

[42] Elliot's "Debates," I, 92ff, gives the documents named here. See also Hamilton, "Hist. Republic," II, 514ff.

motives of State policy. Of the New England States all but Rhode Island were at the outset in favor of the revised proposals. New Hampshire wished neither her imports nor her exports taxed by the States through which much of them had to pass; Massachusetts was worried over the large sum owed her by the general government, and wished provision made for its repayment; and Connecticut was eager to be relieved of the heavy import taxes laid by New York and Rhode Island. All the Middle States could be fairly counted upon to support the new impost plan, though Maryland was lukewarm. In New York, for example, Hamilton, Duane, and others desired a strong national government in and for itself, while many influential citizens who hardly shared this sentiment were eager to have the national debt provided for. As for Maryland, though she had never been trampled by contending armies, though her people held few securities of the United States, and though she was still sullen over the question of the Western lands, Madison believed that her desire for national tranquillity would bring her into line. Of the Southern States, Virginia and the Carolinas all needed protection against the commercial dominance of New England. It was true that in Virginia, a counter-motive existed in certain quarters in the shape of an unwillingness to surrender the privilege of taxing North Carolina by import duties, but this rendered North Carolina's wish to obtain immunity from the demands of other States the greater. South Carolina was impoverished by the war, which had taught her how exposed her position was; and she was a creditor of the United States. Georgia also was weak, and was threatened by Spanish and Indian aggressions.[43]

Yet the moment was less favorable than Madison believed. The issue between the believers in a closely cohesive nation and the advocates of a loose confederacy had by now been fairly joined, and the resentment of the determined champions of State sovereignty and independence was already a considerable obstacle. This was

[43] Washington wrote the States that it was their duty to grant the impost without hesitation, and warned them against a "spirit of disunion, or obstinacy and perverseness." He pursued: "This is the moment to give such a tone to our Federal government as will enable it to answer the ends of its institution. According to the system of policy the States shall adopt at this moment, it is to be decided whether the Revolution must ultimately be considered as a blessing or a curse; a blessing or a curse, not to the present age alone, for with our fate will the destiny of unknown millions be involved. . . ." He added that any obstinate State would be responsible for all the consequences. Edmund Randolph wrote Madison that the first effect of his message upon the Virginia Legislature was to increase the hope of the liberal group for the passage of the impost act, but that he feared the final consequences would be bad: "For the murmur is free and general against what is called the unsolicited obtrusion of his advice." (Washington, "Writings," X, 261 note.)

evident in Congress itself before the session of 1783 had proceeded far. "The purse," said Arthur Lee, "ought never to be put into the same hand with the sword. I will be explicit; I would rather see Congress a rope of sand than a rod of iron." [44] "If the Federal compact is such as has been represented," said John Mercer, "I will immediately withdraw from Congress and do everything in my power to destroy its existence." [45] Quotations from other Virginians, not in Congress, show in how far Madison was deceived as to the sentiment of his own State. George Mason, writing the instructions for the legislators representing Fairfax County, condemned the impost plan and the Congressional arguments supporting it. Examine them carefully, he said, and they will evince plainly a lust for power. They are just like the arguments used for the ship money, and to justify the arbitrary measures of the Stuarts. Let these new powers be added to those which Congress already has, "and the Constitutions of government in the different States will prove mere parchment bulwarks to American liberty." R. H. Lee wrote from Chantilly a month later in the same terms. Arguments could always be found to serve an inordinate thirst for authority; if Congress grasped the purse, she would presently have the sword as well, and then the rule of rotation in office would also be smashed. It is no wonder that the Virginia Legislature in the spring of 1783 rejected the new impost plan by a great majority. Instead, it laid its own impost duties, on the same scale as that asked by Congress, created its own officers to collect them, and provided for their payment into the national treasury.[46]

In New York two essayists, first "Calca" and then "Rough Hewer," filled many newspaper columns with the arguments used by Mason and Lee in Virginia. Greene wrote from South Carolina that the people there hated Robert Morris and Congress, holding that they had been grossly neglected by both in their financial distress; he thought that they leaned towards an independence of

---

[44] Silas Deane took the same view, writing April 1, 1783: "If my advice is of any weight with our great men in Connecticut, let them liquidate, and apportion the public debt, without loss of time, and let each State take its proportion, and manage its own revenues. The great object with Congress is to make a common purse or treasury to be supplied by imposts, duties, etc., laid by themselves, and collected and disposed of by officers of their appointing independent of the several Legislatures, but if our Assembly are wise and mean to be in fact independent they will never submit to a system which will prove as fatal in its consequences, as that which we have happily opposed; no, let each State guard well the strings of its own purse." . . . "Corr. and Journals" of S. B. Webb, III, 9-11.

[45] Gilpin, "Madison Papers," I, 357, 511.

[46] R. H. Lee, "Letters," II, 283-85; Rowland's "Mason," II, 48-52; 59-60.

the Congressional connection.   In Connecticut, which Madison had
accounted safe, the new impost scheme was for the moment curtly
rebuffed.

Delaware, in June, was the first State to comply with the request
of Congress; and on August 25, Pennsylvania became the second,
by a unanimous vote of the Assembly.   In both States the grant of
the impost was coupled with the grant of the State's current quota
of the Federal requisition.   In August also, South Carolina went
as far as Virginia had done, adopting the impost schedule, but
placing its collection in the hands of State officers, and appropri-
ating the revenues to the payment of South Carolina's quota under
the Federal requisitions.   In Massachusetts a severe struggle
occurred.   Nearly forty towns had instructed their representatives
to vote against the impost plan.   But the House carried the impost
bill by a majority of seven, and it defeated an amendment to forbid
any use of the receipts to settle the half-pay accounts of the officers
by a majority of ten; while the Senate passed the bill almost
unanimously.   The town meeting in Boston, in answer to complaints
from some other towns, asserted that "if we ever mean to be a
nation, we must give the power to Congress, and funds too." [47]   But
after these initial successes the progress of the measure grew slower
and slower.

By the latter part of 1785 nine States had in some form accepted
the impost: all the New England States except Rhode Island, all
the Middle States except New York, and all the Southern States
except Maryland and Georgia.   Some, like Virginia and South Carolina, had accepted it in a very imperfect manner, but Congress
correctly felt that once all had acquiesced in the principle, it would
be possible to induce the States which had passed defective laws to
amend them.   Rhode Island had at first ignored the proposals of
Congress, passing her own tariff act; she had then rejected them;
and finally she had enacted a conglomerate, but almost wholly bad
law, complying only in a small part with the Congressional requirements.   She imposed the duties as requested, with some additions;
but she insisted upon collecting them through her own agents, and
she consented to use only $8000 a year from the proceeds towards

---

[47] In Connecticut, the impost proposal passed the House by a majority of fifty-one.
"Never did people in general feel more satisfaction at any public measure," wrote a
Hartford correspondent to the Pennsylvania *Packet* of June 8, 1784, "than in conse-
quence of this act"; Connecticut was always sound.

payment of the foreign debts of the nation, reserving the rest to discharge that part of the country's domestic debt which was held in Rhode Island. The influence of Howell and Ellery was evident in this enactment, which was of course preposterous from a Federal point of view; it was simply a plan for State revenue.

As for the request for the supplementary funds, that was now dead. Five of the States which had granted the impost—Massachusetts, New Hampshire, New Jersey, Virginia, and South Carolina —had manifested their unwillingness to make this additional concession to Congress. All in all, Congress had reason to feel decidedly discouraged.

Congress knew by this time that the success of the revised impost plan was becoming a desperate necessity. At the beginning of the year 1786 a grand committee was appointed to inquire into the fiscal affairs of the nation, and the best means of discharging its debts; and its report, showing that although since October 1, 1781, requisitions totaling $15,670,000 had been made, the response had been insufficient to pay the interest on the foreign borrowings, was presented at the beginning of February. Indeed, the amounts paid in reached only $2,419,000, of which Georgia and North Carolina had contributed not a cent. For the fourteen months ending December 31, 1785, the receipts from the States had been at the rate of less than $400,000 yearly, though it was estimated that in 1787 more than $2,500,000 would be required to maintain the government and meet the interest on the public debt. Moreover, in 1787 the first instalment on the principal of the public debt fell due. Thereafter it would cost a million a year to reduce it. Under the circumstances, even R. H. Lee began to understand that Congress could not obtain the needed moneys unless there was some real expansion of its powers; and the wiser statesmen and thinkers believed in the necessity of arming it with a right to coerce any State that failed to pay its requisition. Indeed, in 1784 the Virginia Legislature, following New York, had resolved that Congress ought to enforce the payment of balances due from any State by distraint on its or its citizens' property.

After some hesitation, Congress took the action urgently recommended by a committee which Rufus King headed, and eloquently pleaded again with the States to adhere without reservations to the impost plan. This appeal was effective in three of the four States

which had hitherto blocked the reform. On February 15, after five
years of opposition, Rhode Island consented. By the beginning of
May Rufus King could inform John Adams that Maryland and
Georgia also had yielded.[48]   New York alone refused to fall into
line, for when her Legislature passed the impost act, it was with
amendments which made passage a defeat. The Legislature insisted
that the collection be kept in State hands, and that the duties must
be payable in bills of credit of New York State. Congress, learning
of the action of New York in August, 1786, felt that almost its last
hope was gone, and this was the fact, for its effort to induce
Governor Clinton to call a special legislative session was quite
unavailing.[49]   To its appeals the executive turned a deaf ear, alleging there was no crisis.

Concurrently with the efforts of Congress to wring a stable revenue
from the States ran its efforts to obtain from them a sufficient control over shipping to enable it to wage commercial warfare with
nations discriminating against the United States. The British
restrictions were especially resented; moreover, great quantities of
English goods were flooding the country, stifling our infant manufactures and draining away our specie. Madison stated in September, 1783, that Congress would have to undertake some defensive
plan, and the commercial sentiment of the North thereafter veered
steadily in favor of determined action by the central government.
The concrete proposals of Congress to meet the situation were formulated early in 1784 and submitted to the States under date of April
30. It asked that, for fifteen years, power be given it to prohibit
the shipment of any goods into or out of any American port in
vessels owned or navigated by foreigners; unless the foreigners
were citizens of a nation with which the United States had a treaty
of commerce. Furthermore, Congress desired power for the same
period to prohibit foreigners in this country from importing, unless
by special treaty, any goods from another land than their own.
This program was calculated to appeal to men who saw the danger

---

[48] Rufus King, "Life and Corr.," I, 172-74.

[49] The result in New York bore out the prediction Schuyler had made in a letter to
Hamilton three years before (May 4, 1783). He wrote then that "although our Legislature seems still inclined to confer powers on Congress adequate to the proper discharge of the great duties of the sovereign council of these States, yet I perceive with
pain that some, chagrined at disappointment, are already attempting to inculcate a
contrary principle, and I fear it will gain too deep a root to be eradicated, until such
confusion prevails as will make men deeply feel the necessity of not retaining so much
sovereignty in the States individually." For the petition signed all over New York
city in behalf of the impost, see Hamilton, "Hist. Republic," III, 171-72.

of our defenseless economic condition, and even Rhode Island, it was said, would make little objection.[50]

Yet when Congress a year later looked about, it found little had been accomplished. The proposal was therefore modified to meet the objections which, it was understood, had been raised in various States. Congress now asked for authority to control the foreign and coastal trade, and to fix the duties upon importations; but with the proviso that all enactments for these purposes should have the consent not only of nine States in Congress but of nine Legislatures, that they should be limited in duration, and that the duties should be collected in the names of the States in which they were paid, and should be held for the use of those States.[51] This new scheme was given encouraging support all over the nation. Its advocates could point not only to the more and more irksome British discriminations, but to the aggressions of the Barbary states, whose cruisers were by this time fully launched upon their course of aggression. But their hopes were to be dashed.

As was to be expected, men found on March 3, 1786, when a Congressional committee reported on the subject, that the State enactments had been as various and conflicting as those which followed the request for the Continental impost. Four States, Massachusetts, New York, New Jersey, and Virginia, had passed such acts as Congress had recommended. In the first, for example, a Boston town-meeting in the spring of the previous year, the mechanics as well as the shipping interests being strongly for the measure, had drawn up an address to other ports, dwelling upon the British restrictions, and asking that Congress be empowered to regulate commerce, in order "to secure reciprocity; and to form a national establishment." Governor Bowdoin had insisted that it was the duty of the State to vest Congress with the required authority, and the Legislature had promptly responded. In Virginia, Madison's influence had been sufficient. Three other States, Connecticut, Pennsylvania, and Maryland, had passed the desired laws, but had fixed two different dates from which they were to be operative; so that the duration of the powers of Congress would differ in different parts of the country. New Hampshire had granted the

[50] Bates, 101; Gilpin, "Madison Papers," I, 572 ff., shows Madison's shrewd estimate of Great Britain's policy of monopolizing our trade. "The supposed contrariety of interests among the States, and the impotence of the Federal Government, are urged . . . as a safeguard against retaliation."
[51] Journals Cont. Congress, Ed. 1823, IV, 546-47.

power of regulating trade, by restrictions or duties, her act being of insufficient scope. Rhode Island and North Carolina had vested Congress with authority over imports alone, the former for twenty-five years, the latter for an indefinite term; and North Carolina had stipulated that when all the States had complied with the Congressional proposal, it should become part of the Articles of Confederation. The three remaining States had done nothing whatever.

The Congressional committee could recommend but one course—that Pennsylvania, Maryland, and Connecticut should amend their laws to make the new powers of Congress commence the day Congress began exercising them; that New Hampshire, North Carolina, and Rhode Island should give their acts due breadth and free them from clogging conditions; and that the laggard trio, Delaware, South Carolina, and Georgia, should take favorable action on the Congressional demand.[52]

This appeal brought a remarkable, though not a sufficient, response. South Carolina, indeed, acted before it could have heard of it, her law dating from March 11. Delaware promptly assented, and Georgia passed her law on August 2, 1786. No State had now failed to take at least partial action. Of those whose enactments had been faulty, Rhode Island on March 13, 1786, voted Congress full power over both imports and exports, and though she attached the condition that the law should not take effect until Congress obtained authority to regulate interstate trade as well, her action was deemed satisfactory. But New Hampshire and North Carolina, by failing to amend their enactments, remained at the close of 1786 the great obstacles to the full success of the reform. It was desirable that other States should recast their legislation to conform perfectly with the proposal of Congress, but of these two alone could it be said that amendment was indispensable. Congress made a last appeal to them, but the hope for a vigorous national government was now seen to lie with the Federal Convention.

IV.   Congress and the Peace Treaty

Congress had now been rebuffed and humiliated in its efforts to gain a stable revenue from the States, and to seize the only economic weapon available for retaliation against European injuries to our

[52] Elliot's "Debates," I, 108ff.

commerce and manufactures. Meanwhile, another acute problem, pregnant with new humiliations for the national government, had been raised: the problem of enforcing the provisions of the treaty of peace with Great Britain.

The treaty had required not a little of American justice and magnanimity. Its fourth article declared that creditors on either side should meet with no lawful impediment to the recovery of their debts at full sterling value. The fifth article required the United States to "earnestly recommend" that the various Legislatures restore all estates, rights, and properties confiscated from British subjects, and from persons resident in districts occupied by the British, when these latter persons had not borne arms against the United States. Persons of any other description—e.g., loyalists who had fought on the British side—were to have full liberty to go to any part of the United States and remain a year for the purpose of recovering their estates and property. Congress was bound to intercede in their favor also, asking the States to restore them their rights and property freely, they refunding to any new owners the price paid for the property. Finally, the sixth article stipulated that no further confiscations of British or loyalist property, and no further prosecutions of loyalists, should take place anywhere. In fine, the United States engaged to do three things without reference to the willingness or unwillingness of the States. It was to see that British debts were paid; to protect loyalists traveling or residing in America for a year; and to stop all confiscations and punishments. One thing Congress was to call upon the States to do. It was to ask them to restore all estates and rights to British subjects, to Americans who had accepted British protection in New York, Charleston, and other occupied places, and to American loyalists who had not fought in the British armies. The British knew that an earnest recommendation by Congress was not a national law. But they also knew that the Revolution would have broken down if the States had not generally accepted Congressional recommendations as laws, and that it had been upon a Congressional recommendation in 1777 that confiscation had become general.

The news that Congress was required to recommend not only that prosecutions stop, but that the loyalists be allowed by legal process to regain what had been taken from them, provoked a violent and nation-wide controversy. John Adams had been willing to offer generous terms to "the wretches how little soever they deserve it, nay, how much soever they deserve the contrary"; but there was little popular feeling with him. For a time after the peace the violent and radical element had its way in most States. Many who had skulked during the war, of course, exhibited the most fury now. But the bitterness left among even brave and liberal people by the conflict was great—greater than the bitterness between North and South after the Civil War. The patriots could not forget that their towns had been burned, their countrysides laid waste, their sons or brothers killed in battle or marshalled into hideous prison ships. The Tories and British civilians knew well what to expect. Before the opening of 1783 they had generally deserted Charleston and Savannah, and had begun leaving New York city. The richest went to England. The common folk flocked to the British possessions in North America, in such numbers that within a few years they swelled the population of Canada and the Bermudas by 60,000.[53]

Congress did its part with promptness. On January 14, 1784, it issued a proclamation asking the States to restore all estates, rights, and properties confiscated from British subjects, upon terms —as the treaty had provided—equitable to Americans who had purchased the confiscated properties. But when the Legislatures took up the question, it was urged that the loss of the British and loyalists was nothing compared with the damages sustained by patriot towns and individuals. Falmouth, New London, Fairfield, Norfolk, Charleston, and other coastal towns had been laid in ruins, and Franklin had declared in discussing peace terms that if the accounts were strictly balanced, America's would be much the heavier. The loyalists, it was asserted, would provoke mob outrages if allowed to settle, and would not become whole-hearted supporters of the republic. Considering that, as Jeremy Belknap said, "their mouths were full of curses against their king," this last objection was empty, but timorous men, and selfish men with their eyes fixed upon loyalist estates, urged it vehemently.

Riots against the Tories followed their attempts to return; some especially shocking disorders at Worcester, Mass., Stamford, Conn., Woodbridge, N. J., and in New York city and Charleston might be

---

[53] Flick, "Loyalism," Ch. 9. The author estimates that out of a population of 180,000 in New York State, 90,000 were loyalists, and 35,000 emigrated at the close of the Revolution; p. 182.

listed. Throughout the Carolinas a swift vengeance was visited upon many of those who had assisted Tarleton or served with the murderous bands of Tories in the partisan warfare of that section. In New England, wrote Belknap,[54] "we flew into a passion, and in the face of the treaty resolved in town meetings not to admit the refugees; though, had we not been so rash, they would have been glad to have come among us on the same terms that the Gibeonites were spared, in the days of Joshua." George Mason tells us [55] that in Virginia he everywhere heard men say: "If we are now to pay the debts due to British merchants, what have we been fighting for all this while?" Caroline County, in this spirit, addressed the Legislature upon "the impolicy, injustice, and oppression of paying British debts." [56] In South Carolina in the summer of 1784 the notorious Tory fighter, Love, taking advantage of the safety guaranteed by the treaty, and supported by his native effrontery, appeared in the region of Ninety-six, where his misdeeds were well known. When he was thrown into jail and prosecuted before the Court of Sessions, the presiding judge, Aedanus Burke, annulled the case, and declaring that conscience alone could punish the prisoner, dismissed him. Burke was perfectly right. But the rough men in the courtroom heard his judgment with anger, took the law into their own hands, and hanged Love to a neighboring tree.

Not every State, but almost every State, was guilty of grave infractions of the treaty. It was in the South that opposition to the compact was greatest, for in addition to the Tory outrages there, the South saw a grievance in the fact that large numbers of negroes had escaped from bondage by taking protection under the British flag. Laurens, helping negotiate the treaty, inserted a clause prohibiting the British from "carrying away any negroes or other property" when they evacuated our territory; but when they set sail, the British sent these black refugees away. This was the humane course, and was unselfish; Carleton, to facilitate the payment of just American claims for indemnity, caused accurate lists of the transported negroes to be made. Some 5000 are said to have left Savannah alone.[57] But the Southern States were highly irritated

---

[54] *Mass. Hist. Soc. Colls.*, Series V, Vol. II, 282.
[55] Rowland's "Mason," II, 46.
[56] Cf. Hamilton, "Hist. Rep.," III, 25 ff.
[57] Van Tyne, "Loyalists," 289; see F. A. Ogg, "Jay's Treaty and The Slavery Interests," Annual Report Am. Hist. Ass., 1901, I. The infractions of the treaty on both sides are thoroughly treated by S. F. Bemis in "Jay's Treaty."

by the loss of so many workers. In South Carolina Rutledge was attacked for not having made it impossible for the British to carry them off; and in Virginia the Legislature angrily denounced the violation of the treaty.

After Yorktown, Virginians were inflamed by what they had suffered from the invaders in the closing stages of the war. In the last days of 1782, the House of Delegates defended the justice of the confiscation laws, and unanimously resolved "that all demands and requests of the British court for the restitution of property confiscated by this State, being neither supported by law, equity, or policy, are wholly inadmissible; and that our delegates be instructed to move Congress that they may direct their delegates, who shall represent these States in a general Congress for adjusting a peace or truce, neither to agree to any such restitution, nor submit that the laws made by any independent State of the Union be subject to any adjudication of any power or powers on earth." Put bluntly, this was the preposterous demand that no treaty be made which might conflict with any law by any State. British merchants and agents who quitted Virginia and Maryland at the beginning of the Revolution left property there, including debts, to the amount of £3,000,000 sterling. They had no sooner begun to return after the peace than on July 2, 1783, the Governor of Virginia ordered all loyalists or British citizens to leave the State forthwith. In October the Legislature, while preventing the immigration of refugee Tories from other States to Virginia, removed the restrictions on factors and merchants. But the laws which prevented British creditors from collecting debts, or recovering other property, continued in full force.

The Carolinas and Georgia were as harsh and unreasonable as Virginia. North Carolina refused to retrace the steps it had taken for the confiscation of loyalist property, passing in October, 1784, a law directing the sale of such holdings, and thirteen months later an act to secure the buyers of confiscated estates in their titles. The confiscations and amercements ordered by the Jacksonborough Legislature of South Carolina in 1782 have already been described, and Jay regarded the ordinances of the following year for the sale of confiscated estates as a flat violation of the treaty. Not until 1786 was a bill carried which finally closed up "the business of confiscation and amercement." An equally heinous contravention of the treaty was the law of 1784 forbidding suit for any debt contracted by any citizen of the United States before February 26, 1782, and until the beginning of 1785, and prescribing the repayment of such debts by instalments. The application of this law should have been limited to American creditors. In South Carolina as well as in Virginia, when the return of British citizens provoked outrages, the Governor—instead of bending every effort to sustain the laws—transgressed the treaty by ordering the newcomers to abandon their property and get out. The British also complained that the Jacksonborough act of confiscation was retroactive to July 4, 1776; and that houses and lands, initially Tory-owned, but which actually belonged to British merchants, not to Tories, when the Act was passed, were sold under it in 1784 without respect for the treaty's guarantees. As for Georgia, the British Government succinctly alleged that:

Laws and regulations similar to those which have passed in South Carolina exist in this State, with degrees of peculiar and manifest aggravation; the judges from the bench having declared that no suit shall be proceeded on, if brought by a British subject; while, on the other hand, they allow British subjects to be sued by their creditors.

Among the Middle States, the treaty violations by New York were easily the worst. Jay admitted that the Trespass Act of March, 1783, which the Legislature was at such pains to continue in force against the well-founded objections of the liberals, was an early and odious infringement upon plain British rights. The British Government in 1786 spoke of it with especial indignation:

By virtue of this law, actions to an enormous amount were immediately instituted against British subjects, who, relying implicitly on the treaty of peace and the faith of nations, were encouraged to remain in New York upon its evacuation for the purposes of collecting their debts, and settling or extending their commercial affairs; and in cases where those who had occupied the premises were not to be found, the demands were made on the lodger, the late servant, or the agent of these occupiers. These suits have been prosecuted with the utmost severity, and being determinable by juries of interested men . . . it is no wonder that verdicts for exorbitant rents and damages have in every instance been found against the defendants.[58]

By the Legislature of January, 1784, a long series of infractions of the treaty was placed upon the statute books. One bill was framed to disfranchise loyalists, and was drawn in terms which made it affect persons guiltless of any real offense against the United

[58] In the prosecutions of the loyalists for occupancy of Whig premises, cutting timber, or other trespass, more than one million dollars was claimed in damages. Jones, "Hist. N. Y.," II, 251-55; Flick, "Loyalism," 159; Dip. Corr. of U. S., 1783-89, Ed. 1855, II, 581 ff., which gives in full Lord Carmarthen's very cogent list of the British grievances.

States.[59] A resolution was passed, calling on the Governors of the other twelve States to interchange lists of banished persons with each other and with New York, in order that no refugee might find a spot to rest upon American soil. Still another resolution was introduced declaring, quite gratuitously, that notwithstanding the recommendation of Congress, New York could not comply with the fifth article of the British treaty.[60] The confiscation of the estates owned by the Society for the Propagation of the Gospel was —simply because it held a royal charter—proposed, but was too plainly villainous to pass. Moreover, a bill called the Alienation bill, which would have at once expelled from the State all remaining loyalists, was prepared, and when it was not pushed forward with the energy the radicals thought proper, mass-meetings attested their indignation.

New Jersey, which in 1781 had suspended the sale of confiscated estates, passed an act on December 16, 1783, to continue it. This, of course, was not a violation of the treaty, but simply a rebuff to the Congressional recommendation. Petitions condemning the harsh treatment the Tories were suffering in New York, and inviting them to come live peaceably among the tolerant inhabitants of New Jersey, found many signers in Amboy, Piscataway, New Brunswick, and a few other towns, and to these places the erstwhile loyalists went in troops. In Pennsylvania and Delaware the number of Tories was great, and that of the lukewarm even greater, so that after the treaty of peace loyalists and British subjects were leniently treated. The British Government, however, complained of the Pennsylvania act which for a short time, till the autumn of 1784, restrained the recovery of old debts. "Not only a uniform opposition has been made to the payment of interest, but the lawyers, dreading the resentment of some of the most violent among their countrymen, have refused to engage in the recovery of these unpopular demands; and . . . not one action for the payment of an old British debt has been prosecuted in this State." In Maryland

---

[59] Hamilton always spoke with special bitterness of the law depriving certain groups of the ballot and other civil rights, which, as he said, was "an attempt to transfer the sceptre from the hands of government to those of individuals, to arm one part of the community against another, to enact a civil war."

[60] It must be remembered that New York's Confiscation Act of 1779 had been peculiarly harsh. The Council of Revision had vetoed it because it was obscure and contradictory, convicted certain persons by name without a trial, tended to subject loyal inhabitants to gross oppression, and was in part "repugnant to those plain and immutable laws of justice which no State can with honor throw off." The Assembly repassed it over this veto 28 to 9 (*Assembly Journal*, 1779, 102ff); and now the State still stood by it.

also, the moderates, after a wave of anti-loyalist feeling had swept the State in 1783, triumphed. Legislation embodying some objectionable features was opposed by Charles Carroll of Carrollton and Robert Goldsborough, and in 1786 there was nothing of which the British could complain save that, as in Virginia, they were not allowed freely to collect the pre-war debts owed them.

As we should expect, the New Englanders, who since 1776 had been touched directly by the war along only the southern and Maine coasts, showed the most enlightened spirit. Early in 1784 a committee of the Massachusetts House, headed by Samuel Adams, reported that no one who had borne arms against the United States, or had lent money to the enemy for war purposes, should ever be permitted to return to Massachusetts, but this view did not prevail. The State did no more than to confirm her previous confiscatory legislation, and to pass an act (November, 1784) outlawing the interest which had accrued on British debts from 1775 to 1783.[61] New Hampshire, instead of making it easy for evicted loyalists to re-purchase their confiscated possessions, voted the spring of the same year a law for the speedy sale of the seized estates; but it did no more. Rhode Island's laws interfering with the obligation of contracts were of course a violation of the treaty, but then a madness lay upon Rhode Island, and the British were far from being the worst sufferers. Indeed, the shore towns of New England soon began to realize that the peopling of Nova Scotia was raising up a rival on the fishing banks; and that the loyalists, if permitted to take up their homes among them, would have brought wealth in their hands.

The passing away of wartime resentments, the awakening of a sentiment of justice and magnanimity, alone did much to break down these evil laws. Respect for the pledged word of the nation was a powerful influence; while the aggressive attitude of the British Government, which refused to evacuate the lake posts or pay for the negroes carried away until the United States fulfilled its treaty obligations, was an important factor in obtaining a reform. There is no question that the British very early infringed the treaty, but the American violations were so heavy that Jay said

[61] The Massachusetts Legislature in the fall of 1785 repealed all legislation against Tories and refugees. See the *Centinel*, November 19, 1785, for hostile comment; N. Y. *Packet*, January 16, 1786. Lord Carmarthen's complaint of treaty violations in 1786 contained only one count against a New England State—Massachusetts—and the New Englanders said that it was misstated. *Mass. Hist. Soc. Proceedings*, IX, 7-9.

he hardly thought it surprising or culpable in the English to retain the Northwestern posts.[62]　In the fall of 1784 Monroe, during a tour to Montreal, Niagara, and Lake Erie, learned that the British meant to hold these posts until Virginia and New York, regarded as the most flagrant offenders, repealed their obnoxious laws.[63]　In 1785 Adams wrote from London that the American demands would not be met while there remained in force any State law suspending suits for recovering British debts.[64]　In February, 1786, Lord Carmarthen sent Adams a detailed list of the offenses of the States, and when Congress received it, most of the allegations contained therein were found to be correct.　The result was that Congress resolved, in vigorous language:

> that the Legislatures of the several States cannot of right pass any act or acts for interpreting, explaining, or construing a national treaty, or any part or clause of it; nor for restraining, limiting, or in any manner impeding, retarding, or counteracting the operation and execution of the same; for that on being constitutionally made, ratified, and published, they become in virtue of the Confederation, part of the law of the land, and are not only independent of the will and power of such Legislatures, but also binding and obligatory on them.[65]

With a copy of this resolution, Congress sent each State a request that it repeal its laws, if any, transgressing the treaty, and even if no repeal was necessary, pass a declaration that the treaty was the full law of the State.

The two States whose assent to this request was most important and least probable were New York and Virginia.　Already, in 1784, Hamilton in New York had made himself a champion of the position taken by Congress on the treaty.　He had argued against the Trespass Act upon the ground, in part, that it was a violation of the treaty.　It might be objected, he said, that Congress had no control over the internal affairs, the police power, of New York. Not at all; the authority of Congress was unquestionable.　In memorable language, he maintained that "the sovereignty and independence of the people began by a Federal act; that our external sovereignty is known only in the Union—that foreign nations only recognize it in the Union; that the Declaration of Independence was the fundamental constitution of every State, all of which was acceded

---

[62] Two early American violations, in New York and South Carolina, occurred simultaneously, on March 17, 1783; one Pennsylvania violation on March 12, 1783; but the British were already averse to evacuating the western posts, as Haldimand's dispatch of August 20, 1783, showed, and they violated the treaty of November 25 by taking Negroes from New York. Dip. Corr. of U. S., 1783-89, 1855 ed., II, 642-44.
[63] R. H. Lee, "Letters," II, 297-99.
[64] Dip. Corr. of U. S., 1783-89, II, 500-01.　Nor would the Maryland bank stock be recovered, nor American negroes paid for.
[65] This was widely published; N. Y. *Packet,* April 27, 1787.

to by the Convention of New York. . . ." Hence, Hamilton concluded that "Congress had complete sovereignty; that the Union was known and legalized in the Constitution of New York previous to the Confederation, and that the first act of the State government accepted it as a fundamental law; from which reflections we are taught to respect the sovereignty of the Union, and to consider its constitutional powers as not controllable by any State." [66] The Confederation was an abridgement of that sovereign power, which gave to Congress the full power of making war, peace, and treaties, and the exclusive power to do so; this power must be respected. For the general public Hamilton stated his arguments in the essays of Phocion, which were read in all parts of America. As he said of his original pamphlet, "the force of plain truth carried it along the stream of prejudice, and the principles it held out gained ground in spite of the opposition of those who were too angry or too much interested to be convinced." Chancellor Kent, then a young man, wrote long after that no hasty production of the press ever had a truer success, and that "the rising generation readily imbibed those sentiments of temperate civil liberty and of sound constitutional law, which Hamilton had so clearly taught."

In Virginia also the constitutional powers of Congress found powerful defenders. The Legislature of that State had, like New York's, resolved in 1784 that it could not comply with the treaty. That is, it had declared that it had "no inclination to interfere with the power of making treaties with foreign nations, which the Confederation hath wisely vested in Congress; but it is conceived that a just regard to the national honor and interest of the citizens of this Commonwealth, obliges the Assembly to withhold their coöperation in the complete fulfillment of the said treaty." In the Senate a remonstrance against this was signed by seven men, Henry Lee, William Lee, Burwell Bassett, John Brown, Nathaniel Harrison, and William Fitzhugh, who believed Virginia bound in honor to execute the treaty.[67] Nearly all the great men of the State—Madison,

---

[66] But the State government flatly refused to regard the national treaty-making power as "not controllable." The two houses resolved in the spring of 1784 "That while this Legislature entertain the highest sense of national honor, of the sanction of treaties, and of the deference which is due the advice of the United States in Congress assembled, they find it inconsistent with their duty to comply with the recommendation of the said United States, on the subject matter of the fifth article of the said definitive treaty of peace." Jones, "Hist. N. Y.," II, 493-94.

[67] Md. *Journal*, July 23, 1784. They further argued that as for the slaves taken away by the British, Congress had already asked payment for them; that the removal of the slaves had not been approved by the British Government, which Franklin thought would certainly pay for them; and that in any event, it was politic to fulfill the treaty.

George Mason, Washington, Monroe (who was not altogether firm), and young John Marshall—were for a repeal of the laws contravening the treaty. R. H. Lee, who thought both nations to blame, wrote in 1785 that it was the peculiar duty of a republic to square its conduct with the principles of virtue. The chief influence in the opposite scale was that of Patrick Henry, but Madison believed that if Henry could be defeated on the issue of full religious freedom, he could be defeated on this. In the end, however, the view that the treaty was absolutely binding upon the States was beaten in both Virginia and New York, under circumstances which accentuated the check to federalist principles.

This rebuff to Congress came in both States during 1787. Hamilton, now thirty years old, was still fighting sturdily in New York for the principles he had laid down in 1784, and entered the Legislature which met in January with the determination to vindicate them. His measure to abrogate all laws conflicting with the treaty he supported by a careful speech. No other State, he argued, had so much to gain as New York from a strict observance of the treaty. The British retention of the western posts, by its injury to trade and in other ways, cost the inhabitants of the State £100,000 a year.[68] Some men were apprehensive that the bill would restore confiscated estates, and while he was sure it would not, he was willing, if they insisted, to add a provision guarding against any such effect. If New York, so much concerned in enforcing the treaty, failed to pass the general repeal asked by Congress, other States very little interested could point to her stubbornness as a reason for declining. Three years earlier, he had compared the course of the Americans in making a solemn national treaty and then evading it by State laws to the treachery of the Roman general who, having promised Antiochus to restore half his vessels, sawed them in two before their delivery, and of the Platæans, who, having promised the Thebans to give up their prisoners, killed them and restored them dead. He repeated again that the world had its eyes upon America, and looked to it for an exemplification of the spirit of liberty working in practical affairs; the habits of nations, like those of men, were formed in infancy and youth, and it was important to habituate the American States to

---

[68] New York was so eager in 1783 to lay hands upon these posts that it instructed Hamilton, then in Congress, that it wished them garrisoned by New York troops. Hamilton, believing that Continental troops should be used, disregarded these instructions; Hamilton, "Hist. Rep.," II, 554 ff.

rectitude and tolerance. These arguments swayed the House, but the bill died in the upper chamber.

In Virginia an effort to repeal the anti-debt laws violating the treaty was made in the legislative session of the winter of 1784-85, and failed only, as has been noted, by the fact that the sudden freezing of the James prevented the return of certain legislators and the fulfillment of all legal forms before adjournment.[69] At the session of 1785-86 another effort at repeal was beaten by direct and bitter opposition. During the debates, Madison tells us, no pains were spared to abuse the treaty by attacks upon Congress, the New England States, and John Adams and its other negotiators. At the autumn meeting of the Legislature in 1787 George Mason, ably seconded by George Nicholas, took up the request of Congress regarding it. On November 17 the committee of the whole resolved that all laws repugnant to it ought to be repealed, but that the operation of the repeal should be suspended until the executive was informed by Congress that the other States of the Union had passed similar acts of compliance. Patrick Henry, in his dissatisfaction proposed that the annulment of the laws be suspended, not until all the other States had complied with the treaty, but until Great Britain did so. His amendment, and another which would have postponed the payment of debts to British subjects until they could be paid in a time and manner suited to "the exhausted situation of this Commonwealth," were happily defeated. The resolution was passed, and a committee brought in a bill which repealed every part of the statutes conflicting with the peace treaty.

It was unfortunate enough that this bill contained a clause keeping it ineffective until Congress should inform the Governor that all other States had made it possible for British creditors to recover their debts; but still further to emasculate it, Patrick Henry and his associates brought forward the same amendment that had failed, by a majority of 33, when the mere resolution was under consideration—the amendment that the law should not take effect until Eng-

---

[69] The subject had been discussed for a year. A member of Congress wrote to a Virginia legislator, December 10, 1783: "I am, myself, *principled against* refugees and British debts. I think the former will make wretched Republicans, and to the latter, in my opinion, all just title has been forfeited. But let us see what the faith of America as a nation, and her interests as a people, require, and leaving all prejudice against those people aside, act in conformity thereto. Our conduct, or rather the conduct of some very wild and unthinking people scattered throughout the United States, has hurt us much in the eyes of all Europe, where that article in favor of refugees is considered very humiliating to Great Britain, and such as our honor and interest call on us to explain and adhere to liberally." (Md. *Journal,* January 2, 1784.) See A. C. McLaughlin, "Western Posts and Br. Debts," Am. Hist. Assn. Reports, 1894.

land had restored the northwestern posts and the runaway slaves or their equivalent. Virginia legislatures were always mercurial bodies. From some cause, probably either an outburst of popular sentiment or an outburst of Henry's oratory, the Assembly suddenly changed front, and, passing the amendment by a majority of 49, virtually destroyed the law.[70]

V.　State Indifference to Congress

Congress had now failed to win from the States an acknowledgment of its power to make a valid treaty of peace, even as it had failed during the war to obtain from them the money and men sorely needed, and as it had failed since the war to wring from them a dependable revenue or the partial control of American commerce. Its humiliation was complete. It was plain that the only hope for a vigorous national government lay in a wholly new Constitution.

One indication of a declining respect for Congress, it must be noted, had lain in the steady diminution after the Revolution of the influence and worth of its personnel. This diminution had unfortunately begun to be marked soon after the adoption of the Articles of Confederation. The States in many instances found their ablest men reluctant to enter the membership of a body which had so little real power, while some deliberately elected mediocre men when they might with a little trouble have prevailed upon others to accept. As Hamilton noted, each State in order to promote its internal prosperity tried to place its best men in its own offices. When they had made their choice of delegates, the delegates often considered their private affairs more important than those of Congress, and devoted themselves so little to public business that Congress found it difficult to obtain a quorum. The Articles provided that no State could cast a vote unless represented by two or more delegates, and that on important questions the assent of nine States was required. Upon the impressive and momentous day when Washington resigned his commission and received the thanks of Congress (December 23, 1783), the ceremony was preceded by the passage of resolutions, proposed by Williamson of North Carolina and seconded by Jefferson, urging upon the Governors of six States that the safety and credit of the Union required the immediate attendance of their dele-

---

[70] Journals, 50 ff.; Henry, "Henry," II, 325-26; Beveridge, "Marshall," I, Ch. 6.

gates. A few months later, on the anniversary of Lexington, Congress adopted a long formal complaint that several States were represented by two delegates only. Under these circumstances, almost complete unanimity was required in conducting the more important transactions. Were all the States represented by two men each, five of the twenty-six delegates might tie an equal number of State votes, and defeat any important measure. The case was much worse when several States were represented by nobody. "Of eleven States now on the floor of Congress, nine being represented by only two members from each, it is in the power of three out of the twenty-five, making one-eighth of the whole, to negative such a measure."

Complaints continued to emanate from Congress. On August 7, 1785, it was pointed out that many States were still either unrepresented, or represented by only two men, and it was voted that once a month the Secretary should send the Legislatures a list of the States represented and unrepresented, and of the members from each. But this prodding was fruitless. Between October, 1785, and the following April, there were only three days when nine States were on the floor. Rufus King, saying that it was a farce to continue waiting, proposed an ultimatum—that Congress should resolve upon adjournment *sine die* if the situation did not mend within a given time.[71]

From the first Monday in November, 1784, to July 29, 1785, the attendance in Congress is noted in the journal 169 times. The best-represented States in this period were Virginia (delegates present 162 times), Massachusetts (152), and New York and South Carolina (146 each). Five States were represented on from 30 (Delaware) to 115 (Maryland) occasions each. On only six occasions were as many as twelve States represented at once, while on forty occasions there were less than nine on the floor. As King said, the States cared too little about the Union to maintain their delegations, and men from whom a genuine interest might have been expected cared little more. Oliver Ellsworth, public-spirited and conscientious, was a delegate for six years, but he went to Philadelphia only five times in all, and his total service in Congress aggregated only about eighteen months. In 1786 Congress debated whether a member had the right to withdraw without permission from Congress or his State. Such a withdrawal often meant that a State quite dropped out of the list of those voting. Yet New York, Virginia, and Maryland affirmed the

[71] King, "Life and Corr.," I, 133-34.

absolute right of withdrawal, and four other States—New Hampshire, Rhode Island, Connecticut, and Georgia—were divided. Eleven men voted that members had the right, and eighteen that they had not.[72]

The early Congresses included the best talent of the nation that was not actively busied in the field, in the diplomatic service, or in the Governors' chairs. But the later Congresses were Congresses of small men. It is sufficient to compare the Congress of 1774-75 with that which we find sitting in 1782, and the latter with the Congress of 1786. The States sent to the first a galaxy which included the two Adamses, Sherman and Deane, Jay and Duane, Galloway, Cæsar Rodney, McKean, Samuel Chase, Washington, Patrick Henry, R. H. Lee, and the two Rutledges. In the Congress sitting in 1782 there was only a handful of delegates of such eminence—Hamilton, Charles Carroll, Madison, Lee, McKean, Duane, and Rutledge.[73] The remainder were men of merely local reputation—men like Gilman and Livermore of New Hampshire, Wolcott and Huntington of Connecticut, l'Hommedieu of New York, Clymer of Pennsylvania, Hanson of Maryland, Blount and Nash of North Carolina, and Telfair and Few of Georgia. Four years later a further decline was seen. The choice of such men reflected more than carelessness in the State Legislatures—it reflected the progress in them of a spirit of unwillingness to make Congress a body of great collective wisdom and energy. Haring of New York, for example, Manning of Rhode Island, and Pettit of Pennsylvania were well known to be enemies to a strong central government.[74]

Not merely by withholding consent to the proposals of Congress, and refusing to let it exert general powers, did the States show their want of national spirit. They showed it also by the vigor and self-confidence with which they pursued measures of their own infringing on the proper field of Congress. Madison's rhetorical questions in the Constitutional Convention showed how deeply this hurt men like himself. "Has not Georgia, in direct violation of the Constitution, made war with the Indians and concluded treaties? Have not Virginia and Maryland entered into a partial compact? Have not Penn-

[72] N. C. State Records, XVII, 497; Brown's "Ellsworth," 53-54.
[73] Hamilton in 1780 lamented the diffident, timid air shown by the Congress in its relations with the States, and its want of tact in dealing with the army; "Works," I, 227-28.
[74] Worthington C. Ford notes (Journals Cont. Cong. IV, 8) that "In civil matters the formation of State governments under Constitutions prepared the way [in 1776] for a decline in the energy and influence of the Continental Congress."

sylvania and New Jersey regulated the bounds of the Delaware? Has not the State of Massachusetts at this time a considerable body of troops in pay? Has not Congress been obliged to pass a conciliatory act, in support of a decision of their Federal Court, between Connecticut and Pennsylvania, instead of having the power of carrying into effect the judgment of their own court?"

For Georgia to make war and conclude treaties was nothing unusual. The Constitutions of a number of States gave their governments just these powers. When Congress sent commissioners to negotiate the treaty of Fort Stanwix with the Six Nations, many difficulties were deliberately thrown in their way by New York, and the agents had to exert much firmness and perseverance to overcome them. Congress was vested by the Articles with the power of regulating American relations with the Indians, but several States illegally insisted upon doing the same in their own fields; and so fixed did the practice become that one of Washington's first energetic acts as President was to call a halt upon Georgia's brazen violation of the Constitution in continuing it.[75]

Virginia, Maryland, South Carolina, and Pennsylvania borrowed or tried to borrow money abroad exactly as if they were sovereign nations; and after the war Maryland negotiated herself for the recovery of her stock in the Bank of England, instead of entrusting the negotiation to the American Minister, John Adams. Virginia's diplomatic activities became so extensive that the legislature provided for a clerk of foreign correspondence. Her legislature also ratified the peace treaty. When Patrick Henry was negotiating with Spain in 1778 for Spanish approval of the erection of a fort on the Virginia border, he promised from Virginia in return "the gratitude of this free and independent country, the trade in any or all its valuable productions, and the friendship of its warlike inhabitants."[76] Nine States, from Massachusetts on the north to South Carolina on the south, organized their own navies, and some States established their own systems of privateering. Several States fitted out their own armies, and used them for State purposes. In the instance of George Rogers Clark, Virginia waged a campaign to enlarge her own bounds

---

[75] R. H. Lee, "Letters," II, 297-99. As an example of the uncertainty of Congress as to its own powers, see Sparks, "Letters to Washington," IV, 68-69.

[76] "Another consequence of this disordered state of things was the negotiation of commercial leagues, growing out of geographical causes, between the States of New Jersey and Pennsylvania, and of Maryland and Virginia, in direct contravention of the sixth article of the Confederation." Hamilton, "Hist. Rep.," III, 148.

without the knowledge of Congress; and she paid all the immediate expenses of the expedition herself, though she later insisted upon repayment by Congress. The ill-starred descent of the Massachusetts army in 1779 upon the Penobscot forts was followed by a long wrangle before Congress, which had not authorized it, would pay the bills. Much of the war in the South, in the early part of the Revolution, was waged without the knowledge or direction of Congress.[77]

In all, the view that the United States in Congress assembled constituted a nation, vested with all the attributes of sovereignty, had much less currency from 1776 to 1787 than might be inferred from the writings of statesmen like Hamilton, Madison, and Washington. The view was very general that Congress was simply a meeting of the ambassadors of thirteen independent and sovereign, but leagued, nations. Congress, said Randolph, was "a mere diplomatic body . . . always obsequious to the views of the States"; it is, said Adams, "not a legislative assembly, nor a representative assembly, but only a diplomatic assembly." The New York merchants, petitioning for the impost plan, and praising Congress as the chain and soul of the nation, nevertheless asserted: "Our confederacy is formed of thirteen independent republics. . . ."[78]

When individual delegates had any quarrel with Congress as a body, they always fell back upon their diplomatic privileges, insisting that they were responsible only to their own States. In April, 1778, Dr. Thomas Burke expressed himself with heat upon some question, and then broke the quorum of Congress by unceremoniously withdrawing. On being sent for, he spoke so violently that Congress declared him in contempt of its dignity. Burke thereupon asserted that Congress was not the judge of his conduct, but North Carolina, and he submitted the case to North Carolina, whose Legislature of course sustained him.[79] The Continental government was regarded as a "foreign" government by some State Rights supporters, and the epithet was actually applied to it in the Massachusetts Legislature.[80] This view so impressed itself upon the French that in 1781, some months before Yorktown, it was suggested at the French court that the thirteen States should send thirteen agents or em-

[77] Van Tyne, *Amer. Hist. Review,* XII, 539-41.
[78] N. Y. *Packet,* March 7, 1785. Even the government of Connecticut spoke of that State as a "republic."
[79] N. C. State Records, XIII, Introduction.
[80] Austin, "Gerry," I, 407-15; 495-99.

bassies to attend the congress at Vienna, in order to make peace with Great Britain. Vergennes was hastily informed that this would be a violation of the Articles, and that Congress would not consent to have America regarded as a baker's dozen of nations.[81]

In 1785 Congress seemed to Washington a nugatory body, the Confederation little more than a shadow without substance, and the nation steadily descending from its once high vantage point "into the vale of confusion and darkness." During this and the following year many men within and outside Congress still cherished the hope that by amendments to the Articles the body might be given a sufficient dignity and authority. Governor Bowdoin, in his message to the Massachusetts Legislature in 1785, proposed a Continental convention—of which there had been much talk in 1784—to draw up a compact vesting in Congress "All the powers necessary to preserve the Union, to manage the general concerns of it, and promote its common interest"; the States to confirm the compact. In response, the Legislature urged Congress to call a convention of all the States, "to revise the Confederation, and report to Congress how far it may be necessary, in their opinion, to alter or enlarge the same, in order to secure and perpetuate the primary objects of the Union." Bowdoin was requested to send a letter on this subject, together with a copy of a circular to all the States, to Congress. However, the three Massachusetts delegates, Gerry, Holton, and King, audaciously withheld the letter and circular from Congress, submitting a number of objections to Bowdoin. Even admitting the necessity of vesting more power in Congress, they asked, should the powers not be temporary, would it be wise to make amendments in any fashion not prescribed by the Confederation, and, if a convention were called, ought it not to be restricted to certain definite ends? They feared, they added, that a convention would produce "an exertion of the friends of aristocracy" for an aristocratic government.[82]

This is not the place to rehearse the familiar story of the calling of the Federal Convention, and its triumphant execution of a momentous task. The basic question facing this Convention was the question of how the new Federal Government should give effect to its authority in the fields assigned to it. Should it operate through the

[81] Adams, "Works," VII, 450-52.
[82] Hamilton, "Hist. Rep.," III, 135ff.

State governments, trying to impel them to carry out its will?—the principle upon which some other modern confederacies have rested. Or should it act upon men, not States, and legislate directly for its own citizens? The Convention was too wise to hesitate long for an answer. The advocates of a coercive clause were quickly overthrown. Madison in a letter to Jefferson following the adjournment of the Convention explained its action with his characteristic succinctness. "It was generally agreed," he said, "that the objects of the Union could not be secured by any system founded on the principle of a confederation of sovereign States. A *voluntary* observance of the Federal law by all the members could never be hoped for. A *compulsive* one could evidently never be reduced to practice, and if it could, involved equal calamities to the innocent and the guilty, the necessity of a military force, both obnoxious and dangerous, and, in general, a scene resembling much more a civil war than the administration of a regular government. Hence was embraced the alternative of a government which, instead of operating on the States, should operate without their intervention on the individuals composing them; and hence the change in the principle and proportion of representation." [83]

Had the Convention made the error of writing into the Constitution the principle of "compulsive observance" of the Federal will by the States, the nation would quickly have faced that civil strife of which Madison spoke. Instead, the basic assumption was made that while there were two sovereignties, no State enactment was for a moment valid if it conflicted with the Federal Constitution or the Federal statutes passed in accordance with the Constitution. Federal laws were to be enforceable throughout the whole land, peaceably but firmly and perfectly, by the judicial machinery of the whole land. State laws, if unconstitutional, were to be nullified not by Federal threats against the State capitals, not by the march of troops, but by the simple action of the State and Federal judges, sitting quietly on their benches, in ignoring them.

Not only the nation, but the States, took a new birth from the ratification of the Federal Constitution. They were instantly and utterly cut off from a whole field of activities in which they had no proper function, and compelled to concentrate their energies upon

[83] "Letters," Ed., 1865, I, 344. See A. C. McLaughlin, "Confederation and Constitution," Ch. 15.

true State questions. We have shown that their record with regard to purely domestic problems was upon the whole good, not bad. They had made fairly consistent progress in constitutional, financial, humanitarian, and administrative paths, and they could begin the new era with justified self-confidence and hope.

CHAPTER FOURTEEN

FACING WESTWARD: CONCLUSION

In less than a generation, 1760-1790, the compact belt of settlement which flanked the Atlantic coast approximately doubled in area. At the beginning of this period there were perhaps 1,500,000 people in the colonies, and at its close the United States held almost 4,000,-000. The former date found the white population confined to the southeastern parts of New York and Pennsylvania, and about half of the present area of North Carolina and Virginia; in North Carolina it stretched a narrow finger of settlement up the Wateree only as far as Camden, and in Georgia another finger up the Savannah as far as Augusta. Considerable portions of even Massachusetts, New Jersey, and Maryland remained to be settled. From Albany, from Lancaster, and from Hillsborough in North Carolina the traveler might strike west and plunge immediately into the primeval forest, wholly untouched by man. But despite the interruption of two wars, immigration, the fecundity of the people, and the irresistible call of the west wrought their changes with amazing rapidity. By 1790 the tide of population had covered all of what is now Virginia, the two Carolinas, New York southeast of Fort Stanwix, and the lower half of Pennsylvania, where it was spilling over into Ohio. Outposts of settlement had been thrown forward into central Tennessee, and in Kentucky an irregular patch of colonization was fast covering the middle part of the State.[1]

Even by 1791 the population of what we may strictly call the West remained small, but it was rapidly increasing. Of the 4,000,000 Americans, not more than 150,000 dwelt beyond the watershed of the Alleghenies.[2] What is now Tennessee then contained at the utmost 60,000 people; a few of them in the Mero or Nashville

[1] The first census gave the United States 3,929,000 people. Consult W. S. Rossiter, "A Century of Population Growth in the United States." There is an excellent map in E. B. Greene's "The Foundations of American Nationality," 530, showing population in 1790.

[2] Channing, III, 528, says 125,000 at the utmost in 1790; but this may represent too small an allowance for the Tennessee country. An imperfect return by the Governor in 1791, with five districts missing, gave 35,691 people in Tennessee; see Winterbotham's "United States," III, 234.

district, but most of them in the east, adjoining the Carolina line. The Kentucky country, then part of Virginia, had 73,677 people, of whom there were 200 in the hamlet of Louisville and 844 in Lexington. The settlement of Ohio did not begin in earnest until 1788, when Marietta and Cincinnati were founded. However, the western reaches were filling up during Washington's first administra- tion at an accelerating pace. The settlers in Kentucky doubled in numbers in a half dozen years following 1784. By every trail and pass new families were coming. The four or five thousand people in a thin fringe along the north bank of the Ohio were the advance corps of an army that within a few years was to move north till the whole State was sown with farms and towns.

I. SETTLEMENT OF THE WEST

The process of planning new commonwealths in the West had begun long before the Revolution. Even after the royal proclamation of 1763 forbidding settlement beyond the Appalachian watershed, the British government was not hostile to a well-regulated colonization of new lands. Shelburne, the author of the proclamation, knew that the West was certain to be inundated by white emigrants, and took the side of other intelligent British statesmen who wanted settlement encouraged as fast as Indian titles could be purchased and the good will of the red men secured.[3] Unfortunately, there was another school of British politicians—the Rockingham Ministry of 1765 was dominated by it—which wished the trans-Allegheny region set apart as a permanent Indian reservation, from which white land-hunters should be excluded. Its policy was not adopted, but it was able to prevent the actual application of the opposite plan. Land speculation was a fever of the day, in which most active Americans desired to participate. Many schemes for the establishment of a fourteenth Colony were broached before 1776, some American, some Anglo-American, but none reached fruition.[4]

[3] For the report on western affairs upon which Shelburne founded his recommenda-
tion for this proclamation, see Shortt and Doughty, "Constitutional Documents of
Canada," 97. A discussion of the proclamation and the policy will be found in C. W.
Alvord, "The Mississippi Valley in British Politics," I, 199 ff. This work, with
C. W. Alvord and C. E. Carter's "The Critical Period, 1763-65," and their "The
New Régime, 1765-67," offers materials for a full understanding of the West in
British hands.
[4] For Franklin's interest in settling the West by British colonists, urged as early as
1754, see Works, Smyth Edition, III, 358. The beginnings of Anglo-American discus-
sion of the subject are treated in G. H. Alden, "New Governments West of the
Alleghenies Before 1780."

A number of wealthy and influential Virginians immediately after the Seven Years' War planned a colony occupying a tract of ten and a half million acres bordering the Mississippi in what is now Illinois, Kentucky, and Tennessee, and in 1763 petitioned the Crown for a grant. Washington and five of the Lees were included.[5] But the Crown, which did not want to strengthen Virginia's claim to a region that it regarded as imperial territory, refused. Later, General Phineas Lyman of Connecticut and certain military associates had a plan for a series of colonies along the Mississippi.[6] Still more important was the scheme for a colony in the Illinois country with which George Croghan's name is identified.[7] The ultimate participants included Sir William Johnson, Governor William Franklin, Benjamin Franklin, Joseph Galloway, and men of prominence in the Middle Colonies. Shelburne discussed the project with Benjamin Franklin, and drafted a famous memorandum in which he proposed the establishment of colonies at Detroit, in the Illinois country, and on the lower Mississippi. But a new Ministry came into power in 1768, Lord Hillsborough began his disastrous administration of the Provinces, and these sensible plans perished forthwith.[8] Still another proposal which progressed almost to success was that for the Vandalia Colony, comprising most of what is now West Virginia and a part of Kentucky, the chief promoter of which was Samuel Wharton of Philadelphia. The Board of Trade and Plantations went so far in 1773 as to approve the grant asked for, and had it not been for the Revolution, the formal transfer might soon have followed.[9]

The actual creation of the Vandalia Colony would have produced a clash between Virginia and the Crown, for the Virginians on the basis of their Charter claimed all this region. The land speculations of Governor Dunmore and other influential men of the Province, with the uncontrollable push of Virginia settlers into the west, at this juncture brought on Lord Dunmore's War with the Indians.[10] The Virginia troops, mustered the summer of 1774 under the Gov-

[5] The petition and other documents are printed in Alvord and Carter, "The Critical Period," 19 ff.
[6] Alvord and Carter, "The New Régime," 260 ff.
[7] See A. T. Votwiler's "George Croghan and the Westward Movement, 1741-1782," in *Pa. Mag. of Hist. and Biog.*, 1922.
[8] Documents illustrating Hillsborough's policy are printed in N. Y. Col. Docs., VIII, 19 ff.
[9] F. J. Turner, "Western State Making in the Revolutionary Era," *Amer. Hist. Review*, I, 70.
[10] Dunmore's War is treated in Roosevelt's "Winning of the West," I, ch. 8; Archibald Henderson's "Conquest of the Old Southwest," 196 ff.; and R. G. Thwaites and L. P. Kellogg, "Documentary History of Dunmore's War."

ernor and Andrew Lewis, really fought their campaign in defiance
of imperial regulations, and in defence of Virginia's title to the
western country; and their victory over the savages at the battle of
the Great Kanawha opened up the tracts south of the Ohio to the
migration of the Virginians and Pennsylvanians.   It also made
possible a new and quite irregular attempt to found a colony in
Kentucky.   Ten years earlier Daniel Boone, a North Carolina
frontiersman, had undertaken an exploring expedition into Kentucky in behalf of a group formed by Richard Henderson, a scion
of an aristocratic Virginia family which had come to North Carolina
for its rich and cheap lands.   In the months of peace following
Lord Dunmore's War, Judge Henderson established the Transylvania Company, and for the sum of £10,000 sterling in money and
goods, bought from the Cherokees the region bounded by the Ohio,
Kentucky, and Cumberland Rivers.   He intended to form a proprietary Colony under the crown there, and from the four distinct
settlements which the region contained he called together a convention to draft a compact with the proprietors.   But the royal
governors of Virginia and North Carolina issued proclamations
denouncing his enterprise, and when the Virginians took their
government into their own hands, they promptly annulled Henderson's title.   The plan for Transylvania died, and when the settlers
sent delegates to the Virginia Provincial Convention, the county of
Kentucky was born in its place.[11]

Meanwhile, the region later called Tennessee received its first
large body of settlers during the sixties.   Defying the royal proclamation, late in the decade many Virginia and North Carolina families pushed into the fertile valley of the Holston River, where they
could squat upon land which did not cost even entry fees.   The
rebellion of the Regulators and their defeat at the Alamance sent a
fresh tide across the mountains.   James Robertson led a vanguard
of 16 families to the Watauga Valley in 1771, and literally thousands
followed; we are told that one church congregation in the Regulators' district was reduced from 606 to 14 members.   A convention
of the Watauga settlers was held, and drew up articles of association
which led Governor Dunmore to declare that they had "to all intents
and purposes, erected themselves into, though an inconsiderable,
yet a separate state."   Governor Martin of North Carolina called

[11] Henderson, "Conquest of the Old Southwest," ch. 15; G. W. Ranch's "Boones-
borough" in the Filson Club Publications.

upon them to return immediately, but they ignored him and adopted the laws of Virginia as their own. Thus affairs stood when the Revolution broke out.[12]

The close of the Revolution saw the title to the Northwest, thanks principally to the expedition of George Rogers Clark, placed in American hands. It saw also the safety of the settlers in the Kentucky and Tennessee country fairly assured, for the time being, by successful campaigns undertaken against the Cherokees in 1776 and 1781, and the Chickamaugas in 1779.[13] The idea of regional autonomy had been greatly strengthened by the Revolution. It had been a rebellion against a distant authority in behalf of a greater self-government. At the very beginning of the war the inhabitants of the region about the headwaters of the Ohio, including the site of Pittsburgh, had petitioned Congress asking that it be made independent as Westsylvania, "the fourteenth Province of the American Confederacy." Pennsylvania and Virginia were quarreling over this district, but the people wanted to be governed neither from Philadelphia nor Williamsburg.[14] Congress naturally refused to offend either State by acting. Now, immediately after the peace with England, vigorous movements for new States developed in both the Kentucky and Tennessee country.

The Watauga and Holston settlers had defied the North Carolina Government when it was in royal hands, and now they defied it in American hands. In a convention held in August, 1784, they formed an association, and the following December adopted a temporary Constitution and gave their commonwealth the name of Frankland, later changed to Franklin. John Sevier was chosen Governor, and when next spring the North Carolina authorities inquired into the secession of these four western counties, he wrote a defiant letter stating that the Tennesseeans had become convinced that they were being altogether disregarded by North Carolina, and were acting from "necessity and self-preservation" in setting up a sovereign State. This was not true, for the North Carolina legislature had just made the four western counties into the District of Washington,

---

[12] See Henderson, *op. cit.*, ch. 13; Martin's proclamation is in the N. C. Col. Recs., IX, 825; for a treatment of the Watauga Association, see J. W. Caldwell, "Const. Hist. of Tennessee."

[13] Channing, III, 361 note, refuses to recognize Clark's conquest as a decisive factor in Great Britain's determination to relinquish the Northwest. For a description of the Indian tribes south of the Ohio, see *Tenn. Hist. Magazine*, I, 21 ff.

[14] The Westsylvania Memorial is in Cummins, "Hist. of Washington County, Pa.," 187.

with a judiciary and a brigadier-general to organize their defense. Nevertheless, the settlers did suffer manifold difficulties in obtaining needed laws, justice on appeal, prompt action in the face of Indian threats, and fair consideration of economic question. Much farther to the west the Nashville region had received its first settlers in 1780, a swarm from the parent hive on the Watauga, who under the leadership of James Robertson beat back the savages and planted one hamlet after another. They were so completely unprotected by North Carolina or the United States, and so hard hit by the closing of the Mississippi, that in 1788 they made overtures to the Spanish authorities for an alliance or annexation. For a time Sevier and his Franklin followers maintained their position. A Constitution, based on North Carolina's, was adopted the fall of 1785. But the infant "State" was weakened by internal dissensions, and by the combined firmness and moderation of the North Carolina authorities. Governors Caswell and Joseph Martin insisted upon complete submission to the laws of North Carolina, and by the end of 1787 the secessionist movement was dead.[15]

Greater strength was manifested by the struggle for separation occurring at the same time in the Kentucky country immediately to the north. Here too the settlers found the capital at Richmond too far distant, and believed their interests were neglected. As early as May, 1780, nearly 700 inhabitants signed a memorial to Congress asking it to form them into a separate State. But the procedure of the majority was as law-abiding and moderate as that of the Tennesseans was arbitrary and illegal. In 1784, under the menace of an Indian attack, a convention was held at Danville to consider measures for repulsing it, and found that no man in Kentucky was empowered to mobilize the militia for an immediate offensive. Chafing under this and other hardships, the settlers determined to ask Virginia to grant them the right to organize as a new State.[16] Another convention at the close of the year, to which delegates were elected by the military companies, adopted an address to the Kentuckians which gave seven reasons for separation. The people had no agency with authority to embody the militia, and none able to execute the laws; they were ignorant of many Virginia statutes until long after their passage; they could not prosecute suits in the Court of

---

[15] G. H. Alden, "The State of Franklin," *Amer. Hist. Review,* VIII.
[16] R. M. McElroy, "Kentucky in the Nation's History," gives the history of the movement for separation.

Appeals at Richmond without great loss; the cost of participation in the distant Virginia government was excessive; and their commercial interests could never correspond with Virginia's. A third convention in August, 1785, sent an address to the Virginia Assembly. For their part, the Virginians were by no means hostile. Early in 1786 they responded with an act requesting the Kentuckians to hold still another meeting to decide whether they wanted Statehood upon certain generally fair conditions, including the assumption of part of Virginia's debt.

Then followed a series of confused events in Kentucky. A new Indian war broke out, changes were asked in the conditions laid down by Virginia, and other factors conspired to cause a wearisome delay. Virginia was unwilling to consent to the separation of Kentucky until Congress had agreed to admit her as a new State. But as the delay dragged on, a considerable party of Kentuckians, seeing how weak the Confederation was and angered by the evidence that it was ready to surrender the navigation of the lower Mississippi, began actively to oppose entrance into the Union. Led by General James Wilkinson, an unprincipled settler in the region, they demanded immediate severance from Virginia, an independent government, a treaty with Spain for the navigation of the Mississippi, and a reservation of the question of a connection with the United States to the future. While most of the settlers were too loyal to enter Wilkinson's plot, the majority regarded it with some indulgence as a means of bringing pressure to bear upon Congress.[17] A convention which met in September, 1787, petitioned Congress for admission to the United States, but the old national government refused to act, handing the question over to the new Federal Congress. It was hence not until 1792 that Kentucky finally became the fifteenth State, adopting her Constitution in April and entering the Union in June.

The year 1787, in which the Federal Constitution was drafted, was also the year in which the destinies of the West received their most definite shaping. Congress not only adopted its ordinance for the government and future of the Northwest Territory, but granted the Ohio Company, which had been founded by General Rufus Putnam, the Rev. Manasseh Cutler, Winthrop Sargent, and other New Englanders, the right to purchase 1,500,000 acres for a million

[17] There was also a Spanish conspiracy in Tennessee; the subject is treated in the *Tenn. Hist. Mag.* for December, 1917.

dollars.[18]   South of the Ohio, this year Kentucky was turning her back upon Wilkinson and the other unprincipled men who had been negotiating with Spanish agents, and was preparing to enter the Union.   Still farther south, this was the year in which the last embers of the secessionist movement in the Tennessee country were quenched by North Carolina.   South Carolina's cession of her western claims was made in 1787, and it was only a question of time till North Carolina followed her example.   When she finally did so, the creation of the Territory South of the Ohio followed in May, 1790, upon the same basis as the Northwest Territory, save that there was to be no exclusion of slavery.   The first governor sent to the Northwest Territory was General Arthur St. Clair, a man of high character but weak administrative capacity; the first governor of the Southwest was William Blount of North Carolina, a competent administrator but a man of defective character.

All the old States with large unoccupied areas made haste, while the Revolutionary War was still raging, to encourage their settlement.   Georgia established a land office for that purpose in June and North Carolina in November, 1777; Virginia in May, 1779; and Pennsylvania in April, 1781.[19]   The land of these commonwealths could almost be had for the asking.   Georgia by her first law (1777) gave every head of a family 200 acres, with 50 more for every member of his family and for every slave up to ten in number.   A settler with a household of five, and ten slaves was thus entitled to 950 acres free.   This legislation was followed in 1783 by a less generous enactment, but it endured only two years.   Then the land-hungry emigrants, pouring westward into the rich new counties of Washington, Franklin, and Greene to raise corn, wheat, and tobacco, were delighted by a new law which again allowed every head of a family 200 acres and every other member 50, up to a grand total of 1000, without charge.   Those whose households were small might buy land at three shillings an acre, in the depreciated currency of the time, to make up the maximum acreage.   This system of distribution gave every encouragement to the spread of the plantation, manned by blacks.   The Piedmont or upland country, shut off from the

[18] W. P. and J. P. Cutler, "Life of Manasseh Cutler," I; J. A. Barrett, "Evolution of the Ordinance of 1787" in Univ. of Nebraska Papers; B. A. Hinsdale, "The Old Northwest."
[19] Georgia's land laws are in Marbury and Crawford's Statutes, 316 ff.; Pennsylvania's are in the collection of laws by A. J. Dallas, I, 891 ff., II, 201 ff., etc.; Virginia's in Hening, X, 35-65; North Carolina's in State Records, XXIV, 43-48, etc. (consult index).

lowlands by the dreary pine barren country, had heretofore contained comparatively few slaves, either in Georgia or South Carolina; but the ease with which large holdings were obtained was soon to conspire with the growth of cotton culture to foster slavery.

North Carolina was almost equally generous. Any man might have 640 acres if his survey was bounded in any part by vacant lands, and 1000 acres where it fell within lands already preëmpted —that is, where he did not get first choice from an attractive stretch. For this he was to pay only about sixpence an acre in depreciated currency, together with the fees; though if his allotment happened to exceed 640 acres for himself and 100 acres for every member of his family, the charge for the excess area was greater. Virginia's act of 1779 gave every family on the western waters 400 acres free, while if more was wanted, it had a preëmption right to 1000 acres adjoining, for which the charge was only two cents an acre. Anyone, moreover, could go to the land office, and buy unlimited tracts at eight shillings an acre in depreciated money. Great land companies were formed in Europe and America, and huge Virginia stretches were bought up by speculators to be held for a future profit. The poor homeseeker, thus shut out of some of the best farming country, had to purchase at an advance, become a renter, or remove farther west. In Pennsylvania the old proprietary holdings were being sold in 1784 at two shillings an acre, and the land beyond the Alleghenies at eight pence.

Lands, moreover, were given away in enormous quantities as bounties for Revolutionary service.[20] North Carolina by an act of 1780 offered each volunteer 200 acres, and the following year increased the amount to 640 acres. Georgia's record shows how many different forms these compensations in land might take. Her soldiers of the Continental Line received "continental certificates" good for farms; men who had enrolled for emergency service were given "minute men certificates"; men who, after being driven from their homes, served as soldiers, were allowed "refugee certificates"; those who had merely remained in the State, maintaining their American allegiance, when others had fled, were entitled to "citizens' certificates" for 250 acres apiece; and there were "marine certificates"

---

[20] Military grants by the State are comprehensively treated in M. N. Oldfield's "Federal Land Grants to the States," Univ. of Minnesota Studies, No. 2, ch. 4. North Carolina's bounty laws are in the State Records, XXIV, 339, 42. Virginia gave privates 300 acres and officers more, up to 15,000 acres for major generals; Hening, X, 331, 375. Pennsylvania gave privates 200 acres, and major-generals 2,000; Laws of Commonwealth of Pa., II, 89 ff., 272 ff.

for men in the State's naval force.[21] We have seen how in Pennsylvania the greed of speculators who bought up the land certificates of needy soldiers affected the course of politics and the administration of the State finances.

All the settlers were attracted by the same reward, fertile lands, easily cleared, costing little or nothing; but what we may call the forces of impulsion behind them were varied. Many were Europeans fleeing from economic or governmental injustice; many were veterans left uprooted by the war. Some were tenant farmers of the East, or overseers of Tidewater plantations, tired of being landless. A number of Virginia farmers moved west to escape the institution of slavery, and gave thanks when they reached the free soil of Ohio, while on the other hand, many Southerners and even some New Englanders emigrated to buy large areas and stock them with slaves. The canny Yankee would sell out at home, stop in Maryland to purchase negroes, and settle on a plantation in Kentucky or Tennessee. There rapidly grew up in Kentucky the same distinct cleavage between the slaveholders of the Bluegrass country and the hill farmers which existed in Virginia between the Tidewater planters and mountain settlers. But whatever the impelling motive, the stream that poured west down the Ohio, along the Wilderness Road through the Cumberland Gap, and down the Holston and Tennessee Rivers, swelled with only occasional checks from the Indian menace.

The rapid development of a fringe of new commonwealths had an unmistakable influence upon national polity. The early efforts at western State-making all tended to strengthen the central government and the feeling of nationalism. The settlers of the would-be States of Westsylvania and Franklin, in appealing to Congress for recognition, urged it to assume full control over the western lands. One element in Kentucky turned its eyes for a time toward New Orleans, but only for a time, while the people of what is now West Virginia consistently desired a stronger national authority as their best protection. Drawn from every part of the Confederacy, the western settlers were naturally inclined to be more loyal to the nation than to the locality; while the fact that the older States could regard the West as a common possession increased their sense of unity.

[21] Stevens's "Georgia," Vol. II, Book V, ch. 2.

But the influence of western development upon the government and institutions of the States as such was equally pronounced. Two characteristics plainly stamped the nascent commonwealths beyond the Appalachians, democracy and radicalism.[22] Democracy suggested many—not all—articles of the Ordinance of 1787: the interdiction of slavery; the provision for full religious freedom; the clear and workable provision for the descent of property, by which the widow of a man who died intestate was to have one-third his property and the children to share the rest equally; and the requirement that education should forever be encouraged. As for the radicalism, it was of the type which has usually marked our frontier communities. It was expressed in the compact between Judge Henderson and the settlers of Transylvania in 1774, under which the self-government of the people was limited only by the Proprietors' veto-power. It appeared in the Constitution adopted by the "State of Franklin," granting a unicameral legislature comprehensive powers. We meet it again in the association drawn up by the settlers of the Nashville region in 1780—the Cumberland compact—which was closely modeled upon the earlier compact of the Watauga settlers. It vested the administration in a committee or court of twelve Triers or Judges, to be elected in the different hamlets by the adult freemen, and to be subject to recall. Looking backward, this rough-and-ready government somewhat resembled the old English court-let; looking forward, it had its resemblance to the modern commission government.

Democracy and radicalism appeared saliently in the government of the frontier commonwealth of Vermont. One of the best features of the Constitution which the Vermonters adopted in 1777 was its provision that any adult freeman might vote or hold office whether he had a pennyworth of property or not, and regardless of his religious tenets. One section of the bill of rights has enabled Vermont to boast that she was the first State to prohibit slavery by constitutional provision. In its main outlines the government followed that of Pennsylvania, for Dr. Thomas Young, of Philadelphia, was one of the principal advisers of the little commonwealth. It comprehended a unicameral legislature, an executive of fourteen heads —Governor, Lieutenant-Governor, and twelve councilors—and a Council of Censors. Happily for Vermont, where the population was homogeneous and party animosities were mild, this faulty frame-

[22] Cf. F. J. Turner, "Significance of the Frontier in American History," Rept. Amer. Hist. Assn., 1893, 199 ff.

work served well enough. The Council of Censors proved an effective body in 1786, when it met and proposed changes in the Constitution which a convention duly accepted, and which greatly improved the instrument. Its form was made clearer, the functions of the three departments were more precisely defined, and the Governor and Council were given not only a qualified veto, but the power to propose amendments to bills.[23]

But while the spirit of the frontier was thus radically democratic, the new West was not destined to produce governments lacking in balance or vigor. For this fact we must in large part thank the national Congress. It instituted territorial governments in both the Northwest and Southwest which were highly centralized and authoritative. Its reasons for doing this, when most of the thirteen original States had made their executives weak and their legislatures unwisely strong, were three in number. The country to be governed, in the first place, was wild and subject to peril from the Indians or irresponsible adventurers; it was necessary to place ample authority in the hands of an agency always alert and ready to act. Again, the impotence and confusion of several State governments on the coast had shown the error of the old policy. But the greatest reason was that the western country was a national domain, in which the supervision and policy of the Federal Government must always be supreme; and the one satisfactory way of exercising national control was through a Federally-appointed Governor of great powers. This Governor appointed all local officers, laid out townships and counties, enforced the laws, commanded the militia, and at the beginning was authorized, together with three Federally-appointed judges, to adopt any laws of the older States, subject to disapproval by Congress. The new States of the West thus learned in their infancy the value of an energetic and powerful executive department, while it may have had a certain value to the older States as an example.[24]

II. GENERAL CONCLUSION

Historians have sometimes written as if, except for a single fundamental consideration, it were a misfortune that the American nation

[23] The records of the Governor and Council of Vermont have been published by the State in eight volumes; L. H. Meader's monograph on "The Council of Censors" covers Vermont's as well as Pennsylvania's experience.
[24] Cf. D. G. McCarty, "Territorial Governors of the Old Northwest," ch. 4. Some provisions of the Northwest Ordinance reflected the political views of fairly conservative easterners; e.g., the property qualifications and the restraints on interference with contracts.

began its career rather as a congeries of thirteen states than as a single unitary state. The colonies plunged into the war in a wavering file, Georgia and New York standing irresolute long after Massachusetts was actually at arms. They would not agree upon a national army of effective character when it might have shortened the war by years. Later they would not consent to a national treasury, a national tariff, or a national foreign policy. At times, some of them struck at their neighbors with unconcealed malevolence; again, some were so wretchedly misgoverned that they did themselves grave injury. To the mind which reflects upon the high abilities and achievements of the principal national leaders, from Washington down, and the contrasting weakness of the petty men who frequently swayed State affairs, the conclusion may seem plain. Had all the revolting colonists from north to south been governed from one center as effectively as all Virginians were governed from Richmond—had it been possible to do this, which assuredly it was not—the Americans might have had an army able to win without foreign help, a sound fiscal system, and a competent diplomacy. The one fundamental loss, these critics would say, would have been the sacrifice of the basis of our admirable federal system, with all that is implied in its nice division of local and national functions. But actually the States served an infinitely larger purpose in the years 1775-1789 than merely making possible our dual system of government.

In the main, this purpose was one of conservation—the States were the agencies through which most of the political and institutional experience gained by the colonists since the planting of British America was preserved. In smaller degree, it was constructive—the States applied new theories to their old practices, and the resulting experimentation was fruitful.

Their very unevenness in entering the Revolution points to a characteristic service in conservation. The process of revolution in its external phase ended when British authority was destroyed; in its internal phase, the reshaping of government and society, no one could say just what was its terminus. By dividing the movement into thirteen parts, each with its own center and character, the States prevented it from going too far in its internal phase. It is usual for revolutions to overshoot their mark—the Puritan Revolution, French Revolution, and Russian Revolution all did so. The moderate element in a revolution never shows sufficient energy to please the radical element; and because it is moderate, it does not have enough decision to hold the radicals back. In Pennsylvania the internal revolution was pushed too far. The moderates were thrown rudely to one side and the radicals set up a government that sometimes acted like a tyranny. But in the country as a whole that did not happen; the clash of conservative Whigs and extremist Whigs occurred on thirteen different stages, with no synchronization, and a consequent abatement of its heat, while the extremists were in general deprived of the support to be had in linking their dubious schemes of internal change with their sound determination to overthrow British rule.

The States preserved, as a heritage from the colonial period, some evils which were only slowly thrown off, such as the restrictions upon suffrage and the connection between church and government. A radical revolution of purely nationalist character might have destroyed them at once. But the States also preserved from the colonial governments a multitude of heritages whose loss would have been an irreparable calamity. The forms and principles of seventeenth century English democracy were there, and all the lessons learned in one hundred and fifty years of partial self-government on American soil, from 1609 to 1776. The revolting colonists took good care to throw away little that was worth saving. The new governments were an organic and uninterrupted growth from the old. When the Federal Constitution came to be written, it was based not merely on the debate and thought of a single summer, as Gladstone in his famous dictum suggested, nor merely on the thought and experience of the Revolutionary era, but on the accumulated results of five generations of political effort in the New World. The States had preserved those results in the only form possible.

The training in self-government which Americans had been striving to enlarge under the crown was suddenly made complete and intensive; and the fact that there were thirteen States to utilize this experience gave assurance that it would be multiform. Colonial practices had varied within rather narrow limits; State practices could differ within very wide limits. Governmental ideas of contrasting nature were now searchingly tested. The American people could observe the comparative happiness of New York under a well-balanced constitution and of North Carolina under one which lacked balance. They could watch the operation in Massachusetts of a government in which the two houses had equal powers, of one in Virginia in which the upper house had limited powers, and one in Pennsylvania in which there was but one house. They could see in Georgia the result of a total divorce between church and state, and in Connecticut the effect of a close connection. Experiments could be attempted, some fruitful, like Maryland's with the electoral college, some barren, like Pennsylvania's with the Censors. Sometimes a majority of the States proved that a given institution was valueless—no sensible man wanted an executive council in the Federal Government.

On the whole, the success of the American people with their State governments was sufficient to justify an increasing measure of self-confidence. They quickly shook off that fear of a despotism, that apprehension that a Cæsar or Cromwell might spring up, which is so hard for us to understand, but which to many was so real and terrible. The State governments would have been better had the Revolution been less a civil war. In the rigor of the struggle hundreds of thousands of loyalists were disfranchised or exiled, and they included many of the best educated and most judicious citizens. Yet in not more than three States does the balance lie on the debit side of the ledger. The dangers to property and order in 1785-86 aroused a wave of alarm which swept the movement for a strong national government to success. Yet State rights men like Clinton and Hancock might justly argue in 1788 that the danger had been only temporary, was exaggerated, and had already been surmounted. The States, as distinguished from the nation, were safe.

Even as the national government was being born, Madison wrote that past history and all evidences of public sentiment made it unquestionable "that the first and most natural attachment of the people" would always "be to the governments of their respective States." [25]

[25] *Federalist*, No. 46.

BIBLIOGRAPHY

(The following bibliography is divided into two parts, the first treating documentary materials and general histories, and the second giving the special sources for each chapter.)

I

The documentary sources now in print are extensive but uneven. A few States, such as North Carolina and Pennsylvania, have published small libraries of material, while others have left even their legislative journals untouched. Students should consult Hasse's "Public Archives of the Thirteen Original States to 1789" in the *Report of the American Historical Association for 1906*, vol. II. The fullest guide to manuscript materials, which need not be summarized here, is the findings of the Historical Manuscripts Committee of the American Historical Association in the *Reports,* indexed under the various States in the general index.

Only a few national collections of documents need be mentioned in a bibliography concerned with State sources. Peter Force's "American Archives" (9 v. 1837-53) is an indispensable array of papers for the years 1774-76. There are various editions of the Journals of the Continental Congress, the best being issued by the Library of Congress under the editorship of W. C. Ford and later Gaillard Hunt, still incomplete. The "Diplomatic Correspondence of the United States, 1783-89" (7 v.; 1833-34), and Francis Wharton's "Revolutionary Diplomatic Correspondence of the United States" (6 v.; 1899), are valuable. Jonathan Elliot's "Debates in the Several State Conventions on the Adoption of the Federal Constitution" (5 v.; 1836-45) also contains the Journals of the Federal Constitutional Convention and Madison's Notes. E. C. Burnett's "Letters of Members of the Continental Congress," to be complete in six volumes, of which the first two appeared in 1921-23, throws light on State history.

The New England States as a group have shown more enterprise in publishing documentary materials than any other section. The New Hampshire Provincial and State Papers, vols. 7, 8, 9, 10, 21, and 22, present legislative records and other sources for the years 1764-1792 (1873-77; 1892-93). Other New Hampshire publications are listed in J. A. Larned, "Literature of American History, A. L. A. Guide" (1902), pp. 8, 9. Of value for Massachusetts history are the "Journals of Each Provincial Congress" (1838), which contains also the journals of the committees of safety; and Alden Bradford's "Speeches of the Governors," with the legislative replies, 1765-75 (1818). The Massachusetts Historical Society is publishing the "Journals of the House of Representatives," 1715-23 (4 v.; 1919-23), an enterprise the State should have undertaken long ago. The Collections of the Massachusetts Historical Society form a rich mine. Especially to be mentioned are the Jeremy Belknap Papers (2 v.; 1877), the Bowdoin-Temple Papers (2 v.; 1897, 1907), the William Heath Papers (3 v.; 1878, 1904-5), the Jonathan Trumbull Papers (4 v.; 1885-1902), and a first volume of the letters of John Adams, Samuel Adams, and James Warren (1917). The "Public Records of the Colony of Connecticut" offer in vol. 15 (1890) the legislative records of 1775-6, including the journal of the Council of Safety, and a continuation of these materials is found in three volumes of the "Records of the State of Connecticut, 1776-81" (1894-1922). The "Records of the Colony and State of Rhode Island," vols. 7-10 inclusive (1862-65), though imperfect, furnish a wealth of matter on Rhode Island 1770-92. For Vermont the two chief sources are the "Records of the Council of Safety and Governor and Council" (8 v.; 1873-80), and the "Vermont State Papers" (1823).

Turning to the Middle States, we find papers indispensable to Pennsylvania history for this period in the Pennsylvania Archives, First Series, vols. 4-11 inclusive (1853-55). The papers of the Governors are in vols. 3 and 4 of the Fourth Series (1900). In vols. 10-16 inclusive of the Colonial Records (1852-53) are the minutes of the Provincial Council 1771-75, the Council of Safety 1775-7, and the Supreme Executive Council 1777-90. The "Votes and Proceedings of the House of Representatives," vols. 5 and 6 (1758-1776) are to be found in large libraries. New York has published the "Messages of the Governors" in ten volumes edited by Charles Z. Lincoln, of which the first covers the colonial period and the second the years 1777-1822 (1909). The State has also issued the "Public Papers of George Clinton to the Evacuation of New York" (11 v.; 1856-61). The "Documentary History of the State of New York" (4 v.; 1849-51), edited with full indexes by E. B. O'Callaghan, and the "Documents Relative to the Colonial History of New York" (11 v.; 1856-61), are both valuable; a supplementary series of four volumes edited by B. Fernow (1877-87) has been added to the latter, of which the final volume contains the proceedings on military affairs of the Provincial Congresses, Convention, and Committee of Safety. There is also the "Journals of the Provincial Congress, Provincial Convention, Committee of Safety and Council of Safety, 1775-78" (2 v.; 1842) which includes the correspondence of these bodies. References to various calendars of New York manuscripts may be found in the A. L. A. Guide, 10, 11.

In the New Jersey Archives, vols. 24-30, first series (1902——), and 1-5, second series (1901-17) are valuable newspaper extracts for the years 1762-82. Henry Stevens's "Analytical Index to the Colonial Documents of New Jersey in the State Paper Offices of England" (1858) is the fifth volume of the Collections of the New Jersey Historical Society, and summarizes many documents of importance in Gov. William Franklin's administration. We have also a "Catalogue of Papers Relating to Pennsylvania and Delaware in the State Paper Office" (1850). The minutes of the Delaware Council, 1776-92, are in the sixth volume of the Delaware Historical Society Papers (1887).

The publishing record of the Southern States is the most uneven of all. We find in volumes 11, 12, 16, and 21 of the "Archives of Maryland" (1892-1901) the Journal of the Maryland Convention, 1775, and the Journal and Correspondence of the Council of Safety, 1775-77, and the State Council, 1777-79. The "Correspondence of Horatio Sharpe," royal governor till 1769, is in volumes 6, 9, and 14 of the "Archives" (1888-95). As for Virginia, we have the "Collections of the Virginia Historical Society," edited by R. A. Brock (new series; 11 v.; 1882-92); the "Calendar of Virginia State Papers" (11 v.; 1875-93); the "Proceedings of the Conventions of 1775-76" (1816); and the "Journals of the House of Delegates" (1776-90; 4 v.; 1827-28), which supplements the "Journals of the House of Burgesses, 1619-1776," edited by J. P. Kennedy and H. R. McIlwaine (1905-15). The "Legislative Journals of the Council of Colonial Virginia" (3 v.: 1918-19) were also edited by H. R. McIlwaine.

The most enterprising Southern State in the publication of documentary materials has been North Carolina. Of the ten volumes of her "Colonial Records," edited by W. L. Saunders, volumes 9 and 10 (1890) cover the years 1771-76; of the "State Records," edited by Walter Clark, volumes 11 to 28 inclusive (1895-1907) cover the years 1776-1790. They are indispensable to a study of the period. The second and third volumes of the Collections of the South Carolina Historical Society (1858-59) contain the journal of the Council of Safety for 1775-76. Some papers of the Council of Safety, General Committee, and Provincial Congress are in the *South Carolina Historical and Genealogical Magazine*, vols. 1-4, 8, 9 (1900-08). In the "Colonial Records of Georgia," volume 12 (1907) offers the minutes of the Governor and Council, 1771-82; volume 15 (1907) the journal of the Commons House, 1769-82; and volume 17 (1908) the journal of the upper house, 1763-74. In the "Revolutionary Records" (1908) of the same State, volume 2 furnishes the minutes of the Executive Council and journal of the land court, 1778-85, while volume 3 has the journal of the Assembly, 1781-84. The journal of the Council of Safety and Provincial Congress are in the first volume of the "Revolutionary Records."

Collections of State laws for this period are easily accessible. Students should consult W. H. Crawford and Horatio Marbury, "Digest of the Laws of the State of Georgia, 1755-1800" (1802); South Carolina's "Statutes at Large 1682-1838" (10 v.; 1836-73), edited by Thomas Cooper and David J. McCord; the statutes of North Carolina in the "State Records," vol. 23; W. W. Hening's "Virginia Statutes at Large, 1619-1808" (13 v.; 1819-23); Maxcy's edition of the "Laws of Maryland" (3 v.; 1811); A. J. Dallas's "Laws of Pennsylvania 1700-1801" (1797-1801) and J. T. Mitchell and Henry Flanders's "Statutes at Large of Pennsylvania 1682-1801" (11 v.; 1896-1906); "General Statutes of New Jersey" (3 v.; 1896); the "Laws of the State of New York, 1777-1801" (5 v.; 1886-87); the "Acts and Laws of Massachusetts, 1775-1789," in three volumes, printed year by year, but each volume paged continuously; the "Index to the Laws of New Hampshire, 1679-1883" (1886), and A. P. Cross, "Index to the General and Special Legislation of the State of Vermont" (1894).

The State and local historical societies number scores. A guide to the contents of their thousands of volumes is offered in A. P. C. Griffin's "Bibliography of American Historical Societies" (1907, second ed.). The publications of the Massachusetts Historical Society, American Antiquarian Society, New York Historical Society, Pennsylvania Historical Society, and Virginia Historical Society are the most notable.

GENERAL HISTORIES

Several State histories are of peculiar value because written by men who lived during or soon after this period. Jeremy Belknap's "History of New Hampshire" (3 v.; 1784-92) is still one of the best of all State histories. Thomas Hutchinson's "History of the Province of Massachusetts Bay, 1749-74" (1828) is an able book, based in part on documents since lost. George R. Minot's "History of the Insurrection in Massachusetts in 1786" (1788) is an analysis of the causes and events of Shays's rebellion, by a capable Massachusetts jurist. Benjamin Trumbull's "Complete History of Connecticut . . . to 1764" (2 v.; 1818) has merit, but does not compare with Belknap.

On New York history we have two good works by loyalists. William Smith's "History of the Late Province of New York" (N. Y. Hist. Soc. Colls., first series, vols. 4 and 5; 1829-30), written by a Tory lawyer whose manuscript diary in the New York Public Library is also a valuable source, comes down to 1762. It is supplemented by Thomas Jones's "History of New York During the Revolutionary War" (2 v.; 1879). David Ramsay's "History of South Carolina" (2 v.; 1809) is topical, not chronological, and comes down to Jefferson's administration. His "History of the Revolution of South Carolina" (2 v.; 1785) is dull but valuable because based on personal impressions and conversations with participants in the war. John D. Burk's "History of Virginia" (3 v.; 1804-05), written with advice from Jefferson, comes down only to 1776, but was continued by Skelton Jones and L. H. Girardin in an additional volume (1816); the continuation covers the years 1776-81, embodies many documents, and is detailed on the events leading up to the Revolution. Hugh Williamson's "History of North Carolina" (2 v.; 1812) stops with 1771 and is almost worthless. J. S. Jones's "A Defence of the Revolutionary History of North Carolina" (1834) closes with the Declaration of Independence, but is indispensable for its brief period.

Later State histories are for the most part poor or indifferent, with a few scientific and vigorous works. The best continuous history of Massachusetts is John S. Barry's "History of Massachusetts" (3 v.; 1855-57), based on the authorities available when written and showing good judgment, but out of date. Alden Bradford's "History of Massachusetts" (3 v.; 1822-29) is restricted to the years 1764-1820, and is less valuable. The standard history of Rhode Island until recently was S. G. Arnold's "History of Rhode Island, 1636-1790" (2 v.; 1859-60). I. B. Richman's "Rhode Island, A Study in Separatism" (1905) is an excellent short study, and Edward Field's "Rhode Island and Providence Plantations at the End of the Century" (3 v.; 1902) contains a wealth of material, sometimes ill digested. A good short history of New Hampshire is F. B. Sanborn's "New Hampshire: An Epitome of Popular Government" (1904), while a fuller account is offered in Everett S. Stackpole's "History of New Hampshire" (4 v.; 1917). Alexander Johnston's "Connecticut: A Study of a Commonwealth-Democracy" (1887) is a brief outline based on thorough study, but developing a mistaken thesis. George L. Clark's "A History of Connecticut" (1914) is a good popular work, "Connecticut as a Colony and as a State," edited by Forrest Morgan (4 v.; 1904) contains much material, badly proportioned and sometimes uncritical. By far the best book for the period is Richard J. Purcell's "Connecticut in Transition, (1918), the emphasis of which is on the years after 1800. Local histories for the New England States are numerous and often valuable. A good example is the "History of Concord, New Hampshire," edited by James O. Lyford (2 v.; 1903).

An admirable State history is D. S. Alexander's "Political History of the State of New York" (3 v.; 1905-09), which begins with the year 1774; it is supplemented by his "Four Great New Yorkers" (1923), dealing with the times of Roosevelt, Cleveland, Platt, and Hill. The work shows clear insight and is written with vigor and sparkle. Jabez D. Hammond's "History of Political Parties in the State of New York" (4th ed., 2 v.; 1846) takes 1789 as its starting point. E. H. Roberts's "New York" (2 v.; 1887) is a rather superficial work. Isaac S. Mulford's "Civil and Political History of New Jersey" (1848) comes down only to 1789, and covers the last years but sketchily. A large and ill-planned compilation is offered in "New Jersey as a Colony and as a State" (4 v.; 1902), by F. B. Lee and others. The fullest history of Pennsylvania is by H. M. Jenkins and others, "Pennsylvania, Colonial and Federal" (3 v.; 1903). For this period it is less useful than A. S. Bolles's "Pennsylvania, Province and State" (2 v.; 1899). A brief history, brightly written and full of ideas, but capricious in emphasis, is S. G. Fisher's "Pennsylvania, Colony and Commonwealth" (1897). It gives little attention to events after 1783. The student cannot neglect W. H. Egle's "Illustrated History of the Commonwealth of Pennsylvania" (1876), an assemblage of county histories by various writers, generally reliable. For Delaware there are but two general histories, the three volumes by H. C. Conrad

(1908) and the compendious, ill-arranged, and badly written two volumes by Thomas Scharf (1888).

Scharf also wrote an outstanding "History of Maryland" (3 v.; 1879), which is ill-digested and inaccurate, but offers much material not available elsewhere, including important documents. James McSherry's "History of Maryland" (1849) is not of value. W. H. Browne's "Maryland, the History of a Palatinate" (1884), one of the best books in the American Commonwealth Series, extends only to the Revolution. The volume on Virginia in that series, by John Esten Cooke (1883), delightfully written but unscholarly, also gives almost all its space to the years before 1783. R. R. Howison's "History of Virginia" (2 v.; 1846-48) is popular and uncritical. The two volumes of "Sketches of Virginia, Historical and Biographical," by W. H. Foote (1850-55) are really a history of Presbyterianism there. Another work of scattered materials is Henry Howe's "Historical Collections of Virginia" (1845). By all odds the most valuable study of Virginia history during this period is H. J. Eckenrode's "The Revolution in Virginia" (1916). Our fullest history of North Carolina is a set of six uniform volumes (1919), of which R. D. W. Connor has written the first, "The Colonial and Revolutionary Periods, 1584-1783," and W. K. Boyd the second, "The Federal Period, 1783-1860" (1919). They are interesting, accurate, and as thorough as the space allows. Among the older books which they largely displace are John W. Moore's "History of North Carolina" (2 v.; 1880), and S. A. Ashe's "History of North Carolina" (1908), which comes down to 1783. W. D. Cooke's "Revolutionary History of North Carolina" (1853) is sketchy.

The recent five volume history of South Carolina edited by H. G. Cutler (1920) is disappointing; Volume One ends with the year 1830. But in Edward McCrady's four volumes, the two last of which ("South Carolina in the Revolution, 1776-83"; 1901-02) are invaluable, we have one of the best of all State histories. The older works are not worth mentioning, save Ramsay's and R. W. Gibbes's "Documentary History of the American Revolution" (3 v.; 1853), relating especially to South Carolina. As for Georgia, the best known books are W. B. Stevens's "History of Georgia to 1798" (1847-59), and C. C. Jones's "History of Georgia" (1883), both in two volumes, and in the older style of historical authorship. The latter is the better, but it closes with the Revolution, to which most of the second volume is devoted.

Chapter I: The Colonies Before Their Union

General authorities are cited in the "Guide to the Study and Reading of American History," by E. Channing, A. B. Hart, and F. J. Turner (1912), and in Evarts B. Greene's "Foundations of American Nationality" (1922). Works of special value are Carl L. Becker's "The Eve of the Revolution" (1918), G. E. Howard's "Preliminaries of the Revolution" (1905), C. H. Van Tyne's "Causes of the War of Independence" (1922), and J. T. Adams's "Revolutionary New England, 1691-1776" (1923).

A number of monographs treat separate Colonies and their problems with more scientific thoroughness than the general histories. They include W. H. Fry's "New Hampshire as a Royal Province" (1908); Carl L. Becker's "Political Parties in the Province of New York from 1760 to 1775" (1908); W. R. Shepherd, "History of Proprietary Government in Pennsylvania" (Columbia University Studies, 1896); Isaac Sharpless, "History of Quaker Government in Pennsylvania" (2 v.; 1898-99), and "Political Leaders of Provincial Pennsylvania" (1919); E. J. Fisher, "New Jersey as a Royal Province, 1738-1776" (Columbia University Studies, 1911); N. D. Mereness, "Maryland as a Proprietary Colony" (1901); P. S. Flippin, "Royal Government in Virginia" (1919); Charles L. Raper, "North Carolina, A Study in English Colonial Government" (1904); W. R. Smith, "South Carolina as a Royal Province, 1719-1776" (1903); and J. R. McCain's "Georgia as a Proprietary Province" (1917), which comes down only to 1752.

Among monographs on special phases of colonial history may be named Louise P. Kellogg's "The American Colonial Charter," in the Report of the American Historical Association, 1903; E. B. Greene's "The Provincial Governor in the English Colonies" (1898); and A. E. McKinley's "Suffrage Franchise in the English Colonies" (1905).

Chapters II and III: The Revolutionary Transition

Revolutionary history has been subjected to a thorough restudy in recent years. British commercial measures have been regarded in a new light since the publication of George L. Beer's "Commercial Policy of England Towards the American Colonies" (1893), "British Colonial Policy 1754-65" (1907), "Origins of the British Colonial System 1578-1660" (1908), and "Old Colonial System, 1660-1754" (2 v.; 1912). Equally valuable is Arthur M. Schlesinger's "Colonial Merchants and the American Revolution" (1918). Charles M. Andrews's "Boston Merchants and the Non-Importation Movement" (1917) is narrower in scope. The best account of British western policy as a cause of the Revolution is C. W. Alvord's "Mississippi Valley in British Politics" (2 v.; 1917). For religious influences upon the Revolution see A. L. Cross's "Anglican Episcopate and the American Colonies" (1902), W. P. Breed's "Presbyterians and the Revolution" (1876), and M. L. J. Griffin's "Catholics and the American Revolution" (2 v.; 1907-09). An original interpretation of constitutional issues is offered by Charles H. McIlwain's "The American Revolution" (1923).

The best general histories of the inception of the Revolution are the third volume of Edward Channing's "History of the United States" (1912); the first volume of George O. Trevelyan's "The American Revolution" (4 v. to 1778; 1899-1907), a work continued by "George III and Charles Fox" (2 v.; 1912-14); M. A. M. Marks's "England and America, 1763-1783" (2 v.; 1907); George Elliot Howard's "Preliminaries of the Revolution" (1905); C. H. Van Tyne's "Causes of the War of Independence" (1922); H. E. Egerton's "Causes and Character of the American Revolution" (1923); and R. G. Adams's "Political Ideas of the Amercian Revolution" (1922). The sixth volume of Justin Winsor's "Narrative and Critical History of America" contains valuable references. Contemporary accounts not to be neglected are David Ramsay's "American Revolution" (1789) and William Gordon's "Rise, Progress, and Establishment of the Independence of the United States" (4 v.; 1788). David Ramsay's "History of the Revolution of South Carolina" (1785) and John Drayton's "Memoirs of the American Revolution" (1821) bear particularly upon the South.

The list of special monographs in State history for these years is long and varied. For North Carolina we have E. W. Sikes, "Transition of North Carolina from Colony to Commonwealth" (1898); J. S. Bassett, "Constitutional Beginnings of North Carolina" (1894) and "Regulators of North Carolina" (Am. Hist. Assn. Rept., 1894); and W. H. Hoyt's "Mecklenberg Declaration of Independence" (1907). An excellent study of "Sectionalism and Representation in South Carolina" was published by W. A. Schaper in 1901, while W. Roy Smith's "South Carolina as a Royal Province" (1903) covers the destruction of the royal government. H. J. Eckenrode's "The Revolution in Virginia" (1916) and C. H. Ambler's "Sectionalism in Virginia" (1910) are indispensable. Monographs relating to Maryland include J. A. Silver's "Provisional Government of Maryland, 1774-77" (1895), and B. C. Steiner's "Life and Administration of Sir Robert Eden" (1898), both in the Johns Hopkins University Studies. C. H. Lincoln's "Revolutionary Movement in Pennsylvania" (1901) is illuminating. The same may be said of A. C. Flick's "Loyalism in New York" (1901) revealing the importance of Toryism. Among the New England monographs should be mentioned H. A. Cushing's "Transition from Provincial to Commonwealth Government in Massachusetts (1896), a detailed political history of Massachusetts from 1774 to 1780, and Edith A. Bailey's "Influences Toward Radicalism in Connecticut, 1754-75" (1920).

The three outstanding city histories are James Grant Wilson's "Memorial History of New York" (4 v.; 1891-93), Justin Winsor's "Memorial History of Boston" (4 v.; 1880-81), and J. T. Scharf and T. Westcott's "Philadelphia" (3 v.: 1884). Several shorter histories, like Mrs. Ravenel's "Charleston" (1906), are useful.

To list half of the important biographies throwing light on the subject-matter of these chapters would here be impossible. No student can neglect the standard studies of the greater statesmen. Among valuable recent lives stand L. S. Mayo's "John Wentworth" (1921), and D. D. Wallace's "Henry Laurens" (1915). Biographies of minor figures, like J. J. Boudinot's "Life of E. Boudinot" (1896) and I. Q. Leake's "Life and Times of Gen. John Lamb" (1857) are frequently of prime importance. The lives of certain loyalists have a special value: G. E. Ellis's "Count Rumford" (1868), James K. Hosmer's "Thomas Hutchinson" (1896), and E. H. Baldwin's "Joseph Galloway" in the *Pennsylvania Magazine of History and Biography*, 1902. Special attention should be given L. H. Gipson's "Jared Ingersoll: A Study of American Loyalism" (1920).

Chapters IV and V: Constitutional History.

Texts of the State Constitution may be found in Ben: Perley Poore's "Charters and Constitutions" (2 v.; 1877), or, more correctly, in Francis N. Thorpe's "American Charters, Constitutions, and Organic Laws" (7 v.; 1909). For references to the printed journals of the constitutional conventions, see the State Library Bulletin of the University of the State of New York, Additions No. 2, November, 1894, 266 ff.

The standard treatise on constitutional procedure was long John A. Jameson's "The Constitutional Convention" (revised ed. 1887), in part now supplanted by Roger Sherman Hoar's "Constitutional Conventions" (1917). A sketchy summary of State constitutional history is presented in J. Q. Dealey's "Growth of American State Constitutions" (1915). Two dry but valuable essays upon early State Constitutions are contained in the *Annals of the American Academy of Political and Social Science*,

W. C. Morey's "First State Constitutions and Sources of American Federalism" (1893), and W. C. Webster's "State Constitutions of the American Revolution" (1897). Charles E. Merriam's "History of American Political Theories" (1903) should be consulted, and A. N. Holcombe's "State Government in the United States" (1916), while A. C. McLaughlin's "The Courts, the Constitutions, and the Parties" (1912) is valuable. Francis N. Thorpe's "Constitutional History of the American People" (2 v.; 1898) pays special attention to the States. Charles Borgeaud's "Adoption and Amendment of Constitutions" (1895) covers European as well as American practise.

For separate treatment of the ballot in the Constitutions, see "Suffrage in the United States," by Kirk Porter (1918), a dry but accurate monograph, and James Schouler's essay on "The Evolution of the American Voter" in the *American Historical Review*, II, 655 ff. T. R. Powell writes exhaustively on "The Separation of Powers" in the *Political Science Quarterly*, June, 1912, and March, 1913. Charles G. Haines has treated "The American Doctrine of Judicial Supremacy" (1914), and Horace A. Davis "The Judicial Veto" (1914).

The most thorough constitutional history of a single State is Charles Z. Lincoln's "Constitutional History of New York" (5 v.; 1905), while there is also an admirable short "Constitutional History of the State of New York" by J. Hampden Dougherty (1915). For the constitutional history of North Carolina see J. S. Bassett, "Constitutional Beginnings of North Carolina" (Johns Hopkins Studies, Series 12); E. W. Sikes, "Our First Constitution," in the North Carolina Booklet, vol. 7; Frank Nash, "The North Carolina Constitution of 1776 and Its Makers," in James Sprunt Historical Publications, vol. 12; and W. K. Boyd, "Antecedents of the North Carolina Convention of 1835," in the *South Atlantic Quarterly*, 1910. Hugh Blair Grigsby has written an account of "The Virginia Convention of 1776" (1855), especially valuable for its portraits of delegates. For the first Maryland Constitution, see B. C. Steiner's "Western Maryland in the Revolution," Johns Hopkins University Studies, Series 20, B. W. Bond's "State Government in Maryland, 1777-81," Series 23, and J. A. Silver's "Provincial Government of Maryland," Series 13. The best account of the Delaware Constitution is in the Papers of the Historical Society of Delaware, II, No. 17. For that of Pennsylvania see S. B. Harding's "Party Struggles over the First Pennsylvania Constitution," in the Annual Report of the American Historical Association, 1894. Valuable for both Pennsylvania and Vermont is L. H. Meader's study of "The Council of Censors" in the Papers of the Historical Seminary of Brown University, No. 10. On the Connecticut Charter-Constitution see Chapter V of R. J. Purcell's "Connecticut in Transition" (1918); and for the constitutional history of Massachusetts to 1780 see S. E. Morison's "Vote of Massachusetts on Summoning a Constitutional Convention" in the *Proceedings of the Massachusetts Historical Society*, April, 1917.

A separate treatment of the Bills of Rights is found in George Jellinek's "The Declaration of the Rights of Man" (1901) and Max Farrand's "The Delaware Bill of Rights," *American Historical Review*, III, 641. The influence of American Constitutions upon Europe is discussed in H. E. Bourne's "American Precedents in the French National Assembly," *American Historical Review*, VIII, 470. For an illuminating account of the political philosophy of the Revolution, see the second and last chapters of Carl Becker's "The Declaration of Independence: A Study in the History of Political Ideas" (1922).

The best work upon constitutional revision is Walter F. Dodd's "Revision and Amendment of State Constitutions" (1910). The proceedings of the important State revising conventions are in print. The "Journal of the Convention of 1779-80" in Massachusetts was published in 1832. To some extent it is supplemented by the "Journal of the Constitutional Convention of 1820" (1821), which contains much matter on the workings of the original Constitution. The "Journal of the Convention to Revise the Constitution of New Hampshire, 1791-92," was published in 1876. For Pennsylvania, the "Proceedings Relative to Calling the Conventions of 1776 and 1790" were published in 1825, containing the journals both of the Council of Censors in 1784 and the Convention of 1790. Material upon the movement for revision in Virginia is afforded by the "Proceedings and Debates of the Virginia Constitutional Convention of 1829-30" (1830).

A careful study of constitutional revision in Massachusetts will be found in the "Manual" prepared for the Massachusetts Convention of 1917-18 (1917), the essay by S. E. Morison cited, and Charles Francis Adams's "Life of John Adams" (1856). The Essex Result and its history are given in Theophilus Parsons's "Memoir" (1859) of his father, Theophilus Parsons, Sr. The *Proceedings of the Massachusetts Historical Society*, II, 64 ff., contain material on the executive veto in Massachusetts. Lois K. Mathews in "The Expansion of New England" (1909) summarizes the grievances of the District of Maine and Hampshire County against the Constitution of

1780. A thorough history of revision in New Hampshire is offered by J. F. Colby's "Manual of the Constitution of New Hampshire" (1912), and E. C. Bean's "Manual" for the New Hampshire Constitution of 1918 (1918). Timothy Dwight's Travels, vol. I (1821), explain the workings of the Connecticut Constitution. Some pages upon the two revisions in South Carolina will be found in Ramsay's "Revolution of South Carolina," I, as well as his "History of South Carolina," II. The fullest source for revision in Georgia is the first volume of the "Georgia Revolutionary Records."

Chapter VI: Political Development in New England
Newspapers of the period are an indispensable source upon politics, not only for specific information but the insight they give into the spirit of parties. At the end of the Revolution the *Connecticut Courant* and Boston *Gazette* were two of the best journals published in America, and in 1784 the federalist *Massachusetts Centinel* took its place beside them. Other newspapers worth consulting are the *New Hampshire Gazette, Vermont Gazette, Vermont Journal,* Newport *Mercury, United States Chronicle* (Providence), and the *Independent Chronicle* (Boston). The *Connecticut Gazette,* published 1755-1786, was followed by the *Connecticut Journal.* A guide to library files is offered by the *Proceedings of the American Antiquarian Society, 1914——.*
Legislative journals of the Massachusetts House were printed year by year contemporaneously. Those of the Connecticut General Court are in the "Records" of the Colony and State, and those of New Hampshire in the "Provincial and State Papers." The "Vermont State Papers" (1823) contain some early journals of the Assembly, and from 1784 they were printed contemporaneously.
Of the monographic studies a number are indispensable. For Massachusetts, A. E. Morse's "Federalist Party in Massachusetts to the Year 1800" (1909) stands preeminent. The same may be said of Purcell's "Connecticut in Transition" for Connecticut, a State upon which we also have M. Louise Greene's "Development of Religious Liberty in Connecticut" (1905). For Rhode Island the outstanding study is F. G. Bates's "Rhode Island and the Formation of the Union" (1898). Among more general monographs are W. A. Robinson's "Jeffersonian Democracy in New England" (1916), which nominally begins with 1789; S. D. Luetscher, "Early Political Machinery in the United States" (1903); O. G. Libby's "Geographical Distribution of the Vote of the Thirteen States on the Federal Constitution" (1894); P. E. Lauer's "Church and State in New England" (Johns Hopkins Studies, 1892); and Henry Jones Ford's "Rise and Growth of American Politics" (1914) are illuminating. The volumes by Morse and Purcell contain lists of pamphlets and election sermons.
The numerous biographies throw less light on politics than might be expected. We may mention the lives of John Adams, and W. V. Wells's "Life and Public Services of Samuel Adams" (3 v.; 1865), supplemented by R. V. Harlow's "Life of Samuel Adams" (1923). There is no life of Bowdoin, and no worthy life of Hancock. The Samuel Adams manuscripts in the New York Public Library are a much-used source. There is a little material of worth in Noah Brooks's "Henry Knox" (1900) like the long letter on Shays's Rebellion in ch. 9, and in H. C. Lodge's "Life and Letters of George Cabot" (1877). Seth Ames's "Works of Fisher Ames" (2 v.; 1854) present the writings of a zealous Massachusetts Federalist. On the other side, T. C. Amory's "Life of James Sullivan" (2 v.; 1859) is a ponderous biography of a prominent Anti-Federalist leader. The chief value in J. T. Austen's "Elbridge Gerry" (2 v.; 1828-29), the life of another Anti-Federalist, is in the letters. For the social background see E. S. Thomas's "Reminiscences of the Last Sixty-five Years" (2 v.; 1840), and W. J. Bentley's "Diary" (4 v.; 1905-14).
For Rhode Island, W. E. Foster's "Stephen Hopkins" (Rhode Island Historical Tracts, 1884) is especially valuable. In New Hampshire William Plumer did not enter public life till the end of this period, but his son's "Life of William Plumer" (1856) shows political conditions as he found them. Simeon E. Baldwin's "Life and Letters of Simeon Baldwin" (1919) presents Connecticut politics as viewed by a young lawyer after 1786. There are two lives of Gov. Jonathan Trumbull, that by I. W. Stuart (1859), and the much better work by Jonathan Trumbull (1919). W. G. Brown's "Life of Oliver Ellsworth" (1905) and L. H. Boutell's "Life of Roger Sherman" (1896) deal with men more prominent in national than State affairs.

Chapter VII: Political Development in the Middle States
Newspapers are an even more important source for the political history of the Middle States than of New England, for the relations of party leaders and editors were close. The *Pennsylvania Packet* is as valuable for politics as for commerce, which is saying much. There should also be named the *Pennsylvania Gazette,* the *Freeman's Journal* (Philadelphia), the *New York Packet, Advertiser, Independent Journal,* and *Independent Gazetteer,* and the *New Jersey Gazette.*

There has unfortunately been no monographic history of New York politics under George Clinton, but John S. Jenkins's "History of Political Parties in New York" (1846), which begins with the Revolution, and the first volume of D. S. Alexander's "Political History of the State of New York" (1906), cover the period hurriedly. A. C. Flick's "Loyalism in New York During the Revolution" (1901) has much value. While Dixon R. Fox's "Decline of Aristocracy in the Politics of New York" (1919) commences only with the year 1800, it has retrospective passages, as has Howard Lee McBain's monograph on "De Witt Clinton and the Origin of the Spoils System" (1907). For New Jersey the only special study of worth is L. Q. C. Elmer's "Constitution and Government of New Jersey" (2 v.; 1849-72). S. B. Harding's "Party Struggles Over the Pennsylvania Constitution" (1894) is supplemented by W. Roy Smith's "Sectionalism in Pennsylvania During the Revolution" in the *Political Science Quarterly*, vol. 24, pp. 208-235 (1909).

We have a particularly large array of biographies of leaders in this section. For New York, the seven-volume life of Hamilton by J. C. Hamilton, entitled "History of the Republic as Traced in the Writings of Alexander Hamilton" (1857-64) is the outstanding work. The lives of Jay by William Jay (2 v.; 1833) and George Pellew (American Statesmen Series, 1890) are both good. William Kent's "Memoirs and Letters of James Kent" (1898) embodies autobiographical material on the struggles between federalists and anti-federalists at the close of this period. Gouverneur Morris after 1777 gave his services to the nation, not the State, but the lives by Jared Sparks (3 v.; 1832) and Theodore Roosevelt (1888), and the "Diary and Letters," edited by Anne Cary Morris (2 v.; 1888) throw light on New York affairs. Isaac Q. Leake's "Memoir of the Life and Times of Gen. John Lamb" (1857) is invaluable. For New Jersey history, Theodore Sedgwick's "William Livingston" (1833) has original papers of value, though it is an old-fashioned biography. Almost every prominent figure in Pennsylvania politics has had his biographer. Burton Alva Konkle's "George Bryan and the Constitution of Pennsylvania" (1922) is impartial and illuminating. High rank must be given to Charles J. Stillé's "Major-General Anthony Wayne" (1893) and "Life and Times of John Dickinson" (1891); and to William B. Reed's able "Life and Correspondence of Joseph Reed" (2 v.; 1847). Among other works are Konkle's "Life and Times of Thomas Smith, 1745-1809" (1904), which treats of the career of a colonel, legislator, and judge; L. Harley's "Life of Charles Thomson" (1900); and William H. Smith's "St. Clair Papers" (2 v.; 1882). Glimpses of the social background are found in J. F. Watson's entertaining but untrustworthy "Annals of Philadelphia," revised by W. P. Hazard (1898), the "Extracts From the Diary of Christopher Marshall, 1774-81," edited by William Duane (1877), Alexander Graydon's "Memoirs" (1811), and the "Diary of Jacob Hiltzheimer, 1765-98" (1893). For Delaware the leading biography is William Thompson Read's "Life and Correspondence of George Read" (1870).

Chapters VIII and IX: Political Development in the South
Files of Southern newspapers for this period are few. Chief value attaches to those of the *Maryland Journal*, published in Baltimore by William Goddard, a noted journalist, and the *South Carolina Gazette* (the name varies slightly in form at different periods) which had been founded in 1733 and paid close attention to politics.

Monographs on Maryland history are numerous and excellent. B. W. Bond's "State Government in Maryland, 1777-81" (Johns Hopkins Studies, vol. 23, 1905), George Petrie's "Church and State in Maryland" (*Idem*, vol. 10, 1892), and B. C. Steiner's "Western Maryland in the Revolution" (vol. 20, 1902) are all careful studies from the sources. For Virginia, Eckenrode's "The Revolution in Virginia" is the principal guide. In addition, we have C. H. Ambler's "Sectionalism in Virginia from 1776 to 1861," of which the first chapter treats this period; J. A. C. Chandler's "History of Representation in Virginia" (Johns Hopkins Studies, vol. 14, 1896) and "History of Suffrage in Virginia" (*Idem*, vol. 19, 1901); James Parton's "Thomas Jefferson, A Reformer of Old Virginia" (*Atlantic Monthly*, July, 1872); Eckenrode's "Separation of Church and State in Virginia" (1909) and Gaillard Hunt's "James Madison and Religious Liberty" (American Hist. Association Report, 1901); and the interesting characterizations of political leaders in Hugh Blair Grigsby's "The Virginia Federal Convention of 1788" (2 v.; 1890-91).

Especially valuable monographs upon North Carolina are H. M. Wagstaff's "State Rights and Parties in North Carolina 1776-1831" (Johns Hopkins Studies, vol. 24, 1906), and Stephen B. Weeks's "Church and State in North Carolina" (*Idem*, vol. II, 1893). W. D. Cooke's "Revolutionary History of North Carolina" (1853) is a sketchy treatise on military affairs. The only important monograph touching South Carolina politics in this period is William A. Schaper's "Sectionalism and Representation in South Carolina" (1901). McCrady's two fine volumes on South Carolina in the Revolution (1901-02) unfortunately conclude his work, and a continuation beyond 1783 is highly desirable. Ulrich B. Phillips presents a study of "The South Carolina Federalists" in the *American Historical Review*, vol. 14, 1909. By the same author we have "Georgia and State Rights" (1902), which begins with the year 1788, but contains retrospective material.

Biographies are again numerous. The best in the Maryland field is B. C. Steiner's "Life and Correspondence of James McHenry" (1907). Kate M. Rowland's "Life of Charles Carroll of Carrollton" (2 v.; 1898) is as valuable as could be expected in the case of a statesman who was accustomed to destroy all his letters. Henry Wheaton's "Account of the Life, Writings, and Speeches of William Pinkney" (1826) is much better than the "Life of William Pinkney" by his nephew, William Pinkney (1853). A good account of Samuel Chase would fill a decided lacuna. It is not necessary to mention at length the well-known lives of Washington, Jefferson, Madison, Henry, and R. H. Lee; Moncure D. Conway's "Life and Papers of Edmund Randolph" (1888); R. H. Lee's "Memoir of the Life of Richard Henry Lee" (2 v.; 1825); Kate M. Rowland's "Life of George Mason" (2 v.; 1892); and the first two volumes of Albert J. Beveridge's "Life of John Marshall" (1916). Lyon G. Tyler's "Letters and Times of the Tylers" (3 v.; 1884-96) is a valuable collection of materials commencing with the outset of the Revolution.

Much the best biography for North Carolina's history is G. J. McRee's "Life and Correspondence of James Iredell" (2 v.; 1857-58). F. M. Hubbard's "Life of William R. Davie" is one of the best essays in the Library of American Biography edited by Jared Sparks (2d series, vol. 15, 1844-48). In the *North Carolina Booklet* will be found brief biographies of outstanding Revolutionary figures in North Carolina, such as T. M. Pittman's "John Penn" (vol. 4). A biography of John Rutledge is much needed. A series of his letters is printed in the *South Carolina Historical and Genealogical Magazine*, 1917, and there is a sketch in Henry Flanders's "Lives and Times of the Chief Justices" (2 v.; 1881). David Duncan Wallace's "Life of Henry Laurens" (1915) is thorough, but Laurens had little to do with State politics after 1777. A sketch of Alexander Gillon is presented in the *South Carolina Historical and Genealogical Magazine*, vol. 9 (1908). In addition, the student may consult Joseph Johnson's "Traditions and Reminiscences of the American Revolution" (1851); John Drayton's "Memoirs of the American Revolution" (2 v.; 1821); William Moultrie's "Memoirs of the American Revolution" (2 v.; 1802); William Gilmore Simms's "Life of Francis Marion" (1844); and G. W. Greene's "Life of Nathanael Greene" (3 v.; 1867-71). C. C. Jones's "Biographical Sketches of the Delegates from Georgia to the Continental Congress" (1891) is disappointing.

Chapter X: Progress in Liberalism and Social Reform

For social changes the most illuminating single source is the newspapers. Files of early magazines, particularly the *Columbian* and *American Museum*, should be consulted. Early volumes of travel are important: Brissot de Warville, "New Travels in the United States" (1792); F. J. de Chastellux, "Travels in North America in 1780-82" (1828); Charles H. Sherrill's "French Memories of Eighteenth Century America" (1915); Thomas Coke's "Journal of His Fourth Tour" (1792); Thomas Cooper, "Some Information Respecting America" (1794); W. Mathews's "Historical Review of North America" (2 v.; 1789); and Henry Wansey's "Excursion to the United States in 1794" (2d ed.; 1798). W. Winterbotham's "Historical, Geographical, Commercial, and Philosophical View of the American United States" (4 v.; 1795) is valuable.

The best general treatises on slavery are Henry Wilson's "Rise and Fall of the Slave Power in America" (3 v.; 1872-77), colored by strong Northern prejudices; Ulrich B. Phillips's "American Negro Slavery" (1918), fair in tone; J. Z. George's "Political History of Slavery" (1915), a sketchy work; G. W. Williams's "Negro Race in America" (2 v.; 1883); W. E. B. DuBois, "Suppression of the African Slave Trade" (1904); and G. M. Stroud, "Sketch of the Laws Relating to Slavery" (2d ed.; 1856).

Among the monographs on special phases of slavery are G. H. Moore, "Slavery in Massachusetts," which shows that there was little anti-slavery sentiment in Massachusetts before the Revolution; B. C. Steiner, "History of Slavery in Connecticut" (Johns Hopkins Studies, vol. II, 1893); W. D. Johnston, "Slavery in Rhode Island, 1755-76," in Rhode Island Historical Society Pubs., n. s., vol. 2; A. J. Northrup's brief essay on "Slavery in New York" in N. Y. State Library Report for 1900; E. V. Morgan, "Slavery in New York," Amer. Hist. Association Papers, V (1891); H. S. Cooley, "Slavery in New Jersey" (Johns Hopkins Studies, vol. 14, 1896); E. R. Turner, "Slavery in Pennsylvania" (1911); Richard R. Wright, Jr., "The Negro in Pennsylvania" (1912); J. R. Brackett, "The Negro in Maryland" (1889); William

Pinkney, "Speech in the Maryland House of Delegates, 1789"; Philip Slaughter, "The Virginia History of African Colonization" (1855); J. C. Ballagh, "History of Slavery in Virginia" (1902); B. B. Munford's "Virginia's Attitude Toward Slavery" (1909); and J. S. Bassett's "Anti-Slavery Leaders of North Carolina" (Johns Hopkins Studies, vol. 16, 1898).

Upon church and state, see S. B. Weeks's "Church and State in North Carolina" (1810), (Johns Hopkins Studies, vol. II, 1893); R. B. Semple's "Rise and Progress of the Baptists in Virginia," enlarged by G. W. Beale (1894); Philip Schaff's "Church and State in the United States" (1888), a treatise on the first amendment to the Constitution; Isaac Backus, "History of New England, With Particular Reference to . . . the Baptists," a work by a liberal-minded minister (3 v.; 1777-96); E. W. Carruthers, "Life and Character of the Rev. David Caldwell" (1842); W. H. Foote's "Sketches of North Carolina" (1846) and "Sketches of Virginia" (1855), both on the Presbyterian Church; J. M. Buckley's "History of Methodism" (1897); C. C. Tiffany, "History of the Protestant Episcopal Church" (1895); F. L. Hawkes, "Contributions to the Ecclesiastical History of the United States." (2 v.; 1836-39); Thomas O'Gorman, "History of the Roman Catholic Church in the United States" (1897); H. J. Eckenrode's "Separation of Church and State in Virginia" (1910); and C. F. James, "Documentary History of the Struggle for Religious Liberty in Virginia" (1900).

For reforms in the criminal law, see the pamphlet by William Bradford, "An Inquiry How far the Punishment of Death is necessary in Pennsylvania" (1793). See also the essays by Dr. Benjamin Rush in the American Museum, volumes II and IV. Consult J. B. McMaster, "Old Standards of Public Morals" (*Amer. Hist. Review,* II, 515) for corruption in political life.

The only satisfactory treatise on American prison reform is O. F. Lewis's "Development of American Prisons and Prison Customs, 1776-1845" (1923). Students should also consult F. H. Wines's "Punishment and Reformation" (enlarged edition, 1919); the first reports of the Prison Discipline Society; the anonymous "Account of the State Prison in the City of New York, 1801"; Harry E. Barnes, "History of the Penal, Reformatory, and Correctional Institutions of New Jersey"; G. Haynes, "Pictures from Prison Life"; F. C. Gray, "Prison Discipline in America"; "Penal and Charitable Institutions of Pennsylvania" (2 v.; 1897); F. B. Sanborn, "The Poor Laws of New England," in the *North American Review,* April, 1868; and John Cummings, "Poor Laws of Massachusetts and New York" (1895).

Among the general authorities on education are Paul Monroe, "Cyclopædia of Education" (1911-13); E. G. Dexter, "History of Education in the United States" (1904); Ellwood P. Cubberley, "Public Education in the United States" (1919); Richard G. Boone, "Education in the United States; Its History" (1889); and F. P. Graves, "Education in Modern Times" (1913). It is impossible here to list the dozens of monographs upon education in the various States; the general histories just named and the A. L. A. Guide contain references to them.

Chapter XI: Financial History of the States

The fullest work upon American financial history is A. S. Bolles's "Financial History of the United States" (3 v.; 1879-85), the first volume of which covers the years 1774-89; a treatise of great research and good judgment. D. R. Dewey's "Financial History of the United States" (1903), Chapter II, is valuable. The best monograph on this period is C. J. Bullock's "Finances of the United States, 1775-89," written with special reference to the national budget. Two useful biographies are E. P. Oberholtzer's "Robert Morris, Patriot and Financier" (1903), and W. G. Sumner, "The Financier and Finances of the American Revolution" (2 v.; 1891), which is ill-arranged but full of material nowhere else easily procurable.

Two conflicting views of the Continental and State paper issues are represented by Samuel Breck's "Historical Sketch of Continental Paper Money" (1843), which defends them as in effect only a moderate tax upon the people, and Henry Bronson's "Historical Account of Connecticut Currency, Continental Money, and Finances of the Revolution" (New Haven Colony Historical Society Papers, I; 1865), which is more scholarly, and harshly criticizes the issues. Henry Phillips's "Historical Sketches of the Paper Currency of the American Colonies Prior to the Adoption of the Federal Constitution" (2 v.; 1865-66) is full of material. J. W. Schuckers's "Brief Account of the Finances and Paper Money of the Revolutionary War" (1870) is a good sketch, though only a sketch, coming down to 1790. W. G. Sumner's "History of American Currency" (1874), gives a few pages to the Continental paper money, the Bank of North America, and the paper money agitation of 1785-86. A better book is A. Barton Hepburn's "A History of Currency in the United States" (revised edition, 1915). W. M. Gouge's "Short History of Paper Money and Banking in the United States" (1833) is badly arranged, but still a standard authority.

Of works by contemporaries several are valuable. Tench Coxe's "View of the United States of America" (1794) is a series of papers published 1787-94, exhibiting the position of American commerce and manufactures. Peletiah Webster's "Political Essays on the Nature and Operation of Money, Public Finance, and Other Subjects" (1791) criticizes the paper issues harshly, treats of tender acts, and covers taxation. Timothy Pitkin's "Statistical View of the Commerce of the United States" (1835) has good tables.

The four standard works thus far published on banking, none of which is of great value for State financial history, are W. G. Sumner's "History of Banking in the United States" (1896), Charles A. Conant's "History of Modern Banks of Issue" (1896), J. J. Knox's "History of Banking in the United States" (1900), and C. F. Dunbar's "Theory and History of Banking" (1896).

For State finances see T. Pitkin's "History of the United States" (2 v.; 1828); American State Papers, Finances, I; J. H. Hollander, "Studies in State Taxation," referring especially to the Southern States (Johns Hopkins Studies, vol. 18, 1900); C. H. J. Douglas, "Financial History of Massachusetts" (Columbia University Studies, 1891); D. C. Sowers, "Financial History of New York" (Columbia Studies, vol. 17); H. S. Hanna, "Financial History of Maryland, 1789-1848)) (Johns Hopkins Studies, vol. 25); A Citizen of Maryland, "Short History of the Public Debt of Maryland" (1845); W. Z. Ripley, "Financial History of Virginia, 1609-1776" (Columbia University Studies, vol. 4); W. L. Royall, "History of Virginia Banks" (1907); W. K. Boyd, "Currency and Banking in North Carolina, 1790-1836" (Trinity College Historical Papers); W. F. Dodd, "Effect of the Adoption of the Constitution on the Finances of Virginia" (*Va. Hist. Magazine*, vol. 10); Louise A. Reams, "Taxation in Virginia During the Revolution" (Richmond College Hist. Papers, June, 1917); T. R. Snively, "Taxation of Negroes in Virginia" (Univ. of Virginia Publications, 1916).

Chapter XII: State Quarrels and Friendships
Wm. Gordon's "Rise, Progress, and Establishment of the Independence of the United States" (4 v.; 1788) gives some attention to ill-feeling between men of different Colonies. So does Joseph Galloway's "Historical and Political Reflections on the Rise and Progress of the American Rebellion" (1780). The *Federalist* is much concerned with it; see especially No. 23. The principal materials, however, are to be found in the "Works" of John Adams, especially volumes 2, 7, and 9; Madison's "Writings" (Hunt ed.), volumes 1 and 2; Monroe's "Writings," volume 1; Washington's writings and Jared Sparks's "Letters to Washington" (4 v.; 1853); and the collected works of R. H. Lee, Gouverneur Morris, Rufus King, Dickinson, Hamilton, and Patrick Henry. The "Correspondence and Journals of S. B. Webb," edited by W. C. Ford (3 v.; 1894), the "Army Correspondence of John Laurens" (Bradford Club, 1867), Alexander Graydon's "Memoirs" (1811), and William Moultrie's "Memoirs" (2 v.; 1802) are enlightening contemporary documents.

For boundary disputes, in addition to the footnote references, see D. Goodloe's "North Carolina and Georgia Boundary," in *North Carolina Booklet*, volume 3; "Report of the Committee on the Western Boundary of Maryland" (in the Fund Publications, Maryland Historical Society, No. 29); Neville B. Craig, "The Olden Time" (2 v.; 2846-48) for matter on the Pennsylvania boundary disputes; C. W. Bowen, "Boundary Disputes of Connecticut" (1882), a scholarly monograph; and the Regents' Boundary Commission, "Report upon the New York and Pennsylvania Boundary" (1886), with the two supplementary volumes of documents, "Report on the Boundaries of the State of New York" (1874-84). The bearing of the western lands upon State relations is best treated in H. B. Adams, "Maryland's Influence upon Land Cessions in the United States" (Johns Hopkins Studies, III, 1885), corrected and supplemented by chapter 2 of B. W. Bond's "State Government in Maryland" (Johns Hopkins Studies, XXIII, 1905). See also the references for chapter 14 of this book.

The Wyoming question may be studied in Charles Miner, "History of Wyoming" (1845), a gossipy but full book; George Peck, "Wyoming; Its History, Stirring Incidents, and Romantic Adventures" (1858); S. G. Fisher, "The Making of Pennsylvania" (1896); Octavius Pickering, "Life of Timothy Pickering," vol. 2 (4 v.; 1867-73); Fairfield County Historical Society Reports, 1896-97; O. J. Harvey, "History of Wilkes-Barre" (3 v.; 1909-10); and the documentary records of Pennsylvania. For the Vermont question see the "Records of the Governor and Council of Vermont" (8 v.; 1873-80); the "Vermont State Papers" (1823); the "Collections" of the Vermont Historical Society, especially volume 2, which contains extracts from the Haldimand Papers, the "Proceedings" of the same body; B. H. Hall's able "History of Eastern Vermont" (2 v.; 1858); Hiland Hall, "History of Vermont" (1868); and Ira Allen, "Natural and Political History of the State of Vermont" (1898). The best single work on the Mississippi question is F. A. Ogg's "The Opening of the Mississippi:

A Struggle for Supremacy in the American Interior" (1904), which contains references for further study. See also chapter 7 of Gaillard Hunt's "Life of James Madison" (1902).

The first chapter of the "History of Transportation in the United States Before 1860" by Caroline E. MacGill and others (Carnegie Institution; 1917) treats modes and difficulties of communication. Commercial relations may also be studied in W. Hill's "First Stages of the Tariff Policy" (Publications of the Amer. Econ. Association, VIII, No. 6), W. C. Fisher's "American Trade Regulations Before 1789" (Amer. Hist. Association Papers, III, 467-493), and Victor S. Clark's "History of Manufactures in the United States, 1607-1860" (Carnegie Institution, 1916).

Chapter XIII: Relations of the States with Congress

The principal general studies of the growth of nationality 1783-89 are familiar. They are John B. McMaster's "History of the People of the United States" (vol. 1; 1883); George Bancroft's "History of the Formation of the Constitution" (2 v.; 1882); John Fiske's "Critical Period of American History" (1888); Edward Channing's "History of the United States," volume 3 (1916); and A. C. McLaughlin's "The Confederation and the Constitution" (American Nation Series, 1905). Material of value may be found in John Brown Scott's "The United States: A Study in International Organization" (Carnegie Endowment for International Peace; 1920). The principal sources are equally well known. Supplementing the Journals of Congress, Elliott's "Debates," and the *Federalist*, we have Max Farrand's "Records of the Federal Convention" (3 v.; 1911), and the "Documentary History of the Constitution" (State Department; 1894).

Commercial problems as they affected the idea of union are treated in Eugene A. Schuyler's "American Diplomacy and the Furtherance of Commerce" (1886), and in S. F. Bemis's work on "Jay's Treaty" (1923), especially chapter 2. State laws on commerce are summarized in the British Privy Council Report contained in the "Collection of Interesting and Important Reports and Papers on Navigation and Trade of Great Britain . . . in the West Indies and America" (1807). Excellent studies of the British debts, and the British seizures of slaves, are found in the Annual Reports of the American Historical Association—A. C. McLaughlin's "British Posts and Western Debts" (1894), and F. A. Ogg's "Jay's Treaty and the Slavery Interests" (1901).

Bearing directly on the writing and adoption of the Constitution are Max Farrand's "The Framing of the Constitution" (1913) and "Fathers of the Constitution" (1920), and Allen Johnson's "Union and Democracy" (1915). Charles A. Beard's "Economic Interpretation of the Constitution of the United States" (1913) summarized the conclusions to which one school of writers had long been tending. J. F. Jameson's "Essays in the Constitutional History of the United States" (1889) offers five papers on such topics as the development of the executive departments, and the movement for a second constitutional convention. A study of the relations between the States and Congress in 1774-75 is presented in Albion W. Small's "Beginnings of American Nationality" (Johns Hopkins Studies, vol. 8, 1890), based on a close study of the Journals of Congress. A fuller study of the same subject is given in C. H. Van Tyne's "Sovereignty in the American Revolution," in the *American Historical Review*, volume 12. G. T. Curtis's "History of the Constitution" (2 v.; 1854) is valuable.

The ratification of the Constitution is discussed in O. G. Libby's "Geographical Distribution of the Vote of the Thirteen States on the Federal Constitution" (1894), which showed how clear was the economic cleavage between rural and commercial interests; S. B. Harding, "Ratification of the Constitution in Massachusetts" '(1896), which also contains much matter on State politics; A. E. Morse, "The Federal Party in Massachusetts to 1800" (1909); J. P. Warren, "The Confederation and the Shays's Rebellion" (*American Historical Review*, vol. II, 42 ff.); J. C. Welling, "Connecticut Federalism," in "Addresses, Lectures, and Other Papers" (1904); F. G. Bates, "Rhode Island and the Formation of the Union" (1898); J. B. McMaster and F. B. Stone, "Pennsylvania and the Federal Constitution" (1888); H. B. Grigsby, "History of the Virginia Federal Convention of 1788" (2 v.; 1890-91), supplemented by A. J. Beveridge's "Life of John Marshall," chapters 9 and 10 of volume 1 (1916), and C. H. Ambler's "Sectionalism in Virginia" (1910); U. B. Phillips, "The South Carolina Federalists," in the *American Historical Review*, vol. 14 (1909); and C. L. Raper, "Why North Carolina at First Refused to Ratify the Federal Constitution" (American Historical Association Report, 1905).

Chapter XIV: Facing Westward; Conclusion

Much material on both the Northwest and Southwest is to be found in the publications of State historical societies. For western North Carolina and Tennessee see the James Sprunt Historical Monographs (1900———) and *Tenessee Historical Maga-*

zine (1915————). For western Virginia and Kentucky see the *Virginia Magazine of History and Biography* (1893————) and *Register of the Kentucky Historical Society* (1902————). The *Proceedings* of the Mississippi Valley Historical Association, *Transactions* of the Illinois State Historical Society, *Collections* of the Illinois State Historical Library, *Publications* of the Indiana Historical Society, *Collections and Researches* of the Michigan Pioneer and Historical Society, and *Collections* of the Wisconsin State Historical Society, are all valuable.

The most scientific account of the westward movement before 1775 is contained in C. W. Alvord's "Mississippi Valley in British Politics," before mentioned. It is supplemented by the two volumes by Alvord and Carter cited in the notes, G. H. Alden's "New Governments West of the Alleghenies Before 1780" (1897), M. M. Quaife's "Chicago and the Old Northwest, 1673-1835" (1913), and Justin Winsor's "The Westward Movement: The Colonies and the Republic West of the Alleghenies, 1763-1798" (1897), a careful book, but dull. Roosevelt's "Winning of the West" (4 v.; 1889-96) covers the years 1763-1807. It is written with engaging vigor and color, but is not wholly accurate, and slights social and economic aspects of Western settlement. F. J. Turner's "Significance of the Frontier in American History" (Wisconsin Historical Society, 1894) and "Western State Making in the Revolutionary Era" (*American Historical Review,* 1895-96) are essays of interpretative depth. Archibald Henderson's "The Conquest of the Old Southwest" (1920) is the condensed result of thorough research.

The best State histories bearing material on western expansion are volume 1 of the Centennial History of Illinois, C. W. Alvord's "The Illinois Country" (1920); Logan Esarey's "History of Indiana" (1915); Robert M. McElroy's "Kentucky in the Nation's History" (1909), which gives a chapter to Transylvania; R. H. Collins's "Kentucky" (2 v.; last ed., 1882), a full history of the gazetteer type; John Haywood's "Civil and Political History of Tennessee" (1823); and James G. Ramsay's "Annals of Tennessee" (1853), a documentary record. Humphrey Marshall's "History of Kentucky" (2 v.; 1824) is partisan but valuable as the work of a man who entered Kentucky in 1780. The histories of Ohio by Rufus King (1888) and Michigan by T. M. Cooley (1885) in the American Commonwealth Series are good. W. H. Foote's "Sketches of North Carolina" (1845) is ill-arranged and deals mainly with the western part of the State. J. W. Caldwell's "Studies in the Constitutional History of Tennessee" (1895) is a series of essays.

Bearing particularly upon the westward movement in the older States are F. W. Halsey's "Old New York Frontier" (1901); O. Turner's "Pioneer History of the Holland Purchase in Western New York" (1850) and "Pioneer Settlement of Phelps and Gorham's Purchase, and Morris's Reserve" (1851); Boyd Crumrine's "Washington County, Pennsylvania" (1882); L. K. Mathews's "Expansion of New England," before mentioned; S. Kercheval's "History of the Valley of Virginia" (1902); and L. P. Summers's "History of Southwest Virginia, 1745-86" (1903).

Upon the Ordinance of 1787 there exists a small library. B. A. Hinsdale's "The Old Northwest" (1888) is comprehensive. D. G. McCarty's "Territorial Governors of the Old Northwest" (1910) offers a good summary of constitutional and administrative history. J. A. Barrett's "Evolution of the Ordinance of 1787" (1891) and P. J. Treat's "National Land System, 1785-1820" (1910) are excellent monographs. H. B. Adams's "Maryland's Influence upon Land Cessions to the United States" (Johns Hopkins Studies, vol. 3, 1885), has been mentioned. Thomas Donaldson's report on "The Public Domain" (1884), made for the Public Land Commission, is useful but ill-digested.

Biographies and monographs are too numerous to be named in full. There are lives of Manasseh Cutler, by W. P. and J. P. Cutler (1888), and Rufus Putnam, by Mary Cone (1886); while we have Rowena Buell's "Memoirs of Rufus Putnam" (1903). The best lives of Boone are by Reuben Gold Thwaites (1911) and Stewart Edward White (1922). A. B. Hulbert has written "Boone's Wilderness Road" (1903) and "Pilots of the Republic" (1905). F. M. Turner's "Life of Sevier" (1910) is much superior to James R. Gilmore's "John Sevier as a Commonwealth Builder" (1887) or his "Advance Guard of Western Civilization" (1888), the latter dealing with James Robertson. A sketch of St. Claire's life precedes W. H. Smith's "St. Claire Papers" (2 v.; 1882). Lord Dunmore's War and the border war of the Revolution are treated in C. W. Butterfield's "Girty Family" (1890). S. B. Weeks's "Joseph Martin" (American Historical Association Report, 1893) is valuable for Tennessee history. R. G. Thwaites and L. P. Kellogg have compiled a "Documentary History of Dunmore's War" (1905), and the Spanish conspiracies are dealt with in F. A. Ogg's "The Opening of the Mississippi" (1904).

INDEX

Acts of Trade. *See* Commerce.

Adams, John, on Caucus Club, 13; radical, 15; on ecclesiastical alignment, 21; on committees of correspondence, 31; and McDougall, 55; on outrages, 66; on army before Boston, 69; on assumption of government, 88; and Pennsylvania, 98-103, 106, 150, 250*n.*, and Locke, 121; as political scientist, 121; influence on State Constitutions, 122-125, 161; and Paine, 123; on attitude of South, 123*n.*; and resolution for State governments, 125; and suffrage, 140; on Virginia, 143; on overthrow of conservatives, 145; and popular vote on Constitution, 177; and Massachusetts Constitution, 179, 211; on Reed, 258; on Livingston, 302; on Chase, 313; on J. Rutledge, 370; and education, 467, 468; on taxation, 492; on prejudice against New England, 550, 551; and Washington, 551; provincialism, 555; and Dickinson, 555*n.*; and free trade, 557; on diplomatic impotence, 564*n.*; on spirit of Congress, 607; on policy of Congress, 608-610; and Maryland, 611; on price-fixing, 617; and confederation, 624; and apportionment, 625; and equal vote in Congress, 625; and loyalist rights under treaty, 645; on treaty violations, 652.

Adams, Mrs. John, on Hancock, 215.

Adams, John Quincy, on Hancock-Bowdoin campaign, 220.

Adams, Samuel, Junto, 13; radical, 15; and town meetings, 30; committees of correspondence, 31; intercolonial committee, 32; essays (1773), 33; and independence, 33*n.*; and delegates to Congress, 35; and Quakers, 100; Constitutional Convention, 179, 211; on need of Constitution, 181; as State leader, 208; faction and opponents, 210, 212, 213; in General Court, 214; and

Shays's rebels, 218; and ratification, 235; and Lieutenant-Governorship, 242, 243; Governor, 243; and Hancock, 243; and religious establishment, 422; and loyalist treaty rights, 561.

Albany, population, 49.

Allen, Ethan, at siege of Boston, 68; Ticonderoga, 79; and Congress and Vermont, 581; and Wyoming, 589.

Allen, James, on paper money, 251.

Allen, John, proscribed, 254.

Allen, William, proscribed, 254; and College, 264, 265.

Alsop, John, Continental Congress, 57; and commercial amendment, 283.

Alston, Joseph, income, 369.

American Revolution, preliminaries in Massachusetts, 4; Pennsylvania conservatism, 9; local grievances, 16-26; principal causes, 24, 38; and Imperialism, 26, 38; New England preparations, 66-71, 79, 80; preparations elsewhere, 71-74, 81-83; general war, 108; discontent of troops, 258, 260, 266, 267, 278; provincialism in army, 548-551; military remissness of States, complaints, 574-576; problem of keeping up army, 611-616, 626; problem of supplies, 616; commutation of half pay, 634, 635; Newburgh Address, 635; States and expenditures, 659; bounty land, 672.

Ames, Fisher, and ratification, 235; on State imposts, 556.

Amis, Thomas, Spanish seizure, 346.

Annapolis, retains capital, 317; and paper money, 532.

Annapolis Convention, New York, and, 284, 289; origin, 317, 512.

Arbuthnot, Marriot, Charleston siege, 375.

Aristocracy, colonial, 12, 42; overthrow, 444. *See also* Entail; Primogeniture.

Armstrong, John, and Wyoming, 279.

ilation, 605; and treaty violations, 649, 651.

Jefferson, Thomas, on ease of transition, 1, 125; declaration on taking up arms, 15; and extra-legal agencies, 27; resolutions (1774), 62; and military preparations, 73; and North's offer, 76; and Locke, 121; Virginia Constitution, 124, 144; on reform, 144; on legislative domination, 167; and constitutionality, 170n.; on Constitutions, 171; on idealization of "fathers," 172; and constitutional revision, 193, 194; in State service 206; war powers, 207; and Luther Martin, 313; as progressive leader, program, 324, 325, 334; redrafting legal code, 327, 453, 454; and moving capital, 327; and aristocracy, 327, 441; as Governor, loss of leadership, 328, 329, 333, 334; and British invasion, 329-333; inquiry into conduct, 333; and confederate impost, 336; on British debts, 337; influence of "Notes", 339; and Randolph, 340; and Potomac improvement, 341; on Madison and Mason, 357; and ratification, 409; and religious freedom, 433, 434, 436; and entail, 441; and primogeniture, 442; and slave trade, 445, 446; and slavery, 449; influence of Beccaria, 455; and prison reforms, 462; and education, 467, 468; on State debts, 478, 481; on taxation, 494; on State broils, 555; and free trade, 557; and federal monetary unit, 568; on monetary confusion, 570; Northwestern Ordinance, 596; plan for confederation, 622.

Jenifer, Daniel of St. Thomas, and State Senate, 309; Federal Convention, 318; and State loan, 505; on loyalist confiscations, 509n.

Johnson, James (or Zachariah Johnston), and ratification, 350.

Johnson, Joseph, on war impoverishment, 394.

Johnson, Reverdy, on Luther, Martin, 314.

Johnson, Thomas, fee controversy, 22; Continental Congress, 62; war powers, 207; Governor, 309:; career, 312; and independence, 313; and ratification, 319; on tax arrears, 513n.; and paper money, 530, 532.

Johnson, Sir William, Illinois scheme, 666.

Johnston, Hannah, courtship, 360.

Johnston, Samuel, Provincial Convention, 41; Provincial Congress, 91; on constitution-making, 130; and suffrage, 131, 140; and framing Constitution, 141; ability, 358; career and character, 359; on radical control, 363; Continental Congress, 378; on provision tax, 379; candidacy for Governor, 382, 385; and treaty of peace, 386, 389; State Senator, 387, 410; Governor, 406; and ratification, 408, 410; and religious freedom, 438; on tax collection, 513.

Johnston, Zachariah. *See* Johnson, James.

Jones, Allen, and framing Constitution, 141; conservative leader, 361; Speaker, 364n.; in Assembly, 387; and ratification, 408; on South Carolina, 576n.

Jones, (?) Gabriel, and Virginia ratification, 350.

Jones, N. W., political power, 14; agitation, 48.

Jones, Thomas, of New York, on Scott, 55.

Jones, Thomas, of North Carolina, and religious establishment, 142; conservative leader, 359; and intolerance, 438.

Jones, Willie, Provincial Convention, 41; and framing Constitution, 138; as radical leader, 140, 361; control of House, 364, 364n.; and loyalists, 365; and Federal Convention, 406; and ratification, 408-410.

Judd, William, and Wyoming Valley, 589.

Judiciary colonial, and grievances, 3-5, 17, 20, 31, 32; Maryland, 92; Georgia, 93, 109; question in framing Constitutions, 139, 166; North Carolina, 142, 364; New York, 161; and power to declare acts void, 168-170; New Hampshire, 184; South Carolina, 202; Pennsylvania, 263.

Junto, in Massachusetts, 13, 212.

Kaimes, Lord, on colonies and union, 553.

Kalm, Peter, on disjunctive spirit, 545.

Kempe, J. T., confiscation, 444.